Management: Application and Cases

Mosley | Mosley | Pietri

D1254944

CENGAGE
Learning·

Australia • Brazil • Japan • Korea • Mexico • Singapore • Spain • United Kingdom • United States

Management: Application and Cases

Supervisory Management, 8th Edition
Mosley | Mosley | Pietri

© 2011 South-Western, Cengage Learning. All rights reserved.

Executive Editors:
 Maureen Staudt
 Michael Stranz

Senior Project Development Manager:
 Linda deStefano

Marketing Specialist:
 Courtney Sheldon

Senior Production/Manufacturing
Manager:
 Donna M. Brown

PreMedia Manager:
 Joel Brennecke

Sr. Rights Acquisition Account Manager:
 Todd Osborne

Cover Image:
Getty Images*

*Unless otherwise noted, all cover images used by Custom Solutions, a part of Cengage Learning, have been supplied courtesy of Getty Images with the exception of the Earthview cover image, which has been supplied by the National Aeronautics and Space Administration (NASA).

For product information and technology assistance, contact us at
Cengage Learning Customer & Sales Support, 1-800-354-9706
For permission to use material from this text or product,
submit all requests online at cengage.com/permissions
Further permissions questions can be emailed to
permissionrequest@cengage.com

This book contains select works from existing Cengage Learning resources and was produced by Cengage Learning Custom Solutions for collegiate use. As such, those adopting and/or contributing to this work are responsible for editorial content accuracy, continuity and completeness.

Compilation © 2011 Cengage Learning

ISBN-13: 978-1-133-44251-6

ISBN-10: 1-133-44251-X

Cengage Learning
5191 Natorp Boulevard
Mason, Ohio 45040
USA

Cengage Learning is a leading provider of customized learning solutions with office locations around the globe, including Singapore, the United Kingdom, Australia, Mexico, Brazil, and Japan. Locate your local office at:
international.cengage.com/region.

Cengage Learning products are represented in Canada by Nelson Education, Ltd.
For your lifelong learning solutions, visit **www.cengage.com /custom.**
Visit our corporate website at **www.cengage.com.**

Printed in the United States of America

CUSTOM TABLE OF CONTENTS

CASES

PART 1

Overview

1

Supervisory Management Roles and Challenges

Ariel Skelley/Blend Images/Getty Images

Many supervisors in positions like Jackie Schultz's face the common challenge of achieving results through the efforts of others.

Supervisors are linking pins who are members of, and link or lock together, independent groups within an organization.
—*Rensis Likert*

CHAPTER OUTLINE

Preview

JACKIE SCHULTZ, PANERA BREAD SUPERVISOR For Panera Bread, bread continues to bring in the dough … pun intended. With 2008 sales volume of more than $1 billion and profits of $167 million from its 1300-store chain, Panera Bread continues to outperform in the casual dining industry. With its mission statement "A loaf under every arm," CEO/owner Ronald Shaich states that the centerpiece of Panera's vision is the highest quality experience for its customers—quality ingredients, quality preparation, quality presentation, and quality service. Let's take a closer look within one of its stores to see how it happens.

Jackie Schultz joined Panera in one of its Southeast stores as an associate (as Panera employees are called) while a high school senior in 2004. A quick learner, she cross-trained for multiple associate jobs (Panera has nine areas of certification) and, within six months, was named an associate trainer. After a year, she was promoted to shift supervisor and training specialist, the position she presently holds while working on her degree at a local university.

Jackie is one of three supervisor/managers who report to the overall store manager (Exhibit 1-1) and who have prime responsibility for the associates' delivery of Panera quality to the restaurant floor. Associates in Jackie's store are a diverse group: The 21 employees are mostly under 25, with the youngest being 17 and the oldest nearly 50.

Thirteen of the 21 employees are females, 13 are white, 7 are African American, and 1 is Asian. Twenty work full time (25 or more hours), one works part time, seven attend college, all are high school graduates or equivalent, and three are parents.

The core of Jackie's daily job is seeing that Panera's commitment to quality is reflected in her associates' job performance. To control quality, Panera has standardized procedures for all important store activities. Its stores have consistent procedures for baking, food/beverage displays, customer greeting, order taking, cashiering, handling food, preparation and placement of food on a tray, kitchen and store sanitation, cleanliness, and others. Name an activity that is related to quality within the store, and Panera has an in-place procedure to achieve it.

Our associates are well trained and highly motivated in keeping up their performance. The challenge comes when we're shorthanded or really busy. We often have large groups come in—tennis players participating in national/regional tournaments at local

EXHIBIT 1-1
Partial Organization Chart for Panera Bread

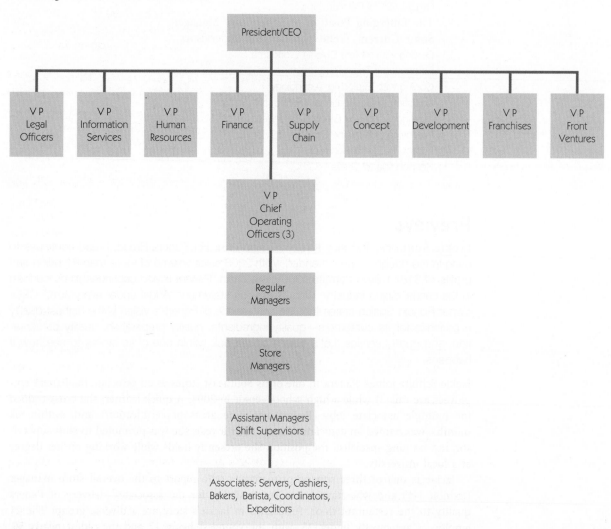

courts, or sometimes we get a busload of tourists or a high school group, such as cheer-leaders. That's when our quality is tested. I will be right in there with my associates, on the line myself as needed, having someone redo a customer's order, clean a spill in the dining area, or bus a table. Regardless of how busy the store is, it's important for our customer's experience to be great. Greeting with a smile and making the connection is what we're about. We want to provide an everyday oasis for all of our customers.

Schultz wears a number of hats during the typical day, which is characterized by many different activities and multitasking—coordinating, communicating with, and encouraging associates; pitching in and helping on the line as needed; visiting customers; handling phone calls; meeting with a supplier or a corporate visitor; and meeting with her own general manager. Some store manager meetings may be formal, regarding such topics as new Panera policies to be relayed to associates or discussing food costs, new products, or profitability. Schultz may initiate a meeting with her own manager to get a question answered, to nominate an associate for special recognition, or to mention problems or concerns. She also spends time in her training role, encouraging and helping associates cross-train for certification in different associate jobs, as this is one objective that upper management has for each store. The certification system is completed by associates online, in the store. "I encourage my associates to be certified in as many areas as they can, as it helps them understand the whole store concept, which makes them more valuable, and in fact, earns them more money." Jackie's certification in all nine store areas enhances her own credibility as a supervisor.

Recognition plays an important part in associates' buy-in to the Panera concept. There are formal recognition forms, such as a hat pin for reaching certification, formal "Wow" recognition by the store manager for special performance, and recognition with gift certificates at the three or four meetings attended by all employees, called "Bread Bashes." Schultz believes strongly in giving praise and recognition on her shift, especially when she sees someone doing something special.

I'm really big on verbal praise. It might be a "Thank you for helping that couple," to praise for an associate who without being asked brings an elderly couple's food to their table, or a "Wow, I loved the way your bakery display is so clean, organized, and has a waterfall effect." Recognition is especially important for new associates. I'm glad that I was an associate before I went into management. I know where they're coming from, what they appreciate, and how different everyone is. For example, I understand associates' different learning styles, such as visual, auditory, and hands-on. Visual learners can pick things up from a computer screen or out of a book of drawings and illustrations. To others you may be able to explain it, and they'll get it. Others learn best by actually doing it. It's important for a supervisor to clue into their preferences.

Looking back at how her management style has changed over the past four years, Jackie feels that she was perhaps too "soft" when she first assumed the supervisor role at age 18, and that being that young was a disadvantage. She recalls discussing with her dad the fact that associates seemed to test her authority quickly following her promotion to supervisor. He said, "Jackie, you're the youngest, you've not been there long, you're a female, you're 4′10″, and you also happen to be half Asian. What do you expect?" Now she feels at ease in her role, enjoys leading others, and has no trouble being assertive as called for, as when discussing an associate's tardiness or failure to follow a procedure or even when having to give a written reprimand. Her biggest assets are her communication skills, sensitivity to others, and technical expertise.

Jackie sums up her supervisory role as similar to that of a coach/facilitator in helping associates perform at their best. Many associates have developed a special relationship with repeat customers. She states, "We've had customers send cards or gifts for special occasions to our associates, like when they've graduated, gotten married, or had a baby. Our store is a special place."[1]

This case illustrates well the many aspects of a supervisor's job and some of the major challenges that supervisors face. Note that:

1. Jackie performs a broad set of duties, ranging from scheduling work, assigning tasks, coordinating work flow, monitoring performance, training, providing recognition, and disciplining when necessary.
2. She interfaces with people from multiple groups, including her associates, fellow supervisors, manager, corporate personnel, suppliers, and customers.
3. She uses a variety of skills, including her interpersonal skills, computer expertise, and technical skills/understanding of the primary tasks performed by associates.

Jackie faces a common challenge of supervisors—obtaining results through others. In a sense, her effectiveness is determined by how successful her personnel are. One way of looking at the supervisor's job, then, is to think of it in terms of "helping your people be as good as they can be." This preview case indicates some of the many factors that affect the work of supervisors and managers at all organizational levels, such as the need for excellent communication skills, the use of technology, and recognition of workforce diversity. At no time has the job of supervision been recognized as being so important. Likewise, at no time has it been more challenging. In reading this material, you will be introduced in more depth to the roles and challenges of being a supervisor.

The Need for Management

Whenever a group of people work together in a structured situation to achieve a common objective, they form an **organization**. The organization may be a student group, a business firm, a religious group, a governmental institution, a military unit, a sports team, or a similar group. The main objective of such organizations is to produce a product or provide a service. Other organizational objectives may be to provide satisfaction to members, employment and benefits to workers, a product to the public, and/or a return to the owners of the business (usually in the form of a profit). To reach these objectives, management must perform three basic organizational activities: (1) **operations**, or producing the product or service; (2) **marketing**, or selling and distributing the product; and (3) **financing**, or providing and using funds. These activities must be performed in almost all organizations, be they large corporations or small entrepreneur shops, whether they operate for profit or not for profit.

What Is Management?

Organizations are the means by which people get things done. People can accomplish more working together than they can achieve alone, but to combine and coordinate the efforts of the members of the organization, the process of management is required. Without management, people in the group would go off on their own and try to reach the organization's objectives independently of other group members. If small organizations lacked management, the members' efforts would be wasted. If management were absent in larger, more complex organizations, objectives would not be reached and chaos would result. In summary, *managers are needed in all types of organizations*.

Management can be defined as the process of working with and through people to achieve objectives by means of effective decision making and coordination of available resources. The basic resources of any organization are **human resources**, which are the

organization

A group of people working together in a structured situation for a common objective.

operations

Producing an organization's product or service.

marketing

Selling and distributing an organization's product or service.

1 *Explain why management is needed in all organizations.*

financing

Providing or using funds to produce and distribute an organization's product or service.

management

Working with people to achieve objectives by effective decision making and coordinating available resources.

human resources

The people an organization requires for operations.

EXHIBIT 1-2
How Management Combines the Organization's Resources into a Productive System

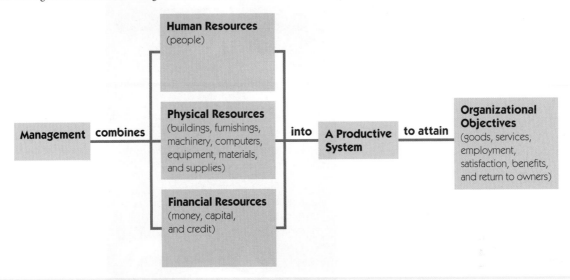

physical resources

Items an organization requires for operations.

financial resources

The money, capital, and credit an organization requires for operations.

people involved; **physical resources**, which include buildings, furnishings, machinery, computers, equipment, materials, and supplies; and **financial resources**, such as money, capital, and credit. Exhibit 1-2 shows *the vital task of management: combining resources and activities into a productive system to attain organizational objectives.*

Consider this situation:

Pete Bolton, entrepreneur, operates a one-person shoe repair shop. Pete performs all the necessary activities, including repairing shoes, serving customers, ordering equipment and supplies, maintaining equipment, keeping records, paying bills, and borrowing money. He does it all. Would you say that Pete is performing management?

Our position is that he is not. On the one hand, he certainly employs *physical* and *financial resources*. On the other hand, while he does interact with customers, they are not an employed resource, because they do not perform work. The only *human resource* that Pete utilizes is himself. Now consider a new scenario for Pete:

Business is so good that Pete leases the adjacent office and removes the wall, creating five times more floor space for the shop. He hires four employees: Three perform shoe repairs and one is a counter clerk/repairer. Whereas in the first situation he was a doer, performing all activities himself, in the second situation Pete must manage, guide, and direct others who perform tasks. The skills required for Pete to perform successfully in the new situation differ markedly from those required in the first. Pete must now perform "management."

This simple example explains why many individuals perform successfully in nonmanagement positions such as entrepreneurs, technicians, operators, and professionals but often fail when placed in positions of supervision. The material you are reading will help you succeed in the second situation!

2 *Describe the different levels of management.*

Levels of Management

Except in very small organizations, the different levels of management are usually based on the amount of responsibility and authority required to perform the job. Individuals at

Darama/Corbis

Supervisors help their employees learn, grow, and develop so that company objectives can be reached.

authority

Given the right to act in a specified manner in order to reach organizational objectives; the right to tell others how to act to reach objectives.

responsibility

Occurs when key tasks associated with a particular job are specified.
The obligation of an employee to accept a manager's delegated authority.

top management

Responsible for the entire or a major segment of the organization.

middle management

Responsible for a substantial part of the organization.

higher levels of the organization have more authority and responsibility than those at lower levels. **Authority** is the right to tell others to act or not act in order to reach objectives. **Responsibility** is the obligation that is created when an employee accepts a manager's delegated authority.

Large organizations usually have at least three levels of management, plus a level of operative employees. These levels are generally referred to as (1) *top management,* (2) *middle management,* and (3) *supervisory management.* In large organizations, there may be multiple levels of top and middle management.

Self–Check

In the chapter preview, for example, note that five levels of management exist at Panera Bread. The president/CEO and vice president levels comprise top management, the regional manager and store managers comprise middle management, and supervisors comprise the supervisory management level.

Exhibit 1-3 shows that authority and responsibility increase as one moves from the nonmanagerial level into the managerial ranks and then into the higher managerial levels. The titles and designations listed are only a few of those actually used in organizations.

Although the duties and responsibilities of the various management levels vary from one organization to another, they can be summarized as follows. **Top management** is responsible for the overall operations of the entire organization or oversees a major segment of the organization or a basic organizational activity. **Middle management** is responsible for a substantial part of the organization (perhaps a program, project,

EXHIBIT 1-3

How Management Authority and Responsibility Increase at Higher Levels

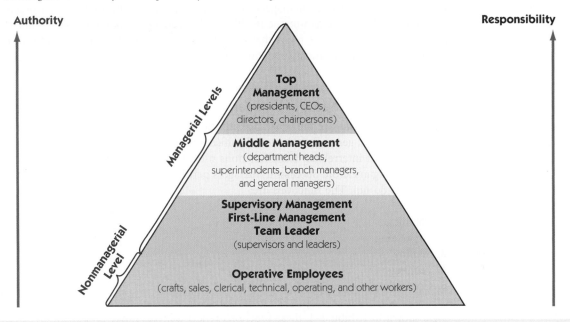

supervisory
management

Controls operations of
smaller organizational
units.

division, plant, store, or department). Finally, **supervisory management** has control over the operations of a smaller organizational unit (such as a production line, operating unit, office, or laboratory). Managers in this last group, such as Jackie Schultz of Panera Bread (see chapter preview), are in charge of nonmanagerial or rank-and-file employees, and are the managers with whom most employees interact.

Our focus is primarily upon the first level of managers, who may be called *supervisory managers* or simply *supervisors*. It is this group that is the organization's primary link with most of its employees. At BP Group, the large multinational energy company, they number 10,000 and are called first-level leaders, overseeing operations at retail outlets; managing crews at chemical plants, refineries, or drilling platforms; or supervising professionals in research and development (R&D), human resources, marketing, or accounting. About 75 percent of BP employees report to them, and as one BP executive states "in aggregate their decisions make an enormous difference in BP's turnover, costs, quality, safety, innovation, and environmental performance."[2] A study of 17,000 federal agency employees concluded that "frontline supervisors" are important determinants of federal agency performance: "they are key figures in building and sustaining an organization culture that promotes high performance and they influence many factors of agency performance and effectiveness."[3] In some organizations, the term "team leader" may be used interchangeably with "first-line supervisor." In other organizations, it refers to a position quite different from that of a supervisor. For example, in organizations that use self-directed work teams, the work team itself performs many functions considered "supervisory" or "managerial," such as planning, scheduling, and evaluating its own work, and assigning tasks to members. "The team leader of such a group is a working team member who facilitates the team's effectiveness by encouraging members, helping resolve problems, scheduling and leading team meetings, serving as the team's spokesperson with other organizational groups, and so on. Although these types of team leaders lack the formal authority of a traditional supervisor, their roles are similar in many ways."[4]

What Do Managers Do?

It is now time to see what managers do that makes them so necessary to an organization's success. We first examine the functions managers perform, then look at some roles managers play. Note at this point that not all managers spend the same amount of time performing each management function or playing each role.

Functions Performed by Managers

managerial functions

Broad classification of activities that all managers perform.

Managerial functions are the broad classification of activities that all managers perform. There is no single, generally accepted classification of these functions, but we believe that five separate but interrelated basic functions must be performed by any manager at any level in any organization. Successful managers perform these functions effectively; unsuccessful ones do not. The functions are:

1. Planning
2. Organizing
3. Staffing
4. Leading
5. Controlling

As shown in Exhibit 1-4, these functions reflect a broad range of activities.

EXHIBIT 1-4
The Management Functions in Action

PRIMARY FUNCTION	EXAMPLES
Planning	Determining resources needed
	Setting daily, weekly, monthly performance objectives
	Developing work schedules
	Anticipating and preparing for problems before they occur
Organizing	Making sure members understand roles and responsibilities
	Deciding who is best suited to perform a given task
	Assigning tasks to team members
	Coordinating members' activities
Staffing	Interviewing and selecting potential employees
	Securing needed training to upgrade members' skills
	Helping employees grow and develop through coaching, job rotation, broadening of assignments
Leading	Communicating relevant information to members
	Coaching, encouraging, supporting members
	Praising, recognizing, rewarding for work well done
	Building employee acceptance of change
Controlling	Observing and monitoring employee performance
	Ensuring employee compliance with standards, procedures, rules
	Identifying and resolving crises, problems that occur
	Following up to ensure implementation of decisions

planning

Selecting future courses of action and deciding how to achieve the desired results.

organizing

Deciding what activities are needed to reach goals and dividing human resources into work groups to achieve them.

staffing

Recruiting, training, promoting, and rewarding people to do the organization's work.

leading

Guiding, influencing, and motivating employees in the performance of their duties and responsibilities.

controlling

Comparing actual performance with planned action and taking corrective action if needed.

Planning. **Planning** involves selecting goals and future courses of action and deciding how to achieve the desired results. It also encompasses gathering and analyzing information to make these decisions. Through planning, the manager establishes goals and objectives and determines methods of attaining them. All other basic managerial functions depend on planning because it is unlikely that they will be successfully carried out without sound and continuous planning.

Organizing. Deciding what activities are needed to reach goals and objectives, deciding who is to perform what task, dividing human resources into work groups, and assigning each group to a manager are tasks that make up the **organizing** function. Another aspect of organizing is bringing together the physical, financial, and human resources needed to achieve the organization's objectives.

Staffing. The process of recruiting, selecting, training, developing, promoting, and paying and rewarding people to do the organization's work is called **staffing**. This basic function is sometimes regarded as a part of the organizing function, but we think it is important enough to be considered separately.

Leading. The **leading** function involves guiding, influencing, and motivating employees in the performance of their duties and responsibilities. It consists of coaching and empowering employees, facilitating their activities, communicating ideas and instructions, and motivating employees to perform their work efficiently. Typically, middle managers and supervisory managers spend a larger proportion of their time in leading—that is, "working with their people directly"—than do top managers.

Controlling. The **controlling** function involves comparing actual performance with planned standards and taking corrective action, if needed, to ensure that objectives are achieved. Control can be achieved only by setting up standards of performance, checking to see whether they have been achieved, and then doing what is necessary to bring actual performance in line with planned performance. This function must be executed successfully to ensure that the other management functions are effectively performed.

How the Functions Are Related

Although the five management functions must be performed by managers in all types of organizations and at all management levels, they may be performed in different ways and given different emphasis by various managers. One or more functions may be stressed over another at a particular level. For example, planning is done most often by top management, and leading and controlling are common among supervisory managers. Yet the functions are interrelated, interactive, and interdependent, as shown in Exhibit 1-5. Although they may be performed in any order, the functions tend to be performed in the sequence indicated by the numbers in the exhibit.

Roles Played by Managers

The preceding discussion of the management functions might lead you to believe that the manager's job is orderly, well organized, systematic, and harmonious, but this is just not so. In performing these functions, managers engage in a great many varied, disorganized, fragmented, and often unrelated activities. These activities may last for a very short time or may extend over a longer period.

roles

Parts played by managers in the performance of their functions.

In carrying out these activities, managers play **roles** as if they were actors, and these roles change rapidly and frequently. A landmark management study identifies 10 roles, grouped as follows: (1) interpersonal roles, (2) informational roles, and (3) decision-making roles.[5]

EXHIBIT 1-5
How the Management Functions Are Related

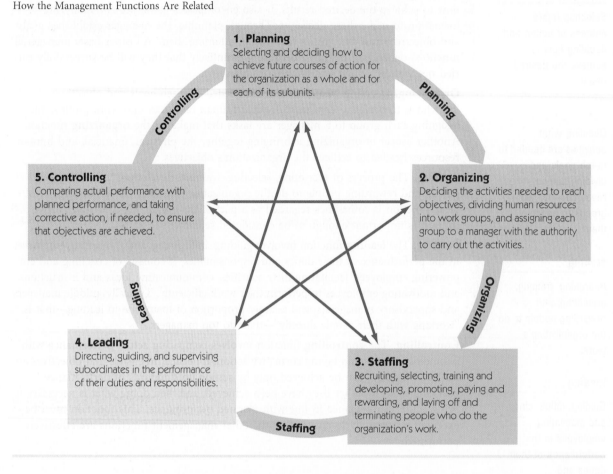

1. Planning
Selecting and deciding how to achieve future courses of action for the organization as a whole and for each of its subunits.

2. Organizing
Deciding the activities needed to reach objectives, dividing human resources into work groups, and assigning each group to a manager with the authority to carry out the activities.

3. Staffing
Recruiting, selecting, training and developing, promoting, paying and rewarding, and laying off and terminating people who do the organization's work.

4. Leading
Directing, guiding, and supervising subordinates in the performance of their duties and responsibilities.

5. Controlling
Comparing actual performance with planned performance, and taking corrective action, if needed, to ensure that objectives are achieved.

Exhibit 1-6 shows how each might be carried out by a supervisor like Jackie Schultz (chapter preview).

Like managerial functions, these roles are given varying degrees of emphasis by managers in different organizations and at different levels in the same organization. Managers vary in how they interpret the roles, the time they devote to them, and the importance they assign to them. With training and experience, supervisors can learn to perform these duties effectively.

Skills Required for Effective Management

4 *Explain the basic skills required for effective management.*

You may be wondering at this point what basic skills managers need to perform the managerial functions and play the managerial roles most effectively. Although many skills are needed, a few of the most common ones are:

1. Conceptual skills
2. Human relations skills
3. Administrative skills
4. Technical skills

EXHIBIT 1-6
Roles Played by
Managers

ROLE	WHAT IS INVOLVED	EXAMPLES
INTERPERSONAL ROLES		
Figurehead	Representing the unit as its symbolic head.	Greeting department visitors, attending meetings and ceremonies, representing company on community boards
Leader	Helping personnel reach organizational and personal goals.	Motivating, encouraging, supporting associates; providing feedback about performance; building morale.
Liaison	Maintaining relationships between the unit and outsiders.	Meeting with departmental heads, supervisors, suppliers, and customers.
INFORMATIONAL ROLES		
Monitor	Seeking out useful information that is especially relevant for the unit/ organization.	Attending professional meetings, learning about forthcoming changes.
Disseminator	Providing relevant information to appropriate organization members.	Routing reports and information to employees and others; copying departmental head on memos sent to employees.
Spokesperson	Representing employees to supervisors and vice versa; representing the unit to others.	Representing the department at weekly meetings; speaking out against changes that adversely affect employees.
DECISION-MAKING ROLES		
Entrepreneur	Tackling problems; seeking changes to improve unit.	Introducing new equipment, encouraging improved methods, promoting innovation by employees, taking risks.
Disturbance handler	Responding to crises/problems that arise.	Resolving employee conflicts, soothing employees' resistance to change.
Resource allocator	Allocating the unit's resources.	Preparing a budget, deciding which associates receive new equipment, which are offered overtime work.
Negotiator	Negotiating differences with employees, managers, and outsiders.	Negotiating with a difficult customer, bargaining for favorable terms with employees, other departments, own department head, and others, getting better terms from a supplier.

Source: "Roles Played by Managers" adapted from The Natures of Managerial Work by Henry Mintzberg. Copyright © 1973 by Henry Mintzberg. Reprinted by permission of Henry Mintzberg.

The relative importance of these skills varies according to the type of industry in which managers work, the organization to which they belong, their level in the managerial ranks, the job being performed, and the employees being managed. Exhibit 1-7 shows an estimate of the relative importance of these skills at different management levels.

Self-Check

Which roles are being performed when Jackie Schultz of Panera Bread (see chapter preview) performs each of the following tasks?

1. *Visits a competitor store, Atlanta Bread Company, to observe their operations*
2. *Reconciles a situation with a customer who is unhappy with his meal/service*
3. *Meets with store manager to voice her and her associates' disapproval of a new policy regarding overtime pay*
4. *Compliments an associate for special service to a customer*

HISTORICAL INSIGHT

Taylor's "Scientific Management" and Fayol's "Management Principles"

Historically, evidence of early management practice is easy to find. It was required to organize and build the Roman Empire and other civilizations. China's Great Wall, Egypt's pyramids, and other massive architectural feats stand today as concrete examples of successful management. The same can be said of the great amount of planning and organization required in building massive, effective organizations, including governments, religious institutions, and armies.

Early approaches to managing consisted primarily of trial and error. Businesses were small, entrepreneurial ventures with personal oversight by owners or foremen, each achieving efficiency in his or her own most effective way. In the mid-1800s, the advent of the factory system changed that approach. Inventions of machinery and tools caused production to shift from "made by hand" to "made by machine" and enabled mass production. In the United States, the expansion of transportation (railroads) and communications (telegraph, telephone, and postal systems), the development of Western frontiers, and the building of mechanized plants created larger organizations and the need for more systematic management. It was during this changing of the organizational landscape toward larger organizations in both the United States and Europe that two key figures, American Frederick W. Taylor (1856–1915) and Frenchman Henri Fayol (1841–1925), began careers that would lead them to be considered major pioneers in management. Both were engineers, but their careers focused on two distinct management areas: Taylor at the operating level, Fayol at the executive level.

Taylor and Scientific Management. Taylor's business career took him through positions of physical laborer, foreman, head engineer, and private consultant until his death in 1915 at age 59. It was during his work at Midvale Steel, a large Philadelphia foundry, and later at Bethlehem Steel, that he began to research ways to improve efficiency. Operating in a production environment with few substantiated "rules of thumb," Taylor systematically conducted numerous experiments involving efficiency. These included time study; determining physical weight loads that workers could efficiently handle during a day; efficiencies of equipment, such as optimum shovel head size; and many others. His theme was that through proper work methods, workers could produce more work while earning higher pay, benefiting both employers and workers. Taylor's systematic approach was called "Scientific Management," and through papers presented at professional meetings and word of successful applications, his system gained much recognition. He was elected head of the prestigious American Society of Mechanical Engineers, became a consultant, taught courses at Harvard, and traveled extensively, presenting his new gospel of efficiency. He spawned a number of other "efficiency" associates who themselves gained national popularity, including Carl Barth (inventor of the slide rule), Frank Gilbreth (motion study), and Henry Gantt (production charts).

Taylor's books, *Shop Management* and *Principles of Scientific Management*, laid the groundwork for his system. His "Scientific Management" distinctly shaped management practice during the critical period when American industry was shifting from smaller, manager-owner firms to larger-scale operations. Ford Motor Company, for example, used Taylor's ideas in building its Highland Park, Michigan, plant, which opened in 1910.

FPG/Hulton Archive/Getty Images

Taylor and Fayol were pioneers in the study of management in early 20th century mass production work environments like this 1917 Detroit aircraft factory.

Fayol and Management Principles. Like Taylor, Frenchman Henri Fayol began his career in technical work when, following his graduation as a mining engineer, he joined a large iron mining/foundry operation, Commentary-Fourchambault, in 1860. Earning a reputation for developing ways to fight underground fires, Fayol was promoted to several management positions and, in 1888, was named managing director, today's equivalent of CEO. When he took over, the company was in severe financial straits and its key mineral/ore deposits severely depleted. Fayol succeeded in turning the company's fortunes around. It was during his long experience as a top manager of a full-scale, fully integrated enterprise of 9,000 employees that Fayol developed his ideas about management. Unlike Taylor's operational focus, Fayol built a theory of management from the perspective of an executive. He felt that management was sufficiently important that it should be studied and theories developed; then, this being done, it could be taught and studied in universities. The body of management theory he developed included "principles" of management, including principles for planning, organizing, staffing, and controlling. He felt that all managers in all organizations must perform certain basic management functions, very similar to the functions just presented in this chapter.

Like Taylor, Fayol was a writer and paper presenter at meetings. His major work, *General and Industrial Management*, was published in 1916, nine years before his death in 1925. Unfortunately, it was not until the 1940s that an English translation of his book would lead to proper recognition of his work in the United States. Many of Fayol's ideas form the framework for contemporary management theory, most notably those dealing with the planning and organizing functions.

Source: Frederick W. Taylor, The Principles of Scientific Management (New York and London: Harper and Brothers, 1911); Henri Fayol, General and Industrial Management, trans. Constance Storrs (New York: Pitman, 1949; originally published in French, 1916); Daniel Wren, The Evolution of Management Thought, 3rd ed. (New York: John Wiley and Sons, 1987), especially Chapters 7, 11, and 12, which discuss Taylor, and Chapter 10, which discusses Fayol.

EXHIBIT 1-7
The Relative Importance
of Managerial Skills at
Different Managerial
Levels

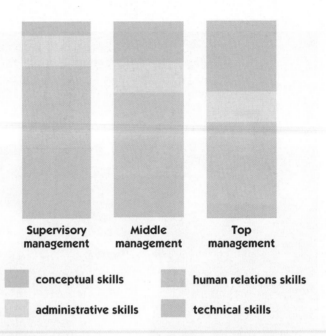

	Supervisory management	Middle management	Top management

conceptual skills   human relations skills

administrative skills   technical skills

Conceptual Skills

conceptual skills

Mental ability to
become aware of and
identify relationships
among different pieces
of information.

Conceptual skills involve the ability to acquire, analyze, and interpret information in a
logical manner. All managers need to understand the environments in which they operate, as well as the effects of changes in those environments on their organization. In
other words, managers should be able to "see the big picture." Top managers particularly
need strong conceptual skills because changes affecting the organization tend to be more
important at their level than at other managerial levels. About one third of their time is
spent using conceptual skills.

Human Relations Skills

**human relations
skills**

Understanding other
people and interacting
effectively.

Human relations skills consist of the abilities to understand other people and to interact
effectively with them. These skills are most needed in performing the leading function
because they involve communicating with, motivating, leading, coaching, empowering,
and facilitating employees, as well as relating to other people. These skills are important
in dealing not only with individuals, but also with people in groups and even with relationships among groups. These skills are important to managers at all levels, but especially to supervisory managers, who spend almost one half of their time using human
relations skills.

Recall that Jackie Schultz (chapter preview) considered her human relations skills to
be one of her biggest strengths as a supervisor.

Administrative Skills

administrative skills

Establishing and
following procedures
to process paperwork
in an orderly manner.

Administrative skills are the skills that permit managers to use their other skills effectively in performing the managerial functions. These skills include the ability to establish
and follow policies and procedures and to process paperwork in an orderly manner. By
lending *coordination, order,* and *movement* to tasks, administrative skills underlie the
ability some people have to "make things happen" and "get things done." These skills
are very similar to those possessed by good students, who are well organized and get
things done efficiently.

Technical Skills

technical skills

Understanding and being able to supervise effectively specific processes required.

Technical skills include understanding and being able to supervise effectively the specific processes, practices, or techniques required to perform specific duties. Technical skills are more important for supervisors than for top managers, since supervisors are closer to the actual work being performed. They must often tell—or even show—employees how to perform a job, as well as know when it is done properly.

A head nurse in a hospital, for example, must have some degree of technical understanding of proper equipment use, nursing procedures, medication, chart maintenance, and other important aspects of a nurse's job. We are not saying that the head nurse or any other supervisor must necessarily be a technical expert, but that a supervisor needs a basic understanding of the work being done to perform the managerial functions and roles effectively.

The four skills we have just discussed form the basis for a wide variety of important management actions. For example, effective time management requires *conceptual* and *administrative* skills to prioritize activities and efficiently dispose of required paperwork; being an effective trainer requires the *technical* skills or an understanding of the subject matter and the *human relations* skills of being sensitive and able to communicate effectively with a trainee; political know-how requires *conceptual* and *human relations* skills to identify the potential implications of actions and to build strategic relationships.

emotional intelligence (EI)

The capacity to recognize and accurately perceive one's own and others' emotions, to understand the significance of these emotions, and to influence one's actions based on this analysis; an assortment of skills and characteristics that influence a person's ability to succeed as a leader.

More recently, the concept of *emotional intelligence* has become a popular way to view a specialized skill set involving people's emotions. It involves use of both conceptual and human relations skills. **Emotional intelligence, or EI** as it is often referred to, is the capacity to recognize and accurately perceive one's own and others' emotions, to understand the significance of these emotions, and to influence one's actions based on this analysis. Examples of emotional intelligence might be controlling one's anger when under duress, reading an employee's facial expressions and body language as expressions of disappointment or anger, or perhaps ending a team meeting because of diminished

Supervisors often use both their human relations and their technical skills in discussions with employees.

energy/interest by participants. Studies of emotional intelligence have linked it with leadership success. You will learn more about emotional intelligence in Chapter 6.[6]

In summary, effective supervisory management requires all of the skills—conceptual, human relations, administrative, and technical. The appropriate mix, however, depends on the level of management and the circumstances surrounding the managerial situation.

Self-Check

Which of the four skills are reflected when a supervisor performs these tasks?

1. *Prepares a to-do list for next week*
2. *Completes paperwork required for employee to attend a training seminar*
3. *Conducts a weekly performance review meeting with a new employee*
4. *Completes her unit's daily performance report*

The Transition: Where Supervisors Come From

5 *Explain where supervisors come from.*

Each year, several hundred thousand nonmanagers become supervisors or managers. Skilled operators or technicians become supervisors, teachers become principals, ministers become pastors, nurses become head nurses, and salespersons become sales managers. Most of these positions are filled by current employees.

Internal promotions make sense for at least three reasons. First, an inside candidate understands the organization and its culture. In addition, if promoted within the same department, he or she will know the tasks required, the personnel, fellow supervisors, and likely the new boss. Second, management has firsthand knowledge of the employee's record of accomplishment and can use this as a predictor of success. Third, to promote someone internally serves as a reward and as an incentive for those employees who have an interest in management and demonstrate management potential.

Unfortunately, organizations commonly make two crucial mistakes when selecting supervisors. One is to automatically select the best present performer. Although the best performer may have excellent technical skills, as you saw earlier, other skills, especially human relations skills, are also important.[7] Frequently, outstanding technical performers have unreasonably high expectations or little patience with nonproducers. Moreover, they may find it difficult to let go of their old positions, at which they were so good. Instead, they continue to perform their unit's operating work, neglecting the supervisory responsibilities of their position.

One of the authors was scheduled to interview a maintenance supervisor of a large paper manufacturer. His assistant informed the author that he was running late for the interview because of an equipment breakdown. An hour or so later he entered the office, sleeves rolled up, with grease covering his hands. "Sorry about missing the appointment; I'll be right with you after I wash up," he said. The author learned from this supervisor's crew that for this supervisor, almost every breakdown was a "major one." He micromanaged, insisted on being notified of every development, and continually took over his technicians' jobs, especially the most challenging ones. His crew members had little opportunity for skill development and little initiative. As one stated, "Our best work is done when he [the supervisor] is out of the plant, like on vacation." Note in Exhibit 1-8 that micromanagement/failure to delegate is one of the primary reasons supervisors/managers fail.

Another crucial mistake made by organizations stems from inadequately preparing the employee to assume a supervisory position. Unfortunately, it is common to hear a supervisor say that the transition to supervisor went like this: "When I left work on

EXHIBIT 1-8
Why Supervisors and
Managers Fail

There are many reasons why supervisors and managers fail to be effective. Formal research about manager failure has focused on "derailment," referring to managers selected by their organizations for a rapid advancement but who don't make the grade. Typically it is people issues, such as items 1 and 2 below, that bring them down. In our own experiences in conducting manager/supervisor training workshops, we typically ask attendees to identify bosses they've had who have been ineffective. This list below shows common reasons given.

Ten Reasons Supervisors/Managers Fail

1. Insensitive to others; dominating, intimidating, bullying style
2. Feeling of superiority; arrogant, cold, indifferent to employees
3. Unwilling to listen
4. Unable to get people to work as a team
5. Betrayal of team's trust—deceptive, untruthful, manipulative
6. Micromanagement; failure to delegate
7. Out for self; overly political, not sharing credit, pushing one's own career
8. Too nonassertive; hands-off; won't address performance problems/issues
9. Lack of technical skill/understanding
10. Boss-related issues; unable to get along, overdependence, unwilling to disagree

Source: Also, see Robert D. Ramsey, "The Most Important Skills for Today's Supervisors," Supervision, November 2007, 3–6; Chuck Williams, Management (Mason, OH: Thomson South-Western, 2008), 14–15; E. Van Velsor and J. Brittain, "Why Executives Derail: Perspectives across Time and Cultures," Academy of Management Executive, November 1995, 62–72.

Friday, I was a lab technician. With absolutely no training or warning, on Monday morning I learned I was a lab supervisor." Ideally, an organization should take great care when identifying potential candidates for supervisory positions and, once candidates are chosen, should help new supervisors make the transition. Before a permanent position is assigned, promising potential supervisors can be identified, assessed, and trained. Thus, such candidates may fill in as temporary supervisors when the supervisor is absent because of illness or vacation or may occupy a "lead" position that actually entails some supervisory responsibility. Fortunately, organizations are doing a much better job nowadays of identifying people with supervisory potential and preparing them through appropriate training to help them make a successful transition.

Supervisory Relationships

6 *Clarify the different relationships supervisory managers have with others.*

If we are to understand the role of supervisory managers in organizations, we must look at some of the relationships they have with different individuals and groups. For example, supervisors are legally a part of management and interact upward with other members of management. However, they are often not accepted as peers by those managers, who come from outside the organization—usually with more education—and have higher social status and position. Before their promotion, supervisors typically worked as peers with those they now supervise.

The three major types of relationships that supervisors have, as shown in Exhibit 1-9, are (1) personal, (2) organizational, and (3) external. These comprise the supervisor's **relationships network**, the major individuals and groups with whom the supervisor interacts.[8]

relationships network

The major individuals and groups with whom the supervisor interacts.

Personal Relationships

At one time it was believed that managers and employees left their personal problems at home when they entered the workplace. We now recognize that people bring their

EXHIBIT 1-9
The Supervisor's Network of Relationships

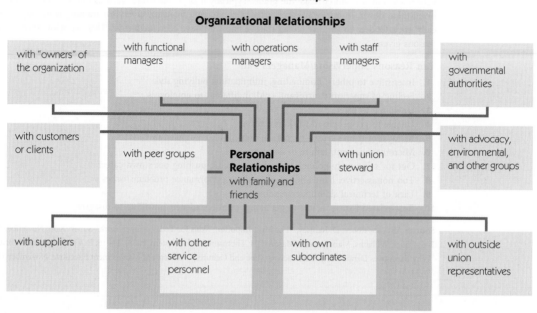

problems—as well as their pleasures—to their jobs. Supervisors' relationships with their families and their friends determine their attitudes and frame of mind as they perform managerial duties. Their attitudes, in turn, influence the relationships they have with other people, both inside and outside the organization.

Organizational Relationships

Within the organization, supervisory managers have varied and often conflicting relationships with several organizational entities. As shown in Exhibit 1-10, these are the supervisor's employees, the supervisor's peer group supervisors, the union steward (if the company is unionized), and the supervisor's managers.

Supervisor-to-Employee Relationships Supervisory managers must relate to their own employees and to people from other units who perform some type of service for them. As Exhibit 1-10 illustrates, a manager-to-employee relationship exists where the supervisor facilitates and directs nonmanagerial personnel.

Relationships with Peer Supervisors and Union Steward There are essentially two sets of horizontal relationships: those with other supervisory managers and those with the union steward or other representative(s) of the employees. Supervisors need the feeling of support and reinforcement that comes from associating with other supervisors who are considered their equals or peers. Yet the relationship can result in competition or even conflict if they seek to be promoted to the same job at the next higher level.

In a unionized organization, employees select a **union steward** to represent them in their dealings with management. Although the steward is a supervisor's peer—legally, if not organizationally—he or she does represent the supervisor's employees. Therefore, the association between the supervisor and the union steward may be competitive or even

union steward

A union member elected by other members to represent their interests in relations with management.

EXHIBIT 1-10
The Flow of Supervisors'
Organizational
Relationships

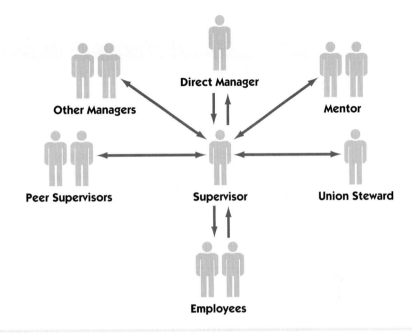

combative. This association provides supervisors with a challenge but can also be frustrating. For example, a supervisor will probably attempt to motivate employees to improve productivity, whereas a union steward may encourage them to maintain the status quo for fear that their jobs will be eliminated.

Supervisor-to-Manager Relationships Supervisors have a *reverse* manager-to-employee relationship with their immediate manager. As a result of downsizing, reengineering, empowering, and similar new managerial approaches, this relationship is being upgraded. In addition to a supervisor's direct manager, staff managers in other departments, such as legal and research, may also tell supervisors what to do. Functional executives, such as the controller and the human resource manager, may also interact with supervisors in handling certain activities. Often, supervisors have an upper manager who serves as **mentor** and acts as advocate, teacher, and advice giver.

External Relationships Supervisory managers must also deal with people outside the organization. Some of the people who must be served or catered to are the owners of the business, customers or clients, suppliers, higher-level union representatives, governmental authorities, and leaders of environmental and advocacy groups. These relationships can be quite difficult and frustrating for supervisors, who represent their organizations but usually do not have the authority to make decisions and enforce them.

mentor

An experienced manager who acts as an advocate and teacher for a younger, less experienced manager.

The Emerging Position of Supervisory Managers

7 *Discuss the emerging position of supervisory managers.*

Peter Drucker, world-renowned management consultant, author, and academic, correctly predicted 30 years ago that important changes in the role of supervisors would occur as a result of organizations' quest for improved quality. He noted that top management, of necessity, would conclude that the commitment and involvement of rank-and-file employees in improving quality would make them central in leading the quality charge. The result would be greater authority or empowerment for rank-and-file employees to make key decisions on their own, including such things as planning,

EXHIBIT 1-11
Changing Views of
Supervisor's Job

TRADITIONAL VIEW OF SUPERVISOR'S JOB	EMERGING VIEW OF SUPERVISOR'S JOB
Supervisor-focused work unit	Team-focused work unit
Dominant role	Supportive role
Technical skills emphasis	Facilitation skills emphasis
Seeking stability	Encouraging change
Telling, selling skills	Listening skills
Personal responsibility for results	Shared responsibility for results
Personal problem solving	Team problem solving
Narrow, vertical communication	Broader, horizontal, external communication
Fear, pressure used to motivate employees	Pride, recognition, growth used to motivate employees
Autocratic decision style	Participative decision style

determining the resources needed to perform their jobs best, and interfacing directly with people who affect their job, such as customers, suppliers, and service department personnel. Under this scheme, Drucker reasoned, the supervisory role would shift. No longer would supervisors effectively manage by fear and the pressure of "my way or the highway" management. Instead, they would assume supportive, facilitating roles as leaders, teachers, and coaches.

Several other trends have fueled the shift in supervisory roles that Drucker predicted. One is the trend toward leaner organizations with fewer levels of management. Another is organizations' present commitment to helping employees at all levels grow and develop. The resulting shift in the role of supervisory managers looks like that shown in Exhibit 1-11.

Self-Check

Does Jackie Schultz's style as a supervisor (see chapter preview) fit the traditional or emerging view of the supervisor's job?

No matter what type of role supervisors play, their goals are the same—getting out production, maintaining quality, holding down costs, maintaining high morale, and otherwise serving as management's representative while also acting as a spokesperson for employees. Although the knowledge and skills required today to perform most supervisory jobs have greatly increased from, say, 25 years ago, the central objective has remained the same—to obtain quality and quantity production while maintaining good human relationships.

A study of supervisors in two plants within the same company illustrates this point.[9] One plant followed traditional organizing practices: The supervisor had authority to supervise, to determine working conditions, to plan the work and schedule it, and to control it. In the other plant, "team advisors" were used instead of supervisors, with the focus being on facilitation rather than traditional direction of the work teams. As it turned out, "exceptional" and "average" supervisors at both plants, whether they were called supervisors or team advisors, exhibited characteristic behaviors.

"Exceptional" supervisors:

1. Were competent, caring, and committed both to getting the job done and to supporting their employees.
2. Pushed for high quality, provided clear direction, and motivated employees with timely, accurate feedback.
3. Willingly shared information with personnel, even if the system didn't require it.
4. Were committed to teamwork and employee participation in the department's decisions.
5. Shared skills and knowledge willingly and saw their role as one of coach rather than driver.
6. Understood what was involved beyond their own units, from the broader perspectives of the plant.
7. Took the initiative in implementing changes and new approaches.

Supervisors considered only "average" in the two differently organized plants also exhibited similar behaviors. These supervisors:

1. Set narrowly defined goals and had more specific performance standards.
2. Were less attuned to the plant's overall goals and focused more narrowly on their own unit.
3. Provided less information or feedback about performance to their work groups.
4. Were less flexible, less innovative, and less willing to change.
5. Maintained tighter controls and were uncomfortable practicing participative management.

Note that the "exceptional" supervisors exhibited behaviors that were more consistent with the emerging view of the supervisor's job (Exhibit 1-11).

Some Current Trends Challenging Supervisors

8 *Discuss some trends challenging supervisors.*

As shown earlier, today's supervisors must be prepared to adjust to the many current trends that will challenge their best performance. Among the more significant of these trends are (1) dealing with a more diverse workforce, (2) emphasizing team performance, (3) coping with exploding technology, (4) adjusting to occupational and industry shifts, (5) meeting global challenges, (6) improving quality and productivity, (7) improving ethical behavior, and (8) responding to crises.

Dealing with a More Diverse Workforce

diversity

Refers to the wide range of distinguishing employee characteristics, such as sex, age, race, ethnic origin, and other factors.

Diversity refers to the wide range of characteristics that distinguish employees, such as sex, age, race, ethnic origin, and other factors. At no time in our history has our workforce been so diverse, and this trend is expected to continue. Our comments here focus only on broad trends regarding gender, race, ethnicity, and age.

According to the U.S. Department of Labor, in 2008, white males represented 44.5 percent of all U.S. workers. However, the shifting U.S. population calls for decreasing numbers of whites, and by 2016, only about 27 percent will be white males. Hispanic employment will have increased by 32 percent, Asian employment by 28 percent, and African-American employment by 20 percent. Overall, women will account for almost 47 percent of the total workforce by 2016.[10] Although men and women are entering the workforce at about the same rate, men, who have been in the workforce longer, are retiring at a faster rate. Thus, like racial and ethnic minorities, women will continue to occupy many types of jobs and positions that were previously the domain of men, including supervisory and management positions.

More diverse work groups are becoming the norm in today's organizations.

glass ceiling

Invisible barrier that limits women from advancing in an organization.

Providing opportunities for women is particularly challenging, as there appears to be a **glass ceiling** in many organizations. These ceilings are considered invisible barriers that limit the advancement of women into higher levels of the organization. Thus, supervisors will be expected to design programs to attract and to develop women and minority employees and to provide them with a full range of opportunities for growth and development, the same as they do for all other employees.

Along with changes in gender, race, and ethnicity, the workforce is aging, as is the rest of the U.S. population. Those in the 55 or older age group made up 18 percent of the 2008 workforce, but their number will increase by more than 10 million employees and comprise 23 percent of the projected workforce by 2016.[11] Being able to effectively manage such diverse individuals requires greater supervisory skills than was the case with the more homogeneous work groups of past decades.

Emphasizing Team Performance

empowerment

Granting employees authority to make key decisions within their enlarged areas of responsibility.

As organizations seek to equip employees to function on their own, less direct supervision is required. This **empowerment** results in supervisors increasingly working with work groups or teams. These teams make suggestions for improvements in activities to make things run smoothly and to accomplish goals effectively.

When supervisors work with these teams, their roles are changed. No longer are they "bosses"; instead, they become leaders, facilitators, or **team advisors,** who share responsibility with the team for maintaining cost, quality, and prompt and effective delivery of products. Therefore, supervisors must provide further training to their teams to manage the production process more effectively.

team advisors

Share responsibility with team for cost, quality, and prompt delivery of products.

Coping with Exploding Technology

Most working Americans now earn their living by creating, processing, utilizing, and distributing information, and the computer revolution shows no sign of slowing. As innovations in computer and other communications technology have displaced thousands of workers who used different skills, new opportunities are opening up for those who have the required education, training, and temperament. Conversely, employees with outdated skills are being replaced in the workplace.

Computer-based information technologies continue to revolutionize how organizations function, affecting how tasks are performed, customers served, and people supervised.

Jackie Schultz (chapter preview) uses the Panera Bread intranet daily to access menu and product information, view her store's performance, and help train her associates. Panera's corporate software system can help forecast the number of customers based on historical data and even local weather forecasts. She uses e-mail and text messaging to communicate with her own manager and corporate personnel, in addition to associates and suppliers.

The primary effect of exploding technology on supervisors will be the need to keep personally abreast of changes that can potentially improve effectiveness, improve training of employees, and overcome employees' resistance to change. Change brings with it uncertainty, and because most people resist that which is uncertain, overcoming employee resistance to technological change becomes an increasing part of the supervisor's job.

Adjusting to Occupational and Industry Shifts

The previously mentioned technological advancements, along with cultural and marketing changes, have resulted in shifts in occupation and industry mixes. First, emphasis on the traditional industries has declined, with a concurrent shift toward more people-related activities such as services and marketing. Along with these shifts, many organizations have been **reinventing** themselves, dramatically changing their size, organizational structure, and markets. Many of the large companies have also been **reengineering** their activities. A common reengineering approach is to ask, "If we blew this place up and started over, what would we do differently to improve cost, quality, service, or speed? What should we eliminate? What can we do that would make things easier for our customers?" Not only are manufacturing companies reengineering, but so are many service companies, such as Sears and Taco Bell. These and other activities resulted in another trend, called **downsizing,** in which an organization strives to become leaner and more efficient by reducing its workforce and consolidating departments and work groups.

With the recession that began in 2008, downsizing has become necessary as organizations adapted to the resulting decreased demand for services and products. However, organizations also downsize to become more efficient. Results often include eliminating 10 to 20 percent—or more—of a company's jobs, especially at the management level. This means that frontline workers—and their supervisors—must handle more diverse tasks, think more creatively, and assume more responsibility. On the downside, those same people must work harder and therefore are under more pressure.

In an effort by organizations to avoid health care expenses and other costs associated with maintaining a large workforce, and to aid in transitions during downsizing, temporary workers have been in much demand. They account for about 5.7 million employees, or 4.1 percent of the U.S. workforce, with temporary services firms, such as Manpower and Kelly, becoming the number one U.S. job producer from 2004 to the projected 2014 period.[12]

Supervisors face numerous challenges when integrating temporaries into their teams of permanent employees, who often view temporaries as obstructing their own overtime, commissions, or higher pay. Temporaries, knowing their assignment are only for a few

---

reinventing

Organizations dramatically changing such elements as their size, organizational structure, and markets.

reengineering

"It means starting over.... It means asking and answering this question: If I were creating this company today, given what I know and given current technology, what would it look like?" Rethinking and redesigning processes to improve dramatically cost, quality, service, and speed.

downsizing

Eliminating unnecessary levels of management; striving to become leaner and more efficient by reducing the workforce and consolidating departments and work groups.

days, weeks, or months, typically know little about the organization and often show little inclination to be included as team members.

Meeting Continued Global Challenges

As business activities have become more global, those interested in supervisory management need to understand that they may have to operate in a one-world market. In fact, we estimate that up to one-half of all college graduates will work in some type of international activities in the future. Although we usually think of product exports as autos, movies, or computers, exports of financial information and other services are growing even faster.

A result of the global challenge is the large number of U.S. businesses, such as Random House, Magnavox, Wilson Sporting Goods, Uniroyal, and others, that are foreign owned. This changing ownership may lead to differing cultures and management styles, especially at supervisory levels. U.S. production facilities have also moved to Mexico, China, and other countries where low wages and high productivity lead to a competitive advantage. When supervisors move to those areas to supervise local workers, or when a foreign company acquires a domestic company, supervisors must learn to adapt to cultural differences and find ways to adjust to nontraditional styles.

Improving Quality and Productivity

No organizational theme has run deeper in the past decade than has the search for improved quality and productivity. Global competition has been the primary force behind this interest. The view of quality being embraced today reflects a comprehensive organizational approach to customer satisfaction through continuous improvement in organizational processes.[13] Almost all major firms similar to that of Panera Bread (chapter

Richard Vogel/AP Photo

Many U.S. production facilities have relocated to other countries. This trend will likely extend into the foreseeable future and will continue to have an effect on management ideologies and style.

preview), have adopted some form of quality management focus that addresses not only such processes as product design and manufacturing, but also marketing, purchasing, human resource management, and others. The supervisor, as management's direct link with employees, plays an important role in an organization's quality initiatives. It is the supervisor who is challenged to find ways to gain employee commitment to high-quality performance.

Equally important as achieving better quality is achieving improved productivity, which is a measurement of the amount of input needed to generate a given amount of output. Because productivity is the basic measurement of the efficiency of people and processes, it becomes a challenge for supervisors to improve through having people work better and smarter.

Improving Ethical Behavior

The downfall of major organizations, such as Enron, Arthur Andersen, Tyco, World-Com, HealthSouth, Bernard L. Madoff Investment Securities, and South Korea's Daewoo, has dramatically called attention to the issue of organization ethics. Although the problems in these companies resulted primarily from the behaviors of upper-level managers, the vulnerability of organizations to ethical misdeeds was clearly exposed. The result is that organizations have raised the "ethics" bar for all employees and management levels—including supervisors—for a wide range of issues, not just financial ones. These include accuracy and truthfulness in reporting results, reporting employee discrimination and sexual harassment, responsibility for supporting employee development, and due vigilance in reporting what can be viewed as unethical requests and behavior by others.

ethical dilemmas

Situations in which the supervisor is not certain of the correct behavior.

In this environment, supervisors will likely continue to face **ethical dilemmas** in which they are not sure of the correct action in a given situation involving themselves or their employees.[14]

Responding to Crises

Dealing with crises—events that have a major negative or potentially negative impact on entire organizations or on individual managers or supervisors—has always been part of managerial life. Recently, however, the scope of such events has been dramatically increasing. As the first management interface with operating employees, supervisors are particularly challenged to maintain production and morale during such times.

One such crisis was the collapse of the U.S. and global credit markets in 2008 and the economic recession that followed. Major corporations were humbled, including Citibank, Merrill Lynch, Lehman Brothers, General Motors, Chrysler, Circuit City, and many others, large and small. Consider the impact on employees of the auto companies, their suppliers, and their dealerships—uncertainty as to which brands, plants, and dealerships would remain viable. Downsizings have occurred throughout many large industries and organizations, such as Pepsico, Dow Chemical, Boeing, GE, and Disney, as well as smaller organizations. However, crises also take other forms, such as mergers and acquisitions, illegal mismanagement, and even acts of terrorism or natural disasters. The World Trade Center attacks of September 11, 2001, resulted in the indirect or direct loss of 55,000 jobs. Hurricane Katrina, which hit Louisiana, Mississippi, and Alabama in 2005, negatively affected 145,000 businesses and 2.5 million employees.[15]

Add to these extraordinary crises those associated with technological outages, equipment breakdowns, job accidents, incidents of workplace violence, and sudden loss of key suppliers/customers, and one can view the supervisor's role as increasingly one of addressing workplace crises.

Final Note: The Supervisor and Leading

In the pre-1990 years, managers who were adept at planning, organizing, staffing, and controlling—and not so effective in leading—could function effectively. Unlike the relatively stable environment then, today's management challenges make effective "leading" essential. Managers and supervisors must do more with fewer personnel, integrate more diverse team members, ask personnel to reach increasingly higher performance levels, and continuously implement change. No longer do they rely on authority as the primary means to achieve these goals, but on influence and persuasion. In short, their leadership is being tested at much higher levels than ever before, and the results have not been satisfactory, according to many critics of U.S. business, who say, "We need more leaders and fewer managers." What they really mean, given the new, dynamic environment, is that we need managers at all levels who are better at performing leadership.

Note the title of this book: *Supervisory Management: The Art of Inspiring, Empowering, and Developing People.* While coverage is provided of the other four management functions—planning, organizing, staffing, and controlling—the largest number of chapters are devoted to leading. These include a chapter on leadership itself as well as chapters on communicating, motivating, coaching, resolving conflict, implementing change, and managing teams, all of which are essential leadership tools.

Chapter Review

1. **Explain why management is needed in all organizations.**

   Management is needed whenever people form organizations. An organization is a group of people in a structured situation with a common purpose. People form organizations because they realize they can achieve more by working together than they can alone.

   Management is the process of working through people to achieve objectives by making effective decisions and by coordinating the development and use of scarce human, financial, and physical resources.

2. **Describe the different levels of management.**

   Large organizations usually have at least three levels of management. Top management oversees the overall operations—or a major segment of the organization or one of the basic organizational activities; middle management is responsible for a smaller part, such as a division or department; and supervisory management controls a smaller organizational unit.

3. **Discuss what managers do.**

   Managers at all levels do essentially the same things, but to different degrees. First, they perform the same functions—namely, planning, organizing, staffing, leading, and controlling. In performing these functions, managers engage in many varied and often unrelated activities that require them to play different roles. In playing interpersonal roles, a manager may act as a figurehead, a leader, or a liaison between different groups. Informational roles include acting as a monitor, disseminator, and/or spokesperson. Finally, decision-making roles require the manager to be an entrepreneur, a disturbance handler, a resource allocator, and/or a negotiator.

4. **Explain the basic skills required for effective management.**

   Effective managers need various skills to perform their functions and play their roles. Conceptual skills are needed in acquiring, interpreting, and analyzing information in a logical manner. Human relations skills involve understanding other people and interacting effectively with them. Administrative skills provide the ability to get things done by using other skills effectively. Technical skills consist of understanding and being able to supervise the processes, practices, or techniques required for specific jobs in the organization.

5. **Explain where supervisors come from.**

   By far most supervisory positions are filled through internal promotion. This has several advantages. Insiders understand the organization and its culture, and when promoted within their own department, the tasks, personnel, and other supervisors are familiar as well. Managers know something about the potential supervisor's capabilities through his or her record of accomplishment. In addition, internal promotion serves as a reward and incentive for present employees who desire to move up. Organizations can help to ensure a successful transition to supervision by identifying, assessing, and training potential supervisors and observing how they perform in temporary supervisory assignments.

6. **Clarify the different relationships supervisory managers have with others.**

   Supervisory managers are involved in at least three sets of relationships. First, they have personal relationships with their families and friends. Second, they have sometimes conflicting organizational relationships with lower-level employees, fellow supervisors, and higher levels of management. Third, they have external relationships with outsiders, such as business owners, customers or clients, suppliers, union representatives, governmental authorities, and leaders of environmental and advocacy groups.

7. **Discuss the emerging position of supervisory managers.**

   The role of supervisory managers has drastically changed during the past 25 years. In the traditional role, supervisors had strong technical expertise, had much authority over employees, and were key problem solvers. Pressure was often the tool used to motivate employees. The emerging role of supervisors has resulted from organizational trends toward greater organizational emphasis on quality, empowerment of employees, downsizing of management ranks, and commitment to employees' growth and development. These trends have given employees authority to plan their own work, to determine the resources they need, and to resolve job problems themselves. While still responsible for achieving results, supervisors have shifted toward leading, facilitating, and supporting employees, in contrast to the dominant, authority-laden traditional role.

8. **Discuss some trends challenging supervisors.**

   As the supervisory position grows in importance, it is becoming more complex because of many trends that are challenging supervisors' abilities to perform their jobs. The more important trends challenge supervisors to (1) deal with a more diverse workforce, (2) emphasize team performance, (3) cope with exploding technology, (4) adjust to occupational and industry shifts, (5) meet global challenges, (6) improve quality and productivity, (7) improve ethical behavior, and (8) respond to crises.

Key Terms

organization, p. 6

operations, p. 6

marketing, p. 6

financing, p. 6

management, p. 6

human resources, p. 6

physical resources, p. 7

financial resources, p. 7

authority, p. 8

responsibility, p. 8

top management, p. 8

middle management, p. 8

supervisory management, p. 9

managerial functions, p. 10

planning, p. 11

organizing, p. 11

staffing, p. 11

leading, p. 11

controlling, p. 11

roles, p. 11

conceptual skills, p. 16

human relations skills, p. 16

administrative skills, p. 16

technical skills, p. 17

emotional intelligence (EI), p. 17

relationships network, p. 19

union steward, p. 20

mentor, p. 21

diversity, p. 23

glass ceiling, p. 24

empowerment, p. 24

team advisors, p. 24

reinventing, p. 25

reengineering, p. 25

downsizing, p. 25

ethical dilemmas, p. 27

Questions for Review & Discussion

1. Why do people form organizations?
2. Identify the five functions every manager must perform and briefly explain each.
3. Why is management needed in organizations?
4. What are the three levels of management found in most large organizations? Describe each, giving its responsibilities.
5. Identify the four skills that managers need. Can someone be weak in one of these skill areas and still function effectively as a supervisor? Explain.

6. How are most supervisory positions filled? Explain why this is so.
7. What are the three types of supervisory relationships? Explain.
8. Identify each of the trends challenging today's supervisors and explain how each affects supervisors.
9. What are some reasons why "leading" is such a critical skill for supervisors and managers today?

Interpersonal Skill

Information

Skill Builder 1-1

Analysis of Supervisor/Management Job Descriptions

The purpose of this exercise is to have you view some actual job descriptions for supervisory/management positions as listed by real organizations.

Instructions:

1. Think about a supervisory/management position that interests you. The position must be a first-line supervisor/manager position of your choice. In addition, you may include the type of industry in your search, such as banking supervisor, nursing supervisor, recreation manager, hotel maintenance supervisor, etc.
2. Visit Monster.com at http://www.monster.com.
3. Type the name of the supervisory/management position in the "Search Jobs" box. You may leave blank the "U.S. Locations" box, which will result in a nationwide search. Clicking "Search" will likely result in numerous listings, depending on how general or specific your "Search Job" supervisory/management listing was.

(Continued)

Technology

4. Scroll the listings, viewing job titles and the names of the organizations for which there are position vacancies. Find a position/organization that looks of interest, and click the job title. You will then find the company's job description for the position.
5. Select and print out job descriptions for three different organizations, noting the differences in responsibilities, duties, and requirements. What conclusions about supervision/management and the organizations can be drawn from these?
6. Write a report, one-half to one page in length, to your instructor, commenting on the differences noted. Include printouts of the three job listings.
7. Be prepared to discuss your results in class, individually or in teams, as determined by your instructor.

Skill Builder 1-2

Interpersonal Skill

Information

The Personal Interest Inventory

Directions: Each of the following questions is worth a total of 3 points. For each question, assign more points to the response you prefer and fewer points, in order of preference, to the others. For example, if one response receives 3 points, the other two must receive 0; if one receives 2 points, then the others must receive 1 and 0; or each may receive 1 point. Enter your scores in the Score Matrix.

1. Which activity interests you most?

     1 a. Working with your hands
     2 b. Working with people
     0 c. Reading books

2. Which skills would you invest time in learning?

     0 a. Research and writing
     2 b. Organizing and leading
     1 c. Crafts and art

3. Which job activities would you enjoy most?

     0 a. Counseling and coaching
     2 b. Building and doing
     1 c. Thinking and planning

4. Which trait is most characteristic of you?

     2 a. Helper
     1 b. Doer
     0 c. Scholar

5. Which would you most enjoy doing?

     2 a. Talking with people
     0 b. Writing a book
     1 c. Building a house

6. How do you prefer to use your spare time?

     0 a. Outdoor projects
     2 b. Social activities
     1 c. Thinking

7. Which of these traits is most important to you?

     1 a. Physical coordination
     2 b. Ability to deal with people
     0 c. Mental ability

8. Which jobs most reflect your interests?

     2 a. Teacher, social worker, counselor
     1 b. Engineer, surveyor, craftsman
     0 c. Researcher, historian, author

(Continued)

9. Which ability is your strongest?

___0___ a. Communication skills

___1___ b. Creative thinking

___2___ c. Physical skills

10. Which tasks do you perform best?

___1___ a. Operating and maintaining

___0___ b. Communicating and motivating

___2___ c. Developing and planning

11. Which occupation interests you most?

___2___ a. Pilot

___1___ b. Judge

___0___ c. Politician

12. Which of the following is most interesting to you?

___1___ a. Helping others

___1___ b. Thinking things through

___1___ c. Using your hands

13. Which skills could you learn with the least effort?

___0___ a. Leading and negotiating

___2___ b. Artwork and handicrafts

___1___ c. Language and theoretical reasoning

14. What tasks appeal to you most?

___2___ a. Developing new theories

___0___ b. Helping people with problems

___1___ c. Developing a skill

15. What assignment appeals to you most?

___1___ a. Working with ideas

___1___ b. Working with people

___1___ c. Working with things

16. Which is your greatest attribute?

___2___ a. Creativity

___0___ b. Competence

___1___ c. Sensitivity

17. For which occupation do you have a natural talent?

___1___ a. Counselor

___2___ b. Builder

___0___ c. Scientist

18. Which subject interests you most?

___3___ a. Practical arts

___0___ b. Philosophy

___0___ c. Human relations

19. To which group would you prefer to belong?

___0___ a. Scientific society

___1___ b. Outdoor group

___2___ c. Social club

20. How do you like to work?

___0___ a. In a group, discussing and recommending solutions

___2___ b. Alone, using ideas and theories

___1___ c. Alone, using tools and materials

SCORE MATRIX

QUESTION	THINGS	PEOPLE	IDEAS
1.	a.	b.	c.
2.	c.	b.	a.
3.	b.	a.	c.
4.	b.	a.	c.
5.	b.	c.	a.

(Continued)

QUESTION	THINGS	PEOPLE	IDEAS
6.	a.	b.	c.
7.	a.	b.	c.
8.	b.	a.	c.
9.	b.	c.	a.
10.	a.	b.	c.
11.	a.	c.	b.
12.	b.	c.	a.
13.	b.	a.	c.
14.	c.	b.	a.
15.	c.	b.	a.
16.	c.	a.	b.
17.	b.	a.	c.
18.	a.	c.	b.
19.	b.	c.	a.
20.	c.	a.	b.
	TOTAL	TOTAL	TOTAL

Instructions: The Personal Interest Inventory should give you some insight into the strengths you would bring to a management position. Basically, if you enjoy an activity, it is likely to be something that you do well. The three areas shown in the Score Matrix—things, people, and ideas—correspond to the following skills, which managers must use in doing their job:

Things: Technical skills
People: Human relations skills
Ideas: Conceptual skills

1. After scoring your inventory, break into groups of three to five and discuss your profiles. To what extent are they similar? Different? Are any of the areas dominant in the group? Underrepresented? Discuss.
2. Generalize about the kinds of supervisory jobs that might call for

   a. High technical skill
   b. High human relations skill
   c. High conceptual skill

3. Are your answers on this inventory consistent with the type of management job that you have in mind? If there are inconsistencies, what do they mean?

Source: Based on an exercise designed by Billie Stockton, Anita Bullock, and Anne Locke, Northern Kentucky University, 1981.

Interpersonal Skill

Information

Skill Builder 1-3

Effective and Ineffective Supervisors

Instructions

1. Think of all the supervisors for whom you've ever worked—part time or full time. If you have not worked for a supervisor, consider some of your teachers or perhaps a coach.
2. Select two—one who was most effective and one who was least effective—and list the behaviors of each.
3. In groups of three to five classmates, share your lists and discuss. Were there common behaviors? Select a spokesperson to present your discussion results to the class.

Coach X: Effective Hospital Administrator?*

Assume that you are a member of the search committee that is evaluating applicants for the position of administrator of a 300-bed, community-owned hospital in your city. In examining the applicants' resumes, you note that most have had experience in health care settings, many having previous experiences as administrators or assistant administrators.

One application, however, is quite different. It is from one of the most successful college football coaches in the country, someone we will call X. Being a sports fan, you have seen this person many times on national television as his teams have consistently placed in the top 10 NCAA ratings. He has won five national championships in the past 15 years. His school leads major colleges in athlete graduation rates; throughout his 30-year coaching career, his programs have not been charged with a single NCAA violation. He has won the national coach-of-year title four times. He has mentored countless assistant coaches who themselves have become successful. His former players have been among the NFL's biggest stars. He has charisma and is a gifted motivational speaker. No one is more highly respected in the profession. Serving also as athletic director during the past five years, he oversees a $57 million budget and 400 employees, and the university's athletic department is one of the most profitable in the country. His university's sports teams annually win the award given to the university having the best overall team performance across all sports. He has served with distinction as head of the National

Association of College Coaches and is often selected to represent his peer coaches on significant NCAA issues. Presidents Bush and Obama have named him to important presidential commissions. He has often been courted by Democrats and Republicans as an easily winnable gubernatorial or U.S. Senate candidate. Why is he interested in the position of head administrator of the hospital? In his application, he states that it was always his ambition to change careers by age 55. While acknowledging his lack of experience in the health care field other than through hospital stays with family, players, and friends, he would love the challenge of hospital management.

INSTRUCTIONS:

1. Respond to the following question: Would X be someone whom you would consider as a viable potential candidate for the hospital administrator position, despite his limited technical expertise?
   ____Yes ____No   Why?
2. Suppose that the position being sought was that of supervisor of the hospital's computer technology department. Would your answer be the same? Why?
3. In groups of four to six, discuss your answers, and be prepared to report highlights of your discussion to the overall class.

*Any association of Coach X as presented in this case with a real person or persons is coincidental.

PART 2

Planning and Organizing

2

Fundamentals of Planning

Radius Images / Jupiter Images

Effective planning is critical to personal and professional success, whether you are dealing with a short-term project or the long-term objectives of an organization like Waterkeeper Alliance, featured in the chapter preview.

LEARNING OBJECTIVES

After reading and studying this chapter, you should be able to:

1. **Discuss some of the more important points about planning.**

2. **Explain the steps involved in planning.**

3. **Explain how planning differs at top, middle, and supervisory management levels.**

4. **Explain how the hierarchy of objectives works.**

5. **Discuss some important guidelines in setting objectives.**

6. **Differentiate the various kinds of standing and single-use plans.**

7. **Draw a simple PERT chart.**

If you don't know where you're going, any road will get you there.
—*Author Unknown*

After you have made up your mind just what you are going to do, it is a good time to do it.

—*Josh Billings*

CHAPTER OUTLINE

Preview

EFFECTIVE PLANNING: A NONPROFIT PERSPECTIVE Now that you have seen some of the roles played by supervisors and some of the challenges they face, it is time for you to see how they play these roles and meet these challenges.

Waterkeeper Alliance, an international, grassroots, nonprofit organization, "connects and supports local Waterkeeper programs to provide a voice for waterways and their communities worldwide .... Each Waterkeeper program reflects the needs of the waterbody and community it represents. The common thread for each Waterkeeper program is a full-time person who serves as the Waterkeeper, the public advocate for that body of water."[1]

Nonprofit organizations, such as Waterkeeper Alliance (WA), face many similar challenges to those dealt with in profit-driven businesses. While the means of facing these challenges may differ depending on the organization's core mission, almost any organization is fundamentally concerned with how to fulfill its mission while increasing revenues, keeping costs down, and maintaining positive cash flows, especially during flat or declining economic periods. Typically, local nonprofit directors' and staff members' planning efforts are critical to achieving positive results on a national or international scale.

Let's take a closer look at one of WA's 191 local affiliates to see how their planning process helps manage these challenges to fulfill its mission.

Casi Callaway has been the Director of Mobile Baykeeper (MBK), formally known as Mobile Bay Watch, since 1998. During the early days, Casi's primary goals related to affiliating with a larger, recognized organization and developing a strong, active board. With regard to the first objective, the MBK mission of "providing citizens the means to protect the beauty, health and heritage of the Mobile Bay watershed"[2] fit well with WA's mission, so one of Casi's earliest planning efforts was to apply to be an affiliated member of WA. In 1999, WA accepted MBK's proposal, which was an important point in the nonprofit's early stage of growth because a key advantage of this international association was Casi's ability to float a question or plan by a cadre of seasoned veterans who have likely had the same or similar experiences to gather their feedback.[3]

In addition to WA's assistance, Casi recognized the need for a knowledgeable, connected, and active board. For an environmentally focused nonprofit operating in a predominantly conservative geographic region, this could have potentially been a "deal breaker." However, Ms. Callaway is a tenacious, intelligent, persevering, and high-energy young woman who quite adeptly analyzed the situation and chose to focus on commonalities that could ultimately align environmental and conservative interests alike. Her plan was to recruit conservative men, well known and respected in their local communities, who were also avid fishermen and hunters. Her reasoning was sound: Who is likely to be more concerned about the quality of the local watersheds and animal habitats than outdoorsmen keenly interested in preserving the wilderness for their children and grandchildren? The strategy worked like magic. Her efforts have been so well received that, over time, Casi has diversified the board membership to include women and environmentalists. She even recruited Jimmy Buffet, a local favorite songwriter, to be an honorary board member and give a benefit concert![4]

Ms. Callaway has played an instrumental role in transforming the organization from a loosely organized coalition to an operationally sound community stakeholder. During 2004 to 2006, MBK operated with a staff of two. As the organization became more formal in terms of structures, policies, and procedures, it became apparent to Casi that MBK needed to focus its efforts on planning strategically. Specifically, a formal vision statement identifying key performance areas, which could then be linked to long-, intermediate-, and short-term goals and plans, was necessary to manage properly the organization's growth and direction for the next five years. She decided to contact an external consultant to facilitate MBK's strategic planning process.

Board involvement is voluntary, so efficient use of members' time is important to encourage continued participation. Therefore, Casi and the consultant worked together to develop a series of structured questions to be sent to the board members to gather relevant data prior to the one-day strategic planning session. The questions ranged from "What do you see as MBK's strengths and weaknesses?" to "What do you perceive the appropriate size of MBK in terms of membership, scope of budget, and number of staff?" Once the data were collected and tabulated, the key performance areas emerged to form the core agenda for the planning event. Not surprisingly for an organization in the growth stage of development, guidelines for effective decision making, organizational structure (in terms of board size/responsibilities and staff capacity), membership development, marketing, and fundraising were the top performance concerns identified. Long- (3 to 5 years), intermediate- (1 to 3 years), and short-term (1 week to 1 year) goals for each of the performance areas were also provided by the board members and were included in the initial report used during the planning event.

At the retreat, which was held offsite at a board member's bay house, the board was organized into teams based on interests and expertise to address each of these broad performance areas and associated goals. The idea was for each team to take an initial stab at "fleshing out" the performance area by prioritizing the goals, linking them into a hierarchy (broad/long term to specific/short term), creating goals statements (communicating what and why), and developing initial action plans (identifying how and when), all of which were presented to the full board for feedback, modifications, and additional work. At the end of the retreat, each team was tasked to begin implementing the agreed upon short-term plans, with the expectation of giving a progress report at the next board meeting to ensure goal accomplishment in each major area.[5]

Five years after the initial planning event, tremendous strides have been made in all key performance areas. According to Casi, one of the biggest is the guidelines that were developed to improve decision making at the program level. Once these decision guidelines were implemented, the process of prioritizing and choosing among the issues and campaigns became much more efficient and effective. Another improvement is a more inclusive, broad-based board. Members are more diverse as far as geographic locations, professional backgrounds, and gender. Broad board scope provides additional expertise and continuous learning opportunities for Casi and her staff, ranging from improved financial accounting to enhanced marketing and public relations strategies. To illustrate, MBK had approximately 2,500 members at the time of the strategic planning retreat. Due to enhanced marketing and fundraising efforts, today membership levels exceed 3,500—that equates to roughly 250 or so new members a year!

As a result, the MBK budget has grown approximately 50 percent over the past five years. Collectively, the strides made in these key performance areas have enabled Casi to expand her staff from two full-time members (in 2004) to four full-time and two part-time staff members, which translates into additional productivity. None of this would have been possible, according to Casi, without effective planning! In fact, at the time of this publication, MBK was embarking on another formal strategic planning event to be ready for the next five years.[6]

Many managers see themselves as being strictly "fire fighters"—handling first this problem, next another, and then another. As the chapter preview illustrates, supervisors in all types of organizations and at all levels must become more proficient at planning— perhaps the most neglected function of management at all levels.

Planning involves selecting future courses of action for your organization and deciding how to achieve the desired results. This chapter builds on that definition. We focus on the first of the management functions—planning—and show that much planning must precede effective empowerment of employees and achievement of improved quality.

Some Important Points about Planning

1 *Discuss some of the more important points about planning.*

Suppose you and a group of friends decide to take a weekend camping trip. Effective planning requires answers to the following kinds of questions: What constraints impact the group, such as the distance you can travel or the funds you have available? What activities most interest the group, such as hiking, boating, fishing, or mountain biking? What camping sites are available to choose from, and which activities are offered at each? What supplies and equipment will be needed, and does the group have the means to obtain them? Only after questions such as these are answered can you do more effective planning. Then your group can decide when and where to go, what time to leave, who will bring what, and perhaps even when to schedule your planned activities. Your plan should also anticipate contingencies such as weather and occupancy of sites. Should rain be forecast, might you postpone the trip to a later date? If not, might you bring rain gear or have games available for indoor use? Might you reserve a site in advance or, if not, have a nearby backup site in mind?

As you can see, the trip's effectiveness depends greatly on the quality of planning that you and your group put into it. Supervisory planning works much the same way. Supervisors do planning—both routine and detailed—as an ongoing part of their jobs. This may include plans for scheduling work, developing and living within budgets, making job assignments, and so on. They must also plan for major events that happen infrequently, such as when a department manager of a major department store plans for an annual inventory count or when a pizza store manager knows a week in advance that she must deliver 300 freshly baked pizzas to a convention of 600 people.

Basic Steps Involved in Planning

2 *Explain the steps involved in planning.*

Planning means deciding what will be done in the future; in other words, planning is forward looking. A manager must have a lot of discipline to set aside the time needed

EXHIBIT 2-1
The Three Planning
Steps

to solve present problems and to plan for the future. As you can see, much planning is intellectual—a "between the ears" activity that involves hard work. Effective managers must use conceptual, human relations, administrative, and technical skills. Planning is normally an example of a conceptual skill, but it also requires other skills, especially to get the plans adopted and implemented.

Planning covers a wide variety of activities, from simple to complex, and from short to long term. In all cases, however, the three basic planning steps are:

1. Setting an objective or goal.
2. Identifying and assessing present and future conditions affecting the objective.
3. Developing a systematic approach to achieve the objective (the *plan*).

These are shown in Exhibit 2-1.

Three additional steps must also be taken to achieve effectively the objective or goal established in step 1, although they are not exactly planning steps. These include the following:

4. Implementing the plan (organizing, leading, staffing).
5. Monitoring the plan's implementation (controlling).
6. Evaluating the plan's effectiveness (controlling).

These last three steps illustrate how closely planning is related to the other managerial functions, especially controlling.

The *first step in planning—setting an objective or goal*—addresses the issue of what one hopes to achieve. Notice in the chapter preview that the strategic planning process involved identifying the organization's key performance areas as well as long-, intermediate-, and short-term goals associated with each.

The *second planning step—identifying and assessing present and future conditions affecting the objective*—recognizes important variables that can influence objectives. In the camping trip example given earlier, these would include such factors as equipment needed, weather, and site availability. Since planning involves the future, certain assumptions about the future must be made.

The *third step of planning is developing a systematic approach to achieve the objective*. This third step becomes the *plan*. It addresses such issues as the how, when, who, and where of the plan. The plan's complexity and importance are major factors in determining how formal and detailed this final step must be. For example, a plan to build a new 200-bed–wing expansion for a hospital would be much more formal and detailed than a plan to shut down a paper-making machine for routine maintenance. Many daily plans are routine, however, and are carried about in supervisors' heads rather than being committed to paper.

Planning Is Most Closely Related to Controlling

Of the managerial functions, planning is probably most closely related to controlling. As you will see in more detail in a later chapter, the steps in controlling are as follows:

1. Setting performance goals or norms.
2. Measuring performance.

3. Comparing performance with goals.
4. Analyzing results.
5. Taking corrective action as needed.

Note carefully the first step in the preceding list. It involves planning!

Many Managers Tend to Neglect Planning

Poor planning results in disorganized and uncoordinated activities, thus wasting time, labor, and money, but since thinking is often more difficult than doing, many managers —including supervisors—tend to slight planning. It is very tempting to forgo thinking about the future in order to get busy performing a task or solving present work problems. Thus, it is not unusual for a supervisor to spend the day fighting one "fire" after another—seemingly never catching up. The result is frequently unsatisfactory. Consider the following example:

> *Henrietta Green, one of my supervisors, had a hectic schedule and was about to be driven up a wall. She said: "Today I had three no-shows because of the weather, and my department is absolutely swamped. I'm pitching in myself, but I've also got to conduct a tour for some of our home office staff personnel after lunch. I'm supposed to meet with our industrial relations people on a case that goes to arbitration next week. To cap it off, Barbara Brown is asking for a transfer out of the department and wants to talk about it today. She and two of the other workers can't get along. This afternoon, I've got to have some important figures ready for the cost accounting department. On top of all this, I'm supposed to supervise my 19 people, three of whom are new hires who are just being broken in. What a day! But recently, they all seem to be like this."*

Is it any wonder that this supervisor forgoes planning when her typical daily schedule is so demanding? Ironically, many of the short-run crises that confront supervisors could be greatly eased by proper planning. As shown in Exhibit 2-2, when a supervisor devotes too little time to planning, short-run problems are likely to result, including impossible deadlines, unforeseen obstacles, crises, and crash programs. These problems preoccupy the supervisor, leaving little time to devote to planning—and the cycle goes on and on!

contingency planning

Thinking in advance about possible problems or changes that might arise and having anticipated solutions available.

Contingency Planning Anticipates Problems

It is important for supervisors to build flexibility into their plans by preparing contingency plans. **Contingency planning** means having anticipated solutions in advance for

EXHIBIT 2-2
The Nonplanner's Cycle

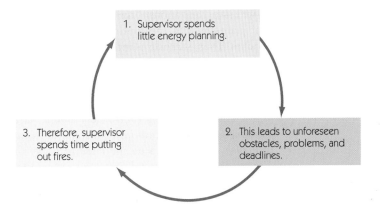

1. Supervisor spends little energy planning.

2. This leads to unforeseen obstacles, problems, and deadlines.

3. Therefore, supervisor spends time putting out fires.

problems or changes that may arise and being prepared to deal with them smoothly when they do arise.

> Consider the emphasis on contingency planning and preparedness after Hurricane Katrina hit the Gulf Coast region in August of 2005. Many federal, state, and local governmental entities were harshly criticized for their ill-preparedness and response to the storm and the devastation that occurred. Due to increased public scrutiny, government at all levels is addressing future potential disasters and developing more effective emergency response plans (ERP).

> The city of Fairhope, a resort retirement community situated along the shores of Mobile Bay in south Alabama, is one such municipality. The city's mayor and departmental managers have learned through experience with hurricanes Frederick (1979), Ivan (2004), and Katrina (2005) the importance of having contingency plans in place to address a variety of possible problems. According to James Gillespie, the city's Administrative Superintendent, "The public sector has to deal with expectations that are different from those in the private sector. A municipality must aim to accommodate and assist all citizens, which involves proactively developing an emergency response plan for the worst scenario imaginable and devising alternative options based on that position. Dedication and love for your town is what drives city employees—you have to take care of your town and plan for your citizens, you can't afford to wait and react. The city hires people to do a job with the caveat that they must be willing to operate outside their job descriptions when an emergency arises."[7]

You might think of contingency planning as the responses to the "What if … ?" questions that describe serious events. Thus, contingency planning separates effective managers from ineffective ones. Proper anticipation of a problem may prevent it from happening. If you are to be a good contingency planner, you will need to ask yourself the following questions and find answers to them:

1. What might happen that could cause problems within my area of responsibility?
2. What can I do to prevent these events from happening?
3. If these events do occur, what can I do to minimize their effect?
4. Have similar situations occurred in the past? If so, how were they handled?

In Exhibit 2-3, you can see how managers at FEMA utilize contingency planning to help improve their effectiveness.

scenario planning

Anticipating alternative future situations and developing courses of action for each alternative.

A variation of contingency planning is **scenario planning**, which involves anticipating alternative future situations and developing courses of action for each alternative. Scenario planning has a long-term focus and is typically associated with planning at upper levels within organizations. Front-line managers are becoming more involved with this type of planning with the continuing emphasis on utilizing participatory management approaches. Thus, scenario planning is a necessary tool for most managers today.[8] Consider the City of Fairhope again and what issues it now has to be prepared for that were not critical issues 15 years ago.

> To enhance the police department's flexibility and response in the field, the department uses a disaster planning control tool similar to a yes/no command flow chart when planning for future critical incident scenarios. Once a possible scenario has been identified, such as a gunman on the loose in a city's hospital or at one of its schools, the disaster planning command center is used to establish responsibilities, devise reporting relationships, identify assigned areas, preset critical contact information, and allocate vehicles for transportation. Next, critical incident drills are performed to simulate a gunman on the loose. The officers soon realized the significance of scenario planning

EXHIBIT 2-3
FEMA Tricks Out New
Trailers for Next
Disaster[9]

EMMITSBURG, Md.—They're clean, shutterless and decorated with a rainbow of beige hues. They're mobile homes built for future disaster victims and, so far, have safe levels of formaldehyde.

The six newly designed mobile homes were rolled out Thursday by federal officials to replace the much-criticized travel trailers used in the wake of Hurricane Katrina in 2005. Many people said living in the earlier models made them sick.

The mobile homes—including one travel trailer—were built as part of a program to develop new disaster housing solutions for the Federal Emergency Management Agency.

After Katrina, 1 million people lost their homes in Louisiana and Mississippi. FEMA sent thousands of mobile homes into the region only to learn later of high levels of formaldehyde, a chemical used in the glue for building materials that can lead to breathing problems and is also believed to cause cancer. Residents of FEMA-issued trailers reported frequent headaches, nosebleeds and other ailments.

The new models—which range in price from $45,000 to $75,000—were toured by federal officials in Emmitsburg, Md. The trailers have been tested and meet FEMA standards for safe formaldehyde levels.

Students at the National Emergency Training Center in Emmitsburg will live in the units and test them for the next six to 12 months, said Jack Schuback, the FEMA official who is overseeing the project.

One thing they will watch is whether formaldehyde levels increase over time. Schuback said cooking and smoking can sometimes increase the level of formaldehyde in the air.

There is no industry standard for the amount of formaldehyde allowed in travel trailers. The government sets standards for indoor air quality for materials used to build mobile homes, but not for travel trailers.

Government tests in 2007 found an average of 77 parts formaldehyde per billion parts of air in FEMA trailers issued after the 2005 hurricanes. FEMA's standard for the new trailers is 16 parts formaldehyde or less per billion parts of air.

Getting these units built without using much formaldehyde was one of the challenges, Schuback said.

One of the prototypes—the D&D Hybrid Park Model—is two bedrooms, one bathroom with walls insulated with 100 percent sheep wool. The wool absorbs the formaldehyde, said D&D chief executive officer Bill Hanblin.

The travel trailer prototype—made by Texas-based Frontier RV—is the first to have a device that circulates fresh outside air into the trailer, said Ryan Buras, a housing program specialist at FEMA. This one-bedroom trailer is also handicap-accessible with a bathroom three times larger than the typical travel trailer bathroom.

The other four units are made by Arkel International LLC of Baton Rouge, La., Heston Group of New Orleans, Lexington Homes Inc., of Lexington, Miss., and TL Industries of Elkhart, Ind.

If a major hurricane or flood left people homeless—as happened after Katrina—FEMA could order units similar to those being tested, Schuback said.

The government's disaster housing strategy—which was adopted during the Bush administration—says disaster victims can be housed in trailers only as a last resort, even though Bush officials promised to never use them again. The strategy says that if mobile homes are used, they must meet FEMA's new standard and disaster victims can use them no longer than six months.

By FEMA's count, 2,570 trailers and mobile homes are still being used in Louisiana and 1,500 in Mississippi to house victims of hurricanes Katrina and Rita.

Source: Eileen Sullivan, "FEMA tricks out new trailers for next disaster," Associated Press, May 14, 2009. Reprinted by permission.

when a real situation arose; in less than six minutes, the police were at the scene and ready to respond to a gunman loose in Thomas Hospital. The disaster command planning center concept has been so successful for the city's police force that other department managers like Dan McCrory have picked up on it—"It provides preplanning information at your fingertips! Fairhope is in the vector for jumbo jets flying to Brookley Field. If a plane crashed in Fairhope, we would need fire, morgue, triage, and other support from nearby cities and towns. The command center has been very useful in helping us think through what we would do if this situation actually happened."[10]

Companies must have contingency plans for providing supplies, parts, and other necessities in the aftermath of a disaster, such as a flood, earthquake, or hurricane.

strategic planning

Has longer time horizons, affects the entire organization, and deals with its interface to its external environment.

mission

Defines the purpose the organization serves and identifies its services, products, and customers.

3 *Explain how planning differs at top, middle, and supervisory management levels.*

objectives

The purposes, goals, and desired results for the organization and its parts.

strategies

The activities by which the organization adapts to its environment to achieve its objectives.

operational planning

Consists of intermediate- and short-term planning.

Planning Differs at Different Management Levels

Management planning differs according to the level of management at which it occurs, as shown in Exhibit 2-4. Top managers are more involved in **strategic planning**, which has longer time horizons, affects the entire organization, and deals with the organization's interaction with its external environment. Strategic plans include:

1. The **mission**, which defines the fundamental purpose the organization attempts to serve and identifies its services, products, and customers.
2. The overall **objectives** that drive the organization, such as profitability, customer satisfaction, employee relationships, environmental protection, or other critically important ends to be sought.
3. **Strategies**, the activities by which the organization adapts to the important factors that comprise its external environment, including consumers, customers, suppliers, competitors, and social, political, economic, and technological conditions.

Middle and supervisory level managers are more concerned with operational planning. **Operational planning** consists of intermediate- and short-term planning that facilitates achievement of the long-term strategic plans set at higher levels. As shown in Exhibit 2-4, these plans operationalize the plans made at higher levels and are much narrower in scope and much shorter term than those formed at higher levels. As one supervisor related:

Planning? Sure, I spend time planning. But most of my department's goals, objectives, and schedules are handed down to me from above. My planning is more along these lines: How can I get better performance from my work group members? How can I cut down turnover and absenteeism? Given my group's workload for the week, or for the day, what's the best way to attack it? Whom should I assign to various jobs?

EXHIBIT 2-4
Planning at Three
Management Levels

LEVEL	PLANNING PERIODS	WHAT IS PLANNED
Top managers	Strategic long-term, intermediate-range plans of 1 to 5 or more years	Growth rate Competitive strategies New products Capital investments
Middle managers	Intermediate- and short- range plans of 1 month to 1 year	How to improve scheduling and coordination How to exercise better control at lower levels
Supervisors	Short-range plans of 1 day, 1 week, 1 to 6 months	How to accomplish performance objectives How to implement new policies, work methods, and work assignments How to increase efficiency (in costs, quality, etc.) Employee and supervisor vacations

Take last week, for example. Four of my people were out—two sick and two on vacation—and I had to do a lot of planning in order to figure out who'd work where and when. Things seemed to go a lot more smoothly because I'd put in some time anticipating the problems. I've learned to plan on having a few people out "sick" on the opening day of hunting season!

As you can see, all managers need to plan, regardless of their position in the hierarchy. Although planning at the supervisory level generally is less complex and involves less uncertainty than planning at higher levels, it is still crucial that such planning be done effectively.

Self–Check

What are some other examples of events for which supervisory managers must plan?

Importance of Setting Objectives

Objectives are crucial to effective planning. As one of the opening quotations in this chapter implied, only if you first know where you are heading can you effectively plan to get there.

What Are Objectives?

As previously stated, objectives are the goals that provide the desired purposes and results for an organization and its parts. Plans are aimed at achieving objectives. They answer the question "What do I want to accomplish?"

Is there a difference between an *objective* and a *goal*? Management experts disagree on this matter. Some say that goals are broad and nonspecific, whereas objectives are narrow and specific. Others reverse the distinction just given. Still others do not distinguish between the two. Since the terms *goal* and *objective* are often used interchangeably, we will treat them as synonyms in this book.

Objectives Serve as a Stimulus for Motivation and Effort

If you follow organized sports, you know that athletes frequently have objectives they try to achieve. For example, baseball players may strive to hit .300; basketball players may attempt to average 20 points; and football quarterbacks seek to average 50 percent pass completions. A weekend golfer may step up to the first tee with an 85 in mind. A Friday-night league bowler may shoot for an average of 150. Just as athletes are motivated by goals or objectives, so are people in the world of work.

> *Richard Ost owns three small drugstores in some of Philadelphia's most notorious neighborhoods. Yet he brings in over $5 million each year. His primary goal is to operate more efficiently to serve his customers better. "I didn't go to pharmacy school to count to 100," said Richard Ost, pharmacist and owner of the Philadelphia Pharmacy. He employs three pharmacists and fills 750 prescriptions a day, an astounding 292% over the national average, for 3,800 customers each month. Since he has a small staff, he relies on an automated pharmacy workflow system that makes it possible for him to handle his heavy volume. "The more that technology can take over basic operations and facilitate communications with other health care professionals, the better job I can do serving patients," noted Ost.[11]*

In summary, objectives provide a stimulus for effort; they give people something to strive for. If Ost had no set goal—if he simply planned to go out and sell—he would have no benchmark for determining whether he was doing well or poorly.

Hierarchy of Objectives

4 *Explain how the hierarchy of objectives works.*

hierarchy of objectives

A network with broad goals at the top level of the organization and narrower goals for individual divisions, departments, or employees.

In any organization, objectives are first needed at the top management level. Once top management has determined broad objectives or goals, other levels of the organization, including supervisory management, reflect these in objectives or goals of their own, thus creating a **hierarchy of objectives**. Exhibit 2-5 presents a hypothetical hierarchy of objectives for a firm, Computronix.

Computronix's overall organizational objectives are increased profits, improved market share, new product introductions, and cost effectiveness, as well as others not mentioned. Note how one of these, the cost-effectiveness objective, is reflected at progressively lower organizational levels. At the division level, the Computronix's Dixon Division general manager's objectives address cost effectiveness by seeking a 5 percent reduction in production costs and implementing a new inventory control system. The Dixon Division maintenance department reflects the plant's 5 percent production cost reduction through the objectives of reduction of equipment downtime, and the work unit objectives reflect the maintenance department head's objectives, and so on down the line. The diagram in Exhibit 2-5, though simplified, shows how the individual worker can be linked to top corporate levels through objective setting.

Unified Planning through Objectives

unified planning

Coordinating departments to ensure harmony rather than conflict or competition.

A major advantage of organizational objectives is that they give managers at lower levels guidance in developing their own operational plans and coordinating their own activities. Ideally, top management's objectives should give tactical plans at lower levels unity of purpose. **Unified planning** means ensuring that plans at all organizational levels are in harmony, rather than at cross-purposes, with one another. Unified planning is especially

EXHIBIT 2-5
Hierarchy of Objectives for Computronix

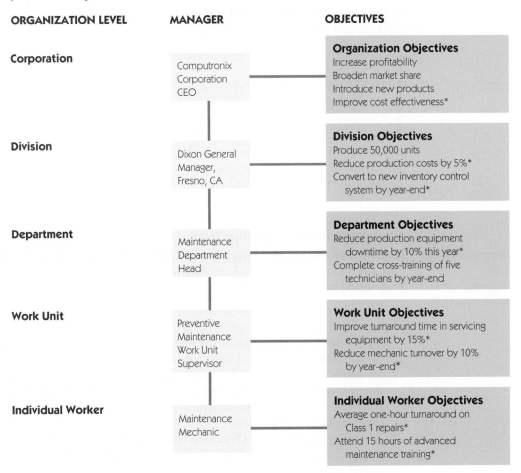

ORGANIZATION LEVEL	MANAGER	OBJECTIVES
Corporation	Computronix Corporation CEO	**Organization Objectives** — Increase profitability; Broaden market share; Introduce new products; Improve cost effectiveness*
Division	Dixon General Manager, Fresno, CA	**Division Objectives** — Produce 50,000 units; Reduce production costs by 5%*; Convert to new inventory control system by year-end*
Department	Maintenance Department Head	**Department Objectives** — Reduce production equipment downtime by 10% this year*; Complete cross-training of five technicians by year-end
Work Unit	Preventive Maintenance Work Unit Supervisor	**Work Unit Objectives** — Improve turnaround time in servicing equipment by 15%*; Reduce mechanic turnover by 10% by year-end*
Individual Worker	Maintenance Mechanic	**Individual Worker Objectives** — Average one-hour turnaround on Class 1 repairs*; Attend 15 hours of advanced maintenance training*

*Objectives directly linked to improved cost effectiveness.

important where coordination is required among departments or work units. Many supervisors are extremely dependent on other departments in accomplishing their own objectives. Continuing with our hypothetical example in Exhibit 2-5, a lack of unified planning at Computronix's Dixon Division has led to difficulties!

"This is ridiculous! They are trying to cut me down," stormed Juan Fernandez, supervisor of the processing department at the Dixon Division. The division was under the gun to reach its monthly production quota, and Fernandez's department absorbed a lot of the pressure. Fernandez continued: "If we don't process quota, the division doesn't make quota. It's as simple as that. But those jerks in maintenance are killing me. Last week, they were supposed to shut me down for PM [preventive maintenance]. But what happened? Absolutely nothing! They couldn't get to me because they were caught shorthanded. You tell me why they had to send three of their technicians to a training school last week. I built my whole departmental schedule around last week being slack. They knew I was scheduled for PM last week. There's no way they're shutting me down for even 1 minute during the next 3 weeks."

Dixon has a problem here! Fernandez doesn't want to shut down for maintenance, but he risks some downtime later if his equipment doesn't receive the proper preventive maintenance. The lack of unified planning at lower levels may cost Dixon its objectives. It has already strained the relationships among personnel in the plant.

Self-Check

What action would you take now if you were Juan Fernandez? What should be done to prevent this type of situation in the future? You might reflect on the chapter preview about MBK to identify an effective means of prevention.

As you will see shortly, other types of plans may also be established to aid in unified planning at lower levels. These other types of plans—policies, procedures, and rules—are more specific than objectives and spell out the methods used at lower levels.

Guidelines for Setting Objectives

5 *Discuss some important guidelines in setting objectives.*

Objectives set out for employees what they must do to make their performance acceptable. Since all supervisors should set objectives in their departments, the following guidelines should prove helpful to managers at all levels.

1. *Select key performance areas for objectives.* Since objectives focus attention and effort, the more important areas will suffer if there are too many objectives. Instead of having 15 objectives, select four or five key areas of performance, such as quality, quantity, customer relations, and cost controls, that really count!
2. *Be specific, if possible.* The objective "to have good quality" probably means different things to you and to your employees. "To produce parts with a 99 percent acceptance rate by the inspection department" is more specific, and it gives the worker a tangible measure of progress.
3. *Set challenging objectives.* Objectives should not be set so low that they can be met through "average" effort. Instead, they should require some stretching, but they should not be so difficult to achieve that an employee is discouraged from attempting to achieve them.
4. *Keep objective area in balance.* Effort expended in one performance area frequently affects another. The quality of work required influences the quantity of work, and the quantity of work may affect employee safety. Therefore, objectives may be needed in each of these areas to balance them properly.
5. *Objectives should be measurable.* If you want to determine whether employees are achieving objectives, there should be some way of measuring the extent to which those objectives are being attained.
6. *Involve employees in setting objectives.* What do employees consider the key performance areas of their job? What do they think is a challenging but fair objective in a given area? When possible, ask these questions. There are times, however, especially during periods of financial difficulties and other crises, when it is not feasible or desirable to involve employees in objective setting.
7. *Follow up.* Once objectives have been set, supervisors tend to let up. Frequently only the supervisor knows the results of a worker's performance. Discuss progress with employees. Sharing results and discussing employees' progress will improve their commitment and demonstrate your own.

Self-Check

Note the quality objective in guideline 2: "to produce parts with a 99 percent acceptance rate by the inspection department." Do you see any problems with making this the only objective? Explain.

Types of Plans

6 *Differentiate the various kinds of standing and single-use plans.*

Once objectives have been set to determine *what* needs to be accomplished, plans can be developed to outline *how* the objectives can be attained. These plans fall into two categories: *standing plans* and *single-use plans.*

Standing Plans

standing plans or repeat-use plans

Plans that are used repeatedly over a period of time.

Standing plans, or repeat-use plans, are those that are used repeatedly over a period of time. The three most popular types of standing plans are *policies, rules,* and *procedures.*

policy

Provides consistency among decision makers.

Policies A **policy** is a guide to decision making—a sort of boundary on a supervisor's freedom of action. That is, it is a way to provide consistency among decision makers. For example, suppose that an *objective* of Computronix is "to operate our divisions so as to achieve high safety." Note that this objective tells the "what." A *policy* for achieving this objective at the various divisions could be that "all flammable substances will be stored and handled in a manner consistent with federal, state, and local regulations." Another policy might be: "Each division shall emphasize safety performance of employees through a well-designed promotional campaign." Within the Dixon Division of Computronix, an overall policy established by the general manager might be: "Each operating department shall hold safety meetings at least once every three months to encourage adherence to rules and solicit employee safety suggestions." Other examples of policies are shown in Exhibit 2-6.

Supervisory managers fit into the policy picture in two key ways. First, they play an important part in implementing organizational policies that have been established by higher management. Second, they create policies within their departments as guides for their own work groups. Here are some examples:

1. *Absence notification.* "Employees who will be absent should notify me in advance, assuming this is feasible."
2. *Decision making.* "Employees are encouraged to make decisions on their own within their area of responsibility."

EXHIBIT 2-6
Examples of Policies

Compensation policy: "This company shall establish and maintain wages on a level comparable to those paid for comparable positions in other firms in the community."
Overtime policy: "Supervisors shall offer overtime opportunities first to the most senior employees in the department."
Grievance policy: "Each employee shall have an opportunity for due process in all disciplinary matters."
Purchasing policy: "Where feasible, several sources of supply shall be utilized so as not to be solely dependent on one supplier."
Supervisory policy: "Managers shall periodically hold group meetings with employees for the purposes of discussing objectives, explaining new developments that may affect employees, responding to questions, and, in general, encouraging more effective and accurate communications within the organization."

Self-Check

What are some other examples of supervisory policies? Can you think of any examples of policies established by the teacher of this course?

Policies established by upper-level managers should be put into writing since they must be enforced at operating levels by supervisors. Also, they often form the basis for legal proceedings against the organization and its management. Supervisory policies like the ones just mentioned, however, may be communicated orally. Some policies may be unwritten, implied, or based on past practices because "that's the way things actually happen."

It was Mary Hicks's first week on the job. Her supervisor, Clara Sanchez, had been very helpful in showing her the ropes. Each day, Mary had shown up for work a few minutes before starting time—just to make sure she was on time. She noticed, however, that at least a third of the employees drifted in 5 to 10 minutes late. This was true not only in her department, but also in others throughout the building. On asking one of her coworkers about this, she was told, "Yeah, they don't get really upset about 5 or 10 minutes, just so it's not the same person all the time."

The preceding example describes a practice that has become so widespread that supervisors may treat it as a policy. Supervisors must keep in mind that action or even inaction may come to be thought of as policy by employees and serve as a guide to their behavior.

Policies are relatively permanent but should not be set in stone. Circumstances change, and management must from time to time reexamine the appropriateness of its policies.

rule

A policy that is invariably enforced. Rules are inflexible requirements and are much stronger than guidelines. It is important for supervisors to know when they can be flexible in promoting the objectives of their company and when they have to enforce rules.

Rules Like policies, rules provide guidance. But a **rule** is stronger than a policy in that the guidance given by a rule is final and definite. Rules are inflexible and *must* be obeyed, under threat of punishment. If you work in an organization that has the rule "No smoking on the premises," you cannot smoke, and that is that. Note the difference between a policy and a rule as shown in these examples:

1. *Policy:* "Employees who violate the no-smoking rule are *subject to discharge.*"
2. *Rule:* "Employees who violate the no-smoking rule are *automatically discharged.*"

Why distinguish between rules and policies, especially when the distinction is sometimes a fine one? First, as a supervisor, you must know when you do not have flexibility. Second, too many rules can result in overmanagement. Taking too much discretion away from the employees leads them to say, "Well, let me look in the rule book and see what I'm supposed to do."

Self-Check

What are some examples of rules that you can think of? Can a supervisor establish his or her own rules? Give an example.

Although rules have an important place in organizations, their overuse can lead to problems. When there are too many rules, supervisors lose their individualism and may

Rules are inflexible requirements and are much stronger than guidelines. It is important for supervisors to know when they can be flexible in promoting the objectives of their company and when they have to enforce rules.

use the rules as crutches. Or they may offer weak, apologetic reasons when they enforce the rules. For example, consider the following dialogue:

Supervisor: "Catherine, I'm sorry to have to write you up for punching in three minutes late."

Catherine: "But you know I was actually here 10 minutes early and just forgot to punch in. I was at my desk all the time. I can't afford to get laid off half a day for being written up."

Supervisor: "Sorry, Catherine. It doesn't seem fair to me, either, but I've got to stick by the rule book. A rule's a rule."

Procedures The need for procedures arises when an organization or a department requires a high degree of consistency in activities that occur frequently. Procedures are established to avoid "reinventing the wheel" and to ensure that an effective sequence is followed. A **procedure** outlines the steps to be performed when a particular course of action is taken. Organizations have procedures for obtaining leaves of absence, ordering parts through central purchasing, taking weekly inventory, processing an employee's grievance, and so on.

procedure

Steps to be performed when a particular course of action is taken.

> ## Self-Check
> *Can you think of a procedure for a regular activity that takes place in each of the following organizations: airline, hospital, retail store, college? Procedures used in driving a car? Preparing a payroll?*

single-use plans

Developed to accomplish a specific purpose and then discarded after use.

Single-Use Plans

Single-use plans are developed to accomplish a specific purpose and are then discarded. Unlike policies, rules, and procedures, single-use plans detail courses of action that won't be performed on a repetitive basis. Examples of single-use plans are programs, projects, budgets, and schedules. These plans are more numerous and diversified than standing plans.

Programs We hear and read about programs daily—such as your city's pollution control program, a voter registration program, and so on. A **program** is a large-scale plan that involves a mix of objectives, policies, rules, and smaller projects. A program outlines the specific steps to be taken to achieve its objectives and the time, money, and human resources required to complete it. It is essentially a set of single-use plans carried out over a period of time. Other examples of programs are:

1. A tourism marketing program undertaken by your state.
2. A research program undertaken by drug producer Pfizer to develop vaccines for major diseases, such as AIDS and Parkinson's.

Projects A **project** is a distinct, smaller part of a program. For example, a state's tourism program involves many projects, such as selecting a tourism committee, benchmarking several states with outstanding tourism programs, promoting public attractions, and upgrading the welcome centers that greet transit visitors on interstate highways. Each project has its own objectives and becomes the responsibility of personnel assigned to oversee it.

Budgets Most individuals, families, or organizations use some form of budgeting. A well-planned budget serves as both a planning and a controlling tool. Simply stated, a **budget** is a forecast of expected financial performance over a period of time. A departmental budget covers such items as supplies, equipment, scrap, overtime, and personnel payroll.

Schedules A **schedule** is a plan showing activities to be performed and their timing. Scheduling techniques range from a simple note or appointment book used to schedule your day to sophisticated schedules for such major challenges as building a new plant or launching a space shuttle. Two scheduling approaches with which you should be familiar are the Gantt chart and PERT network.

The **Gantt chart** is a visual progress report that identifies work stages or activities on a vertical axis and scheduled completion dates horizontally. It is named after its developer, Henry Gantt, a management consultant who introduced the basic idea in the early 1900s. Since then, Gantt charts have been used extensively as a planning tool. Exhibit 2-7 illustrates a simplified Gantt chart. Note the specific activities that proceed from contract negotiation to job start-up and the scheduled times for each. Also note that one activity, long lead purchasing, can be carried on simultaneously with development of a manufacturing schedule. In actual practice, Gantt charts may include movable strips of plastic to represent bars, with different colors to indicate scheduled and actual progress. At a glance, a manager or supervisor can see whether a project is on time, ahead of schedule, or behind schedule. Although the Gantt chart is helpful as a planning tool, it does not show directly how the various activities involved in a job depend on one another. It is in showing such dependencies of activities that PERT network analysis can be helpful.

Program Evaluation and Review Technique (PERT) is a management scheduling tool that shows relationships among a network of activities and events to determine the completion time of a project. Typically, PERT is used on highly complex, one-time projects, such as building a skyscraper or completing the prototype of a new jet aircraft, and requires the use of a computer. However, its principles are relevant for many supervisors, especially in planning and scheduling various aspects of their jobs.

---

program

A large-scale plan composed of a mix of objectives, policies, rules, and projects.

project

A distinct part of a program.

budget

A forecast of expected financial performance over time.

schedule

A plan of activities to be performed and their timing.

Gantt chart

Identifies work stages and scheduled completion dates.

Program Evaluation and Review Technique (PERT)

Shows relationships among a network of activities to determine the completion time of a project.

7 *Draw a simple PERT chart.*

EXHIBIT 2-7
Example of Gantt Chart
Showing Activities
Needed in Production
Start-Up

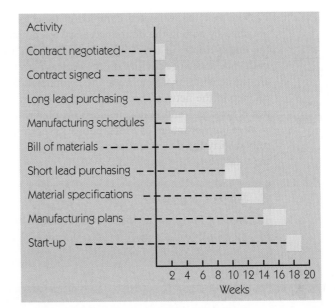

Let's examine a PERT chart that can be applied at the supervisory level. Suppose that you are a maintenance supervisor and your department has to overhaul an important machine. You have determined that the following activities must be done to complete the job:

A. Remove the machine from its foundation.
B. Haul the machine to the repair shop.
C. Dismantle the machine.
D. Order and receive new replacement parts from the manufacturer.
E. Repair the machine.
F. Test-run the machine.
G. Build a new machine foundation.
H. Move the repaired machine to the factory floor.
I. Secure the machine to the new foundation.

Now, assume that you are asked to estimate when the machine can be ready for use again. The PERT network of events and activities involved in your analysis is shown in Exhibit 2-8. The numbered squares represent events at which the different activities to complete the job *begin* and are *completed*. For example, Event 2 marks the completion of Activity A and the beginning of Activities B and G. The lines represent the activities to be performed. The hours represent your estimate of how long each activity will take to complete based on your experience or on information supplied by others.

EXHIBIT 2-8
PERT Network for
Completing Machine
Overhaul

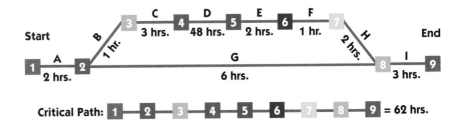

Note that the estimated completion time for the job is 62 hours. This total time is obtained by adding the hours necessary to complete the series of activities that comprise the *longest* route, in terms of time, to complete the job. This route is called the **critical path**. The series of activities on the critical path include A, B, C, D, E, F, H, and I. These are the activities that determine the completion time for the job. Activity G is not a critical step in the network because it can be begun and completed independently of Activities B through I and is not included on the critical path.

A major advantage of PERT networks, even for simple problems, is that they graphically display the dependent parts of a total job. The supervisor thus has a better grasp of the total job to be completed.

critical path

The series of activities in a PERT network that comprise the longest route, in terms of time, to complete the job.

Self-Check

Suppose that it takes you four hours rather than the two hours estimated to repair the machine (Activity E) as shown in Exhibit 2-8. Will this cause your project to be completed later than planned?

Chapter Review

1. **Discuss some of the more important points about planning.**

    Supervisors do planning as an ongoing part of their jobs. They must include planning for scheduling work, developing and living within budgets, and making job assignments.

2. **Explain the steps involved in planning.**

    Planning is deciding what will be done in the future. The three planning steps are (1) setting an objective or goal, (2) identifying and assessing present and future conditions affecting the goal, and (3) developing a systematic approach to achieving the goal. Properly done, planning helps managers accomplish the four other management functions of organizing, leading, staffing, and controlling. Of these functions, planning is most closely linked to controlling. Because it is a difficult and time-consuming process, many supervisors tend to neglect planning. Instead of planning, they scurry about solving one problem, then another, seemingly too busy to plan anything. Effective planning anticipates many problems so that they are more easily handled when they occur. Contingency planning is thinking about anticipated problems in advance and having potential solutions available.

3. **Explain how planning differs at top, middle, and supervisory management levels.**

    Planning differs for top, middle, and first-level management. Top managers spend a greater proportion of their time developing strategic long-term and intermediate-range plans of one to five or more years. Strategic plans include the organization's mission, objectives, and strategies and interfacing with its external environment. Middle-level and supervisory managers perform operational planning—intermediate-range and short-range plans of one year to one day—that operationalize strategic plans.

4. **Explain how the hierarchy of objectives works.**

    Objectives are crucial to effective planning. Once established, objectives provide a stimulus for individual effort. The objectives set at one management level reflect the objectives of the next higher operational level. This network of objectives is called a hierarchy of objectives. Objectives permit unified planning and coordination at lower management levels.

5. **Discuss some important guidelines in setting objectives.**

   Among the guidelines for setting objectives are (1) setting them in only selected, key performance areas; (2) making them specific; (3) making them challenging rather than easy; (4) balancing them properly, as may be the case with volume and quality; (5) stating them in measurable terms; (6) involving employees in setting them; and (7) following up on results.

6. **Differentiate the various kinds of standing and single-use plans.**

   After objectives have been established, plans can be developed throughout the organization. Standing, or repeat-use, plans direct action that deals with recurring situations. They include policies, rules, and procedures. A policy is a guide to individual decision making. Policies allow some flexibility, whereas rules are final and definite as to what action must be taken. A procedure outlines the steps that should be taken to complete a given action, such as applying for vacation leave or processing a grievance. Single-use plans are one-time plans that are discarded on completion. Examples of these are programs, projects, budgets, and schedules.

7. **Draw a simple PERT chart.**

   Two important types of schedules are Gantt charts and PERT charts, each of which provides a visual display of activities to be performed and the time frames involved.

Key Terms

contingency planning, p. 43

scenario planning, p. 44

strategic planning, p. 46

mission, p. 46

objectives, p. 46

strategies, p. 46

operational planning, p. 46

hierarchy of objectives, p. 48

unified planning, p. 48

standing plans, or repeat-use plans, p. 51

policy, p. 51

rule, p. 52

procedure, p. 53

single-use plans, p. 53

program, p. 54

project, p. 54

budget, p. 54

schedule, p. 54

Gantt chart, p. 54

Program Evaluation and Review Technique (PERT), p. 54

critical path, p. 56

Questions for Review & Discussion

1. What are the three basic steps in planning? Why do supervisors tend to slight the planning function?
2. How does planning differ among top, intermediate, and supervisory management levels?
3. What are some guidelines for setting objectives?
4. What is meant by a hierarchy of objectives? Explain.
5. What is the difference between a policy, a rule, and a procedure?
6. What is a Gantt chart? How does it differ from a PERT chart?
7. What is contingency planning? Explain.
8. Distinguish between objectives and strategies.

Resources

Interpersonal Skill

Skill Builder 2-1

Testing Your Planning Skills (Group Activity)

The general manager (GM) of the Marshall Biscuit Division of Lancaster Colony Corporation has just named you as chairperson of the first annual blood drive, to be conducted at the plant site. A strong believer in the company's participation in community affairs and himself a member of the local Red Cross board of directors, the GM has committed the division's employees to the blood drive. Your committee will set the exact dates for the drive, which is to be held in three or four months. As chairperson, you have been assigned a team of four other company employees to plan and implement the project. All members are highly respected, competent people, representing a true cross-section of the employees: One is a production worker who is responsible for operating the ovens; another, an engineer, represents the professional segment; the human resources manager represents the management group; and a payroll clerk represents the administrative office group. The GM was given your name by your boss, who expressed confidence in your ability to lead a successful donor campaign at the plant. At 27, you are the youngest person on the committee and anxious to do a good job. You have called the first committee meeting, which you have advertised as a "preliminary planning meeting," to identify key factors that must be planned for if the committee is to meet its objective of having a successful blood drive at Marshall Biscuit.

Instructions:

1. Make a list of what you consider the key planning issues to be identified by the committee at this initial planning meeting.
2. Of the items on your list, which two or three do you believe are the most crucial? Why?
3. Identify major problems that could prevent accomplishment of your objective. What contingency planning could be done to avert them or minimize their impact?
4. To help in your preparation for the planning meeting, identify 6 to 10 steps that you feel will be needed to achieve a successful blood drive. These steps might be such things as:

   a. Determine a date.
   b. Identify a location.
   c. Secure commitment from Red Cross.

   Draw a PERT chart that shows the sequence and relationship of the activities identified. (You need not be concerned with the length of time needed for each activity.)
5. Compare your responses to questions 1, 2, 3, and 4 with those of other students. To what extent do they agree with you?

Resources

Interpersonal Skill

Information

Skill Builder 2-2

Determining Priorities: Put Savings First

During 2008, the savings rate in the United States was precariously low, even negative at times. However, personal savings is a key means of ensuring a stable future for you and your family. Take a moment to test your personal planning skills with the following personal budgeting activity.

Instructions:

Step 1.   Visit the website http://finance.yahoo.com/how-to-guide/banking-budgeting/12832, to get started. You will find a five-step program that includes a handy preset budget form that you may easily modify for your purposes.

Step 2.   For one month, track your personal income and expenses using a pocket-sized notebook and pen or a personal electronic device. Regardless of how small the purchase price is, be sure to track ALL expenditures for one month. Record all items and break them into categories. For example, your income may possibly be categorized as: money earned waiting tables, monthly student loan income, and money provided by family. Some common expense categories would include rent, car insurance, gas, and so on.

Step 3.   Analyze your monthly habits to determine where your money is going. Do you have money left over at the end of the month, spend all that you make, or finance your current lifestyle with unsecured debt (credit cards)? Begin to think about ways to reduce your expenses or increase income stream(s). The website, http://finance.yahoo.com/how-to-guide/banking-budgeting/12832, has some suggestions that may work for you.

Step 4.   Set a savings goal for yourself; remember to use the goal-setting principles you learned about in this chapter to guide your efforts. For example, you want to be realistic about what you can achieve, and if you are not currently a saver, look for discretionary expenses you could eliminate to free up even small amounts. For example, just finding an extra $30 per month equals $360 per year. As you become a savvy saver, you can create a more challenging goal.

Step 5.   Think about alternative ways to achieve your goal. Pick one that will work for you and stick to it! One suggestion is to visit various financial planning websites, such as http://finance.yahoo.com/banking-budgeting, to benchmark plans that have worked for others. One strategy shared by some financial advisors, including Susie Orman, is to have your local bank or credit union electronically transfer your savings goal each month from your checking to your savings account. This strategy ensures that you pay yourself first, and in most cases, if you don't see the money in your account, you won't miss it!

CASE 2-1

Island Shades

Terry Allen has an idea for a new business. She would like to start a retail operation that would provide high-quality eyewear to discriminating consumers. The business, Island Shades, would use a focused differentiation strategy, catering to middle- and upper-income individuals ranging in age from 16 to 50 years. These customers would range from avid outdoors people to birdwatchers to Sunday drivers. She envisions carrying high-end sunglasses (Gucci, Prada, Oakley, Ray Ban, Costa Del Mar, etc.) and custom-prescription sunglasses. She will stock a wide assortment of styles and a variety of colors.

Although Terry will stock some affordable options in each product category, the bulk of her inventory will be priced at $100 or greater. She estimates that she will need to invest $75,000 to $95,000 in inventory to begin her business and ensure she has the variety and quality her discerning customers will expect. She estimates that her monthly sales will start at $15,000 and fluctuate depending on the seasonal peaks and valleys. For instance, the first, second, and fourth quarters of the year will be much more lucrative than the third quarter due to ski season, summer activities, and the holiday season. Terry expects to average $35,000 per month in sales over this time period. Currently, she is also planning to pay a consultant to develop an interactive website enabling customers to purchase merchandise online. The initial quote for the up-front cost for development is $4,000, with an ongoing annual fee of $300.

Terry believes that the perfect location for this retail store is in the Palacio, an upscale and trendy shopping village just off a major interstate highway in a mid-sized city with a population of 295,000. (The population for the greater metropolitan statistical area is 500,000.) Palacio is centrally located within the city and easily accessible from several high-end neighborhoods. One key factor in choosing this location is that other upscale retail shops and restaurants currently operate at Palacio, which attracts the desired target market. Terry believes that she will need around 2,000 to 2,500 square feet. Terry recently checked with a local leasing agent and found out the following information:

A 2,400-square foot corner unit is open.

The rent is $3,300 per month. (Taxes and insurance charges are included.)

The build out cost is $16.00 per square foot.

The lease term is 3 to 5 years with several different renewal options.

Terry wants a comfortable, friendly atmosphere that is alluring without being stuffy. The quote she received for build out cost would enable her to accomplish this objective. It includes displays, but furniture and accessories would be additional. Terry estimates that these features would run an additional $5,500. Space is available now and going quickly. Even though it is August, she would like to get started and sign a lease agreement.

Terry is quite aware that she will be working long hours at the beginning. She plans to be open Monday through Saturday from 10:00 a.m. to 7:00 p.m. These hours will allow her to operate when potential customers are eating lunch and dinner and browsing at Coldwater Creek, Anne Taylor, Adventure Outdoors, and so on. Based on these hours of operation, Terry believes she needs two to three part-time employees who would rotate shifts. She is planning on tapping the local high schools and universities to recruit quality part-time employees. Based on the data she has gathered, she expects to pay between $8 and $10 an hour. Since she is relying on part-time employees, there would be no need to pay benefits such as medical and dental.

Questions

1. Analyze Terry's goal and plan based on the concepts you learned in this chapter. Are there additional key performance areas that Terry could identify for action? Is her goal realistic?
2. Do you agree with Terry's view that Island Shades will be successful? Why or why not?
3. Would you recommend any changes or modifications to her goal or plan? Discuss.
4. Present a summary of your analysis and recommendations to the class.

Source: Prepared by Don C. Mosley, Jr. and Charles Warren, Mitchell College of Business, University of South Alabama, Mobile, AL. The company and individual names and some of the case information have been changed for privacy purposes.

3

Decision Making, Problem Solving, and Ethics

Every business leader, such as Facebook's founder and CEO Mark Zuckerberg, has to take care with making decisions to maintain the organization's success.

LEARNING OBJECTIVES

After reading and studying this chapter, you should be able to:

1. Explain the role of decision making in the supervisor's job.

2. Discuss why supervisors need to make so many decisions.

3. Define decision making and identify at least four elements involved.

4. Discuss how decisions are made.

5. Name some factors to keep in mind when making decisions.

6. Decide whether to use the individual approach or the group approach when making decisions.

7. Discuss some ways of improving decision making.

8. Explain the role of ethics in the organization's and supervisor's decision making.

It is management's public responsibility to make whatever is genuinely in the public good become the enterprise's own self interest.
—Peter F. Drucker

Ethics is a code of values which guide our choices and actions and determine the purpose and course of our lives.
—Ayn Rand

All the analyst really requires for the solution to a problem is: first, the painstaking assembly of all the phenomena; second, exhaustive patience; and third, the ability to comprehend the whole problem with a fresh and unbiased imagination.
—Ellery Queen

CHAPTER OUTLINE

Preview

FACEBOOK

> *I'm here to build something for the long term. Anything else is a distraction.*
> —MARK ZUCKERBERG

For those of you who don't know Mark Zuckerberg, he may be the most powerful person in his mid-20s on the planet. He is the founder and CEO of the immensely popular social networking site, Facebook, although Zuckerberg would disagree with the aforementioned title. He explains that Facebook is actually a world-changing tool to facilitate information flows among users and their friends, colleagues, and family members, and by the way, its applicability transcends the college crowd. His vision centers on a concept he refers to as the "social graph." As described by Newsweek reporter Steven Levy, "[Facebook] is a mathematical construct that maps the real-life connections between every human on the planet. Each of us is a node radiating links to the people we know. 'We don't own the social graph,' [Zuckerberg] says. 'The social graph is this thing that exists in the world, and it always has and it always will. It's really most natural for people to communicate through it, because it's with the people around you, friends and business connections or whatever. What [Facebook] needed to do was construct as accurate of a model as possible of the way the social graph looks in the world. So once Facebook knows who you care about, you can upload a photo album and we can send it to all those people automatically.'"[1]

Zuckerberg initially created the bare-bones site while a college sophomore at Harvard, and it was an instant success—after only two weeks, 4,300 users were on board. Just like nodes within a social grid, word spread rapidly, and people at other universities were requesting sites for their schools. Facebook began changing the social paradigm for students everywhere! In fact, Mark's idea was so successful that he quit Harvard and moved west with his partners to solicit investment monies. One executive suggested that Mark's plan was akin to those of Google or eBay at similar stages of development. His plan was to use the investment capital to grow Facebook, which he in fact did. In 2005, the social graph expanded to include high schools, and in 2006, to "work networks." In addition, Zuckerberg has filled Facebook with a variety of applications. However, he has held firm on his fundamental principle of inclusiveness by allowing anyone to create applications that can piggyback on Facebook's infrastructure. This decision further fuels the Facebook mystique.[2]

In 2007, Facebook had a presence in two locations, operated with roughly 300 employees, and had revenues of approximately $100 million. Fast forward to 2009, and Facebook is in seven U.S. cities and three foreign countries with 200 million active users. Facebook has 900 plus employees and is expected to exceed $300 million in revenues.[3]

Although no one can deny the popularity of Facebook, some wonder whether Mark Zuckerberg is still making the right decisions. For example, he turned down a $1 billion purchase offer from Yahoo, even though he was aware of the fate of similar sites, such as Friendster.[4] A huge controversy brewed last year over Facebook Beacon, the program that "automatically alerted users' friends of their activities on selected sites, including eBay and Fandango."[5] The backlash resulted in scaled back features just weeks after its release. Additional challenges loom on the not-so-distant horizon for Mark and his management team to effectively address. One key issue that must be addressed for long-term growth and survival: Can Facebook be an integral part of the lives of graduates in older generations? On the flip side, will increased numbers of older individuals result in "unhipness" and actually drive the core college-age users away?[6] One thing is for sure, Mark's decisions will be grounded in his business philosophy: "I'm here to build something for the long term. Anything else is a distraction."[7]

We will discuss the subject of decision making in considerable detail. Decisions must be made about people, processes, and priorities, to name just a few issues! Keep Mark Zuckerberg's problem in mind because we will return to his situation throughout the chapter.

Role of Decision Making in Supervisory Management

1 *Explain the role of decision making in the supervisor's job.*

Managers must make decisions whenever they perform any of the five management functions—planning, organizing, staffing, controlling, and leading. Without decision making, the entire management system would cease to exist. For example, in *planning,* the supervisor must decide which objectives to seek, which policies to establish, and what rules to institute. In *organizing,* choices must be made as to who gets what authority and how duties and responsibilities are grouped. In *staffing,* decisions must be made concerning employee selection, placement, training, and development; performance appraisal; compensation; and health and safety. In *controlling,* if actual performance does not conform to planned performance, decisions must be made about how best to bring them together. The function of *leading* entails deciding how best to communicate with and motivate employees.

The decisions that managers make often must be made quickly—and frequently with little information, or even conflicting information. Then, those decisions must be carried out to achieve the department's objectives!

Decision Making: The Heart of Supervisory Management

Decision making is central to the supervisor's job. Supervisors must continually decide what is to be done; who is to do it; and how, when, and where it is to be done (see Exhibit 3-1). As we will show throughout the chapter, although these decisions may be discussed separately, they are interrelated. One decision is affected by, and builds on, previous ones. For example, what your department produces determines what types of production facilities are needed. Decisions about production, in turn, influence the types of employees needed and the training and compensation they should receive. All of these decisions affect the amount of resources budgeted for the department.

Why Supervisors Need to Make So Many Decisions

2 *Discuss why supervisors need to make so many decisions.*

Supervisory managers—even more than managers at other levels—are involved in directing employees' behavior toward achieving the organization's goals, as well as those of the employees themselves. Supervisors must make more decisions more frequently—and often more quickly—than other managers, since they're operating on a production-

EXHIBIT 3-1
Decision Making Is the Heart of Supervisory Management

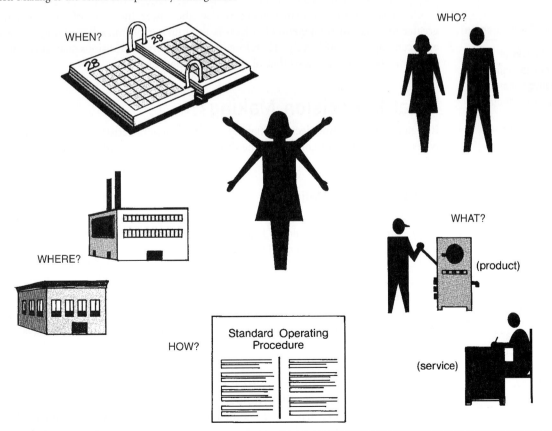

oriented, day-by-day, person-to-person basis. These decisions involve a variety of activities, as the following example illustrates.

Wilma Malone, nursing supervisor at Alquippa Medical Center, had been at work for only three hours, but she had already made several major decisions. For example, she had

1. *Signed up to attend a one-day course on time management, to be offered the following week;*
2. *Assigned performance ratings to five of her new nurses on their performance appraisal forms;*
3. *Approved vacation requests for two nurses in her department;*
4. *Referred to the floor physician a patient's request to be taken off a prescribed medication;*
5. *Resolved a dispute between one of the nurses and a floor orderly;*
6. *Selected Jane Moore to serve as her replacement when she was to take her vacation in three weeks; and*
7. *Requisitioned supplies needed by her department.*

In addition, she made a handful of other minor decisions. The young trainee assigned to Malone said, "Are you always this busy, or is it just because it's Monday morning?" Malone replied, "It's all a normal part of a supervisor's job."

Employees look to their supervisors for more direction, assistance, guidance, and protection than do subordinates of managers at higher levels. Also, in general, supervisors spend more time socializing with others in the organization since they have more employees than other managers. All of these activities require decision making.

One basic truism of management is that the lower the level of management, the greater the **span of management,** which is the number of immediate employees a manager can supervise effectively. Therefore, supervisors make decisions that affect not only their own behavior, but also that of many other people.

span of management

The number of immediate employees a manager can supervise effectively.

3 *Define decision making and identify at least four elements involved.*

What Is Decision Making?

It is now time to define decision making, discuss its characteristics, look at some selected types of decisions, and consider some differences between decision making and problem solving.

Decision Making Defined

Have you known people who couldn't ever make up their minds? They might say, "I really don't know what to do. If I do this, such and such will happen. If I do that, then something else might happen." They just can't make decisions.

The word *decide* comes from a Latin word meaning "to cut off." When you make a decision, you first consider a matter causing you some uncertainty, debate, or dispute, and then make a choice or judgment that more or less results in a definite conclusion. You cut off further deliberation on the matter. Thus, **decision making** is the conscious consideration and selection of a course of action from among two or more available alternatives in order to produce a desired result.

decision making

Considering and selecting a course of action from among alternatives.

Elements Involved in Decision Making

There are several facts you should know about decision making. The most important ones are (1) a decision may not be needed, (2) decisions involve the future, (3) the process is a conscious one, and (4) there must be more than one alternative solution.

A Decision May Not Be Needed A wise decision maker begins by asking, "Is a decision needed?" It may seem strange to include this question in a discussion of decision making, but it is important. In many supervisory situations, no decision is needed, and decision making would be in vain. If a given event is inevitable or if higher management is going to act in a certain way regardless of the supervisor's wishes, then making a decision is a waste of time. Some things cannot be changed regardless of the supervisor's wishes or actions.

Decisions Involve the Future Surely you have heard others say, "If only I had done this, then that wouldn't have happened." They assume that if they had made a different decision, it would have resulted in a happy marriage, a rapid promotion, or a killing in the stock market. It is said that hindsight is 20/20, but the supervisor's world is no place for Monday-morning quarterbacking. Rather, it's a place to prepare for today or tomorrow. Because a supervisor's decision making is oriented toward the future, it always contains an element of uncertainty.

Decision Making Is a Conscious Process Decision making involves a conscious process of selection. No decisions are needed about breathing or digestion, because these are unconscious, reflexive actions. In making a decision, the individual consciously (1) becomes aware of a want that needs to be satisfied, (2) seeks relevant behavioral alternatives, and (3) evaluates them as a basis of choice, as shown in Exhibit 3-2.

Decision Making Involves More Than One Alternative As indicated earlier, for a true decision to be made, there must be two or more available alternatives to choose from, including the possibility of doing nothing. Frequently, there are only two choices, as in a "yes or no" or "to do or not to do" situation. The decision to do nothing is sometimes the worst decision.

Most decision situations involve several alternatives with varying expected outcomes. You may not be aware of some of the alternatives and may not have decision authority over others. For other alternatives, you must estimate expected outcomes. You then evaluate each outcome in terms of its desirability. Sometimes there are no desirable alternatives. In such cases, you have to decide between two undesirable ones.

EXHIBIT 3-2
Decision-Making
Process

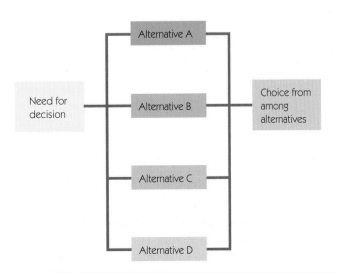

Types of Decisions to Be Made

Although there are many ways of classifying decisions, we will discuss only one at this point—namely, categorizing decisions as either programmed or unprogrammed.

Programmed decisions are those that are routine and repetitive. Since such decisions tend to be similar and must be made frequently, supervisors usually establish a systematic way of handling them. Here are some examples of this type of decision:

programmed decisions

Routine and repetitive decisions.

1. How to handle an employee who reports to work late or is absent without permission.
2. How to schedule work, shifts, vacations, and other time variations.
3. How to determine which employees need training and what type of training should be given to them.
4. How frequently to do maintenance servicing of machinery and equipment.

The effective supervisor handles these decisions in a systematic way and may even set up a decision framework, including guidelines such as policies, procedures, or rules to be followed.

Unprogrammed decisions are those that occur infrequently. Because different variables are involved, requiring a separate and different response each time, establishing a systematic way of dealing with such decisions is difficult. Some examples of unprogrammed supervisory decisions include the following:

unprogrammed decisions

Decisions that occur infrequently and require a different response each time.

1. Whether to buy an important piece of machinery or equipment, especially an expensive, complex piece.
2. How to react to a union representative who says that a grievance will be filed if you give a written reprimand to a certain worker for a work-related violation of safety rules.
3. How to handle a severe accident or explosion.
4. Whom to promote to a supervisory position.

How Decision Making and Problem Solving Relate

In one of his educational films, Joe Batten, a well-known management consultant, has a manager say, "We have no problems here, just opportunities. Each problem should be considered an opportunity." Although we don't necessarily agree with that conclusion, it does give us a chance to show how decision making and problem solving are related. An **opportunity** is a set of circumstances that provides a chance to improve a situation or help reach a goal. A **problem** is an existing unsatisfactory situation causing anxiety or distress that must be addressed.

opportunity

A chance for development or advancement.

Effective supervisors must be able to identify problems and their cause(s), to analyze complex and involved situations, and to solve problems by removing their cause(s). However, placing too much emphasis on problems can prevent one from identifying opportunities. After all, solving a problem only eliminates or neutralizes a negative situation. Progress or advancement comes from seeking and identifying opportunities; recognizing the emotions, needs, and motivations of the people involved; and analyzing ways of satisfying them. Here are some examples of "opportunity" decision making at the supervisory level:

problem

An existing unsatisfactory situation causing anxiety or distress.

1. Replacing a piece of equipment that, although it is still functioning well, can be upgraded to increase efficiency.
2. Improving an already effective preventive maintenance system.
3. Cross-training employees to broaden their skills and raise morale.

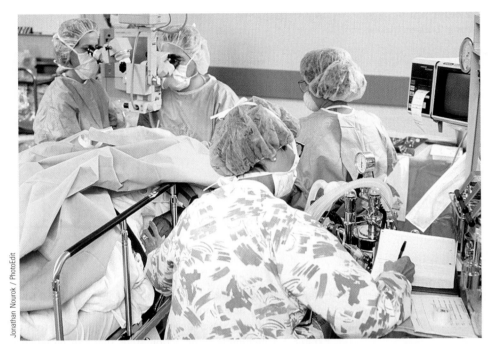

Imaging the numerous decisions required of a nurse working in a supervisory position in a hospital helps us understand what decision making is, the types of decision that must be made in a workday, and how decision making and problem solving relate to one another.

4. Creating a new position for a highly skilled technician who has recently left the employ of a competitor.

5. Instituting the most innovative new processes and techniques.

Stop & Think

What other examples of "opportunity" decision making can you think of?

How to Make Decisions

4 *Discuss how decisions are made.*

Exhibit 3-3 shows that the decision-making process involves six basic steps. We have already mentioned most of them.

Step 1: Define the Idea or Problem

Peter Drucker once stated that a decision is only as good as the correct definition of the problem. In other words, the right cure for the wrong problem is just as bad as the wrong cure for the right problem. However, it is not always easy to know what the problem is or which opportunity is the best one to seek. When you have a fever, it is only a symptom of the true problem—an infection or other disorder. Likewise, as a supervisor, you remember that low morale, high turnover, many complaints or grievances, waste, and declining sales are not the real problem. They are only symptoms of the real problem.

EXHIBIT 3-3
Steps in Decision Making

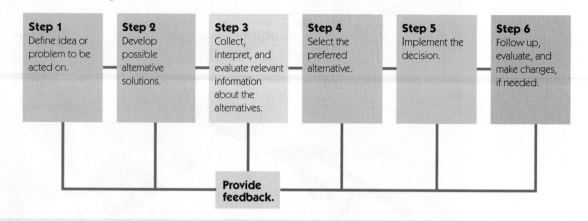

If the decision to be made involves solving a problem, its cause, or the factors that are creating it, must be determined. Without identifying the cause (or causes), it is difficult to solve the problem because you may be treating its symptom rather than the root cause (s). Exhibit 3-4 highlights some action steps that can be taken to identify the source of elusive problems.

EXHIBIT 3-4
How to Identify the Source of Elusive Problems

Every supervisor, manager, and foreman has experienced it. Something's wrong—but you can't quite put your finger on it. Something doesn't feel right. But what is it?

Profits may be down. Or production off. Or performance flat. Or morale is in the dumps. But why? There's definitely a problem. But what is it? Where is it? Guess who gets to figure it out? If you are reading this article, you do!

Supervisors are, first and foremost, "fixers." If something is not clicking in your factory, shop, office, department or division, it's your job to find out why and get things back on track. That's why there is a little bit of detective in every effective supervisor.

All successful managers know that discovering what's really wrong or pinpointing the exact problem and its source isn't a matter of extrasensory perception or lucky guesses. It is the result of close attention, systematic investigation, probing analysis and intuitive insight.

How does it work? Following are 10 action steps many successful managers take to identify the exact source and origin of elusive problems in the workplace. They may help you root out problems, sooner rather than later, as well:

1. *Ask. Some managers think they have to know or come up with all the answers.* They're wrong. Even though you are the "boss," you don't have to detect and dissect every problem all by yourself. It's OK to ask others (e.g., colleagues, employees, customers) "What's wrong?" Everyone has a stake in surfacing and solving hidden problems in the workplace. There are lots of ways to inquire about problems and solutions. Hold brainstorming sessions. Conduct individual interviews. Initiate question-driven interdisciplinary dialogues and discussions. Don't be afraid to try a variety of approaches. The important thing is to ask the right people the right questions at the right time (usually sooner, rather than later). You may be amazed by what you can find out merely by asking. Too many problems remain unidentified because no one ever asks, "What's really going on here?" Dumb questions may be nonproductive, but questions never asked are much worse.

2. *Let someone else do the asking.* Employees won't always tell their supervisors bad news—even if it is true. They may not want to upset the boss, betray confidences or be viewed as an informant. In some toxic organizational cultures, "whistle blower" is looked down on as "stool pigeon," which translates to "traitor." What often works best is to bring in a respected third party to pick employees' brains and ask around about what's not working. Workers may open up more to an objective outsider than to their own supervisor. This approach succeeds only if the outsider has universal

credibility and is trusted by all parties involved. Widely respected former managers, union representatives, retirees, or outside third parties with a reputation for integrity are the best choices.

3. *Check out rumors.* Rumors are usually just gossip—part venting and part entertaining. But sometimes, rumors are more. They can be true. Rumors can be symptoms of a problem. Clues to a problem. Or the problem itself. In any case, it's worth tracing down ugly or dangerous rumors to their source and determining their credibility. If a rumor proves to be the root of what's wrong, simply setting the record straight may be all it takes to eliminate the problem and move on.

4. *Pay attention to veteran employees.* Novices and newcomers are seldom the source of serious problems within the organization. They are not usually allowed enough latitude to do significant damage. Besides, they are normally under close scrutiny to see if they are going to work out.

5. *Test the communication systems.* More organizational problems are caused by poor communication, miscommunication, or lack of communication than by any other source. That's why any supervisory sleuthing to uncover an internal problem should include a communications audit.
   The questions to ask and answer include:

   • Are employees at all levels getting the information they need?
   • Is the information accurate and consistent?
   • Are employees receiving needed information in a timely manner?

   The easiest, quickest, and best way to resolve, eliminate, or prevent internal problems is to make sure that all operations are completely transparent. This requires open, accurate, and complete information flowing freely in all directions throughout the honeycomb of the organization. Poor communication is always a problem. Better communication is always the solution.

6. *Revisit policies and procedures.* The legendary comic strip hero, Pogo, once proclaimed, "We have met the enemy and he is us." He could have been talking about overorganized organizations (particularly business organizations) that become so obsessed with their own rules, regulations, and rituals that these trappings take on a life of their own—actually displacing or replacing the organization's core mission and purpose. Sound familiar?

7. *Re-examine expectations.* What you expect is what you get. Right? Not always. Expectations can be stepping stones—or stumbling blocks. When expectations, goals, quotas, or targets are unreasonably high, workers eventually get frustrated. Often, they just give up and start going through the motions. This is a sure-fire recipe for trouble in the workplace. Conversely, if expectations are too low, there is no challenge. Workers quickly get bored and inattentive, which leads to sloppy work—and mistakes. It is only when expectations stretch employees, but remain reachable, that they promote continuous growth and drive peak performance.

8. *Review the reward system.* Reward symbols (bonuses, perks, gifts, prizes and recognition awards) are designed to honor the best and challenge the rest (the wannabes, also-rans and near-misses). But it doesn't always work that way. If you reward the wrong workers or distribute the wrong rewards in the wrong way, the system can backfire. The result is likely to be disappointment, jealousy and resentment, rather than motivation, incentive and challenge. When the reward system is the problem, the solution may be as simple as asking 3 employees what rewards are most appropriate and appreciated and allowing workers to help choose the most worthy recipients.

9. *Re-evaluate vendors.* Vendors are part of the extended family of your organization and a vital factor in its success or failure. A new vendor who is unfamiliar with your operation or a current vendor who lowers quality measures or standards or changes delivery or maintenance systems can send ripples of readjustment throughout your organization. It doesn't take much variation by a vendor to slow things down and disrupt operations. Sometimes, when something goes wrong inside the organization, the cause lies outside the organization. As a supervisor, it's your job to track down the source of the problem wherever it is.

10. *Look to the competition.* Occasionally, what appears to be an internal problem is really a different kind of trouble altogether. If your organization is slipping behind, it may not mean you are doing something wrong. It may just be that the competition is doing something "righter." When you are doing everything as well as ever and still are losing ground, the competition is flat-out beating you. It's time to discover what your competitors are doing differently and figure out a way to equal or surpass their success.

The 10 steps above provide a systematic checklist for defining and finding the source of problems in the workplace. But what if you exhaust the list and still haven't discovered what's wrong? If your staff, team, or crew is still having a problem and you can't find the source by looking inside and outside the organization, what's left? Where else can you look?—In the mirror. Remember Pogo?

EXHIBIT 3-4
Continued

Look at your own leadership. Is your attitude, management style, planning, execution, or follow-through falling short? If you are the problem, you have to be the solution. How? Change, quit, or wait to be ousted. It's that simple.

All good supervisors have to be problem-solvers. In business, as in the medical model, the basis for any solution (cure) is an accurate diagnosis. To succeed as a problem-solver, you have to learn to be a good diagnostician. The first rule is don't guess or rush to judgment. Be methodical and thorough. Take your time in identifying what's wrong. Misdiagnosis in management—as in the medical profession—is the first step to malpractice. And there is no malpractice insurance for supervisors.

Source: Adapted from Ramsey, Robert D. "How to identify the source of elusive problems." Supervision 70.1 (Jan 2009): 10(4). Academic OneFile. Gale. University of South Alabama (AVL). 7 July 2009. Reprinted by permission of National Research Bureau.

Step 2: Develop Alternatives

alternatives

Possible courses of action that can satisfy a need or solve a problem.

The second step is to develop alternative ways of solving the problem or taking advantage of the opportunity. **Alternatives** are possible courses of action that can satisfy a need or solve a problem. Several choices are usually available if you are able to identify and develop them. It is easier to choose from a few alternatives than from many, so reduce the number to as few as is feasible. Also, be aware that, if choices are limited, they may include only undesirable ones.

This is the stage in which you decide whether you should make the choice or channel it to some other person who has the authority or expertise to make it. If you decide that it is your "call," one choice is to do nothing, hoping that the problem will go away or solve itself in time. You must be careful, though, that this doesn't become an excuse for not making a difficult choice. If it does, you may get a reputation for being indecisive—the "kiss of death" to many promising supervisory careers.

Step 3: Collect, Interpret, and Evaluate Information About Each Alternative

5 *Name some factors to keep in mind when making decisions.*

Usually there are many sources from which to gather information affecting a decision. Sometimes standing orders, policies, procedures, and rules provide relevant information. In fact, these documents may have already made the decision for you—or at least may indicate how you should decide. Other sources of information include your own experience, company records and reports, discussion with the people directly and indirectly involved, and personal observations.

Perhaps you've heard the saying, "Tell me what you want to prove, and I'll get you the data to prove it." The effective evaluation of alternatives involves looking *objectively* at the pros and cons of each one. Choices can be evaluated in many ways. The information can be written down on a type of balance sheet, as shown in Exhibit 3-5, with the reasons for each alternative on one side and the reasons against it on the other. Or a process of elimination can be used in which the undesirable (or less desirable) choices are dropped.

Step 4: Select the Preferred Alternative

cost/benefit analysis

Estimating and comparing the costs and benefits of alternatives.

Finally, you reach the point where you must make a choice. You look at your conclusions from step 3 and then logically and rationally pick the alternative you think is most desirable for all concerned from objective, ethical, and practical points of view.

Selecting the preferred alternative involves cost/benefit analysis and risk analysis. Using the technique of **cost/benefit analysis,** you estimate what each alternative will cost in terms of human, physical, and financial resources. Then you estimate the expected benefits. Finally, you compare the two estimates. You choose the one with the greatest payoff, where the ratio of benefits to cost is most favorable.

EXHIBIT 3-5
Evaluating Alternatives

risk

The possibility of defeat, disadvantage, injury, or loss.

Analysis of risk is inherent in decision making. **Risk** is the possibility of defeat, disadvantage, injury, or loss. Prudent decision makers try to minimize risk by effectively forecasting outcomes and considering all variables.

Step 5: Implement the Decision

Effective decision making doesn't stop when you choose from among alternatives. The decision must be put into operation. For example, you might need to obtain and allocate some equipment and supplies. Or you might need to develop methods and procedures. Or you might have to select, train, or even terminate some employees. This is a difficult part of decision making because you must face and deal with people who may not like your choice. Many good supervisory decisions are ineffective because of the way they're implemented.

Step 6: Follow Up, Evaluate, and Make Changes—If Needed

This last step in the decision-making process involves exercising management's control function. It determines whether the implementation of the decision is proceeding smoothly and achieving the desired results. If not, and the decision can be changed or modified, it should be. If it can't be changed, then you must live with it and try to make it succeed.

6 *Decide whether to use the individual approach or the group approach when making decisions.*

Approaches to Decision Making and Problem Solving

Two approaches that are particularly useful in both decision making and problem solving are the Myers-Briggs Type Indicator and the Vroom-Yetton model. The Myers-Briggs Type Indicator is the better known and is used throughout the world.

The Myers-Briggs Type Indicator®

Myers-Briggs Type Indicator® (MBTI®)

Helps identify an individual's personal style related to decision-making and problem solving.

The 126-item **Myers-Briggs Type Indicator® (MBTI®)** helps identify an individual's personal style.[8] Although it measures eight dichotomies of personality types, we will concern ourselves with only the four internal dimensions: (1) sensing versus (2) intuition and (3) thinking versus (4) feeling. These four are directly related to decision making and problem solving. (The Myers-Briggs concept is based on the work of scholar-physician Carl Gustav Jung, born in Switzerland and a contemporary of Sigmund Freud. Isabel Myers and her mother, Katherine Briggs, further refined and added to the basic theory.)

According to Myers and Briggs, people who rely primarily on *sensing*, or becoming aware of things through the five senses, tend to be patient, practical, and realistic. Those who rely primarily on *intuition* tend to be impatient, idea and theory oriented, and creative. Although everyone uses both ways of perceiving, Myers and Briggs indicates that at an early age, we develop a preference for one method over the other. Therefore, we tend to use our favorite approach and slight the one we enjoy less. Thus, people develop a set of traits based on whether they prefer sensing or intuition, as shown in the top half of Exhibit 3-6.

People who trust and prefer *thinking*, or using a rational, logical process to come to impersonal conclusions, are quite skillful in dealing with matters that require logic, objectivity, and careful examination of facts. On the other hand, those who trust and prefer *feeling*, or using innate processes that take into account one's own and others' values and beliefs, tend to be adept at working with other people and successful in applying skills in interpersonal and human relations. Such people are normally tactful and appreciative and have the ability to empathize with other people's problems and feelings. The bottom half of Exhibit 3-6 compares thinking and feeling types.

Although experience and growth opportunities can help develop weaker dichotomies, most people have two developed dimensions. The ideal is to maintain a balance by developing capability in all four. This is especially important for decision making, since all four dichotomies can be valuable in the decision-making method described earlier.

Sensing, which helps in developing and facing facts as well as being realistic about the nature of the problem or opportunity, is helpful in step 1, recognizing a problem or opportunity. *Intuition*, on the other hand, is used in areas where creativity is needed to see possibilities and develop opportunities. It is therefore helpful in step 2, developing alternative courses of action.

Because *thinking* is impersonal and logically considers the consequences of cause and effect, it is helpful in step 3, evaluating the alternatives. *Feeling* comes into play when it is necessary to consider the values and ethics of others and the impact of the final decision on them. This provides sensitivity in selecting the preferred alternative and implementing it.

Stop & Think

Reflect on the chapter preview. What type of MBTI® decision style do you think Mark Zuckerberg possesses? Why?

Ideally, as a result of new experiences such as working in a team or being coached through training, we can develop balance and function effectively in all dichotomies. Although she is retired now, a bank officer who developed such balance while we were consulting with her bank is profiled next.

EXHIBIT 3-6
Characteristics of
Different Personality
Types

HOW DO YOU PREFER TO TAKE IN INFORMATION? THE S–N DICHOTOMY	
SENSING	**INTUITION**
People who prefer Sensing like to take in information that is real and tangible—what is actually happening. They are observant about the specifics of what is going on around them and are especially attuned to practical realities.	People who prefer Intuition like to take in information by seeing the big picture, focusing on the relationships and connections between facts. They want to grasp patterns and are especially attuned to seeing new possibilities.
Characteristics associated with people who prefer Sensing:	*Characteristics associated with people who prefer Intuition:*
• Oriented to present realities • Factual and concrete • Focus on what is real and actual • Observe and remember specifics • Build carefully and thoroughly toward conclusions • Understand ideas and theories through practical applications • Trust experience	• Oriented to future possibilities • Imaginative and verbally creative • Focus on the patterns and meanings in data • Remember specifics when they relate to a pattern • Move quickly to conclusions, follow hunches • Want to clarify ideas and theories before putting them into practice • Trust inspiration

HOW DO YOU MAKE DECISIONS? THE T–F DICHOTOMY	
THINKING	**FEELING**
People who prefer to use Thinking in decision making like to look at the logical consequences of a choice or action. They want to mentally remove themselves from the situation to examine the pros and cons objectively. They are energized by critiquing and analyzing to identify what's wrong with something so they can solve the problem. Their goal is to find a standard or principle that will apply in all similar situations.	People who prefer to use Feeling in decision making like to consider what is important to them and to others involved. They mentally place themselves into the situation to identify with everyone so they can make decisions based on their values about honoring people. They are energized by appreciating and supporting others and look for qualities to praise. Their goal is to create harmony and treat each person as a unique individual.
Characteristics associated with people who prefer Thinking:	*Characteristics associated with people who prefer Feeling:*
• Analytical • Use cause-and-effect reasoning • Solve problems with logic • Strive for an objective standard of truth • Reasonable • Can be "tough-minded" • Fair—want everyone treated equally	• Empathetic • Guided by personal values • Assess impacts of decisions on people • Strive for harmony and positive interactions • Compassionate • May appear "tenderhearted" • Fair—want everyone treated as an individual

Note: While the names of some of the MBTI® preferences are familiar words, the MBTI® meaning of the preferences is somewhat different from everyday use. Remember:

• "Extrovert" does not mean "talkative" or "loud."
• "Introvert" does not mean "shy" or "inhibited."
• "Feeling" does not mean "emotional."
• "Judging" does not mean "judgmental."
• "Perceiving" does not mean "perceptive."

A Well-Balanced Myers-Briggs Profile

Linda Dean Fucci was secretary/treasurer at Auburn National Bank in Auburn, Alabama. Her duties included investment portfolio management, shareholder relations, asset liability management, strategic planning, accounting procedures, budgeting, tax planning, and control. In 1994, her duties were expanded to include the departments of data processing, marketing, and electronic services. She was also promoted to senior vice president of the bank's holding company.

After graduating from Southern Union Junior College with a grade point average (GPA) of 4.0, she completed flight training to the level of commercial pilot and flight instructor. Linda has always regretted not completing a Bachelor of Science degree in business, but this lack has not been a barrier to her career achievement. For example, she graduated from Louisiana State University's Graduate School of Banking of the South—one of the premier schools in the country for bankers on a fast career track—in 1986 with a GPA of 2.73 (out of 3.0). In a graduating class of 353 bankers, she not only ranked ninth in academic achievements but also was elected class president. The Alabama Senate passed a resolution of commendation for that achievement. Her previous bank president, William Walker, singled her out in a speech at a state banking meeting as the best chief financial officer at the time of any bank in the state.

Linda's decision-making style is intuitive-thinking. Although these two dimensions are her strongest, she is quite flexible. Through experience and effort, she has developed the sensing and feeling sides as well. In a confidential employee survey evaluating the effectiveness of the top-level Auburn National Bank officers, Linda received an excellent rating. Under the heading of "Additional Comments," one of the employees made this observation: "Linda is a great officer of the bank, representing us in a highly professional manner. She is a great manager and leader, earning a high degree of respect from her employees. She is my mentor. When I grow up, I want to be just like her."

Asked to describe her management philosophy and core values, Linda responded with the following impromptu remarks:

Maybe because I came up through the ranks, I can remember what it was like to be at all different levels. I can remember being unsure of myself and how different reactions made me feel. I try not to reprimand when people make mistakes but to understand and teach. I try never to make them feel "stupid." I do not think that people make errors intentionally....

I think that people need to feel important. Sometimes all it takes is a title. I do not like to call people "clerks." Doesn't "funds management assistant" sound better than "clerk"?

I try to provide my employees with as much knowledge as I can. I sincerely believe that shared knowledge is increased power. The more people in my department know, then the better they do their jobs and the better I, my department, and the whole organization look. I don't think anything makes me feel better than to teach someone something and then see them excel at putting it to use.

Once my employees have learned enough to progress to a given level, I try to leave them alone to get their jobs done. I know they will make some mistakes, but I also think they will learn more this way.

I try to give lots and lots of credit. Whenever I am praised for something done in my department, if others had a hand in it, I give them credit. On the other hand, I try not to pass on the blame. We deal with that back in the department.

I try always to be honest with the employees in my department.

I guess it all comes down to treating others the way I want to be treated; putting myself in their place and feeling how they feel; sensing what is difficult for them to say, to do, and trying to make it easier.

I believe in participative management. I have seen it work in our institution. People are experts in different areas, and the pooling of that expertise creates an exceptional organization. People work harder for a plan they have had a part in than a plan simply dictated to them.

Source: Discussions and correspondence with Linda Dean Fucci.

Carl Jung saw type development as a lifelong, never-ending process. People grow and develop problem-solving and decision-making processes if they have the ability to learn from experience. In our profile of Linda Fucci (intuitive-thinking), we saw an example of development of the sensing and feeling dimensions. As a result, she has the ability to use the appropriate dimension at the appropriate time, thus gaining good balance and wholeness in problem solving and decision making.

The Vroom-Yetton Model

Vroom-Yetton model

Provides guidelines on the extent to which subordinates are involved in decision making or problem solving.

The **Vroom-Yetton model** provides guidelines on the extent to which subordinates are involved in decision making or problem solving.[9] This involvement may run the gamut from consensus decision making by a natural or self-managing work team, a committee, or an ad hoc task force to the manager making the decision with minimal or no involvement of others. The assistance of subordinates may occur at any of the decision-making steps.

The extent of employee involvement is a contingency call based on the situation, the quality of information available to the decision making, the importance of subordinates' acceptance of the decision, and the time to make the decision.

Participation Exhibit 3-7 defines five alternative participation styles, as developed by Vroom and Yetton. There are two autocratic approaches (A and B), two consultative

EXHIBIT 3-7
Managers' Participation Styles for Making Decisions

PARTICIPATION STYLE	DESCRIPTION
A	You solve the problem or make the decision yourself, using the information available to you at the present time.
B	You obtain any necessary information from subordinates, then decide on a solution to the problem yourself.
C	You share the problem with the relevant subordinates individually, getting their ideas and suggestions without bringing them together as a group. Then *you* make the decision.
D	You share the problem with your subordinates in a group meeting, in which you obtain their ideas and suggestions. Then *you* make the decision.
E	You share the problem with your subordinates as a group. Together you generate and evaluate alternatives and attempt to reach agreement (consensus) on a solution. You can provide the group with information or ideas, but you do not try to press them to adopt "your" solution, and you are willing to accept and implement any solution that has the support of the entire group.

Note: A & B = autocratic, C & D = consultative, E = group consensus.

Source: Figure 9.3 from Leadership and Decision-Making, by Victor H. Vroom and Philip W. Yetton, © 1973. Reprinted by permission of the University of Pittsburgh Press.

approaches (C and D), and one group consensus approach (E). These five approaches represent the varying degrees of participation by others a manager uses in decision making.

Appropriate Style A manager can use a decision tree in determining which approach to use. One example of such a tree is shown in Exhibit 3-8. The questions shown at the top help the decision maker determine the characteristics of a given decision situation.

To use the model for a particular situation, you start at the left-hand side of the tree and work toward the right. When you encounter a box, answer the corresponding question and proceed to the next appropriate box. The decision style designation you finally reach will suggest which of the participation styles from Exhibit 3-7 you should probably use.

There are other parts of Vroom's and Yetton's theory that are too detailed to present here. This classic model has been the subject of much attention and is being tested and evaluated by many management researchers.[10]

Two cases at the end of this chapter will give you an opportunity to put the model to use. Although a model such as the one just discussed can help in selecting the best decision-making method, a manager's personal style also has a major impact on the method chosen. (Exhibit 3-9 shows how to use the model in making the decision on a student banquet date.)

Creative Problem Solving

More organizations and individual managers are involving subordinates in decision making and problem solving, particularly using styles similar to D and E in the Vroom-Yetton model. As a senior technician and union leader in a paper mill told one of the

EXHIBIT 3-8
Decision Tree,
Governing Group
Problems

1	2	3	4	5	6	7
Is there a quality requirement such that one solution is likely to be more rational than another?	Do you have sufficient information to make a high-quality decision?	Is the problem structured?	Is acceptance of decision by subordinates critical to implementation?	Is it reasonably certain that your subordinates would accept the decision if you were to make it by yourself?	Do subordinates share the organizational goals to be obtained in solving this problem?	Is conflict among subordinately likely in preferred solution?

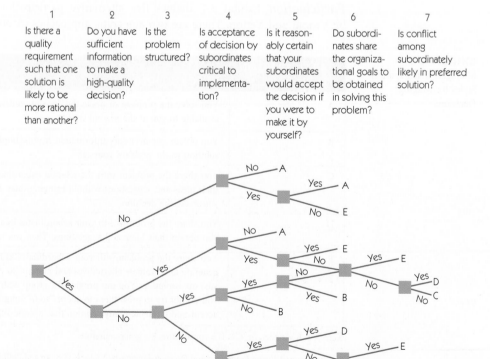

EXHIBIT 3-9
The Vroom-Yetton Model: Which Decision Style to Use

Decision Problem

As president of the Student Management Club at State University, you must make a decision concerning a date for the annual student banquet.

Q1 Is there a quality requirement such that one solution is likely to be more rational than another?

Ans Yes. One solution is likely to be more rational since there are various dates that will be unsatisfactory because of competing activities.

Q2 Do you have sufficient information to make a high-quality decision?

Ans No. You may have certain information on competing dates for some officially scheduled university activities, but there may be some other kinds of activities going on that you are unaware of.

Q3 Is the problem structured?

Ans Yes. Selection of a given date for a banquet to be held within the next month is a well-structured decision problem.

Q4 Is acceptance of the decision by your subordinates critical to implementation?

Ans Yes. If the subordinates (and others) don't show up, the banquet is a failure.

Q5 Is it reasonably certain that the decision would be accepted by your subordinates if you were to make it by yourself?

Ans No. You might accidentally select a date that would not be suitable to your subordinates. For example, the day you select could be one on which subordinates have a major exam or term papers due the following day.

Q6 Do members share the view that the banquet date is important?

Ans Yes. Members have shown good attendance at meetings and consider the banquet the highlight of the year. Awards are presented, next year's officers are announced, and so on.

Optimum Decision Style

As president, you should share the problem with members as a group, with the group generating and evaluating alternatives, and should attempt to arrive at a consensus decision.

---

authors, "Management used to tell us what to do; now they ask us." One of the primary reasons for this trend is the concept of synergy.

The Concept of Synergy and Some Processes of Creative Problem Solving

7 *Discuss some ways of improving decision making.*

synergy

The whole is greater than the sum of the parts.

Synergy means that the whole is greater than the sum of the parts. This concept is especially applicable in the use of teams and ad hoc task forces in problem solving. Assume that an ad hoc task force of five persons is presented with a complex problem that has an impact on the entire organization. If the team reaches a synergistic solution to the complex problem, then mathematically, synergy can be defined as $1 + 1 + 1 + 1 + 1 = $ more than 5.

Increasingly, this type of synergy is being achieved by teams throughout the world. This emphasis on synergistic teamwork is recognized in the United States by Rochester Institute of Technology's College of Business and *USA Today*'s Quality Cup Awards. These awards are presented in five categories to teams that have made outstanding contributions in products or services. The categories are manufacturing, service, nonprofit, government, and organizations with fewer than 500 employees.

creativity

Creativity is the process of developing something unique or original.

Developing Creativity

Scientists generalize that the right hemisphere of the brain captures our intuitive impulses. If we think of ourselves as problem solvers/decision makers, the right side of the brain generates ideas and is where imagination originates. Right-hemispheric functions are frequent catalysts for solution alternatives.

Alternatively, the brain's left hemisphere functions in logical, analytical, and linear ways, allowing the decision maker to evaluate his or her intuitive, imaginative alternatives. This is where judgment enters into the process. Although the brain has a multifunctional capacity, the decision maker may allow his or her preferred brain functioning to dominate and can allow left-side evaluation and analysis to encroach on right-brain intuitive ideas prematurely.

To gain the maximum benefit from ad hoc task forces, quality circles, self-managing work teams, or any problem-solving effort, the brain's left-hemisphere functions must be restrained initially. The key to doing so is to make use of the concept of deferred judgment. This is the idea behind brainstorming, and the secret is to develop right-hemispheric skills and to use them appropriately. After the ideas are generated, it is helpful to use analytical brain functions to evaluate and judge which insights are good, cost effective, and so forth. Using right-hemisphere functions as thought generators and following them with left-brained functions results in powerfully effective "whole-brained" creativity. Three techniques that are very useful in the idea generation process are brainstorming, the Crawford Slip technique, and the nominal grouping technique.

Brainstorming

brainstorming

Freely thinking of ideas without evaluating the ideas as they are generated.

One of the most effective techniques in creative problem solving is brainstorming. **Brainstorming** refers to a group of individuals responding to a question such as "How can we improve communication?" without evaluating the ideas as they are generated. The ideas are offered and recorded, no matter how silly they may appear and without regard to the rank of individuals or the value of any idea. Sorting out the value of respective ideas comes later. Larry Hirschorn, management consultant and writer, has suggested four excellent guidelines when using this powerful technique:

1. The group favors quantity over quality.
2. Team members refrain from judging anyone's contributions; they can ask questions later, in the evaluation part.
3. Team members avoid censoring.
4. Pride of authority is minimized; team members should feel free to offer variants and build on one another's ideas.[11]

Brainstorming is especially useful in developing alternatives during step 2 of the decision-making or problem-solving process. In most cases in creative problem solving, the team will draw from a number of alternatives in putting together the action plan. In addition to identifying possible solutions, brainstorming is also useful in these dimensions of creative problem solving:

- Defining all possible problems
- Redefining problems
- Determining all possible causes for a problem
- Listing all possible actions for implementing the chosen solution

Unfortunately, based on the observations of the authors, formally appointed committees and management meetings with subordinates rarely use brainstorming in their deliberation. For example, a faculty committee spent the allotted time for a meeting (two hours) debating the pros and cons of the second idea presented. On the other hand, ad hoc task forces and problem-solving teams tend to use brainstorming in a more creative and effective manner.

Stop & Think

Why do you think formal committees or bosses meeting with their subordinates seldom use brainstorming in problem-solving endeavors?

The Crawford Slip Technique

The **Crawford Slip technique** was developed by Professor C.C. Crawford at the University of Southern California. It makes use of two elements that are important in achieving creativity—fluency and flexibility. **Fluency** is the ability to let ideas flow out of your head like water over a waterfall, and **flexibility** is the ability to use free association to generate or classify ideas in categories. Materials needed are a number of 3″ × 5″ scratch pads and a number of empty boxes distributed among the participants. The process starts by telling participants that they are about to engage in a new type of problem solving that will generate 50 to 100 new ideas.

For example, this technique was used with the top management of Baldor Electric Company, a very successful company listed on the New York Stock Exchange. Unfortunately, one of the large motors it produced was losing money. The following series of steps was initiated to deal with the problem.[12]

1. Participants were asked not to pause to evaluate ideas and not to generate such thoughts as "We've tried this before."
2. Every participant was given a 3″ × 5″ scratch pad.
3. In this technique, the leader presents a problem in how-to form. In the case of Baldor Electric, the problem presented was, "How can we reduce costs on our 300 series motors without affecting quality?"
4. Each person would write down as many answers to the problem as time would permit. After an idea was written on a slip, it was placed in the idea bank (box) anonymously.
5. After 10 minutes, the idea boxes were collected and task forces established. In the case of Baldor, there were three task forces. Idea slips were distributed to them like cards dealt from a deck.
6. Each task force was charged with arranging the ideas in categories, using judgment (left side of the brain) to throw out weak ideas and then developing the good ideas and presenting recommendations to the larger group.

The CEO of the company then judged what ideas were most relevant to solving the problem and decided to implement them. Please note that although there was considerable participation in the process, *one person made the final decision*. In many instances, this is a desirable approach in using participative management.

Nominal Grouping Technique

The **nominal grouping technique (NGT)** also makes use of brainstorming, and we have found the technique to be very effective in developing creativity and generating useful information. Nominal grouping is a structured group technique for generating ideas through round-robin individual responses, group sharing without criticism, and written balloting. The authors have found it to be exceptionally beneficial to use nominal grouping in working with organizations. Exhibit 3-10 identifies the steps in nominal grouping when it is used in this manner. The following example illustrates the steps in the process.

Two of the authors were asked to participate in a management development program for a branch plant of a corporation headquartered in our home state. The plant, located in another state, was struggling to achieve a break-even point, and the executive vice president hired us to conduct management training sessions. The authors were rotating training sessions, and the report after the first session was that the "canned management training was similar to placing a Band-Aid on a festering boil." During the break, the employees complained about issues and problems the training program did not directly address. A consultation with the executive vice president resulted in a change in strategy for the next session.

EXHIBIT 3-10
Steps in Nominal
Grouping

Divide into groups of six or nine persons.

Without interaction, list the strengths you feel are associated with Question 1, and then list the problems for Question 2.   (Time: 6 minutes.)

Select a recorder.

a. The recorder asks each member, one at a time, to read from his or her card one strength associated with Question 1. *Example:* What are the strengths of this plant?

b. The recorder writes each strength exactly as it is read.

c. Those having the same strength should raise hands. The recorder checkmarks each strength once for each person raising a hand.

d. When all Question 1 strengths are recorded, the procedure is repeated for Question 2 problems. *Example:* What are the problems preventing this plant from reaching its potential effectiveness?

Discuss the two lists. Clarify, defend, elaborate, or add other items as needed.   (Time: 5 minutes.)

Without interaction, each member lists on an index card the *five* items he or she considers most important with reference to Question 1; do the same for Question 2.

The recorder collects and records the votes.

Using the nominal grouping process, the 25 participants (supervisors, managers, and staff personnel) were asked to respond to two questions:

1. What are the strengths of the plant?
2. What are the problems preventing this plant from reaching its potential effectiveness?

Twelve strengths were generated, and 55 problems were initially identified. Through nominal voting, the top five problems were prioritized; task forces from the participants were formed, and action plans were developed to solve the plant's more pressing problems.

Stop & Think

Because in this process only five problems were addressed, speculate on what happened to the majority of the other problems.

If your answer was, "They dissipated," you are correct.

Developing and implementing the action plans were catalysts in shifting the plant from a low performer to a high performer within a year.

8 *Explain the role of ethics in the organization's and supervisor's decision making.*

Ethical Considerations Play a Part

Supervisors must be particularly concerned with ethical considerations when making decisions and solving problems. They should have a true concern for the well-being of others, both inside and outside the organization. Therefore, supervisors should not only obey all laws and conform to the ethical codes of practice established by their employer and society, but also have a personal set of ethical principles that guides their actions. However, the difficult question is, what is and what isn't ethical?

ethics

Are the standards used to judge the "rightness" or the "wrongness" of one person's behavior toward others.

Ethics are the standards used to judge the "rightness" or "wrongness" of one person's behavior toward others. As this concept of ethical behavior is the individual's personal *ethic,* it is the highest and most rigid level of behavior. The next highest level is adhering to professional and organizational *codes of ethics,* which are statements of what is and isn't acceptable behavior. The lowest level is the *legal level,* where we are all expected to adhere to the "law of the land."

> *Making a profit with no regard for the repercussions of operating methods can be disastrous. Ethical operations will take into account many factors including the impact on the overall economic well-being of the local community and the community at large. The reputation of a fine organization and its financial standing can be soiled quickly by operating in an unethical manner.*

> *For example, Arthur Andersen, who headed one of the most respected accounting firms in the world, was a zealous supporter of high standards in the accounting industry. A stickler for honesty, he argued that an accountant's responsibility was to investors, not to the clients' management.*

> *During the early years, it is reported that Arthur Andersen was approached by an executive from a local rail utility to sign off on accounts containing flawed accounting or else face the loss of a major client. Arthur Andersen refused in no uncertain terms, replying that he would not sign the accounts "for all the money in America."*

> *For many years, Arthur Andersen's motto was "Think straight, talk straight." There is no doubt that Arthur Anderson was one of the most respected accounting firms in the world. This organization was built on being trustworthy. Its accounting expertise was highly valued. At the same time, it demonstrated high ethical standards and integrity that was beyond reproach. For decades, its accomplishments were rock solid.*

> *Unfortunately, a huge lapse in ethical judgment by key management personnel regarding Enron erased the company's entire reputation. Its history of a highly prized reputation in professional accounting was damaged forever. Today, it is no longer a viable accounting firm.*

> *Scandals involving Arthur Anderson and Enron are examples of ethically challenged organizations. Both of these companies were great at one time. Sadly, they stumbled along the way to success. They misplaced their ethics, with devastating results.*[13]

Even after passage of the Sarbanes-Oxley Act, a response to the Enron debacle, media stories abound of mismanagement, fraud, and deceit (e.g., Bernie Madoff and Mark Bloom). So what is the best approach to ensure ethical decision making in organizations today? That is the focus of the next section.

Stop & Think

Consider the numerous media stories highlighting unethical business behaviors. Which one in your opinion is the most troublesome? Why?

ethical organizations

Organizations composed of three pillars: ethical individuals, ethical leaders, and sound structures and systems.

Ethical Organizations

Why is the topic of ethics so important for business managers to consider? To answer this question, business professors Marc Orlitzky, Frank Schmidt, and Sara Rynes looked at 52 studies on corporate social responsibility over a 30-year period. They found that well-run, profitable businesses also boasted solid social and environmental records.[14] In short, it makes economic sense! So how does a company manage ethics and social responsibility to differentiate itself from its competitors? Exhibit 3-11 shows that **ethical organizations** are composed of three pillars: ethical individuals, ethical leadership, and sound structures and systems.

In 2009, financier Bernard Madoff was convicted of operating an enormous and lengthy Ponzi scheme, defrauding his clients of tens of billions of dollars.

EXHIBIT 3-11
The Three Pillars of Ethical Organizations

The Ethical Organization

Ethical Individuals
- Act with integrity
- Behave honestly
- Inspire trust
- Treat people right
- Play fair
- Have high level of moral development

Ethical Leadership
- Be a role model
- Uphold ethical values in the organization
- Communicate about ethics and values
- Reward ethical behavior
- Swiftly descipline unethical behavior

Structures and Systems
- Corporate culture
- Code of ethics
- Ethics committee
- Chief ethics officer
- Ethics training
- Whistle-blowing mechanisms

Source: Adapted from Linda Klebe Trevino, Laura Pincus Hartman, and Michael Brown, "Moral Person and Moral Manager," *California Management Review*, 42, No. 4 (Summer 2000), 128–142. Copyright © 2000, by The Regents of the University of California. Reprinted by permission of The Regents.

Ethical Individuals Ethical individuals are honest and act with integrity. Ethical people can be trusted by others and can be relied upon to make the "right" choice, even in very challenging circumstances. To illustrate, consider the strength of Sherron Watkins's character, the person responsible for blowing the whistle on the aforementioned Enron and Arthur Anderson.

> *Were Sherron Watkins's actions worth the fallout? Since then, as one of America's most famous whistle-blowers, she has argued in published articles and speeches that her actions were not only justifiable, but ultimately beneficial. Watkins insisted that businesses must be judged on more than just the profits they create, and that "we need to reward the good, ethical ones." Although many people were hurt by her actions, she feels vindicated that her insistence on morality in business has lessened the chance that corruption will be rewarded.*[15]

Managers may not be faced with the type of ethical dilemma Sherron Watkins had to deal with on a daily basis, but ethical issues do arise in the workplace. What separates people like Sherron from the rest of the pack is a firm belief in treating others fairly, with respect, and with dignity. Sometimes it is as simple as following the golden rule, treating others as you would like to be treated. However, as the collapse of Enron shows, simply hiring ethical individuals such as Sherron is not enough—it is only part of the solution. Leadership is at the core of initiating a vision of ethical behavior and setting the tone for what is and is not considered appropriate behavior.

Ethical Leadership Look at Exhibit 3-11 again—this particular pillar is at the center of the ethical organization for a reason. Leaders guide the way; they are the visible face of the organization to internal as well as external stakeholders. As such, they are role models for others. This is especially true for supervisors. Your employees observe how you communicate with others, handle interpersonal conflict, and appraise others' actions, and even see some actions of which you are unaware! For example, if you openly communicate with your employees about ethics and important values, they will, over time, develop a sense of trust and a certain level of respect for you. If you act swiftly to deal with unethical behavior, this sends a direct message regarding what will and will not be tolerated. As a result, your employees' behaviors will become more consistent with the expectations that you have set. Consider the following story about Dan Amos.

> *Dan Amos, CEO of Aflac, joined the company in 1973. During his tenure, the company has grown into an international powerhouse in the insurance industry. Amos inherited a company that was founded on ethical principles, like many of the World's Most Ethical Companies. "This company was founded with the premise that if you take care of your employees, they will take care of the company. This principle has proven true for more than 50 years as Aflac has grown from a small family business to a Fortune 500 company," says Amos. One of the aspects that helps the company continue to thrive is Amos' transparent leadership. "As a public company there is a responsibility to tell people what is happening regardless of whether the news is particularly good or bad," Amos admits. "At Aflac, it is our custom to tell the people what we are doing and why we are doing it to limit any surprises in the future. As a publicly traded company, our actions impact the lives of shareholders and since they own our company, they have a right to know what lies ahead." This isn't just rhetoric—Amos can regularly be heard around the office telling employees, "Bad news does not improve with age." Amos notes that Aflac's ethics program isn't just intended for upper levels of management. Rather, an ethical culture is taught from the top down.*[16]

Stop & Think

Structures and Systems In addition to having ethical individuals and leaders, it is important that corporations create and sustain cultures that support ethical behavior. Developing a values statement or code of ethics is a good starting point, but to ensure this document has teeth, it is necessary to appoint a chief ethics officer to chair an ethics committee responsible for conducting ethics training and developing whistle-blowing mechanisms, such that the true spirit of the ethics document permeates throughout the entire organization.

Creating an ethical corporate culture is not easy. *Ethisphere* publishes a list of the world's most ethical companies each year. They utilize expert professors, government officials, lawyers, and organizational leaders to identify the initial pool of organizational candidates and develop and apply ethical criteria to generate a short list of potential winners. The winners of the World's Most Ethical Companies Awards are truly ethical leaders in their industries. (You may visit http://ethisphere.com to view winners for previous years or the current candidates.)

> *Each of these companies will have materially higher scores versus their competitors. They are the companies who force other companies to follow their leadership or fall behind. These are the companies who use ethical leadership as a profit driver. And each of these companies embody the true spirit of Ethisphere's credo, "Good. Smart. Business. Profit."*[17]

External monitoring by watchdog groups is certainly a behavioral influence on organizations, but better internal monitoring is likely the key determinant of organizational change. As little as a decade ago, U.S. companies had few people to inspect thousands of manufacturing sites. Their superficial audits "didn't get at the root causes of problems," says Auret Van Heerden, executive director of the nonprofit Fair Labor Association.

> *Today, Van Heerden says, more corporations are strengthening their monitoring and teaching suppliers how to better run their plants and manage workers.... Nike (a 2008 Ethisphere Award Winner) is a seasoned veteran of audits. In the 1990s, the company was a favorite target of activists because of foreign sweatshops run by its suppliers.*

> *Now Nike inspects many of its 1,000 suppliers' factories worldwide. It grades them from A to D and warns poorly run sites to improve or get dropped, says Nike Vice-President Dusty Kidd.*[18]

Xerox (another 2008 Ethisphere Award Winner) has developed and implemented structures and systems to ensure honest, ethical interaction with another key stakeholder group—its employees.

> *Speaking with David Frishkorn, Director of Business Ethics & Compliance at Xerox, reveals a unique approach that Xerox employs in their ethics program. Many companies will place a strong emphasis on tone from the top, and stop there. Frishkorn prefers a different approach. "When everyone focuses on tone from the top, you can have somebody standing there, yelling and shouting, but if they're not respected, or if the message isn't properly received, or if the environment is one that is contrary to what the words from the top are, it's not going to be effective," says Frishkorn. "The real test of the tone*

*from the top is that it's received well and that the employees commit to the program."
To that end, Frishkorn says that Xerox helps employees get involved in the ethics program through a basic monthly survey that asks simple questions such as, "Do you think
it's an ethical environment?", "Do you know about the helpline?", and "Would you call
the helpline?" These fundamental questions help the compliance team get an accurate
reading of the corporate environment. "There is ample opportunity and space in that
survey for people to write in comments, and that's where we actually get a lot of the
'good' data," Frishkorn says. "So when something monumental happens that is either
good or bad from the employees' perspective, relative to the ethics at Xerox, we can
pick up on that pretty quick in the write-in comments."[19]*

Stop & Think

Think of your own organization or, if you are not currently employed, a past employer
or your school. Evaluate how ethical your organization is using the three pillars just described. Does your employer give equal weight to developing and sustaining all three
pillars?

Chapter Review

1. **Explain the role of decision making in the supervisor's job.**

   This chapter focused on managerial decision making, which is the conscious selection of a course of action from among available alternatives to produce a given result. All employees, but especially managers, must make decisions.

2. **Discuss why supervisors need to make so many decisions.**

   Programmed decisions are routine and repetitive and enable management to develop
   a systemic way to make them. Unprogrammed decisions occur relatively infrequently, and a separate decision must be undertaken each time.

3. **Define decision making and identify at least four elements involved.**

   The five steps in managerial decision making are (1) recognizing a problem or opportunity, (2) developing alternative courses of action, (3) evaluating the advantages
   and disadvantages of the alternatives, (4) selecting a preferred alternative and implementing it, and (5) evaluating the decision results.

4. **Discuss how decisions are made.**

   The decision-making method used is also influenced by the decision maker's personal problem-solving type or style. According to the Myers-Briggs Type Indicator,
   individuals have two ways of perceiving information and two ways of evaluating it.
   The four combinations of sensing-thinking, intuitive-thinking, sensing-feeling, and
   intuitive-feeling have a definite influence on problem solving and decision making.
   Ideally, a balance will be developed by using all four dimensions in decision making.

5. **Name some factors to keep in mind when making decisions.**

   To what extent should a manager involve others in the decision-making process?
   The Vroom-Yetton model helps answer the question by examining the key characteristics of given decision situations and identifying various decision-making styles.

A particular decision style can be selected based on answers to questions about the characteristics of the given situation. Some techniques for involving others in creative problem solving are brainstorming, the Crawford Slip technique, and the nominal grouping technique.

6. **Decide whether to use the individual approach or the group approach when making decisions.**

   The more effective supervisors use ethical value judgments in making decisions. Ethics are the standards used to judge the "rightness" or "wrongness" of actions or decisions when dealing with other people or organizations. Ethical value judgments have a wide range of consequences involving the decision maker, employees, stockholders, and the community in general, and therefore, as much consideration should be given to people and their problems as to economical and financial factors.

7. **Discuss some ways of improving decision making.**

   Decision-making can be improved by individuals working together to achieve synergy. Brainstorming, The Crawford Slip, and the Nominal Grouping Techniques are tools supervisors can use to enhance creativity and achieve synergy during the decision-process.

8. **Explain the role of ethics in the organization's and supervisor's decision making.**

   Ethical organizations are composed of three pillars: ethical individuals, ethical leaders, and ethical structures and systems. Although ethical leadership is at the center of a well-grounded organization, a lack of one or more of these key elements makes an organization vulnerable to unethical tendencies and practices.

   Supervisors must be particularly concerned with ethical considerations when making decisions and solving problems. They should have a true concern for the well-being of others, both inside and outside the organization. Therefore, supervisors should not only obey all laws and conform to the ethical codes of practice established by their employer and society, but also have a personal set of ethical principles that guides their actions.

Key Terms

span of management, p. 66

decision making, p. 66

programmed decisions, p. 68

unprogrammed decisions, p. 68

opportunity, p. 68

problem, p. 68

alternatives, p. 72

cost/benefit analysis, p. 72

risk, p. 73

Myers-Briggs Type Indicator (MBTI), p. 74

Vroom-Yetton model, p. 77

synergy, p. 79

creativity, p. 79

brainstorming, p. 80

Crawford Slip technique, p. 81

fluency, p. 81

flexibility, p. 81

nominal grouping technique (NGT), p. 81

ethics, p. 82

ethical organizations, p. 83

Questions for Review & Discussion

1. Peter Drucker states that a big decision-making error supervisors frequently make is failing to get a handle on a problem. Often, managers plunge in prematurely. Why do you think many managers make this common mistake?

2. Discuss the following statement: It's better for a manager to try to carry out a poor decision for the sake of worker confidence. You can't build worker confidence by continually admitting the poor decisions you make.

3. What are the pros and cons of decisions made by groups such as committees and task forces as compared to decisions made by one person?

4. Is it possible for someone to be a good decision maker but a poor supervisor? Explain.

5. One supervisor says that she finds procrastination to be a big help in her decision making. Do you agree or disagree? Why?

6. Is it possible to operate as an ethical organization without one or more of the three pillars? Discuss.

Resources

Information

Systems

Skill Builder 3-1

Coast Guard Cutter Decision Problem

You are the captain of a 210-foot medium-endurance Coast Guard cutter, with a crew of 9 officers and 65 enlisted personnel. Your mission is general at-sea law enforcement and search and rescue. At 2:00 this morning, while en route to your home port after a routine two-week patrol, you received word from the New York Rescue Coordination Center that a small plane had ditched 70 miles offshore. You obtained all the available information concerning the location of the crash, informed your crew of the mission, and set a new course at maximum speed heading for the scene to commence a search for survivors and wreckage.

You have now been searching for 20 hours. Your search operation has been increasingly impaired by rough seas, and there is evidence of a severe storm building to the southwest. The atmospherics associated with the deteriorating weather have made communications with the New York Rescue Coordination Center impossible. A decision must be made shortly about whether to abandon the search and place your vessel on a northeasterly course to ride out the storm—thereby protecting the vessel and your crew, but relegating any possible survivors to almost certain death from exposure—or to continue a potentially futile search and incur the risks it would entail.

Instructions: You have contacted the weather bureau for up-to-date information concerning the severity and duration of the storm. While your crew members are extremely conscientious about their responsibility, you believe that they would be divided on the decision of leaving or staying.

Review the decision processes in this chapter in Exhibit 3-7 and decide which comes closest to what you would do if you were the captain in this situation. Circle your choice:

A   B   C   D   E

Source: Vroom/Jago, The New Leadership: Managing Participation in Organizations, 1e, pp. 42–43, © 1988 Pearson Education, Inc. Reproduced by permission of Pearson Education, Inc.

Resources

Information

Systems

Skill Builder 3-2

New Machines Decision Problem

You are the manufacturing manager in a large electronics plant. The company's management has always been searching for ways of increasing efficiency. They have recently installed new machines and put in a new, simplified work system, but to the surprise of everyone, including yourself, the expected increase in productivity was not realized. In fact, production has begun to drop, quality has fallen off, and the number of employee separations has risen.

You do not believe that there is anything wrong with the machines. You have had reports from other companies that are using them, and the reports confirm this opinion. You have also had representatives from the firm that built the machines go over them, and they report that the machines are operating at peak efficiency.

You suspect that some parts of the new work system may be responsible for the change, but this view is not widely shared among your immediate subordinates—four first-level supervisors, each in charge of a section, and your supply manager. The drop in production has been variously attributed to poor training of the operators, lack of an adequate system of financial incentives, and poor morale. Clearly, this is an issue about which there is considerable depth of feeling within individuals and potential disagreement among your subordinates.

This morning you received a phone call from your division manager. He had just received your production figures for the last six months and was calling to express his concern. He indicated that the problem was yours to solve in any way that you thought best, but that he would like to know within a week what steps you plan to take.

You share your division manager's concern about the falling productivity and know that your people are also concerned. The problem is to decide what steps to take to rectify the situation.

Instructions: Review the decision processes in this chapter in Exhibit 3-7 and decide which comes closest to what you would do if you were the manager in the above situation. Circle your choice:

A B C D E

Source: Case IV from Leadership and Decision-Making, by Victor H. Vroom and Philip W. Yetton, © 1973. Reprinted by permission of the University of Pittsburgh Press.

Information

Technology

Skill Builder 3-3

Identifying Your Problem-Solving Style

Instructions: Indicate the response that comes closest to how you usually feel or act. If you really cannot choose, two answers being an absolute toss-up, leave that question unanswered. There are no correct or incorrect answers.

1. Which are you more careful about, (a) what people's rights are or (b) how people feel?
2. Which phrase do you feel best describes you, (a) having common sense or (b) having vision?
3. Are you more likely to be impressed by (a) principles or (b) emotions?
4. Which phrase best describes your preference as to how to get a job done, (a) using techniques that have proved effective in past situations or (b) experimenting with new and different approaches?
5. In making decisions, which is more important to you, (a) standards or (b) feelings?
6. Which do you think is worse, (a) not having a clear grasp of details or (b) not having a clear grasp of the big picture?
7. Do your friends see you as basically more (a) hardheaded or (b) warmhearted?
8. Are you basically more interested in (a) data or (b) ideas?
9. If another person says something that is incorrect, which would you normally do, (a) point out the error or (b) ignore it?
10. Which kind of person would you prefer as a roommate, (a) someone who's very practical, with both feet on the ground, or (b) someone who's always having new ideas?
11. Are you best described as (a) drawing conclusions in a logical, objective way or (b) drawing conclusions based on feelings or emotions?
12. In making decisions, are you more likely to decide based on (a) the real facts and data or (b) your hunches?
13. As a student, would you prefer taking (a) fact-oriented courses or (b) theory-oriented courses?
14. Which do you feel is the greater error, (a) to be too sympathetic or (b) to be too firm?
15. Assume that a party contains two rooms of people, and in each room are the same types of people. Which room would you be drawn to, (a) a room with sensible people or (b) a room with imaginative people?
16. Which of the following terms best describes you: (a) objective or (b) compassionate?
17. Which do you value more highly, (a) a strong sense of reality or (b) a strong imagination?
18. Which role has the greater appeal to you, (a) being a judge or (b) being a peacemaker?
19. In which of these activities have you more interest: (a) production or (b) design?
20. Would you describe yourself as (a) more firm than merciful or (b) more merciful than firm?

(Continued)

Score Sheet
Instructions: Record your answers to each question in the appropriate box. Then add the total number of checks in each column. If you have an equal number of points for Sensor and Intuitor, circle the Intuitor; if an equal number of points for Thinker and Feeler, circle the Feeler.

Resources

Interpersonal Skill

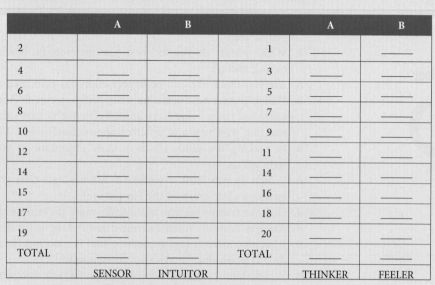

	A	B		A	B
2	___	___	1	___	___
4	___	___	3	___	___
6	___	___	5	___	___
8	___	___	7	___	___
10	___	___	9	___	___
12	___	___	11	___	___
14	___	___	14	___	___
15	___	___	16	___	___
17	___	___	18	___	___
19	___	___	20	___	___
TOTAL	___	___	TOTAL	___	___
	SENSOR	INTUITOR		THINKER	FEELER

The Keirsey Temperament Sorter is very similar to the MBTI® in terms of question content, terminology, and personality types. To find out your complete personality type (using all four dimensions), you may visit http://www.keirsey.com/ to complete a multiquestion instrument and receive a preview of your complete personality profile online. Simply proceed to http://www.keirsey.com/sorter/register.aspx to register and complete the online instrument.

Information

Skill Builder 3-4

The $100,000 Investment Decision

Assume that a wealthy entrepreneur has provided a $2 million fund for the management department at your school to be used in improving students' decision-making skills. The department has decided to use this course as the vehicle for student development in decision making.

Divide the class into teams of five to seven students. Each team is given $100,000 to invest for a period of five years. At the end of that period, a member of each team will have six months to liquidate the team's investment(s).

The $100,000 principal, along with 50 percent of profits, will be returned to the management department. The remaining 50 percent will be divided among team members. The department will cover any loss of principal up to $75,000.

Each team's assignment is as follows:

Technology

1. Following the steps of the decision-making process, reach a decision about what your investment(s) will be. Write out your reasoning for each step in the decision-making process and turn in the report to your instructor.

2. Prepare a 10-minute PowerPoint presentation and discuss with the rest of the class why your decision will reap the best return in five years.

At the end of the exercise, class members will vote on which team seems to have made the best investment decision(s).

Supervisor Creativity—Supportive Behavior Assessment 3-1

Leadership

Supervisor Assessment Exercise 3-1: Supervisor Creativity—Supportive Behavior For each of the following questions, using a six-point Likert scale ranging from "never" (1) to "always" (6), select the answer that best describes how frequently your supervisor is engaged in the following behaviors.

My functional manager/supervisor

1.	attempted to get materials I needed to do my job.	____
2.	worked persistently to secure resources I needed to be innovative in my work.	____
3.	Served as a good role model for creativity.	____
4.	provided valued rewards for my creative work.	____
5.	publicly recognized my innovation efforts.	____
6.	encouraged me to set innovation goals.	____
7.	praised my creative work.	____
8.	'stood up' for my innovative efforts.	____
9.	praised my creative work.	____
10.	took pride in my work and accomplishments.	____
11.	bolstered my confidence in my creative potential.	____
12.	encouraged me to collaborate with others in my work.	____
13.	stressed the importance of idea sharing among colleagues.	____
14.	actively sought work interaction with outside members.	____
15.	tried to obtain work-related information necessary for my job.	____
16.	encouraged me to communicate openly with people in other departments.	____

Scoring and Interpretation The high score on this instrument is a 96 ($6 \times 16 = 96$). The low score is a 16 ($1 \times 16 = 16$). The mid-point is 56.

Sum up your total points. A score of 76 or higher suggests superior creativity and supportive behavior skills. A score of 56 to 76 indicates above average creativity and supportive behavior skills. A score below 56 suggests that there is room for improvement.

Source: Adapted from Pamela Tierney and Steven M. Farmer. The Pygmalion Process and Employee Creativity, Journal of Management, Jun 2004, Vol. 30, pp. 413–432. Copyright © 2004 by Sage Publications. Reprinted by permisison of Sage Publications.

When Your Personality and Job Don't Match—Time for a Change

Cynde Greer began working for a well-known federal agency as soon as she graduated from high school. Not unlike many young people first starting out, her decision was based on the hourly pay and good benefits. But after working there for a very short period of time, she realized she didn't really like the job or the organization. The environment was very bureaucratic, stifling, and unfair. Cynde said, "My manager would give me work to do, and because of my work ethic, I would do the job to the best of my ability. After a while, my manager was giving me more work than the others, and I asked why. The manager said, 'I know you will do it and do it right.' So right then I knew if you show any drive, initiative, and know-how, you are NOT going to be promoted! They promote the people that can't get along with others and don't do the work!"

Without a college degree, she didn't think she could find a better job, so she continued to work at the federal agency. Over time, the negative environment really wore on Cynde's mental state. As she describes, "It is hard to work somewhere for 18 years where the only type of feedback you get is negative. We were never complimented on our work or told we were doing a good job." Finally, the last straw was when her manager came to her and told her that of her two days off each week, she would have to give up Fridays. That was the turning point. Although she only needed to put in two more years of service to be eligible for early retirement, she knew she was too angry and stressed out to make it. So she quit.

As a member of a dual-income family, she started looking for another job. One day on the radio, she heard an advertisement for massage therapy school. She had always enjoyed getting a massage and pampering herself, so she decided to apply. Cynde was accepted and immediately knew she had made the right decision. Cynde said, "It just felt right! The day I gave my first massage, I got such positive feedback. I had not had that in my previous job. Helping others has always been important to me, and with massage therapy, you can see the transformation—the help you are

providing people is apparent immediately. I thrived on the positive feedback."

Although Cynde truly felt her career move was the right decision, she and her husband, John, had to figure out if they could financially handle the $10,000 or so initial investment (including the cost of school) necessary to get Cynde started as a massage therapist after graduation. Based on their calculations, Cynde would have positive cash flows within the first year of operation that would enable her to effectively manage the debt she would incur. John's best estimate on break-even was about eight years. This estimate included the assumption of additional investments (e.g., continuing education units [CEUs], equipment, etc.). They decided to go for it!

Three main types of legitimate massage therapy exist. The first type is somewhat "spiritual" in the sense that the body's aura and energy are emphasized. The second type is focused on recreational massage or "spa therapy," which is often experienced at resorts. The third type is medical or health related. Cynde wanted her business mission to be the latter, helping people with pain management. She rented a 325-square foot facility for $300 per month. Cynde did the painting, decorating, and website herself to keep her costs down. She initially tried joining business associations and various advertising strategies but soon realized the best way to get dependable customers was simple word of mouth.

After three years in business, Cynde is doing well. She charges $65 per hour with rate differentials for more or less time. Financially, she is making double what most therapists make. Her clientele is composed of individuals 35 years of age and older, with 85 percent being women and 50 percent being recurring customers. The business flows are somewhat seasonal—Christmas and spring are the most active periods. From January to May, her schedule is quite full, with summer being the slowest period. Cynde believes she has done better than most, even during economic downturns, because of her mission. People with pain don't take breaks. Her services are always in demand—so much so that in addition to her clients, she is now teaching classes at the massage therapy school! Her massage classes include Swedish, spa, sports, chair, and special populations (e.g., pregnancy), as well as courses in business management and laws/licensing. In addition, she sublets her facility off and on to another therapist when she is not using it. Even though the sublet brings in additional revenues, it is not a dependable arrangement.

At this point, Cynde is faced with another decision to make. What to do next? She has identified four possible alternatives.

1. Implement a stability strategy and continue operating just as she is currently.
2. Grow the business through independent contractors. She has spoken to her landlord and believes she can get the space next door, which is between 1,000 and 1,200 square feet. While the rent is negotiable, Cynde believes she may be able to negotiate a rate between $700 and $1,000 per month. The space is already set up for dividers, so she could conceivably put two to four other therapists in the space in separate areas. In addition to a bathroom, it has an area for a washer and dryer, which would enable Cynde to launder on site the sheets, blankets, and towels used by her clients. Cynde would rent each space for $600, which would include the use of her established business name, the space, utilities, and washing/drying services. Each therapist would handle all of his or her own customers, including appointments, billing, supplies, etc.
3. Grow the business by hiring employees. Assuming she could get the space next door under the same terms and conditions described in alternative 2, Cynde would hire one to two massage therapists, rather than using independent contractors. The employee could be paid $15 per hour to be on site for six to eight hours five days a week and could earn tips from clients.

Since she is now teaching at the massage school, Cynde believes she will be in a position to offer an opportunity to the best graduates.

4. Diversify the business by becoming a full-service salon. This alternative would require moving to a different, larger, and more visible business location. The facility would need two separate entrances—one for massage therapy services and one for traditional salon services. Her daughter is thinking about cosmetology school, and this would be an opportunity for Cynde and her daughter to work together, with her daughter ultimately having something tangible as a career alternative. The full-service salon would provide hair styling, manicures, pedicures, a variety of massages (e.g., health, sports, spa), and personal care products. The salon would employ full-time employees as well as utilize independent contractors.

Questions

1. What type of MBTI® decision style do you think Cynde has? Explain.
2. Based on your answer to question 1, what are Cynde's strengths and blind spots when making important decisions?
3. Help Cynde with steps 3 and 4 of the decision process (e.g., see Exhibit 3-3) by gathering information from the library and the Internet, visiting and interviewing similar types of businesses locally, and so on. Using this information and what you have learned from this chapter, how would you advise Cynde to proceed? Discuss.

Source: Prepared by Don C. Mosley, Jr. and Charles Warren, Mitchell College of Business, University of South Alabama, Mobile, AL.

4

Fundamentals of Organizing

LEARNING OBJECTIVES

After reading and studying this chapter, you should be able to:

1. Understand the stages of organization growth.

2. Identify the advantages and disadvantages of the functional, product, and matrix departmentalization approaches.

3. Explain the principles of unity of command and span of control.

4. Describe the difference between line and staff.

5. Understand how to avoid excessive conflict between line and staff.

6. Explain the three types of authority found in organizations.

7. Distinguish between centralization and decentralization.

8. Discuss the benefits and costs of downsizing.

9. Explain the four types of contemporary organizational approaches.

10. Understand the relationship between management philosophy, strategy, and newer forms of organization.

Rayman/Digital Vision/Jupiter Images

New businesses, like John Moody's, often begin as one-person organizations inspired by the business owner's personal interests.

The only things that evolve by themselves in an organization are disorder, friction, and malperformance.

—*Peter Drucker*

Preview

JOHN MOODY'S GROWING ORGANIZATION Our story begins in a small Midwestern city of 75,000. Our main character is John Moody, 29, a high-school graduate and veteran, who has been working in a large paper mill on the outskirts of the city since his discharge from the service. John has held the same semiskilled job at the operative level since he started at the mill. His wife's relatives believe he is a lazy person with a low IQ who will never amount to much. Actually, John is quite an intelligent person, but his basic satisfaction in life comes from the challenge of building and creating things in his garage workshop. Although he assumes that he will never get rich, he feels his take-home pay is sufficient to take care of the necessities of life and to support his hobbies. Even though his job at the mill is not very challenging, he gets all the challenge he needs from tinkering around in his workshop.

Unfortunately, the country has begun to slide into an economic recession, which is adversely affecting the paper industry. Several mill employees, including John, are laid off because of excessive inventory buildup. John signs up for unemployment compensation and decides to spend time building a new boat trailer in his garage. He puts a lot of thought and effort into the task. The result is an excellent trailer—such a fine one that several of his friends talk him into building trailers for them for 20 percent more than his expenses.

Even at this price, his boat trailer sells for less than those sold in local stores. Before long, so many requests are coming in that John finds himself spending all his time in his garage. At this point, John decides to work full time building boat trailers as long as he can make a living doing so.

Organizing is one of the key functions of any manager or supervisor. In this chapter, we present concepts, principles, and a frame of reference for understanding this function. We do so by expanding on the John Moody preview case throughout the chapter to illustrate the stages of growth in most organizations and the principles of organizing.

Many first-level managers understand organization only from a narrow vantage point—their immediate department or perhaps one or two levels above them. We believe that it is equally important to be able to see and understand the organization from a much broader standpoint. The more completely supervisors understand the big picture, the better equipped they are to work effectively as key members of the management team. Consequently, organizing is presented from a broad, overall perspective in this chapter. Failure to understand the organizing function from a broader viewpoint can lead to the following problems:

1. Excessive violation of the unity of command principle.
2. Failure to develop additional departments or work groups when needed.
3. Unclear and improper assignment of duties and responsibilities to new employees.
4. Ineffective use of organizational units and inadequate development of human resources because of improper decentralization of authority.
5. Excessive and unhealthy conflicts between departments and between line supervisors and staff personnel.

The Four Stages in Growth of an Organization

1 *Understand the stages of organization growth.*

To see the organizing function of management in operation, let us study the growth and development of John Moody's hypothetical manufacturing business. Usually, a business organization grows in four stages. Stage 1 is the one-person organization, stage 2 is the organization with assistants added, stage 3 is the line organization, and stage 4 is the line-and-staff organization. Not all organizations go through all of these stages. Many skip the first stage and go directly to stage 2. For clarity's sake, however, we'll discuss each stage.

Stage 1: The One-Person Organization

From our reading of the preview case, we see that John Moody's business is in the first stage of organizational growth—that is, a one-person operation (Exhibit 4-1). This means that John alone performs the three basic activities common to all manufacturing operations: financing, producing, and selling.

EXHIBIT 4-1
John Moody's
One-Person
Organization

John Moody
Owner and Operator

Finance
Production
Sales

Stage 2: The Organization with Assistants Added

After 3 months, so many orders are coming in that John Moody cannot fill them. In the past few years, the federal government has built a number of dams near John's town, creating four new lakes in the region. Fishing has been good, and there is a large demand for boats and boat trailers. John is now making more money per day than he did when he was with the mill. To keep pace with the orders, he hires Ray Martin, a former army buddy, to help build the trailers. For a small monthly salary, John also hires his wife, Nancy, to keep the books and handle the financial details. Before the month is out, Ray has mastered his job so well that he and John are producing more boat trailers than they have orders for. At this point, John and Ray start thinking about hiring someone as a salesperson. Ray's brother, Paul, has just graduated from college with a major in marketing. After hearing about John's business from John and Ray, Paul decides that it has possibilities. With the assurance of an opportunity to buy into the business in the future, Paul starts to work for John as a salesperson.

Exhibit 4-2 shows that John Moody has had to hire three assistants to help carry out the three primary activities of his business. This stage is a critical one; over 50 percent of new businesses fail in their first year of operation from lack of capital, ineffective management, or both.

Paul Martin proves to be an excellent salesperson, and the business continues to grow. To keep up with the increasing volume of orders, John hires additional people. Also, the business moves to a larger building. As Exhibit 4-3 shows, after two years, John has 18 people working for him. His net income is such that Nancy has quit working, but John finds himself so busy that he cannot enjoy his higher income. More important, he feels that he is losing control of the business. The increased costs per trailer support this belief.

EXHIBIT 4-2
John Moody Hires Assistants

John Moody
Owner and Manager

| **Nancy Moody** Finance | **Ray Martin** Production | **Paul Martin** Sales |

EXHIBIT 4-3
John Moody's
Organization after Two
Years

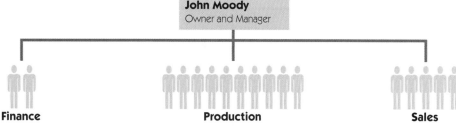

John Moody
Owner and Manager

Finance   **Production**   **Sales**

Stop & Think

Before reading further, look at the organization chart in Exhibit 4-3. Can you explain why John Moody is losing control of his business?

In desperation, John Moody asks the Martin brothers for advice about his problem. Paul Martin recalls that in one of his college courses, the instructor talked about the management principle of span of control. This principle holds that there is a limit to the number of people a manager can supervise effectively. In Paul's opinion, the solution is to select managers for the areas of finance, production, and sales.

Paul's solution seems so simple that John Moody wonders why he didn't think of it himself. He places Beth Fields—his best accountant—in charge of finance, Ray Martin in charge of production, and Paul Martin in charge of sales.

Stage 3: The Line Organization

line organization

An organization concerned with the primary functions of the firm—in this case, production, sales, and finance.

Exhibit 4-4 shows that John Moody has selected a manager for each of the three major departments, and his span of control has been reduced from 18 to three employees. Beth Fields is responsible for two employees, Ray Martin for nine employees, and Paul Martin for four employees. In effect, John Moody's business is now structured as a **line organization.** This means that each person in the organization has clearly defined responsibilities and reports to an immediate supervisor.

There are two advantages to having a line organization at an early stage of a business organization's growth:

1. Quick, decisive action on problems is possible because authority is centralized—it is in the hands of John Moody and his three managers.
2. Lines of responsibility and authority are clearly defined. Everyone knows what his or her job and obligations are. Thus, evasion of responsibility is minimized and accountability is maximized.

As a result of the line organization and the capabilities of each manager, the unit cost of making each boat trailer is lowered. Under the leadership of sales manager Paul Martin, the business expands its sales territory to cover most of the states in the

EXHIBIT 4-4
The Span of Control in John Moody's Line Organization

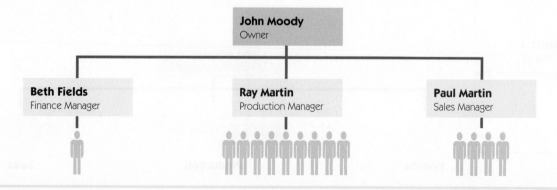

Midwest. As sales increase, production also increases. New people are added in both sales and production. The line organization develops to accommodate the increased growth. Keeping in mind the principle of span of control, John Moody adds new sections in production and sales whenever the volume of business justifies the new additions. He now also finds time to concentrate more on such tasks as developing plans for the future, coordinating the work of the three departments, and supervising his managers.

After 10 years, John Moody's business is employing over 150 people. During this period, John has promoted Ray Martin to be in charge of five production department heads. Exhibit 4-5 shows that this move has created an additional level of management in the production department. The department heads, in turn, are each responsible for four production supervisors. Each production supervisor is responsible for 10 production workers. Similarly, John has made Paul Martin sales manager in charge of three regional sales managers, each of whom is supervising eight salespersons.

Stage 4: The Line-and-Staff Organization

Unfortunately, increasing sales require John Moody's business to add more people to meet production quotas, so the profit on each unit produced declines. Finally, Beth Fields, the head of finance, reports to John that each $1.00 in sales is costing $1.10. In other words, a boat trailer that the business sells for $300 is costing $330 to manufacture. Although the business is now financially sound, John is aware that, with the way things are going, it will not take long for the business to go bankrupt. He, therefore, decides to call in a reputable management consultant.

EXHIBIT 4-5
John Moody's Line Organization after 10 Years

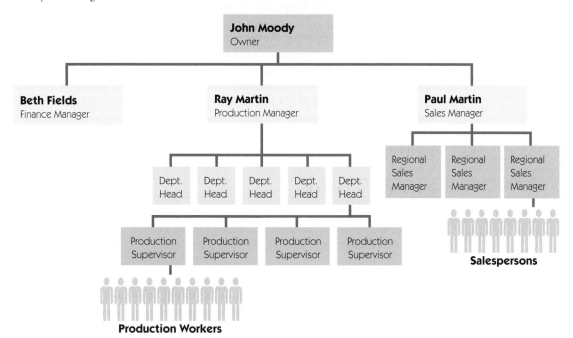

Stop & Think

Before reading the consultant's recommendations, decide what you think is the primary problem or problems causing manufacturing costs to increase in John Moody's business. The management consultant interviews managers from different levels in the company. After several days of investigation, the consultant makes the following report to John Moody:

line-and-staff organization

An organization structure in which staff positions are added to serve the basic line departments and help them accomplish the organization objectives more effectively.

My investigation reveals that you have made a mistake that many companies make: You are operating purely as a line organization, whereas at your stage of growth, you need to adopt a **line-and-staff** *organization. This means that you need to hire several staff experts to perform some of the activities your line managers presently do. As it now stands, your organizational structure tends to overload your managers. They are, in effect, wearing too many hats. More specifically, I have found evidence of the following three kinds of inefficiency:*

1. *Your supervisors are doing their own hiring, firing, and disciplining. Consequently, you have no uniform way of screening, selecting, promoting, and disciplining employees. Moreover, a number of the supervisors are hiring friends and relatives for their departments, and other employees believe that favoritism is rampant throughout the company.*
2. *The several department heads independently purchase materials and supplies for their departments. This duplication of effort has caused excessive space and dollars to be tied up in raw materials inventory. In addition, this practice has opened the door for waste and pilferage of supplies and materials.*
3. *Your department heads and supervisors are involved in method and layout studies, maintenance and repair work, scheduling and dispatching, and, to cap it off, quality control—all on top of their primary jobs of supervising the work and motivating their employees. The old proverb that "a jack of all trades is master of none" is certainly borne out by the situation I find in your plant.*

My primary recommendation, therefore, is that you hire a human resources specialist to screen and select new employees, a production control manager to do all the purchasing and inventory control, and an industrial engineering manager to do method and layout studies and the like. [Their relationship to the organization is shown in Exhibit 4-6.] By adding these three staff specialists, you will give your department heads and supervisors a chance to concentrate on their primary job of overseeing production and motivating their employees. Equally important, you should receive immediate benefits and cost savings by eliminating inefficiencies and installing improved ways of operating.

Stop & Think

What adjustments will the supervisors need to make to accommodate the consultant's recommended changes? Do you think these changes will help or hinder the supervisor in the job of motivating and managing his or her crew?

The consultant went on to report that, in the future, additional staff people would be needed if the company's rate of growth continued. He also stated that the company might want to consider diversifying by adding product lines that would require similar skills.

EXHIBIT 4-6
John Moody's Line-and-Staff Organization

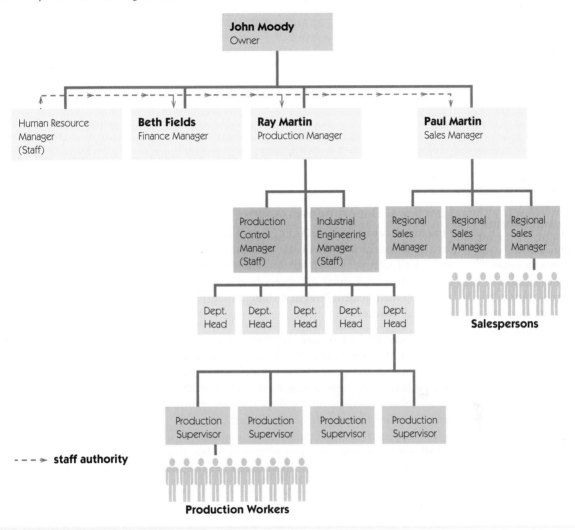

---

departmentalization

The organizational process of determining how activities are to be grouped.

2 *Identify the advantages and disadvantages of the functional, product, and matrix departmentalization approaches.*

John Moody accepted the consultant's recommendations, and his line-and-staff organization went on to achieve not only record sales, but also record profits and growth. Ultimately, any growing business needs to pass into this fourth stage. Unfortunately, many do not, and some suffer the consequences of decline and bankruptcy.

Departmentalization

The process of determining how activities are to be grouped is called **departmentalization.** There are many ways that these activities may be organized. For example, types of departmentalization include organizing by function, product, service, process, territory, customer, and matrix. Note that most organizations use a combination of these forms; that is, most organizations will use more than one of these approaches in their groupings. However, usually organizations use a functional approach at the top and other approaches at lower levels. Because three of these forms are more complex and are

used extensively, we provide elaboration for functional, product, and matrix departmentalization.

Functional Departmentalization

functional departmentalization

A form of departmentalization that groups together common functions or similar activities to form an organizational unit.

Functional departmentalization groups common functions or similar activities to form an organizational unit. Thus, all individuals performing similar functions are grouped, such as all sales personnel, all accounting personnel, all nurses, all computer programmers, and so on. Exhibit 4-7 shows how functional departmentalization would be used at the top management level in dividing the three major business functions—production, sales, and finance.

Advantages of Functional Approach The primary advantages of the functional approach are that it maintains the power and prestige of the major functions, creates efficiency through the principles of specialization, centralizes the organization's expertise, and permits tighter top-management control of the functions. For example, having all library-related activities on a college campus reporting to a common "library director" permits unified library policy to be carried out.

This approach also minimizes costly duplications of personnel and equipment. Having all computers and computer personnel in one department is less expensive than allowing several departments to have and supervise their own computer equipment and personnel.

Disadvantages of Functional Approach There are also many disadvantages to a functional approach. Some of these are that responsibility for total performance rests only at the top, and since each manager oversees only a narrow function, the training of managers to take over the top position is limited. Organizations attempt to remedy this by transferring managers so that they become "rounded," with experience in several functions. Coordination between and among functions becomes complex and more difficult as the organization grows in size and scope. Finally, individuals identify with their narrow functional responsibilities, causing subgroup loyalties, identification, and tunnel vision.

Product Departmentalization

At some point, the problems of coordination under a functional approach become extremely complex and cumbersome, especially when rapid, timely decisions must be made. The functional approach is slow and cumbersome because there is no single manager accountable for all the given activities, with the result that considerable coordination and communication are required before decisions can be reached. Consequently, some products that top management feels have the most potential may not receive the attention they

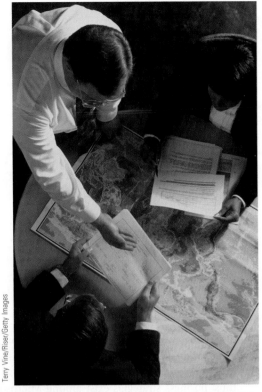

Terry Vine/Riser/Getty Images

Types of departmentalization can vary widely according to the activities being grouped. Sales organizations, for example, often structure groups according to territories.

deserve. And no one person is accountable for the performance of a given product line. What can be done to resolve this dilemma? One solution for many organizations is to shift to smaller, more natural semiautonomous mini-organizations built around specific products, each with its own functional capabilities. This is known as **product departmentalization,** in which all the functions associated with a single product line are grouped. Exhibit 4-8 is an example of product departmentalization.

Some of the advantages of product departmentalization are that attention can be directed toward specific product lines or services, coordination of functions at the product division level is improved, and profit responsibility can be better placed. Also, it is easier for the organization to obtain or develop several executives who have broad managerial experience in running a total entity. Microsoft has reorganized into five product divisions: Client (Windows product family); Server and Tools (consists of software server products, services, and solutions); Online Services Business (includes an online advertising platform, personal communications services, and online information offerings); Microsoft Business (consists of Microsoft Office suites, Microsoft Dynamics, and Unified Communications); and Entertainment and Devices (includes Xbox, Zune digital music and entertainment device, Mediaroom, mobile and embedded device platforms, Surface computing platform, and Windows Automotive). A president has been selected to head each business segment (Client—Steven Sinofsky; Server and Tools—Bob Muglia; Online Services Business—Qi Lu; Microsoft Business—Stephen Elop; and Entertainment and Devices—Robert Bach) and is responsible for managing the functions of a stand-alone operation with its own marketing and sales, finance, development, and so on. By

product departmentalization

A form of departmentalization that groups together all the functions associated with a single product line.

EXHIBIT 4-8
Example of Product Departmentalization

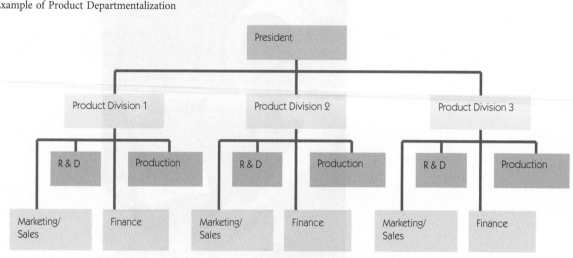

dispersing the accountability among the presidents of the newly created business divisions, Microsoft intends to be more responsive and better prepared to deal with competitive threats. The reorganization also recognizes that different patterns of growth and, thus, business strategies exist among Microsoft's divisions.[1]

Some of the disadvantages of product departmentalization are that it requires more personnel and material resources, it may cause unnecessary duplication of resources and equipment, and top management assumes a greater burden of establishing effective coordination and control. Top management must use staff support to create and oversee policies that guide and limit the range of actions taken by its divisions.

Matrix Departmentalization

matrix departmentalization

A hybrid type of departmentalization in which personnel from several specialties are brought together to complete limited-life tasks.

Matrix departmentalization is a hybrid type of departmentalization in which personnel from several specialties are brought together to complete limited-life tasks. It usually evolves from one or more of the other types of departmentalization and is used in response to demands for unique blends of skill from different specialties in the organization. The matrix structure is used not alone but in conjunction with other types of departmentalization. Say, for example, that a company had to complete a project requiring close, integrated work between and among numerous functional specialties. The project could be designing a weapons system or building a prototype for a supersonic aircraft. The traditional approaches to organization we have discussed do not easily provide for the flexibility to handle such complex assignments, which involve expertise from numerous functional areas of the organization. As shown in Exhibit 4-9, a project manager is given line authority over the team members during the life of the project.

The matrix organization provides a hierarchy that responds quickly to changes in technology. Hence, it is typically found in technically oriented organizations, such as Boeing, General Dynamics, NASA, and GE, in which scientists, engineers, or technical specialists work on sophisticated projects or programs. It is also used by companies with complex construction projects. Under this system, team members' functional

EXHIBIT 4-9
Example of Matrix
Departmentalization

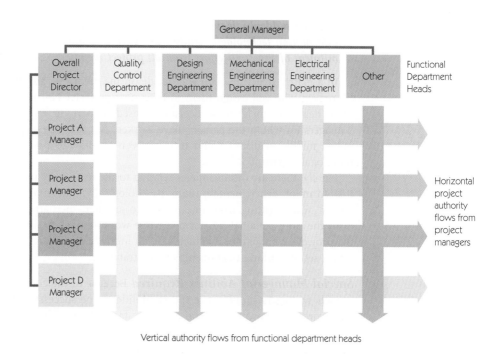

Vertical authority flows from functional department heads

departments maintain personnel files, supervise administrative details, and assemble performance reports while their members are on assignment.

Advantages of the Matrix Approach One advantage of the matrix approach is that it permits open communication and coordination of activities among the relevant functional specialists. Another advantage is that its flexibility enables the organization to respond rapidly to change. This response to change is the result of a self-imposed and professional desire to respond—not a response to a hierarchically managed change effort. The use of this approach is essential in technologically oriented industries.

Disadvantages of the Matrix Approach One disadvantage of matrix departmentalization relates to the lack of clarity and coordination in assigned roles. Conflict may occur when the requirements of the project team result in decisions contrary to the philosophy and viewpoint of the home office. For example, a project team might want the authority to make most decisions on-site, while the home office wants tight control. Another possible source of conflict is the assignment of team members to more than one project; someone must determine how to allocate such team members' time on each project. Such situations require *facilitators,* who intervene to resolve clashes resulting from conflicting priorities.

Jean Johnson was a professor of management at Mid-Atlantic University.

For the past year, she had been teaching in the management department and working half-time on an interdisciplinary project to improve the university's information technologies. For the life of the project, she had two bosses—the project director and the chairman of the management department.

Until recently, this dual reporting had not caused any problem, but within the last month, the chairman of the management department had been putting increasing pressure on Jean to teach an additional course for the fall term. A professor had resigned suddenly, leaving the department shorthanded. The dilemma was that the information technologies study was nearing completion and required a major commitment of time and effort from all project members.

In a matrix structure, who will decide on the members' advancement and promotion? Moreover, who will assign them to their next projects? Normally, the functional department head will make these decisions, based in part on reports received from project managers for whom the persons have worked. But functional specialists are often caught in the middle in disputes and torn between loyalties to project managers and to their functional department heads.

Finally, there are disadvantages relating to the temporary nature of assignments under this form of departmentalization. Psychologically, one may never feel that one has "roots" while drifting from one project to another—perhaps unrelated—project. Moreover, the close personal ties formed while working on a project team may be severed at the project's completion, in which case an individual's reassignment requires establishing a new set of working relationships with strangers.

Special Managerial Abilities Required Because of the complexities of the matrix approach, managers should have special abilities to be successful. They should be adept at teamwork and coordination and also have facilitation skills.

Two Important Organizing Principles

3 *Explain the principles of unity of command and span of control.*

Two important principles involved in the organizing function were illustrated in the case of John Moody's organizations. These are unity of command and span of control (or span of management). Let us now discuss these principles in detail.

Unity of Command

unity of command principle

States that everyone should report to and be accountable to only one boss.

The **unity of command principle** states that everyone in an organization should report to and be accountable to only one boss for performance of a given activity. This supervisor should be responsible for evaluating performance, passing down orders and information, and developing employees to become better employees in the organization. It is to this person that employees should turn for help in carrying out their duties and should communicate any deviations, either positive or negative, in implementing their duties. In sum, the supervisor is responsible only for motivating his or her employees to achieve effective results and for taking action when employees deviate from planned performance.

Adherence to the unity of command principle is important for five reasons:

1. It prevents duplication and conflict when orders and instructions are passed down.
2. It decreases confusion and "passing the buck" because everyone—including managers—is accountable to only one person for a given assignment.
3. It provides a basis whereby a supervisor and his or her employees can learn about each other's strengths and weaknesses.
4. It provides an opportunity for a supervisor and employees to develop supportive relationships and to realize their individual and group potential in achieving organizational objectives.
5. It promotes higher morale than is generally found in organizations that do not follow the unity of command principle.

Unfortunately, some managers only give lip service to this principle, although their organization chart seems to reflect it. One of the authors of this book was working with

Catherine Yeulet/istockphoto.com

Following the unity of command principle, the supervisor is solely responsible for motivating his or her employees to achieve company goals.

a branch plant of a large company to tailor a management development program. Among other things, this author was examining the leadership styles practiced by key managers and their effect on employees. To determine those leadership styles, the author interviewed managers at all levels. The results showed that the plant manager, though unusually capable and generally effective, made one mistake with his employee managers: He violated the unity of command principle by periodically conducting inspections throughout the plant and making on-the-spot suggestions to operative employees. Often, he made these suggestions when the employees' supervisor was not present. As a result, operative employees were following instructions that their immediate supervisors were unaware of. Moreover, employees would stop working on their assigned duties to carry out the instructions of the plant manager. This practice caused a problem for supervisors, as illustrated by Exhibit 4-10.

As a result of this one error, a serious morale problem had developed. Many of the plant manager's otherwise effective managerial practices were being undermined. When this situation was called to his attention, he was quite surprised. It seems that he had slipped into this habit without being fully aware of its long-range consequences. When this manager thereupon began passing his suggestions and instructions through lower-level managers, morale improved.

Although employees should have only one supervisor, they may, of course, have relationships with many people. For example, in a line-and-staff organization, line supervisors and department heads will have many contacts with staff personnel. These contacts are necessary so that both line and staff personnel can accomplish their duties. Later in this chapter, we will explain how these relationships can be developed without violating the unity of command principle. The important thing to remember is this: If a conflict results from a staff request and a line manager's command, the employee should have a single manager to turn to for clarification or a final decision.

EXHIBIT 4-10
Violating the Unity of Command Principle

Span of Control

Before World War II, experts maintained that the span of control should be three to eight people, depending on the level of management. In those days, one of the first things an organizational consultant examined when a company was having problems was the span of control at various levels. Today the three-to-eight-people limit is no longer accepted as universally applicable. This is why we state the **span of control principle** simply as follows: There is a limit to the number of people a person can manage effectively. Just as you can span only a limited number of feet and inches with your arms, your mental reach can span only a limited number of the problems, situations, and relationships that make up the activities of management.

span of control principle

States that there is a limit to the number of people a person can supervise effectively.

Narrower Span of Control at the Top One thing we can say without qualification: The higher the managers are in an organization, the fewer people they should have reporting directly to them. There are at least three reasons for relating span of control to management level:

1. Top-level managers must solve a variety of different, nonrecurring problems. Much mental concentration is required to solve such problems.
2. Middle managers must spend much of their time doing long-range planning, working with outside interest groups, and coordinating the various activities of the organization. They cannot afford to be tied down by the excessive burden of supervision created when a large number of people report directly to them.
3. First-level managers, by contrast, tend to be concerned with more clearly defined areas of operation. Although they are responsible for a certain amount of coordination with other departments, most of their contacts are directly with their immediate employees. Hence, they are able to supervise more people than are higher-level managers.

Different Approaches to a Supervisor's Span of Control Exhibit 4-11 depicts three different approaches to a supervisor's span of control, leading to quite different jobs for

EXHIBIT 4-11
Narrow, Wide, and Very
Wide Spans of Control

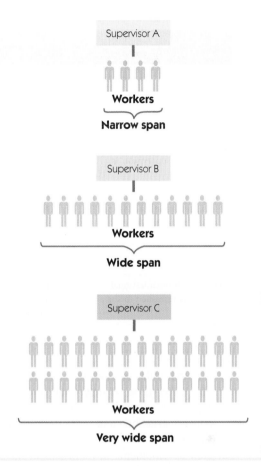

supervisors A, B, and C. Can we say that one of these approaches is best? No, because the correct size of a supervisor's span of control depends on a number of circumstances, as shown in Exhibit 4-12.

Companies that follow a policy of a narrow span of control are often hampered in achieving effective results. If an organization of, say, a thousand people rigidly adheres to a span of between three and seven, this tall, narrow organizational structure (with many, many management levels) will have some disadvantages. Numerous supervisory managers will be required, resulting in high payroll costs. Communication will have to pass up and down through many levels, increasing the possibility of distortion. Over-supervision may restrict decision making by employees and limit their opportunities to achieve their full potential. On the other hand, an advantage of tight control is that the work can be closely directed, so the company can hire relatively less skilled people.

Tendency toward Wider Spans of Control Over the years, many companies have tended to broaden their span of control at all levels. There are at least four reasons for this trend:

1. Higher educational attainment, management and supervisory development programs, vocational and technical training, and increased knowledge generally on the part of the labor force have improved the abilities and capacities of both managers and employees. The greater the supervisor's capacity, the more people he or she can supervise.

EXHIBIT 4-12
Factors Contributing to
a Narrow or Wide Span
of Control

FACTOR	NARROW SPAN INDICATED	WIDE SPAN INDICATED
How physically close are the people performing the work?	Dispersed, perhaps even in different geographical locations	Very close, perhaps all in one physical work area in a building
How complex is the work?	Very complex, such as development of a manned space station that will orbit the earth	Rather routine and simple, such as an assembly-line operation
How much supervision is required?	A great deal. So many problems arise that the supervisor needs to exercise close control.	Little. Workers are well trained and able to make normal job decisions easily.
How much nonsupervisory work is required of the supervisor?	Much. The supervisor spends much time planning, coordinating, and performing nonsupervisory tasks.	Little. Not much planning and coordination is required of the supervisor. The supervisor spends most of his or her time supervising employees.
How much organizational assistance is furnished to the supervisor?	Much. The supervisor may do his or her own recruiting, training, and controlling.	Much. The supervisor may be aided by a training department, quality control department, etc.

2. Research indicates that in many situations, *general* supervision is more effective than *close* supervision. A supervisor practicing general supervision delegates authority and supervises by results, whereas a supervisor practicing close supervision provides detailed instructions and often does the same type of work as the workers he or she is supervising.
3. New developments in management have permitted businesses to broaden their span of control and supervise by results, without losing control. For example, by using enhanced technologies, an organization can process information more quickly and develop more efficient information-reporting systems.
4. Finally—and sometimes this is the primary reason—wider spans of control save the company money.

Relationships between Line and Staff

4 *Describe the difference between line and staff.*

line personnel

Carry out the primary activities of a business.

staff personnel

Have the expertise to assist line people and aid top management.

Line personnel carry out the primary activities of a business, such as producing or selling products and/or services. **Staff personnel,** on the other hand, use their expertise to assist the line people and aid top management in various areas of business activities. Line departments, therefore, are like a main stream. Staff departments are like the tributaries serving and assisting the main stream, although they should not be thought of as being secondary to the line departments. Both line and staff people are important.

Stop & Think

Of the various jobs you've held, which were "line" and which were "staff"?

Once a business has reached the fourth stage of growth and is no longer a small organization, it becomes more complex and difficult to coordinate. A line and staff

EXHIBIT 4-13
Line and Staff Contacts

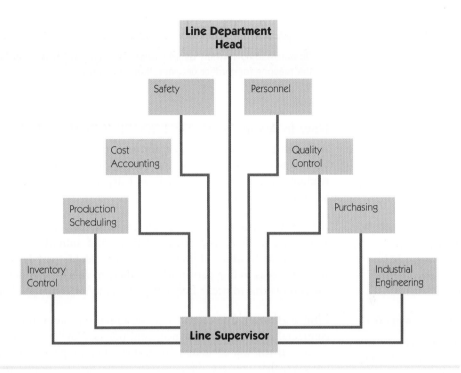

structure that places competent specialists in certain positions, such as human resources management, legal and governmental departments, research and development, and public relations, will help eliminate confusion, duplication, and inefficiency. However, a growing organization must be continually alert to pitfalls and potential trouble spots.

Conflicts between Line and Staff

One common problem in most large organizations is excessive conflict between line and staff personnel and between different departments. Differences in viewpoint between people and departments are natural, inevitable, and healthy, but excessive conflict can disrupt an entire organization. As shown in Exhibit 4-13, many line and staff contacts are normal.

There are many reasons excessive conflict can develop between line and staff personnel within an organization. Exhibit 4-14 summarizes some reasons for conflict between line and staff personnel.

EXHIBIT 4-14
Some Reasons for
Conflict between Line
and Staff Personnel

- Staff personnel give direct orders to line personnel.
- Good human relations are not practiced in dealings between line and staff personnel.
- Overlapping authority and responsibility confuse both line and staff personnel.
- Line people believe that staff people are not knowledgeable about conditions at the operating level.
- Staff people, because of their expertise, attempt to influence line decisions against line managers' wishes.
- Top management misuses staff personnel or fails to use them properly.
- Each department views the organization from a narrow viewpoint instead of looking at the organization as a whole.

Stop & Think

Before reading further, decide what you think might be done to decrease or eliminate the reasons for conflict between line and staff personnel.

How to Avoid Excessive Line-Staff Conflict: Delineating Authority

5 *Understand how to avoid excessive conflict between line and staff.*

6 *Explain the three types of authority found in organizations.*

advisory authority

Authority of most staff departments to serve and advise line departments.

line authority

Power to directly command or exact performance from others.

functional authority

A staff person's limited line authority over a given function.

Although conflict between line and staff people is not likely to be eliminated, a major way to avoid it is to ensure that people clearly understand the authority/responsibility relationships between individuals and departments. There are three types of authority: advisory, line, and functional.

Advisory Authority The primary responsibility of most staff departments is to serve and advise the line departments. This type of authority is called **advisory authority** or the *authority of ideas.* However, some staff people may be so zealous in their efforts to sell their ideas to line personnel that they, in effect, hand out orders. If the line supervisor permits this to occur frequently, the unity of command begins here to break down.

Line Authority The second type of authority, **line authority,** is the power to directly command or exact performance from others. Having this power to command does not mean that you will elicit effective performance simply by giving out orders. It does mean, however, that you are directly responsible for the results of a certain department or group of workers. Line authority is not restricted to line personnel. The head of a staff department has line authority over the employees in his or her department.

Functional Authority The third type of authority, **functional authority,** is usually a restricted kind of line authority. It gives a staff person a type of limited line authority over a given *function,* such as safety or quality, regardless of where that function is found in the organization. For example, a staff safety specialist may have functional authority to insist that line managers follow standard safety procedures in their departments. The staff safety specialist may have top management's blessing to dictate to lower-level line managers exactly what they must and must not do concerning any matter that falls within the realm of safety. A quality control inspector may tell a line worker that certain parts need to be reworked. A human resources specialist may say to a line supervisor that the latter cannot fire a certain employee. A cost accountant may notify line departments that certain cost information must be furnished weekly, and so on.

Stop & Think

Can you think of some other common examples of functional authority?

Are you thinking that functional authority seems to violate the unity of command principle? It does! For this reason, it is important that all individuals clearly understand what functional authority is. Top-line managers have the major responsibility for defining the nature of functional authority. Moreover, it is important for line personnel to exercise their right to appeal to higher management levels when they have disagreements with staff personnel. Functional authority is necessary, but it can be dangerous if it is granted indiscriminately. Normally, it is given only to a staff area where there is a great deal of expertise and the staff expert's advice would be followed anyway.

Ed Young/Documentary/Corbis

Behind-the-scenes functions of research (accounting, quality control, and safety) are found in many companies. What kind of authority would a staff person have working in this environment?

decentralization

The extent to which authority is delegated from one unit of the organization to another.

7 *Distinguish between centralization and decentralization.*

Another way to avoid excessive conflict between line and staff people is to have effective communication between people and between departments. Key managers overseeing both line and staff people can improve the communication process by periodically bringing line and staff people together to discuss problems that cut across departmental lines. This example may inspire lower-level managers to do the same thing with their key employees. Thus, the danger of seeing only part of the picture will be minimized.

Decentralization versus Centralization

The concept of decentralization is closely related to the concept of delegation. Briefly, delegation is the process by which managers allocate duties and authority downward to the people who report to them and assign responsibility for how authority is used.

An example of delegation occurred when John Moody called in assistants to help him do a better job than he could do alone. He assigned his assistants duties in finance, production, and sales.

Both delegation and decentralization are concerned with the giving of authority to someone at a lower level. **Decentralization** is the broader concept, as it refers to the extent to which authority is delegated from one level or one unit of the organization to another. In a *decentralized* organization, middle and lower levels of management make broader, more important decisions about their units. In a *centralized* organization, upper management makes most of the important decisions that concern all levels or units within the organization.

Factors Affecting Decentralization

No organization is completely centralized or decentralized. Decentralization is a relative concept and depends on a number of factors, including the following:

1. *Top-management philosophy.* Some top managers have a need for tight control. They put together a strong central staff and want to make the most important decisions themselves. Others believe in strong delegation and push decisions to the lowest levels of their organization.

2. *History of the organization's growth.* Organizations that have grown by merging with other companies or acquiring them tend to be decentralized. Those that have grown on their own tend to be centralized.

3. *Geographic location(s).* Organizations that are spread out, with units in different cities or regions, tend to be decentralized so that lower-level managers can make decisions that fit their territory or circumstances.

4. *Quality of managers.* If an organization has many well-qualified, well-trained managers, it will likely be decentralized. If it has few, top management will centralize and make the most important decisions.

5. *Availability of controls.* If top management has an effective control system—good, timely information about performance at lower levels—the organization will tend to be decentralized. Without a good flow of control information for monitoring results, it will tend to be centralized.

6. *The economy.* Generally, there is a tendency toward more centralization during poor economic times, such as a recession, and more decentralization during good economic times.

7. *Mergers, acquisitions, and joint ventures.* Unfortunately, many mergers, acquisitions, and joint ventures fail to achieve expected synergies and positive outcomes because they do not effectively plan and implement an early strategy to integrate different organization cultures, to evaluate old ways of operating, and, when appropriate, to develop new ways of functioning. Certainly, not dealing with decentralization versus centralization can have a negative impact on the organization and its managers and supervisors.

8. *The external business environment.* Generally, in relatively certain or stable business environments, there is a tendency toward more centralization because the focus tends to be internally on improving efficiencies of operations. In dynamic, turbulent business environments, more decentralization occurs, because rapidly responding and adjusting to environmental stimuli is most important. With product life-cycles in some tech industries of less than 12 months, organizational flexibility and rapid response are critical for survival.

Stop & Think

In your opinion, which factors are most significant in determining whether an organization is centralized or decentralized? Why?

Effect of Decentralization on Organizational Structure

The degree to which an organization is decentralized will have a direct effect on the number of levels within the organization. The trend in the United States is toward reducing

EXHIBIT 4-15

Layers of Management Reflecting a Centralized versus a Decentralized Structure

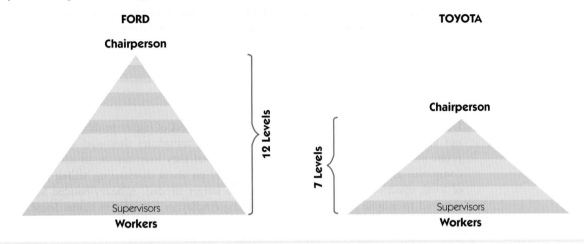

the number of levels of management and decentralizing. While Toyota, which is relatively decentralized, has only seven levels of management, this trend has not been as emphasized by Ford and GM. As shown in Exhibit 4-15, Ford Motor Company, which is relatively centralized, has 12 layers of managers and supervisors between the operational employees and the chairperson. GM was even more cumbersome. Now, with the U.S. government–supported restructuring of GM, it will be interesting to see what new structure will emerge.

Downsizing

8 *Discuss the benefits and costs of downsizing.*

In their book *In Search of Excellence,* Thomas Peters and Robert Waterman noted that one of the attributes of excellent companies is a simple organizational structure with a lean top-level staff. In a 1988 article, management theorist Peter Drucker predicted that by 2008, a typical large business would have half the levels of management and one-third the managers of its 1988 counterpart.[2] Drucker's forecast is coming true throughout the United States and Canada. **Downsizing** is the process of eliminating unnecessary levels of management and employees, thus reducing the number of staff personnel and supervisors.

downsizing

Eliminating unnecessary levels of management; striving to become leaner and more efficient by reducing the workforce and consolidating departments and work groups.

Benefits of Downsizing

One of the major benefits of downsizing is the tremendous cost reductions that occur almost immediately. Perhaps even more important are the improvements that take place in the way the organization is managed. Turnaround time in decision making is speeded up, and communication usually improves in all directions. Moreover, the organization becomes more responsive to customers and provides faster product delivery. Downsizing also removes the tendency for each level to justify its existence by close supervision and by frequently asking for reports and data from lower levels. Without excessive interference and stifling of creativity at lower levels, line managers have more opportunity to develop and use their authority to make decisions affecting the bottom line. In the final analysis, all of these things translate into higher profits. These concepts are illustrated next.

A. T. Kearney analyzed management layers among both highly successful companies and others whose performance was not above average in their industry. The 15 not-so-successful companies typically had at least four more organizational layers than the 26 successful ones. Interviews confirmed that more layers in the organization in-hibit productivity because the decision-making process is slower and the chances are greater that opportunities will be lost.[3]

Costs of Downsizing

Downsizing has some costs that can wreck the prospect of higher profits if the process is not accomplished ethically and efficiently. Some companies downsize so rapidly and prune staff and middle management so much that they lose control. In addition, some companies are very insensitive in the way they go about downsizing, telling a number of loyal, effective managers that they are no longer needed. A heavy-handed approach can lead to morale problems with remaining employees for years to come. Some other potential disadvantages are increased workloads, diminished chances of promotion, and threatened job security for those remaining.

Perhaps the greatest costs are the least known—the social costs. Research shows that when employees lose their jobs because of downsizing, domestic problems increase. Fifteen percent lost their homes, despite an increase in the number of hours their spouses worked. Moreover, the suicide rate for laid-off workers is 30 times the national average.[4] Because of these costs, downsizing can never be painless, but thoughtful planning can minimize the pain.

Impact on Remaining Supervisors and Managers

Remaining managers and supervisors must adapt to fuzzier lines of authority and must develop skills in team building. In tall, narrow structures, middle managers and supervisors are accustomed to carrying out orders, and suddenly they must operate differently. As a first-line supervisor in an International Paper Company mill told one of the authors: "They used to tell us what to do; now they ask us." With the increasing emphasis on quality and service management, a supervisor has to function more as a coach, a facilitator, an expediter, and a team developer.

Stop & Think

Due to numerous internal and external environmental factors, downsizing has become a "preferred" course of action for many organizations. Is downsizing an ethical business practice? Why or why not?

Ways to Get Beyond Downsizing

Without question, downsizing has a negative impact on employee morale, and, according to an American Management Association survey, just 45 percent of firms that have downsized have seen corporate profits increase.[5] Thus, it is important to look on downsizing not as an end in itself but as a means to an end. The way to get back to health is to focus on the remaining employees by developing a strategy of support for survivors and a strategic plan for growth and development for the organization.

However, it is important not to go back to a traditional management and organizational design based on principles of command, control, and compartmentalization.[6]

Photographer's Choice /Getty Images

After a layoff or restructuring, supervisors may find themselves functioning as coaches to help boost morale and restore a cooperative team atmosphere among the surviving employees.

reengineering

"It means starting over.... It means asking and answering this question: If I were creating this company today, given what I know and given current technology, what would it look like?" Rethinking and redesigning processes to improve dramatically cost, quality, service, and speed.

This danger can be negated by (1) developing effective work teams and (2) using a process called *reengineering*.

Reengineering is a reaction to the way many organizations do work today using the traditional methods of command, control, and compartmentalization. In a world of rapid change, firms that focus on division or specialization of labor with a resulting fragmentation of work end up with vertical structures built on narrow pieces of a process. Consequently, decisions are slow, and people look upward to their department heads and bosses for answers, rather than looking horizontally to internal and external customers to solve problems and get answers.[7]

When Michael Hammer and James Champy, two of the world's leading experts on reengineering, were asked for a quick definition, they gave this answer: "It means starting over.... It means asking and answering this question: If I were recreating this company today, given what I know and given current technology, what would it look like?"[8] Their more formal definition of reengineering is "the fundamental rethinking and radical redesign of business processes to achieve dramatic improvements in critical, contemporary measures of performance such as cost, quality, service, and speed."[9]

Reengineering can be very expensive, and so firms should not use it for everything. If you have an unprofitable business, it may be better to close it, or, if quality is a problem, focus on improving the quality rather than starting over. The general guideline is to save reengineering for big challenges that really matter, such as new product development or customer service. Although by one estimate, 50 percent of reengineering efforts fail to achieve the goals set for them, when it is done properly, reengineering has a big payoff. For example, Union Carbide used reengineering to save $400 million in three years.[10]

As Hammer and Champy have documented, the following types of changes occur when a company has successfully reengineered business processes:

- Work units change from functional departments to process teams.
- Jobs change from simple tasks to multidimensional work.
- Roles change from controlled to empowered.
- Job preparation changes from preparation to education.
- Focus of compensation shifts from activity to results.
- Advancement criteria change from performance to ability.
- Values change from protective to productive.
- Managers change from supervisors to coaches.
- Organizational structure changes from hierarchical to flat.
- Executives change from scorekeepers to leaders.

Contemporary Organizational Perspectives

9 *Explain the four types of contemporary organizational approaches.*

The Inverted Pyramid

The creation of the **inverted pyramid** has been attributed to Nordstrom, a very successful specialty retailer. Nordstrom's structure is very flat with few levels and employs a bottom-up management philosophy. The sales and sales support personnel, who are in direct contact with the customer, make the key decisions. The chart portrays "helping hands" symbolizing that all other levels are there to help and support the sales personnel to better serve and satisfy the customer. Exhibit 4-16 shows Nordstrom's inverted pyramid and the helping-hand concept.[11] The success of Nordstrom's management philosophy and empowered personnel permeates beyond sales through the entire organization and is reflected in the end results. Nordstrom has been able to outperform both Macy's and Saks by utilizing more effective inventory management. Nordstrom holds inventory for an average of 62 days, while Macy's holds it for 119 days, and Saks for 140. The faster inventory turnover has freed up more cash so that Nordstrom does not need to borrow to finance new projects. The outlook for Nordstrom, even in turbulent times, seems to be optimistic.[12]

inverted pyramid

A structure widest at the top and narrowing as it funnels down.

EXHIBIT 4-16
Nordstorm's Inverted Pyramid

Source: Based on description found in Robert Spector and Patrick D. McCarthy, *The Nordstrom Way: The Inside Story of America's #1 Customer Service Company* (New York: Wiley, 1996).

The Wagon Wheel

wagon wheel

An organization form with a hub, a series of spokes radiating from the hub, and the outer rim.

Management consultant and author Nancy Austin points out that the **wagon wheel** is even more unorthodox than the inverted pyramid. In her words, "There are usually three main parts to these innovative formats: the hub of the wheel; a series of spokes, which radiate from the hub; and, finally, the outer rim. Customers are at the center. Whether you call the hub 'customers' or 'customer satisfaction,' customers show up inside the chart! Next come the spokes—business functions (finance, marketing, engineering) or teams (new-product development, customer satisfaction, suppliers). Keeping it all together on the outer rim—where the rubber meets the road—are the chief executive and the board, who are placed there to make sure everybody has at his or her fingertips everything needed to serve customers. Here, too, managers are coaches and supporters, not naysayers and devil's advocates. The stubborn 'Us vs. Them' antagonism spawned by the old hierarchical mentality begins to even out a bit."[13]

Team Structures

team structure

Utilizes permanent and temporary cross-functional teams to improve horizontal coordination and cooperation.

Team structure utilizes permanent and temporary cross-functional teams to improve horizontal coordination and cooperation. Exhibit 4-17 provides an example of the team structure. Teams provide speed and flexibility to meet the challenges associated with increasingly dynamic business environments. Take, for example, a retail store such as Family Dollar. Each employee has been hired to perform a particular task, such a stocking, running the register, or managing the store, but as Vernon Mason, an Assistant Manager with Family Dollar, shares, "We cross-train all of our employees so they can perform a variety of jobs on an as needed basis. When the truck arrives and we're pressed for time to get the stock out, we need everyone on board and able to do the task that needs to be done right then."[14] Teams provide supervisors the opportunity to utilize the diverse talents of each member to achieve effective outcomes.

Network Structures

network structure

Sometimes referred to as a modular structure; includes a central business unit, or "hub," that is linked to a network of external suppliers and contractors.

As Exhibit 4-18 illustrates, a **network structure,** sometimes referred to as a modular structure, includes a central business unit or "hub" that is linked to a network of external suppliers and contractors. With technology, such as the Internet, companies can operate efficiently and effectively with a virtual network by focusing only on those core activities they do quite well. Many companies, such as Apple, Ashley Furniture, and Nike, outsource noncore business activities to reduce costs, speed production, utilize outside expertise, or some combination thereof.

EXHIBIT 4-17
Example of Team-Based Structures

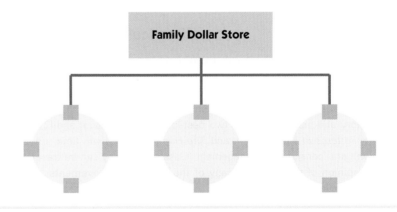

Family Dollar Store

EXHIBIT 4-18
Example of a Virtual
Network

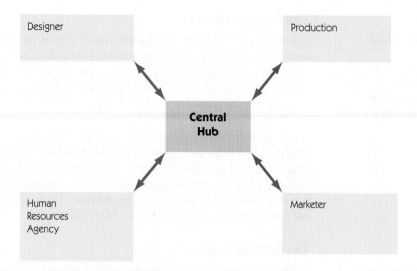

Designer

Production

**Central
Hub**

Human
Resources
Agency

Marketer

Stop & Think

Is it possible to integrate the contemporary organizational structures with the more traditional (functional, product, and matrix forms) ones? Explain.

Management Philosophy, Strategy, and Organization

10 *Understand the relationship between management philosophy, strategy, and newer forms of organization.*

Earlier in the chapter, we discussed the impact management philosophy has on the organization. Management philosophy is particularly significant when we discuss the newer forms of organizations, involving more decentralization, empowerment, team development, quality improvement, and networking. In a world of rapid change and global competition, more and more firms are shifting to increased decentralization, team development, and empowerment.

HISTORICAL INSIGHT

Historical Insight

During the 1960s and 1970s, Dr. Rensis Likert and his team of researchers and consultants at the University of Michigan's Institute for Social Research Survey Research Center made tremendous contributions to management theory and practice. Likert's two best-known books, *New Patterns of Management* and *The Human Organization,* are considered management classics, and, in the opinion of the authors, many of the concepts are quite valid today.[15]

One concept that is especially relevant to this chapter is the researchers' conclusion that two causal variables affecting both intervening variables and results are (1) management philosophy and leadership behavior and (2) organization structure. It follows that if, over time, an organization is having difficulties, they can be traced back to the causal variables where improvements and perhaps changes need to be made.

Exhibit 4-19 shows the *internal systems model* developed by Likert. The model groups the dimensions of a company's human organization into three broad categories of variables: *causal, intervening,* and *end result.*

1. *Causal variables.* Causal variables determine the course of developments within an organization and the results achieved by the organization. They include only those independent variables that can be altered or changed by the organization and its management. Causal variables include the structure of the organization, and management's policies; decision, business, and leadership strategies; skills; and behavior.
2. *Intervening variables.* Intervening variables reflect the internal state and health of the organization. They include the loyalties, attitudes, motivations, performance goals, and perceptions of organization members and their capacities for effective interaction, communication, and decision making.

EXHIBIT 4-19
Variables

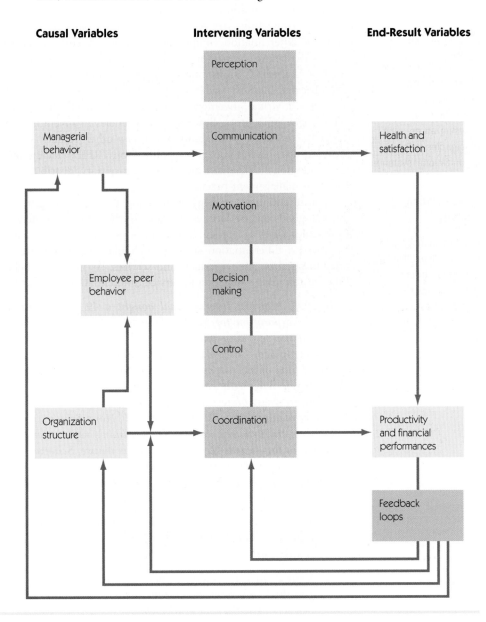

3. *End-result variables.* End-result variables are dependent variables that reflect the achievements of the organization, such as productivity, costs, scrap loss, and earnings.

You can see that causal variables affect intervening variables and that intervening variables, in turn, affect the end results. Thus, an organization running into such difficulties as declining sales and profits or high turnover and absenteeism can usually trace the problem to deficiencies in variables of this sort: organizational structure or top management's policies, decisions, and leadership philosophies, strategies, and behavior.

Strategy and Structure: The Fit Perspective

Competitive Strategies Michael Porter identified that managers in organizations use a variety of competitive strategies to be effective. Two important ones are the cost leadership and differentiation competitive strategies. A **cost leadership strategy** attempts to lower costs below competitors by focusing on creating efficiencies within organizational systems. Walmart is an example of an organization following a cost leadership strategy. They became the cost leader in the retail arena through the utilization of technology to create a virtual inventory system, which effectively lowered their cost structure below their competitors. By creating efficiencies in inventory management, they single-handedly redefined profitability for every other retailer in the industry. Currently, Walmart uses radiofrequency identification (RFID) technology, tagging products to create additional efficiencies and improve inventory, distribution, customer management, and theft management practices.

A **differentiation strategy** is used by managers to gain a competitive advantage through goods and/or services that are clearly unique or different from the competition. Companies such as Harley Davidson, Apple, Publix, and Samsung have successfully employed a differentiation strategy such that consumers are willing to pay a higher price to purchase their products and services. As illustrated below, Marriot's brand, the Ritz-Carlton, uses a quality and service differentiation strategy to achieve success.

cost leadership strategy

Attempts to lower costs below competitors by focusing on creating efficiencies within organizational systems.

differentiation strategy

Used by managers to gain a competitive advantage through goods and/or services that are clearly unique or different from the competition.

In 1995, Marriott International bought a 49 percent interest in the Ritz-Carlton Hotel Corporation for $200 million in cash and assumed debt. In 1998, Marriott bought the rest, and under Marriott's leadership, the high standard of excellence was continued. "Ritz-Carlton maintains a database on the preferences of nearly one million of its customers, detailing their likes, dislikes, family and personal interests, preferred credit card, etc. Each employee is responsible for identifying and recording guest preferences. The goal is to customize service and thereby create a lasting relationship with the customer."[16] Horst Schulze, the Ritz-Carlton's past president, is credited with catalyzing the chain's reputation for quality and service. In regard to the awards received during his tenure, Schulze stated, "We are not resting on the momentary glory or satisfaction of these awards. ... It is our intention to not only serve you with genuine care and comfort, but to fulfill all your needs in our hotels and give you complete service excellence all of the time."

"Today every employee, from housekeeper to server to manager, is committed to the ultimate dream and vision.... 100 percent guest satisfaction." The tailored features of the Ritz-Carlton's focus on quality, service, and guest satisfaction include:

1. *In the 2-day orientation program for new employees, the training manager emphasizes that, "you serve but you are not servants"; rather, "you are ladies and gentlemen serving ladies and gentlemen."*

2. *In addition to the orientation program, 100 additional hours of training are provided to employees.*

3. *When processes are improved or reengineered in one hotel, the information and concepts are shared with all hotels.*

4. *Every worker is empowered to spend up to $2,000 to fix any problem a guest encounters.*

Patrick Mene, director of quality, has reported that employees do not abuse this privilege: "When you treat people responsibly, they act responsibly." Are employees achieving the goal of 100 percent guest satisfaction? In the eyes of one customer, they are. "They not only treat us like a king when we hold our top-level meetings in their hotels, but we just never get any complaints," said Wayne Stetson, the Staff Vice President of the Convention and Meetings Division of the National Association of Home Builders in Washington, D.C.[17] *The Ritz-Carlton is a hotel that has created a culture where the employees practice their credo. As they say in the business world, "they walk their talk."*

Structure Fits Strategy Exhibit 4-20 shows why it is important for an organization's structure to "fit" its strategy. The cost leadership strategy attempts to lower costs below competitors by focusing on creating efficiencies within organizational systems. As such, a centralized, vertical structure that focuses employee efforts internally is best suited to ensure stable operations. The characteristics associated with a vertical, functional structure are clear lines of authority, centralized decision making, and a focus on rules and procedures. In contrast, the differentiation strategy attempts to gain a competitive advantage through goods and/or services that are clearly unique or different from the competition. Innovation, flexibility, and responsiveness are keys to ensuring this strategy is successful. Therefore, a horizontal structure that facilitates employee cooperation and coordination is the best fit. Other characteristics of a decentralized organization include decentralized decision making, informal interactions, and adaptive response.

Stop & Think

Do you agree that it is important for the firm's structure to fit its strategy? Why or why not? Would you expect Apple and United Parcel Service (UPS) to operate with similar or dissimilar strategies and structures? Explain.

EXHIBIT 4-20

Organizational Strategy and Structure: A Fit Perspective

Functional Structure

Functional with Interdepartmental Task Forces, Integrators

Divisional Structure

Horizontal Teams

Strategic Goals

Strategic Goals:
Differntiation, innovation, flexibility

Strategic Goals:
Cost leadership, efficiency, stability

Chapter Review

1. **Understand the stages of organization growth.**

   This chapter focused on concepts that give supervisory managers a better understanding of their organization. A continuing case illustrated several phases of organization growth, from a one-person organization to a line-and-staff organization. It is important for a growing company to evolve from a line organization to a line-and-staff organization. This evolution allows the company to take advantage of specialization in such areas as human resources, quality control, purchasing, maintenance, scheduling, and safety. It also allows line managers and supervisors to concentrate on supervising and motivating their employees.

2. **Identify the advantages and disadvantages of the functional, product, and matrix departmentalization approaches.**

   The span of control principle emphasizes that there is a limit to the number of people a person can effectively manage. As one moves down the organization chart from top-management to supervisory management levels, the span of control should increase. The reasons for tying span of control to management level are (1) top management requires the freedom to solve a variety of different, nonrecurring problems; (2) higher-level managers must spend much of their time doing long-range planning, working with outside interest groups, and coordinating the various activities of the business; and (3) supervisory managers tend to be concerned with more clearly defined areas of operation.

3. **Explain the principles of unity of command and span of control.**

   Two important management principles for organizations are unity of command and span of control. Following the unity of command principle is important because it prevents duplication and conflict when orders and instructions are passed down. It also decreases confusion and "passing the buck" and provides a basis for managers and their employees to develop a better understanding of what they expect of each other. Finally, it promotes higher morale than is found in organizations that excessively violate the unity of command principle.

4. **Describe the difference between line and staff.**

   Although both line and staff personnel are important, their duties differ. Line personnel carry out the primary activities of a business, such as producing or selling products and/or services. Staff personnel use their expertise to assist the line people and to aid top management in various business activities.

5. **Understand how to avoid excessive conflict between line and staff.**

   A line-and-staff organization sometimes leads to excessive conflict between line and staff departments. Conflict can be minimized by ensuring that people understand the authority/responsibility relationships between individuals and departments.

6. **Explain the three types of authority found in organizations.**

   The three types of authority found in organizations are advisory authority (common in staff departments), line authority (direct command authority over employees), and functional authority (limited line authority in a narrow area of specialization). Another way to avoid excessive conflict is to have effective communication between people and between departments.

7. **Distinguish between centralization and decentralization.**

   The concept of centralization versus decentralization is important in understanding organizations. Some factors that influence the extent of centralization or decentralization are top management's philosophy, the history of the organization's growth, its geographic location(s), the quality of managers, and the availability of controls. Computer technology has increased the ability of higher management to shift in either direction. The trend, however, seems to be in the direction of decentralization.

8. **Discuss the benefits and costs of downsizing.**

   Many organizations are currently being streamlined by downsizing, or by reducing the number of administrative levels. Although rapid downsizing can get out of control and there is unavoidable cost to the staff and supervisors who are laid off, the benefits to the organization in the form of cost reduction, faster decision making, and improved communication outweigh the costs. As a result of downsizing, supervisors often have more authority and responsibility, on the one hand, but they are also called on to act more as leaders, coaches, facilitators, and team developers.

9. **Explain the four types of contemporary organizational approaches.**

   The four types of contemporary organizational approaches include the inverted pyramid, wagon wheel, teams, and network structures. In an inverted pyramid, first-line supervisors are empowered to address issues in a timely manner and make important decisions. With the wagon wheel, the customer is the focal point, emphasizing customer services. The team structure highlights the benefits of individuals cooperating and collaborating together in order to achieve synergistic outcomes. The network structure utilizes technologies to create and maintain virtual relationships. While each of the contemporary options has unique qualities, all of them enable managers to be responsive and flexible when adapting to changing environmental conditions.

10. **Understand the relationship between management philosophy, strategy, and newer forms of organization.**

    The newer forms of organization that are being developed, the inverted pyramid and the wagon wheel, emphasize the role and importance of the customer and empowerment of employees who are close to the customer. Creative leadership is particularly valuable in developing innovative forms as a result of growth and new challenges.

Key Terms

line organization, p. 100

line-and-staff organization, p. 102

departmentalization, p. 103

functional departmentalization, p. 104

product departmentalization, p. 105

matrix departmentalization, p. 106

unity of command principle, p. 108

span of control principle, p. 110

line personnel, p. 112

staff personnel, p. 112

advisory authority, p. 114

line authority, p. 114

functional authority, p. 114

decentralization, p. 115

downsizing, p. 117

reengineering, p. 119

inverted pyramid, p. 120

wagon wheel, p. 121

team structure, p. 121

network structure, p. 121

cost leadership strategy, p. 124

differentiation strategy, p. 124

Questions for Review & Discussion

1. Outline the four stages of organizational growth, and relate them to an organization with which you are familiar.
2. What two important management principles affect the successful operation of a growing organization? Do you think John Moody's difficulties could have been avoided if he had understood these principles? Discuss the advantages and disadvantages of functional, matrix, and product departmentalization.
3. What is the relationship between levels of management and span of control? Explain the advantages and disadvantages.
4. Distinguish between line and staff functions. Are they always easily identified in various types of business enterprises? Justify the existence of both line and staff departments.
5. What conflicts may arise between line and staff personnel? What reasons can you give for these problems? How does effective communication ease the conflict?

6. What are the three types of authority? Do they all exist in all four stages of functional growth?
7. What are some factors that favor centralization or decentralization?
8. How can a company minimize the negative effects of downsizing?
9. What are the potential benefits and potential drawbacks of reengineering?
10. What contemporary organization form would be the easiest to implement in a traditional functional organization?
11. Discuss the relationship between management philosophy, strategy, and forms of organization. If you were the owner/manager of 10 convenience stores in the same city, what type of strategy and structure would you use? If you were the owner/manager of 10 Certified Public Accountant (CPA) offices in various cities, what type of strategy and structure would you use?

Information

Skill Builder 4-1

YDL (You Deserve Luxury) Corporation
YDL Corporation designs and builds luxury, high-end yachts and mobile coaches. The company's niche market is wealthy individuals who can afford to pay millions to travel in style. Many of YDL's clients are famous celebrities, such as singers, actors/actresses, and royal families. The company's mission is as follows:

We are an international design and production firm intent on creating the highest quality yachts and mobile coaches for discerning clients. We work in partnership with our key stakeholders to deliver a high-end product that is tailored to meet our customers' needs. Thus, we recognize the importance of and emphasize building solid relationships with our customers, employees, and suppliers alike. Our promise is to deliver quality, on-time.

YDL continues to grow even when other businesses' sales are declining. YDL's core competencies are quality and service, and it prides itself on their ability to adapt to customer and market changes. It employ between 125 and 150 total employees, depending on order levels. YDL's administrative and production facilities are located in California.
Answer the following questions:

1. What type of business strategy do you think YDL is pursuing? Explain.
2. What form of departmentalization (organizational structure) do you believe YDL utilizes? Why?

esources

Interpersonal Skill

Skill Builder 4-2

Reducing Costs in an Accounting Firm (Group Activity)

Divide the class into groups of five to seven students, each group representing the managing partners of an accounting firm. Discuss the following situation and report to the class on what your group's plan is, and how you would communicate it to employees.

There are 30 employees in your organization, and for the past year, sales and profits have been down. In fact, for the past six months, the firm has been operating at a loss.

Two months ago, a larger accounting firm acquired your firm in a friendly takeover. Its philosophy is to treat your smaller organization as a semiautonomous division of the accounting company, providing only general guidance and managing by results.

The accounting company CEO has asked your group, the managing partners, to develop a plan to reduce costs. It is important to note that 90 percent of your budget goes to salaries. The accounting company CEO also wants to know how you will communicate the plan to employees.

Source: The Synergistic Group, consulting files, 6 Schwaemmle Drive, Mobile, AL 36608.

Systems

Interpersonal Skill

Skill Builder 4-3

Google's Organizational Structure (Group Activity)

Google has experienced dramatic growth in a relatively short period of time, moving from an entrepreneurial venture to a publicly traded company seemingly overnight. All the reports and stories about the internal operations in the media suggest Google is a loosely structured network of creative energy. Form teams of three to five students. Your assignment is to conduct Internet research to uncover Google's true form of departmentalization (organizational structure). Each team's assignment is to prepare a brief report of its findings to present to the rest of the class.

Information

Technology

CASE 4-1

John Moody Is Facing Reorganization

When we last heard from John (See Exhibit 4-6), his organization was in a mature stage of organizational development. His business had grown from a single entrepreneur to a large, vertical, line-and-staff organization. Unfortunately, the economy is experiencing a recession, which is impacting the demand for John's products. His costs are exceeding his revenues, and he cannot afford to continue operating at a loss long-term.

Perform the following tasks

1. Using the information about John's company in the chapter, particularly the organizational chart in Exhibit 4-6, analyze his current situation. Consider whether John's strategy and structure are still useful.

2. Prepare a report to include your recommends regarding what should be done to turn this situation around. You should include an organizational chart in your report reflecting your recommendations.

5

Delegating Authority and Empowering Employees

Melanie Stetson Freeman/The Christian Science Monitor via Getty Images

In empowered organizations, teams thrive when leaders delegate some authority and people are able to learn from each other.

The greatest challenge in life is to be who you are and to become what you are capable of becoming.

—*Robert Louis Stevenson*

The second greatest challenge is to assist and empower other people to become what they are capable of becoming.

—*Donald C. Mosley, Sr.*

Preview

LARRY S. BONINE, INTERNATIONAL LEADER IN EMPOWERMENT, TEAM BUILDING, AND CREATING HIGH-PERFORMANCE LEARNING ORGANIZATIONS Peter Senge in his influential book, *The Fifth Discipline*, offers a very important insight and observation that is essential in understanding the "why" of effective delegation, empowerment, and team building.

> *"Learning organizations are possible because, deep down, we are all learners. No one has to teach an infant to learn. In fact, no one has to teach infants anything. They are intrinsically inquisitive, masterful learners who learn to walk, speak, and pretty much run their households all on their own. Learning organizations are possible because not only is it our nature to learn, but we love to learn. Most of us at one time or another have been part of a great "team," a group of people who functioned together in an extraordinary way—who trusted one another, who complemented each others' strengths and compensated for each others' limitations, who had common goals that were larger than individual goals, and who produced extraordinary results. I have met many people who have experienced this sort of profound teamwork—in sports, or in the performing arts, or in business. Many say that they have spent much of their life looking for that experience again. What they experienced was a learning organization. The team that became great didn't start off great—it learned how to produce extraordinary results."*[1]

The first chapter of Senge's book is titled, "Give me a lever long enough ... and single-handed I can move the world." Reflecting on that quote, Larry Bonine is the leader who comes to mind. This author first met Larry while serving as one of two facilitators for the first formalized public sector partnering project, the construction of the Oliver Lock and Dam on the Black Warrior River in Alabama.[2]

Larry is tall (6'4") and lanky, and even with a quick and ready smile, he conveys a certain commander/leadership aura and presence. During our work with the U.S. Army Corps of Engineers (USACE), we were told that Colonel Bonine was a West Point graduate and a sure bet to make general if he stayed in the military. It was not until later that we learned that Larry was not a West Pointer, but actually a graduate of Tennessee Tech University. He certainly looks like a West Pointer and has the charismatic/transformational leadership quality you would hope to find in a West Pointer. One of Larry's early role models was Raymond Cronwell, Assistant Professor of Military Science at Tennessee Tech, whose leadership and military bearing had a major positive influence on Larry's decision to make the Army his first career.

Larry's first Battalion Commander, an autocratic, Theory X leader who believed people must be directed or threatened with punishment to get them to put forth adequate effort, also had a major influence on Larry; he learned what he did *not* want to be like as an officer. Fortunately, his next commander used just the opposite leadership style and provided a great positive learning experience for him. While serving as a company commander in Germany and Vietnam, Larry continued to be blessed with good commanding officers and role models.

When Larry first had the opportunity for a higher command and was given a choice of Battalion Commander or District Commander, he chose the district assignment. At the time, he was younger than anyone he supervised and had no experience building dams. Rather than trying to hide his inexperience, he confessed to the experienced personnel that he needed their guidance and wanted to know what he could do to help and empower them. They responded with a high degree of creativity and performance. Later, Colonel Larry Bonine was District Engineer for USACE in Mobile, Alabama, the Corps' largest district, running from Panama to North Georgia. When Larry arrived to take command, the district had a reputation for being bureaucratic, with excessive red tape and a lack of timely decision making. Bonine's leadership produced a number of initiatives that served as catalysts for change and renewal, not only in the Corps, but also in the construction industry in general.

Early in Larry's tenure, professional training and education were provided to all district employees in teamwork and leadership. The cultural change initiative was called the Mobile Team Express; all employees who achieved a certain level of training were presented, by the Colonel, with a railroad engineer's hat labeled "Mobile Team Express." The internal team building and partnering continues to this day.

It was the lack of teamwork that prompted Dan Burns, Chief of Construction of the Mobile district, to approach Colonel Bonine with the idea of trying partnering in the public sector. Partnering is a variation of team building and strategic planning that emphasizes shared leadership, open communication, and solving problems at the lowest level possible. As Burns explains the situation:

> *"Frequently, the time consumed between the initiation of a project and the final resolution of all administrative problems and financial responsibilities is two or three times the duration of the actual field work. Over 40 percent of my time as chief of construction has been involved in dispute resolution and conflict management; [we felt] there had to be a better way, [and so decided] to investigate the concept of partnering utilized in the private sector."*[3]

At the time Burns made these comments, the Corps had a backlog of disputes with contractors that many times would result in costly litigation. In the words of Larry Bonine:

> *"My first encounter with partnering came in 1988, while I was District Engineer for the Army Corps of Engineers in Mobile, Alabama. We had plans to construct the Oliver Lock and Dam, on the Black Warrior River in Alabama. The district Chief of Construction, Dan Burns, approached me with the notion to try private sector*

partnering as a tool to reduce claims and facilitate communication for the project. Although none of us had any experience with partnering, it sounded like a good idea. We tried it and the concept was a tremendous success. Later, I briefed the other District Engineers in the Corps on partnering. Colonel Chuck Cowan, then District Engineer in Oregon, picked up on the partnering concept and gave it the push it needed to become Corps policy. Enough can't be said to describe Chuck's impact on partnering. His personal energy and commitment, coupled with the enthusiasm of the construction industry in the Northwest, demonstrated [that] the time for Public Sector Partnering had arrived."[4]

The second partnering effort was the construction and operation of a tactical and operational control center at Cape Canaveral. The partners were the U.S. Air Force Systems Command, USACE, the Harris Company, and the W & F Construction Company. At the initial workshop, a major problem identified was the lengthy response time on cost-saving–value engineering proposals by the contractor. The average response time was 15 months, so the contractor rarely submitted cost savings ideas. The partners developed a plan to change the turnaround time from 15 months to 15 days.

The facilitator of the workshop recalls considerable skepticism on the part of the Air Force and contractor participants that the command office of the Corps in Mobile would approve the plan. This skepticism was present despite the fact that lower-level engineers from the Corps had participated in developing the action plan. Actually, this type of empowered creative thinking and problem solving by those most involved in the project was exactly what Larry Bonine and Dan Burns were expecting when they initiated partnering in the public sector. They strongly supported the plan, and in the first three months of the project, approximately $400,000 in cost savings were generated as a result of contractor-initiated engineering proposals. This high-visibility project turned out to be a group success.

As a result of partnering success in the Mobile district and other districts, Commanding General Harry Hatch emphasized two major initiatives in USACE in the 1990s: (1) concern for the environment and (2) partnering. The U.S. Navy heard about partnering, visited Mobile, adopted its partnering model and approach, and used it in projects from Guam to the U.S. East Coast. The Associated General Contractors of America were influenced by the Mobile model, developed partnering guidelines, and ultimately presented the Excellence in Partnering Awards for outstanding projects. These are just some of the reasons why, when I think of Peter Senge's quote, "Give me a lever long enough …" I think of Larry Bonine.

Larry retired from the USACE as a full colonel. Because of his excellent reputation and experience, he had a number of interesting opportunities but chose to work for an international engineering firm, Parsons-Brinckerhoff.

After several years with Parsons-Brinckerhoff, Larry received an offer to become Director of the Arizona Department of Transportation. He continued to lead through team building and partnering, and after five years, the Arizona Department of Transportation was known as one of the country's leading learning organizations. During this time, Larry and his leadership team would spend two days each month with his middle managers teaching and implementing enlightened leadership management concepts and practices. For example, the five disciplines of a learning organization were taught and discussed thoroughly. These disciplines are systems thinking, personal mastery, mental model, building a shared vision, and team learning. Larry is quite proud that leaders from the Arizona department have been selected to head other organizations. Tom Warren was selected to head the Utah Department of Transportation, and Mary Peters is a top executive in the U.S. Department of Transportation Federal Highway Administration.[5]

authority

Given the right to act in a specified manner in order to reach organizational objectives; the right to tell others how to act to reach objectives.

responsibility

Occurs when key tasks associated with a particular job are specified. The obligation of an employee to accept a manager's delegated authority.

job descriptions

Provide information to employees about the important job-related tasks.

1 *Recognize the importance of delegation.*

2 *Explain what is involved in the delegation process, including authority, responsibility, and accountability.*

delegation of authority

The process by which leaders distribute and entrust activities and related authority to other people in an organization. The three key aspects of organization are (1) granting authority, (2) assigning duties and responsibilities, (3) requiring accountability.

accountability

The obligation that is created when an employee accepts the leader's delegation of authority.

Today, Larry is founder and president of the Pinnacle Leadership Group and continues to be an international leader in empowerment, team building, and creating high-performance learning organizations. His group accomplishes this by offering consultation services, designing in-house training and development courses, and offering a two-and-half–day leadership course in Scottsdale, Arizona. Comments from a recent participant attest to the value of the course and Larry's continuing influence as a change agent:

> *"Best leadership course I've been to ... combines all the leadership training I've experienced in a 25-year military career with the best ideas of partnering ... and packs it into a two-and-half day program."*

> —ROBERT KEYSER, COLONEL, U.S. ARMY CORPS OF ENGINEERS, MOBILE DISTRICT COMMANDER

Concepts and Definitions

A number of leaders are intelligent and well educated yet, unlike Colonel Larry Bonine, they do not practice true empowerment. The authors are convinced that mastering the art of delegation and empowerment is essential to a leader's growth, development, and effectiveness. Consequently, we want to start with concepts and definitions to ensure we understand the process of delegation and empowerment.

Role of Delegation

Delegation is the process by which leaders distribute and entrust activities and related authority to other people in an organization. The three key aspects of delegation are (1) granting authority, (2) assigning duties and responsibilities, and (3) requiring accountability.

- *Authority* is the right to do something. When authority is delegated, an individual or team is given the power or right to act in a specified manner in order to reach organizational objectives. For example, a department chair at a university is given the authority to recruit faculty members to fill vacant positions without the president of the university having to interview each candidate to make a final decision.
- *Assigning duties and responsibilities* occurs when key tasks associated with a particular job are specified. In mid- to large-size organizations, **job descriptions** provide information to employees about the important job-related tasks. Due to the dynamic nature of business today, managers may assign nontraditional duties and responsibilities. For example, production employees in a southeastern furniture manufacturing plant are given the responsibility of projecting a positive image of the company both on the job and in the community. Since the plant competes for most of its production personnel from the surrounding rural area with other manufacturers, a positive corporate image is a key differentiating factor.
- *Accountability* is the obligation that is created when an employee accepts the leader's **delegation of authority**. **Accountability** flows upward, such that the delegatee is responsible to the next higher level of management to effectively carry out the assigned duties and responsibilities.

Decentralization

Although closely related to the concept of delegation of authority, decentralization is the broader concept, in that it refers to the extent to which authority is delegated from one level or unit of the organization to another, rather than from one individual to another.

The Role of Authority

3 *Understand the role of authority.*

Since authority is constantly being used, its nature and role should be well understood. As mentioned earlier, authority is the *right* to do something or to tell someone else to do it to reach organizational objectives. If no one in an organization had authority, employees could come to work and leave when they wanted, and they could carry out their assignments in any way they wanted, rather than in the way prescribed by higher authority. Without a system of authority, an organization could not function. The following are some examples of higher authority in action.

A police officer gives a motorist a ticket for driving 45 mph in a 30-mph zone. The officer's authority derives from the city council.

In 1999, Henry Ford III, as chairman of Ford Motor Company, fired Jacques Nasser as its president. Ford's authority came from the company's board of directors, which got its power from the stockholders.

The department manager at Macy's assigned the work shifts for her personnel during the Christmas holidays. Her authority was delegated by the store manager.

In each of these examples, the individual exercised the right to exert authority over others. That authority came with the position and resulted from delegation by a higher-level manager.

Chip Henderson/Index Stock Imagery/ Photolibrary

Delegating allows employees an opportunity to learn by doing. It also allows the supervisor to perform other tasks, and it improves control. As a result, more work gets accomplished!

Sources of Authority

There are two contradictory views regarding the source of a manager's authority: the formal theory and the acceptance theory.

formal theory of authority

Authority exists because someone was granted it.

Formal Authority View   According to the **formal theory of authority,** authority is conferred; authority exists because someone was granted it. This view traces the origin of authority upward to its ultimate source, which for business organizations is the owners or stockholders. The head nurse in a hospital has authority granted by the nursing director, who has been granted authority by the hospital board, which has been granted authority by the stockholders (if a private hospital) or the public (if a public hospital). The formal theory is consistent with the definition of authority we presented in the previous section.

Stop & Think

You may be reading the material in this book because it has been assigned by an instructor. What is the source of the instructor's authority to make such an assignment, to give exams, and to assign a grade in the course?

acceptance theory of authority

A manager's authority originates only when it has been accepted by the group or individual over whom it is being exercised.

Acceptance of Authority View   The **acceptance theory of authority** disputes the idea that authority can be conferred. Acceptance theorists (chiefly behaviorists) believe that a manager's authority originates only when it has been accepted by the group or individual over whom it is being exercised. Chester Barnard stated this position. He wrote, "If a directive communication is accepted by one to whom it is addressed, the authority for him is confirmed or established."[6] Thus, acceptance of the directive becomes the basis of action. Disobedience of such a communication by an employee is a denial of its authority for him or her. Therefore, under this definition, the decision about whether an order has authority lies with the person to whom it is addressed and does not reside in "persons of authority" or those who issue those orders, as implied in this example:

Jan was a manager in a large publishing company that had initiated a participative management by objectives process. Jan's immediate supervisor asked her to set objectives for her area and develop a one-year plan to accomplish those objectives. Jan consulted her employees and developed what she perceived as difficult but attainable objectives.

When her boss reviewed the objectives, he discovered he disagreed and revised them drastically. He then called Jan in and dictated that she accept the altered objectives. Jan responded that the objectives would be impossible for her staff to achieve and she could not agree to them in good conscience. At this point, Jan refused to accept her boss's authority, and, although her boss eventually capitulated, it caused some future difficulties in their relationship.[7]

Stop & Think

Do you agree with Jan's position in this example? Why or why not? Assuming that Jan was correct in feeling that the revised objectives would be impossible to attain, how might she have handled the situation differently?

A female supervisor in a traditionally male role may find her power tested by her subordinates.

We have defined authority in line with the position taken by the formal theorists—that authority is a right a manager has been formally granted by the organization. As we will shortly point out, though, the acceptance theorists seem to confuse authority with power or leadership, which involves the ability of a manager to influence employees to accept his or her authority.

The behaviorists, however, do make the point that *to be effective*, managers are certainly very dependent on acceptance by others of their authority.

The Role of Power

4 *Understand the role of power and why it is a great motivator.*

The leader's possession of authority is not always sufficient in itself to assure that subordinates will respond as the leader's desires. In such cases, a leader must use some other approach, as the following example illustrates.

Mary Fleming was named supervisor of the Number 2 paper machine at the northern mill of a large national company.[8] *She was the first female supervisor to be named to such a traditionally male position. The position carried much authority with it, but Mary was intelligent enough to realize that her authority alone would not get her workers to accept her and meet performance standards.*

Several of the employees tested her immediately by taking extended work breaks and making some snide remarks within her hearing about the department's "skirt supervisor." Mary ignored this behavior the first few days and felt that the worst thing she could do was to overreact and come on too strong. But the resistance persisted. Mary had a meeting with Carl White and Pete Antheim, the two senior members of the department, and asked for their advice about handling the situation. White and Antheim seemed flattered by being consulted and told Mary they'd handle the situation. The problems never recurred, and six months after the incident, Mary's group was highly supportive of her leadership, and the "female department head" issue had been forgotten.

EXHIBIT 5-1
Authority–Power
Combinations

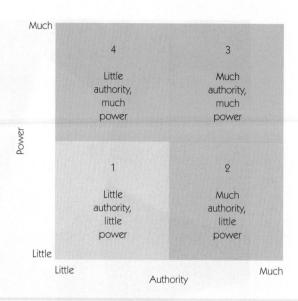

We will now study this example with an eye toward the authority-power combinations illustrated in Exhibit 5-1. Mary used a leadership strategy that played a key role in getting her into quadrant 3, where she had both authority and power. **Power** is the ability to influence individuals, groups, events, and decisions, and is closely related to leadership. In an earlier example in this chapter—where Jan refused to accept impossible objectives dictated by her boss—we see an example of quadrant 2 in operation. Jan's boss had considerable authority but little power to influence Jan to accept his edict. In other cases, staff personnel have little authority but much power to influence line managers (quadrant 4).

The belief of Sir Dahlberg Acton that "power tends to corrupt, and absolute power corrupts absolutely" is widespread in today's culture. In recent years, however, there has been an increasing awareness that power is not necessarily all bad—that the use of power may be essential for the effective accomplishment of individual, organizational, and social goals. Interest in power has also been generated by David McClelland's research showing that a high need for power is an important characteristic of successful managers.

power

the ability to influence individuals, groups, events, and decisions.

How Power Is Obtained

As shown by J.R.P. French, Jr., and Bertram Raven in one of the earliest—and still most useful—studies, power can be obtained from many sources.[9] Six of these sources have been translated into types of power, classified as follows:

1. **Reward power** arises from the number of positive rewards (money, protection, etc.) that a leader is perceived as controlling.
2. **Coercive power** results from people's perceived expectation that punishment (being fired, reprimanded, etc.) will follow if they do not comply with the orders of a leader.
3. **Legitimate power** develops from internalized values that dictate that a leader has an inherent right to influence subordinates. According to this view, one has an obligation to accept that influence simply because a person is designated as a boss or leader.

4. **Control-of-information power** derives from the possession of knowledge that others do not have. Some people exercise this type of power by either giving or withholding needed information.

5. **Referent power** is based on people's identification with a leader and what that "leader" stands for or symbolizes. Personal charisma, charm, courage, and other traits are important factors in the exercise of referent power.

6. **Expert power** results from a leader's expertise or knowledge in an area in which that leader wants to influence others.

Do not infer from this discussion that a given leader draws upon all of these types of power. Rather, leaders find their own sources of strength from many of these types. We can say that more effective leaders draw more on referent power and expert power, and practice more open communication in information sharing.

How Power Can Be Used

Some leaders believe that if a manager has power and shares it with others (delegates it), it is diminished. Actually, the best way to expand power is to share it, for power can grow, in part, by being shared. Sharing power is different from giving it or throwing it away—delegation does not mean abdication.

Effective leaders have a high need for power, but that need is directed toward the benefit of the organization as a whole. In addition, the need for power is stronger than the need to be liked by others. Thus, as a leader you must be willing to play the influence game in a controlled way. This does not imply that you need to be authoritarian in action. On the contrary, it appears that power-motivated leaders make their subordinates feel stronger rather than weaker. A true authoritarian would have the reverse effect, making people feel weak or powerless.

The Role of Empowerment

5 *Explain the role of empowerment and indicate ways to increase empowerment.*

empowerment

Granting employees authority to make key decisions within their enlarged areas of responsibility.

Empowerment essentially is the granting of authority to employees to make key decisions within their enlarged areas of responsibility. The driving idea of empowerment is that individuals closest to the work and to customers should make the decisions. Similar to Colonel Larry Bonine, D. Michael Abrashoff is another military leader who has been a model of progressive leadership in empowerment. In 1997, Abrashoff was commander of the USS Benfold, "a $1 billion warship with the world's most advanced computer-controlled combat equipment, revolutionary radar technology, a stack of missiles capable of taking out precise targets on land, sea, or air, and a crack crew of 300 highly skilled, totally committed sailors." The ship spearheaded some of the most critical missions in the Desert Storm confrontation with Iraq.

Abrashoff's leadership led to the Benfold's being the best ship in the Navy. "In fact, the ship won the prestigious Spokane Trophy for having the best combat readiness in the fleet—the first time in at least 10 years that a ship of its class had received that honor." Excerpts from an article best describe the commander's philosophy and grass roots leadership principles and the concepts he practices:

I divide the world into believers and infidels. What the infidels don't understand (and they far outnumber the believers) is that innovative practices combined with true empowerment produce phenomenal results.

He continues,

I'm lucky, all I ever wanted to do in the Navy was to command a ship. I don't care if I ever get promoted again, and that attitude has enabled me to do the right things

Reuters/Corbis

The USS Benfold, which engaged in critical missions during Operation Desert Storm in Iraq, was led by Commander Michael Abrashoff, who carried out successful delegation and empowerment in a very challenging environment.

for my people instead of doing the right things for my career. In the process, I ended up with the best ship in the Navy, and I got the best evaluation of my career. The unintended benefit? My promotion is guaranteed.

When you shift your organizing principle from obedience to performance,... the highest boss is no longer the guy with the most stripes, it's the sailor who does the work. There is nothing magical about it.... In most organizations today, ideas still come from the top. Soon after arriving at this command, I realized that young folks on this ship are smart and talented, and I realized my job was to listen aggressively to pick up all of the ideas that they had for improving how we operate. The most important thing a captain can do is to see the ship from the eyes of the crew.[10]

Why Leaders Fail to Delegate

Many good and intelligent people have difficulty delegating authority when in leadership positions, particularly in the early stages of their careers. Our culture has a major influence on why this occurs so frequently.

In the formative years, success in school and in summer jobs depended primarily on the individual's efforts. Achievement and success did not come from inspiring, developing, and working with other people. Grades were determined primarily by hard work and self-discipline. Moreover, those who went to college had a high need for achievement and usually chose difficult majors. The majority who chose fields such as accounting, finance, and banking usually had a keen sense of responsibility, were very conscientious, and were good with details. A survey of bank leaders attending the Louisiana State University Banking School indicated that most of the participants had personality types that incorporated

6 *Understand why some leaders are reluctant to delegate and why employees may not welcome delegation.*

these qualities. One class of 65 bankers was given a home-study problem of identifying their primary weakness that needed improvement to increase their effectiveness as a bank leader. They were also asked to develop and implement an action plan to turn the weakness into a strength. The weakness that appeared most frequently in the banking class was delegation. The Action Plan to improve delegation by a vice president of lending is found in Exhibit 5-2.

Stop & Think

How many people do you know who follow the guide "if you want it done right, do it yourself"? Do you follow this guide? What negative consequences will this trait have for effective delegation and empowerment if you are a leader?

EXHIBIT 5-2
Action Plan of James
McKenney, Vice
President of Lending

I. Statement of my objective
To greatly improve my efficiency and effectiveness in carrying out the delegation process with the leading officers reporting to me.

II. Analysis of the problem or objective
   A. At the banking school when we discussed the 16 problem styles (Myers-Briggs profiles and analysis), I discovered that the characteristics of my type could lead to being a very effective leader if a few potential blind spots can be overcome. It seems that those who are sensing/thinking types (as I am) are so conscientious that our attitude is "If you want it done right, do it yourself." This statement definitely applies to me.
   B. When I was recently promoted to this position, the president of the bank gave me a number of positive reasons for my promotion. He also cautioned me that with my increased responsibilities, I could expect to get involved in activities as previously, but he wanted me to focus on developing the skills and knowledge of our loan officers and improve bottom line results.
   C. I realize that most of my life I earned good grades in high school and college because of individual effort. This carried over to my work habits as a loan officer, but I now realize that to be a successful supervisor, I need to develop my team and make use of coaching and empowerment.

III. Development of alternative solutions
   A. Start having biweekly meetings for one hour after banking hours.
      1. At our first meeting we will jointly develop objectives that enhance and reinforce the bank's financial goal.
      2. At our subsequent meetings we will review our progress and discuss any problem loans.
   B. Set up a participative individual management-by-objectives program. This plan will allow individual bank officers to set performance objectives that support our lending division's objectives. During this process I will play the role of coach and mentor, and after the initial meeting, set up performance review sessions with each officer every six months or as needed.
   C. Once every six months at our biweekly meeting we will conduct a brainstorming session to identify our strengths and any problems, issues, or missed opportunities we need to address.
   D. I will explore educational opportunities available for our officers, including scheduling several officers for our state banking school or the Banking School of the South.

IV. Final action plan
I have begun implementing all of the alternative ideas (A, B, C, and D in Section III). Prior to sending this to you, I met with our president and CEO and discussed the ideas. He was most enthusiastic and supportive and is presenting the concept to our executive committee for possible implementation in all divisions of our bank.

Source: This example is based on the experiences of Don Mosley when he served as coordinator and instructor for the management and leadership segment of the Banking School of the South at Louisiana State University. The name is fictional to ensure no embarrassment to the actual banker.

The late industrialist Andrew Carnegie once said, "When a man realizes he can get others in to help him do something better than he can do it alone, he has taken a big step in his life." The following are some other reasons why many leaders have difficulty delegating:

- Many leaders like to control but feel that when they delegate they surrender some of their power and authority. Pfeffer, Cialdini, Hanna, and Knopoff (1998) found that managers tended to assign higher evaluations of work quality to their employees when the managers themselves were more involved in the production.[11] Because empowerment dilutes work supervision, many managers may make inaccurate evaluations of their workers' abilities, skills, and output.
- Some leaders do not delegate because of a lack of trust in others.
- Closely related to the above point, because leaders are being held accountable for results, they don't delegate out of fear employees will make mistakes. Research by Yuki and Fu (1999) found that one determinant of managerial delegation was the strength of the manager–subordinate relationship. Managers delegated more to employees who they perceived to be competent, who shared their task goals, and who had longer tenure.[12]
- Others do not delegate because they are insecure and are afraid that their employees will do so well that they will be recognized and promoted ahead of the leader.
- A legitimate reason why some leaders don't delegate is they correctly assess that employees need more training, coaching, and experience in certain assignments.

Why Employees May Not Welcome Delegation

Of course, there are also reasons why employees may not welcome delegation:

1. **Ambiguous or Unclear Duties and Responsibilities.** When delegating authority, the manager must clearly communicate to the employee the employee's duties and responsibilities, the need for and importance of the assignment, and why the employee was selected. In one case, the plant had been downsized so drastically that workers were being assigned responsibilities and duties that middle managers had previously performed. In this type of environment, change occurs rapidly, so there is always the chance that newly delegated responsibilities and duties will be poorly communicated, which can lead to negative outcomes.

2. **Fear of Failure.** Even if assignments are communicated so individuals understand what comprises their new duties, other problems may arise. Many managers misdiagnose the job maturity level of their employees and assign them tasks that are too difficult. This mistake may result in the employee being unfairly criticized during their performance review or perhaps even fired. A company that one of the authors worked with in a consulting capacity had a national presence and was growing rapidly; it promoted internally as a means of filling newly created positions and to motivate its existing employees. One individual was promoted to manager of his work department because he had excelled as an operating-level employee and possessed the technical expertise that was needed. However, he had not had an opportunity to develop other skills needed in the new management position, such as team building, communication, conflict management, and leadership skills. His inability to employ a diverse skill set with his employees ultimately led to his being replaced as head of the work department.

3. **Increased Stress.** Finally, increased delegation can mean increased stress on employees. Even when effective communication and appropriate training are provided, employees may still resist delegation and empowerment. Management efforts to

downsize or restructure the organization to be more competitive can lead to employee role overload. During the 1990s, the following comments seemed quite common: "They call it empowerment and say we get a chance to be a real part of this organization. I call it doing more work for the same amount of money." Some employees prefer not to be empowered. As Hackman and Oldham's Job Characteristics Model points out, the level of participation an individual is comfortable with is not just dependent on effective job design, communication, and training. Meaningful participation also depends on that person's need for growth and development. Managers must assess an employee's job maturity level and need for growth when selecting an employee for delegation.[13]

Facing Adaptive Challenges

7 *Know how to face adaptive challenges.*

Ronald A. Heifetz's book, *Leadership Without Easy Answers*, is an innovative and creative contribution to leadership.[14] In this book and in a follow-up article in the *Harvard Business Review* by Heifetz and Donald Laurie, a concept of adaptive challenges and work is presented. In their words:

> *To stay alive, Jack Pritchard had to change his life. Triple bypass surgery and medication could help, the heart surgeon told him, but no technical fix could release Pritchard from his own responsibility for changing the habits of a lifetime. He had to stop smoking, improve his diet, get some exercise, and take time to relax, remembering to breathe more deeply each day. Pritchard's doctor could provide sustaining technical expertise and take supportive action, but only Pritchard could adapt his ingrained habits to improve his long-term health. The doctor faced the leadership task of mobilizing the patient to make critical behavioral changes; Jack Pritchard faced the adaptive work of figuring out which specific changes to make and how to incorporate them into his daily life.*

> *Companies today face challenges similar to the ones confronting Pritchard and his doctor. They face adaptive challenges. Changes in societies, markets, customers, competition, and technology around the globe are forcing organizations to clarify their values, develop new strategies, and learn new ways of operation. Often the toughest task for leaders in effecting change is mobilizing people throughout the organization to do adaptive work.*

> *Adaptive work is required when our deeply held beliefs are challenged, when the values that made us successful become less relevant, and when legitimate yet competing perspectives emerge. We see adaptive challenges every day at every level of the workplace—when companies restructure or reengineer, develop or implement strategy, or merge businesses. We see adaptive challenges when marketing has difficulty working with operations, when cross-functional teams don't work well, or when senior executives complain, "We don't seem to be able to execute effectively." Adaptive problems are often systemic problems with no ready answers.*

> *... But the locus of responsibility for problem solving when a company faces an adaptive challenge must shift to its people. Solutions to adaptive challenges reside not in the executive suite, but in the collective intelligence of employees at all levels, who need to use one another as resources, often across boundaries, and learn their way to those solutions.*[15]

reframing

Examining the situation from multiple vantage points to develop a holistic picture.

Reframing and Training **Reframing** and training is one way to face adaptive challenges at work. It helps organizations and individuals to change values and behaviors and to identify new approaches and strategies. The essence of reframing is examining

Increased delegation can sometimes overwhelm employees.

the "situation from multiple vantage points to develop a holistic picture. Effective leaders change lenses when they don't make sense or aren't working."[16] Leadership training and development have a major impact in getting leaders/managers to change. In the final analysis, the motivation to change and improve effectiveness in delegation and empowerment rests with the individual—both leader and follower.

Achieving Effective Delegation and Empowerment

8 *Indicate ways to achieve effective delegation and discuss the roles of various parties in achieving effective delegation.*

When the authors conduct workshops regarding leadership, team building, and partnering, we start by asking participants, "What is the most effective way you learn that produces the most insight, growth, and development?" Although we have received different answers, a core group of people always responds by saying that experience and, especially, mistakes are the best learning tools. We then ask, "What is the implication of saying, 'We know of people who have had 1 year of experience 20 times?'" Usually, someone correctly assesses that although those individuals have experience, they really haven't learned from that experience. Thus, the key to learning from experience, including both successes and failures, is to go through a disciplined reflection on that experience.

Exhibit 5-3 shows the **experiential learning** model and highlights the importance of using feedback to gain insights in learning from experience. The use of this model, particularly in a coaching or mentoring environment, is very helpful for achieving successful delegation, empowerment, and results.

experiential learning

Using an integrated process of experiencing, identifying, analyzing, and generalizing to gain insights in learning.

Coaching and Teaching

Two of the most significant ways of empowering and developing people are coaching and teaching. This area is so significant to the leadership process that we have an additional chapter covering the topic, so at this point, we will only introduce the process.

EXHIBIT 5-3
The Experiential Learning Model

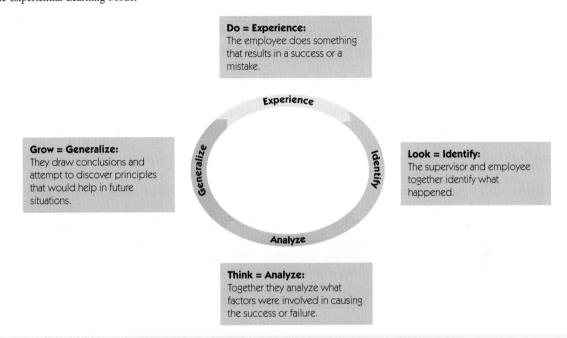

Do = Experience:
The employee does something that results in a success or a mistake.

Grow = Generalize:
They draw conclusions and attempt to discover principles that would help in future situations.

Look = Identify:
The supervisor and employee together identify what happened.

Think = Analyze:
Together they analyze what factors were involved in causing the success or failure.

Experience

Generalize

Identify

Analyze

There are many different ways to coach and teach. The forthcoming story describes a way that may have been the catalyst for Dwight D. Eisenhower's becoming General of the Army and President of the United States. As a student at West Point, Eisenhower excelled as a football player until a football injury ended his career. After a bout with despondency, he regrouped and directed his energies to becoming head cheerleader. During this period, he was not known for excelling in his studies and graduated in the middle of his class.

Most of his initial assignments after graduation involved coaching the football team; from all reports, he was a good coach. Fortunately, he was then assigned to Panama and reported to General Fox Conner, a graduate of West Point, who saw great leadership potential in young Eisenhower. In World War I, Conner had served as General Pershing's operations officer in France and was considered one of the smartest men in the army.

After the war, in 1922, Conner took command of the 20th Infantry Brigade in the Panama Canal Zone. He requested that Eisenhower be assigned to his command as executive officer; Conner's old boss, U.S. Army Chief of Staff John Pershing, granted the request. Conner was a great teacher and coach for Eisenhower, and since their duties were light, they spent a lot of time in a teacher/coach/student relationship.

Conner insisted that Eisenhower read serious military literature and forced the younger man to think about what he was reading by asking probing questions. Eisenhower read memoirs of Civil War generals, then discussed with Conner the decisions Grant, Sherman, and others had made. What would have happened had they done this or that differently? What were the alternatives? Eisenhower was anxious to please, so anxious that he read *Clausewitz on War* three times—a difficult enough task to complete even once and made more difficult by Conner's insistent questioning about the implications of Clausewitz's ideas.

Conner and Eisenhower also discussed the future. Conner insisted there would be another war in 20 years or less, that it would be a world war, that America would fight with allies, and that Eisenhower had better prepare himself for it. He advised Eisenhower to try for an assignment under Colonel George C. Marshall, who had been with Conner on Pershing's staff. Marshall, Conner insisted, "knows more about the techniques of arranging allied commands than any man I know. He is nothing short of genius." Indeed, Conner's highest praise was "Eisenhower, you handled that just the way Marshall would have done."[17]

Many years after Eisenhower was identified as a world class leader, he stated that his three years under Conner were "a sort of graduate school in military affairs.... In a lifetime of association with great and good men, he is the one figure to whom I owe an incalculable debt." In fact, Eisenhower has stated frequently that Conner influenced him more than anyone he ever served under.[18]

In the fall of 1924, Eisenhower was transferred back to Ft. Meade to coach football. He was greatly disappointed because he had his heart set on attending the infantry school; however, the Chief of Infantry turned down his request without discussion. The infantry school was a prerequisite for the Command and General Staff School (C & GSS) at Ft. Leavenworth, Kansas, and only the best and brightest of officers were selected to attend. Finally, Conner used his influence with the war department to get Eisenhower to the C & GSS. Even then, the infantry command tried to discourage him. An aide to the Chief of Infantry wrote advising Eisenhower to stay away from C & GSS because "you will probably fail," in which case the failure would make him useless as an infantry officer.[19] Eisenhower then wrote Conner expressing some self-doubts and asking his advice on how to prepare himself. In his reply, Conner said, "you may not know it, but because of your 3 years' work in Panama, you are far better trained and ready for Leavenworth than anybody I know."[20]

Conner was right. Eisenhower persevered, and through hard work, diligent study, and the development of a good mind, Eisenhower finished number one out of a class of 275 of the best young officers in the Army.

Stop & Think

Do you agree or disagree on the importance of coaching and teaching in the empowerment and development of individuals? If you agree, identify and reflect on who influenced you the most in the role of coach, teacher, and mentor. Specifically, share with someone else how you were influenced.

Benefits of Delegation

9 *Recognize the benefits of delegation.*

- **Employee Development.** Through delegation, employees can learn from their experiences. When managers enable their employees to succeed and/or make mistakes on their own, a valuable learning opportunity is created. The manager can assist the individual in analyzing the situation and evaluating the reasons for the success or failure, so the employee can grow from the experience.
- **Improved Control.** Contributing to the benefit of employee development, managers who delegate effectively emphasize results, not specific actions, and provide feedback when appropriate.
- **Improved Time Management.** Leaders who choose not to share their power may find they are so consumed with "putting out fires" that they have very little time to devote to truly important or long-term tasks. Conversely, managers who effectively delegate tasks to their subordinates have more time to spend on planning and trouble shooting.

- **Enhanced Power.** When employees are empowered, the environment created results in more people being knowledgeable and concerned about the organization's objectives. This concern leads to a sense of responsibility or ownership in the work itself.

Seven Habits of Unsuccessful Executives

We want to conclude this chapter with some interesting insights from leadership theorist Sydney Finkelstein, Professor of Management at the Tuck School at Dartmouth College. He wrote an article, "The Seven Habits of Spectacularly Unsuccessful Executives." Two of the seven habits are directly related to the concepts covered in this chapter, and others are indirectly related. The seven habits are as follows:

1. They see themselves and companies as dominating their environment.
2. They identify so completely with the company that there is no clear boundary between their personal interests and the corporation's interests.
3. They think they have all the answers.
4. They ruthlessly eliminate anyone who isn't 100 percent behind them.
5. They are consummate spokespersons obsessed with the company image.
6. They underestimate obstacles.
7. They stubbornly rely on what worked for them in the past.[21]

Stop & Think

Which two habits are directly related to the concepts in this chapter? Why?

Finkelstein goes on to say, "Most of the great destroyers of value are people of unusual intelligence and talent.... Nearly all of the leaders who preside over major business failures exhibit four or five of these habits."[22]

In our chapter review, we discuss the two habits most directly related to concepts in this chapter and how they relate to all leaders, not just to high-level executives.

Chapter Review

1. **Recognize the importance of delegation.**

   The delegation process is a partnering process between a supervisor and employees, bosses, and colleagues. Experiential learning is an important part of delegation, allowing employees to grow and develop by "learning through experience." Effective delegation is essential to performing the supervisory management job successfully. In addition to developing people, delegation (1) allows the supervisor to do other things, (2) accomplishes more work, and (3) improves control.

2. **Explain what is involved in the delegation process, including authority, responsibility, and accountability.**

   The process of delegation has three aspects: granting authority, assigning responsibility, and holding people accountable for results. Because accountability is essential to maintaining effective control over results, a person who delegates an assignment should not be able to escape accountability for poor results. Controls to ensure effective delegation can include personal observation by the delegator, periodic reports by the delegate, and statistical reports concerning output, costs, and grievances.

3. **Understand the role of authority.**

   Authority is the *right* to do something or to tell someone else to do it, to reach organizational objectives. If no one had authority, employees could do just what they liked in no prescribed manner; they could come and go as they pleased. Without a system of authority, an organization could not function.

4. **Understand the role of power and why it is a great motivator.**

   Power is the ability to influence individuals, groups, events, and decisions, and is closely related to leadership. Power can be used for good or evil by leaders. Successful leaders have (1) the ability to influence others and (2) a greater need for power than for being liked or needing to do tasks alone. They also believe that to expand power, they need to share it with other members of the organization through delegation and empowerment.

5. **Explain the role of empowerment and indicate ways to increase empowerment.**

   The driving role of empowerment is that individuals closest to the work and to the customers should make the decisions. When implemented properly, empowerment becomes an important way to improve organizational performance. Coaching and teaching are important in carrying out successful empowerment. Also critical to the process is sharing information with everyone and, where appropriate, using self-directed work teams.

6. **Understand why some leaders are reluctant to delegate and why employees may not welcome delegation.**

   Despite the benefits of effective delegations, some supervisors fail to do so for a variety of reasons. For example, because of his or her accountability to a manager, a supervisor may closely monitor or even perform an employee's work. Also, many leaders or supervisors like control and do not want to surrender their power and authority. On the other hand, many employees do not welcome delegation. They may feel the duties and responsibilities are not clearly communicated; they may not understand the importance of the assignment or why they were selected. Also, there is the *fear of failure* factor. Other problems may arise that the employee is not prepared to solve, leading to an employee being unfairly criticized. With more responsibility frequently comes *increased stress* to get the job done correctly. Therefore, some employees may still resist delegation and empowerment.

7. **Know how to face adaptive challenges.**

   Reframing and training, related to the concept of coaching and teaching, is one way to face adaptive challenges at work. It helps organizations and individuals to change values and behaviors and to identify new approaches and strategies.

8. **Indicate ways to achieve effective delegation and discuss the roles of various parties in achieving effective delegation.**

   One of the solutions to ineffective delegation is to emphasize management training and development. However, effective delegation also requires knowing when to delegate, understanding how the delegation process operates, and taking the time to train employees. Although higher management should be supportive and supervisors should delegate clearly, it is the responsibility of employees to function on their own and turn to their supervisors for help when there is a *major* problem.

9. **Recognize the benefits of delegation.**

   The first of four benefits is *employee development*. The manager can assist the individual in analyzing the situation and evaluating the reasons for the success or failure, so the employee can grow from the experience. The second benefit is *improved control*. Managers who delegate effectively emphasize results, not specific actions, and provide feedback when it is appropriate. *Improved time management* is the third benefit. Rather than leaders having their time consumed with "putting out fires," they can effectively delegate tasks to their subordinates and have more time for planning and trouble shooting. And finally, the fourth benefit is *enhanced power*. When employees are empowered, an environment is created resulting in more people being knowledgeable and concerned about the organization's objectives, which in turn leads to a sense of responsibility.

Key Terms

authority, p. 136	accountability, p. 136	power, p. 140
responsibility, p. 136	formal theory of authority, p. 138	empowerment, p. 141
job descriptions, p. 136	acceptance theory of authority, p. 138	reframing, p. 145
delegation of authority, p. 136		experiential learning, p. 146

Questions for Review & Discussion

1. Discuss four reasons delegation is important.
2. Describe the process of delegation.
3. Explain the interrelationships among authority, responsibility, and accountability.
4. Why do some supervisors fail to delegate effectively? If this situation were a common problem in an organization, what could be done to increase supervisors' skills in delegating effectively?
5. What are the roles played in effective delegation?
6. In what way or ways can higher management affect the delegation process?
7. In what way or ways can employees affect the delegation process?
8. Do you think Commander Abrashoff's approach and philosophy would be successful in the private sector? Why or why not?
9. Do you agree or disagree with McClelland that power is the great motivator? Support your position.
10. How does a firm set boundaries to create autonomy and empowerment?

Information

Skill Assessment 5-1

Delegating Tasks to Subordinates

For each of the following questions, select the answer that best describes your approach to delegating tasks to subordinates. Remember to respond as you *have* behaved or *would* behave, not as you think you *should* behave. If you have no managerial experience, answer the questions assuming you are a manager.

When delegating to a subordinate, I:

		USUALLY	SOMETIMES	SELDOM
1.	Explain exactly how the task should be accomplished.	____	____	____
2.	Specify the end results I expect.	____	____	____
3.	Feel that I lose control.	____	____	____
4.	Expect that I'll end up doing the task over again myself.	____	____	____
5.	Only delegate routine or simple tasks.	____	____	____
6.	Clarify to subordinates the limits of their authority.	____	____	____
7.	Establish progress report dates with the subordinate.	____	____	____
8.	Inform all who will be affected that delegation has occurred.	____	____	____

Scoring Key and Interpretation For questions 2, 6, 7, and 8, give yourself 3 points for *Usually,* 2 points for *Sometimes,* and 1 point for *Seldom.*

For questions 1, 3, 4, and 5, give yourself 3 points for *Seldom,* 2 points for *Sometimes,* and 1 point for *Usually.*

Sum up your total points. A score of 20 or higher suggests superior delegation skills. A score of 15 to 19 indicates that you have room for improvement. A score below 15 suggests that your approach to delegation needs substantial improvement.

Source: Stephen P. Robbins and Phillip L. Hunsaker, Training in Interpersonal Skills, 3rd ed., p. 181, © 2003. Reproduced by permission of Pearson Education, Inc., Upper Saddle River, New Jersey.

Information

Skill Assessment 5-2

Do You Delegate as Much as You Can?

By assigning duties in a more efficient way, delegating not only can create greater overall productivity but also can reduce overload and burnout of managers. To learn whether you are a good delegator, answer "yes" or "no" to each of the following questions:

_____ Do you often work overtime?

_____ Do you take work home evenings and weekends?

_____ Is your unfinished work increasing?

_____ Are daily operations so time-consuming that you have little time left for planning?

_____ Do you keep control of all the details needed to do a job?

_____ Do you frequently have to postpone long-range projects?

_____ Are you distracted by constant emergencies?

_____ Do you lack confidence in your subordinates' abilities to shoulder more responsibility?

_____ Do you find yourself irritable and complaining when the work of your group doesn't live up to expectations?

_____ Do conflict, friction, and loss of morale characterize the atmosphere of your work group?

_____ Do your subordinates defer all decisions to you?

_____ Do you instruct your subordinates to perform certain activities, rather than accomplish certain goals?

_____ Do you feel that you're abdicating your role as a manager if you ask for your subordinates' assistance?

_____ Have subordinates stopped presenting their ideas to you?

_____ Do operations slow down much when you're away?

_____ Do you believe that your status and the salary you earn automatically mean that you have to be overworked?

If nine or more of your answers are affirmative, it's likely that you're not delegating enough. If so, identify the negatives, and work on eliminating them. Here are the most common reasons for not delegating:

- Lack of patience. (It takes longer to explain it than to do it myself.)
- Insecurity. (I'm so eager to prove myself that I refuse to delegate.)
- Inflexibility. (I'm convinced that nothing can be done properly unless I do it myself.)
- Inadequacy. (I'm afraid of being shown up.)
- Occupational hobby. (I'm so attached to some aspect of the job that I just don't want to give it up.)

Source: From "Do You Delegate as Much as You Can?" in *Nation's Business.* Originally published July 1996. Reprinted by permission. uschamber.com, September 2009. Copyright © 1996, U.S. Chamber of Commerce.

Skill Builder 5-3

Resources

Delegating Simulation

Problem: Mary Manager has taken a deep look at herself and her department and has decided she must delegate more to her employees for the following reasons: (1) She has consistently worked more than 40 hours a week for several years. (2) The pressure of trying to get everything done has put her on edge with some of the staff. (3) She has not been sleeping well because of worry. Last night she spent three hours formulating a list of responsibilities she might delegate to her five employees. The list is as follows.

A. A weekly report that takes 50 minutes to prepare. This report could easily be delegated to Roberto, but it would reveal certain departmental figures that have not been revealed to employees in the past. There is nothing secret about the data, but Mary feels she might lose control if everybody knows what goes on.

B. A weekly fun job that Mary has always enjoyed. Kaylee would love to do the job (she would probably do it better than Mary), but Mary wants to keep it because it

Interpersonal Skill

Information

Systems

keeps her closer to her employees and facilitates communication. This job usually takes about an hour.

C.   A very routine weekly stock or supply room count that takes an hour and a half. Mary has delegated this job before, but she always winds up taking it back because the grumbling from the employee disturbs her more than doing the job herself. Besides, sometimes the count is wrong and she ends up doing the job herself anyway.

D.   A very short (15-minute) meeting every day at 4:00 p.m. to exchange information with her staff. Mary has refused to delegate this because she fears losing power/ respect with her employees. Terrance would be able to facilitate the meeting effectively and not be overloaded.

E.   A daily (10-minute) delivery job of a special report to top management. Mary has kept this to do herself because it gives her a chance to have a cup of coffee and she can play a little politics with middle and top management executives.

F.   A special routine meeting each month that many managers already delegate to an employee. It would be excellent training for Meredith to have this assignment. Mary has kept it to herself, however, because she is afraid that something will happen at the meeting that she won't know about.

Instructions: Indicate which one is the most critical activity for Manager Mary to delegate, the next most critical activity, and so on. Next, assemble into teams of five to six members and try to reach a consensus regarding a team list of priorities to present to the class.

Individual Rankings

A.   A weekly report _____
B.   A weekly fun job _____
C.   A very routine weekly stock of supply room _____
D.   A very short daily meeting _____
E.   A daily delivery job _____
F.   A special routine meeting each month _____

Rationale: _____
_____

Team Rankings

A.   A weekly report _____
B.   A weekly fun job _____
C.   A very routine weekly stock of supply room _____
D.   A very short daily meeting _____
E.   A daily delivery job _____
F.   A special routine meeting each month _____

Rationale: _____
_____

Source: Adapted from Elwood N. Chapman, Supervisor's Survival Kit, Second Edition, 1975, pp. 108–109 (Science Research Association, Inc.)

Resources

Interpersonal Skill

Information

Systems

Skill Builder 5-4

Developing a Delegation Action Plan

The purpose of this exercise is to have you think of an actual delegation back on the job or at school. Identify at least one activity that you presently perform that would be a potential candidate for delegation to one or more of your team members.

A. Activity

_____
_____
_____
_____

B. What are the potential benefits of delegating this activity to one or more of your team members?

_____
_____
_____
_____
_____

C. What are the potential obstacles to delegating this activity?

_____
_____
_____
_____
_____

D. Develop a plan using the multistep delegation process you learned about in this chapter for putting the delegation in place. Your plan might address such things as to whom you will delegate the authority, how you will communicate the delegation, what information your delegate will need to perform the activity, whether others need to be informed, and your strategy for overcoming the obstacle and control/feedback mechanisms to assure the delegation is carried out effectively.

_____
_____
_____
_____
_____
_____
_____
_____
_____

Pair up with another student in the class and role play the delegation meeting. Your partner will play the role of the employee. Be sure to put yourselves "mentally" in the actual setting with your partner providing realistic responses to your request(s). When you finish the role play, your partner should provide you with feedback regarding the strengths and weaknesses of your action plan to improve the actual meeting. Afterward, you and your partner should swap roles and go through the same process.

CASE 5-1

Joyce Wheat's Problem

Joyce Wheat was quite pleased when she graduated from Florida Atlantic University with a degree in health care management. While pursuing her degree, she had been employed by a regional retirement community management company as an environmental services employee. She was a very efficient worker and had been promised an opportunity to move into management upon completion of her degree. After graduation, Joyce entered the rapidly growing company's management training program. From there, she was placed in a much busier facility in Jacksonville as an assistant manager. As an achievement-oriented person, Joyce saw this as the first step toward her long-range goal of becoming an environmental services manager and eventually holding the title of regional manager.

In her position as assistant manager, things went well. Wheat was familiar with all operations, and she practiced close supervision, stayed on top of things, and really stressed high production and friendly service. Approximately one year later, she was promoted to manager at another busier location that was one of the top five most efficient and profitable locations within the company. In fact, the previous manager had been promoted to regional manager and was Wheat's boss.

At this stage of her career, Joyce was well ahead of schedule in her long-range program of becoming a regional manager. She had anticipated spending a minimum of two to three years as an assistant before having an opportunity to advance to manager, but the company was growing so rapidly that new managers were in demand. Her next career objective of becoming a regional manager seemed well within reach, since the industry and company were growing at a rapid rate.

Joyce surmised that what had worked for her as an assistant manager would also work for her as a manager. She was not really concerned that the assistant manager and five supervisors who would be reporting to her were older and more experienced. After all, results were what counted. At her first meeting, she stressed her high expectations and set as an objective "to increase productivity by 10 percent in three months." The yearly objective was to be 20 percent. Joyce expected "excellent" ratings for all her staff by the residents. She indicated that she believed strongly in the management principle of follow-up. Not only would she be closely following up on their work, but she would also expect them to do the same with their employees.

Two months later, overall productivity at her facility was down by 7 percent, and staff ratings had dropped to average. Wheat was beginning to worry. It seemed that the more she stressed excellence, increased productivity, and efficiency and tried to follow delegated assignments closely, the more resistance she encountered. Although the resistance was not open, it was definitely present. In fact, she sensed hostility even from the night shift, a group with which she had always been close.

At the end of three months, productivity was down by 10 percent, and staff evaluations were the worst they had ever been.

INSTRUCTIONS:

Meet in groups of six or seven people. Make a diagnosis of what the problem is, and identify the critical issues involved. What are the main reasons that this problem exists within organizations? Select one member of your team to present what the team thinks Wheat's boss should do. After all teams have presented, the class should vote on which approach offers the best solution.

CASE 5-2

The Autocratic Manager

The plant manager of a paper mill has contacted your consulting firm to help diagnose why production has dropped in the last 18 months. Moreover, he wants a proposal from your firm on what can be done to turn things around. The partial organization chart indicates there are seven levels of management and the mill employs 410 people.

This mill is a key one in a company that has many mills located throughout the country. The manufacturing process goes through several stages before turning out finished products. The mill employs a relatively large number of engineers, and most managers have an engineering background. The mill is unionized.

The plant manager has four years to go to retirement and wants to leave the firm with a reputation as a "manager who achieves effective results." He is a dynamic individual and has tended to use either an autocratic or a benevolent autocratic approach in managing. He took over the mill six years ago when production was low and a permissive management climate existed. He immediately shifted to a more autocratic management system, and for four years, production was high.

He is convinced that the reason for the current problem is that people at the foreman and supervisory level are not doing their jobs effectively. He thinks the solution is to develop detailed job descriptions for these positions and initiate a foreman management development program that will teach the foremen to get more work out of the unionized employees.

You suggest that interviews be conducted at different levels before making a diagnosis and developing a recommended plan of action. Below are the results of interviews discussing the question, "What problems are preventing this mill from reaching its potential effectiveness?"

RESULTS OF TOP MANAGEMENT INTERVIEWS:

a. The problem is that we must get commitment from foremen to management's higher performance expectations.
b. The greatest concern is abdication of responsibility by foremen. They fail to insist on top performance, and they tend to let employees do what they want. Once we get hourly people under control, we will see an improvement and increased production.

RESULTS OF MIDDLE MANAGEMENT INTERVIEWS:

a. Overmanagement from the top level to the supervisory level and undermanagement from the supervisory level down.
b. Too many levels of management.
c. Bypassing of middle management to supervise employees directly.
d. Dictatorial system of management in mill.
e. Supervisors and foremen oversupervised.
f. Foremen not given enough authority.
g. Fault-finding atmosphere in mill.
h. Employees will not accept foreman's job.
i. Up and down communication problems.

RESULTS OF INTERVIEWS WITH FOREMEN:

a. Inability to make decisions because authority is not delegated or is taken away.
b. If you do make a decision, you don't get backing from your bosses. Example: Night foremen have the ability to make 90 percent of the decisions the dayshift foremen are required to consult someone else about.
c. Too much pressure and threats from above.
d. Constant criticism when we have equipment or people problems, but no praise when we run above standard.
e. Low morale and poor attitudes. People cover their tracks and have the attitude that "it's everyone's problem but mine."
f. Communication problems, especially with higher management.

INSTRUCTIONS:

1. Why do you think the autocratic approach worked effectively for four years in this situation?
2. Diagnose the problems and/or issues facing this mill.
3a. Develop a PowerPoint presentation and present your consulting team's set of recommendations to the class.

(Continued)

CASE 5-2 (*Continued*)

3b. Develop a set of recommendations that you or your consulting team will present to the mill manager. Include suggestions regarding his leadership style. (Role play the presentation, keeping in mind that the manager is paying your consulting fee.)

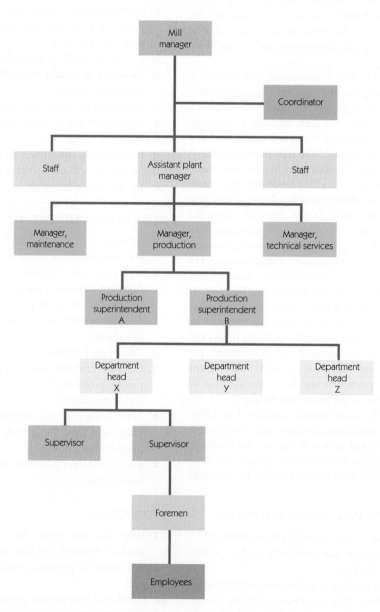

Source: Developed from the consulting files of the Synergistic Group LLC, Mobile, AL.

PART 3

Leading

6
Communication

The *Boston Herald* has undergone many changes in the last several years, but good internal communication skills have helped pave the way for employees to adjust to the changes.

Rick Friedman/Corbis News/Corbis

LEARNING OBJECTIVES

After reading and studying this chapter, you should be able to:

1. Describe the five components of the communication process model.

2. Explain the forms of electronic communication technology.

3. Explain the different ways in which nonverbal communications influence supervisory communication.

4. Identify the three basic flows of formal communication in an organization.

5. Explain the managerial communication style matrix.

6. Identify and explain how organizational, interpersonal, and language barriers affect supervisory communication.

7. Identify five specific actions supervisors can take to improve their communications.

8. Show how a supervisor can use feedback to improve communication.

9. Define and illustrate active listening skills.

No one would talk much in society if they knew how often they misunderstood others.
—Johann Wolfgang von Goethe

When it comes to communication, my rule of thumb is it's not what you tell 'em but what they hear.
—Red Auerbach

Too many people think they are wonderful with people because they have the ability to speak well. What they fail to realize is that being wonderful with people means being able to listen well.
—Peter Drucker

CHAPTER OUTLINE

Preview

A SUPERINTENDENT SPEAKS ABOUT COMMUNICATION AND HIS JOB Bob Greim is a long-time employee of the *Boston Herald*, and he has held a number of supervisory positions at the daily newspaper over the years. In 2003, Bob managed the printing production for the Herald, which had a circulation of 263,000 at the time. He oversaw seven foremen who directly supervised 70 to 80 print production employees. Because of the very fast pace of his work environment—working round the clock to produce an entire issue every 24 hours—Bob recognized that the need to communicate and share information effectively was magnified.

As such, Bob utilized a number of communication tools to keep the work flowing smoothly. He found written communication to be essential for the transitions between day- and night-shift workers. When he would arrive in the morning, he expected to receive reports from his night foremen that were detailed and clear. These reports were essential to Bob's decision making and functioning, and they enabled him to respond accurately to any questions his superiors might have had about the pressroom operation. Therefore, when selecting a candidate for an open position for a foreman, Bob always made sure he chose a person who had the ability to communicate clearly and provide sufficiently detailed information. Bob himself also honed his skills at writing reports for the foremen when he left work at night, and trusted that they would read what he had written and understand what needed to be done.

Face-to-face communication was also an important aspect of Bob's work habits. He was required to attend a daily management meeting at 11:00 A.M., where he was routinely called upon to participate intelligently with correct information and solutions to problems. Bob acknowledges that these meetings were not always directly relevant to his work and perhaps not as productive for him personally as they could have been. However, he saw a benefit in having these team meetings, as people from all units within the paper—from editorial to advertising to operations—shared their needs and issues, developed sensitivity toward fellow team members, and learned to work cooperatively and share responsibility for problems instead of finger pointing. Commented Bob, "We have had some real success at the *Herald,* and I'd like to think it's due, in part, to interacting well—up, down, and across."

In recent years, however, Bob's communication skills have been challenged as never before. As with many newspapers around the world, the *Boston Herald*'s circulation has decreased significantly over the past six years. After being promoted to production manager, Bob faced the daunting task of managing the paper's 300 production employees through several downsizings. Ultimately, the production function was eliminated after the paper's management decided to outsource it. As Bob noted, these were particularly stressful, challenging times, trying to maintain production and employee morale. Many who lost their jobs had been with the *Herald* their entire working careers.

Bob offers this advice for managers facing similar predicaments: "I tried to be forthright, open, and honest about what was coming," he says. "It was along the lines of 'Here's our situation, so we need to figure out what will work best.'" Bob spearheaded the paper's negotiations with the union throughout each downsizing and ultimate production shutdown, negotiating severance pay, health care, and unemployment compensation benefits. At the time of our 2009 interview, he managed the *Herald*'s risk management and safety functions and served as production liaison with the outsourcing firm—positions that still require his expertise in verbal and written communication.[1]

Source: From Zaremba. *Organizational Communication,* 1E, p. 142. Copyright © 2003 South-Western, a part of Cengage Learning, Inc. Reproduced by permission. www.cengage.com/permission

ommunication is a critically important managerial skill. A typical workday finds supervisors assigning jobs, discussing coordination efforts with people from other departments, having discussions with their own bosses, attending meetings, listening to and counseling employees—the list could go on and on. Studies of managers and supervisors show that they spend 70 to 80 percent or more of their time directly communicating with others in meetings, on the telephone, online, or informally while walking around. Consider the management functions of planning, organizing, leading, and controlling—communication is essential in performing these. Moreover, the emerging supervisor role of teacher, leader, and coach depends heavily on effective communication. Studies of managers and supervisors, like Bob Greim of the *Boston Herald,* reinforce how important communication skill is in performing their jobs successfully.[2]

What Is Communication?

1 *Describe the five components of the communication process model.*

Many supervisors think that communication is just a matter of "telling it like it is." When communication breakdowns occur, they are more likely to place the blame on others rather than themselves. Supervisors with such attitudes fail to recognize the downside of this narrow view of their communication responsibilities. To really understand a supervisor's role in communication, let us first learn about the basic communication process.

EXHIBIT 6-1
Communication Process
Model

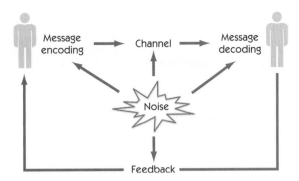

communication process model

Model of the five components of communication and their relationships.

sender

Originates and sends a message.

messages

Words and/or nonverbal expressions that transmit meaning.

channel

The means used to pass a message.

receiver

The ultimate destination of the sender's message.

feedback

The response that a communicator receives.

Communication Process Model

Rather than define communication in words, we will use a model that illustrates the **communication process** (see Exhibit 6-1). The five elements of the model are (1) message encoding, (2) the channel, (3) message decoding, (4) feedback, and (5) noise.

The Sender Encodes the Message

Encoding is the process by which a **sender** converts ideas into symbols, such as words or gestures that are capable of communicating. Each day, supervisors such as Bob Greim (see chapter preview) send hundreds of encoded **messages** to their employees, managers, other supervisors, personnel from other departments, and people outside the organization. These messages consist not only of spoken and written words, but also nonverbal messages such as tone of voice, appearance, placing a watch on a desk and smiling or frowning, or showing up on time—or late—for an important meeting.

The Channel The **channel** is the means used to pass the message. Channels include face-to-face communication, the phone, written forms (such as e-mails, memos, reports, or newsletters), and group meetings. Note in the chapter preview the importance Greim placed on his 11 A.M. meeting of superintendents and on written messages to and from his foremen. A sender's choice of channel is often very important.

> *One supervisor related how after his maintenance crew had completed an important machine repair, the plant manager chewed him out for taking too long to complete the job. "I didn't mind getting chewed out as much as I minded the way he did it," said the supervisor. "He did it by e-mail, and copied the whole plant."*

The Receiver Decodes the Message

Decoding is the process by which a **receiver** converts into an idea(s) the communication symbols encoded by the sender. Just as a sender's skill at encoding is important to effective communication, so also is the receiver's skill in decoding the sent message. Receivers give meaning to a message based on such factors as their interpretation of words, familiarity with the subject matter, perception of the sender's intent, ability to listen, and the meaning they attribute to the sender's nonverbal signals.

Feedback

The message that we send in response to someone else's communication is called **feedback**. An advantage of the face-to-face communication channel is its immediate feedback and the number of feedback cycles allowed. Note in Exhibit 6-2 the information

EXHIBIT 6-2
Communication
Feedback

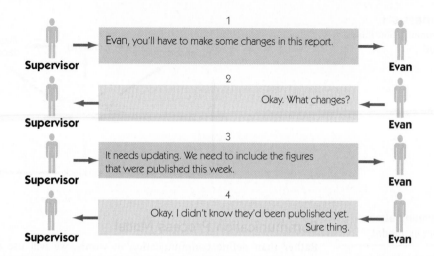

1
Supervisor → Evan, you'll have to make some changes in this report. → Evan

2
Supervisor ← Okay. What changes? ← Evan

3
Supervisor → It needs updating. We need to include the figures that were published this week. → Evan

4
Supervisor ← Okay. I didn't know they'd been published yet. Sure thing. ← Evan

exchanged between the supervisor and Evan in just a matter of seconds, with each assuming the role of encoding, decoding, and providing feedback. Most importantly, a supervisor's decision about the feedback needed to achieve the communication goal determines the appropriateness of the communication channel used, be it a one-to-one meeting, a larger group meeting, a voicemail or e-mail, or a handwritten note.

Noise

Noise consists of the potential barriers to effective communication in each phase of the communication process model. An example of noise at the "encoding" stage might be a supervisor's choice of words. Suppose your boss told you by voicemail that she just talked with an important customer and that you need to follow up with the customer *"right away."* Does *right away* mean now, immediately after you hear the voice message? Or does it mean that you can do it several hours later? The nonspecific use of language is but one form of noise. Later in the chapter, you will learn more about "noise" when we discuss communication barriers.

Electronic Communication Technology

2 *Explain the forms of electronic communication technology.*

Communication practices at the supervisory level are being greatly impacted by advancements in electronic communication technology. Just as computer fluency has become an essential employee requirement in many jobs, it has also become a prerequisite for more supervisory positions. Increasingly, supervisors use electronically linked computer networks within their organization (intranets) and external to their organization (the Internet) to access and transfer information, and, importantly, to communicate through e-mail. **E-mail** refers to messages and documents created, transmitted, and read entirely on computer (see Exhibit 6-3).

e-mail

Refers to messages and documents created, transmitted, and read entirely on computer.

Sharon Olds, sales supervisor for AutoFin, a large auto leasing company, uses electronic communication extensively, sending and receiving more than 50 e-mails daily. We've all heard on our phones a voice say, "This call may be monitored for quality ...." Monitoring calls by her 12 associates is how Sharon spends a major part of her day, listening to associates contact customers by phone to sell extended leases, vehicles, and extended warranties. Although her office is relatively close to the associates' cubicles, e-mail allows her to be spontaneous, reduces time involved in walking to see if someone

EXHIBIT 6-3
E-mail Tips

Here are some tips to help make your e-mail more effective.

1. Use e-mail only for relatively simple, clear-cut messages. Don't use it when questions or information need discussion or clarification, or when the subject is sensitive or emotional.
2. Use a descriptive subject line
3. Use short lines and short paragraphs, especially the first and last paragraphs.
4. For routine and positive messages, be direct, getting to the point in the first or second sentence.
5. For a message that contains emotional content, an indirect approach may be best, with some information leading up to the message. However, reconsider whether e-mail is the appropriate medium.
6. Avoid full caps for your text—it is the equivalent of shouting.
7. Treat an e-mail as a permanent record. It can be intentionally or mistakenly forwarded to others, and about 40% of companies monitor employees' e-mails. Be careful of what you write!

Sources: Marie Flatley and Kathryn Rentz, Business Communication (New York: McGraw-Hill/Irwin), 2010, pp. 30–33; Scott Ober, contemporary Business Communication (Boston, MA: Houghton Mifflin Company, 2009), pp. 58–92.

is available, and enables easy record keeping. She uses e-mail to pass on to her team members information about policy and procedure, but she also uses it to recognize individual and group performance. Sharon also uses other electronic technology, such as PowerPoint software when making presentations to associates or her own boss, and has used instant messaging as part of a problem-solving team whose members worked at different locations.

instant message (IM)

Use of intranet or Internet technology that allows people to receive messages in real time.

text message

A written message sent by cell phone that uses abbreviations.

An **instant message (IM)** uses intranet or Internet technology that allows people to receive messages in real time. It is similar to a phone conversation but in writing. It can include a group of people who type individual messages seen by everyone in the "chat room." A **text message** is a written message sent by cell phone; it typically uses abbreviations, such as "cu2mor" ("see you tomorrow"). Advances in voice communication technology have also considerably affected supervisory communication. Regardless of location, cellular phones enable a supervisor to keep in touch with employees and others. Digital pagers accomplish the same. Voicemail enables supervisors to leave and hear recorded voice messages. Teleconferences enable communication with people in different locations simultaneously; videoconferences provide the additional benefit of visual communication.

Amanda Phillips, sales manager for ADT, the large national home and business security system company, supervises eight salespeople who work a four-state area and reside in three different locations. Her major daily means of communication with them is by e-mail and cell phone. A weekly team meeting is attended physically by some members; others participate through a remote cell phone conference call.[3]

Importance of Nonverbal Messages

3 *Explain the different ways in which nonverbal communications influence supervisory communication.*

Nonverbal messages are a rich communication source. Studies show that only about 10 percent of emotional meaning is communicated verbally; the other 90 percent is communicated nonverbally.[4] In other words, your impression of someone's emotions, such as anger, happiness, or fear, is formed more strongly from that person's tone of voice, facial expression, or other nonverbal means than from the words the person uses. Exhibit 6-4 shows some of the important relationships between verbal and nonverbal messages.

Note that supervisors must be careful that their verbal and nonverbal signals are consistent and do not give an impression not intended. Moreover, being sensitive to and observing the nonverbal messages sent by others is also quite important.

EXHIBIT 6-4
How Nonverbal
Communication
Impacts Verbal
Communication

Several important ways that nonverbal messages impact verbal communications are as follows:

1. **Repeating/Complementing.** Examples: pointing while giving directions; yawning while saying you're worn out; smiling while saying, "Nice job getting this out on time."
2. **Contradicting.** Examples: acting nervous and fidgeting when you say you're under control; yawning when you say you're interested; avoiding eye contact when saying "Your job is safe."
3. **Substituting.** Examples: a raised hand substitutes for "I have a question"; the index finger pointed indicates "Over there"; a head shake says "No"; a head nod says "Yes."
4. **Emphasizing.** Examples: pounding a table when stating a disagreement; gritting your teeth when saying you're angry; raising your voice to make an important point.

Can you add some other examples to each of these?

voice signals

Signals sent by placing emphasis on certain words, pauses, or the tone of voice used.

body signals

Nonverbal signals communicated by body action.

facial signals

Nonverbal messages sent by facial expression.

object signals

Nonverbal messages sent by physical objects.

space signals

Nonverbal messages sent based on physical distance between people.

time signals

Nonverbal messages sent by time actions.

touching signals

Nonverbal messages sent by body contact.

4 *Identify the three basic flows of formal communication in an organization.*

Nonverbal signals fall into seven categories:

1. **Voice signals.** Emphasis on certain words, pauses, or tone of voice. For example, can you say "Nice job, Evans" in such a way that it's actually a putdown?
2. **Body signals.** Slumped posture, clenched fist, or the act of kicking a piece of equipment.
3. **Facial signals.** Smile, frown, raised eyebrow, smirk, or degree of eye contact.
4. **Object signals.** Office furniture, such as desks or chairs, plus carpet, plaques and awards on the wall, or clothing or jewelry worn.
5. **Space signals.** Huddling close, being distant, or sitting beside someone.
6. **Time signals.** Being on time, being available, or saving time. An interview was scheduled for a potential medical school intern at Johns Hopkins Hospital. The interview was scheduled for 11:00 A.M., but transportation was affected by a severe snowstorm. The student arrived at 1:00 P.M. for the interview, feeling his lateness would surely be acceptable. He was told, "What if a patient was in a life and death situation and you were on call and did not come in?" He was not given an interview.[5]
7. **Touching signals.** Shaking hands, sympathetic pat on the back, or touching someone to gain attention.

Stop & Think

Steve Jobs, co-founder and CEO of Apple Computers and former CEO of Pixar Animation Studios, often dresses very casually at work. He frequently wears jeans. A coat and tie are exceptions rather than standard attire. Jobs explains this as his personal style. In what ways does a manager's attire communicate?

Flows of Communication

To put the supervisor's communication role in perspective, we need to examine the flows of communication in an entire organization. Here we will look at communication *within* the organization, rather than with outside groups such as customers, suppliers, or government agencies. Exhibit 6-5 shows that formal communication flows in several directions: (1) downward, (2) upward, and (3) laterally or diagonally. A

EXHIBIT 6-5
Flow of Formal Communication in an Organization

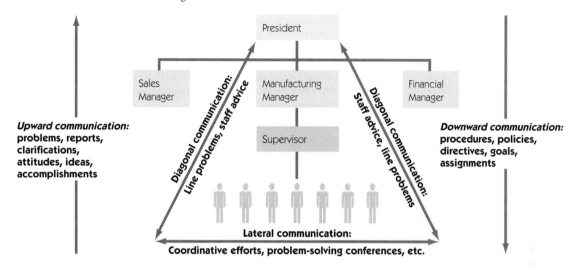

fourth flow is the flow of informal communication, commonly known as the **grapevine.**

The Vertical Flows: Downward and Upward Communication

Downward communication originates with managers and supervisors and passes down to employees. Tremendous amounts of communication constantly flow in this direction. Examples of downward communication include announcements of goals and objectives, policies, decisions, procedures, job assignments, and general information.

> *A recent study of 336 organizations showed that up to two thirds of their employees do not understand or even know their organization's mission and strategies. About 30 percent of the organizations indicated that this information was only available to their upper management.*[6]

Studies show that employees consistently rate their direct supervisor as their preferred choice of communication channel. A recent study showed that nurses' perceptions of their supervisors' communication effectiveness affected the nurses' productivity, turnover, and overall nursing effectiveness.[7] Exhibit 6-6 lists communications that employees *like* to receive from their supervisor. Take a few seconds to examine the list before reading further. Do any items on this list strike you as being more crucial than others? "Knowing where you stand" is often listed by employees as their single most important need.

Upward communication flows from lower to upper organizational levels, as shown in Exhibit 6-7. It may consist of progress reports on a job; requests for help or clarification; communication about employees' concerns, attitudes, and feelings; or ideas and suggestions for improvements on the job.

Unfortunately, many supervisors do not seek these forms of upward communication, especially progress reports, from their employees. Neither do they obtain information about their employees' true attitudes, feelings, or suggestions for improvements. Japanese managers have a much better reputation than American managers for being receptive to workers' needs and opinions, especially in the area of job improvements. In one year, for instance, Toyota implemented over 60,000 new ideas that were received from workers at its five U.S. manufacturing plants.

EXHIBIT 6-6
Communications
Employees Like to
Receive from Their
Supervisor

Role clarifications. What's expected of you, how much authority and responsibility you have, and your job assignments.

Praise and recognition. A supervisor's commendations on a job well done, compliments about you in the presence of third parties, and expressions of appreciation.

Constructive criticism and feedback. Tactful criticism that demonstrates interest and implies a personal and professional concern on the part of the supervisor.

Demonstration of interest. Communications reflecting interest in your professional growth and development, efforts to work with you to do a better job, and giving you undivided attention during conversation (as opposed to lack of eye contact or partial attention).

Requests for information or assistance. Asking your opinion and advice, and consulting with you about relevant matters on the job.

Information that:

a. Makes you feel important because you're "in the know"
b. Pertains to your department's progress, to other work team members, to plans for the department, and to contemplated changes
c. Pertains to aspects of the overall organization, such as sales, forecasts, objectives, outlook for the future, and general internal changes of which the supervisor is aware
d. Pertains to promotions, merit increases, desirable job assignments, and favors that can be granted by the supervisor

EXHIBIT 6-7
Upward
Communication from
Employees to
Management

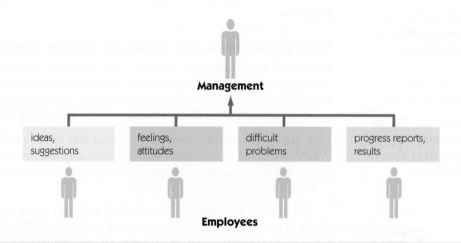

In addition to requesting oral or written progress reports, other means of encouraging upward communication from employees include suggestion systems, an open-door policy, attitude and morale surveys, group or individual meetings at which employees are encouraged to speak up, and hotlines where employees can anonymously solicit answers to questions or report unethical practices.

One superintendent who we know holds a weekly supervisors' meeting to review work progress, discuss job changes, and resolve problems in the department. When issues are being discussed, he often makes sure that he gets others' opinions before giving his own. As he states, "I know personally that if this group knows how I feel about something, more of them will tell me what I want to hear. I like to get their views first. Some will come right out and ask what I think, as if once I tell them, the discussion should end."

Stop & Think

Dramatic changes are taking place to make the workforce much more diverse, including increasing percentages of foreign workers and of U.S. workers of African American, Hispanic, Asian, and Native American descent. In what ways do these changes affect the *downward communication flow* from manager/supervisor to work team members and the *upward communication flow* from team members to manager/supervisor?

5 *Explain the managerial communication style matrix.*

Managerial Communication Matrix Now that you have a good understanding of the vertical communication flows, you can better understand each supervisor's communication relationship with his or her team members. As shown in Exhibit 6-8, The Managerial Communication Matrix, a supervisor's basic communications with team members consist of disclosing information (downward communication) and receiving information from them (upward communication). A supervisor can be considered high as an information discloser and high as an information receiver (box 4), high in one but not the other (boxes 2 and 3), or low in both (box 1).

When you work for a high discloser, you hear frequently about performance expectations, standards, your boss's likes and dislikes, where you stand, and about the goings-on in the organization.[8] Low disclosers communicate less frequently and openly about such matters.

High information–receiving supervisors are accessible and maintain an environment that encourages feedback from employees. They are apt to spend much of their time listening to employees' discussions about performance progress, problems being experienced, and ideas and feelings about organizational and personal issues. In contrast, low

EXHIBIT 6-8
The Managerial
Communication Matrix

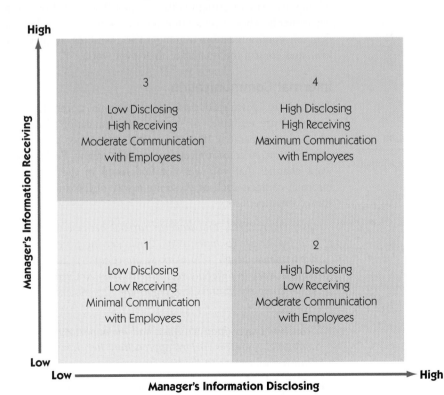

information–receiving supervisors are less accessible and tend to create a less encouraging upward-communication environment.

What would you like your own boss's style to be? In our workshops and seminars, about 90 percent of managers and supervisors state a strong preference in working for a high discloser, high receiver (box 4). When seminar participants are told they must choose their boss's style as being either high disclosing, low receiving (box 3) or low disclosing, high receiving (box 2), most choose box 3 (high disclosing, low receiving). This reflects the importance managers place in knowing clearly their boss's performance expectations and his or her evaluation of their performance. To determine where you fall on the matrix, complete Skill Builder 6-1 at the end of this chapter.

Lateral–Diagonal Flows

lateral–diagonal communication

Flows between individuals in the same department or different departments.

Lateral–diagonal communication takes place between individuals in the same department or different departments. This form of communication has become more important in the past 25 years for several reasons. First, organizations have become greatly specialized. Members of staff departments such as purchasing, human resources, cost accounting, maintenance, and others interact regularly with line personnel. This may be to provide services, coordinate, advise, and sometimes actually give directives.

> In the chapter preview, note the importance of Bob Greim's 11:00 A.M. daily meeting with superintendents from editorial, printing, advertising, and circulation to share information and concerns.

A second reason is the increased use of teams. Cross-functional, problem-solving teams composed of personnel from different departments have become an increasingly necessary approach to address problems that cut across organizational lines. One form of employee empowerment is the use of self-managed or autonomous work teams *within* departments. These teams often meet as a group on a daily basis and are highly dependent on communications among their members as they budget, schedule, and assign jobs, and control the quality of their *own* work.

Informal Communication

informal communication

Separate from a formal, established communication system.

The upward, downward, and lateral–diagonal communication flows that we have just presented are examples of formal communication. **Informal communication** is that which exists separately from the formal, established communication system. Some examples of informal communication are given below. Each example represents a social network channel that you will not find listed in the company's organization chart. Yet, informal contacts such as these are a way of life and can be a valuable communication source for supervisors.

> Lisa, Diane, Fred, and Roberto carpool because they all work for the same company and live about 35 miles away. Their driving time is usually spent talking about their departments, people who work at the company, and other job-related matters. Because they all work in different departments, they are very much "in the know" about a number of company matters long before the formal company communication channels carry them.

> Branch manager Juan Vasquez had an important request of his General Manager for additional resources. Before approaching her, however, he sought advice from a fellow branch manager as to the best strategy.

The Grapevine The best-known informal communication method is the grapevine, also called the *rumor mill*. It is called a grapevine because, like the plant it is named after, it is

Coworkers having lunch together is a common setting for informal communication.

tangled and twisted and seemingly grows without direction. Yet some surveys have found the grapevine to be employees' major source of information about their company, and it has been found to be surprisingly accurate. In fact, studies show that in many situations, over 75 percent of grapevine information is correct.[9]

Purposes Served by Informal Communication Informal communication accomplishes a number of purposes. Among these are (1) providing a source of information not ordinarily available, (2) reducing the effects of monotony, and (3) satisfying personal needs such as the need for relationships or status. Some people, in fact, take great pride in their unofficial knowledge of company matters.

Living with Informal Communication Effective supervisors realize that informal communication serves important purposes. A supervisor must be aware that, unless employees are informed through formal channels, the informal channels will take up the slack. Keeping employees well informed is the best way to manage the grapevine, although it can never be eliminated. It will tend to be especially active when employees are concerned about job security or status.

Note in the chapter preview that Bob Greim of the *Boston Herald* chose a timely, open approach in communicating plans for downsizing and ultimately outsourcing his production employees' jobs.

6 *Identify and explain how organizational, interpersonal, and language barriers affect supervisory communication.*

Barriers to Effective Supervisory Communication

Now that you understand the communication process, let's explore some typical communication barriers that a supervisor faces on the job. These barriers may be organizational, interpersonal, or language related.

Organizational Barriers

Three types of organizational barriers to communication are (1) layers of hierarchy, (2) authority and status, and (3) specialization and its related jargon.

Layers of Hierarchy Have you ever asked someone to give a message to a third person and found that the third person received a message totally different from the one you sent? The same thing occurs in organizations. When a message goes up or down the organization, it passes through a number of "substations" at each layer. Each layer can add to, take from, qualify, or completely change the original message! At higher levels of management, messages are usually broad and general. At lower levels, these broad messages must be put into more specific terms. That's frequently the fly in the ointment, especially when lower and top levels have a gap of understanding between them.

Exhibit 6-9 illustrates this effect. Loss of information accuracy does not only occur as messages pass downward; even more serious losses occur in upward communication. Poor performance, grievances, and issues at lower levels may not be accurately conveyed. The stops along the way are subject to different interpretations, addition or elimination of parts of the message, or often, discontinuation of the intended flow. In 1986, the spacecraft Challenger disaster resulted in the death of seven astronauts and a severe setback for NASA's space program because upper officials who made the launch decision had not received from lower levels their grave concerns about the shuttle's safety.[10] The same can be said about the large information gap between Federal Emergency Management Agency (FEMA) field representatives, FEMA top management, and the White House during the aftermath of Hurricane Katrina.

Authority and Status The very fact that one person is a boss over others creates a barrier to free and open communication.

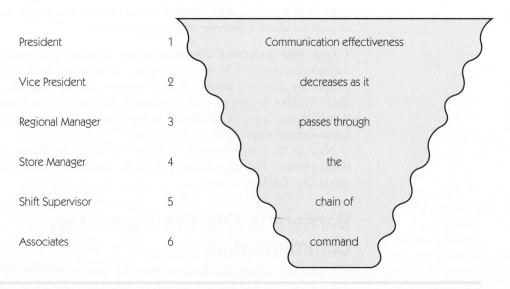

EXHIBIT 6-9
Communication and the Chain of Command

President	1	Communication effectiveness
Vice President	2	decreases as it
Regional Manager	3	passes through
Store Manager	4	the
Shift Supervisor	5	chain of
Associates	6	command

Stop & Think

Recall your feelings, as a student in elementary or high school, when you were told to report to the principal's office. Even if you had done nothing wrong, you were probably still very anxious and defensive about the visit.

Conference room patter among the construction superintendents was loose and jovial. Some made negative remarks about the major agenda item, which was to push for early completion of the project on which they were assigned. One person joked about another being the one to tell the boss that everyone felt the present schedule wouldn't be met, much less an advanced one. However, when the Operations Vice President walked in, the mood shifted dramatically. The vice president did most of the talking. When he asked whether everyone bought into the new schedule, the superintendents' silence implied that they had.

The above scenario happens throughout all levels of management everywhere. Because managers exercise power over employees' performance evaluations, rewards and penalties, and favorable and unfavorable distribution of resources and job assignments, employees will not be so likely to give them unwelcome information or information that makes them look bad. In the earlier Challenger example, several announced launches had been postponed, adding to the pressures on lower-level managers not to disappoint their bosses. Accordingly, there is a built-in tendency for information about problems being experienced, employee frustrations, and disagreements to not be communicated openly and accurately.

Specialization and Its Related Jargon The *principle of specialization* states that employees are more efficient when each performs just one task or only certain aspects of a task. For example, accountants do accounting work, salespersons sell, industrial engineers prepare efficiency studies, and safety specialists see to it that working conditions are safe.

Today's increased specialization, however, also creates problems. Specialists have their own technical language or jargon, interests, and narrow view of the organization. Many special terms used by accountants, computer technology personnel, marketing specialists, and other groups are foreign to people in other departments. This can severely hamper communication.

Interpersonal and Language Barriers

Even if the three organizational barriers just discussed did not exist, a supervisor's communication can still be distorted by interpersonal and language-related problems. Three important barriers are differing perceptions, language-related factors, and linguistic styles.

perception

How one selects, organizes, and gives meaning to his or her world.

Differing Perceptions **Perception** is the process by which we select, organize, and give meaning to our world. All of us have a special way of filtering things around us based on our culture, needs, moods, biases, expectations, experiences, and so on.

Thus, a major barrier to communication results from the increasingly diverse workforce. Broad differences in age, race, sex, education, nationality, and other factors result in quite different perceptions and interpretations of what is seen and heard, and they often result in different styles of communicating. This poses a much stronger communication challenge to supervisors than if all team members had similar backgrounds and shared similar characteristics with their supervisor.

One factor limiting our perception is that we can't grasp the whole situation at a given time. Some matters receive greater attention than others, while some matters receive none at all. Those matters we do focus on usually serve some immediate purpose. A person's needs, moods, cultural and social influences, and attitudes all come together to determine which things are important and what they mean.

In a factory accident, for example, the following persons might "see" the accident quite differently: a supervisor, who may have lost a valuable worker; a safety manager, whose safety record may have been blemished and who will have to conduct an investigation; a fellow worker, who is the injured worker's best friend; a company nurse who attends to the injured worker; and a human resources manager, who is concerned with worker's compensation and finding a replacement for the injured worker. Depending on whom you communicated with, might each have a different perspective of the accident?

When we go about interpreting things around us, we have a tendency to put similar things in the same category, to make them easier to handle. This tendency is called **stereotyping.** Stereotyping poses a formidable communication challenge, given the increasing diversity of employees. There are strong negative stereotypes for various nationalities, races, religions, sexes, occupations, and other groups in our society. As a supervisor, you must be aware that your and your employees' attitudes, biases, and prejudices—both positive and negative—strongly influence communications with others.

stereotyping

The tendency to put similar things in the same categories to make them easier to deal with.

Language-Related Factors

A primary communication barrier is posed by the lack of a common primary language. More than 47 million Americans (almost 20 percent of the U.S. population) age 5 years or older speak a language other than English at home. Spanish is the dominant second language spoken in the United States, with Chinese being next. The recent influx of immigrants from Mexico, many of whom speak little or no English, has led many organizations to offer classes in both English and Spanish to increase communication effectiveness.[11]

In the Pacific Northwest, Hispanics comprise more than 60 percent of firefighting crews employed by private contractors. During a raging wildfire in southern Oregon, leaders of a fire crew got word to evacuate immediately a fire line that was being dug. The problem, however, was that all crew firefighters digging the line in the area were Hispanic, and none understood the instructions given in English. After much shouting and arm waving, someone was found to translate the message into Spanish and the crew was successfully evacuated.[12]

No one knows the specific number of U.S. workers having limited or no English skills, but estimates show that there may be as many as 10 million illegal Hispanic immigrants, making this total number significant. Throughout the United States, they are employed in many smaller entrepreneurial organizations in agriculture, trades, manufacturing, service, and not-for-profit sectors. Managers and supervisors with English- and Spanish-speaking skills are a hot commodity in many parts of the country, as are human resource personnel who are capable of conducting bilingual hiring, testing, orienting, training, and safety sessions. Sometimes managers themselves take the initiative to address the language barrier. Since most of his 50-employee organization is Hispanic, Bruce Frye, owner of Fresno, California–based Frye Roofing, went back to school to learn Spanish.[13]

Growing diversity in the United States results in differing linguistic styles that can be barriers for successful communication. Supervisors need to be aware of these differences to manage their employees effectively.

Even when people speak the same language, language is still a major communication barrier. The fact that people interpret words differently can be traced to a lack of precision in the use of language.

Suppose as you and a nursing supervisor colleague are talking, one of your nurses passes by and you say to your colleague, "That's Judy Snead; she's a really good nurse." What does "good" mean to you? It might mean that Judy is a sympathetic listener who spends a lot of time talking with patients and being cheerful and friendly. To your fellow supervisor, a "good" nurse may be one who is knowledgeable and competent and goes about her or his work without trying to make much conversation.

> *Misinterpretation of the word "empty" by maintenance personnel led to 50 to 60 oxygen canisters labeled "empty" being shipped in the cargo hold of ValuJet Flight 592 en route to Atlanta from Miami on May 11, 1996. Unfortunately, the "empty" canisters were still highly volatile. They were routinely packed in cardboard boxes and stored in the plane's cargo hold without required safety measures. The canisters ignited in flight, causing the plane to crash in the Florida Everglades, killing 110 crew members and passengers. Subsequent investigations resulted in grounded ValuJet flights, adverse publicity, and severe financial repercussions for ValuJet, and a fine of $2 million for Sabretech, the airline maintenance firm responsible for shipping the canisters.[14]*

Supervisors often use imprecise language when more precise language is necessary. Suppose a supervisor tells an employee, "You must improve on your absenteeism, as it has been excessive. Otherwise, you'll be disciplined." What does "improve on your absenteeism" and "excessive" mean? What "discipline" does the supervisor have in mind?

Stop & Think

How many times out of 100 possibilities would each of the following frequencies mean if an event happened: Often_____   Seldom_____   Every Now and Then_____
Usually____   Rarely_____
Compare your answers with someone else's. What's the message here about language?

Another language barrier is that words have multiple meanings and not all people have the same level of language skill, as exemplified in Exhibit 6-10. Many terms familiar to a veteran employee, for example, may be over the heads of a new crop of employees going through an orientation program. In some cases, people even try to "snow" others by using terms they know the others will not understand!

Linguistic Styles Linguistic styles greatly reflect the continuing diversity in the United States and the ways employees communicate at work. Linguistic style refers to typical patterns in our speech, including such factors as volume, speed, and pauses; being direct or indirect; asking questions; and using body language with speech. Differences in linguistic styles are important communication barriers, especially among different cultures, where the styles vary greatly. For example, Asian workers tend to communicate very formally and show much respect toward their bosses by speaking softly.[15] They also use lengthy pauses to assess what is said. Americans, on the other hand, often forgo formality and view pauses as signs of uncertainty or insecurity. Brazilians and Saudis favor closer physical speaking distances than do Americans. An American supervisor may find a Brazilian employee's desire for a close speaking distance aggressive, when, in fact, for the employee, it is a normal physical distance. Another cultural linguistic style difference involves eye contact.

> *Several years ago, Barbara Walters interviewed Libyan leader Colonel Muammar al-Gaddafi for a national U.S. television audience. She was reportedly taken aback because during the interview he refused to look directly at her as he spoke. Walters considered this insulting, as if the intent was to demean her. Her reaction was attributable to differences in linguistic style of the two cultures. In al-Gaddafi's culture, not looking directly at her was a sign of respect.*

Linguistic style may also vary among subcultures. Among some Native Americans, a child's continued eye contact with an adult is a sign of disrespect. Important differences

EXHIBIT 6-10
Multiple Interpretations of Words

FIX the machine to its foundation. (anchor)
FIX that nitpicking cost accountant. (give just due)
FIX the cash register. (repair)
FIXING to go to the storeroom. (getting ready to)
FIX our position regarding overtime policy. (establish)
FIX you up with that young engineer. (arrange a date)
A banquet with all the FIXIN'S. (special effects, side dishes)
FIX things up with the salespeople. (make amends, patch up a quarrel)
If we don't make quota, we're in a FIX. (a pickle, a bad position)
FIX the game (pay off someone to affect the outcome, rig it)
FIX your hair before seeing the boss. (arrange, make orderly)
FIX the department meal on Friday. (cook, prepare)
FIX the company's mascot dog. (neuter)

EXHIBIT 6-11
Linguistic Styles of Men and Women

A number of popular books about the different linguistic styles of men and women have been written in recent years. Among them are Deborah Tannen's *You Just Don't Understand: Women and Men in Conversation* and John Grey's *Men Are from Mars, Women Are from Venus*. Some of their ideas, greatly simplified, are shown here.

	WOMEN	MEN
Object of talk	Establish rapport, make connections, negotiate inclusive relationships	Preserve independence, maintain status, exhibit skill and knowledge
Listening behavior	Attentive, steady eye contact; remain stationary; nod head	Less attentive, sporadic eye contact; move around
Pauses	Frequent pauses, giving chance for others to take turns	Infrequent pauses; interrupt each other to take turns
Small talk	Personal disclosure	Impersonal topics
Focus	Details first, pulled together at end	Big picture
Gestures	Small, confined	Expansive
Method	Questions; apologies; "we" statements; hesitant, indirect, soft speech	Assertions; "I" statements; clear, loud, take-charge speech

Source: From Guffey. *Business Communication* 5e. © 2006 South-Western, a part of Cengage Learning, Inc. Reproduced by permission. www.cengage.com/permissions.

exist between linguistic styles of American males and females, as shown in Exhibit 6-11. American males may find swearing and racy joke telling acceptable among themselves, but females often find this offensive. Furthermore, women's linguistic styles tend to be more indirect, expressive, and polite, whereas men's styles are more direct and assertive. Women view conversation as a means for establishing a "connection" and intimacy with others; men see conversation as a negotiation through which they seek to establish or maintain status and independence.[16]

Improving Supervisory Communications

7 *Identify five specific actions supervisors can take to improve their communications.*

As we've indicated, communication is too critical to your success as a supervisor to be left to chance. Improving your skills in communication will help you accomplish your "task" and "people" goals. Some specific things you can do are (1) set the proper climate with your employees, (2) plan your communication, (3) use repetition to reinforce key ideas, (4) encourage the use of feedback, and (5) become a better listener.

Set the Proper Communication Climate

A supervisor doesn't communicate in a vacuum. Communications take place within the entire supervisor–employee or supervisor–group relationship. A supervisor and his or her workers each bring a store of experiences, expectations, and attitudes to the communication event. These mental pictures strongly influence the meaning each person assigns to the messages sent and received. Thus, the setting is very important for good communication.

What type of setting best contributes to effective communication? We believe that two important factors are (1) mutual trust between the supervisor and employees and (2) a minimum of status barriers.

Establish Mutual Trust Trust helps communication in two ways. First, if an employee trusts you, he or she is more willing to communicate honestly and openly. Second, if employees trust you, they are less likely to distort your motives and make negative assumptions about your communications. If you fight for your employees' interests by bargaining with higher management, if you discipline fairly and consistently, and if you respect your employees' abilities, you are more likely to be trusted by them. You'll be considered a source of help in reaching their goals.

Minimize Status Barriers Status barriers consist of those factors that call attention to the fact that the supervisor ranks higher than his or her employees. Status barriers may be such things as dress, formality, office arrangement, and so forth. Generally, the best communication occurs in a setting where people are relaxed and comfortable and status differences are reduced. For example, the way a supervisor arranges his or her office furniture has much to do with establishing a relaxed setting. Being seated across from a supervisor's desk is more formal than being able to sit at right angles or side by side.

> *One supervisor says he likes to discuss certain sensitive matters away from his own turf to make an employee feel more comfortable and less nervous. By design, supervisors may communicate in the employee's work area or in a neutral situation such as over a cup of coffee or lunch.*

> *President of Honda of America, Shoichiro Irimajiri wore no tie and ate in the company cafeteria. On the front of his white overalls, which were just like those everyone else in the plant wore, was his nickname, "IRI." He had no private office but worked at a desk in the same work area as the 100 others in his white-collar work group. This represented a distinct effort to diminish the status differences between him and all other employees.*

Plan for Effective Communication

How many times have you completely blown a communication situation by not being prepared for it? After it's over, you think "Now why didn't I say this?" or "I never should have said such and such."

Anticipate Situations If you are a supervisor, many of your contacts will occur without much warning and may not allow much planning. Yet you can anticipate a number of situations. For example, you can give thought to the following situations before they occur:

1. Giving employees their performance evaluations.
2. Disciplining employees and making work corrections.
3. Delegating authority for a job and communicating job assignments and instructions.
4. Persuading employees to accept changes in the job or work environment.
5. Trying to sell an idea to your boss or to other staff members.

If you understand how complex good communications are, you'll be more aware of the existing barriers and try to minimize their effects. To be understood by your team members, you must put yourself in their shoes and try to see things from their viewpoint. An old North American Indian prayer expresses the thought this way: "Lord, grant that I may not criticize my neighbor until I've walked a mile in his moccasins."

Select the Proper Channel Part of communication planning involves determining the appropriate communication channel or medium that will be used to convey the message. As mentioned earlier, common options include a personal or group meeting, a telephone call, a memo or letter, an e-mail, or an electronic conference.

One-on-one, face-to-face communication is the richest channel available to supervisors and managers.

information richness

Amount of verbal and nonverbal information that a channel carries.

Generally, supervisors and managers prefer face-to-face communication because that channel is high in **information richness**—the amount of verbal and nonverbal information that a communication channel carries. As shown in Exhibit 6-12, face-to-face communication is the richest channel because it enables nonverbal messages and offers spontaneous feedback. The one-on-one, face-to-face setting is the richest communication form, followed by small-group meetings and telephone messages. Telephone messages have no visual contact but still enable nonverbal information to be passed through tone of voice, inflection, pauses, and volume. A voicemail message, however, loses much potential information richness because it lacks opportunity for immediate feedback.

Lower information richness channels include the written communication forms: e-mails, memos, and letters. These channels lack nonverbal communication, and they do not provide a direct opportunity for spontaneous feedback. They are useful for delivering straight-forward messages and presenting impersonal information, such as data, routine policy, and announcements, especially when a permanent record is useful. However, written messages are clearly less suited when the content deals with complex or emotional issues or when clarification of the writer's intent is necessary to interpret properly a message's meaning. The e-mail message sent to 400 company managers by Neal Patterson, CEO of Cerner, a 3,000-employee software company, had a devastating effect. Some excerpts:

We are getting less than 40 hours of work from a large number of our KC-based EMPLOYEES. The parking lot is sparsely used at 8:00 A.M.; likewise at 5:00 P.M. As managers you either do not know what your EMPLOYEES are doing or YOU do not CARE. You have created expectations on the work effort which allowed this to happen inside Cerner, creating a very unhealthy environment. In either case you have a problem and you will fix it or I will replace you. NEVER in my career have I allowed a team which worked for me to think they had a 40-hour job. I have allowed YOU to create a culture which is permitting this. NO LONGER....

You have allowed this to get to this state and you will fix it or I will replace you ... You have 2 weeks. Tick Tock.[17]

EXHIBIT 6-12
Communication Channel Richness

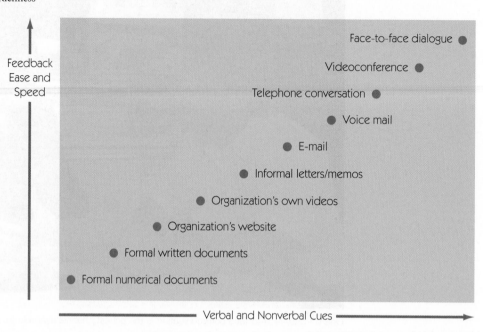

Source: Adapted from Hellriegel/Slocum/Woodman. Organizational Behavior, 10E. © 2004 South-Western, a part of Cengage Learning, Inc. Reproduced by permission. www.cengage.com/permissions.

Patterson later said he was "trying to light a match under them" and "expecting them to take it with a grain of salt." The message was leaked throughout the company intranet and then found its way to the Internet. Its harsh tone shocked thousands of employees and outside readers, especially financial analysts and investors. Within three days, the company stock dropped more than 25 percent. Patterson later apologized to all, wishing he had never hit the "Send" button. But the damage had been done. The message to supervisors and managers is this: Be careful in choosing your message channel!

If you must communicate a personal, sensitive message where empathy and listening are required, such as one involving a transfer, promotion, or performance coaching, face-to-face communication is likely called for. On the other hand, if the message is straightforward or routine, involves much data or detail, or must serve as a record, then written communication is called for. A very important message may call for both written and spoken channels to be used together.

Consider the Receiver's Frame of Reference Earlier we discussed how each of us has unique filters that influence the way we interpret the world around us. Obviously, the better attuned you are to your subordinates' and others' patterns of evaluation, the more effective your communications to and from them will be. Effective communication, then, requires you to step into the shoes of others and visualize situations from their perspective.

A supervisor must frequently ask questions like these:

1. How is this person *like* me?
2. How is this person *different* from me?
3. How is this person *similar* to other employees?
4. How is this person *different* from other employees?
5. How will this person react if I say such and such?

Given increased organizational diversity, these questions are especially important. You don't find the answers to these questions by reading employees' biographical data from personnel files. The only way to discover employees' different motives, needs, attitudes, and ways of interpreting things is to interact with them directly, be sensitive to these differences, and use effective feedback and listening techniques.

Reinforce Key Ideas through Repetition

Let's begin this section with a simple experiment. Say aloud the following sequence of numbers: 84, 97, 62, 58, 84, 73, 32, 45, 84. Now glance away from the numbers and repeat as many as you can. It's a good bet that one of the numbers that made an impression on you was written more than once.

Repeating a message plays an important part in communicating effectively. This is especially true when certain parts of a message may be more important than others. Repetition, or redundancy, improves the reader's recall and reduces the chance that incorrect assumptions will be made by the receiver. For example, you might state a complicated message in several ways, using examples, illustrations, or comparisons. You can also say the same thing several times, but in different words. Here, for instance, is how a supervisor might communicate an instruction to an employee.

Danny, we just got a telephone order for a 42-by-36–inch fireplace screen in our KL–17 series. I know you haven't done one up like it since last year, when that customer in Idaho gave us so much trouble. That's the same style a different customer wants, with black and gold trim as shown in this catalog clipping. And you heard me right: He wants it 42 inches high by 36 inches wide. We don't get many like that—higher than wide, I know. (Hands Danny the written specifications for the screen.) Can you get it out in the next week?

Note how the supervisor used a past example and a catalog to clarify the style of the fireplace screen and how the supervisor repeated the required measurements, even though he also provided written specs.

Encourage the Use of Feedback

8 *Show how a supervisor can use feedback to improve communication.*

Two ways a supervisor can encourage employees to provide feedback are (1) to create a relaxed environment and (2) to take the initiative.

Create a Relaxed Environment Earlier in this section, we discussed the importance of establishing a favorable setting for communication. Having a relaxed setting is especially important in obtaining feedback from an employee. As a supervisor, you certainly should not look down on employees for asking questions or for openly stating their opinions, suggestions, or feelings on a subject. A defensive attitude on your part discourages feedback. As you've learned about channel richness, how you communicate also determines, to a large extent, the amount of feedback you will receive, with face-to-face communication being the richest medium.

In ancient times, an Asian king hated to hear bad news. Whenever a courier reported bad news or an unfortunate event to the king, the king became furious and had the courier beheaded. After three couriers bit the dust, the king began hearing only good news! The moral here for supervisors is that they must be receptive to all information, both good and bad, from their employees, or they, too, will be surrounded by a smokescreen.

Take the Initiative Although the type of communication used and the setting for the communication are important in determining what feedback is obtained, a supervisor still must take the initiative in getting responses from the work group. For example, after giving a job assignment, you might ask "Do you have any questions?" or "Did I leave anything out?" An even better approach would be to say, "To make sure I've gotten my message across, how about repeating it to me?" Frequently this approach produces a number of clarifications that someone might otherwise be unwilling to request for fear of looking stupid. You must be careful, however, not to use a patronizing tone of voice or to put too much of the burden of understanding on the employee. Remember—effective communication is a two-way street. Finally, you can set the stage for further feedback with a comment such as, "If anything comes up later or if you have some questions, just let me know." A participative leadership style relies heavily on good two-way communication, which is a form of feedback. When a supervisor allows team members to make decisions or to express opinions, their responses are a form of feedback. This style helps a supervisor better understand the team members' thinking.

Feedback can also help you learn how to send messages better in the future. When you discover that your initial message wasn't clear or that your use of persuasion was not effective, you can refine future messages. A summary of tips about feedback appears in Exhibit 6-13.

EXHIBIT 6-13
Tips About Feedback

- Generally, feedback is better where there is a trusting relationship between people. If a person doesn't trust you, he or she is not likely to level with you or share feelings very readily. As a result, you are told only what you want to hear instead of what you *should* hear. For example, the person may say, "Yes, sir, things are going okay on the Anders job," when in reality, there is a lack of progress or some severe problem. Or the person may say, "I certainly agree with you, boss," when in reality the person doesn't agree with you at all but doesn't want to upset you or risk being chewed out.
- Some people give feedback readily, but others need some encouragement. Examples of the latter type are people who are timid, quiet, or insecure or have learned that "it's best to keep your mouth shut around here." *Asking* such people for their ideas, suggestions, or feelings may elicit feedback. For example, you can say, "Dale, how will this new policy affect your group?" or "What do you think about … ?"
- Complimenting people for providing feedback reinforces their willingness to *continue* providing feedback. When you say, "I appreciate your honesty in discussing this" or "Thanks, Joan, for raising some issues that need to be clarified," you are encouraging the other party to give feedback in the future.
- When you are giving instructions, it is a good habit to ask the listener if he or she has any questions. For example, you can ask, "Is this clear, Tom? Do you have any questions?" Some supervisors end their instructions with "Now, Tom, let's see if we're together on this. In your own words, run by me what it seems I've just said." If the instructions are given over the telephone, you can say, "Okay, Tom, read back to me those seven dates I just gave you so we can make sure we're together on this."
- When you have potentially negative feedback to give, it is helpful to begin by saying, "Sarah, may I offer a suggestion about … ?" or "May I give you my impression of … ?" or "Can I share my feelings about … ?" This approach is less pushy, and the message will be received with less defensiveness than if you bluntly blurt out the negative information.
- Nonverbal signals and body language offer a wide variety of feedback. Frowns, nervous fidgeting, nods of the head, and other facial expressions and body movements give us a lot of information. Frequently, however, we overlook these signals completely because we are not looking at the other person or because we are absorbed in our own thoughts and messages.

Become a Better Listener

It has been said that Mother Nature blessed human beings with two ears and only one mouth as a not-so-subtle hint that, unfortunately, we often ignore. "How to Be a Good Listener" has become a popular subject and is being taught today in many elementary and high schools throughout the country. One of Dr. Stephen Covey's *Seven Habits of Highly Effective People* is "Seek first to understand, then to be understood."[18] Studies of managers show that, on average, they spend a larger percentage of their work day (about 60 percent) on listening than in the other communication forms—speaking, writing, or reading.[19] Test your listening skills by completing the test in Exhibit 6-14.

Stop & Think

> Our own research reveals that of the four communication skills (writing, speaking, reading, and listening) that managers and supervisors most frequently use, listening is the skill in which they have had the least training. Why do you think this is so?

9 *Define and illustrate active listening skills.*

active listening

A listening technique for understanding others and encouraging open feedback.

reflective statement

The listener repeats, in a summarizing way, what the speaker has just said.

Active Listening Techniques   A particular listening technique that is essential for good listening is called **active listening** (also known as *feeling listening, reflective listening,* and *nondirective listening*). Active listening requires the listener to make a response that states what he or she has heard. It is used by psychologists, psychiatrists, counselors, and others when it is especially important to understand how someone feels and thinks. We think that active listening is of great value to supervisors as a method for understanding employees and for encouraging more open feedback.

The **reflective statement** is a form of active listening in which you repeat the gist of the sender's message as you understand it.

Suppose the speaker is Joan Chavez, one of your team members. She tells you:

Chavez: "I have a little problem. It's about Klaric, our new guy. You asked me to help him transition into the team, but people have asked, 'Where'd we dig this guy up?' He has no clue about fitting in, and the others seem to resent him for that. While he's technically okay, he doesn't seem to care about being part of the team."

An effective reflective statement would summarize, using your own words, what you think Chavez has just told you. For example, a reflective statement would be:

You: "So while he's competent, you feel that he's not making much progress fitting in as a team member."

This statement tosses the communication ball to Chavez to clarify her statement if needed or to elaborate. A reflective statement may also go beyond the speaker's words and reflect your interpretation of the speaker's feelings. For example, picking up on Chavez's body language, facial expression, and tone of voice, you might have said:

You: "So it seems that you're pretty frustrated about his not fitting in."

Note that Chavez has not stated a frustration in the words of her message. However, your reading between the lines, combined with her nonverbal message, may strongly

EXHIBIT 6-14
Rate Your Listening Habits

As a listener, how frequently do you engage in the following listening behaviors? Place a check in the appropriate column, and determine your rating based on the scale at the bottom of the page.

LISTENING HABIT	VERY SELDOM 10	8	6	4	ALMOST ALWAYS 2
1. Faking attention, pretending to be interested when you're really not.	_____	_____	_____	_____	_____
2. Being passive—not asking questions or trying to obtain clarifications, even when you don't understand.	_____	_____	_____	_____	_____
3. Listening mainly to what a speaker says rather than his or her feelings.	_____	_____	_____	_____	_____
4. Allowing yourself to be distracted too easily.	_____	_____	_____	_____	_____
5. Not being aware of the speaker's facial expressions and nonverbal behavior.	_____	_____	_____	_____	_____
6. Tuning out material that is complex or contrary to your own opinion.	_____	_____	_____	_____	_____
7. Drawing conclusions, having your mind made up before hearing the speaker's full line of reasoning.	_____	_____	_____	_____	_____
8. Allowing yourself to daydream or wander mentally.	_____	_____	_____	_____	_____
9. Feeling restless, impatient, eager to end the conversation.	_____	_____	_____	_____	_____
10. Interrupting the speaker, taking over the conversation to get in your own side of things.	_____	_____	_____	_____	_____

YOUR TOTAL SCORE: _____	
90–100	Superior
80–89	Very good
70–79	Good
60–69	Average
50–59	Below average
0–49	Far below average

suggest it. In response to your reflective statement about her feelings, assume that Chavez further elaborates:

Chavez: "Well, the thing that gets me most, I guess, is that I don't know how I could have messed up in evaluating him."

Now you have gained further insight into what Chavez is communicating.

EXHIBIT 6-15
Tips for Better Listening

- Try to avoid doing most of the talking yourself. Give the other person an opportunity to speak.
- Avoid distractions. Close your office door or move to a quieter area.
- Act interested in what the other person says. Don't doodle, write, or work on something else. Give the employee your full attention.
- Ask questions. As long as the questions aren't considered nosy or brash, this will help keep you interested and encourage the employee to give more details.
- Summarize what you think someone has said. "What you're saying is …." This will reinforce what you have heard and enable the other person to correct any misunderstanding on your part.
- Be empathetic. Try to put yourself in the speaker's shoes.
- Don't lose your temper or show signs of being upset by what the speaker is saying. Try to listen with an open mind.
- Don't interrupt. Let the person finish speaking before you respond.
- Use active listening techniques—reflective statements and probes—to ensure your understanding of key points, to help the speaker talk, or to steer the conversation in certain directions.
- After an important conversation or meeting, jot down notes to yourself about the main points discussed.

probe

Directs attention to a particular aspect of the speaker's message.

The **probe** is more specific than the reflective statement. It directs attention to a particular aspect of the speaker's message. For example, in the above scenario, your response to Chavez could be any of the following: (1) "He doesn't seem to fit in at all?" or (2) "You say the other guys seem to resent him?" Note that these probes are more specific than the reflective statement, and they allow you to pursue what you feel may be important.

Other Listening Fundamentals A number of other important techniques can help your listening effectiveness. These are presented in Exhibit 6-15. As you can see, good listening is hard work. But it is an essential tool for the supervisor!

Chapter Review

1. **Describe the five components of the communication process model.**

   Supervisors spend anywhere from 70 to 80 percent of their time in some form of communication. The communication process consists of five parts: message encoding, a channel, message decoding, feedback, and noise.

2. **Explain the forms of electronic communication technology.**

   Among the new forms of electronic communication that are impacting communication at the supervisory level are e-mail, instant messages, text messages, mobile phones, digital pagers, voicemail, teleconferencing, and videoconferencing.

3. **Explain the different ways in which nonverbal communications influence supervisory communication.**

   "Meaning" lies in people rather than in words, and nonverbal messages communicate our emotions more strongly than words. Six categories of nonverbal communication signals are voice, body, object, space, time, and touching.

4. **Identify the three basic flows of formal communication in an organization.**

   In any organization, there is a tremendous volume of formal communication that flows in three directions: downward, upward, and laterally or diagonally. Downward communication includes announcements of goals, objectives, policies, decisions, procedures, job assignments, and general information. Upward communication consists of progress reports from employees; their requests for assistance; communication about their attitudes, feelings, and concerns; and ideas and suggestions for job improvement. Lateral–diagonal communication occurs between persons within a department or in different departments. It typically involves contacts between line and staff members and among team members in natural, cross-functional, and self-managed teams.

5. **Explain the managerial communication style matrix.**

   The managerial communication style matrix reflects supervisors' behaviors toward disclosing information and receiving information. Supervisors who are high disclosers are active downward communicators to their employees. Supervisors who are high information receivers are open, accessible, and receptive to upward communication from their employees.

6. **Identify and explain how organizational, interpersonal, and language barriers affect supervisory communication.**

   A number of organizational, interpersonal, and language barriers can hamper a supervisor's effectiveness in communication. Organizational barriers include the levels of hierarchy through which a message must pass, the authority and status of managers, and the jargon of specialized departments. Interpersonal and language barriers include people's differing perceptions, the general imprecision of language, and different linguistic styles.

7. **Identify five specific actions supervisors can take to improve their communications.**

   There are several ways to improve supervisory communication. First, a supervisor should establish the proper setting when communicating with employees. The proper setting is a climate where the trust level is high, the supervisor is viewed as a source of help, and status barriers are minimized. Second, a supervisor should plan his or her communication. This involves determining in advance a communication strategy and channel choice that will enable the supervisor's communication objective to be reached. Third, a supervisor must consider the receiver's frame of reference. This requires looking at things from the receiver's view, which can be difficult. Fourth, a supervisor should use repetition to reinforce key ideas. Finally, a supervisor should encourage and induce feedback and become a better listener.

8. **Show how a supervisor can use feedback to improve communication.**

   Two ways in which a supervisor can encourage employees to provide feedback are by (1) creating a relaxed communication environment and (2) taking the initiative to encourage feedback from others. A favorable feedback environment makes team members feel comfortable and relaxed and encourages open expression of their true feelings. Supervisors can take the feedback initiative by asking questions and creating situations that encourage or require their employees to communicate.

9. **Define and illustrate active listening skills.**

   Active listening, known also as *feeling listening, reflective listening,* or *nondirective listening,* is a method of encouraging feedback from others. Two forms of active listening are reflective statements and probes. Reflective statements restate back to the speaker a summary of what the listener has heard the speaker express. Probes are more specific reflective statements that direct attention to a *particular* aspect of the sender's message.

Key Terms

communication process model, p. 163

sender, p. 163

messages, p. 163

channel, p. 163

receiver, p. 163

feedback, p. 163

e-mail, p. 164

instant message (IM), p. 165

text message, p. 165

voice signals, p. 166

body signals, p. 166

facial signals, p. 166

object signals, p. 166

space signals, p. 166

time signals, p. 166

touching signals, p. 166

grapevine, p. 167

downward communication, p. 167

upward communication, p. 167

lateral–diagonal communication, p. 170

informal communication, p. 170

perception, p. 173

stereotyping, p. 174

information richness, p. 179

active listening, p. 183

reflective statement, p. 183

probe, p. 185

Questions for Review & Discussion

1. What are the five components of the basic communication process model? Define each. Identify some of the important forms of electronic communication discussed in the text.
2. Explain the six different ways in which nonverbal signals influence supervisory communication.
3. Identify the three major flows of communication in an organization.
4. Explain the managerial communication style matrix. What are some purposes served by informal communication?
5. What are some examples of linguistic style communication differences that you have experienced? Explain.
6. How does planning aid communication effectiveness? Can you give a personal example?
7. Explain how a supervisor can use feedback to improve communication.
8. Define and give an example of active listening.

Information

Interpersonal Skill

Skill Builder 6-1

Assessing Your Information-Disclosing and Information-Receiving Style
Instructions: Please read the 16 items listed and circle the answer that best characterizes you.

TO WHAT EXTENT DO YOU:	NOT MUCH LIKE YOU			MUCH LIKE YOU	
1. Make known your position on issues	1	2	3	4	5
2. Ask others for their advice about matters	1	2	3	4	5
3. Compliment/give recognition to others	1	2	3	4	5
4. Act friendly, approachable	1	2	3	4	5
5. Offer constructive criticism to others	1	2	3	4	5
6. Indicate willingness to explore differences of opinion	1	2	3	4	5
7. Keep people informed about things you know are going on	1	2	3	4	5
8. Invite feedback about your own behavior or thinking	1	2	3	4	5

(Continued)

Skill Builder 6-1 (*Continued*)

TO WHAT EXTENT DO YOU:	NOT MUCH LIKE YOU			MUCH LIKE YOU	
9. Make clearly known your expectations of others	1	2	3	4	5
10. Try to avoid distractions when listening to others	1	2	3	4	5
11. State your disagreement with opinions when they differ from your own	1	2	3	4	5
12. Hear out a position fully before making a judgment or decision	1	2	3	4	5
13. Provide adequate details when instructing or explaining	1	2	3	4	5
14. Ask questions of others to obtain information	1	2	3	4	5
15. Tell people when they've done something that irritates you	1	2	3	4	5
16. Keep an open mind to others' ideas and suggestions	1	2	3	4	5

Scoring: To calculate your information-disclosing score, add the results of items 1, 3, 5, 7, 9, 11, 13, 15 = _____ Information-Disclosing Score Total.

To calculate your information-receiving score, add the results of items 2, 4, 6, 8, 10, 12, 14, 16 = _____ Information-Receiving Score Total.

Instruction: Break into groups of three to five other students, compare your results, and discuss. Select a spokesperson to report the results of your discussion.

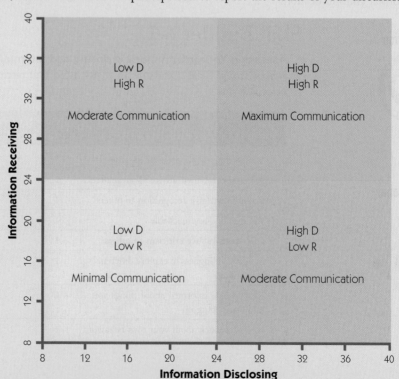

Information

Interpersonal Skill

Skill Builder 6-2

Listening Skills Practice

For this exercise, three-person teams will be used. One person will be the sender, another the listener, and the third the observer.

1. The sender speaks to the listener for 30 to 45 seconds on one of the following subjects:

   a. How I most like to spend my spare time
   b. What I plan to be doing five years from now
   c. What I most like about my job, school, or life (select one)
   d. The type of person I best get along with
   e. What I think the ideal job would be and why
   f. Other topics selected by speaker

2. The listener responds, making a statement that reflects accurately the main ideas communicated by the sender.
3. The observer gives his/her critique of the listener's reflective statement and the listener's nonverbal behavior while listening.
4. Sender, listener, and observer jointly discuss steps 1, 2, and 3.
5. The three parties rotate roles and repeat steps 1, 2, 3, and 4. This should be done until each party has served at least once in each role.

Information

Interpersonal Skill

Technology

Skill Builder 6-3

Using Repetition as a Communication Tool

This exercise is a study of the use of repetition as a communication tool.

Instructions:

1. Go to http://www.usconstitution.net/dream.html and download the text of Dr. Martin Luther King's famous "I Have a Dream" speech.
2. Print a copy of the speech.
3. Drop to paragraph 11, which begins "I say to you my friends …"
4. Read the rest of Dr. King's speech, and write a short analysis of his strategic use of repetition.
5. Bring your analysis to class and be prepared to discuss it with your classmates.

CASE 6-1

Room 406*

It was 4:56 P.M. on the surgical floor of Collins Memorial Hospital. Nurse Rhoda Fleming, an efficient head nurse with 15 years of experience, was in charge of the floor that afternoon. As is the case in many hospitals, she had responsibility for several patients herself as well as assuming supervisory responsibilities over other floor nurses. Making a final room check of her own patients prior to the arrival of her 5:00 P.M. relief, in Room 406 she found that Mr. Henry Youstra, who had undergone surgery the week before and not done well, had died. She pulled the sheet over the face of the body and made a mental note to tell her relief to empty the room for a new patient, bed space being especially important at this time in the hospital.

After finishing her check she returned to the floor desk. The evening shift supervisor, Anne Simmons, had already arrived, and was waiting at the desk.

"Hi, Anne. 406 just died, so that room's all set to go again. Too bad. We can certainly use the space, though."

"That's for sure. Has 411 had her shot yet? Dr. Alpers really climbed on me yesterday about it. You know how he is."

"No, not yet. You'd better do that right away."

"Does the office know that 406 is ready?"

"No, you'll need to call them after you get things taken care of."

Nurse Supervisor Fleming then left, and Simmons gave 411 her shot and went about other duties, dropping in on her own patients, and chatting with nurses on the shift.

At 5:45 P.M. she called the office and told them that room 406 was ready for occupancy, though she had not checked the room herself. She was told that a patient would be moved from recovery and would ultimately occupy 406.

Visitors' hours began at 7:00 P.M. at the hospital. As she had been doing three times daily throughout the week, as the fourth floor elevator doors opened, Mrs. Henry Youstra walked out and went down the hall to visit her husband.

At 8:00 P.M., the end of visiting hours, Nurse Supervisor Simmons checked each of her assigned patient rooms to see that visitors had left. In room 406 she found Mrs. Youstra dead on the floor beside the bed containing her husband's body.

Questions

1. Explain how "noise" impeded accurate communication between Shift Supervisors Fleming and Simmons in this incident.
2. What barriers to communication existed in the situation?
3. How might this miscommunication have been avoided?

*Adapted from William V. Haney, Communication Patterns and Incidents (Homewood, IL: Richard D. Irwin, 1960) pp. 71–72.

7

Motivation

Curt Pickens/istockphoto.com

Like Sharon Olds, all supervisors play a key role in motivating their employees.

Give me enough medals and I'll win you any war.

—Napoleon Bonaparte

Journalist: "Your Eminence, the Vatican is such a huge place. About how many people work here?"
Pope: "About half, my son."

—Anonymous

CHAPTER OUTLINE

Preview

SHARON OLDS: MOTIVATOR Since Sharon Olds became a sales supervisor at AutoFin, her department has consistently reached or exceeded its goals. When she took over her present supervisory position, Sharon knew that she faced a strong challenge given the diverse ages, education levels, marital statuses, cultures, and needs of her personnel. Her department ranked in the middle of the pack from a performance standpoint. She felt that AutoFin was a solid organization to work for, with very good pay and benefits. Job security was excellent, assuming an employee met or came close to production quotas, which, although difficult, could be attained with hard work. Working conditions were excellent once employees became accustomed to spending 90 percent of their work time on the phone with customers.

Sharon felt the biggest difference she could make was to soften the impersonal, bottom-line attitude of upper management. "Although an excellent company to work for, we are very bottom-line oriented. While our success comes from our people, top management is seen as impersonal and numbers oriented," Sharon says. "They give an impression of being less concerned with employees. My job is not only about making numbers, but also having my people feel good about themselves and our department. Motivating people is an important key to my job."

A summary of some of Sharon's interactions reveals how she approaches the task of motivating her personnel:

1. Sharon uses weekly staff meetings as an opportunity for her associates to grow and learn from each other. For example, at each meeting, she has three or four members report to the larger group about a particular customer contact that began on a negative note and was turned into a positive outcome by the associate.

2. Sharon actively works to encourage and support her newest associates. After monitoring one particularly difficult conversation in which a new associate handled a sour, rude customer in a patient, highly professional manner, Sharon e-mailed the associate: "Jan, we should use the tape of your Miami phone call as the textbook example in effective communication. Great job!"

3. Sharon works hard at recognizing outstanding employee performance. When one associate set a weekly record for extended customer lease contracts, Sharon e-mailed her lauding the achievement and copied the department manager and other associates. Sharon also congratulated the associate personally on her accomplishment and, at the weekly associates' meeting, led the team in giving her a round of applause.

4. Sharon finds a variety of ways to give recognition. When one associate shared at a team meeting suggestions for improving the customer database, Sharon e-mailed the suggestion to her own boss and recommended that all departments adopt the suggestion, crediting the employee for the suggestion. Sharon also championed the idea with her fellow supervisors. The recommendation was eventually implemented, and Sharon persuaded her boss to send a personal letter of appreciation to the employee.

5. Sharon particularly enjoys coaching and helping her lead associate learn the ropes. The associate ultimately wants to become a supervisor. Sharon often seeks his advice and will delegate to him special broadening assignments. When Sharon was sick with the flu, she had the associate represent the department at a special meeting of supervisors and her own manager. She could tell that he was quite pleased to do this.

6. Although eager to praise for good performance, Sharon will not back off from addressing performance problems. However, she does so tactfully and with concern for her associates' feelings. Several weeks ago, her 57-year-old associate, one of her highest producers, achieved only one-half of her daily quota on two consecutive days. When Sharon approached her to discuss it, instead of first bringing up the matter, Sharon began with some small talk. The employee herself brought up the issue with, "I guess you see where I've gotten off to a slow start this week...."

7. Sharon is extremely sensitive about the best way to treat her associates. When one walked in 20 minutes late for the second time in a week, Sharon noted his hurried entrance but withheld acknowledgment or eye contact. She talked with him within the hour about his tardiness, preferring not to address it immediately. During the eventual discussion, Sharon listened patiently to his explanations, which she considered plausible. She reinforced the reasons why punctuality was important and insisted that he be on time. The next day when the employee arrived on time, Sharon made sure she saw him, greeting him with a friendly "Good morning," and asked if she could fix him a cup of coffee.

8. Sharon works hard to make her associates feel like part of the team and to share team identity. She informs everyone about the team's progress toward sales goals. At meetings, her language consists of "we" and "us." Once each year, she orders sandwiches and pizza and treats her associates to lunch in the conference room. Sharon intentionally avoids bringing up work-related issues, preferring the lunches to be social occasions. She and her lead associate feel that the lunches are effective in establishing camaraderie.

Source: Personal interview; names of company and persons disguised.

Motivation: Some Fundamentals of Understanding Human Behavior

motivation

Willingness to work to achieve the organization's objectives.

The chapter preview demonstrates that understanding and motivating employees is the core of effective supervision. Perhaps you've heard people say that no one can motivate someone else. What they mean is that **motivation** comes from within. It is the result of a person's individual perceptions, needs, and goals. We define motivation as the willingness of individuals and groups, as influenced by various needs and perceptions, to strive toward a goal. Enlightened managers and supervisors like Sharon attempt to integrate the needs and goals of individuals with the needs and goals of the organization.

The quest for high quality and quantity of work, safety, cost effectiveness, compliance with company policies and procedures, and punctuality are important issues that supervisors face each day. For example, the cost of absenteeism is approximately $660 per employee, or about $25,000 annually for small companies and more than $10 million for larger organizations.[1] A global study of 85,000 employees in 18 countries across four continents showed that only 14 percent considered themselves "highly engaged"—that is, they felt involved and enthusiastic about their work (Exhibit 7.1). The most engaged workers were found in Mexico, Brazil, the United States, and Belgium, in that order. Countries in which workers reported the least engagement were Japan and Italy. Although U.S. employees rank among the most engaged workers, there is still much room for improvement. A recent survey of approximately 80,000 U.S. employees found that about 20 percent considered themselves "disengaged". This is consistent with an earlier Gallup poll of U.S. workers, which showed that 54 percent were only "moderately engaged" and that 19 percent were so negatively engaged that their companies might be better off when they call in sick.[2]

In our management seminars, supervisors and managers are asked to anonymously rate on a scale from 1 (lowest) to 10 (highest) the motivational level of employees whom they supervise. The anonymous ratings are collected and written on a flip chart

EXHIBIT 7-1

Determining Employee Engagement

The Gallup Poll is the most widely used measure of employee engagement, having been administered to over a million employees and more than 80,000 work units. Referred to as "Q12," the 12-question survey resulted from hundreds of focus groups and thousands of employee interviews. The 12 questions shown below are scored on a scale of 1 to 5, depending on a responder's weak or strong agreement. According to Gallup, there is a very strong correlation between a high score and superior job performance. Note the important role that one's supervisor plays in determining how each question would be answered:

1. Do you know what is expected of you?
2. Do you have the materials and equipment you need to do your work right?
3. At work, do you have the opportunity to do what you do best every day?
4. In the last seven days, have you received recognition or praise for doing good work?
5. Does your supervisor, or someone at work, seem to care about you as a person?
6. Is there someone at work who encourages your development?
7. At work, do your opinions seem to count?
8. Does the mission/purpose of your company make you feel your job is important?
9. Are your associates (fellow employees) committed to doing quality work?
10. Do you have a best friend at work?
11. In the last six months, has someone at work talked to you about your progress?
12. In the last year, have you had opportunities to learn and grow?

Source: "Feedback for Real," Gallup Management Journal, March 15, 2001 at http://gallup.com/content/811/feedback-real.aspx; also Workforce Managment Online, October, 2003 at http://www.workforce.com/section/09/article/23/53/40.html.

or board. Only rarely do scores higher than 8 appear; the average tends to be in the 5 to 6 range. When asked why ratings tend to be so mediocre, participants respond with comments such as "People today just don't seem to care as much," or "Some employees just want their paycheck and will do just enough to get by," or "There's no pride or commitment to their work." A survey of 250 executives found that nearly one-third cited "motivating employees" as their biggest people challenge, outdistancing "finding qualified staff," "training," "retaining staff," and "resolving staff conflict."[3]

Few social scientists would deny that people often act emotionally, but many would dispute that most people behave irrationally and unpredictably. They would argue that if more people understood the *why* of human behavior, other people's behavior would seem more rational and predictable. Why don't more people have pride in their work? Why do they just do enough to get by? Why are others outstanding performers? The answer often lies in their motivation.

HISTORICAL INSIGHT

The Hawthorne Studies

You may already be familiar with Frederick Taylor's "scientific management" approach, which emphasized efficient employee work methods as the basis for achieving higher performance. In the late 1920s and early 1930s, other researchers discovered the importance played by employees' psychological attitudes toward their work.

The Hawthorne Studies were conducted at the Hawthorne Plant of Western Electric, a Chicago plant of 30,000 employees that was the manufacturing arm of giant AT&T. The studies began in 1924 as an experiment to determine whether increases in lighting would affect worker productivity. Researchers studied two groups of workers, one called the research group and the other called the control group. In the research group, lighting levels were increased in stages over a period of months. In the control group, lighting levels remained the same. Researchers were confused to note that not only did productivity increase steadily throughout the study period for the research group, but it also increased for the control group where no lighting changes had been made! Perplexed, the researchers introduced a new lighting variable in the research group; they reduced lighting to levels below those at which the experiment began. They were again stumped by a continued productivity increase. Baffled, the researchers regrouped. What was going on here to cause the higher performance?

Further research conducted at Hawthorne yielded some answers. In another study, six 15- and 16-year-old girls agreed to participate in the research and were put to work producing relay assemblies, a telephone component. The work area was separated from other plant areas to enable researchers to observe the employees and keep detailed records. For 2½ years, a series of changes in the girls' working conditions were introduced, including shorter workdays and workweeks, periodic rest breaks, free lunches and snacks, and changes in starting and quitting times. And, perhaps you have guessed the results. Throughout the entire 2½ years, their output increased from 2,400 to 3,000 relays weekly per worker. Moreover, their attendance and morale also increased steadily.

What do you think was causing these improvements? Subsequent experiments and an extensive interview program with workers throughout the plant attributed the improvements to psychological factors within the experimental groups. By being singled out to participate in the experiments, the workers selected felt "special" and important, causing them to operate under motivational conditions quite unlike other Hawthorne workers. Management had directed attention toward them, and their results became more meaningful. An important result of the Hawthorne Studies was the discovery of a powerful motivational force that ushered in the beginning of the human relations era of management.[4]

Levels of Motivation

1 *Identify the three levels of employee motivation.*

Broadly, when we say that someone is or is not motivated to engage in a certain behavior, we can refer to three distinct, but often related, levels as shown in Exhibit 7.2.[5] One level is the direction in which the individual behaves. Does an employee behave in desirable ways?

Does an AutoFin associate:

- Spend 90 percent of his or her time on the phone with customers?
- Key into his or her computer the result of each contact as it occurs, as instructed by management?
- Attempt to sell a warranty agreement to each customer who extends the lease or purchases the vehicle outright?
- Cooperate with other associates by providing them with needed information about customer contacts they may have shared?

A second motivation level relates to *how hard* the individual works to perform the behavior(s). An employee may be aware of the need for the behavior, but how much energy and effort does he or she exert to perform it properly?

A welder at Inland Marine's Yard 2, John knows that he should secure his safety harness when he works at heights three feet or more above ground, as this company safety requirement is regularly discussed at weekly safety meetings held by his supervisor. However, because he is experienced, John feels that this requirement is often a nuisance, so he usually "forgets." He'd rather put his energy into welding, which is what he is paid to do, he says. As John's supervisor states, John just isn't motivated to be conscientious or exert effort in following established safety rules.

For many supervisors, it is this second motivational level—getting employees to put effort into what they do—that provides the biggest challenge. Retail department store managers often complain that salespeople don't put energy into keeping their areas neat and orderly. A restaurant manager keeps watch, making sure bartenders don't spend too much time talking with friends or customers they've developed a relationship with while overlooking the beverage needs of others. A branch bank manager laments that a teller may not try hard to make eye contact with customers, smile, call the customer by name, or attempt to cross-sell a certificate of deposit or loan.

The third and final motivational level reflects an employee's *persistence*. In the face of adversity, obstacles, or roadblocks, how hard does an employee keep trying? Some employees may be highly motivated when conditions are favorable, but what happens in the face of adversity or roadblocks? When an employee isn't feeling well in the morning, will she call in absent? If she shows up, will she still persevere and perform the job well? If her equipment acts up, will she be motivated to find a makeshift way to get the work done?

Frito-Lay is filled with tales of salespeople going to extraordinary efforts to meet their customers' needs. These include braving the fiercest of weather to ensure their daily contacts with stores that they serve, or going to great lengths to help a store clean up after a hurricane or fire. Letters about such acts pour into Dallas headquarters.[6]

EXHIBIT 7-2
The Three Levels of Motivation

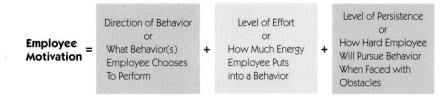

| **Employee Motivation** = | Direction of Behavior or What Behavior(s) Employee Chooses To Perform | + | Level of Effort or How Much Energy Employee Puts into a Behavior | + | Level of Persistence or How Hard Employee Will Pursue Behavior When Faced with Obstacles |

Intrinsic and Extrinsic Motivation

intrinsic motivation

Behavior that an individual produces because of the pleasant experiences associated with the behavior itself.

Intrinsic motivation is that behavior that an individual produces because of the pleasant experiences associated with the behavior itself. Employees who are intrinsically motivated feel satisfaction in performing their work. This satisfaction may come from any of several factors, including enjoying the actual work done, the feeling of accomplishment, meeting the challenges, and so on.

Anne Marie Bains has strong intrinsic motivation in her work as a pharmaceutical sales representative. She enjoys traveling and the freedom of planning her calls. But the highlight is the actual time she spends communicating with health care professionals—getting to know them on a professional basis, gaining their confidence, and sharing with them information about her company's products.

extrinsic motivation

Behavior performed not for its own sake, but for the consequences associated with it. The consequences can include pay, benefits, job security, and working conditions.

By contrast, **extrinsic motivation** is performed not for its own sake, but rather for the consequences associated with it. The consequences can include such factors as the pay, the benefits, the job security, or working conditions.

As loan collector for a local bank, Ben Harrison dislikes "putting the squeeze" on people, as he calls it. But because his job brings in money for the bank, he feels secure, can earn a nice bonus by reaching collection goals, and has excellent benefits, and the bank is located only a few minutes from his home.

Ben is extrinsically motivated. It's not what he *does* in his job that he finds satisfying, but the indirect factors of pay, benefits, and working conditions.

The Motivation–Performance Link

2 *Explain the relationship between performance and motivation.*

Many supervisors mistakenly assume that performance is directly related to an employee's level of motivation. Initially, one might conclude that the more highly motivated an employee is, the higher that employee's performance will be. This is not necessarily the case. Unquestionably, direction of behavior, level of effort, and persistence affect an employee's performance. However, the motivation–performance link is just not that simple.

As shown in Exhibit 7.3, in addition to an individual's motivation, personal abilities and skills and level of organizational support also influence performance.

It is possible that an employee with low motivation may indeed outperform a more highly motivated but less-skilled employee. New employees in particular often have strong motivation, but their performance will not be as good as that of more experienced personnel. Also, an employee's performance depends largely on what we call "organizational support." We all are familiar with sports examples of highly motivated players whose "performance" is below par, despite excellent skills and strong motivation.

EXHIBIT 7-3
Factors Affecting an Individual's Job Performance

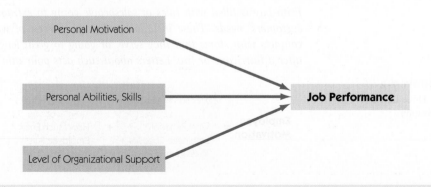

Consider the National Football League (NFL) quarterback who last year made all-pro but this year has three rookie offensive linemen and no pass protection, the outstanding pass receiver who this year is handicapped by a rookie quarterback, or the pitcher whose infield leads the majors in errors. It works similarly in nonsports organizations. The level of organizational support, such as quality physical and financial resources with which to work, timely assistance, and upper management support, also strongly influence an individual's performance.

We conclude this discussion by stating that, *things being equal, employees who are more highly motivated will have higher performance.* However, things are seldom truly equal, which challenges the supervisor's diagnostic skills when examining the true cause of a performance-related problem.

Since the 1960s, much research has been done on the behavior of people at work. Some significant theories have been developed that are important to anyone in a position of leadership who wants to avoid unnecessary friction arising from human relationships in an organization. For a person of action, such as a supervisor who has to work with and through people, an understanding of motivation theory is essential. Kurt Lewin, famous for his work in the study of groups, once said that there is nothing so practical as good theory. The remainder of this chapter will focus on the important theories of motivation, with emphasis on their application to effective supervision.

3 *Understand and explain Maslow's hierarchy of needs theory and the principle underlying his theory.*

Maslow's Hierarchy of Needs Theory

One theory that is particularly significant and practical was developed by psychologist Abraham H. Maslow and is known as the hierarchy of needs. Of all motivation theories, it is probably the one best known by managers. The key conclusion drawn from Maslow's theory is that people try to satisfy different needs through work.[7]

Principles Underlying the Theory

hierarchy of needs

Arrangement of people's needs in a hierarchy, or ranking, of importance.

The two principles underlying Maslow's **hierarchy of needs** theory are that (1) people's needs can be arranged in a hierarchy, or ranking, of importance, and (2) once a need has been satisfied, it no longer serves as a primary motivator of behavior. To understand the significance of these principles to Maslow's theory, let us examine the hierarchy of needs shown in Exhibit 7.4.

EXHIBIT 7-4
Maslow's Hierarchy of Needs

Pyramid (bottom to top)	Ways of Satisfying the Need on the Job
Self-Fulfillment or Self-Actualization	Learning new skills, growing and developing, feeling a sense of accomplishment, exercising responsibility.
Ego or Esteem	Praise, recognition, promotion, getting one's name in the company paper as "employee of the month," being given more responsibility, being asked for help or advice.
Social or Belonging	Work groups, group meetings, company-sponsored events.
Safety or Security	Safe working conditions, pensions and benefits, job security, fair treatment, fair grievance system.
Physiological or Biological	Pay, rest breaks, clean air.

physiological or biological need

The need for food, water, air, and other physical necessities.

Physiological or Biological Needs At the lowest level, but of primary importance when they are not met, are our **physiological** or **biological needs**. "Man does not live by bread alone," says the Bible, but anything else is less important when there is no bread. Unless the circumstances are unusual, the need we have for love, status, or recognition is inoperative when our stomach has been empty for some time. When we eat regularly and adequately, we cease to regard hunger as an important motivator. The same is true of other physiological needs, such as those for air, water, rest, exercise, shelter, and protection from the elements.

safety or security need

The need for protection from danger, threat, or deprivation.

Safety or Security Needs When our physiological needs have been reasonably well satisfied, **safety** or **security needs** become important. We want to be protected from danger, threat, or deprivation. When we feel threatened or dependent, our greatest need is for protection or security. Most employees are in a dependent relationship at work, so they may regard their safety needs as being very important. Clune Construction, a Chicago and Los Angeles interior construction firm that is listed as a "Best Place to Work," addressed the security/safety needs of its 200 employees when, in 2009, it guaranteed that there would be no layoffs, despite the economic recession.[8] Also, arbitrary or autocratic management actions such as favoritism, discrimination, or the unpredictable application of policies can be a powerful threat to the safety of any employee at any level.

social or belonging need

The need for belonging, acceptance by colleagues, friendship, and love.

Social or Belonging Needs **Social or belonging needs** include the need for belonging, for association, for acceptance by colleagues, and for friendship and love. Although most supervisors know that these needs exist, many assume—wrongly—that they represent a threat to the organization. Fearing group hostility to its own objectives, management may go to considerable lengths to control and direct human efforts in ways that are detrimental to cohesive work groups.

When employees' social needs, as well as their safety needs, are not met, they may behave in ways that tend to defeat organizational objectives by becoming resistant, antagonistic, and uncooperative.

ego or esteem need

The need for self-confidence, independence, appreciation, and status.

Ego or Esteem Needs Above the social needs are the **ego or esteem needs**. These needs are of two kinds: (1) those that relate to one's self-esteem, such as the need for self-confidence, independence, achievement, competence, and knowledge; and (2) those that relate to one's reputation, such as the need for status, recognition, appreciation, and respect from one's colleagues.

> *During World War I, General Douglas MacArthur, a 38-year-old brigadier general, had recently been named commander of a battlefield brigade in Europe. On the eve of a major battle in France, he met with the battalion commander. In an effort to inspire the men, MacArthur asked that when the signal was given to start the charge, the commander, a major, be the first one out to lead the charge, in front of his men. MacArthur said, "If you do this, your battalion will follow you, and you will earn the Distinguished Service Cross, and I will see that you get it." MacArthur then paused, looked at the major for several long moments, and said, "I see that you are going to do it. You have it now." With that, MacArthur removed from his own uniform his Distinguished Service Medal and pinned it on the major's uniform. The following day, proudly wearing his as yet unearned Distinguished Service Cross, the major was the first to lead the charge, his troops behind him, and they achieved their battlefield objective.[9]*

Unlike the lower-level needs, ego needs are rarely fully satisfied, because people, once they have become important, always seek more satisfaction of such needs. A few years ago, the typical organization offered few opportunities for lower-level employees to

Fun activities often arise out of the work environment, which helps employees meet their own social or belonging needs.

satisfy their ego needs. However, well-managed and innovative companies are doing a better job in this regard today.

> *Southwest Airlines is continuously ranked as one of the best U.S. companies to work for. Employees frequently use descriptions of their employment as, "Working here is truly an unbelievable experience. They treat you with respect ... empower you ... use your ideas to solve problems ... they encourage you to be yourself."[10] Still, the conventional method of organizing work, particularly in mass-production industries, gives little consideration to these aspects of motivation.*

Self-Fulfillment or Self-Actualization Needs At the top of Maslow's hierarchy are the **self-fulfillment** or **self-actualization needs**. These needs lead one to seek realization of one's own potential, to develop oneself, and to be creative.

self-fulfillment or self-actualization need

The need concerned with realizing one's potential, self-development, and creativity.

> *John B., age 64, is about three years from taking company retirement. He enjoys woodworking and has become quite good at it, his bowls and carved figures having won several awards at arts fairs. John is one of the most knowledgeable technical service representatives in the company, but he continually turns down overtime work on weekends. "The extra money just isn't worth it to me anymore," he says. "I'd much rather spend my time working in my shop or showing my work at an arts and crafts show." John recently was asked on short notice to be flown over a weekend to a customer location to help resolve a difficult problem that the site could not resolve. He accepted. As he stated, "It wasn't the money, it was the fact that nobody else could resolve it and I looked forward to the challenge."*

It seems clear that the quality of work life in most organizations provides only limited opportunities to fulfill self-fulfillment/actualization needs, especially at lower organizational levels. When higher-level needs are not satisfied, employees compensate by trying to further satisfy lower-level needs. The needs for self-fulfillment may remain dormant.

Stop & Think

Reflect on the examples of motivation described in this chapter's preview. Which need levels of employees are reflected in each of these?

Qualifying the Theory

Maslow's theory is a relative rather than an absolute explanation of human behavior. You should be aware of the following four important qualifiers to his theory:

1. The needs hierarchy is based on U.S. cultural values. Though the five needs are universal, the sequence of the hierarchy may differ, depending upon the culture. Cultures such as those in Chile, Venezuela, and Japan value job security and lifelong employment much more strongly than achievement-oriented, individualistic cultures such as the United States and Great Britain.
2. The priorities of some individuals may differ. For example, an artist may practically starve while trying to achieve self-actualization through the creation of a great work of art.
3. Needs on one level of the hierarchy do not have to be completely satisfied before needs on the next level become important.
4. Unlike the lower levels, the two highest levels of needs can hardly ever be fully satisfied. There are always new challenges and opportunities for growth, recognition, and achievement. A person may remain in the same job position for years and still find a great deal of challenge and motivation in his or her work.

Bob Buschka, a computer programmer for a large bank in a Midwestern state, has held his position for 20 years, turning down several promotions. He is considered one of the top programmers in banking in the area. The bank sends him to various schools to keep him growing and developing on the job. "We know what a gem he is," says his boss, "and we give him lots of room to operate—special key projects, training and developing new programmers, and keeping up with the new applications to our industry."

Herzberg's Theory

4 *Differentiate between Herzberg's dissatisfiers and motivators.*

In the 1960s, a researcher named Frederick Herzberg conducted in-depth interviews with 200 engineers and accountants from 11 different firms in the Pittsburgh, Pennsylvania, area.[11] Those interviewed were asked to recall an event or series of related events that made them feel unusually good and unusually bad about their work and how much the event(s) affected their performance and morale. Prior to Herzberg's study, a common assumption was that factors such as money, job security, and working conditions were all strong positive motivators and pretty much worked the same way: If these things were not satisfied at work, people would be negatively motivated; if they were satisfied, people would be positively motivated. Herzberg's findings disproved this assumption and helped us better differentiate among various motivational factors.

Dissatisfiers and Motivators

dissatisfier or hygiene factors

Factors that employees said most affected them negatively or dissatisfied them about their job, including low pay, low benefits, and unfavorable working conditions.

satisfier or motivator factors

Factors that employees said turned them on about their job, such as recognition, advancement, achievement, challenging work, and being one's own boss.

Herzberg found that two different lists emerged, one for factors that made the engineers and accountants feel unusually good and the other for factors that made them feel unusually bad. What people said most affected them negatively, or *dissatisfied* them (called **dissatisfier** or **hygiene factors**) about their jobs, were things such as low pay, low benefits, unfavorable working conditions, poor job security, and poor company policy/administration. The things that *turned them on* (called **satisfier** or **motivator factors**) tended to be recognition, advancement, achievement, challenging work, being one's own boss, and the work itself (see Exhibit 7.5).

A survey of 372 managers seemed to reinforce Herzberg's theory, as 76 percent said that personal achievement and job enjoyment *most* motivated them, in contrast to only 30 percent who cited financial rewards.[12] Note that the satisfier/motivator factors are found at the highest levels of Maslow's hierarchy, whereas the dissatisfier/hygiene factors are at the lower levels.

Stop & Think

Try to answer Herzberg's survey questions yourself. Think about a particular job you have held in the past or presently hold. If you haven't had a job, think of your schoolwork.

1. What specific incident or event (singular or recurring) gave you the most satisfaction?
2. What caused the most dissatisfaction?

Herzberg reasoned that the dissatisfier factors are what people take for granted about their jobs, so their presence is not particularly stimulating. For example, consider an employee who said that the most dissatisfying thing about his job was that the work area was too hot. Assume that the company addressed this issue and installed a cooling system throughout the plant. Six months later, would this employee be likely to say that one of the most satisfying things about the job was the cool plant? Not likely.

EXHIBIT 7-5
Herzberg's Satisfier/
Motivator and
Dissatisfier/Hygiene
Factors

SATISFIER/MOTIVATOR FACTORS	
+ Recognition	"The boss says I've done a good job."
+ Advancement	"I was promoted to team leader."
+ Challenging work	"I solved a really tough job problem."
+ Being one's own boss	"I was given a free hand to do my job."
+ Work itself	"I got to design the new system."
DISSATISFIER/HYGIENE FACTORS	
− Pay	"I'm not paid fairly for what I do."
− Benefits	"This company doesn't pay tuition or medical benefits."
− Working conditions	"It's so hot in the plant it's often unbearable."
− Job security	"With the seasonal work, I never know for sure if I'll have a job."
− Company policy/administration	"We have so much red tape to go through."

Conversely, factors that cause *strong dissatisfaction* do not tend to be such things as the lack of responsibility or challenge in a job or absence of recognition. If a company seeks to eliminate dissatisfaction, it must address factors including wages, working conditions, and security. Note that supervisors often have greater ability to influence motivator factors such as recognition, assigning challenging jobs, and empowering employees than they do hygiene factors of pay, benefits, working conditions, job security, and company policy. A recent study of the Irish health sector examined it from Herzberg's perspective. It found that health sector managers have limited control over employees' pay, job security, and work load, much of this being determined by the "system." Although managers have a greater degree of control over motivational factors of achievement, recognition, and responsibility, the study concluded that managers were not effectively using these motivational tools.[13]

Link to Intrinsic and Extrinsic Motivation

Earlier in the chapter, we discussed the subject of intrinsic and extrinsic motivation. Note that the factors associated with positive motivation were intrinsic to the job, whereas those causing job dissatisfaction were extrinsic to it. When people felt good about their jobs, it was usually because something had happened that showed they were doing their work particularly well or were becoming more expert in their professions. In other words, good feelings were keyed to the specific tasks that they performed, rather than to extrinsic factors such as money, security, or working conditions. Conversely, when they felt bad, it was usually because something had happened to make them feel that they were being treated unfairly.

The crux of Herzberg's theory is that dissatisfiers and satisfiers are each important in their own way. Dissatisfier factors, such as good pay, benefits, working conditions, and job security, must first be addressed by management as a motivational base to prevent employee dissatisfaction. Once dissatisfaction is removed, management will get more "bang for its motivational effort" by focusing on employees' opportunities for responsibility, recognition, advancement, and challenge in their jobs.

> *Walter Vaux was a young chemical engineer toiling in the lab when his boss walked in. "You're doing a wonderful job," he remembers the supervisor saying. "I'm so glad you're part of the department." It was just a few words, but the input was such a valuable motivator that Vaux, now retired, still talks of the lesson he learned—it takes more than cash. "Many other bosses have just taken my contributions for granted and felt that their response was more money. The real motivator was genuinely realizing my successes and telling me so."[14]*

Qualifying Herzberg's Theory

Herzberg's results have been replicated in other studies involving nonprofessionals, such as food service workers, assembly line workers, and others. However, you should bear in mind some important qualifications to Herzberg's theory:

1. Money *can* be a motivating factor, especially when it is tied to recognition and achievement.
2. For some people, especially professionals, the absence of motivating factors such as recognition, advancement, and challenge can constitute dissatisfaction.
3. Critics contend that a built-in bias of Herzberg's findings is that when asked about something on the job that is positive, a person is biased toward mentioning something in which his or her behavior is the focal point, such as a feeling of achievement, meeting a job challenge, and so on. Conversely, when asked about

dissatisfiers, a person is likely to mention extrinsic factors over which he or she has no control, such as pay or working conditions.

Despite these qualifications, we feel that Herzberg's theory is valuable as a general guide to understanding behavior at work. It also helps set the stage to understand better job design theory, discussed later in this chapter.

Other Motivation Theories

5 *Understand and explain expectancy theory.*

This section explores other motivation theories with which you should be familiar. These include expectancy theory, goal-setting theory, equity theory, reinforcement theory, and job design theory.

Expectancy Theory

expectancy theory

Views an individual's motivation as a conscious effort involving the expectancy that a reward will be given for a good result.

The theories of Maslow and Herzberg focus primarily on the individual and his or her needs as dominant employee motivation factors. **Expectancy theory** is more dynamic. It views an individual's motivation as a more conscious effort involving the interplay of three variables: (1) expectancy that effort will lead to a given performance result; (2) probability of reward(s) associated with the performance result; and (3) the value of the reward to the individual.[15] Expectancy theory states that most work behavior can be explained by the fact that employees determine in advance what their behavior may accomplish and the value they place on alternative possible accomplishments or outcomes. Some writers have termed this a "payoff" or "What's in it for me?" view of behavior. Developed by Victor Vroom of the University of Michigan, expectancy theory is illustrated in Exhibit 7.6.

Let us take a look at how expectancy theory operates. Suppose that Maria's boss says, "If you are able to complete the project by Monday, Maria, I'll recommend you for a promotion to supervisor. I realize that it will mean you will be putting in some heavy work without pay, but think about it and let me know your answer." There are three important factors involved. As shown in Exhibit 7.7, one is the Effort → Performance relationship—Maria's expectancy that if she puts in the extra effort, she can realistically complete the project by Monday. The second factor is the Performance → Reward relationship—the likelihood that if she does complete the project by Monday, Maria will actually be promoted to supervisor. In other words, does Maria's supervisor really have the influence to get her the promotion? The final factor is the value Maria places on being promoted to supervisor. Suppose the last thing in the world she wants is the responsibility and pressure of being a supervisor! In expectancy theory, then, the three factors—the Effort → Performance link, the Performance → Reward link, and the value of the reward—all interface to determine someone's motivation.

EXHIBIT 7-6
Expectancy Theory

Motivation =	Expectancy that increased effort will lead to a given performance level (Effort → Performance link)	×	Probability that a performance level will lead to a given reward (Performance → Reward link)	×	Value attached to reward

Thomas Northcut/Digital Vision/Getty Images

Motivating employees through rewards is one aspect of expectancy theory.

EXHIBIT 7-7

Ways to Apply
Expectancy Theory

1. Hire people who have adequate skill levels.
2. Set clear, recognizable performance goals.
3. Make sure employees know what is expected.
4. Continually stress employee training and skill development.
5. Use performance feedback and coaching to help employees gain skills.
6. Have employees share knowledge and expertise with others.
7. Give employees special jobs or assignments that stretch their abilities.
8. Celebrate performance successes.
9. Reward performance achievement.
10. Develop trust in your commitments by others; do not overpromise rewards.
11. Emphasize multiple rewards such as praise and recognition, being assigned desired work, receiving special training, and attending a conference.
12. Determine what different individuals value as rewards (financial, social, being in the know, learning a new skill, etc.) and help make these happen.

Note that the perceptual process plays a critical role in maximizing employee motivation, according to expectancy theory:

1. An employee must *perceive* that he or she has a good chance of achieving the targeted performance level.
2. An employee must *perceive* that if he or she does reach the performance level, he or she will actually receive the reward.
3. An employee must *perceive* the reward to be something valued.

The authors are familiar with one Chicago manufacturer that used tickets to cultural and social events as rewards for a program that tried to improve daily attendance among its hourly workforce. The program had little impact. As one manager stated, rewards with a more targeted appeal, such as free dinners at Chicago restaurants or tickets to professional sporting events, would have been stronger motivators. Often, however, employees may not grasp the reward potential of assignments given by their supervisors. American Express managers are taught to "label and link" when delegating or giving assignments. This means telling why the assignment is important to the individual receiving the assignment.[16]

Supervisors can do a number of things to apply the principles of expectancy theory: (1) they can train and coach employees to reach desired performance levels (the Effort → Performance link); (2) they can deliver on their commitments (the Performance → Reward link); and (3) they can reward performance in ways meaningful to employees (the reward). Exhibit 7.8 illustrates a wide range of rewards that managers can provide, many of which are cost-free.

Here are some ways that Sharon Olds (see chapter preview) uses expectancy theory:

Each of Sharon Olds' sales associates has a sales goal to book 35 monthly customers to a new lease contract or purchase of their present vehicle. At that point, a financial incentive kicks in. Sharon works especially hard on the Effort → Performance aspect of expectancy theory by helping associates to be confident that if they work hard, they <u>will</u> *actually achieve the 35 customer rate and higher.*

Among the tools Sharon employs are continuous sales training of her associates, publicizing achievement levels and success stories, and performance feedback and coaching. "I do my best to make them feel that they have the right stuff and my support to succeed. It is especially important for new associates to know that if they work hard each day, they will achieve the necessary successes with customers. My full-timers have done

EXHIBIT 7-8 Manager's List of Potential Rewards	Raises and bonuses
	Social functions
	Outings
	A night on the town
	A nice meal or lunch courtesy of the manager
	Lunch as a group that the manager buys
	Dinner
	Day off or time off
	Picnics for teams
	Tickets to sports, special events
	Direct oral praise to individual, one to one
	Direct praise to individual in presence of others
	Direct praise/recognition at group events
	Peer recognition
	Letters of recognition to file or place where customers can see them
	Passing on customer compliments and commendations in voice mail or in writing
	Written praise
	Certificates and plaques
	Shirts, phones, pins, hats, cups, jackets, and so on, all with the name of the company on them
	Opportunity to attend conference, special training course
	A parking space
	Additional responsibilities
	Personal call or visit from CEO or senior executive
	New furnishings or equipment
	Being assigned more favorable jobs
	Allowing people to bid on projects/tasks they prefer

Source: Reprinted from Peter Meyer. "Can You Give Good, Inexpensive Rewards? Some Real-Life Answers," November–December 1994, pp. 84–85. Copyright © 1994, Reprinted with permission from Elsevier.

it before and know that they can get there, so my job is more one of encouraging them and rallying them."

Sharon also works hard to reinforce the rewards received by top performers. She knows that the financial incentive is an important reward for most, but for others, it is the fact that they have achieved a high level of success. "That's why I like to make it a big deal when someone gets there, like e-mailing everyone in sight about it," she says. "For many, that is as satisfying or more satisfying than the extra money."

Goal-Setting Theory

6 *Explain how supervisors can use goal-setting theory to motivate employees.*

goal-setting theory

Theory that task goals, properly set and managed, can be an important employee motivator.

Task goals, in the form of clear and desirable performance targets, form the basis of Edwin Locke's **goal-setting theory** of motivation.[17] Goals are important not only in the planning process, but also as an important motivational factor. Locke's basic premise is that task goals can be highly motivating—if they are properly set and if they are well managed. Performance goals clarify the expectations between a supervisor and an employee and between co-workers and subunits in an organization. They also establish a frame of reference for task feedback and provide a foundation for self-management. In these and related ways, Locke believes goal setting is of primary importance in enhancing individual motivation and job performance and has spent much research since the 1970s substantiating that theory.

Listed here are the major ways in which a supervisor can use goal setting as a motivational tool:

1. Set specific goals. Specific, concrete goals consistently lead to better performance than general ones, such as "do your best," or no goals at all.
2. Set challenging but reasonably difficult goals. Be careful, though, not to set unrealistic goals that employees feel they have little chance of reaching. Several years ago, one professional football team posted in the dressing room the following offensive team goals: "Never allow our quarterback to be sacked; always score when inside the red zone (opponent's 20-yard line); never give up a fumble." Because they were unattainable, these goals were likely perceived as meaningless by the team's offensive players.
3. Ensure timely feedback to employees about goal achievement. This may be easier in certain situations, such as sales or production work, than in others.
4. Where practical, strengthen employees' commitment by allowing them to participate in goal setting. A key step in MBO (Management by Objectives) is involving employees in establishing their own key performance goals.
5. When multiple goals are established, make sure employees understand their priorities. For example, is meeting a quality goal more important than meeting a quantity goal or cost-effectiveness goal?
6. Reinforce goal accomplishment. When people reach or exceed goals, ensure timely rewards and recognition.

T. Paul Bulmahn, Chairman of ATP Oil and Gas, a 55-employee, Houston, Texas, offshore development company, wanted his company to grow, so he tried something he had not done before. At the company Christmas luncheon in 2004, he gave his employees a special challenge: triple daily production by the end of 2005 and boost the reserve replacement rate by 200 percent and everyone would go to Sweden and get new Volvo 760s. No kidding!

While it would surely be a challenge, employees committed to the task. However, the progress they made through the fall took a turn for the worse when hurricanes devastated the company's Gulf of Mexico operations. So Bulmahn extended the time frame another quarter, until March 2006. And darn if they didn't put forth a Herculean effort and achieve their goals!

Employees were ecstatic. Thirty-nine of the 55 employees with their spouse or a friend flew to Sweden with Bulmahn and selected Volvos; the others opted instead for a cash payment of $25,000. Bulmahn stated that he issued the challenge because the company had reached a point where it needed to move forward. Achieving the challenging goal of tripling production in a little over a year has put ATP in another league, he said. And doing it without an acquisition was unheard of.[18]

Equity Theory

7 *Define equity theory.*

equity theory

Theory that when people perceive themselves in situations of inequity or unfairness, they are motivated to act in ways to change their circumstances.

Employee motivation can also be viewed in terms of how fairly or "equitably" an employee feels he or she is rewarded as compared to others. **Equity theory** states that when people find themselves in situations of inequity or unfairness, they are motivated to act in ways to change their circumstances.

Two factors determine whether one is in an equitable situation. One is the inputs, such as the skill, education, experience, and motivation, that an employee brings to the job situation. The second consists of the rewards that a person receives for performance, including pay, advancement, recognition, or desirable job assignments. Think of equity theory, then, as an input/output comparison that responds to this question: Given what I bring to a job as compared to what others bring, are the rewards that I receive fair as compared to theirs? If you asked this question of yourself and answered no, according to equity theory, you would likely act to reduce the inequity in several ways. Three options are as follows:

1. You can try to *increase your reward level* by making a case with your supervisor or relevant others, appealing to higher management, or filing a grievance;
2. You can *decrease your input level* by putting in less job effort, taking longer breaks, or being less cooperative; or
3. If you cannot restore equity in your present job, you can *leave the situation* by asking for a transfer or seeking a position with another employer.

reinforcement theory

Based on the law of effect, holds that behaviors that meet with pleasant consequences tend to be repeated, whereas behaviors that meet with unpleasant consequences tend not to be repeated, and rewards and punishments are used as a way to shape the individual.

Equity theory typically addresses broad, overall organizational issues such as pay and benefits, working conditions, and advancement. However, equity theory is quite relevant to individual supervisors. First, some supervisors may be in a position to influence employee pay and promotion when supervisors feel that these are inequitable. Second, supervisors can provide rewards through job assignments, assignment of newer resources, and recognition. In these and other situations, the message is clear: Employees must feel that rewards are equitably distributed; otherwise, they will be motivated to reduce the inequity.

Reinforcement Theory

8 *Define and explain reinforcement theory.*

Reinforcement theory uses rewards and punishments that follow a person's behavior as a way to shape that individual's future behavior.

Based on the law of effect, it holds that behaviors that meet with pleasant consequences tend to be repeated, whereas behaviors that meet with unpleasant consequences tend not to be repeated. To the extent that a supervisor has a degree of control over the reward and discipline system for employees, he or she has some control over the law of effect. Suppose that a worker's attendance has been spotty recently. Reinforcement theory can work in two ways: (1) You can *positively reinforce* (praise, reward) the worker's favorable behavior (showing up on time), thereby encouraging him or her to repeat it, or (2) you can *discourage* the worker's unfavorable behavior through punishment (scolding, writing a disciplinary warning, assigning nondesirable work duties), thereby encouraging him or her not to repeat it.

Advocates of reinforcement theory argue strongly that positive reinforcement often is more effective than punishment in getting people to behave in desired ways.

> *Take, for example, an employee who is punished for not treating a customer well. When the employee is called on the carpet, she might not necessarily know what specifically she must do to improve. Moreover, she might not be in a situation where she feels like listening, even if told. She might respond by associating "customer" and "punishment" and try to avoid customers altogether.*

> *If, on the other hand, when the employee does something right, the supervisor says, "I couldn't help but notice how patient and understanding you were in helping that customer work out her refund; I wanted to compliment you," then we are likely to get an employee out looking for customers to treat well. The specific behaviors (patience, understanding) lead to rewards that satisfy a person's need to enhance his or her self-image.*[19]

Organizations and supervisors have available a wide range of potential reinforcers, as listed earlier in Exhibit 7.8. Note that in addition to the more obvious raises and bonuses, a wide range of nonfinancial rewards was included. Eileen Rogers of Allegra Print and Imaging Company in Scottsdale, Arizona, keeps a supply of $2 bills on hand. Whenever a client expresses satisfaction with an employee's behavior, Rogers gives the employee a $2 bill and delivers a compliment in front of the entire team. Many post the bills near their desks, and one star employee is close to wallpapering her area with them.[20]

Most organizational "award" systems are based on management's recognition of employee performance. However, a system wherein customers, clients, and fellow workers recognize employees can be a powerful reinforcement tool. At American Equity Underwriters (AEU), a subsidiary of Charlotte-based AmWINS Group, a "WOW" board posts messages from clients who praise individual AEU employees for special efforts.

Unfortunately, one of the most effective and least used tools is the simple "thank you," according to Malcolm Baldrige Award Examiner and management consultant Kevin McManus. He encourages supervisors to do a Thank You Assessment (TYA) of their own behavior by asking employees to count the number of times they hear a sincere "thank you" or "I appreciate that" from the supervisor in a given time period. As McManus states:

> *Failing to use this simple tool sends a powerful message to people, just as effectively using it does.… We spend lots of money trying to learn better ways to motivate people through the use of gift certificates, plaques, and tickets to sporting events given out to only a select group of people. At the same time, we fail to say "thank you" to each of our people every day in a manner that means something to them.… Saying "thank you" is free and it is a form of recognition that can be distributed at any time.*[21]

One recent survey showed that 75 percent of employees felt that praise from the boss was the strongest motivator they receive. An independent study conducted by management search firms wanted to find out why upper-level managers left their jobs. The leading reason, given by 34 percent of respondents, was "limited praise/recognition," compared to only 25 percent who said "compensation."[22] Recall how Sharon Olds used praise and recognition to reinforce associates when they performed their jobs well. Indeed, when praise is properly used, it is one of the most effective reinforcers a supervisor has.

Direct praise is one way to reward employee performance.

Motivating through Job Design: The Job Characteristics Model

9 *Explain the job characteristics model.*

job characteristics model

Approach to job design that focuses on five core job elements that lead to intrinsic motivation and then positive work outcomes.

Job design can be used to explain why some supervisors and managers face a more daunting task in motivating employees than others. How a job is designed refers to the number, kind, and variety of tasks that individual workers perform to complete their individual job. The **job characteristics model** of job design is composed of five core job elements that lead to intrinsic employee motivation and other positive work outcomes.[23]

The five important structural characteristics of a job's design, according to the job characteristics model, are:

1. Skill variety: Extent to which the job requires a worker to use a broad range of skills and talents to perform the job successfully.
2. Task identity: Extent to which the job requires a worker to complete a whole, identifiable piece of work.
3. Task significance: Extent to which the job substantially impacts the work or lives of others.
4. Autonomy: Extent to which the job entails substantial freedom and decision making in carrying it out.
5. Feedback: Extent to which the job itself provides information about whether it is performed successfully.

To understand the model, examine Exhibit 7.9. The left side (column 1) of the model lists the five core characteristics. The middle column (column 2) shows the important psychological states enabled by the five characteristics. Note that the first three characteristics—the job's skill variety, identity, and significance—combine to create *meaningful work*. Autonomy enables a *feeling of responsibility*, and feedback enables *knowledge of a job's results*. On the far right, column 3 shows how each of the three psychological states (column 2) leads to high motivation, high-quality performance, high job satisfaction, and low absenteeism/turnover.

EXHIBIT 7-9
Job Characteristics Model

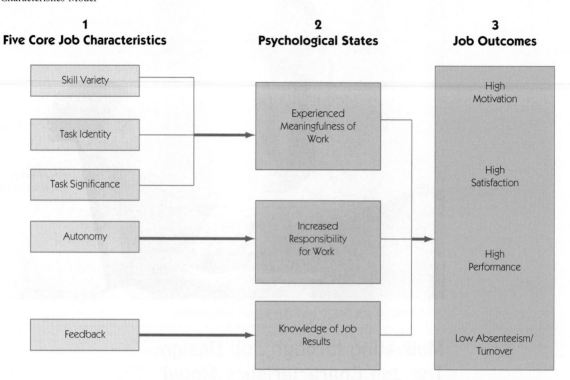

1
Five Core Job Characteristics

2
Psychological States

3
Job Outcomes

Skill Variety

Task Identity

Task Significance

Autonomy

Feedback

Experienced Meaningfulness of Work

Increased Responsibility for Work

Knowledge of Job Results

High Motivation

High Satisfaction

High Performance

Low Absenteeism/ Turnover

Source: Adapted from J. R. Hackman, "Work Design," in J. R. Hackman and J. L. Suttle, eds, Improving Life at Work (Goodyear Publishing, 1977), p. 159. Reprinted with permission.

To help understand the five characteristics, let's assume that you work the first window of a two-window drive through at a local McDonald's.[24] We'll take each of the five characteristics in sequence:

1. Variety: low. You greet the customer, punch in the order on a computer screen, and collect the customer's money. You repeat a few standard phrases such as "Welcome to McDonald's. May I take your order? Drive to the next window please."
2. Task identity: low. Others cook the food, prepare the order, and hand the customer the completed order.
3. Task significance: low. There's not a lot riding on the tasks you perform.
4. Autonomy: low. You must use a standardized greeting, can't give someone a free item because they were patient, and procedures dictate things such as your appearance, dress, and how you relay the order to the kitchen, use the cash register, and so on.
5. Feedback: some. From customer interaction, the number of cars in the drive through, how long it takes you to process them, and whether your register balances at the end of the shift, you do have some idea of how you're doing. Importantly, though, you don't know if you took and recorded orders correctly because this is determined at the next window!

Given the low scores on these five characteristics, we can conclude that a worker who performs on window #1 at McDonald's will not experience high motivation or job satisfaction.

So, why do organizations make supervisors' jobs of motivating employees all the more difficult by having employees perform boring, nonchallenging tasks? The answer lies in the costs associated with change. These include the need to recruit more qualified personnel, increased costs of employee training, and possibly increased compensation. Moreover, not all employees will necessarily accept increased responsibility, especially if they haven't exercised it for extensive employment periods. Presence of a union contract may also be a discourager.

However, individual supervisors should note that they can take some actions on their own to increase employee perceptions of the importance of their work. One of the authors observed this at a large newsprint producer, plagued with poor quality. A new paper machine superintendent, learning that his personnel had never seen a newspaper produced, chartered buses and arranged tours of a nearby major newspaper customer. The visitors received an on-site tour, interfacing with the newspaper's press room personnel, learning of the importance of high-grade newsprint in the printing process and even viewing some newsprint that had been pulled because of poor quality. This had a major impact on the perceived significance of their jobs

The Different Generations: Some Insights for Motivation

10 *Explain how generational differences affect motivation.*

A generational looking glass can be a valuable tool in learning how people differ in the attitudes they bring to work and what they value. Generation members share certain commonalities of thinking and behavior. Shared economic conditions, world events, pop culture, social experiences, education, and parenting give each generation its own persona. Although a generational perspective may not give you a complete picture of a given individual, it can certainly be helpful. Exhibit 7.10 highlights differences among the generations.

With the recent entry of Generation "Y" employees—those born since 1981—into the working world, the workforce for the first time contains four generations.[25]

traditionalists

Workforce generation born before 1945.

Traditionalists: born before 1945 (10% of work force). Children of the depression and World War, they were typically raised in a home with a stay-at-home parent. Imbued with strong family values, traditionalists themselves had a parent stay at home to raise their own children. Loyal and self-sacrificing, they value hard work, get satisfaction from a job well done, and tend to stay with a company a long time.

Baby Boomers

Workforce generation born between 1945 and 1964.

Baby Boomers: born between 1945 and 1964 (45% of work force). Raised in a period of prosperity in the 1950s and 1960s, baby boomers are the largest generation in history. They were the center of their parents' lives, likely having a stay-at-home parent. They are socially skilled, ambitious, and driven to succeed, which for them is often measured materialistically. They believe in growth, change, and expansion. Boomers grew up to want the best for themselves and their families and seek it through hard work and long hours. They, too, show loyalty toward employers and often have a "live to work" reference frame. They dislike authoritarianism and laziness; having paid their dues through hard work and loyalty, they feel particularly dismayed in today's era of downsizing and reengineering.

Generation Xers

Workforce generation born between 1965 and 1980.

Generation Xers: born between 1965 and 1980 (30% of work force). Children of the workaholic Baby Boomers, Generation Xers did not see as much of their parents as earlier generations. In many cases, both of their parents worked; a tripling divorce rate also meant that approximately half were raised in a one-parent home. Generation Xers learned to function on their own, being highly independent, self-reliant, and individualistic. This generation loves freedom and room to grow. Growing up, they

EXHIBIT 7-10
Characteristics of Different Generations

	TRADITIONALISTS (PRE-1945)	BABY BOOMERS (1945–1964)	GENERATION X (1965–1980)	GENERATION Y (1981–PRESENT)
AGE IN 2009 →	AGE 65+	AGE 45–64	AGE 29–44	AGE 1–29
Formative Events	Great Depression World Wars	Post war prosperity	Globalization Downsizing Tech boom	Networking 9-11 World terrorism Internet
Qualities	Loyal Self-sacrificing	Competitive Optimistic	Independent Individualistic Entrepreneurial Lack loyalty	Diverse Skilled Demanding Sophisticated
Assets	Wisdom Experience Persistence	Social skills	Tech skills Educated	Multitasking Work ethic Technologically savvy
Lack	Technology skills	Technology skills	Social skills	Direction Focus Interpersonal skills
Value	Family Patriotism	Material success Free expression Equity	Skill more than title Work-life balance	Patriotism Family Respect
Style	Directive Take charge Do what's right	Respect authority Micromanage Proactive Work hard	Skeptical Reluctant to network Outcome focused Bend rules as needed	Plunge right in Negotiate Blend work/play Measure own success

Strategies for Managing	Respect their experience
	Value their loyalty
	Use their knowledge/
	   experience to help others
		Give important role
		Value their contributions
		Show respect
		Minimize conflict
			Provide autonomy
			Give quick feedbacks
			Update their tech skills
			Give credit for results
				Train/upgrade
				Assign meaningful work
				Use in teams
				Promote positive, open
				   environment

Source: Adapted from Susan P. Eisner, "Managing Generation Y," *SAM Advanced Management Journal* 70, Autumn, 2005, v. 70, pp. 4–13.

heard their parents' laments about layoffs, downsizing, and managers who didn't treat their parents well. They view the employment relationship as one based on service for dollars paid, rather than loyalty, even if it means frequent employer changes. Generation Xers do not believe in paying their dues to achieve success; to them, success means following the opportunity. Although they possess strong technical skills, they lack the social skills of their parents' generations, not being particularly adroit at networking. They thrive on autonomy that allows them independence to handle their jobs as they see fit; thus, they respond poorly to being micromanaged.

Generation Yers: born in 1981 and later (15% of work force). Generation Yers have been raised in a time of globalism, economic expansion, prosperity, and the Internet. Electronic communication technology—laptops, Blackberries, cell phones, and text messaging —has enabled them to see, learn, and keep in touch more at an early age than any preceding generation.[26]

Generation Yers are the most diverse, highly educated, and technically literate generation. As the first truly global generation, Generation Yers have some values

Generation Yers

Youngest workforce generation, born since 1981

consistent with traditionalists, including patriotism, valuing family and home, a strong sense of morality, and commitment to volunteer service. They like intellectual challenge and strive to make a difference. Emotionally mature, Generation Yers have lived with strong social stressors ranging from pressures to excel in school to parental divorce to being products of one-parent homes. Of all the generations, one expert says, the Generation Yers are the most willing to "rock the boat."

Because organizations have been run by Traditionalists and Boomers, large corporations' strict rules of engagement especially clash with Generation Yers' values of openness and flexibility. They are accustomed to handling information and getting immediate results, and want freedom rather than rigid controls and standardized ways of doing things. Teachers and parents allowed them to speak their minds freely, so why not ask a supervisor questions such as "Why do I need to do it that way?" Growing up with instant messaging and live views of the Gulf, Iraqi, and Afghanistan wars on their televisions, Generation Yers are the ultimate stimulus junkies. They want instant feedback, rapid results, and jobs that offer excitement as well as a paycheck.[27]

You can see in Exhibit 7.10 some of the specific actions supervisors and organizations can take that may have special impact on individuals of a given generation. For example, traditionalists may be strongly motivated by an opportunity to mentor a younger employee or help train other team members; the opportunity to attend a technology training class might be highly valued by younger Generation X or Y employees. In the next section, you will learn some important principles for motivating that cut across all generation types. Peter Sheahan, a most sought after international speaker on Generation Y, says there are three things all generations, and especially Generation Yers, want in a motivating work environment:

1. Having their supervisor's respect;
2. Feeling like they are making a real contribution—their work must have an impact;
3. Having control—"Gen Yers want to customize their careers just like lattes are customized by coffee shops." This may range from flexible work hours to rotation among job assignments.[28]

Lessons from the Theories: Five Steps to Motivating Employees

1 1 *Identify five steps to motivating employees.*

Our intent in this chapter has been to explain a number of popular theories of motivation that can help you understand why people act as they do. You have noted the commonalities and close relationships among many of the theories.

Based on these theories, we feel there are a number of things a supervisor can do to help create a motivating environment for employees. Moreover, these five actions apply broadly to supervisors in all types of organizations. These supervisory actions are:

1. Help make employees' jobs intrinsically rewarding.
2. Provide clear performance objectives.
3. Support employees' performance efforts.
4. Provide timely performance feedback.
5. Reward employees' performance.

Help Make Employees' Jobs Intrinsically Rewarding

Recall Herzberg's finding that employees believed the most satisfying things about their jobs included feeling a sense of accomplishment, challenge, or responsibility. Also, note the job characteristics model's elements of motivation: task variety, task identity, task significance, autonomy, and feedback. Granted, it is more difficult to make dull, repetitive jobs more rewarding, especially when you cannot alter an assembly line or change the nature of the work being done. However, you can do a number of things to make even dull, unchallenging jobs more rewarding, such as:

- Rotate jobs/tasks
- Assign team members to special projects that give them a break from the usual grind or enable them to pick up a new skill
- Have employees train new employees
- Help employees learn skills to prepare them for a more advanced job
- Have employees make a safety presentation at a safety meeting
- Ask for employees' help in resolving problems that you face, such as cost or deadline overruns, relationships with other departments, or ways to improve quality
- Have a customer or end user of your department's product or service speak to your group.

As a supervisor, it is worth your effort to make employees' work provide opportunities for intrinsic satisfaction.

Stop & Think

If you are currently a supervisor, what actions could you take to help make your employees' jobs more intrinsically satisfying? If you are not currently a supervisor, select a job you have held that you considered dull and uninteresting. What actions could your supervisor have taken to make the job more rewarding?

Provide Clear Performance Objectives

In line with expectancy and goal-setting theories, make sure employees clearly understand what is expected of them. If possible, set concrete, specific, challenging goals as discussed in goal-setting theory. Moreover, if these are not set by the system itself or by your own manager, try to obtain your employees' assistance in determining these. Employees are more likely to commit to goals they have had a hand in setting.

Support Employees' Performance Efforts

View yourself as a coach whose job is to support your team members. Help them through intangibles such as building confidence and encouraging them, but also support them in tangible ways through the resources you provide, through your responsiveness to their needs, by obtaining additional training for them, and so on. Be viewed not only as their best cheerleader, but as someone who delivers tangible support as well.

Provide Timely Performance Feedback

Performance feedback is the fuel that employees need to sustain their effort. Although the job itself may provide feedback to them, it is important that you acknowledge their progress. Reason would say this is easier to do in favorable situations, but our experiences with managers and employees indicate it is not. Many employees state that they know things must be going well only because they *do not* hear from their supervisor. Managers must give favorable as well as unfavorable performance feedback. Note that we are not talking here about the feedback that accompanies an employee's 6- or 12-month formal review, but the feedback that occurs on a daily, regular basis. Team or departmental progress should be posted in high-visibility areas where everyone can see it regularly—from the CEO to hourly employees.[29]

Reward Employees' Performance

Be liberal with rewards, making sure they are earned. Reinforce your high performers through the reward system available to you, such as merit increases, praise, recognition, or opportunities to take on a more challenging job. Be creative with rewards, remembering that rewards are valued differently by different individuals.

Chapter Review

1. **Identify the three levels of employee motivation.**

   The three levels of employee motivation are (1) the direction of an employee's behavior, (2) the level of effort, and (3) the level of persistence. Direction of behavior relates to those behaviors the individual chooses to perform. Level of effort dictates how hard the individual is willing to work on the behavior. Level of persistence refers to the individual's willingness to pursue the behavior despite obstacles or roadblocks.

2. **Explain the relationship between performance and motivation.**

   Motivation is an important contributor to employee performance, but it is not the only one. Also involved are an employee's skill and ability and organizational support in the form of physical resources and assistance. We conclude that other things being equal, employees who are more highly motivated will have higher performance records.

3. **Understand and explain Maslow's hierarchy of needs theory and the principle underlying his theory.**

   The principle underlying Maslow's theory of a hierarchy of needs is that needs are arranged in a hierarchy of importance and that, once a need has been satisfied, it is no longer a primary motivator. The lower-level needs include physiological, security, and social needs, and the higher-level needs are esteem and self-fulfillment.

4. **Differentiate between Herzberg's dissatisfiers and motivators.**

   Herzberg's research discovered that motivators are those factors that have an uplifting effect on attitudes or performance, whereas dissatisfier/hygiene factors are those that prevent dissatisfaction but do not motivate by themselves. Motivators are recognition, advancement, achievement, being one's own boss, and the challenge associated with the work itself. Dissatisfiers include pay, benefits, working conditions, job security, and company policy/administration. Motivators relate to the two highest levels of the Maslow hierarchy, self-fulfillment and self-esteem. Dissatisfiers are related to lower-level physiological and security needs.

5. **Understand and explain expectancy theory.**

Expectancy theory views an individual's motivation as a conscious effort involving three variables: (1) expectancy that a given effort can achieve a given performance result; (2) probability that achieving the given performance result will lead to a reward; and (3) the value of the reward to the individual. Supervisors can apply expectancy theory by rewarding performance in ways that are meaningful to employees, by helping employees reach desired performance levels through coaching and training, and by delivering rewards as promised to employees.

6. **Explain how supervisors can use goal-setting theory to motivate employees.**

The basic premise of goal-setting theory is that task goals can be highly motivating if properly set and well managed. To maximize their motivational impact, performance goals should be specific and difficult, but achievable. Ideally, employees should participate in the goal-setting process and, if multiple goals are involved, should understand their priorities. Performance feedback about progress toward goal attainment should be provided, as well as timely rewards and recognition when goals are achieved.

7. **Define equity theory.**

Equity theory states that when people feel they are rewarded inequitably as compared to others, they will act in ways to change their circumstances. They may do this by (1) attempting to increase their reward level, (2) decreasing their input level, or (3) seeking to leave the situation by requesting transfer or leaving their employer.

8. **Define and explain reinforcement theory.**

Reinforcement theory uses rewards and punishment that follow an individual's behavior as a way of shaping future behavior. It is based on the law of effect, which holds that behaviors that meet with pleasant consequences tend to be repeated, whereas behaviors that meet with unpleasant consequences tend not to be repeated.

9. **Explain the job characteristics model.**

The job characteristics model, a form of job design, focuses on five core job elements that are capable of leading to intrinsic motivation and other positive work outcomes. These five elements are (1) skill variety, (2) task identity, (3) task significance, (4) autonomy, and (5) feedback.

10. **Explain how generational differences affect motivation.**

The four generations are Traditionalists, born before 1945; Baby Boomers, born between 1945 and 1964; Generation X, born between 1965 and 1980; and Generation Y, born in 1981 or later. Generalizations based on the common experiences shared during a generation's formative years enable insights into their values, behaviors, and what is likely to motivate them. Traditionalists, the oldest generation, tend to be loyal and hard working, value family, and get satisfaction from jobs well done. Workaholic Baby Boomers are ambitious, driven to succeed, and often materialistic; Generation Xers, raised to fend for themselves, are highly independent, technologically competent, and thrive on autonomy and freedom. Generation Yers, the new workforce entrants, are the Internet generation. Technologically savvy, they are the ultimate networkers, like instant results and feedback and open communications, and value flexibility.

11. **Identify five steps to motivating employees.**

Supervisors, in general, can take five specific steps to motivate employees. They can (1) help make employees' jobs more interesting by enabling greater challenge, accomplishment, or responsibility; (2) provide clear performance objectives; (3) support employees' performance efforts through training, coaching, and assistance; (4) provide timely performance feedback to employees; and (5) reward employees generously for performance accomplishment.

Key Terms

motivation, p. 195

Intrinsic motivation, p. 198

extrinsic motivation, p. 198

hierarchy of needs, p. 199

physiological or biological needs, p. 200

safety or security needs, p. 200

Social or belonging needs, p. 200

ego or esteem needs, p. 200

self-fulfillment or self-actualization needs, p. 201

dissatisfier or hygiene factors, p. 203

satisfier or motivator factors, p. 203

Expectancy theory, p. 205

goal-setting theory, p. 208

Equity theory, p. 209

Reinforcement Theory, p. 209

job characteristics model, p. 211

Tradionalists, p. 213

Baby Boomers, p. 213

Generation Xers, p. 213

Generation Yers, p. 214

Questions for Review & Discussion

1. Identify and explain the three levels of employee motivation. Give an example of each for one of the situations below:
   - Customer associate at Home Depot
   - Bagger at grocery chain
   - Carpenter for construction company
2. Explain the relationship between motivation and job performance. Can you identify a situation in which a factor other than your skill or motivation level affected your performance?
3. Briefly outline Maslow's theory of the hierarchy of needs. What need levels are addressed by:
   - Being promoted from operator to supervisor
   - Setting a new record for individual performance
   - Being selected to attend a special training course
4. In what ways did Frederick Herzberg's research concerning employee motivation correlate with Maslow's hierarchy of needs?
5. In a management seminar taught by one of the authors to supervisors in a large shipyard, one supervisor commented: "We have very little

opportunity to 'motivate' employees. All monetary factors—starting pay, yearly merit increases, and bonuses based on the yard's profits—are controlled by upper management, with no input from supervisors. We don't have anything to motivate with." Do you agree or disagree with this supervisor? Why?

6. What are the elements of goal-setting theory? Explain.
7. What relationship, if any, do you see among expectancy theory, goal-setting theory, equity theory, and reinforcement theory? Explain.
8. Identify the five core elements of the job characteristics model.
9. What are some important characteristics of each of the following generations?
   - Traditionalist
   - Baby Boomer
   - Generation X
   - Generation Y
10. Identify five important steps to motivating employees.

Information

Interpersonal Skill

Skill Builder 7-1

Career Exercise: What Do You Want from Your Job?

Assume that you could create the ideal job for yourself. Examine the 12 items shown below and rank these from most important to least important. In other words, what single item of the 12 is most important to you? Number that item 1. Follow a similar process until you have ranked all items.

YOUR PRIORITY RANK	IDEAL JOB FACTOR
_____	a. First-class working conditions
_____	b. Opportunity to achieve wide recognition for job performance
_____	c. Working in the city/area of your choice
_____	d. A super-competent boss
_____	e. Guaranteed job security (lifetime employment)
_____	f. Exceptional advancement opportunity
_____	g. Salary 20 percent higher than the industry average
_____	h. Challenging, interesting job that you really like
_____	i. Professional, supportive colleagues
_____	j. Working for a prestigious, nationally known organization
_____	k. Outstanding fringe benefits
_____	l. Excellent opportunity to grow and develop job skills

Instructions:

1. Now that you have completed the ranking, to what extent, if any, do your results reflect Maslow's needs theory? Herzberg's motivation–hygiene theory?
2. Meet with a group of four to six classmates and compare your rankings. To what extent were the rankings similar? Dissimilar? What might account for any different rankings given by your group?
3. Present a report to the class that summarizes the results of your group's discussion.

Information

Skill Builder 7-2

Classifying Managerial Rewards

Listed here are 15 actions that an organization's managers can take, each of which addresses one or more potential needs on the Maslow hierarchy. Some have been taken from Exhibit 7.8, "Manager's List of Potential Rewards," but others have been added.

Instructions:

1. For each item, identify the levels on the Maslow hierarchy of needs that the action addresses.
2. Select three items that you personally feel would be most important for you at the present time.

Interpersonal Skill

3. In small groups, discuss your results for items 1 and 2. To what extent did your team members agree on the three items? Why were there differences? Be prepared to report your results to the rest of the class.

ACTION		MASLOW NEED LEVEL(S) ADDRESSED
1.	Day off or time off	_____
2.	Personal call or visit from CEO or senior manager	_____
3.	"Employee of the Month" parking space	_____
4.	Direct oral praise from supervisor	_____
5.	Opportunity to attend special training course	_____
6.	Name in company newsletter	_____
7.	Additional responsibilities	_____
8.	Special task force assignment	_____
9.	Company outing, picnic	_____
10.	Being assigned favorable tasks	_____
11.	Opportunity to attend special seminar	_____
12.	New title, new office, new equipment	_____
13.	Direct praise to individual in presence of others	_____
14.	Receiving bonus for reaching production goal	_____
15.	Being given more responsibility	_____

Information

Skill Builder 7-3

The Job Characteristics Survey: Scoring Your Job

In this exercise, you will visit a website and complete an online survey called the "Job Diagnostic Survey." Based on the job characteristics model that you studied in this chapter, the survey measures the extent to which your job provides intrinsic satisfaction. Scoring the survey results in a score called the motivation potential score (MPS) of your job. If you are presently employed, use your job when you respond to the questions. If not presently employed, select a job you have once held.

Interpersonal Skill

Instructions:

1. Go to http://www.marscafe.com/php/hr2/jds_quiz.php3 and sign in. Click "other" or "college student" for occupation and "other" for your job title.
2. Complete the 15-item assessment.
3. Indicate your score for each of the five job characteristics.

Skill variety	_____
Task identity	_____
Task significance	_____
Autonomy	_____
Feedback	_____

Technology

Indicate your job's motivation potential score (MPS) = _____

The maximum score possible = 9,261

The minimum score possible = 27

4. What conclusions can you draw about your job's motivation potential?
5. In groups of four to six students, discuss your scores and possible ways your job's MPS might be improved.

CASE 7-1

Nucor, The Surprising Performance Culture of Steelmaker Nucor

In the early afternoon, three Nucor electricians got a call from their Hickman, Arkansas, plant colleagues. The Hickman mill's electrical grid had failed, which meant the mini-mill couldn't melt the usual auto parts, appliances, and mobile home parts that it uses to produce steel. But why should an outage in Arkansas concern anyone at plants in other Nucor locations? Here's why. At Nucor, steelworker production bonuses are based not only on what their own mill does, but on how others fare also. When a grid goes out, it hurts all. That's why when Hickman's electrician colleagues called for help, people didn't need top management to tell them to go; they responded on their own. Two electricians from the company's South Carolina plant boarded the first plane they could get to Memphis. Arriving at 11:00 p.m., they rented a car and drove two hours directly to the Hickman mill. The third electrician, from the company's Decatur, Alabama, plant, was in Indiana, visiting another Nucor site. He immediately drove to Hickman. Combined with Hickman staff, they camped out on site and worked 20-hour shifts to mobilize the plant in three days—much less than the anticipated week. They received no extra pay for their effort.

Why would they do such a thing? It's because of Nucor's unique way of motivating their workforce and the strong family bond throughout its employment ranks. First, there's pay. Nucor steelworkers make only about $10 hourly, compared to the typical steelworker's $16 to $21 hourly. Managers also earn salaries as much as 20 percent below what competitors pay. But what a difference incentives can make! Based on production incentives for their mills, Nucor's steelworkers averaged $79,000 in pay and incentives in 2005. Then, in 2005, they participated in company profit sharing, topped by a $2,000 one-time bonus that marked the company's record earnings year. That brought the total to $99,000. Workers' incentives are tied not only to quality production in their own mill, but also to that of other mills and overall company profits. They can track their performance each week, so they know exactly where they stand.

However, it's more than just dollars that make Nucor special. The company became the darling of the late 1980s when its unique "pay for performance" system was implemented under then CEO Ken Iverson. Iverson insisted on a culture that would result in employees feeling like owners. In addition to their pay system, Iverson empowered employees to make critical decisions, implement their ideas, and take risks. The rest is history.

Operating in a single North Carolina location then, and in an underdog role to U.S. Steel and other giants, the lean mini-mill company in 2006 has 13,000 employees in 10 locations and is the largest steel producer in the United States, with revenues of $13 billion. Its 387 percent return to shareholders since 2002 has beaten almost all companies listed in the Standard and Poor stock index.

The Nucor culture also includes some symbolic actions, such as every employee's name being placed on the cover of the annual report. There's something egalitarian in the culture as well, such as present CEO Daniel DeMicco flying commercial jets rather than having his own, finding his own parking space in the headquarters lot like every other employee, or making the coffee when it's his turn. In 2005, when the average CEO pay of big companies averaged 400 times that of the hourly employee, at Nucor, DiMicco's was 24 times that of his steelworkers.

Plant managers' incentives are based on the company's overall return on equity, rather than specific results from their own mill. As one stated, "At Nucor, it's not my plant versus someone else's, as they're all 'our' plants. When one plant has a problem it's everyone's problem."

Questions

1. What are the most relevant concepts from the chapter that are reflected at Nucor? Comment specifically about the following:

   Maslow's hierarchy of needs
   Herzberg's motivation–hygiene theory
   Expectancy theory
   Equity theory
   Goal-setting theory

Source: Nanette Byrnes and Michael Arndt, "What Can You Learn From a Company That Treats Workers Like Owners. Inside the Suprising Performance Culture of Stulmaker Nucor," pp. 56–62. Reprinted from May 1, 2006 issue of BusinessWeek by special permission, copyright © 2006 by the MacGraw-Hill Companies, Inc.

8

Leadership

LEARNING OBJECTIVES

After reading and studying this chapter, you should be able to:

1. Describe factors that affect the leadership style used.

2. Discuss and explain two frequently used leadership models.

3. Determine which leadership style is most appropriate in different situations.

4. Contrast heroic supervisors with developmental supervisors.

5. Contrast transformational leadership with transactional leadership.

6. Discuss and explain the benefits and side effects of adaptive leadership.

7. Discuss how to inspire self-confidence, develop people, and increase productivity.

8. Explain why emotional intelligence is so important for effective leadership.

Robert W. Ginn/Alamy

Supervisors may adopt different managerial styles in an effort to influence their employees to achieve company goals.

Leadership is of the spirit, compounded of personality and vision; its practice is an art.
—*Sir William Slim*

Leadership is action, not position.
—*Donald H. McGannon*

Preview

AN IRREVERENT ATTITUDE AND DIRT CHEAP PRICES—A SUCCESSFUL COMBINATION
Jimmy John's Gourmet Sandwiches (JJ) was founded in 1983 by a guy with two first names—Jimmy John Liautaud. His philosophy was simple: Be honest, good, fast, and affordable. However, in the beginning, it was not easy. Even though Jimmy John started with used equipment, the $200 a month rent for store space prevented him from serving ice in the drinks! It didn't matter, the college kids loved the irreverent attitude and cheap prices … and Jimmy John delivered—truly a recipe for success! Today, JJ has become a major player in the sandwich industry with over 690 store locations, which include a limited number of corporate-owned stores. The bulk of the company's growth, however, has been generated through franchising relationships. In fact, the following spiel to attract potential franchisees can be found on the JJ website.[1]

> *Jimmy John's is growing fast and our team is always looking for hard-working people who crave the world's greatest gourmet sandwiches. And we're not talking success as in "shiny new car" success—we're talking success as in "position of power in a worldwide sandwich empire" success.*

> *When you join the Jimmy John's family, anything is possible. It really doesn't matter if you are a delivery driver or a corporate honcho. If you're an entrepreneurial type who's got a strong sense of responsibility and a sense of humor to match, Jimmy John's offers awesome opportunities for growth and adventure.[2]*

Jimmy Burckhartt (Jimmy) owner of Jimmy & Company (DBA Jimmy John's) is a JJ franchisee and the type of individual JJ corporate is trying to attract to grow its business. Jimmy's innate sense of curiosity and passion for life has proved to be a perfect fit with JJ's business philosophy. Starting a new business from scratch is always challenging, even a franchise, but Jimmy has approached his latest opportunity just like those in the past. Even though he may not have envisioned being a restaurant owner when he first began his career, it seems a perfect match.

Jimmy's initial plan after graduating from high school was to earn a bachelor's degree at the University of Louisiana Lafayette, formerly the University of Southwestern Louisiana. One of the exciting aspects of going off to college is the newness or sense of adventure that one experiences, and Jimmy seized life by the horns, taking a full academic load and joining a social organization. It didn't take long with his zest for life before his social activities took priority over academics. Jimmy switched gears, leaving school and becoming a medical paramedic, and ultimately moving to another state to get a fresh start closer to his sister, who was in medical school. He was employed as a medical flight paramedic for several years and gained an enhanced appreciation for learning that can only come with "real world" experience. With his sister's support and guidance, Jimmy eventually went back to school and earned his bachelor's degree.

Armed with a degree and tiring of shift work, Jimmy initially pursued medical school, because he really felt called to help others. In fact, it was this desire to help people that led to an innocent offer to assist one of the nurses with some home remodeling. Little did he know then that this was the first step toward another career move. Jimmy eventually became a contractor and established a successful business, Touchstone Properties. He typically had 10 houses in the pipeline at any given time, but as is the case with many successful entrepreneurs, Jimmy continued to think about other opportunities to diversify his revenue stream. After researching several franchise opportunities, he was actually advised by one of them to give Jimmy John's a hard look, because they were on the rise. His interest piqued, he pursued the lead, and ultimately landed a franchise in July 2007.

This was the beginning of a new and tumultuous adventure in Jimmy's life. He took three months off from Touchstone Properties to get the new franchise up and running. Sherry, his office manager, was very capable, and they had worked together long enough that he trusted her and knew she could handle things in his absence. Sherry did her best to manage affairs from the office, but with the boss away, the on-site crews' productivity levels waned. By the time Jimmy was able to refocus on his construction business, the projects were nowhere near where they should have been, costing him additional money. Thus, he was forced to come up with an alternative plan to manage both businesses successfully. He decided to focus first on getting the existing projects completed, but he would need someone he could trust to handle the franchise in the meantime. The only logical choice was Sherry, but the problem was she had worked in the restaurant business before and had vowed never to work in it again. Jimmy persuaded Sherry to reconsider and help him through this very difficult time. She agreed in large part because of her compassionate nature and the strength of their work relationship.

With Touchstone Properties making up lost ground, it was not long before Jimmy was transferring monies from the construction business to support the franchise, because food and labor costs were running 100% of revenue. At this time, Jimmy made an important decision. He would fully commit to the franchise once all projects were completed, no longer trying to manage multiple business ventures. Once the transition took place, it took him approximately six months (November 2007 to April 2008) of direct on-site management with the franchise to get food and labor costs below 60% of revenues. However, his initial success would prove to be somewhat short-lived because for the next 12 to 15 months, the economy went into a tailspin and business was up and down. Jimmy struggled through the summer of 2008, but business picked up in the fall. Unfortunately in February 2009, he was at a crossroads. He went to the bank and borrowed all he could; it was enough to make payroll for the next two weeks. He had two weeks to figure out how to make Jimmy & Company succeed. You see, all this time Jimmy had been looking for the silver bullet, the one "big" thing that would put him over the top and ensure long-term viability. What he learned surprised him.[3]

Stop & Think

One thing we need to say about motivation is that it cannot take place in a vacuum. For things to happen, effective leadership must be exhibited. This chapter focuses on effective leadership. We do so by expanding on the Jimmy & Company chapter preview case throughout the chapter to illustrate key theories and concepts. Today many supervisors and managers use a less effective leadership style than they could be using, often because they don't have the necessary skills or don't even realize the benefits of using other styles. They don't realize that the most effective style in one situation may not be the most effective in another. Hence, this chapter addresses a number of questions:

1. Why do some leaders use one style and other leaders use another?
2. What effects do different styles have on employee productivity and morale?
3. What style is most appropriate in a particular situation?
4. Should a particular style be used consistently, or should the style be changed as circumstances change?

Such questions are vital for an organization, since supervisory leadership is one of the primary determinants of organizational performance and productivity.

Leadership: What Is It All About?

leadership

Influencing individual and group activities toward goal achievement.

Leadership is defined as a process of influencing individual and group activities toward goal setting and goal achievement. Leadership is a reciprocal process involving the leader and follower(s). Formal leadership is officially sanctioned by an organization through delegation, while informal leadership is unofficial and accorded someone by organizational members. This chapter provides insights and concepts that will assist supervisors in successfully leading their work groups.

Factors Affecting Leadership Style

1 *Describe factors that affect the leadership style used.*

Three factors, or variables, have a major impact on the choice of leadership style: (1) Theory X or Theory Y management philosophy, (2) the followers' readiness level, and (3) the situation faced by the supervisor. As Exhibit 8-1 shows, these factors are interrelated.

Theory X or Theory Y Management Philosophy A supervisor's management philosophy is basically determined by his or her assumptions about the nature of people. Whether they are aware of it or not, most supervisors have a philosophy that influences their style in working with and through people. This philosophy is affected by several factors. Four critical factors interact to influence a supervisor's view of the nature of people and consequently shape his or her philosophy:

1. The supervisor's personality characteristics;
2. The supervisor's family and early school environment;
3. The supervisor's experience and training in the area of leadership; and
4. The supervisor's present work environment, including the type of work and the general management system.

EXHIBIT 8-1
Factors Affecting Choice
of Leadership Style

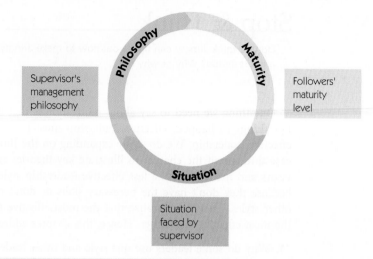

For Jimmy, work has never been about just the paycheck. It has always been more about helping others and the work itself. He is an ambitious person who really enjoys a challenge. His high need for achievement comes naturally and is why "failure" is not in his vocabulary! Coupled with his high need for achievement, Jimmy is also an intuitive personality type, which enables him to be a visionary, seeing all sorts of possibilities, as evidenced by his diverse career interests. He is able to see how the different parts of a business fit together to create a positive servicescape for the customer. As such, Jimmy understands how important each individual employee is to Jimmy & Company's success, but his main focus is coaching people to help them reach their full potential. He has a knack for sizing people up, identifying their strengths, and putting them in positions to succeed.[4]

One of the most widely publicized approaches to the study of management philosophy is Douglas McGregor's concept of Theory X and Theory Y.[5] Based on his consulting and research work in industry, McGregor outlined two contrasting sets of assumptions about the nature of people. A manager's leadership style is influenced by the set of assumptions to which he or she subscribes.

Following are the most significant assumptions of **Theory X**:

1. The average human being has an inherent dislike of work and will avoid it if possible.
2. Because of this human characteristic—dislike of work—most people must be coerced, controlled, directed, or threatened with punishment to get them to put forth adequate effort toward the achievement of organizational objectives.
3. The average human being prefers to be directed, wishes to avoid responsibility, has relatively little ambition, and, above all, seeks security.
4. The average human being cannot be trusted.

Supervisors who accept Theory X assumptions will be more inclined to prefer a structured, autocratic leadership style.

The basic assumptions of **Theory Y** are as follows:

1. The expenditure of physical and mental effort in work is as natural as play or rest.
2. External control and the threat of punishment are not the only means of bringing about effort toward organizational objectives. People will exercise self-direction and self-control in the service of objectives to which they are committed.

Theory X

The average person has an inherent dislike of work and wishes to avoid responsibility.

Theory Y

Work is as natural as play or rest.

3. Commitment to objectives is a function of the rewards associated with their achievement.
4. The average human being learns, under proper conditions, not only to accept but also to actively seek greater responsibility.
5. The capacity to exercise a relatively high degree of imagination, ingenuity, and creativity in the solution of organizational problems is widely, not narrowly, distributed in the population.
6. Under the conditions of modern industrial life, the intellectual potential of the average human being is only partially utilized.
7. The average human being believes that she or he is a winner, so treat her or him like a winner.

Supervisors who hold Theory Y assumptions will be more inclined to prefer a supportive, participative leadership style when the situation calls for it. This last point is important because some people have misconstrued Theory Y by assuming that it always dictates a supportive, participative approach. Although a leader holding Theory Y assumptions about people might prefer a participative approach, the theory does not preclude a tough-minded approach or decisions. For example, Henri Fayol, one of the pioneers of management thinking, used the term "commanding" for what today we call "leading." One of Fayol's principles of command (leadership) is to eliminate the incompetent. However, he indicates that before you take that step, you attempt to develop competence in the employee through training, coaching, counseling, and so on. If these strategies do not work, you eliminate the individual through firing, and everyone knows the action was fair and warranted. This illustration reflects a Theory Y set of assumptions, and the outcome reflects a tough-minded decision.

Edgar Schein, an international expert on organization culture and process consultation, has stated, "Show me an organization that has a key leader with Theory X assumptions about people, and I predict they will eventually screw things up."[6] The authors agree with Schein.

Stop & Think

Which of these Theory X or Y assumptions do you think Jimmy holds concerning his people? Why?

readiness level

The state of a person's drive or need for achievement.

The Followers' Readiness Level **Readiness level** is the state of a person's drive and need for achievement. It results from his or her experience, education, attitudes, and willingness and ability to accept responsibility. These readiness variables should be considered only in relation to a specific task to be performed.

The readiness concept is expressed by the following formula:

$$\text{Readiness} = \text{Ability} + \text{Willingness}$$

If followers are less ready, the leader should use a different style than if followers are more ready. Unfortunately, some supervisors fail to take into consideration the readiness level of their employees.

The majority of Jimmy & Company's employees are under the age of 25. Many never worked in the restaurant business before, and even if they have, they have not worked for someone with such high expectations. Jimmy is not content with just being good; he wants to be the best restaurant—period. For individuals in their late teens or earlier twenties working part-time to pay for their school and social activities, such high performance expectations can be difficult to grasp. Therefore, Jimmy typically has a one-on-one conversation with his new hires soon after they come on board to ensure they have the right attitude and reason for working at Jimmy & Company. You see, Jimmy's philosophy is simple: What you do now, today, ultimately influences what you do in the future. He imparts to his new employees that they need to have pride in what they do, perform their jobs well no matter what, and come to the store every day with a sense of urgency to create the most awesome store in the community. Over time, these actions influence the employees' sense of self-worth, which spills over into other areas of their lives and creates positive career opportunities down the road. As Jimmy states, "If someone is not happy and excited about working here, why spend four to eight hours a day doing something he or she doesn't like? That person needs to find something else that he or she enjoys doing." This straightforward approach has been very effective in terms of employee self-selection decisions—those that are truly committed to Jimmy's vision are the ones that ultimately stay.[7]

The Situation Faced by the Supervisor Common sense dictates that the situation faced by a supervisor should have a major influence on his or her leadership style. A platoon leader directing troops in combat, an airline pilot who suddenly has engine trouble, or a supervisor faced with an immediate safety crisis would certainly not call for a group meeting and get people involved to deal with the emergency.

The nature of the work and the types of assignments must be considered in assessing a situation. Research scientists who perform creative and complex jobs, for example, require more freedom to operate than do workers who perform repetitive, assembly-line work. Finally, a leader's choice of style is influenced by how her or his unit is progressing. For example, a football team with outstanding potential that loses the first three games would get a different leadership response from its coach than a team that had won its first three games.

Two Leadership Models

2 *Discuss and explain two frequently used leadership models.*

Of the many theories and theoretical models regarding leadership, we have selected two that are especially applicable for supervisors. These are (1) Robert Blake and Anne Adams McCanse's well-known Leadership Grid® and (2) Paul Hersey and Kenneth Blanchard's Situational Leadership® Model. Probably more supervisors have been trained using these models than any others. More than a million people have been trained in both the Situational Leadership and Leadership Grid models in 40 countries worldwide.[8] Clearly businesses see these two models as more practical than the theory-based models.

Leadership Grid

Categorizes leadership styles according to concern for people and concern for production results.

Leadership Grid The **Leadership Grid®** in Exhibit 8-2 (originally published as the Managerial Grid by Robert Blake and Jane S. Mouton) shows that a leader has two concerns: production and people.[9] "Concern for Results" is plotted on the horizontal axis of the grid, while "Concern for People" is plotted on the vertical axis. Although the exhibit identifies seven basic leadership styles, theoretically, 81 combinations of "concerns" can be plotted by using the nine-point system in the grid.

authority compliance

The leader has a high concern for production results and uses a directive approach.

If a supervisor is primarily concerned with production and shows little concern for people, he or she is a *9,1* leader (9 in concern for production results and 1 in concern for people). The 9,1 leader is one who structures the work, delegates as little as possible, and usually is an autocrat in getting work accomplished. This style is called **authority compliance** or *task management*.

EXHIBIT 8-2
The Leadership Grid Figure

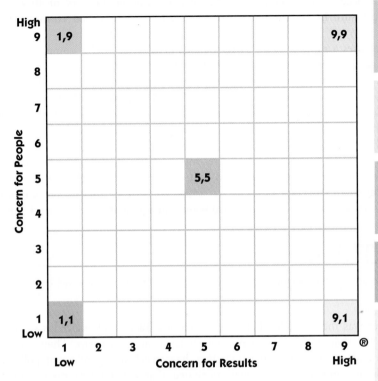

1,9 Country Club Management:
Thoughtful attention to the needs of the people for satisfying relationships leads to a comfortable, friendly organization atmosphere and work tempo.

9,9 Team Management:
Work accomplishment is from committed people; interdependence through a "common stake" in organization purpose leads to relationships of trust and respect.

5,5 Middle of the Road Management:
Adequate organization performance is possible through balancing the necessity to get work out while maintaining morale of people at a satisfactory level.

1,1 Impoverished Management:
Exertion of minimum effort to get required work done is appropriate to sustain organization membership.

9,1 Authority-Compliance Management:
Efficiency in operations results from arranging conditions of work in such a way that human elements interfere to a minimum degree.

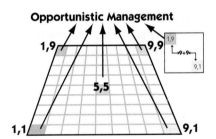

In Opportunistic Management, people adapt and shift to any grid style needed to gain the maximum advantage. Performance occurs according to a system of selfish gain. Effort is given only for an advantage for personal gain.

9+9: Paternalism/Maternalism Management:
Reward and approval are bestowed to people in return for loyalty and obedience; failure to comply leads to punishment.

Source: The Leadership Grid® figure, Paternalism Figure and Opportunism from *Leadership Dilemmas—Grid Solutions*, by Robert R. Blake and Anne Adams McCanse (Formerly *The Managerial Grid* by Robert R. Blake and Jane S. Mouton). Houston: Gulf Publishing Company (Grid Figure: p. 29, Paternalism Figure: p. 30, Opportunism Figure: p. 31). Copyright 1991 by Scientific Methods, Inc. Reproduced by permission of the owners.

Conversely, the supervisor who shows primary concern for people and little concern for production is a *1,9* leader. The 1,9 leader is supportive and somewhat permissive, emphasizing the need to keep employees happy and satisfied. Leaders of this type tend to avoid pressure in getting the work done. This style is called **country club management.**

The *5,5* leader uses a **middle of the road management** style, placing some emphasis on production and some emphasis on people. Usually the unstated agreement in this style is "If you give me reasonable production, I will be reasonable in my demands on you."

The *1,1* leader reflects the poorest of all styles, called **impoverished management.** Supervisors using this type of leadership have completely abdicated the leadership role. If any significant work is done, it is due to the initiative of people working for this leader. In actuality, the leader has retired on the job!

The *9,9* leader believes that the heart of directing work lies in mutual understanding and agreement about what organizational and unit objectives are and about the proper means of attaining them. This type of leader has a high concern for both people and production and uses a participative approach called **team management** to get the work done.

Stop & Think

Which style do you think Blake and associates advocate as the style that works best?

If your answer was the 9,9 style, then you are correct. Blake and associates strongly believe that the 9,9 style is the way to manage in leadership situations. They cite the many managers and supervisors with whom they have worked, regardless of political, religious, or business practices, who have concluded that a 9,9 (team management) leader is using the ideal style.

Hersey and Blanchard's Situational Leadership   It sounds as if we have leadership licked, doesn't it? You may have concluded that the best approach is a high concern for both production and people. But not so fast—a number of people disagree, saying that there is *no one best approach for every situation,* but only a best approach for a given situation.

One of the most popular situational approaches is called the **life-cycle theory of leadership.** It draws heavily on leadership research conducted at Ohio State University. In these studies, leadership behaviors and strategies in a number of different organizations were examined. The researchers concluded that many leadership behaviors fall into one of two areas—task behaviors or relationship behaviors. **Task behaviors** involve clarifying the job; telling people what to do, how to do it, and when to do it; providing follow-up; and taking corrective action. **Relationship behaviors** involve providing people with support, giving them positive feedback, and asking for their opinions and ideas.

These two concepts, along with the concept of the readiness level of followers, are central to understanding the Hersey-Blanchard model.[10] Recall that the readiness level of followers is assessed in relation to their ability to do a *specific* job or task. It encompasses their desire for achievement, experience, education, attitudes, and willingness to accept responsibility. Now that we have a few building blocks, let's examine Hersey and Blanchard's situational leadership model, as shown in Exhibit 8-3.[11]

The Hersey-Blanchard **Situational Leadership® Model** shows the relationship between the readiness of followers and the leadership style based on task and relationship behaviors of leaders. The model consists of four labeled blocks, or quadrants, with a curved line running through each quadrant. At the bottom of the model is a scale showing

country club management

High concern for people.

middle-of-the-road management

Places equal emphasis on people and production.

impoverished management

Management with little concern for people or production.

team management

High concern for both people and production.

3 *Determine which leadership style is most appropriate in different situations.*

life-cycle theory of leadership

Leadership behaviors should be based on the readiness level of employees.

task behaviors

Clarifying a job, telling people what to do and how and when to do it, providing follow-up, and taking corrective action.

relationship behaviors

Providing people with support and asking for their opinions.

EXHIBIT 8-3
The Hersey-Blanchard
Situational Leadership®
Model

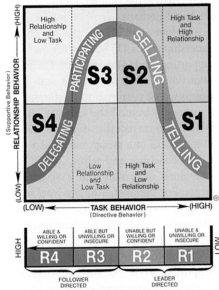

Source: Paul Hersey and Kenneth Blanchard *Management of Organizational Behavior: Utilizing Human Resources,* 8th edition, p. 200. © Copyright 2006 Reprinted with permission of the Center for Leadership Studies. Escondido, CA 92025. www.situational.com All Rights Reserved.

Situational Leadership Model

Shows the relationship between the readiness of followers and the leadership style.

various ranges of readiness: high, moderate, and low. The direction of the arrow on the readiness scale and the direction of the arrow on the task behavior axis indicate that the higher the degree of readiness, the lower the degree of task behavior required.

To use this model, first identify the readiness level of the members of your work group (high, moderate, or low) on the readiness scale. Keep in mind that this point represents your assessment only as to their ability to carry out a *specific* task or assignment. Then draw a vertical line. The point where it intersects the curved line will fall within one of the four quadrants, and the label on that quadrant gives the most effective leadership style for the particular situation.

Hersey and Blanchard use the model to explain not only leadership in dealing with adults, but also parents' leadership in raising children. Let's first illustrate the model using a family situation.

Stop & Think

Assume that a 4-year-old boy is to walk to a birthday party. Although the party is in the neighborhood, it is two blocks away and there are two busy streets to cross. Diagnose the leadership style the child's mother would use to get her son to the party.

If you responded that a high-task and low-relationship style is appropriate, then you are correct. The task involves some danger (crossing busy streets), and the follower is less ready. Hence, the mother should use a structured, high-task approach, accompanying the child and perhaps even holding his hand as they cross the streets.

The four quadrants in the top portion of Exhibit 8-3 can be translated into four basic leadership styles: (1) structuring and telling, (2) coaching and selling, (3) participating and supporting, and (4) delegating. The **structuring and telling style** (S1: high task and low relationship) usually works best with new or less-ready employees and with individuals or groups whose performance is slipping. For example, if a department's costs have increased considerably beyond the standard, then a highly structured, close leadership style would be called for to correct the situation. Thus, the structuring and telling style would be used with an individual or a group that is relatively low in readiness with respect to a given task.

The **coaching and selling style** (S2: high task and high relationship) is best used with individuals or groups that have potential but haven't completely mastered their assignments. For example, a high school football coach with young but talented players should probably use this approach. The coach would have a high concern for both task accomplishment (coaching) and convincing the players through positive reinforcement that they have the ability to win (selling).

An appropriate style to use as individuals or groups mature is the **participating and supporting style** (S3: high relationship and low task). The leader should use more participative management in getting ideas and should involve the followers in setting objectives and solving problems. Think of Maslow's hierarchy of needs theory: As employees gain experience and competence, they have a need for more support for and involvement in their work.

The **delegating style** (S4: low relationship and low task) is one of the more difficult styles for a supervisor to use even when individuals or groups working under the supervisor are exceptionally ready and capable. A primary reason is that the supervisor is held accountable for results and therefore is reluctant to involve employees in her or his work. Perhaps you have heard the expression "If it ain't broke, don't fix it." This saying sums up why the wise supervisor will leave well enough alone as long as results are satisfactory. But what happens when conditions change?

Stop & Think

Suppose you are a supervisor and have a skilled, capable worker who has never caused you any difficulties. For three years, she has been a productive person in your department. Since she has proved to be a capable person, you would probably be using a delegating style in regard to her work. However, in the past two weeks, her work has steadily deteriorated. Projects are late and the work, when completed, is of poor quality. As her supervisor, what leadership style would you use in this situation?

You certainly would not continue to delegate, would you? Most supervisors would shift all the way to a coaching and selling style or even to a structuring and telling style. Depending on what the problem is, either style could be appropriate. This situation shows how a leader might use a different style with an individual or a group, depending on the situation.

Tannenbaum and Schmidt's Leadership Continuum

Robert Tannenbaum and Warren Schmidt are two writers who take a situational viewpoint toward leadership.[12] Their **Continuum of Leadership Behavior,** shown in Exhibit 8-4, is especially useful when a supervisor is considering the degree to which

structuring and telling style

Used with individuals or groups relatively less ready for a given task.

coaching and selling style

Used with individuals or groups that have potential but haven't realized it fully.

participating and supporting style

Best used with ready individuals or groups.

delegating style

Used with exceptionally ready and capable individuals and groups.

continuum of leadership behavior

The full range of leadership behaviors in terms of the relationship between a supervisor's use of authority and employees' freedom.

EXHIBIT 8-4
Continuum of Leadership Behavior

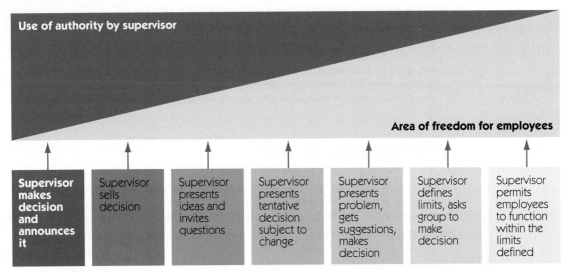

employees should be involved in decision making. The figure is a rectangular block representing a continuum of power, which is divided by a diagonal line into two distinct parts: (1) use of authority by the supervisor and (2) the area of freedom for employees. The more authority the supervisor has, the less freedom there is for employees. Conversely, the more freedom employees are given, the less authority the supervisor uses. The continuum also indicates the range of available behaviors from which the supervisor can draw.

Tannenbaum and Schmidt maintain that each situation calling for a decision may require a different approach. The path the leader chooses to follow should be based on a consideration of the following three types of forces:

1. *Forces in the leader.* These include the leader's value system, confidence in employees, leadership inclinations, and feelings of security or insecurity.
2. *Forces in the employees.* These include the employees' need for independence, need for increased responsibility, knowledge of the problem, attitude toward and interest in tackling the problem, and expectations with respect to sharing in decision making.
3. *Forces in the situation.* These include the type of organization, the group's effectiveness, the pressure of time, and the nature of the problem itself.

These three types of forces can be compared to the three factors affecting leadership (discussed at the beginning of the chapter and shown in Exhibit 8-1). For example, a supervisor's management philosophy is greatly influenced by his or her value system.

The key point to remember is that the successful supervisor is skilled in assessing the appropriate behavior to use in a given situation. Utilizing this approach, how would you deal with the following stop and think question?

Stop & Think

As the result of a dramatic upward shift in sales, the XYZ firm has to rearrange vacation schedules. The previous supervisor consulted individually with employees and, when possible, gave them their first or second choice of vacation time. Because of time pressure, this approach would take too long now. Donna Douglas, the current supervisor, has a lot of confidence in her group of employees. They have a good work record. Drawing from the continuum of leadership behavior, what approach would you recommend that she use in rearranging vacation schedules?

Is One Leadership Style Best?

As we indicated, research supports the thesis that there is no one best style for all situations. However, Hersey and Blanchard and others recognize that, in most situations, the appropriate style is either coaching and selling or participating and supporting. We can learn much from the Blake and associates' thesis regarding the payoffs from utilizing a participative, team approach to managing.

The long-run trend in U.S. industry is for supervisory managers to use more participative styles, although they initially resist the move toward more participation.[13] An explanation for this trend is that employees are becoming better educated and their lower-level needs have been relatively well satisfied. It is only through tapping their higher-level needs, then, that significant motivation will occur. We believe the leadership approaches discussed next (developmental leadership, transformational leadership, adaptive leadership, and servant leadership) are the most affirming of supervisors who hold a Theory Y set of assumptions regarding people. We also believe these approaches are the most rewarding for the employees, the organization, and the supervisors in arriving at win–win outcomes. Although there is some overlap, enough differences exist among the approaches that we present them individually.

Developmental Leadership

4 *Contrast heroic supervisors with developmental supervisors.*

developmental leadership

An approach that helps groups to evolve effectively and to achieve highly supportive, open, creative, committed, high-performing membership.

heroic managers

Managers who have a great need for control or influence and who want to run things.

Earlier in the chapter we noted that no one leadership approach is effective in all situations and that a contingency approach is called for to achieve effective results. In many environments with educated personnel, however, a contingency diagnosis calls more and more for an approach known as *developmental leadership* that is especially effective in managing groups.

Developmental leadership is an approach that helps groups to evolve effectively and to achieve highly supportive, open, creative, committed, high-performing membership. To understand developmental leadership better, let us first examine what David Bradford and Allen Cohen called "heroic management."

Heroic Managers

Heroic managers are those who have a great need for control or influence and want to run things. If they are dynamic and capable, they may do an effective job and produce good results, particularly in the short run. However, it is critical that they do not overcontrol and stymie the development of subordinates. They are depicted very heroically in films, especially those dealing with the Wild West. Some examples are the trail boss who gets the wagon train through to its destination and the sheriff who takes care of the bad guys.

From interviews with managers providing their views of what a good leader is like, Bradford and Cohen developed the following list of characteristics of heroic managers:

EXHIBIT 8-5
The Self-Fulfilling
Consequences of Using
the Heroic Management
Approach

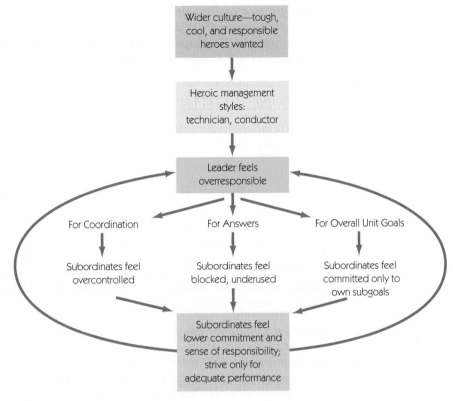

Source: Adapted from *Managing for Excellence.* David L. Bradford and Allen R. Cohen, Copyright © 1984, John Wiley & Sons, reprinted by permission of John Wiley & Sons, Inc.

1. The manager should know at all times what is going on in the department. (In westerns, when asked for information, the trail boss always seems to know what is going on.)
2. The manager should have enough technical expertise to supervise subordinates. (The really good trail boss cannot only outdraw and outshoot anyone around but also handle troublemakers quite effectively with his bare fists.)
3. The manager should be able to solve any problem that comes up or at least solve it before the subordinate does. (If the trail boss cannot handle any problem that arises, he loses face and his leadership position is undermined.)
4. The manager should be the primary (if not the only) person responsible for how the department is working. (The trail boss has total responsibility for the welfare of the group, so shared leadership is out of the question.)

As desirable as these characteristics are, if carried to extremes, they can lead to over-control and lack of development of subordinates, as shown in Exhibit 8-5. Therefore, what is needed is an orientation that focuses on *building heroes* rather than *being a hero*.

Developmental Managers

Building heroes is the goal of developmental leaders. Bradford and Cohen's model of the manager as a developer has three interrelated components: (1) building a shared-responsibility team, (2) continuously developing individual skills, and (3) determining and building a common department vision.[14]

Building a Shared-Responsibility Team In talking about building a shared-responsibility team, we are really talking about shared leadership. Instead of using meetings primarily for reporting and providing information to the group, developmental leaders deal with real issues and actual problem solving.

Stop & Think

Refer to the continuum of leadership behaviors shown in Exhibit 8-4. Which behaviors would support building a shared-responsibility team?

Developing Individual Skills The second component of developmental leadership, continuous development of individual skills, is closely interconnected with the first. One of the best opportunities for individual development is offered by an effective team that deals with real issues. It is no secret that many effective top executives derived considerable development from serving on committees or task forces tackling tough issues. In addition, developmental leaders encourage and seek out opportunities for their people to attend various developmental courses of either a technical or a managerial nature and to increase both knowledge and skills continually.

Shaping a Common Vision Many times, the final component, determining and building a common group vision, is the first step in a manager's movement toward developmental leadership. Bradford and Cohen refer to this as developing the work group's *overarching goal*, which is supportive of the mission and overall goals of the organization. They go on to say that creating a tangible vision makes group members excited about where they are going.

> As noted earlier in the chapter, Jimmy has created a culture centered on the following vision: Have pride in what you do, perform your job well no matter what, understand that what you do today impacts your future, and come to the store every day with a sense of urgency to create an awesome store environment. But as the developmental leadership approach suggests, a common vision is only part of the equation. Fortunately for Jimmy, he is also an effective coach.

> Dale Roberts began working for Jimmy as a delivery driver shortly after the store opened to have something to do while he was between jobs. The job itself was not difficult and the tips were good, so he thought it would be a good fit for a few months. Dale could not have foreseen that 19 months later, he would be the general manager! Jimmy developed Dale slowly during down periods, teaching him how to prep the store in the mornings and close in the evenings. The transition was probably easier because Dale liked the store's "be yourself" environment and has long been passionate about cooking and food. Before long, Dale was promoted to PIC (person in charge), and his responsibilities gradually increased as he learned how to manage schedules, deliveries, time cards, and reports. One reason he was motivated to switch from an hourly position with tips to a salaried employee working 40 to 50 hours a week was the respect and admiration he had for both Jimmy and Sherry. As Dale states, "They're just good people that treat us with respect. If something is on my mind, I know I can go to them and we can talk about it." Dale has become quite confident in performing most of his managerial tasks. The fact that he has developed to a point where he can completely run the store has been a confidence builder. However, he admitted that managing time and people were still challenges for him. Getting everyone to "live the vision" each day can be tricky. Jimmy continues to assist Dale in developing his people skills so that even

Jack Hollingsworth/Photodisc/Jupiter Images

In developmental leadership, the manager needs to have the ability to share a common vision or overarching goal for the group.

when he is in the store and a customer or employee has a question or concern, Jimmy just tells them, "Hey, I'm just the owner. Dale is the manager in charge." This approach not only forces Dale to learn through direct experience, but it is also a source of pride and motivation to know Jimmy has complete confidence in his new General Manager![15]

5 *Contrast transformational leadership with transactional leadership.*

transformational leadership
Converts followers into leaders and may convert leaders into moral agents.

transactional leadership
Leaders identify desired performance standards and recognize what types of rewards employees want from their work.

Transformational and Transactional Leadership

Transformational leadership is one influential theory and way of looking at leadership that has emerged in more recent years; it is closely related to team leadership.

John MacGregor Burns[16] and Bernard Bass[17] were the first to identify and explore the differences between transactional and transformational leadership. Both authors make the case that transformational leadership is a paradigm shift to a more visionary and empowering leadership style, particularly needed in a world of rapid and turbulent change. As Burns states, "the result of transforming leadership is a relationship of mutual stimulation and elevation that converts followers into leaders and may convert leaders into moral agents."

Transactional leadership is a more traditional leadership approach and is similar to an exchange process. For example, a supervisor may implicitly or explicitly get this message across: "If you give me reasonable production, I will keep higher management off your back." Let us first examine transformational leadership and then transactional leadership.

Transformational Leadership

Bass and others have taken Burns' general framework and applied the concepts to the field of management. Their research has resulted in identifying a number of past and current transformational leaders. A recent study found three factors that were an integral part of being a transformational leader—charismatic leadership, individualized consideration, and intellectual stimulation.

The most important factor of transformational leadership is charismatic leadership. *To receive a high score on this factor, a leader would need to instill pride, respect, and esprit de corps and have a gift of focusing on what is really important, as well as a true sense of mission. The second factor,* individualized consideration, *indicates that the leader uses delegated assignments to provide learning and development and gives personal attention to individuals. The third factor,* intellectual stimulation, *indicates that the leader has vision and presents ideas that require rethinking of past methods of operation and allows for development of new ways of thinking.*

Stop & Think

Based on the aforementioned characteristics, who would you consider to be a transformational leader?

Some leaders who have scored exceptionally high on the charismatic leadership factor are R. David Thomas (founder of Wendy's), John F. Kennedy, Dr. Martin Luther King, Jr., Ronald Reagan, Sam Walton (founder of Walmart), and Jack Welch (former CEO of General Electric). Although charisma is important for effective leadership, it may be exercised to meet objectives that do not benefit society—Adolf Hitler and Saddam Hussein are cases in point.[18]

Research today reveals that transformational leaders are not limited to only world-class leaders. In the chapter preview, Jimmy demonstrates many of the characteristics of this type of leader.

Transactional Leadership

Of course, not everyone can be a transformational leader; many leaders fall into the category of transactional leaders. These leaders identify desired performance standards and recognize what types of rewards employees want from their work. They then take actions that make receiving these rewards contingent on achieving performance standards. In essence, this exemplifies an exchange process, a quid pro quo or "I'll do this if you'll do that." The transactional leader operates within the existing culture and employs traditional management strategies to get the job done. Transactional leadership is based on the premise that the leader can positively reward or reinforce employees for their completion of the bargain. For example, if a leader utilized a management-by-objectives system and was able to reward employees who met or exceeded their objectives, this approach would work quite well.

A number of effective leaders demonstrate both transformational and transactional leadership behaviors. One example is Franklin D. Roosevelt, who "illustrated a balance with respect to transformational and transactional leadership.... Roosevelt played the consummate transformational leader with his inspiring addresses, encouragement of intellectual solutions, and fireside chats. He also played the consummate transactional politician in the give-and-take of the balance of powers among executive, legislative, and judicial functions."[19]

Comparison of Transactional and Transformational Leadership One who believes that some people have the ability to grow and develop through levels of leadership and become transformational leaders is George McAleer, former air force pilot and now on the faculty of the National Defense University's Industrial College of the Armed Forces. McAleer agrees with Bass' thesis that transactional leadership can result in lower-order improvements, but if one wants higher-order improvements, transformational leadership is needed. This is the challenge that faces select military officers who are chosen to spend a year at a senior service college such as the Industrial College in Washington, D.C. This year is critical in one's military career: Out of this select group, approximately one in five will become a general or an admiral in the next 5 to 10 years.

In McAleer's words:

"What made them successful up to this point in their careers may not necessarily be the best avenue for them to proceed over the next several years. That's the formidable task my colleagues and I have at the Industrial College. Part of the challenge is encompassed in a course entitled 'Strategic Decision Making.'" [20]

The challenge is to convince these officers that the leadership style that will serve them best in the future as strategic decision makers is transformational. One way to convince them is to contrast the two leadership styles as shown in Exhibit 8-6.

EXHIBIT 8-6
Contrasting Leadership Approaches

TRANSACTIONAL	TRANSFORMATIONAL
Characteristics	
Exchange Process	Relations Orientation
Evolutionary Ideas	Revolutionary Ideas
Within Existing Structure	Emerges in Crisis
Reactive	Proactive
Motivation	
Contingent Reward (Extrinsic)	Inspiration; Recognition (Intrinsic)
Power	
Traditional	Charismatic
Focus	
Outcomes	Vision
Leader	
Specifies Talk	Consultant, Coach, Teacher
Clarifies Roles	Emphasis on Empowering the Individual
Recognizes Needs	Gives Autonomy; Good Listener; Informal
Manages by Exception	Accessible; Model of Integrity
Employees	
Seek Security; Needs Fulfilled	Transcend Self-Interests for the Organization
Separate Organization from Individual	Do More Than They Are Expected to Do
Outcomes	
Expected Performance	Quantum Leaps in Performance

Source: George McAleer's presentation at APT Type and Leadership Symposium, Crystal City, VA, March 5–7, 1993.

Adaptive Leadership

6 *Discuss and explain the benefits and side effects of adaptive leadership.*

adaptive leadership

Organizational members take a hard look at the past to identify what to hold on to, while deciding what needs to go. Employee participation in the change process is the key.

Ronald Heifetz's book, *Leadership Without Easy Answers*, was so well received that he has since coauthored two follow-ups, *Leadership on the Line: Staying Alive through the Dangers of Leading* with Marty Linsky and *The Practice of Adaptive Leadership: Tools and Practices for Changing Your Organization and the World* with Marty Linsky and Alexander Grashow.[21] As these books point out, not all situations require transformational change. **Adaptive leadership** is about organizational members taking a hard look at the past to identify what to hold on to, while deciding what needs to go. Employee participation in the change process is the key, because with adaptive problems, many times the employees themselves are the source. If your people are empowered to evaluate the past and explore new ideas and ways of operating, they will be more motivated to implement the changes. "[A]daptive Leadership requires an experimental mindset approach, not an 'I've got the answer' mindset. It's not enough to have a vision for the future and to identify a critical path for moving forward. Adaptive leaders have to understand that today's plan is simply today's best guess. They must be able to deviate from the plan when they discover realities they hadn't anticipated."[22]

Stop & Think

Based on what you know about Jimmy, would you consider him an adaptive leader? Why or why not?

Amanda Kohn has a unique perspective regarding Jimmy & Company, because she is one of the few employees that has worked in the store since the beginning. She is a family friend of Sherry's and grew up baby-sitting Sherry's children, so when she took the job, she knew what she was signing up for. Her work ethic, people skills, and effervescent personality contribute to her success, such that as soon as she turned 18, Amanda was promoted to PIC (person in charge), providing additional managerial support. When asked about the store's development, Amanda replied, "It takes trial and error to get a sense of what works and what needs to change. We are continuously improving." Before, Jimmy worked seven days a week and never got any time off. "It made a big difference when Jimmy and Sherry decided to promote Dale to General Manager and me to PIC," she shares. "We've created a solid team and the flow of people we have now makes the store feel different." In fact, during one of the in-store interviews, a grandmother, mother, and two children came in to eat lunch and commented on how different Jimmy & Company was from the other local JJ franchise—upbeat, hip, friendly, alive! As Amanda notes, "Every person has the same goal/vision for the store; each day it is about being the best at what we do!" The key has been continuous learning and adaptation to find what works.[23]

Stop & Think

Which would be more challenging for you, switching leadership roles as owner of a construction company to a restaurant or vice versa? Why?

One important issue to be aware of regarding this topic is that many times, adaptive leaders who present tough questions become marginalized within the organization because their views and opinions are not consistent with the current paradigm. Let's face it: People seek comfort in what they know—the familiar. Signals of this resistance include being let go or possibly promoted to a job that has no direct impact on an organization's outcomes.[24] Consider the story of the fall and rise of John Lasseter in Exhibit 8-7.

Adaptive leaders can survive and provide meaningful guidance and direction within traditional command and control environments, but it simply requires an understanding of yourself, the situation, and the people you manage. See the end of chapter case about Kenny the effective supervisor.

Servant Leadership

servant leadership

Defines success as giving and measures achievement by devotion to serving and leading. Winning becomes the creation of community through collaboration and team building.

Although the concept of **servant leadership** has been around for centuries, only recently has it been seriously taught in management and leadership courses. In fact, few supervisory books even mention the concept. Today, however, it is once again recognized as a very powerful and useful concept and philosophy.

The Paradox of Servant Leadership

Bennett J. Sims, Bishop Emeritus of the Episcopal Diocese of Atlanta and president of the Institute for Servant Leadership, provides a beautiful description of the nature of this paradox:

> *The idea of paradox in the abstract is murky, but in a person it can shine like moonlight on tranquil water. Paradox will always need incarnation—embodiment—in order to be real. Logic falls short as a persuader.*
>
> *Consider the paradox of servant leadership. A servant is one who stands below and behind, while a leader's position is above and ahead. Logically then, it is impossible to make these two positions fit a single point in space or in the make-up of one person. But paradox, like servant leadership, is not bound by logic. When paradox is understood as a formula for great truth, then the opposite of a great truth becomes another great truth. Servant and leader combine to form an ideal blend of personal attributes in toughness and tenderness.*[25]

When one of the authors first read this passage by Sims, he immediately thought of an officer he served under in the army. Captain Paul J. Padgent had won a battlefield commission in Korea and was the most highly decorated officer or enlisted man in the 82nd Airborne Division. He carried a pearl-handled revolver, was tough, and had exceptionally high expectations and standards for members of the infantry rifle company he commanded. His troops believed they were the best and would follow him anywhere. An example from a three-month, peacetime, simulated battle in southern Louisiana swamps and forests gives us a clue to his troops' devotion and loyalty. Most of the company commanders had small tents where officers were served individually on plates. Their troops went through a long mess line being served on their mess kits. But in our company, the officers were at the end of the line and followed the troops, and if any item was short, the officers missed it, not the troops. Incidentally, at the end of this three-month field exercise, Captain Padgent's company was singled out as the top-performing company by the umpires.[26]

The United States Marine Corps has a history of training its troops, officers, and noncommissioned officers by placing the well-being of the group before the individual. This notion is an important part of servant leadership and is expounded on in an excerpt from a leadership autobiography by a former student (Exhibit 8-8).

EXHIBIT 8-7
Power and Politics in the
Fall and Rise of John
Lasseter

John Lasseter grew up in a family heavily involved in artistic expression. Lasseter was drawn to cartoons as a youngster. As a freshman in high school, he read a book entitled *The Art of Animation*. The book, about the making of the Disney animated film *Sleeping Beauty*, proved to be a revelation for Lasseter. He discovered that people could earn a living by developing cartoons. Lasseter started writing letters to The Walt Disney Company Studios regarding his interest in creating cartoons. Studio representatives, who corresponded with Lasseter many times, told him to get a great art education, after which they would teach him animation.

When Disney started a Character Animation Program at the California Institute of Arts film school, Disney Studios contacted Lasseter, and he enrolled in the program. Classes were taught by extremely talented Disney animators who also shared stories about working with Walt Disney. During summer breaks from Cal Art classes, jobs at Disneyland further fueled Lasseter's passion for working as an animator for Disney Studios. Full of excitement, Lasseter joined the Disney animation staff in 1979 after graduation from the California Institute of Arts, but he was met with disappointment. According to Lasseter, "[t]he animation studio wasn't being run by these great Disney artists like our teachers at Cal Arts, but by lesser artists and businesspeople who rose through attrition as the grand old men retired." Lasseter was told, "You put in your time for 20 years and do what you're told, and then you can be in charge." He continues, "I didn't realize it then, but I was beginning to be perceived as a loose cannon. All I was trying to do was make things great, but I was beginning to make some enemies."

In the early 1980s, Lasseter became enthralled with the potential of using computer graphics technology for animation but found little interest among Disney Studios executives for the concept. Nonetheless, a young Disney executive, Tom Willhite, eventually allowed Lasseter and a colleague to develop a 30-second test film that combined "hand-drawn, two-dimensional Disney-style character animation with three-dimensional computer-generated backgrounds." Lasseter found a story that would fit the test and could be developed into a full movie. When Lasseter presented the test clip and feature movie idea to the Disney Studios head, the only question the studio head asked concerned the cost of production. Lasseter told him the cost of production with computer animation would be about the same as a regular animated feature, and the studio head informed Lasseter, "I'm only interested in computer animation if it saves money or time."

Lasseter subsequently discovered that his idea was doomed before he ever presented it to the studio head. Says Lasseter, "[w]e found out later that others poked holes in my idea before I had even pitched it. In our enthusiasm, we had gone around some of my direct superiors, and I didn't realize how much of an enemy I had made of one of them. I mean, the studio head had made up his mind before we walked in. We could have shown him anything and he would have said the same thing." Shortly after the studio head left the room, Lasseter received a call from the superior who didn't like him, informing Lasseter that his employment at Disney was being terminated immediately.

Despite being fired, Lasseter did not speak negatively of the Disney organization, nor did he let others know anything other than the project on which he was working had ended. His personal admiration and respect for Walt Disney and animation were too great to allow him to do otherwise.

Lasseter was recruited to Lucasfilm by Ed Catmull to work on a project that "turned out to be the very first character-animation cartoon done with a computer." Not too long afterwards, Steve Jobs bought the animation business from George Lucas for $10 million and Pixar Animation Studios was born. Lasseter became the chief creative genius behind Pixar's subsequent animated feature film successes like *Toy Story*, *Toy Story 2*, *A Bug's Life*, and *The Incredibles*, among others.

In 2006, Disney CEO Robert Iger and Pixar CEO Steve Jobs consummated a deal for Pixar to become a wholly owned subsidiary of Disney. Iger wanted to reinvigorate animation at Disney, and as the top creative executive at Pixar, John Lasseter was viewed as a key figure in achieving this objective. Lasseter "… is regarded by Hollywood executives as the modern Walt [Disney] himself [with capabilities] … that have made Pixar a sure thing in the high stakes animated world." Former Disney Studios head, Peter Schneider, says Lasseter "is a kid who has never grown up and continues to show the wonder and joy that you need in this business." Current Disney Studios chief Dick Cook says that Lasseter is like the famous professional basketball player, Michael Jordan: "He makes all the players around him better."

Lasseter now oversees development of movies at both Pixar's and Disney's animation studios. Says Lasseter, "I can't tell you how thrilled I am to have all these new roles. I do what I do in life because of Walt Disney—his films and his theme park and his characters and his joy in entertaining. The emotional feeling that his creations gave me is something that I want to turn around and give to others."

Source: From Nelson/Quick. Power and Politics in the Rise and Fall of John Lasseter in Instructor's Resource CD-ROM for Nelson/Quick's ORGB 2008 Edition, 1E. © 2009 South-Western, a part of Cengage Learning, Inc. Reproduced by permission. www.cengage.com/permissions

EXHIBIT 8-8
A Distant Drum

Joining the United States Marine Corps at age 17 was the single most important choice I have made for my life. I graduated from boot camp, then from technical school with honors. I was meritoriously promoted and given my choice of duty stations. This was the first real accomplishment I had achieved on my own, and I knew that I didn't even really put forth much effort. It was then that I realized there was a whole world of opportunity available for me, and I was determined to go after a better way of life. I chose El Toro, California, as my duty station. I was proud to be a Marine, and I worked hard in my assigned unit.

I learned innumerable lessons throughout my military service, but the main ones were ingrained during boot camp (the dreaded "Parris Island"), and I live by them still:

1. Tell the truth.
2. Do your best, no matter how trivial the task.
3. Choose the difficult right over the easy wrong.
4. Look out for the group before you look out for yourself.
5. Don't whine or make excuses.
6. Judge others by their actions, not their race, culture, religion, or sexual orientation.

I cannot think of even one important situation in life which cannot be made better by applying these six creeds. I have tried to instill these lessons into my own child, and I am proud to say I believe he lives by them as well.

The exceptional men and women I met and worked with during my military service are still an inspiration to me. I feel a special kinship with each and every Marine I meet.

Source: Cheryl Templet, My Leadership Autobiography, March 1, 1999. A requirement in an MBA Leadership course taught by Donald C. Mosley, Spring Semester 1999, University of South Alabama, Mobile, Alabama.

Characteristics of Servant Leadership

The person to whom we owe the greatest debt for providing us with insights into servant leadership is retired AT&T executive Robert K. Greenleaf. Prior to his retirement, he served seven years as director of management research and led an internal consulting group concerned with the values and growth of people. After his retirement, he worked as a consultant for businesses, foundations, professional societies, church organizations,

Matthew Borkoski/Index Stock Imagery/Photo library

Servant leaders are often empathetic listeners who are committed to the growth of the people they lead.

EXHIBIT 8-9
Ten Characteristics of
Servant Leadership

1. **Listening.** Leaders have traditionally been valued for their communication and decision-making skills. Servant-leaders reinforce these important skills with a focus on listening intently and reflectively to others to identify and clarify the will of a group of people.

2. **Empathy.** Servant-leaders strive to understand and empathize with others. They accept and recognize others for their unique gifts and spirits. One assumes the good intentions of coworkers and does not reject them as people.

3. **Healing.** Learning how to help heal difficult situations is a powerful force for transforming organizations. Servant-leaders recognize that they have an opportunity to help make whole those people and institutions with whom they come in contact.

4. **Persuasion.** Another characteristic of servant-leaders is a reliance on persuasion, rather than using one's positional authority, to make organizational decisions. Servant-leaders seek to convince others, rather than coerce compliance. They are effective at building consensus with groups.

5. **Awareness.** General awareness, and especially self-awareness, strengthen the servant-leader. Awareness aids one in understanding issues involving ethics and values, and it enables one to approach situations from a more integrated, holistic position.

6. **Foresight.** The ability to foresee the likely outcome of a given situation is a characteristic that enables the servant-leader to understand the lessons from the past, the realities of the present, and likely consequences of a decision for the future. It is deeply rooted within the intuitive mind.

7. **Conceptualization.** Servant-leaders seek to nurture their abilities to dream great dreams. This means that one must be able to think beyond day-to-day management realities.

8. **Commitment to the growth of people.** Servant-leaders believe that people have an intrinsic value beyond their tangible contributions as workers. As such, servant-leaders are deeply committed to the personal, professional, and spiritual growth of everyone within an organization.

9. **Stewardship.** Greenleaf's view of organizations is one in which CEOs, staff members, and trustees all play significant roles in holding their institutions in trust for the greater good of society. In effect, everyone has a responsibility for being a good steward within an organization.

10. **Building community.** Servant-leaders seek to build a sense of community among those within an organization.

Source: Larry C. Spears, "Creating Caring Leadership for the 21st Century," The Not-For-Profit CEO Monthly Letter, 5, No. 9, July 1998 (The Robert K. Greenleaf Center for Servant Leadership, 921 East 86th Street, Suite 2000, Indianapolis, IN 46240).

and universities.[27] Greenleaf makes the important point that the servant leader wants to serve first and then lead. The servant leader focuses on meeting the needs of others and responding to problems first by listening. Greenleaf believes that leaders who empathize with others provide a climate in which followers have the ability to grow and develop. Greenleaf also makes the point that leaders "who empathize and who fully accept those who go with them on this basis are more likely to be trusted."[28]

Larry Spears is a scholar who has studied Greenleaf's original writings for a number of years. He is also CEO of the Greenleaf Center for Servant Leadership. He has identified 10 characteristics of servant leadership, shown in Exhibit 8-9.

Stop & Think

Do you think training in servant leadership would be useful for business organizations? Why or why not?

7 *Discuss how to inspire self-confidence, develop people, and increase productivity.*

Core Leadership Functions

The best of the contemporary leadership studies and books support the value of working toward developmental, transformational, adaptive, and servant leadership. Seven leadership functions reinforcing these macro-level approaches are valuing, visioning, coaching, empowering, team building, promoting quality, and listening with empathy. The effective leader is value driven and is able to implement these functions (see Exhibit 8-10). Brief descriptions of the core leadership functions are as follows:

> *Valuing.* Having a good grasp of the organization's values and being able to translate these values into practice and elevate them to higher levels.
>
> *Visioning.* Having a clear mental picture of a desired future for the organization or organizational unit.
>
> *Coaching.* Helping others develop the knowledge and skills needed for achieving the vision.
>
> *Empowering.* Enabling others to move toward the vision.
>
> *Team building.* Developing a coalition of people who will commit themselves to achieving the vision.
>
> *Promoting quality.* Achieving a reputation for always meeting or exceeding customer expectations.
>
> *Listening with empathy.* Clarifying where others are coming from and acceptance of others even with imperfections. Anyone can lead perfect people if perfect people are to be found.[29]

EXHIBIT 8-10

Maureen McNamara: A Profile of an Effective Leader

One who effectively demonstrates the core leadership functions is Maureen McNamara, hospital administrator extraordinaire. Being a hospital administrator is a difficult job today. The industry, in the eyes of one experienced observer, is 10 years behind other industries in employing enlightened leadership and management practices.[30] Maureen attended the Katherine Gibbs secretarial school. The skills she mastered there proved invaluable in her early career, her first job being administrative assistant with the American Mathematical Society. While there, she developed and improved processes and systems for the society. Maureen went on to earn a B.S. in business from the University of Rhode Island and an M.B.A. from Bryant College.

Maureen took a position at Brown University and worked her way through a number of positions in the medical school and at the affiliated hospital. She progressed from management assistant in the department of microbiology and molecular basic science to the dean's office in charge of faculty affairs to assistant administrator for the department of medicine. She was then promoted to associate vice president of operations for the hospital, then to senior vice president of operations, and finally to chief operating officer of the Medical College and hospital. The hospital at that time had 1,500 employees and a budget of $125 million.

Through these positions, Maureen gained insights regarding organization politics and organization inertia and noticed that organizations did not leverage their resources. Each move around the medical school and hospital system gave her increased responsibility, and no matter where she was, she felt she could improve the system and bring people on board.

Her greatest opportunity and challenge came when she was made chief operating officer. She states that she was fortunate to have a CEO who was involved in community and statewide affairs and who allowed her to run the operation. Throughout her career, she confronted issues and problems and took the responsibility for initiating action to solve them.

When going into positions of greater responsibility, it is very important for a leader to know his or her own strengths and to be aware of areas needing help and improvement. Maureen believed her strengths and the reasons for her success were:

- her ability to see the big picture, make connections, and create a vision and mobilize resources to achieve it;
- her ability to inspire others to achieve and grow to an extent they never thought possible;
- her integrity, as well as her direct, candid, straightforward manner; and
- her commitment to always challenge individuals and the organization.

The areas where she perceived she needed help and needed to improve were:

- asking for help (early in her career, she was reluctant to bring others in when she needed help; later this weakness was turned into a strength when she brought in an outside facilitator in organization development [to be discussed later]); and
- listening empathetically and being overly impatient when things did not move or change as fast as she would like.

(Continued)

EXHIBIT 8-10
continued

Her goal and vision were to develop a team approach in delivering health care. In the process of doing so, she wanted to shift the management system to a participative culture and eliminate the undesirable aspects of bureaucracy. Shortly after being made chief operating officer, Maureen faced a major challenge. The union was trying to organize the maintenance and engineering department employees. Maureen had no anti-union feelings; rather, she felt that most unions came into existence to protect employees against poor and arbitrary management practices. She wanted a chance to talk with the 35 employees who made up the department. Prior to meeting with them, she studied the files and backgrounds of each employee. At the meeting she played primarily an active and empathetic listening role. Based on the relationships she built and the approach she took, the union was unsuccessful in two organizing attempts.

Over time, Maureen developed a close relationship with the employees and used their input and participation in an organization development (OD) change program she initiated early in her 10-year stay in senior management. In developing a strategy for the OD change program, she worked closely with Cynthia Bielecki, an excellent and very bright internal staff person in human resources. They decided to bring in an outside consultant to assist them in formulating a shared-leadership approach to improving and managing the organization. They brought in Keith Krewson, who had worked in organization development all of his life and was then in his early 70s. He assisted them throughout the change effort and became a trusted mentor for Maureen.

Some of the innovative steps initiated in the change effort included: changing the organization from within by giving employees ownership of the change process; communicating very early the expectations and goals through oral and written communication and ongoing communication throughout the process; inviting people to apply for two teams—the clinical redesign team and the administrative redesign team; putting on a big party to launch the program and making clear the ground rules and the need to bring in the various stakeholders; going on a retreat into the mountains for team building and action planning; and making herself (Maureen) available to answer questions and having weekly sessions to communicate what was happening.

The outcome was a revitalized organization that became more efficient and effective in delivering patient health care. Leadership expert Joan Goldsmith says it is important for leaders to link commitment with action. She elaborates, "Committed action is sustained over time … and [is] focused on achievement. To encourage committed action, linking leaders radically expand participation and the range of options for organizational direction."[31] Goldsmith's words summarize the success of Maureen McNamara as a leader and team builder. Today, she has her own firm named Bridgework, whose slogan is "Connecting businesses and their leaders to a better future."[32]

Throughout this chapter, we emphasize the importance of values, visioning, empowering, promoting quality, listening with empathy, coaching, and team building. Note the commonality between the core functions and the contemporary approaches to leadership. Also, as we have seen throughout the chapter with Jimmy, leadership of this nature is not restricted to the highest levels of corporate management, but can occur at any level in any size organization.

Like many other managers, Jimmy has strived to achieve the appropriate balance between "driving sales" (task orientation) and "managing employees" (people orientation), and it has not been easy. His values and vision for the store have always been the foundation for the business, but it took time to attract, train, and coach a group of individuals into a cohesive team that bought into his business philosophy. In the meantime, he had to work 80-plus hours, seven days every week, for a year and a half. The secret is to set goals each day that concern your people and your task and take it one step at a time—be patient—which is hard for achievement-oriented people! But over time, this approach enables you to shift from an 80/20 balance between sales and people to a 20/80 split.

When we left Jimmy in the chapter preview, he was facing the most serious professional challenge of his life—enough borrowed cash to keep Jimmy & Company open for two more weeks. Can you predict what happened?

Well, his commitment to the seven core leadership functions, even in the face of extreme adversity (many would have resorted to using a strong task-oriented, command and control style—trying to drive sales), finally paid big dividends. When Dale and Amanda became aware of how dire circumstances were, they felt a sense of urgency. They had developed such strong relationships with Jimmy and Sherry based on mutual trust, respect, and admiration that they simply had to help them figure out how to make it work. It was not an accident that they were developmentally ready to help shoulder the burden at this most critical time. In fact, both Dale and Amanda expressed feeling a "sense of ownership." To understand just how strong those feelings were, consider that Amanda chose to stay in her hometown to go to college rather than attending a university in a different part of the state with many of her friends. She plans to work full-time as a PIC with Jimmy & Company while attending school full-time, playing college soccer, and continuing to help Sherry with baby-sitting.

Jimmy's leadership approach ultimately impacted his company's bottom line. Five months after the cash flow crisis, he is recording record in-store sales, attracting the college students and young professionals in the immediate area, even in one of the toughest economies of the modern era. He just hired a part-time employee whose job it is to visit the local businesses and college campuses to promote and sell catering packages. Jimmy predicts that in a relatively short period of time, he will have the capital to obtain another JJ franchise. His ultimate goal of creating a successful chain of JJ stores is to help Dale or Amanda or others who might want to get set up and take over. Jimmy truly believes that if he can create opportunities to help others, he will have succeeded in life![33]

Stop & Think

Since most of Jimmy's experience has been in health care, construction, and restaurant management, do you think he would be successful if he chose to pursue an opportunity in another industry such as hotel management, banking, or ship building? Why or why not?

8 *Explain why emotional intelligence is so important for effective leadership.*

Emotional Intelligence

An important foundation of successful leaders is a concept called emotional intelligence. **Emotional intelligence (EI)** refers to an assortment of skills and characteristics that influence a person's ability to succeed as a leader. During the 1990s, a healthy dialogue began regarding the true essence of EI. Daniel Goleman, a leading EI researcher, stated, "I.Q. and technical skills are important, but emotional intelligence is the sine qua non of leadership." Goleman and others are proponents of what is referred to as a mixed model of EI that includes the following dimensions: self-awareness, self-regulation, motivation, empathy, and social skill. Goleman suggests that EI not only pinpoints outstanding leaders, but also can be linked to strong performance.[34]

John Mayer and Peter Salovey offer an alternative EI perspective referred to as the four-branch ability model. Their model is a direct response to mixed model proponents, such as Goleman, who suggest that EI is a "catch all" meant to include every human capacity except intelligence quotient (IQ). Mayer and Salovey believe that EI is four distinct skill areas that can be developed in people to enhance their abilities to perceive, process, and manage emotions and behaviors.[35] Exhibit 8-11 provides the four dimensions associated with the four branch ability model. We will briefly summarize each of the four dimensions.

emotional intelligence

The capacity to recognize and accurately perceive one's own and others' emotions, to understand the significance of these emotions, and to influence one's actions based on this analysis; an assortment of skills and characteristics that influence a person's ability to succeed as a leader.

EXHIBIT 8-11
Mayer and Salovey's
Four Branch Model of
Emotional Intelligence

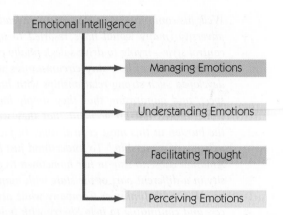

Source: John D. Mayer, Emotional Intelligence Information. (2009, July 31, 2009). The Four Branch Model of Emotional Intellingence. Durham: NH: University of New Hampshire, Retrieved July 31, 2009, from http://www.unh.edu/emotional_intelligence/ei%20What%20is%20EI/ei%20fourbranch.htm. Reprinted by permission of the author.

1. *Perceiving emotion.* The most basic dimension of EI involves accurately perceiving others' emotions through verbal and nonverbal forms of communication. This is the starting point from which one can process the other dimensions.
2. *Using emotions to facilitate thought.* The second dimension is the capacity of the emotions to initiate thinking. When an individual responds emotionally to something, he or she is then cognitively focused. In addition, emotions facilitate as well as hinder creativity and innovation.
3. *Understanding emotions.* "Emotions convey information: Happiness usually indicates a desire to join with other people; anger indicates a desire to attack or harm others; fear indicates a desire to escape, and so forth. Each emotion conveys its own pattern of possible messages, and actions associated with those messages."[36]
4. *Managing emotions.* The last dimension deals with managing emotions. If the information provided by the emotion is understood, then one can "regulate and manage one's own and others' emotions so as to promote one's own and others' personal and social goals."[37]

EI is having a large impact in assessing and evaluating leadership and leaders by researchers and historians. A good example is Doris Kearns Goodwin's work about Abraham Lincoln's presidency. She states that when Lincoln arrived in Washington, he did not have much political experience, but he did have emotional strengths that made him a natural. She writes:

As it turned out, unbeknownst to the country at the time, Lincoln was a towering political genius—not because he had mastered the traditional rules of the game, but because he possessed a remarkable array of emotional strengths that are rarely found in political life. He had what we would call today a first-class emotional intelligence.

To appreciate the magnitude of Lincoln's political success, it helps to understand just how slight a figure he appeared to be when he arrived in Washington. "Never did a President enter upon office with less means at his command." Harvard professor James Russell Lowell wrote in 1863. "All that was known of him was that he was a good stump-speaker, nominated for his availability—that is, because he had no history." His entire national political experience consisted of a single term in Congress that

Emotional intelligence was a major factor in Abraham Lincoln's political success. Lincoln was able to work with people who opposed him. His cabinet included all three of the men he defeated for the Republican nomination.

Bettmann/Corbis

had come to an end nearly a dozen years earlier and two failed Senate races. He had absolutely no administrative experience and only one year of formal schooling. Newspapers described him as a "third-rate Western lawyer and a fourth-rate lecturer, who cannot speak good grammar."

In contrast, his three chief rivals for the Republican nomination were household names in Republican circles. William Henry Seward had been a celebrated senator from New York for more than a decade and governor of his state for two terms before he went to Washington. Ohio's Salmon P. Chase, too, had been both senator and governor, and had played a central role in the formation of the Republican Party. Edward Bates was a widely respected elder statesman from Missouri, a former congressman whose opinions on national matters were still widely sought. All three men, knowing they were better educated, more experienced and more qualified than Lincoln, were stunned when he received the Republican nomination and went on to win the election.[38]

However, Lincoln placed all three defeated candidates in his cabinet. It was a dangerous risk, but Lincoln made sure that he did not have only "yes" men in his cabinet, but some of the best minds in the country. In the introduction to her award-winning book, *Team of Rivals: Political Genius of Abraham Lincoln*, Doris Kearns Goodwin states:

This, then, is a story of Lincoln's political genius revealed through his extraordinary array of personal qualities that enabled him to form friendships with men who had previously opposed him; to repair injured feelings that, left untended, might have escalated into permanent hostility; to assume responsibility for the failures of subordinates; to share credit with ease; and to learn from mistakes. He possessed an acute understanding of the sources of power inherent in the presidency, an unparalleled ability to keep his governing coalition intact, a tough-minded appreciation of the need to protect his presidential prerogatives, and a masterful sense of timing. His success in dealing with the strong egos of the men in his cabinet suggests that in the hands of a truly great politician the qualities we generally associate with decency and morality—kindness, sensitivity, compassion, honesty, and empathy—can also be impressive political resources.[39]

The Influence of Emotional Intelligence at Roadway Express— A Trucking Company

Current researchers and consultants are also publishing important work showing how to change the culture using EI. Ellen Van Oosten of Case Western Reserve and Richard Boyatzis, an early collaborator with Daniel Goleman, give us the story of Roadway Express:

Frank Sims was standing on Roadway Express's shipping dock, watching one of the company's trucks drive away with goods for Specialty Glassware (a pseudonym), one of Roadway's large customers. Frank was worried. The damage problems had been mounting and he was worried about how this might be affecting Roadway's customers. As he walked to his office, Frank began to recall a workshop on emotional intelligence (EI) he had attended recently. Simply recalling the workshop immediately put Frank in a better state of mind: Instead of worrying about the damage and an angry customer, he started to ask himself how he could use what he learned in the workshop to do something constructive and important. As he watched another truck being loaded, an idea began to take shape. What, he wondered, if Roadway's dockworkers and drivers understood how important loading the trucks was for their company? Immediately, he started thinking about how he could engage people in solving the customer's problems.

The dock crew was surprised that the customer's top management would put so much effort into helping them understand the glassware business. He felt good knowing how their efforts fit into the big picture, how important the glassware products were, and how well Specialty Glassware served its own customers' needs. It made them want to be more careful and find ways to help Specialty Glassware succeed. Later on, workers would describe these meetings to new hires as an example of why Roadway was a great place to work.

Leaders like Frank Sims are among the many who can raise the human spirit and make their organizations better. They do so by using their emotional intelligence to create an atmosphere in which people want to do and be their best.... we describe how emotionally intelligent leaders ignite organizations and people to perform better. The article also provides the not insignificant hope that, though EI-based leadership may be rare, it can be developed.[40]

Roadway is a trucking company with more than 20,000 employees and 379 terminals in the United States and Canada. It had a traditional structure that was hierarchical and primarily command and control in the competitive trucking industry. Inspired by Frank Sims' experience, higher management began to look for ways to improve its financial performance, developing a partnership with Case Western Reserve University and designing a tailored program. The leadership program focuses on helping supervisors identify areas for behavioral change and gives them opportunities to apply new habits on the job.[41] Supervisors are also provided with coaches to assist them in mastering five discoveries as shown in Exhibit 8-12.

EXHIBIT 8-12
Boyatzis' Theory of Self-Directed Learning (Goleman, Boyatzis, and McKee, 2002)

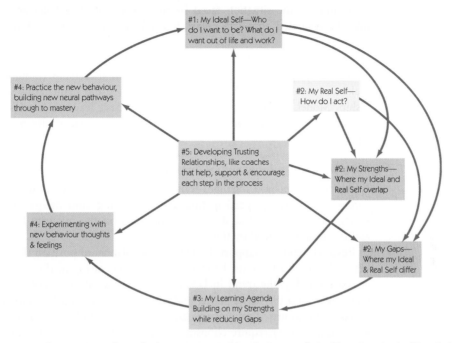

Source: Richard E. Boyatzis, Ellen Van Oosten, "A Leadership Imperative: Building the Emotionally Intelligent Organization," Ivey Business Journal, January/February 2003, p. 3

The culture has changed dramatically, right down to the drivers and mechanics. An example cited in the article noted how a mechanic and driver teamed up to save Roadway $130,000 on one route. Applied to 379 terminals and many routes, it does not take long to see the impact of this one change.

In conclusion, Roadway feels like a new company in an old business. Its people are excited about being leaders and have expanded the ways in which they can make a personal impact. Inspiration and energy have become contagious. A new culture has emerged, one in which people are motivated and innovative. The new Roadway is surpassing many of its competitors in revenue and net profit growth through savvy acquisitions and cost savings during a period that has not been kind to the industry. Roadway's experience is a powerful example of how EI can ignite excitement and inspire better performances from everyone in an organization.[42]

Chapter Review

1. **Describe factors that affect the leadership style used.**

   Leading is a process of influencing individual and group activities toward goal setting and goal achievement. How well this process is carried out has a major impact on both performance and morale.

Three interrelated variables have an impact on the choice of leadership style. These are (1) the supervisor's management philosophy, (2) the followers' readiness level, and (3) the situation faced by the supervisor. The followers' readiness level must be evaluated only with regard to carrying out a specific task or assignment.

2. **Discuss and explain two frequently used leadership models.**

    Two leadership models that are widely used in leadership training programs are Blake and associates' Leadership Grid® and Hersey and Blanchard's Situational Leadership® Model. The Leadership Grid® plots five basic leadership styles. The one Blake and associates recommend as the ideal leadership style is the team management style.

3. **Determine which leadership style is most appropriate in different situations.**

    Hersey and Blanchard highlight four basic leadership styles: structuring and telling, coaching and selling, participating and supporting, and delegating. They make a strong case that the ideal style to use depends on the maturity level of employees and the situation faced by the supervisor.

    Research tends to support the Hersey and Blanchard position that there is no one best style for all situations. However, with the increasing readiness and education of employees today, the trend in U.S. industry is toward using both the coaching and selling style and the participating and supporting style in influencing individual employees and groups. Tannenbaum and Schmidt maintain that each situation calling for a decision may require choosing a solution that balances the three forces found in the leader, the employees, and the situation.

4. **Contrast heroic supervisors with developmental supervisors.**

    Heroic supervision often leads to overcontrol and lack of group development. By contrast, developmental supervision involves the group by using the three interrelated components of (1) building a shared-responsibility team, (2) continuously developing individual skills, and (3) determining a department vision in the form of an overarching goal.

5. **Contrast transformational leadership with transactional leadership.**

    While research supports the thesis that no one leadership style is best for all situations, transformational and transactional leadership styles have emerged as two influential theories. Three important factors of transformational leadership are charismatic leadership (instilling pride, respect, and esprit de corps), individualized consideration (delegating assignments and giving personal attention), and intellectual stimulation (requiring rethinking of past methods and developing new solutions).

    Transactional leadership is a more traditional approach. The transactional leader operates within the existing culture, positively rewarding and reinforcing employees for jobs well done.

6. **Discuss and explain the benefits and side effects of adaptive leadership.**

    Adaptive leadership is about organizational members taking a hard look at the past to identify what to hold on to, while deciding what needs to go. Employee participation in the change process is key, because with adaptive problems, many times the employees themselves are the source. However, adaptive leaders are often marginalized because their views and opinions challenge the status quo.

7. **Discuss how to inspire self-confidence, develop people, and increase productivity.**

   No one single leadership style or model provides a magic formula for inspiring self-confidence, developing people, and increasing productivity. However, by being familiar with all styles, using good common sense, and developing a contingency/situational leadership approach, one can become an effective leader who does realize the preceding objectives. Servant leadership is particularly valuable in inspiring self-confidence, tapping higher-level needs, and developing people.

8. **Explain why emotional intelligence is so important for effective leadership.**

   Research has shown that emotional intelligence is a foundation for successful performance as a leader. There is clearly an assortment of skills and characteristics that influence a person's ability to succeed over the long term. These skills were shown in Exhibit 8-11 and were demonstrated in the leaders profiled in this chapter.

Key Terms

Leadership, p. 227

Theory X, p. 228

Theory Y, p. 228

Readiness level, p. 229

Leadership Grid, p. 230

authority compliance, p. 230

country club management., p. 232

middle of the road management, p. 232

impoverished management., p. 232

team management, p. 232

life-cycle theory of leadership., p. 232

Task behaviors, p. 232

Relationship behaviors, p. 232

Situational Leadership Model, p. 232

structuring and telling style, p. 234

coaching and selling style, p. 234

participating and supporting style, p. 234

delegating style, p. 234

Continuum of Leadership Behavior,, p. 234

Developmental leadership, p. 236

Heroic managers, p. 236

Transformational leadership, p. 239

Transactional leadership, p. 239

Adaptive leadership, p. 242

servant leadership, p. 243

Emotional intelligence (EI), p. 249

Questions for Review & Discussion

1. What is meant by leadership?
2. Briefly discuss the major factors that may influence the choice of an individual's leadership style. Correlate these factors with different leadership styles.
3. Discuss how a supervisor would determine the readiness level of an employee.
4. What leadership actions fall under the category of task behaviors, and what actions fall under the category of relationship behaviors?
5. Do you agree or disagree with Blake and associates that there is one best leadership style? Support your position.
6. Can you identify any transformational leaders from your own experience or reading? Please list the reasons why you placed them in the category of transformational leader. If you cannot identify someone, do you agree with the leaders identified in this chapter—John F. Kennedy, Martin

Luther King, Jr., and George Patton? Why or why not?

7. Can you identify any adaptive leaders based on your experiences or other readings? Under what circumstances will an adaptive leader be most effective? Why?

8. What traits or characteristics regarding servant leadership appeal to you the most?

9. Of the various leadership approaches discussed in the chapter, which one would you most prefer your boss to use in working with you and your group? Explain your reasons.

10. How does transactional leadership differ from the telling and structuring style of Hersey and Blanchard?

11. What are the components of emotional intelligence, and why is emotional intelligence important for effective leadership?

12. Can emotional intelligence be taught to aspiring leaders and integrated into their philosophy and approach? Why or why not?

13. Given what you have learned about Jimmy & Company, how would you describe Jimmy's solution to his situation? Was there a silver bullet?

Skill Builder 8-1

Information

Theory X and Theory Y Attitudes

For each pair of statements, distribute 5 points based on how characteristic each statement is of your attitude or belief system. If the first statement totally reflects your attitude and the second does not, give 5 points to the first and 0 to the second. If the opposite is true, use 0 and 5. If the statement usually reflects your attitude, then the distribution can be 4 and 1, or 1 and 4. If both statements reflect your attitude, the distribution should be 3 and 2, or 2 and 3. Again, the combined score for each pair of statements must equal 5.

Here are the scoring distributions for each pair of statements:

0–5 or 5–0	One of the statements is totally like you, the other is not like you at all.
1–4 or 4–1	One statement is usually like you, the other not.
2–3 or 3–2	Both statements are like you, although one is slightly more like you.

1. ____ People enjoy working.
   ____ People do not like to work.

2. ____ Employees don't have to be closely supervised to do their job well.
   ____ Employees will not do a good job unless you closely supervise them.

3. ____ Employees will do a task well for you if you ask them to.
   ____ If you want something done right, you need to do it yourself.

4. ____ Employees want to be involved in making decisions.
   ____ Employees want the managers to make the decisions.

5. ____ Employees will do their best work if you allow them to do the job their own way.
   ____ Employees will do their best work if they are taught how to do it the one best way.

6. ____ Managers should let employees have full access to information that is not confidential.
   ____ Managers should give employees only the information they need to know to do their job.

7. ____ If the manager is not around, the employees will work just as hard.
   ____ If the manager is not around, the employees will take it easier than when being watched.

8.____   Managers should share the management responsibilities with group members.

____   Managers should perform the management functions for the group.

To determine your attitude or belief system about people at work, add up the numbers (0–5) for the first statement in each pair; don't bother adding the numbers for the second statements. The total should be between 0 and 40. Place your score on the continuum below.

Theory X 0–5–10–15–20–25–30–35–40 *Theory Y*

Generally, the higher your score, the greater your Theory Y beliefs, and the lower the score, the greater your Theory X. Leaders with Theory Y beliefs find it easier to implement participative and empowerment strategies.

Source: From Lussier/Achua. Leadership, Theory, Application, and Skill Development 2E. © 2004 South-Western, a part of Cengage Learning, Inc. Reproduced by permission. www.cengage.com/permissions

Skill Builder 8-2

Information

Diagnosing and Selecting the Appropriate Leadership Style
In each of the following situations, choose the appropriate leadership style. Afterward, your instructor will give you the best and worst answer for each situation.

1. The interdepartmental task force that you manage has been working hard to complete its divisionwide report. One of your task force members has been late for the last five meetings. He has offered no excuses or apologies. Furthermore, he is far behind in completing the cost figures for his department. It is imperative that he present these figures to the task force within the next three days.

   a. Tell him exactly what you expect, and closely supervise his work on this report.
   b. Discuss with him why he has been late and support his efforts to complete the task.
   c. Emphasize when the cost figures are due and support his efforts.
   d. Assume he will be prepared to present the cost figures to the task force.

Systems

2. In the past, you have had a great deal of trouble with one of the people you supervise. She has been lackadaisical, and only your constant prodding has brought about task completion. However, you have recently noticed a change. Her performance has improved, and you have had to remind her of meeting deadlines less and less. She has even initiated several suggestions for improving her performance.

   a. Continue to direct and closely supervise her efforts.
   b. Continue to supervise her work, but listen to her suggestions and implement those that seem reasonable.
   c. Implement her suggestions and support her ideas.
   d. Let her take responsibility for her own work.

3. Because of budget restrictions imposed on your department, it is necessary to consolidate. You have asked a highly experienced member of your department to take charge of the consolidation. This person has worked in all areas of your department. In the past, she has usually been eager to help. Although you believe that she has the ability to perform this assignment, she seems indifferent to the importance of the task.

   a. Take charge of the consolidation yourself, but make sure you hear her suggestions.
   b. Assign the project to her, and let her determine how to accomplish it.
   c. Discuss the situation with her. Encourage her to accept the assignment in view of her skills and experience.
   d. Take charge of the consolidation and indicate to her precisely what to do. Supervise her work closely.

4. Your staff members have asked you to consider a change in the work schedule. In the past, you have encouraged and supported their suggestions. In this case, your staff members are well aware of the need for change and are ready to suggest and try an alternative schedule. Members are very competent and work well together as a group.

   a. Allow staff involvement in developing the new schedule, and support the suggestions of group members.
   b. Design and implement the new schedule yourself, but incorporate staff recommendations.
   c. Allow the staff to formulate and implement the new schedule on their own.
   d. Design the new schedule yourself, and closely direct its implementation.

Source: W. Alan Randolph, Understanding and Managing Organizational Behavior (Homewood, IL: Richard D. Irwin, 1985), pp. 255–257. A complete 20-item Leader Behavior Analysis II questionnaire is available from the Ken Blanchard Companies at 1-800-728-6000.

Skill Builder 8-3

Information

Leadership Characteristics and Skill Assessment

This survey is designed to provide feedback and self-assessment regarding your servant leadership characteristics and your emotional intelligence at work. Read each item listed and decide to what extent you exhibit each characteristic using the following five-point scale:

1—very weak   2—fair   3—average   4—very good   5—excellent

_____ 1. At work I strive to build community within my group.

_____ 2. I do a good job in understanding the personalities of other people, and I usually understand where they are coming from in discussions and problem solving.

_____ 3. I accept the good intentions of others and recognize their unique gifts.

_____ 4. In working with other people, I am trustworthy and have integrity.

_____ 5. In general, I place the interests of my group and customers ahead of my own self-interest unless there is an ethical conflict.

——— 6. I am confident in the work I am doing and have a self-deprecating sense of humor.

_____ 7. I try to listen intently and reflectively to determine where a person is coming from and/or the will of the group.

_____ 8. I tend to pursue goals with optimism, energy, and persistence.

_____ 9. I am committed to the growth and development of people.

_____10. I have developed the skills and feel confident in building and leading teams.

_____11. I rely on persuasion and discussion rather than coercion in team building.

_____12. I am committed and dedicated to providing service to clients and customers.

Instructions: Add your individual scores and divide by 12 to obtain your average.

Scoring scale interpretation:

4.5–5.0	A	Excellent
4.0–4.4	B	Moderately high
3.5–3.9	C	Average
3.0–3.4	D	Below average
2.9	F	Very weak

It would be valuable to have members of your group evaluate you and to compare your self-evaluation with the evaluation from your group.

CASE 8-1

Kenny: An Effective Supervisor

The most effective supervisor encountered by one of the authors of this textbook was named Kenny, and he was maintenance supervisor in a chemical plant of an international corporation.* The author was called in as a consultant because the plant was suffering from the results of the ineffective, autocratic leadership of a former plant manager. Such leadership at the top had adversely affected all levels, resulting in low morale and losses from plant operations. In gathering data about the plant through interviews, questionnaires, and observations, the consultant discovered that one maintenance crew, unlike the rest of the departments in the plant, had very high morale and productivity. Kenny was its supervisor.

In the interview with Kenny, the consultant discovered that Kenny was a young man in his early thirties who had a two-year associate's degree from a community college. The consultant was impressed with his positive attitude, especially in view of the overall low plant morale and productivity. Kenny said that the plant was one of the finest places he'd ever worked and that the maintenance people had more know-how than any other group with which he had been associated. Kenny's perception of his crew was that they did twice as much work as other crews, that everyone worked together, and that participative management did work with them.

The consultant was curious about why pressure and criticism from the old, autocratic manager seemed not to have had any effect on Kenny's crew. The crew gave the consultant the answer. They explained that Kenny had the ability to act as a buffer between upper management and the crew. He would get higher management's primary objectives and points across without upsetting his people. As one crew member described it:

The maintenance supervisors will come back from a "donkey barbecue" session with higher management where they are raising hell about shoddy work, taking too long at coffee breaks, etc. Other supervisors are shook up for a week and give their staff hell. But Kenny is cool, calm, and collected. He will call us together and report that nine items

were discussed at the meeting, including shoddy work, but that doesn't apply to our crew. Then he will cover the two or three items that are relevant to our getting the job done.

Unfortunately, Kenny did have a real concern at the time of the consultant's interview. He was being transferred from the highest-producing crew to the lowest-producing one. In fact, the latter was known as the "Hell's Angels" crew. The crew members were a renegade group who were constantly fighting with production people as well as with one another. The previous supervisor had been terminated because he could not cope with them.

After Kenny was assigned to the new crew, he had to make a decision on the leadership strategies he would use in dealing with them. His initial diagnosis was that the crew had the ability to do the work but lacked the willingness because of a poor attitude.

Through discussion with members of the "Hell's Angels" crew, the consultant learned that on the first day on the job, Kenny called a meeting, shut the door, and conducted a "bull session" that lasted over two hours. Among other things, he told them about his philosophy and the way he liked to operate. He especially stressed that he was going to be fair and treat everyone equally. The crew members were allowed to gripe and complain as long as they talked about matters in the plant, while Kenny played a listening role without arguing with them. In the course of the session, Kenny expressed his expectations of the crew. They, in turn, told him they would do it his way for two weeks to see if he "practiced what he preached."

As you may have surmised by now, Kenny's leadership made the difference. Before the year was out, his new crew was the most productive in the plant. Clues to his success may be found in the following comments made about him by his old crew, his new crew (the former "Hell's Angels" group), the plant's production manager, and Kenny's boss, the plant's maintenance manager.** It should be noted that both the production manager and the maintenance manager are relatively new to their positions and are not part of the former "autocratic management system." As you read these

*The company would not permit use of its name.
**Except for minor editing, the comments are presented as they were made to Donald Mosley.

comments, review what you have learned in the preceding chapters and summarize the principles, points, and concepts from the text that Kenny puts into practice as a leader.

MAINTENANCE MANAGER, KENNY'S BOSS:

- He's very knowledgeable in the maintenance area.
- He has considerable self-confidence.
- He interacts with people in the plant more than other supervisors do and works well with people from other departments.
- He has the ability to motivate his crew and gets along well with them.
- He functions well as a leader in one-on-one situations and in conducting crew meetings. For example, in both cases he lets people know how they stand and provides them with feedback, and together they discuss ways of improving performance.
- He is better organized than most supervisors, and there is less confusion in his department than elsewhere in the company.

PRODUCTION MANAGER:

- He doesn't give the production people any hassle. He doesn't ask a lot of questions about why production wants it done. Instead, he tells the production people what needs to be done and why.
- He's a team player, and he wants to get the job done.
- He's good with people—a great leader—and his crew work well together.
- He's conscientious—he does his job, does it right, and wants others to do the same.
- He goes out into the plant with his people, and he's there with them when they need help and advice.
- His crew doesn't give planners and coordinators a lot of static about what they put into a memo.

KENNY'S OLD CREW:

- He's fair.
- He has a good attitude and a positive outlook.
- He's concerned about and looks out for the welfare of his people.
- He keeps crew problems within the crew and doesn't run to upper management with every little detail.

- He has a broad-based knowledge of our work; people feel confident about his decisions.
- He's a good intermediary between upper management and the crew.
- He gets points across without getting the crew upset.
- When things are tight, he doesn't mind helping his men with the actual work.
- He has a level personality—he doesn't show much emotion.
- He's very supportive of his crew.

KENNY'S NEW CREW (THE FORMER "HELL'S ANGELS"):

- He treats us fairly and equally.
- He takes up for the crew and his men.
- He doesn't threaten you and doesn't come back after a bad job and nit-pick and tell you what you did wrong. He takes a positive approach to solving problems.
- He can be trusted.
- He helps you with your personal problems.
- He's competent at what he does and relates the competency to us.
- He places his employees really well. We're not all like oranges—some are like apples—but he places us where we can do our best.
- He lets us work at our own pace—actually makes us want to work harder.
- He never appears to get angry; he's always the same—cool, calm, and collected.
- He's helpful on the job. He's there, but he's not there—doesn't hang over you, telling you what to do and how to do it. Instead, he wants results but lets us get them our own way.
- He seems to enjoy work and being around us.
- He listens to anything we have to say.

Questions

1. How do you explain Kenny's acceptance by so many other people and the respect they have for him?
2. Can all supervisors operate the way Kenny does and be effective? Explain your answer.
3. Given Kenny's effectiveness in his present job, would you recommend promoting him into high levels of management? Explain.
4. Review the characteristics of transformational leadership (Exhibit 8-6), adaptive leadership, and servant leadership (Exhibit 8-9). Which characteristics apply to Kenny?

9

Group Development and Team Building

Teamwork is a critical factor for success in many work environments, especially in a retail environment such as Family Dollar.

LEARNING OBJECTIVES

After reading and studying this chapter, you should be able to:

1. Identify the stages of group development.

2. Compare the advantages and limitations of groups.

3. Describe the variables that determine a group's effectiveness.

4. Determine what is involved in team building.

5. Describe what made team building successful at Resort Quest.

6. Describe what made team building successful in the nonprofit area.

7. Describe how to work with self-managing work groups.

8. Describe what makes team building successful at SEI.

The essence of [collaboration] is working with people rather than over people or under people.

—Mary Parker Follett

There is nothing permanent except change.

—Heraclitus

CHAPTER OUTLINE

Preview

FAMILY DOLLAR "In 1958, a 21-year-old entrepreneur with an interest in merchandising became intrigued with the idea of operating a low-overhead, self-service retail store. Leon Levine believed he could offer his customers a variety of high-quality, good-value merchandise for under $2. Because he had grown up in his family's retail store, he understood value, quality, and customer satisfaction.

In November 1959, Leon Levine opened the first Family Dollar store in Charlotte, North Carolina, and was on his way to becoming a retailing legend. Right from the start, he had a well-developed philosophy of what Family Dollar would be and how it would operate, a philosophy from which he and his management team have never strayed. The concept is a simple one: "The customers are the boss, and you need to keep them happy."

He created a general floor plan that he used in each of his stores that allowed customers to easily shop for their favorite products in any Family Dollar store. With the stores uniformly laid out and stocked, store managers were able to focus on providing good customer service. This concept for a self-serve, cash-and-carry neighborhood discount store in low- to middle-income neighborhoods proved so successful that today Family Dollar is a chain with over 6,600 stores from Maine to Arizona."[1]

Family Dollar claimed the 359th spot on the 2009 Fortune 500 list and reported an increase of 35.5% in net income for the third quarter of fiscal 2009.[2] Although the company's overall performance is positive, as in many other large corporations, underperforming store units do exist. Thank goodness, because Margaret Gibson just happens to have a knack for turning unprofitable stores around! Known affectionately as the "turn-around lady," Margaret has worked in retail since she was 17 years old. She has been with Family Dollar for over 25 years, during which time she has held a variety of jobs ranging from a front-line employee to district manager. Due to her expertise, she currently floats where needed.

According to Margaret, "There are two keys to turning a store, increasing sales and reducing shrink" (inventory losses). Her most recent "project" involves turning around a store that previously had over $240,000 in shrinkage. The former store manager and all employees were fired by the company, enabling Margaret to start from scratch. She began by hiring nine employees; five had previous dealings with her, which was very important in terms of creating a high-performance team. They understood what they were getting into when they signed on for the job. Margaret openly admits, "I have very high expectations, and I am extremely picky. I don't tell anybody my schedule, because I want to drop in on my days off and see how things are running without me there!" In the beginning, she watched them closer than she does now, but that was part of building an effective team. Initially, morning meetings typically involved Margaret "laying down the law," but she always followed up with some form of positive reinforcement, such as pizza for lunch. She used other positive reinforcement, such as an employee covered dish lunch once a month. Margaret states, "It is important for me to get on their levels and speak to them in a relaxed environment" and vice versa. Such bonding is an important part of team functioning.

A key member of her team is a young man by the name of Vernon Mason who had worked for Margaret before. She was able to persuade him to come on board by promising him she would be flexible with his schedule while he worked on his bachelor's degree in business administration. According to Margaret, "Vernon cares about his job and works extremely hard. He is a self-starter and very dependable. To him, it is more than just a paycheck. Not everyone is cut out to work in retail; it takes a special person, but Vernon has retail in his blood." Margaret learned during their previous stint together that he had a special gift for merchandising, so her goal was to make him assistant manager and teach him the administrative side of the business, especially loss prevention.

Once Vernon mastered the paperwork, he was able to perform every job in the store. In fact, all nine employees are cross-trained to perform all of the store functions except the paperwork. One advantage is that if anyone is ever out for personal reasons, it does not have a negative impact on the team; other employees are able to fill that void. Margaret also assigns each person a specific section of the store based on his or her skills and abilities. Thus, team members feel confident in their abilities to perform their jobs well. This approach to team management pays dividends, especially when the delivery truck arrives, and it only takes Margaret's store half the time to get the stock on the floor compared with other stores within the district.

The team culture is a big reason Margaret has been successful in increasing sales to help turn around this "project" store. Vernon readily admits, "Our store is really a family environment. We do things for the employees to let them know they are doing a good job, like celebrating birthdays. Some have to work two jobs just to make it, but everybody likes their jobs here and is motivated to do well. The employees, in turn, interact with our customers in the same manner. We treat our customers with respect, and we say hello and ask how they are doing. We try to help them find what they need." This family-friendly approach actually attracts the types of customers who respond to those forms of reinforcement, and they continue to come back. In fact, Vernon notes, "Some customers stop to say hello even when they are not shopping!" In addition to heightening sales, Margaret's team has been able to curb shrinkage as well. Family Dollar's average shrinkage is approximately 2.5, whereas, Margaret's store average is 1.91. Such success is motivating for her team, because raises are partially based on inventory management.[3]

EXHIBIT 9-1
External and Internal
Change Forces

External change forces

Educational

Cultural

Social

Organization

Natural
resources

Political/legal

Economic

Technological

Internal change forces

Worker activities/abilities/attitudes

Objectives

Technology,
resources

Policies

Organizational structure

Source: Donald C. Mosley, Paul Pietri, Leon Megginson, Management-Leadership in Action, 5th ed, 1996, HarperCollins, p. 425.

As the chapter preview indicates, creating and maintaining an efficient and effective team can be challenging but quite rewarding. Throughout this chapter, we will cover team-related topics ranging from team formation to team development and change. In addition, we approach teambuilding from several vantage points to assess commonalities as well as differences, but first, the forces that necessitate team functioning are presented.

Forces Causing Change

Numerous factors affect an organization. Continuously changing forces leading to or causing change originate both outside and within the organization, as shown in Exhibit 9-1. You might compare this situation to yourself. You must respond to such external stimuli as the condition of the weather, the requirements of your daily work schedule, and the different needs arising each day. Also requiring responses are the internal stimuli, such as your hunger level, the state of your health, or your attitude. A similar situation exists when we substitute an organization for the individual.

External Change Forces

external change forces

Forces outside the organization that have a great impact on organizational change. Management has little control over these numerous external forces.

Management has little control over the strong impact of numerous **external change forces**. Yet an organization depends on and must interact with its external environment if it is to survive. Specifically, resources, profits, and customers for products and services are all from the outside. Therefore, any force that impacts or changes the environment affects the organization's operations and brings about pressures requiring a change response. External forces—from technological advancements to consumers' changing requirements—cause an organization to alter its goals, structure, and methods of conducting business.

Stop & Think

Suppose you were the director and owner of a 30-bed nursing home. What are some kinds of external change factors that might have an impact on your organization?

internal change forces

Pressures for change within the organization such as cultures and objectives.

Internal Change Forces

Change forces also come from within. **Internal change forces** may result from different organization goals or new challenges, as in the case of Family Dollar. Or, they may be caused by new quality initiatives, changing technologies, or employee attitudes. For example, shifting the goal from short-run profit to long-term growth directly impacts the daily work of most departments and may lead to a reorganization that will streamline overall operations. Changing to automated equipment and robots to perform work previously done by people will cause changes in work routine and just-in-time supplies. Altering incentive programs and personnel policies and procedures may result in different hiring and selection procedures. Employee attitudes about child and/or parent care, insurance needs, or flexible working hours may change daily business practices.

External and internal forces for change are often interrelated, not isolated from one another. At times, this linkage results from the changes in values and attitudes affecting people within the system. Some of these changes from within are from people who have entered the organization. For example, many of the changes now occurring in organizations are the result of the increasing availability of a highly trained workforce, including the need for increased flexibility and responsiveness of the organization to employees' and customers' needs and a flattened hierarchy allowing greater responsibility to be placed with front-line workers.

Planned Change

organizational effectiveness

The result of activities that improve the organization's structure, technology, and people.

For management to plan for change, it must decide what needs to be changed in the organization. In general, management seeks to change things that prevent greater organizational effectiveness. **Organizational effectiveness** results from activities that improve the organization's structure, technology, and people so it can achieve its objectives.

The nature of the problem causing the organization to be less than ideally effective determines the choice of the particular technique used to achieve change. From a choice of alternatives, management must determine which one is most likely to produce the desired outcome. Diagnosing the problem includes defining the outcome that is desired from the change. In general, the desired outcome is either improved employee behavior or activities that will result in improved performance. This can be achieved by changing the organization's structure, technology, and/or people (Exhibit 9-2).

This classification of organizational elements in no way implies a distinct division among elements. According to the systems concept, a change in one element is likely to affect other elements. In general, the more change that is required, the more likely it is that management will change all three elements.

Management must decide the desired outcomes and the type of change programs to use to change the specific organizational element—including those activities needed to get the work done effectively (Exhibit 9-2). Changing the organization's *structure*

EXHIBIT 9-2
Organizational Effectiveness Results from Changing Structure, Technology, and/or People

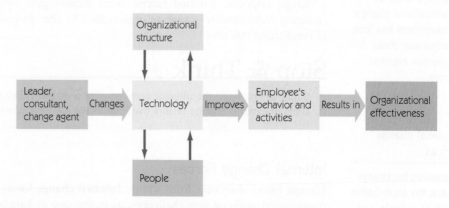

Source: Mosley, Pietri, Megginson, op. cit, p. 429.

EXHIBIT 9-3
Different Responses to
Change

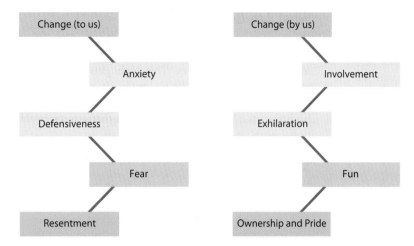

Source: William Walker, management consultant, presentation to the North Mississippi Health Services Board of Directors and staff, May 1, 1999. The Wynfrey Hotel, Birmingham, Alabama.

involves modifying and rearranging internal relationships. This includes such variables as authority–responsibility relationships, communications systems, work flows, and size and composition of work groups.

Changing the organization's *technology* may require modifying such factors as its tools, equipment, and machinery; research direction and techniques; engineering processes; and production system, including layout, methods, and procedures. Changing technology may result from or contribute to changing tasks to be performed. Products and other inputs may be altered. For example, mechanization changes the nature of work performed.

Changing the organization's *people* may include changing recruiting and selection policies and procedures, training and development activities, reward systems, and/or managerial leadership and communication.

Supervisors and employees are likely to support change if they perceive the change as being directed at the real cause of the problem, as being an effective solution, and as not affecting them adversely. Most importantly, those who participate in a change process respond entirely differently than those merely affected by it. Exhibit 9-3 shows these different responses to change.

Next, we turn to the study of group dynamics, which will provide greater insight into creating a climate of positive change.

Importance of Work Groups

synergy

The concept that two or more people working together in a cooperative, coordinated way can accomplish more than the sum of their independent efforts.

To achieve synergy and to gain the most from employees, organizations require groups. **Synergy** means that the whole is greater than the sum of the parts. This is especially applicable when using teams and ad hoc task forces. Assume that a five-person ad hoc task force is given the opportunity to solve a problem that has an impact on the entire organization. If the team reaches a synergistic solution to the problem, then synergy can be mathematically defined as $1 + 1 + 1 + 1 + 1 = $ more than 5. It is important for supervisors to understand the basic concepts of group or team development because work groups or teams produce the synergistic effect needed for management to reach its goals.

What Are Groups?

Groups have been defined in various ways. The definition we prefer is that a **group** is two or more people who communicate and work together regularly in pursuit of one or more common objectives. This highlights the point that at least two individuals must work together to constitute a group. If a group becomes too large, interaction among all members is difficult. This leads to the evolution of smaller groups. Remember, one finding of the Hawthorne studies was that groups could be either supportive of organizational goals or opposed to them overall.

Types of Groups

Groups in organizations are either formal or informal. Formal groups are those created by the organization. The most common example is the group formed by a manager and his or her immediate team members. Informal groups evolve out of the formal organization but are not formed by management. Neither are they shown in the organization's structure. An example would be a friendship group that enjoys discussing sports during lunch.

Formal Groups are deliberately formed by management and are often shown on the organizational chart. For example, command groups are formal groups composed of staff who report to a designated manager, such as a group of vice presidents for worldwide marketing. Committees and task forces are additional examples of formal groups. Later in this chapter, we examine the increasing use of self-managing work teams, another example of formal groups created by management. Exhibit 9-4 illustrates how one manager can be a member of several different groups while employed by one organization.

Informal Groups evolve out of the employees' need for social interaction, friendship, communication, and status. Although not a part of the formal organization, an informal group can sometimes be the same as a formal work team. The group members might give more allegiance to the informal leader than to the formal manager.

Other types of informal groups cross formal work team boundaries and are based on common interests. An informal interest group may come together to seek increased fringe benefits or attempt to solve a particularly broad-based software problem. Another type of informal group is a friendship group. Its members also have common interests, but they are more social in nature. Such groups could include a running team, a band, or the people who gather to chat during a break.

In general, informal groups provide a valuable service by helping members meet affiliation and social needs. Ideally, management tries to create an environment in which the needs and objectives of informal groups are similar to the needs and objectives of the formal organization.

How Groups Develop

B. W. Tuckman developed a model of small-group development that encompasses four stages of growth.[4] A desirable feature of this classical model—which basically has been followed by later researchers[5]—is that it examines the stages in terms of task functions and interpersonal relations, both essential concerns of any group.

Stages of Group Development The stages of group development defined by Tuckman are (1) forming, (2) storming, (3) norming, and (4) performing. There is some overlap between the stages, and the length of time spent in each stage can vary. However, the central concept is that a group will usually remain in a stage until key issues are resolved before moving to the next stage. Sometimes a group appears to have resolved key issues but really

EXHIBIT 9-4
A Manager's
Membership in
Different Groups

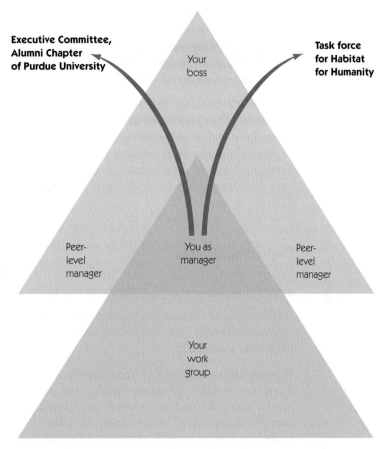

Source: Adapted from W. Alan Randolph, *Understanding and Managing Organizational Behavior* (Homewood, Ill.: Richard D. Irwin, 1985), p. 385.

has not. In this case, after moving to the next stage, the group will have to shift back to the earlier stage to resolve the unsettled issue. The characteristics of each stage follow.

Stage 1: Forming This is the stage in which members first come together and form initial impressions. Among other things, they are trying to determine the task of the group and their role expectations of one another. In this stage, members depend on a leader to provide considerable structure in establishing an agenda and guidelines, since they tend to be unsure of what is expected of them.

Stage 2: Storming The storming stage is typically a period of conflict and—ideally—organization. Conflicts arise over goals, task behaviors (that is, who is responsible for what), and leadership roles. Relationship behaviors emerge, in that people have strong feelings and express them, sometimes in a hostile manner.

It is a mistake to suppress conflict; the key is to manage it. If a group gets through stage 2 successfully, it becomes organized and begins developing norms, rules, and standards.

Stage 3: Norming This is a stage of developing teamwork and group cohesion and creating openness of communications with information sharing. Members feel good about one another and give each other positive feedback, and the level of trust and cooperation is usually quite high. These desirable characteristics of team development result from establishing agreed-on goals and finalizing the processes, standards, and rules by which the group will operate.

If the issues of the earlier stages have not been resolved, the group can regress. Later in this chapter, we will discuss norms in more detail.

Stage 4: Performing This is the stage in which the group shows how efficiently and effectively it can operate to achieve its goals. Information exchange has developed to the point of joint problem solving, and there is shared leadership.

As one organizational behavior text points out, "Some groups continue to learn and develop from their experiences and new inputs.... Other groups—especially those that have developed norms not fully supportive of efficiency and effectiveness—may perform only at the level needed for their survival."[6] Thus, group development, like individual development, is a continuing process.

Evaluating Groups

2 *Compare the advantages and limitations of groups.*

Groups, whether formal or informal, are a fact of organizational life. In this section, we discuss some important advantages and limitations of groups.

Advantages of Groups Among the major advantages of groups are that they (1) provide members with opportunities for need satisfaction, and (2) may function more effectively than individuals.

Provide Opportunities for Need Satisfaction Group membership provides an opportunity for members to satisfy security and relationship needs as well as higher-level esteem and self-actualization needs. Group membership can be highly satisfying. For example, being viewed as a member of a high-performing problem-solving task force brings out feelings of pride. At times, a task you perceive as drudgery may actually turn out to be less distasteful when you are working together in a group.

May Function more Effectively than Individuals Synergy is the concept that two plus two can equal five. This is one of the major potential advantages of groups. The combination of members possessing different perspectives, experiences, and job skills can often work in a team's favor. Moreover, individuals operating as a group may feel a collective responsibility that often leads to higher motivation and commitment.

Limitations of Groups Among the general limitations of groups are that they may (1) encourage social loafing, (2) diffuse responsibility, and (3) be less effective than individuals.

Encourage Social Loafing Social loafing is the term used to describe "taking a free ride" when working with others as a team. We have all known team members who did not pull their weight as part of a team writing a group term paper or putting together a classroom presentation. Generally, social loafing occurs because some members genuinely believe that their contributions to the group are not that significant or they hope for a free ride. Free riders are reinforced when they receive rewards or recognition on an equal basis with those who have carried the greater load.

Diffuse Responsibility

The diffusion of responsibility among members of a group is somewhat related to social loafing and is also one of its major causes. Because each person may be expected to do only a part of a project, no one person may feel totally responsible. Diffused responsibility

Manfred Rutz/Photonica/Getty Images

Employees who work in groups often find they are able to accomplish more than they can by working alone. In addition, working in a group can be a satisfying social experience.

may result in groups assuming positions that individual members would not take if held individually accountable. The "Oh, what the heck" attitude, as well as the idea that "they" will handle it, leads to more liberal risk taking. This also means that the more mundane, routine, and undesirable group tasks may be neglected by individual members in the hope that someone else will complete them.

May be Less Effective than Individuals Although the concept of synergy is an attractive argument in favor of group effort, the sad fact is that sometimes two plus two equals three. One classic study showed this effect dramatically. One would expect a group of three pulling on a rope to exert three times the pulling power that each could attain separately. Such was not the case: Groups exerted a force only two and a half times the average of individual performance.[7]

Thus, as a result of social loafing, diffusion of responsibility, and other factors, groups may not necessarily be more productive and effective than individuals.

Determining Group Effectiveness

3 *Describe the variables that determine a group's effectiveness.*

What are the key factors determining the effectiveness of groups? Exhibit 9-5 highlights the essential variables affecting group satisfaction, goal accomplishment, and productivity. As the model demonstrates, there is a cause-and-effect relationship between leadership (the causal variable), group characteristics (the intervening variables), and the end result variables. Variables affecting group effectiveness are (1) group size, (2) member composition and roles, (3) norms, and (4) group cohesiveness.

Group Size Without question, the size of the work group has an impact on a group's effectiveness. The size of a group depends to a large extent on its purpose. Organizations can take a contingency approach to determining a manager's span of control, which

EXHIBIT 9-5
Model of Group
Effectiveness

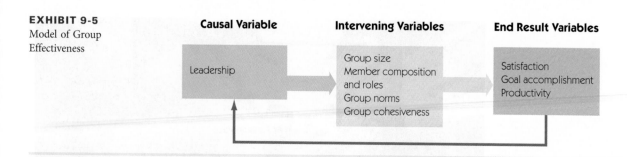

EXHIBIT 9-6
Possible Effects of Size on Groups

CATEGORY/DIMENSIONS	GROUP SIZE		
	2–7 MEMBERS	8–12 MEMBERS	13–16 MEMBERS
Leadership			
1. Demands on leader	Low	Moderate	High
2. Differences between leaders and members	Low	Low to moderate	Moderate to high
3. Direction by leader	Low	Low to moderate	Moderate to high
Members			
4. Tolerance of direction from leader	Low to high	Moderate to high	High
5. Domination of group interaction by a few members	Low	Moderate to high	High
6. Inhibition in participation by ordinary members	Low	Moderate	High
Group Process			
7. Formalization of rules and procedures	Low	Low to moderate	Moderate to high
8. Time required for reaching judgment decisions	Low to moderate	Moderate	Moderate to high
9. Tendency for subgroups to form within group	Low	Moderate to high	High

Source: Adapted from Hellriegel/Slocum/Woodman. Organizational Behavior, 10E. © 2004 South-Western, a part of Cengage Learning, Inc. Reproduced by permission. www.cengage.com/permissions.

influences the size of the natural group. With the increasing use of committees, task forces, quality circles, and self-managing work teams, we need additional guidelines for determining the size of these types of groups. Exhibit 9-6 provides some guidelines on the effects of size on group leadership, members, and group processes.

It has been our experience that the ideal size for a problem-solving group is five to seven members. As Exhibit 9-6 highlights, with this size, there is less chance for differences to arise between the leader and members, less chance of domination by a few members, and less time required for reaching decisions. In company and project workshops, we usually use ad hoc task forces of five to seven to study an issue and report back to the larger group with a recommended plan of action. Almost invariably, the action plan is accepted with only minor modifications. The one time we ran into difficulty was when we used a larger group—14 people—to develop an action plan. In that instance, the reported agreement was later sabotaged by a subgroup of the original group of 14. Their complaint was that the agreement had been rushed through by two of the more dominating members. On the other hand, one study has found that a group of 14 members is the ideal size for a fact-finding group.[8] This shows once again that the ideal size depends on the group's purpose.

Member Composition and Roles The composition of a group has considerable impact on productivity. At the minimum, the ability of members to carry out the mission is a major factor. The more alike members are in age, background, value systems, education, personality type, and so forth, the more similarly they will see things. The literature suggests that for tasks that are relatively simple and require maximum cooperation, homogeneous groups are superior.[9] Conversely, for complex tasks, groups composed of members with widely differing backgrounds are superior because a greater number of different ideas would be generated, increasing the probability of creativity.

Whatever the group's composition, key task and maintenance roles must be carried out if the group is to be effective (Exhibit 9-7). In carrying out the group's activities,

EXHIBIT 9-7

Task and Maintenance Roles in Groups

EFFECTIVE ROLES		INEFFECTIVE ROLES
WORK OR TASK* FUNCTIONS	**GROUP MAINTENANCE* FUNCTIONS**	
Initiating. Proposing tasks or goals; defining need for action; suggesting a procedure or an idea for a course of action.	*Consensus testing.* Checking with the group to see how much agreement has been reached, or now near it is to a united conclusion.	*Displays of aggression.* Deflating others' status; attacking the group or its values; joking in a barbed or semiconcealed way.
Information giving. Offering facts; providing relevant information; giving an opinion.	*Harmonizing.* Attempting to reconcile disagreements; reducing tensions; getting people to explore differences.	*Blocking.* Disagreeing/opposing beyond "reason"; stubbornly resisting group wishes for personal reasons; using hidden agenda to thwart the movement of a group.
Information seeking. Requesting facts; seeking relevant information; checking on meaning; asking for suggestions or ideas.	*Gate keeping.* Helping to keep communication channels open; facilitating the participation of others; suggesting procedures thst permit sharing remarks,	*Dominating.* Asserting authority or superiority to manipulate group or some of its members; hindering others' contributions; controlling through flattery or other farms of patronization,
Clarifying. Interpreting ideas or suggestions; defining terms; clarifying issues before group; clearing up confusions.	*Encouraging.* Being friendly, warm, and responsive to others; indicating by facial expression or remark the acceptance of others' contributions; giving others opportunity for recognition.	*Playboy behavior.* Making a display, "playboy" fashion, of one's lack of involvement, "abandoning" the group while still physically in it; seeking recognition in ways not relevant to group task.
Summarizing. Pulling together related ideas; restating suggestions after group has discussed them; offering a decision or conclusion for group to consider	*Compromising.* When one's own idea or status is involved in a conflict, yielding status; admitting error; disciplining oneself to maintain group cohesion.	*Avoidance behavior.* Pursuing special interests not related to task; staying of subject to avoid commitment, preventing group from facing up to controversy; filibustering.
Reality testing. Making a critical analysis of an idea; testing an idea; testing an idea against some data to see if the idea would work.	*Sharing feelings.* Sensing feelings, moods, relationships within the group; sharing feelings with other members; sharing observations on group processes.	*Sniping.* Ridiculing opinions and ideas of others by word or action; personal criticism.

*The distinction between "task" and "maintenance" roles is somewhat arbitrary. Some of these terms could be classified in either column.

members tend to shift back and forth between these roles naturally. This is especially true in problem-solving groups and in regular work teams where the formal leader is skillful in getting everyone to participate.

Many members in a problem-solving group will play several task or maintenance roles. Unfortunately, ineffective roles or behaviors, such as dominating, can have a negative impact on group effectiveness (see Exhibit 9-7). The skill is for the leader to operate so that members share the leadership role and ineffective behaviors are minimized. Exhibit 9-8 is a questionnaire allowing individual members of a group to assess how well they function in helping the group achieve its goals and in minimizing ineffective behaviors.

EXHIBIT 9-8

Assessing Your Behavior as a Team Member

Instructions:

Select a team you are currently working with or have worked with in the recent past. Assess your behavior on each item for the team that you selected by using the following scale.

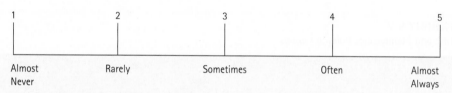

1	2	3	4	5
Almost Never	Rarely	Sometimes	Often	Almost Always

Place the appropriate number value next to each item.

Task-oriented behaviors: In this team, I …

_____ 1.   initiate ideas or actions.

_____ 2.   facilitate the introduction of facts and information.

_____ 3.   summarize and pull together various ideas.

_____ 4.   keep the team working on the task.

_____ 5.   ask whether the team is near a decision (determine consensus).

Relation-oriented behaviors: In this team, I …

_____ 6.   support and encourage others.

_____ 7.   harmonize (keep the peace).

_____ 8.   try to find common ground.

_____ 9.   encourage participation.

_____ 10.   actively listen.

Self-oriented behaviors: In this team, I …

_____ 11.   express hostility.

_____ 12.   avoid involvement.

_____ 13.   dominate the team.

_____ 14.   free ride on others.

_____ 15.   take personal credit for team results.

Total scores of 20–25 on task-oriented behaviors, 20–25 on relations-oriented behaviors, and 5–10 on self-oriented behaviors would indicate that you are probably an effective team player.

Source: Adapted from Hellriegel/Slocum/Woodman. Organizational Behavior, 10E. © 2004 South-Western, a part of Cengage Learning, Inc. Reproduced by permission. www.cengage.com/permissions.

norms

Rules of behavior developed by group members to provide guidance for group activities.

Norms are generally thought of as rules of behavior developed by group members to provide guidance for group activities. Norms, standards, and action plans in an effective team are highly interrelated and are supportive of the organization's goals. However, if a group is not well led, negative norms will result, working against the organization's goals. An example of a negative norm is an informal leader in a construction team sending the message, "Don't rush the work—they'll just give you more to do."

The critical role of leadership is especially important in influencing positive norms. An example of a positive norm is the informal leader in a marketing group sending the message, "Make sure it looks nice—we want to be proud of our work." Business ethics are similar to norms in that they provide guides to behavior. The top leadership of an organization has significant influence on ethical normative values of groups as well as individuals.

group cohesiveness

The mutual liking and team feeling in a group.

Group Cohesiveness is the mutual liking and team feeling in a group. As we have already seen, size plays a major part in the cohesiveness of a group. Another major factor is the frequency of communication.

In the partnering workshops we have conducted, communications were frequently issue-oriented. This led to the development of group cohesiveness. Agreement on overall goals, with the processes and plans to achieve those goals, also enhances group cohesiveness.

Conversely, the major factors preventing group cohesiveness are dysfunctional conflicts, internal power struggles, and failure to achieve goals. However, sometimes a group will be very congenial, agree on goals, and feel like a team, yet fail in its mission.

Three other concepts that play a key role in healthy group development are listening, supporting, and differing. How many times have you been in a group discussion and been cut off in midsentence? How many times have you been thinking about the point you want to make next rather than listening to the other person? Sometimes we find ourselves responding to another person's idea or suggestion with the thought, "That's a great idea—I would never have come up with that." At those moments, it is important to give positive feedback in support of the suggestion if we want to create a supportive group environment for generating ideas. Finally, and perhaps most important for creativity in groups, is the creation of an environment in which people can disagree without being disagreeable. In several of the end-of-chapter activities, you will have an opportunity to solve an unfamiliar problem first on your own and then in a small group. While working in the small group, make a conscious effort to carry out the concepts of listening, supporting, and differing.

Different Approaches to Team Building

4 *Determine what is involved in team building.*

team

A collection of people who must rely on group cooperation.

Now that you have an insight into groups and group dynamics, we focus on teams and team building. Many supervisors are now shifting to the role of team leader, so we will use that term through the chapter. A **team** is a collection of people who must rely on group cooperation if the team is to experience the most success possible and thereby achieve its goals.[10] Experience has demonstrated that successful teams are "empowered to establish some or all of a team's goals, to make decisions about how to achieve those goals, to undertake the tasks required to meet them, and to be mutually accountable for their results."[11]

Unfortunately, a number of teams do not achieve their optimum success and potential. This is often caused by the team leader's leadership style being too autocratic or too permissive in managing the group. Consequently, several of the characteristics of an effective team are lacking. These characteristics are shown in Exhibit 9-9. The following sections illustrate how these characteristics of an effective team are implemented through the use of organizational team building.

Teams and organizations may not be successful because they fail at one or more of the following concepts, first identified by the renowned leadership expert, John W. Gardner:

1. effective leadership at the top of the team and/or organization;
2. effective recruitment of good and talented people; and
3. the creation of an environment so good and talented people grow and develop.

To gain insight into how effective these concepts and characteristics are, we examine team building in various types of organizations.

EXHIBIT 9-9
Characteristics of an
Effective Team

Clear Purpose	The vision, mission, goal, or task of the team has been defined and is now accepted by everyone. There is an action plan.
Informality	The climate tends to be informal, comfortable, and relaxed. There are no obvious tensions or signs of boredom.
Participation	There is much discussion, and everyone is encouraged to participate.
Listening	The members use effective listening techniques such as questioning, paraphrasing, and summarizing to get out ideas.
Civilized Disagreement	There is disagreement, but the team is comfortable with this and shows no signs of avoiding, smoothing over, or suppressing conflict.
Consensus Decisions	For important decisions, the goal is substantial but not necessarily unanimous agreement through open discussion of everyone's ideas, avoidance of formal voting, or easy compromises.
Open Communication	Team members feel free to express their feelings on the tasks as well as on the group's operation. There are few hidden agendas. Communication takes place outside of meetings.
Clear Roles and Work	There are clear expectations about the roles played by each team member.
Assignments	When action is taken, clear assignments are made, accepted, and carried out. Work is fairly distributed among team members.
Shared Leadership	While the team has a formal leader, leadership functions shift from time to time depending on the circumstances, the needs of the group, and the skills of the members. The formal leader models the appropriate behavior and helps establish positive norms.
External Relations	The team spends time developing key outside relationships, mobilizing resources, and building credibility with important players in other parts of the organization.
Style Diversity	The team has a broad spectrum of team-player types, including members who emphasize attention to task, goal setting, focus on process, and questions about how the team is functioning.
Self-Assessment	Periodically, the team stops to examine how well it is functioning and what may be interfering with its effectiveness.

Source: Glenn M. Parker, *Team Players and Teamwork*, p. 33. Copyright © 1991 Jossey-Bass. Reproduced with permission of John Wiley & Sons, Inc.

Team Building in the Sales and Service Sector

The hospitality industry has for some time been one of the fastest growing service sectors in the United States and around the world. One of the many players nationally is a company called Resort Quest, which specializes in selling, managing, and renting properties in beach and ski resorts. Although Resort Quest has long been active in the Destin and Sandestin beach areas of Florida, in 2000, they moved into the Perdido Key area (sometimes called the Lost Key), which is located between Gulf Shores, Alabama, and Pensacola, Florida.

In 1973, only two resort condominiums were in Perdido Key. When Resort Quest placed sales agents on Perdido Key in 2000, there were over 100 resort properties and more were being built. This story is about the development and achievements of a small sales team and what we can learn from their experience.

Leadership at the Top

Pete Mulry is the leader at the top of the sales unit at Perdido Key. Rather than thinking of himself as a traditional hierarchical leader, who exerts power and influence from above, Pete operates as a team leader using shared leadership and serving as a facilitator/coach with the sales team in the achievement of results, which are outstanding. The Perdido Key office has the highest gross sales and profits with the least number of independent sales agents in the entire company.

The background of Pete Mulry provides some interesting insight as to his current success as a team teacher/coach/facilitator. Pete is very dynamic and has spent most of his career as a coach/teacher. He coached baseball, basketball, and football in the Tampa area and was quite successful. He had also completed course work in counseling through the doctoral level when he decided to make a career change.

Jeff Greenberg / PhotoEdit

The hospitality industry is one of the fastest growing service sectors in places like Perdido Key, Florida.

He went to work for Diversified Marketing. With this company, he had the opportunity to manage his own business or move into a sales management leadership program. Pete started out by learning to sell door to door and moved very rapidly from sales into managing his own business, other businesses, and finally, managing the entire company as the number two man.

When he started in Gulf Shores with Diversified Marketing, there were three sales offices, and when he left 10 years later, there were 54 locations. He left Diversified Marketing when he saw the company taking a different direction than where he wanted to go, which was into real estate sales and development. As a leader, he learned that helping enough people get to where they want to go would lead to win-win outcomes and synergistic results. He also observed that excessive micromanagement could keep some young leaders from reaching their potential or even cause them to fail.

When Pete became the leader of the Perdido Key sales team, it was struggling. In a short time, it became an effective, cohesive team with outstanding results, due in large part to Pete's being the causal variable in recruiting, creating a climate for growth, and coaching. This led to significant improvements in communications and teamwork.

Recruitment of Good People

Most of the sales agents have had successful careers and experiences prior to joining the Perdido Key sales team. Kathy, the one I have singled out, is an outstanding individual, as well as a team contributor, and is recognized as an outstanding mentor. She willingly shares information and knowledge with other members of the team.

Kathy At our first meeting, Kathy came across as personable, dynamic, and knowledgeable. According to the experienced agents at Resort Quest, Kathy's strengths are a positive attitude, outstanding knowledge of the amenities of over 100 properties on Perdido Key, and great people skills. Her educational background includes a B.S. in Mechanical Engineering from Florida State University. She told the author that she was surprised at how much her engineering background had helped her in selling condos.

Her first job was with Procter & Gamble in research as a product development engineer. She left Procter & Gamble with an outstanding performance record, including several patents that she developed in the feminine product area, and proved to herself that she could be successful in a large international company.

Stop & Think

Do you see any parallels between Pete Mulry and Margaret Gibson's approach to team development? Why or why not?

The Creation of an Environment for Growth and Development

5 *Describe what made team building successful at Resort Quest.*

Many people will tell you that one of the most difficult tasks in sales is to develop true teamwork and sharing of information. There is a limited supply of potential customers, and each salesperson's compensation directly relates to what he or she sells. It is perceived that each salesperson is competing with the others, and that it is in the best interest of the sales team members to keep information about prospects or sales techniques to themselves. Several members of the Perdido Key sales team have been in organizations where secrecy prevails and cutthroat competition exists. It is refreshing to be in an environment where information is shared and people help each other. Individuals cover for each other in emergencies and nonemergencies. On many occasions, individual and team successes are celebrated by the entire team.

One team member stated that Pete Mulry has the uncanny ability to select people who have the desire to succeed. If they leave the team, they usually do so with a positive attitude about their experience at Resort Quest. One person who left for a better opportunity was Matt Callan, a former Marine pilot, who thanked the team prior to leaving, saying "it has been a great life and learning experience being in this group."[12]

To develop a high performance sales team, Pete Mulry first brought in an outside facilitator, Tim Duncan, to assist in team building. Duncan held some coaching sessions with the team as a whole, as well as with individuals of the team. Based on his experience as a teacher/coach and his insights from his doctoral program, Pete was confident that this step "would help us let down our barriers and our fear of competition." Team members learned to listen, to connect, and to communicate. Over time they began to feel a part of the team and to develop ways to help each other. They moved from the platinum rule of "treat people as they want to be treated" to the golden rule of "treat other people as I want to be treated."[13]

Stop & Think

If you were the team leader, would you make it mandatory for the independent sales agents to attend team meetings or allow voluntary attendance?

A Nonprofit Approach to Teamwork and Team Building

6 *Describe what made team building successful in the nonprofit area.*

The Providence Hospital and Sacred Heart Hospital Cancer Center provides a good example of effective teamwork in every aspect of patient care. Seven doctors of varying specialties are at the center. The three interviewed for this chapter were Dr. Michael Meshad, Dr. Thadeus Beeker, and Dr. Nicole Angel.

Dr. Michael Meshad received his medical education and training at the University of Alabama, in Birmingham, Alabama. He served in Special Forces in the military and was a paratrooper. He enjoys an excellent reputation as an oncologist with an outstanding personality and sense of humor. He was one of the first to see the potential for the center.

Dr. Thaddeus Beeker, a graduate of Wake Forest University, where he played baseball, later received his medical degree from Vanderbilt University. Dr. Beeker was recruited because he has some special talents needed in Mobile. He is the only doctor south of Birmingham, Alabama, who is qualified to do stem cell transplants obtained from the patient's body, as well as other complex treatments. He has the reputation of being on the cutting edge in cancer research and diagnosis. He also treats the whole person and is very interested in receiving feedback on how well patients are doing and how they can do better. Dr. Beeker facilitates communications between doctors, nurses, and staff concerning treatment for cancer patients. One professional who is not under the direct supervision of the Cancer Center, but who has worked with the patients' families, is impressed that Dr. Beeker has asked her to attend his patient visits and has asked her for suggestions on the treatment of the whole person.

Dr. Nicole Angel joined Dr. Meshad and Dr. Beeker in part because she was attracted by Dr. Meshad's reputation and his vision for the center. She likes all of her coworkers and likes the fact that they work as a team. In addition, she states, "The nurses are the best I have ever worked with." One experienced nurse stated, "The doctors trust and respect the nurses, and the patients love the doctors."

The nurses are no small part of this successful team effort. Gail Havard was selected to be Patient Care Manager of the 17 nurses in the Cancer Center and is well received by her former team members. They can depend on her to help them when they are busy, and she is very supportive in working with the team. Gail serves as a mentor to the younger nurses and as coach and advisor regarding diet and the handling of side effects in patients from high-dose chemotherapy. Being a cancer survivor herself, she gives helpful tips concerning living with cancer that are not found in the cancer literature. Gail uses a participative style and consults with and involves her nurses in the decision-making process for new hires. The doctors give Gail excellent evaluations. The outcome is a great nursing team that is both efficient (doing things right) and effective (doing the right things).

The observations summarized below were made over a period of 6 months, through many conversations with doctors, nurses, and staff:

1. The Cancer Center's top priority is taking care of patients.
2. On a scale of 1 to 10 for rating communication among nurses, between doctors and nurses, and among the team, the scores are 9 or 10.
3. The nurses know each job and are able to cover in emergencies or just to help out.
4. The nurses do not hesitate to approach any doctor if they need guidance or prescriptions.
5. Regular meetings are held with the doctors and nurses to discuss opportunities for better patient care.
6. A staff member is provided to interview all patients regarding care, treatment, positives, and any complaints.

Providence Hospital, through its affiliation with nationally established Ascension Health, has worked with Sacred Heart Hospital in Pensacola, Florida, to develop the Cancer Center's treatment program. Then the Cancer Center sought an affiliation with M. D. Anderson Cancer Center in Houston to give Mobile patients access to advice and treatment from the well-known "Andy" Center. The patients will be able to access a second opinion from M. D. Anderson and will have opportunities to participate in clinical trials being conducted at M. D. Anderson and seek records of cancer cases and treatments to determine their best options for treatment. The M. D. Anderson Cancer Center is one of 60 national cancer centers designated by the federal National Cancer Institute to receive additional research funding and to offer more advanced care to cancer patients. Within 24 hours of a local patient's diagnosis, the Cancer Center's physicians are able to hold a conference with M. D. Anderson physicians to discuss the diagnosis and treatment. If a patient needs to go to Houston, his or her medical information will already be in the system, and the Cancer Center can facilitate the trip.[14]

The partnership of Ascension Health, M. D. Anderson, Providence Hospital, and the Sacred Heart Cancer Center team is a giant step toward bringing better diagnosis, timely treatment, and better care to cancer patients through effective teamwork.[15]

7 *Describe how to work with self-managing work groups.*

Self-Managing Work Teams

Today, management is undergoing a transformation, partly because of self-managing work teams that tend to operate by member consensus rather than management direction (Exhibit 9-10). Europe has been in the forefront of experimenting with self-managing work teams, but managers in Canada and the United States are increasingly using teams as building blocks in a corporate renaissance. Estimates suggest that over 500 U.S. manufacturing plants use some form of **self-managing work teams**. Illustrated here is the experience of a small southern plant.

self-managing work teams

Groups that tend to operate by member consensus rather than management direction.

EXHIBIT 9-10
How to Succeed with Self-Directed Work Teams

The self-directed work team is usually thought of as a "leaderless" group of workers who take the place of supervisors and fulfill many management functions.

However, many of the attempts to install self-directed work teams have failed because the teams have neither the skill nor the experience to ensure their successful outcome.

There are some guidelines, if followed, which can increase the success of self-directed teams. Some of the guidelines are not simple and do take some work but they can decrease the mistakes management often makes in trying to develop teams.

1. Have a well thought-out vision of how these teams will fit into the scheme of the entire organization. A common vision of the leadership must be in place and supported by everyone in management with a complete understanding of the concept of teams.

2. With this vision, the entire organization must be prepared to change the culture to support the teams. Teams may be radically counter to what the organization has been doing, so the preparation must be thorough. The change must be a result of incremental steps so everyone will understand the vision and philosophy behind the change. Employee attitudes are sometimes difficult to change, so they will have to have a good idea as to what the teams will do for them and what's in it for them. Management must have a complete understanding of the culture of the organization and how to change it.

3. The organization must have the resources necessary to commit to this type of change in time, money, and people. A large upfront investment will be needed and the time frame will be long-term. People to train and develop the teams will be needed. Either in-house personnel (if they have the skills) or consultants can initially be used, but in the long-term, facilitators and supervisors must be available to help the team. Management must be certain that they have assessed the resources accurately and are willing to commit them to the endeavor.

4. Training is an extremely significant part of developing the teams. Team members must be trained in skills to allow them to function together: conflict management (probably the most difficult skill for team members to learn), assertiveness, communication (listening in particular), problem solving and decision making, and other skills that will enable people to work together effectively. At the same time, facilitators and supervisors must be trained to work with teams. There are new skills supervisors will need to help the teams be successful. It is important they get these skills. Coaching and counseling are skills a supervisor must learn to help the work teams.

5. After the training takes place, it will take time for the teams to get used to one another and develop their new-found skills. When the training is over, the development begins and the development is just as important as the training. Many organizations believe that once the training is over, the teams are ready to function, and this is not necessarily the case. Some teams will take longer to develop than others. Management must have the patience and people available to help this development. In fact, development is an ongoing process and if done correctly, will never end.

6. Performance expectations of the teams must be developed so they will know what is expected of them. The performance standards must be attainable and not "pie-in-the-sky" type standards no one really understands or will be able to achieve. Not only must expectations be developed but also a method to measure these expectations so management can actually see what the teams are accomplishing. Many organizations never measure team performance, and this is a very disastrous mistake.

7. A feedback method to teams must be developed so they can also see what they are doing and make corrections where necessary. The only way there can be continuous improvement in performance is for them to know where they are in relation to the developed standards. If they know, they can and will improve.

8. Boundaries must be set in which the teams will be allowed to operate. This is different from performance expectations in that the teams have to know and understand the limits of their empowerment. Many organizations start right off wanting teams to make "all" the decisions. The problem is the organization doesn't really understand what "all" means and they have problems because the teams are making decisions they should not be making. When management corrects the decision, it causes a setback in team development and long-term effectiveness. Teams should start with narrow boundaries, maybe only simple decisions until they begin to understand and become more comfortable with the decision-making process. As the teams become more sophisticated, they can expand their boundaries and take on more complex decision making. However, teams should only make decisions which affect their immediate team.

9. Do not develop the thinking that self-directed work teams are "leaderless" or never need management intervention. These teams may be able to take over some of the functions of management, but to think they will never need "coaching" or guidance and they will survive on their own will lead to failure of the teams. Supervisors will not be completely replaced, but they will develop a new roll [sic] of coaches and advisors to teams. These advisors, having been trained to work with teams, can help the teams be very successful, or they can cause a serious problem. If they offer the kind of facilitation needed, they can make the difference between success and failure.

These are guidelines to help develop successful self-directed work teams. There are no overnight successes that have been documented as of yet. I doubt there will ever be, but if these guidelines are followed, there can and will be long-term success.

Source: Capozzoli, T. (Feb. 2006). How to succeed with self-directed work teams. Supervision, 67, 2, p.25(2). Reprinted by permission of National Research Bureau.

A small parts plant is owned by a large corporation and employs 320 workers. Most of the self-managed work teams consist of eight to 12 members who select their own leader. At the next level are coordinators, who work with several teams. The coordinators report to an upper-management group called the support team. The coordinators operate primarily as developmental leaders. Their basic leadership practice is to encourage the teams to do things themselves—to be self-managing. Under this structure, there are productivity gains of significantly more than 20 percent.[16]

Even companies that rely on an appointed leader make use of some empowerment concept of self-managed work teams. Michael Lloyd Odom, who received IBM's Global Project Manager of the Year award, is a prime example (only 25 people worldwide have received this award).

One of Mike's projects was running into some difficulty, and he was receiving a lot of negative feedback about one of the team members. Although this team member had good technical skills, he was insecure, and with the layoffs, he feared he was going to lose his job. If there was a problem on the project, he would point a finger and accuse other team members of being at fault. As a consequence, a lot of defensive behavior was taking place within the team.

Mike called the problem employee in and, in essence, held up the mirror and gave him the feedback Mike was receiving from other team members. He also urged the employee to bring any issue or problem to the team as a whole and not to criticize individual members. He emphasized winning or losing *as a team.* He also called in other team members, one at a time, and asked for support in changing this employee's attitude and helping him become a team player. The problem employee was able to turn it around, and the project was successful, meeting or exceeding objectives.[17]

Lessons Learned by Mike Odom

1. "IBM values its people as a key asset. It places a high priority on development of its people. I share the strong belief that people are your greatest asset."
2. "You need to understand the principles of managing a project."
3. "To be successful you have to build a good team; picking a good team is the first step."
4. "You need to be a good coach and work with people to help them understand what it takes to be successful."
5. "A key thing is to understand you are not alone. We are a lot smarter as a team than we are as individuals."
6. "Attitude can make all the difference in the world, not only from the standpoint of the team leader, but from the standpoint of all team contributors."
7. "A team leader's management style can make the difference between a high-performing team and a team that just gets the job done."
8. "I think having good coaching skills is even more important than good technical skills in project management."

Stop & Think

In what type of business environments do you think self-managed teams would be most effective? Easier to implement and manage?

In a team environment, the leader functions like a coach, picking the right members, helping them develop their skills, and recognizing their individual and team achievements.

Team Building in the Financial Sector

8 *Describe what makes team building successful at SEI.*

SEI (NASDAQ: SEIC) is an international provider of asset management, investment processing, and investment operations software for institutional and wealth management funds. The company's clients include banks, investment advisors and managers, institutional investors, and affluent individuals.[18]

As one would imagine, SEI's stock, like most other finance-related businesses, has not performed well during the recent economic meltdown. However, SEI has the potential for strong growth as it emerges from the downturn.[19] Workplace design is one reason for the optimism. Consider the following description of team structures at SEI.

> *When a new employee joins SEI, it is an unusual experience. The new hire is given a map and sent down to a storeroom on the lower floor of the main building. There, the employee is issued a chair and desk, both on wheels, with a computer and phone on the desktop. The map shows where in the complex of nine barnlike buildings on the corporate campus in Oaks, Pennsylvania, the new hire will initially be located. The employee then rolls the desk through the buildings, into the oversized elevators designed for this purpose, and past hallways filled with a provocative (and sometimes shocking) collection of contemporary art.*

> *In a large, open room (filled with similar desks on wheels), the employee finds the spot on the map, nudges neighboring desks aside and pulls down a thick, red wire that snakes down from the ceiling, containing computer, phone, and electrical connections. Once this "python" is plugged in, the company computer recognizes the new employee and routes calls or visitors to the location. Welcome to work.*

The message from Day One is clear. This is an organization that is flexible, creative, and ready for constant transformation. The company is open and not hierarchical. The atmosphere and dress code is business casual. There are no corner offices—or offices at all. There is no need for an open-door policy because there are no doors. Employees are empowered. They can pick up their entire "office" and move to another location to join another team. On average, with the exception of a few anchored departments, they will relocate about twice a year. This may sound unsettling—but that is the point. In a world in which the business environment can change overnight, particularly in financial services, this design gives SEI the flexibility and the mindset to transform itself just as quickly.

While this might not work for every organization, the buildings and artwork at SEI are designed to reflect the culture of the organization. This environment has helped to make SEI a perennial member of Fortune's list of "Best Companies to Work for in America."[20]

Stop & Think

Would SEI's approach work for furniture manufacturers? Shipbuilders? Resort hotel chains? What type of organizations would be best suited for SEI's model?

Chapter Review

1. **Identify the stages of group development.**

    The focus turns to the development of work groups and the types—formal and informal—and stages of development. Formal groups are those formed by management. Informal groups are those that are not part of the official organizational structure and evolve out of employees' affiliation needs. An examination of synergy tells us that two or more people working together in a cooperative way can accomplish more than the sum of their independent efforts, and to achieve synergy, it is important for a group to move through all four stages of group development: forming, storming, norming, and performing.

2. **Compare the advantages and limitations of groups.**

    The primary advantages of groups are that they (1) give members an opportunity for needs satisfaction and (2) may function more effectively than individuals. Some limitations are that they may (1) encourage social loafing, (2) diffuse responsibility, and (3) be less effective than individuals.

3. **Describe the variables that determine a group's effectiveness.**

    Group effectiveness is determined by (1) group size, (2) member composition and roles, (3) norms, and (4) group cohesiveness.

4. **Determine what is involved in team building.**

    Teams are successful if they have effective leadership at the top, effective recruitment of talented people, and an environment permitting good people to grow. The supervisor relies on group cooperation to establish the team's goals and to make decisions to achieve these goals.

5. **Describe what made team building successful at Resort Quest.**

   The leader at the top of the sales team recruited good people and created a climate for growth. This led to improvement in communication and achieved outstanding results.

6. **Describe what made team building successful in the nonprofit area.**

   Communication between doctors, nurses, and staff is very good. The nurses know each task and can cover for each other in emergencies. Doctors and nurses hold regular meetings to discuss how to provide better patient care.

7. **Describe how to work with self-managing work groups.**

   Self-managing work teams have an impact on transforming organizations. Although some individuals and teams occasionally have difficulty coping with increased managerial responsibility, in general, employees in self-managing work teams are more satisfied, and production and quality show improvement. However, any company shifting to a participative team approach needs to ensure that the reward system is supportive or the move could backfire.

8. **Describe what makes team building successful at SEI.**

   The open workplace design makes SEI successful. The workplace design facilitates open communication, egalitarianism, and creativity.

Key Terms

external change forces, p. 265	group, p. 268	Group cohesiveness, p. 275
Internal change forces, p. 265	Formal groups, p. 268	team, p. 275
Organizational effectiveness, p. 266	Informal groups, p. 268	Self-managing work teams, p. 280
Synergy, p. 267	Norms, p. 275	

Questions for Review & Discussion

1. Is change as pervasive as the authors claim? Explain.
2. What are some of the primary reasons people resist change? What are some of the ways a team leader can ensure that change is accepted or at least not resisted?
3. What major changes in the last 10 years have had considerable impact on organizations? Do these changes provide support for or make a case against the use of team building in organizations? Defend your position.
4. Compare and contrast formal groups and informal groups. Explain the importance of leadership in both types of groups.
5. If groups have so many limitations, why are they so popular?
6. Of the factors affecting group effectiveness, do you think there is any order of importance? If so, rank the factors 1 through 4, and explain why you chose to rank them in that order.
7. Identify conditions and organizations where self-managing work teams would *not* be the way to organize. Then identify conditions and organizations where self-managing work teams *would* be the way to organize.
8. How would you deal with an informal leader in a task force who seemed to be totally opposed to the group's objectives?

Resources

Skill Builder 9-1

Team Scavenger Hunt

Introduction Think about what it means to be a part of a team—a successful team. What makes one team more successful than another? What does each team member need to do for their team to be successful? What are the characteristics of an effective team?

Procedure

1. Form teams as assigned by your instructor. Locate the items on the list below while following these important rules:

   a. Your team *must stay together at all times*—that is, you cannot go in separate directions.

   b. Your team must return to the classroom in the time allotted by the instructor.

   The team with the most items on the list will be declared the most successful team.

2. Next, reflect on your team's experience. What did each team member do? What was your team's strategy? What made your team effective? Make a list of the most important things your team did to be successful. Nominate a spokesperson to summarize your team's? That is, helped each team to be effective?

Interpersonal Skill

Source: Adapted from Michael R. Manning and Paula J. Schmidt, *Journal of Management Education*, Building Effective Work Team: A Quick Exercise Based on a Scavenger Hunt. (Thousand Oaks, CA: Sage Publications, 1995), pp. 392–398.

Used by permission. Reference for list of items for scavenger hunt from C.E. Larson and F.M. Lafas, Team Work: *What Must Go Right/What Can Go Wrong* (Newbury Park, CA: Sage Publications, 1989).

Items for Scavenger Hunt Each item is to be identified and brought back to the classroom.

Information

1. A book with the word "team" in the title.
2. A joke about teams that you share with the class.
3. A blade of grass from the university football field.
4. A souvenir from the state.
5. A picture of a team or group.
6. A newspaper article about a team.
7. A team song your group composes and performs for the class.
8. A leaf from an oak tree.
9. Stationery from the Dean's office.
10. A cup of stand.
11. A pine cone.
12. A live reptile.
13. A definition of group "cohesion" that you share with the class.
14. A set of chopsticks.
15. Three cans of vegetables.
16. A branch of an elm tree.
17. Three unusual items that you share with the class.
18. A ball of cotton
19. The ear from a prickly pear cactus.
20. A group name.

Systems

Technology

(*Note*: Items may be substituted as appropriate for your locale.)

Skill Builder 9-2

Interpersonal Skill

Information

Systems

"Win as Much as You Can" Tally Sheet

The detailed instructions for completing this exercise will be provided by your instructor. Basically, for 10 successive rounds, you and your partner choose either an X or a Y on the scorecard. The payoff for each round depends on the pattern of choices made in your group. The payoff schedule is given at the bottom of the scorecard provided.

You are to confer with your partner in each round and make a joint decision. In rounds 5, 8, and 10, you and your partner may first confer with the other partnerships in your group before making your joint decision.

	ROUND	YOUR CHOICE (CIRCLE)	CLUSTER'S PATTERN OF CHOICES	PAYOFF	BALANCE
	1	X Y	_X _Y		
	2	X Y	_X _Y		
	3	X Y	_X _Y		
	4	X Y	_X _Y		
Bonus Round Payoff × 3	5	X Y	_X _Y		
	6	X Y	_X _Y		
	7	X Y	_X _Y		
Bonus Round Payoff × 5	8	X Y	_X _Y		
	9	X Y	_X _Y		
Bonus Round Payoff × 10	10	X Y	_X _Y		

PAYOFF SCHEDULE

4 Xs:	Lose $1.00 each
3 Xs:	Win $1.00 each
1 Y:	Lose $3.00 each
2 Xs:	Win $2.00 each
2 Ys:	Lose $2.00 each
1 X:	Win $3.00
3 Ys:	Lose $1.00 each
4 Ys:	Win $1.00 each

Source: Adapted from an exercise by William Gellermann, Ph.D., in J. Pfeiffer and J. Jones, *Structured Experiences for Human Relations Training*, Vol. II (Tucson, AZ: University Associates, 1974).

CASE 9-1

The Shift to Team Leadership (Group Activity)

You work for a company interested in initiating a team leadership training program, and your plant manager has appointed you to an ad hoc task force to study the feasibility of implementing such a program in your plant. In one of the company's other plants, however, supervisors resisted team leadership, giving the following reasons:

1. Lack of time
2. Leader mind-set ("It's the leader's job to make the major decisions.")
3. Lack of trust in employees
4. Lack of confidence in employees' abilities or judgment
5. Potential for major negative consequences ("too risky," "too costly")
6. Leader's belief that the leader knows best
7. Leader's concern that developed employees will erode leader's base of power ("They're not dependent anymore.")
8. Leader's perception that employees don't desire development ("They don't really care; they only want to do the minimum required.")

INSTRUCTIONS:

1. Divide the class into teams of three to six students.
2. Each team should brainstorm ways to overcome supervisors' predicted resistance to developmental leadership.
3. Each team is to outline an initial training agenda for the developmental leadership program to present to the plant manager.
4. The teams are to present their analysis and recommendations to the plant manager (represented by the instructor or a designated class member).
5. Vote with your class to determine which program appears to have the best chance of success.

(*Note:* Students may not vote for their own team's program.)

CASE 9-2

The AFS Student Organization (Group Activity)

The AFS (All for Students) student organization was created in the mid-1970s and quickly became a popular, co-ed, undergraduate student group. AFS is a multipurpose organization focused on providing good fellowship and friendship among its members, encouraging its members to grow and develop academically, assisting members with career planning and development through seminars, promoting social interest and activities, and participating in charitable and benevolent events within the community.

AFS has historically been one of the top 10 most popular student organizations on campus, continuing to grow and achieve prominence within the university community. Four years ago, AFS actually won the coveted "Challenge Award," awarded to the top student organization each year by the university. Winning the Challenge Award is based on several criteria, including community service hours, university event participation, and head-to-head competition with other student organizations.

AFS's popularity has declined for the past three years. This is evident in the low attendance at regular meetings, the apathy displayed by the current members, and the overall decline in the number of active members on the roster. One potential reason for the situation is that the worsening economy has led many students to take on additional work hours. However, to continue to provide the type and quality of activities and events the membership expects, the AFS Leadership Council was forced to raise dues. Unfortunately, this decision only led to additional defections. The officers on the leadership council have disagreed as to the best remedy for the current situation and have at times been in conflict with one another. They have attempted to initiate several strategies to turn things around, including lowering dues, cutting back programs and events, and stopping the harassment of delinquent members. However, even with an improving economy, nothing has really worked. Many individuals appear to be waiting for the end of the term so changes at the top can be made during elections.

You joined AFS during the current year based on the recommendation of your professor. She said it would be a great leadership opportunity from which you could learn and grow; at the very least, it would serve as a line item on your resume. Several of your friends joined at the same time for similar reasons.

You and your friends recognize the potential of AFS within the university community, but the right leadership and teamwork are needed to restore AFS as a prominent member of the community. Obviously, many of the other members agree, because you and two of your friends, Jen and Terrance, were selected to run for President, Vice President, and Treasurer, respectively. On election night, the membership voted resoundingly for you, Jen, and Terrance to lead AFS for the next school year.

INSTRUCTIONS:

1. Divide the class into teams of three to six students.
2. Each team should brainstorm ways to create an effective team environment in AFS.
3. Each team is to outline an initial plan of action.
4. The teams are to present their analysis and recommendations to the class members.
5. Vote with your class to determine which plan appears to have the best chance of success.

(*Note:* Students may not vote for their own team's program.)

PART 4

Skill Development

10

Meetings and Facilitation Skills

LEARNING OBJECTIVES

After reading and studying this chapter, you should be able to:

1. Explain how technology is enhancing meetings.

2. Explain the four basic purposes of meetings.

3. Differentiate between the leader-controlled approach and the group-centered approach used in meetings.

4. Identify the advantages and disadvantages of meetings.

5. Describe the actions that a supervisor can take before, during, and after a meeting to make it effective.

6. Explain the process of consensus decision making in meetings.

7. Define group facilitation.

8. Explain the role of group facilitator.

9. Differentiate between process consultation and other models of consultation.

10. Specifically identify what can be done to make teleconferencing more effective.

Expert facilitation can help any organization be more successful, whether military or civilian.

Meetings are places where minutes are taken, but hours often wasted.
—*Anonymous*

"You know you're in a bad meeting when you look out the window on a sunny summer day wishing you were the person sitting on the mower."
—*Anonymous*

Preview

CHUCK DANSBY, FACILITATOR "EXTRAORDINAIRE" Facilitators are being called on increasingly to help groups and organizations become more effective. One of the best facilitators around is Chuck Dansby, total quality management supervisor with the Navy's Public Works Center in the San Francisco Bay area. Some public works representatives have suggested that a number of awards received by the center could not have been achieved without expert facilitation. The most prestigious of these awards was the Meritorious Unit Commendation Award issued by the Secretary of Defense.

After graduating from Chattanooga State Technical Institute, Chuck spent 12 years in the Navy, ending his tour as a First Class E6 Petty Officer. In 1988, he joined the Public Works Center, and in 1991 he was named the first quality improvement coordinator. During this time, the center was going through a period of expansion, and Chuck soon found himself operating a quality improvement department with a staff of seven people. Chuck and his team made, as their primary task, helping units and groups to permanently improve their processes. Even though Chuck and his group were in a staff capacity with no command authority, the following comments reveal why various managers called on him for assistance and what they said about him as a facilitator.

Lt. Commander Bryan Johnson asked for Chuck's assistance when he needed to get the environmental group and construction group to work more effectively together. He states, "Chuck was very helpful in teaming with me to get key people to talk through issues and concerns and in getting the groups to cooperate in achieving objectives." He especially appreciated Chuck's ability to ask questions, getting people to brainstorm and rethink alternatives. Program Manager Steve Worthington echoes these observations and states, "Chuck is an excellent listener and is very good at getting people to 'see the big picture.'"

Security Officer Mike Shanlas states, "He gets people to rethink their ways of operating and does it by asking questions. In this manner, people stay focused on the process, and they come out with improved ways of operating. People become indebted to him because he helps them to succeed; he does not set people up for failure."

Contract Manager John Teetsov gives insight as to the ideal quality of a facilitator when he states that Chuck can come into an unfamiliar area and "not knowing the business, can extract the right ideas and answers. Very importantly, he does things in a manner so that the group feels that they are being helped rather than manipulated."

Chuck has attended a number of schools while with the Navy, but the one that had the greatest impact on him as a future effective facilitator was W. Edward Deming's four-day workshop on continual quality improvement. Deming and the course taught Chuck the value of asking the right questions. Today, the Navy's Public Works Center is going through a process of downsizing. To carry out this process in a fair and humanistic manner, Chuck is being called on for his expert facilitation skills in meeting the Public Works Center's greatest challenge.

There is no question that advances in technology are altering the meeting landscape for many organizations and supervisors. As greater numbers of employees work at sites some distance from their supervisor, and perhaps even at home, electronic meetings have become a necessary and valuable communication tool. Computers—including laptops and computer software—cellphones, and videoconference equipment have broadened the communication media available. Meetings conducted through e-mail or web-based computer software are becoming standard for many organizations, and will increase as these tools become more simple and cost effective. For the vast majority of managers and supervisors, though, the face-to-face meeting remains the setting that is most utilized. It is this setting that forms the backdrop for this chapter.

Source: Conversations and correspondence with Chuck Dansby and others with the Navy's Public Works Center, San Francisco Bay area.

Today's supervisors increasingly are being called on to function effectively in meetings, both as leaders and participants. This requires that a supervisor understand certain fundamentals about small group behavior and have certain facilitation skills. The first part of this chapter addresses important information about meetings, including their purposes, approaches, advantages, disadvantages, and some important principles of conducting effective meetings. The second part of the chapter addresses specifics of group facilitation, the skills attributed to Chuck Dansby in the chapter preview.

The Changing Technology of Meetings

1 *Explain how technology is enhancing meetings.*

There is no question that advances in technology are altering the meeting landscape for many organizations and supervisors. As greater numbers of employees work at sites some distance from their supervisor, and perhaps even at home, electronic meetings have become a necessary and valuable communication tool. Computers (including laptops and computer software), cell phones, and videoconference equipment have broadened the communication media available. Meetings conducted through e-mail or web-based computer software are becoming standard for many organizations and will increase as these tools become more simple and cost effective.

Technology changes are also serving as support tools for face-to-face meetings. Power-Point software enables high-quality visual presentation; other packages support participation through voting, immediate electronic tabulation, and display of results. Still other

New technologies enable team members at distant locations to meet more easily without the time or expense of travel.

technology enables electronic display of a working agenda and can record the disposition of each agenda item discussed, including action taken, names of persons responsible for action, dates for completion, and so on. These are visually displayed for all at the meeting to see. McKinsey and Company and Allstate use software packages at their meetings to allow participants' spoken comments at a meeting to be instantly displayed on a computer hooked up to a large overhead projector. Resulting discussion/comments can be identified, linked, or edited onscreen and serve as an immediate basis for meeting minutes.[1]

Mentor Graphics uses software to create an information hub that allows individuals to keep track of documents, procedures, and policies. Chris Sholler, a former general manager at Mentor, states, "We created a wiki using the software to help us track meeting notes, especially for regularly recurring meetings. It stores any documents, meeting minutes, and assigns/tracks action items by sending e-mail reminders to meeting attendees. You can configure it to do a lot of things actually (e.g., track program decisions, identify key stakeholders and their roles for the meeting, create agendas—great for project or program management). It's accessible over the web, but usually through an intranet so only company personnel can reach it."[2] High-tech support tools will continue to impact meeting effectiveness, for all types of meetings, whether all members are physically present in the same room or electronically linked.

For the vast majority of managers and supervisors, the face-to-face meeting remains the setting that is most utilized. Although this is the setting that forms the backdrop of this chapter, most principles presented apply to electronically linked settings also.

Purposes of Meetings

2 *Explain the four basic purposes of meetings.*

Meetings in today's organizations are a fact of organizational life. Estimates are that time spent in meetings ranges from several hours to several days weekly, depending on the organization and position.[3] Depending on the study, estimates suggest there may be as many as 20 million meetings held daily in U.S. organizations.[4] At 3M, for instance, the average manager reports spending 1 to 1½ days weekly in meetings. Unfortunately, 3M managers judge up to half of this time as wasted![5] So much time is devoted to meetings that some organizations, including Nestlé USA, have established a policy of scheduling one day weekly when no meetings are held so as to allow personnel time to "get their work done."[6] Indeed, we have all experienced meetings that are unproductive because irrelevant information is presented, key people are missing, meeting leadership is poor, and nothing meaningful is achieved. To supervisors and most organization members, though, meetings are indeed a fact of organizational life. At Intel, meetings are considered so important that every employee completes an in-house course on effective meetings. In fact, former CEO Andy Grove was himself a course instructor.[7]

Meetings generally are called to achieve one or more of the following purposes (see Exhibit 10-1): (1) to give information, (2) to exchange information, (3) to obtain facts about a particular situation, and (4) to solve a problem.

Information Giving

information-giving meeting

Held to announce new programs and policies or to update present ones.

The **information-giving meeting** is held to make announcements of new programs and policies or to update information on the present ones. Generally, it is closely controlled by the leader or those who are called on to provide information to the group, frequently by means of committee reports. There tends to be little feedback from group members unless they have questions to ask or points to clarify about the information presented. Normally this is the easiest type of meeting to conduct, since its format is highly structured and lends itself well to large groups.

Information Exchange

information exchange meeting

Held to obtain information from group members.

The **information exchange meeting** is called to obtain information from group members and to allow them to provide information to one another.

> *At the* Boston Herald, *a daily 11:00 a.m. meeting of editorial, advertising, circulation, and production superintendents is held to present a status report on the next day's paper. This daily exchange ensures that key managers are knowledgeable about issues that might affect them during the day and helps them get the paper out smoothly.*[8]

EXHIBIT 10-1
Purposes of Meetings

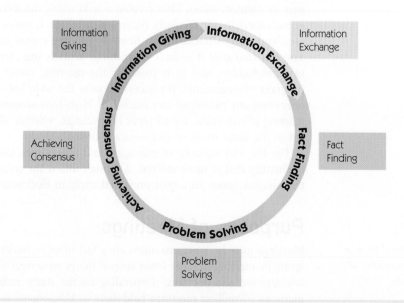

Fact Finding

fact-finding meeting

Held to seek out relevant facts about a problem or situation.

Only relevant facts about a problem or situation should be sought in a **fact-finding meeting.** The meeting leader focuses not on finding solutions but rather on understanding the problem or situation. A supervisor might begin such a meeting as follows: "I called this meeting to discuss the high cost overruns we've been experiencing during the past month. I want to find out as much as I can about your perspective on the causes of this situation. Later, we can consider some steps we can take to reduce these costs." Once the facts have been uncovered, the supervisor will have a better understanding of the situation.

Problem Solving

problem-solving meeting

Held to identify the problem, to discuss alternative solutions, and to decide on the proper action to take.

Typically, the **problem-solving meeting** combines the other purposes of information giving, information exchange, and fact finding. Considered the most challenging of the meeting types, this type of meeting is held to identify the major elements of a problem, to discuss and evaluate alternative solutions, and ultimately to make a decision as to the proper action to take. Topics of problem-solving meetings might include any of the following:

1. improving customer service;
2. reducing absenteeism;
3. determining production schedules or job assignments;
4. finding and remedying the causes of project delays; or
5. implementing a new policy in the best way.

Stop & Think

Lois Kelly, founder and principal of Meaning Maker, a major marketing consulting firm, and former senior vice president of one of the largest public relations firms in the world, says, "Meetings have become 'let me show you my PowerPoint presentation.' The best thing that can happen in corporate America is that there is a ban on PowerPoint. To me a meeting is a place where there is interaction and something gets decided and learned. I have sat through so many meetings where people just go through their slides."[9] What do you think about Kelly's assertion?

Approaches Used at Meetings

3 *Differentiate between the leader-controlled approach and the group-centered approach used in meetings.*

The interactions that take place at meetings vary greatly. Much depends on the purpose of the meeting and the meeting leader's personal style. One of two approaches is generally used in conducting meetings: (1) a leader-controlled approach or (2) a group-centered approach.

Leader-Controlled Approach

leader-controlled approach

Used at meetings of large groups in which the leader clearly runs the show and the open flow of information is impeded.

The **leader-controlled approach,** in which the leader clearly runs the show, is often used at information-giving meetings or when the large size of the group prohibits an open flow of information among members. The leader opens the meeting, makes announcements, or calls on those who have information to present. If anyone in the group has questions to ask or comments to make, he or she addresses them to the leader. The leader may answer the questions or bounce them to someone else. Exhibit 10-2 illustrates this approach. Should a stranger walk in after the meeting has begun, she or he would have no difficulty identifying who is in charge.

EXHIBIT 10-2
Interaction in the
Leader-Controlled
Approach

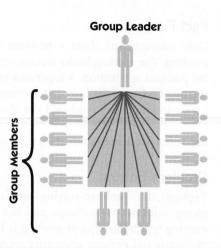

One advantage of this approach is that it is generally easier on the leader, because the fairly rigid structure means that there are few surprises. Another advantage is that this approach allows a large amount of material to be covered quickly. It also lends itself to larger groups.

> *William Pagonis, chief of operations for Sears, Roebuck, requires attendees to stand during his regular briefings. Pagonis boasts that he can cover more material in a 15-minute stand-up meeting than he could in a two-hour seated version.*[10]

An obvious disadvantage of the leader-controlled approach is that it discourages a free flow of information. The fact that comments from the group must go through the leader means that spontaneous, direct remarks may go unmade. The creativity that results from the "piggybacking" of ideas is stifled. Another disadvantage is that members have no real opportunity to get sensitive and emotional issues out in the open and to blow off steam.

Group-Centered Approach

**group-centered
approach**

Used at meetings in
which group members
interact freely and
address and question
one another.

In a **group-centered approach,** group members interact more freely with one another, as shown in Exhibit 10-3. The meeting leader does not dominate the discussions; neither does he or she simply sit back and allow the group to formulate its own direction. Quite the contrary; the leader uses facilitation skills to keep the meeting moving by directing/redirecting focus, asking for clarification, making sure that everyone speaks, summarizing the group's position, testing for consensus, moving the group to the next issue, and so on.

The advantages of the group-centered approach stem from the greater interaction that occurs at the meeting. First, it results in a better understanding of members' viewpoints. Second, if the purpose of the meeting is to solve a problem, the free flow of information may contribute to a better decision. Third, when people can express their emotions or disagreements, they feel better.

One disadvantage of the group-centered approach is that the meeting takes up a great deal more time than does the leader-controlled approach. Another disadvantage is that the increased interaction among members means that the leader's skills are tested more severely. The leader must determine when to move the discussion of a topic along. He or she must make sure that everyone gets a chance to speak and that discussions stay close to the subject. Also, since the leader must deal with diverse personalities, he or she must know how to handle emotions that may arise. A third disadvantage is that this approach is not well suited to large groups because of its interpersonal nature.

EXHIBIT 10-3
Interaction in the
Group-Centered
Approach

Leader

Which Approach Should You Use?

Which approach is better for you, as a supervisor, to use? There is no best answer to this question. The answer depends on such factors as the meeting's purpose, the size of the group, the ability of the group members, the amount of time allowed for the meeting, your skills, and the subjects to be discussed. Remember that you can shift from one approach to the other at a single meeting, depending on the nature of the items on your agenda.

> Yoshi Tanabe's approach at meetings suits his purposes. Take Wednesday's meeting, for instance. The first item on his agenda was the new vacation scheduling procedure. At this point Tanabe was the expert in the room. He made a three- to four-minute presentation on the new procedure and then fielded questions from the group.

> The next topic on the agenda was the need to develop and submit to higher management a plan for the department's participation in the company's 10-year anniversary open house for members of the community. Tanabe used a more open approach for the discussion of this topic. It took up about 20 minutes, with much interaction among the group. Within this time, Tanabe and the group came up with a plan for the department's role during the open house.

Advantages and Disadvantages of Meetings

4 *Identify the advantages and disadvantages of meetings.*

Some supervisors despise attending and conducting meetings. They prefer to communicate on a one-to-one basis. But because meetings are a fact of life for supervisors, it is appropriate at this point to consider the advantages and disadvantages of meetings. Then, in the remainder of the chapter, we will provide pointers on how to make meetings more effective.

Advantages of Meetings

Meetings save time, ensure that the supervisor's communications are consistent, and permit a formal exchange of important information and ideas. Let's explore how these advantages work.

Save Time Suppose you, as a supervisor, have a group of employees whose jobs are *not* performed in the same work area (as is the case with outside sales, delivery services, maintenance, or patient care). To communicate on a one-on-one basis, you would have to move from one location to another during the work period. By having a meeting, you can save a great deal of your personal time that would otherwise be spent tracking down each of your employees.

Moreover, when minutes of the meeting are distributed to members, they serve as a permanent record of what has occurred or been agreed on. In this way, they save time that might otherwise be needed to clarify or repeat what was said.

Ensure Consistency of Information Meetings provide an opportunity for all present to hear the same message. If you communicate separately with each of your team members, you may present the information more effectively to some than to others. Also, some of your team members may ask questions or make comments that help clarify the communication or add a slightly different flavor to it. With one-on-one contacts, the grapevine goes to work, especially if there is a long lapse of time between when you talk with the first team member and when you talk with the last team member.

Permit Formal Exchange of Information Sometimes individual members of a work group have information that *must* be shared with all the other group members. This is particularly true when a problem confronts the work group. In a meeting, a comment made by one member frequently triggers an important idea in another member. This exchange can lead to solutions that might not have been thought of by any one member.

The degree of formality inherent in a meeting can be used to advantage by a supervisor. For example, suppose that you, a supervisor, have been told by the plant manager that production must be increased by 15 percent over the next year, otherwise the plant will be closed. Presenting this information to your work group in a meeting conveys the seriousness of the situation and dramatizes the impact of the message.

Disadvantages of Meetings

Meetings may result in watered-down decisions, may not be cost effective, and may be too impersonal. Let's see how these disadvantages arise.

Many Are Unnecessary Many supervisors claim that they waste too much time in unnecessary meetings. Yet they themselves hold many meetings perceived by their members as unnecessary. Meetings interrupt members' work day, may take them away from higher priority tasks and compete with other activities such as deadline-driven tasks, and can add significantly to job stress. Is the structure provided by a meeting essential to achieving your purpose? Could it be achieved as effectively through other means, such as by telephone, e-mail, or memo? Do all members of your group need the information or just a few? At Intel, most conference rooms are lined with posters reminding those present to adhere to guidelines for effective meetings. Among the posters, one asks, "Is This Meeting Necessary?"[11]

May Not Be Cost Effective Meetings are more expensive than most people realize. When employees are attending meetings, they are not doing their normal jobs. Suppose 10 people, with an average annual salary of $60,000, attend a one-hour meeting. The cost of the meeting includes not only their salaries for that hour, but also costs for vacations, holidays, sick leave, medical insurance, Social Security, travel time, and so on. As shown in Exhibit 10-4, the cost of the meeting is $438. The meeting must therefore provide information important enough to justify the cost associated with it. And Exhibit 10-4 does not include the costs associated with time spent planning for the meeting or traveling.

EXHIBIT 10-4
Meetings Cost!

Many managers overlook the cost of meetings. The following table approximates hourly costs for employ-ees at four salary levels. The hourly rates include only salary and normal benefits. They do *not* include costs of meeting planning and preparation time, travel time/costs, follow-up costs, and the like.

SALARY/BENEFIT HOURLY MEETING COSTS

SALARY	NUMBER OF PARTICIPANTS				
	25	10	8	6	4
$100,000	$1,825	$730	$584	$438	$292
80,000	1,460	584	467	350	234
60,000	1,095	438	350	263	175
40,000	730	292	234	175	117

May Water Down Decisions Unless a meeting is properly conducted and its members are committed to effectiveness, the decisions made at the meeting may simply reflect the *average* input of members, rather than the ideas of the best members. Sometimes opi-nions voiced by the group's brightest or best-informed members may not be accepted by the majority. At other times, knowledgeable members may suppress their own dis-agreements simply for the sake of harmony.

May Become Too Impersonal Meetings may not allow the personal interaction re-quired for many sensitive issues. On a one-on-one basis, employees may communicate readily to their supervisor. But because a meeting involves a more formal setting with many people present, some employees will be reluctant to speak up.

Making Meetings Effective

5 *Describe the actions that a supervisor can take before, during, and after a meeting to make it effective.*

This section presents some ideas that should help you conduct more effective meetings. Some of the actions discussed should be performed *before* the meeting, some *during* the meeting, and some *after* the meeting. As a prelude to this section, we invite you to com-plete Exhibit 10-5.

Factors to Consider Before the Meeting

Two important premeeting steps will ensure an effective meeting: (1) have a clear pur-pose, and (2) preplan the meeting.

Have a Clear Purpose Assuming that a meeting is necessary, you should have a clear purpose for it. Otherwise you will waste everyone's time, including your own. Earlier, we noted that meetings can serve any of several purposes: (1) to give information, (2) to exchange information, (3) to obtain facts, and (4) to solve a problem. Having a clear pur-pose responds to the question that participants ask themselves: "Why are we here?" Hav-ing a clear purpose also enables other premeeting plans to be developed to support the purpose.

Stop & Think

What are the pros and cons of having regular weekly meetings at an established time?

EXHIBIT 10-5
Scoring Your Meeting
Leadership

How would you rate yourself as a meeting leader? For each of the 12 items below, circle the response that comes closest to how you view your own meeting conduct. If you do not conduct meetings, assess the meeting leadership of your own boss or another leader of meetings that you normally attend.

		STRONGLY AGREE	AGREE	DISAGREE	STRONGLY DISAGREE
1.	I assess whether a meeting is the most effective use of everyone's time before calling it.	1	2	3	4
2.	I have in mind a specific objective for each meeting that I call.	1	2	3	4
3.	I plan in advance the details of my meetings, such as who should attend, materials to distribute, meeting place, etc.	1	2	3	4
4.	Where time allows, I plan and distribute an agenda in advance of my meetings.	1	2	3	4
5.	My meetings stick to the published agenda without too much straying.	1	2	3	4
6.	I do not monopolize discussion in meetings.	1	2	3	4
7.	I maintain balanced participation among all meeting members.	1	2	3	4
8.	I encourage discussion of all sides of issues without showing my bias.	1	2	3	4
9.	Participants would say that I keep a meeting moving toward its objectives.	1	2	3	4
10.	At the end of a meeting, I summarize the key ideas presented/actions taken.	1	2	3	4
11.	I maintain and circulate meeting minutes.	1	2	3	4
12.	I follow up in a timely manner on actions taken during meetings.	1	2	3	4

Scoring: Sum your circled responses.

Score of 12–15 = Excellent
        16–19 = Very Good
        20–24 = Good
        25–29 = Average
        30–48 = Below Average

Preplan the Meeting Many meetings are doomed from the start because of poor initial planning. Perhaps another group has reserved the conference room, for example. Or the bulbs in the overhead projector are burned out. Or the people present at the meeting weren't notified that they should bring certain needed information. Or the leader simply hasn't done his or her homework! Proper planning requires you to do some work before the meeting begins. Such work might include the following:

1. Make sure that the people who are to attend the meeting have adequate advance notice (unless it's an emergency meeting).
2. Make sure that key people will be able to attend.

3. Develop and distribute copies of the meeting agenda in advance. This will enable people to bring essential documents with them or to gather information that may prove helpful. See Exhibit 10-6 for agenda planning insights.

4. Let people know in advance if they will be expected to provide information or make a report.

EXHIBIT 10-6

Agenda Planning

Having a well-planned agenda is a critical starting point toward effective meetings. Many organizations have provided meeting "templates," which serve as guides for creating effective agendas. The template may reflect the components of a well-planned agenda and provide an actual physical design that can be used. The sample agenda below illustrates the details of a well-planned agenda for a fact-finding and decision-making meeting.

SAMPLE AGENDA

Date:	March 5, 2010	**Location:**	3rd floor conference room
Meeting called by:	Beth Shapiro	**Attendees:**	See distribution list
Facilitator:	Beth Shapiro, Alice Chang	**Please read:**	Attached memo from Beth on expectations, deadlines, etc.
Note taker:	Bill Smith	**Please bring:**	Memo, So. Am. Strategy Plan

Objectives

- Review past efforts at launching products in South America
- Identify problems or obstacles to product introduction
- Determine possible approaches to overcoming problems
- Assign tasks and establish deadlines

Agenda

Time	Topic	Responsibility
8:30–8:40	• Introductions and review of agenda	Beth Shapiro
8:40–9:00	• Review of past launches in So. America (presentation)	Mario Cisneros
9:00–9:45	• Potential problems and solutions (brainstorming)	Alice Chang
9:45–10:00	• Assignment of action items	Beth Shapiro

Additional Information: This meeting will be the first of two. For this one, the goal is to surface all ideas, so each person should come prepared to contribute. At the end of the brainstorming session, we will decide as a group which solutions to pursue and will assign tasks to the appropriate team members.

Note that the agenda indicates three specific people other than the meeting leader who will have a formal role in the meeting: (1) a note taker (the basis for meeting minutes), (2) a presenter other than the leader, and (3) a resource person who will serve as facilitator for the brainstorming session.

Here are some other helpful agenda planning insights:

1. If possible, distribute an agenda several days before a meeting.
2. Allow an opportunity for members to add topics to the agenda.
3. Indicate the time allotted for agenda topics. This will help time management during the meeting.
4. Where the list of agenda topics is long, begin with routine items.
5. In longer meetings, controversial topics should be addressed sufficiently early in the agenda while group energy is high. Placing controversial items at the end of an agenda when discussion time is limited may give the impression that you are manipulating the group.
6. Build a break into meetings that last longer than 90 minutes. This will allow members to network, address other work-related items, and use the restroom as needed.

Source: Sample Agenda adapted from Deborah J. Barrett, Leadership Communication: (New York: McGraw Hill/Irwin, 2006, p. 216. Other information from http://www.3com/meetingnetwork/reaingroom/meetingguide_anatomy.html

5. Check to see that the meeting room is arranged as you desire and that the visual aids you intend to use function properly.

6. Form a general idea of how long the meeting should last. You may want to indicate this to those who will attend. It is easier to predict the length of information-giving and information exchange meetings, however, than that of meetings held for fact finding or problem solving.

Factors to Consider During the Meeting

When the meeting time arrives, you can take a number of steps to help ensure the meeting's success. Among these are (1) starting the meeting on time, (2) designating someone to take minutes, (3) clarifying your objectives and expectations, (4) keeping the meeting on the desired topic, (5) encouraging participation, and (6) making sure there is closure.

Start on Time Eli Mina, author of *The Complete Handbook of Business Meetings*, says that starting on time is a cardinal meeting principle.[12] There may be occasions when one or two employees do not arrive on time for a meeting. To avoid unnecessary delays, the supervisor should begin the meeting as scheduled. If a supervisor consistently waits for late arrivals, attendees may get the message that it's okay to be late, and successive meetings will start later and later. Such delays waste the time of those who arrive promptly.

Designate Someone to Take Minutes Especially for information exchange, fact-finding, and problem-solving meetings, it is helpful to have someone record the important points discussed and agreed on at the meeting. These points are then outlined in a document called the **minutes** of the meeting, copies of which are distributed after the meeting. If no one takes minutes, those attending the meeting would be well advised to take notes on their own.

minutes

A written record of the important points discussed and agreed on at a meeting.

Clarify Your Expectations Earlier in this chapter, we stated that a meeting was generally called to serve one or more of the following purposes: to give information, to

Prior to a meeting, check to see if the visual aides you intend to use function properly.

exchange information, to obtain facts, or to solve a problem and make a decision. As the leader of the meeting, make sure that you introduce each item on the agenda by stating your purpose for including it. For example:

1. "I'd like to *give you some information* about. ..." [information giving]
2. "Attached to the agenda that I sent each of you was the memo from Human Resources regarding the new benefits. I'd like to *get your reactions* to these new benefits." [information exchange]
3. "The purpose of this meeting is to review the recent changes in our billing policy and their impact on collections. Your input will give me an idea of the success or failure of our new billing policy. In your experience, what has been *the effect of* the billing policy?" [fact finding]
4. "I'd like to get your ideas on what we can do to show our department in its best light during our open house. After hearing your ideas, *I'll put together our plan.*" [problem solving and decision making]
5. "The branch manager wants to know what our department's position is on switching to a week of four 10-hour days, as we discussed in our meeting last week. I can go any way you want to on this. *What do we want to do?*" [decision making]

In each example, the supervisor spelled out and clarified his or her expectations regarding an item on the agenda. Take special notice of examples 4 and 5, in which the supervisor carefully outlined the role of the group in the decision-making process.

Provide Leadership Ineffective leadership ruins many well-prepared meetings. The supervisor must be prepared to demonstrate leadership in the following ways:

1. Keep the meeting moving. *Don't allow a meeting to drag on and on, and don't stray too far from the topic being discussed. If people wander from the topic, you might say, "We seem to have drifted from our major issue. Let's go back ..."*
2. See to it that most or all members contribute to the discussion. *Don't allow one or two people to dominate the meeting. If this happens, call on others first for their comments or reactions.*
3. Summarize the apparent position of the group from time to time. *You might say, "Do I read the group properly? You seem to be saying that ..."*
4. Address various problems related to participant behavior. *Exhibit 10-7 shows how to deal with some inappropriate behaviors.*

Encourage Two-Way Communication In most meetings, the leader's job is to facilitate openness and interaction among group members. This is particularly important when the leader uses the group-centered approach. The leader must be an alert listener and be skilled in helping individuals in the group to express themselves. A key skill is the ability to use questions to involve individual members or the entire group in the communication process. Exhibit 10-8 shows some questioning techniques that can be used by the meeting leader.

6 *Explain the process of consensus decision making in meetings.*

Work to Achieve Consensus Decisions

Given the current trend toward participative management, a particularly important concept is that of consensus decision making.

consensus
_____

The acceptance by all members of the decision reached.

Consensus is frequently misunderstood. It does not mean that members *agree* with the decision; it means that they agree to *accept* it, even though they may not personally favor it. The following example illustrates consensus.

EXHIBIT 10-7

Suggestions for Handling Disruptive and Inappropriate Behaviors at Meetings

TYPE	BEHAVIOR	SUGGESTED RESPONSE
Hostile	"It'll never work." "That's a typical engineering viewpoint."	"How do others feel about this?" "You may be right, but let's review the facts and evidence." "It seems we have a different perspective on the details, but we agree on the principles."
Know-It-All	"I have worked on this project more than anyone else in this room. …" "I have a Ph.D. in economics, and …"	"Let's review the facts." (Avoid theory and speculation.) "Another noted authority on this subject has said …"
Loudmouth	Constantly blurts out ideas and questions. Tries to dominate the meeting.	Interrupt: "Can you summarize your main point/question for us?" "I appreciate your comments, but we should also hear from others." "Interesting point. Help us understand how it relates to our subject."
Interrupter	Starts talking before others are finished.	"Wait a minute, Jim. Let's let Jane finish what she was saying."
Interpreter	"What John is really trying to say is …" "John would respond to that question by saying …"	"Let's let John speak for himself. Go ahead, John, finish what you were saying." "John, how would you respond?" "John, do you think Jim correctly understood what you said?"
Gossiper	"Isn't there a regulation that you can't … ?" "I thought I heard the V.P. of Finance say …"	"Can anyone here verify this?" "Let's not take the time of the group until we can verify the accuracy of this information."
Whisperer	Carries on irritating side conversation.	Walk up close to the guilty parties and make eye contact. Stop talking and establish dead silence. Politely ask the whisperers to wait until the meeting is over to finish their conversation.
Silent Distractor	Reads newspapers, rolls eyes, shakes head, fidgets.	Ask questions to determine the distractor's level of interest, support, and expertise. Try to build an alliance by drawing him or her into the discussion. If that doesn't work, discuss your concerns with the individual during a break.
Busy-Busy	Ducks in and out of the meeting repeatedly, taking messages, dealing with crises.	Schedule the presentation away from the office. Check with common offenders before the meeting to make sure interruptions during the planned time will be minimal.
Latecomer	Comes late and interrupts the meeting.	Announce an odd time (8:46) for the meeting to emphasize the necessity for promptness. Make it inconvenient for latecomers to find a seat, and stop talking until they do. Establish a "latecomers' kitty" for refreshments.
Early Leave	Announces, with regret, the need to leave for another important activity.	Before starting, announce the ending time and ask if anyone has a scheduling conflict.

Source: "Ten Deadly Sins of Poor Presentation" from Presentation Plus by David Peoples, pp. 52–54. Copyright © 1988 John Wiley & Sons, Inc., New York. Reproduced with permission of John wiley & Sons, Inc.

Charles Evans couldn't win support from other team members regarding his position on the team's recommendation about a company parking lot policy. Evans favored a process that allocated preferred parking places for key personnel in the company—some by seniority, some by position. Most other team members favored a process that had no preferred parking.

The team leader stressed the need for a consensus decision that all members could accept. Charles spoke openly about why he felt his approach was best, responded to

EXHIBIT 10-8

Questioning Techniques for Leaders of Meetings

- *Clarifying or elaborating on a point made by someone.*
  Example: "Are you saying that … ?" or "Alice, would you mind giving us a little more detail about the situation? When did it happen?"
- *Calling on someone who is reluctant to talk.*
  Example: "Pete, you've been through more maintenance shutdowns than most of us. What do you think about all of this?"
- *Getting specific facts.*
  Example: "Exactly what were our production figures last month? Can someone give us those figures?"
- *Examining possible alternatives.*
  Example: "What are the pros and cons of converting to the new system?" or "Would we be able to keep up our quality under the new system?" or "What would happen if … ?"
- *Initiating group discussion.*
  Example: "What is your reaction to this new vacation policy?" or "Does this new policy affect anyone here?"
- *Obtaining more participation from the group.*
  Example: "We've heard two alternatives. Are there any more?"
- *Guiding the meeting tactfully in certain directions.*
  Example: "We seem to have already discussed this issue pretty thoroughly and agreed on a course of action. Is everyone ready to move on?"
- *"Testing the water" as to the group's feeling.*
  Example: "What would be your reaction if we went to the system we've been discussing? Would you support it?"

---

questions raised by other team members about his position, and raised many questions about their position. The team leader had given him extra time to survey how other companies in the community handled the situation. Finally, after all issues seemed to have been fully discussed, the team leader said, "I sense that after our full examination of the issue, while not unanimous, the group favors a system that will operate as an open, first-come, first-served system. Is this correct?" No one dissented. She continued, "That, then, is what we will send to the president. Charles, thank you for helping us to more fully explore all aspects of the system that we're recommending. Can you accept the team decision?" Evans reflected, "It was a fair process. I presented my views; they just think differently on this one." He said, "Yes, I can support it, even though I disagree with it." "Good," said the team leader, "We have reached consensus."

Consensus is more difficult when members have personal stakes in decision outcomes and when there is much member diversity. Such is often the case with cross-functional teams. Consensus is not always achievable; some members openly state their intent not to support the group's decision. Perhaps they feel that others do not listen meaningfully to dissenting views or that attacks are made on personality rather than position. At times, the team decision is hurried, or the dissenter feels too strongly pressured or takes the position, "If it's not my way, I won't support it, period." Sometimes members will appear to accept the group's decision but work to sabotage it or divorce themselves from it once the group leaves the meeting room.

Consensus is more likely when a group's members:

1. Openly state their true feelings, ideas, and disagreements.
2. Examine their different views fully.
3. Try to understand underlying reasons behind their differences on an issue.
4. Actively listen to and seek to understand other members' positions.
5. Focus on issues rather than on personalities.

6. Avoid actions that polarize members or lock them into positions. This may be the case with voting or taking sides, especially in early stages of discussion.

Many companies teach skills in consensus decision making to all their employees and team leaders. At Saturn, for example, team members go through a minimum of 92 hours of training in problem-solving and people skills, teaching team members to reach a consensus point they call "70 percent comfortable, but 100 percent supportive."[13] Following discussion of alternatives (or causes), it is sometimes helpful in gaining consensus to determine a group's priorities, especially when several alternatives are available. One approach is the "dot plan." Alternatives are recorded on a flip chart or board. Each team member is given the same number of adhesive dots—say five—in three colors. One color represents high priority, another medium priority, and another low priority. Members then post their assigned dots to the different items. Some teams allow only one dot from one person on any one item; others may allow more passionate advocates to assign more than one. Following posting, a team can easily visualize how its members feel about alternatives. A variant is the "10-4" method used by teams at Bowater Carolina, the large newsprint manufacturer. Under this option, instead of colors, each member may assign a total of 10 points to items but no more than four to a single item. This achieves the same purpose as the dot listings. An example is shown in Exhibit 10-9.

Get Closure on Items Discussed At many meetings that the authors have observed, an item will be discussed, but then the leader will go on to the next item on the agenda, leaving everyone to wonder what has been concluded.

closure

Successfully accomplishing the objective for a given item on the agenda.

Achieving **closure** means reaching a conclusion with respect to a given agenda item that has been discussed. In the following example, notice how a department head achieves closure for a particular agenda item.

Martha Briem, a department head, presented comparative information showing that her department had a quality-rejection rate that was 10 percent higher than that of other departments in the company. She asked for her supervisors' input about possible actions. The discussion lasted about 25 minutes. Then she asked each supervisor to come up with a plan for improving product quality in his or her area and to make a five-minute presentation at a meeting to be scheduled in two weeks.

EXHIBIT 10-9
Eleven Team Members Scoring of Six Alternatives Using the 10-4 System

Item for 10-4 Team Scoring: "Possible Ways to Increase Teamwork in Our Department"

a) Change incentive system so that it reflects part individual, part department results
   3, 1, 2, 1 = 7

b) Include teamwork as an item on performance evaluation system
   2, 3, 1, 3, 4, 4, 3, 4, 3, 4 = 31

c) Develop system for recognizing when someone has been a good team player
   4, 4, 4, 4, 3, 4, 4, 4, 2, 4, 3 = 40

d) Include teamwork-related behaviors as part of everyone's job description
   2, 2, 2, 3, 1, 1, 2, 2 = 15

e) Cross-train members so that they better understand all jobs in the department
   4, 1, 2, 3, 2, 2, 1, 1 = 16

f) Rotate positions occasionally so that members perform each other's jobs
   2 = 2

Key: letter = alternative; numbers = each member's allocation of 10 points; a maximum of 4 points can be awarded to a single alternative.

Ideally, meetings will conclude with consensus and closure.

Factors to Consider After the Meeting

Even though the meeting is over, your work isn't finished. Follow up by making sure that the minutes (if any) are distributed and that any important decisions or responsibilities assigned to specific individuals are carried out.

Distribute Copies of the Minutes Distributing copies of the minutes of the meeting is important for the following reasons:

1. The minutes serve as a permanent record of what has been agreed on and committed to at the meeting.
2. The minutes identify topics on the agenda that have not been dealt with completely or that have been suggested for a future meeting.
3. The minutes permit a smooth transition, allowing you to take up where you left off at the next meeting.

Follow Up on Decisions Made It is crucial that the supervisor follow up on any actions that were agreed on and any decisions that were made during the meeting. The follow-up may consist of personal observations or visits. It may also involve reports that keep the supervisor informed of progress regarding the agreed-on commitments.

> "Oh, I make it a point to follow up on my meetings," stated Luis Santos. "We have a pretty active crowd who say what they think. If I feel that someone has really gotten ticked off or hurt by what was brought up at the meeting, I'll make it a point to try to smooth things out on a one-on-one basis. I also go one-on-one with somebody who said something I wanted to follow up on if I didn't feel the meeting was the place to do it."

More and more organizations are using facilitators to help make their meetings more effective, and they are training team leaders in group facilitation. We examine this important area next.

What is Group Facilitation?

7 *Define group facilitation.*

group facilitation

The process of intervening to help a group improve in goal setting, action planning, problem solving, conflict management, and decision making in order to increase the group's effectiveness.

8 *Explain the role of group facilitator.*

Group facilitation is a process of intervening to help a group improve in goal setting, action planning, problem solving, conflict management, and decision making in order to increase the group's effectiveness. Although an outside facilitator can be helpful, as we saw in the chapter preview, the ideal is for managers and supervisors to gain facilitation skills and utilize shared leadership in carrying out the process.

As organizations cope with the world of increasingly rapid change, the need for facilitation to improve their effectiveness increases. Examples run the gamut from empowering employees, developing shared visions, and creating self-managing work teams to changing to a more participative organizational culture. It is hard to imagine successful change efforts in the areas of total quality management, reengineering, partnering, mergers, or downsizing without some form of facilitation.

Role of the Facilitator

In our discussion of group dynamics and conducting meetings, you were introduced to facilitation challenges and suggestions for handling inappropriate behavior at meetings. A good foundation for being an effective facilitator requires experience and knowledge, not only of dynamics of the group but also of decision making, problem solving, communications, motivation, and leadership. In addition, the core skills shown in Exhibit 10-10 are essential.

An effective facilitator is primarily a helper.

EXHIBIT 10-10
Core Skills for the
Effective Facilitator

- Communication skills—listening and asking the right questions.
- Leadership skills—participative management and developmental leadership.
- Problem-solving skills.
- Group dynamics skills.
- Conceptual and analytical skills.
- Conflict management skills—principled negotiation.
- Process consultation skills—intervention and diagnostic insights.

Process Consultation

9 *Differentiate between process consultation and other models of consultation.*

Among the many roles facilitators must play is that of process consultant. In fact, process consultation skills are identified as being among the core skills of an effective facilitator. This role involves sitting in on team or task force meetings, observing the group's process, and intervening, if needed, to help the group function more effectively. Skill Builder 10-4 is designed to help you better understand when and how to intervene. Increasingly, facilitators are being used in major change efforts of total quality management, reengineering, and partnering. In essence, a facilitator becomes a consultant. The following sections describe three consultation models; we draw extensively from author/consultant Edgar Schein in comparing them.

It is important to keep in mind that the effective facilitator is primarily a helper and wants the group to achieve long-term development and continuous process improvement. Exhibit 10-11 highlights this emphasis by showing the distinction between basic facilitation and developmental facilitation.

Purchase-of-Expertise Model The most widely used form of consultation is the purchase of expert information. The organization, or someone within the organization, decides there is a need to call on an expert to help solve a problem or add a service. For example, someone to initiate an organizational attitude survey or introduce a performance evaluation system may be called. An individual who specializes in conducting marketing surveys or initiating total quality improvement programs may also be needed. Schein points out that this model frequently produces a low rate of implementation of

EXHIBIT 10-11
Basic and
Developmental
Facilitation

CHARACTERISTIC	BASIC FACILITATION	DEVELOPMENTAL FACILITATION
Group objective	Solve a substantive problem or problems.	Achieve group goals along with solving substantive problems while learning to improve processes.
Facilitator role	Help group temporarily improve its processes.	Help group permanently improve its processes.
	Take primary responsibility for managing the group's processes.	Help group assume primary responsibility for achieving goals and managing processes.
Outcome for group	Emphasize dependence on facilitator for solving future problems.	Reduce dependence on facilitator for solving future problems.

Source: Roger M. Schwartz, The Skilled Facilitator: Practical Wisdom for Developing Effective Groups by Roger M. Schwartz, Table 1.1, page 7, adapted as submitted. Copyright © 1994 Jossey-Bass Inc. Reproduced with permission of John Wiley & Sons, Inc.

the consultant's recommendations. Further, this model is based on many assumptions that have to be met for it to succeed, and therein lies its weakness. The assumptions are:

1. The manager has correctly diagnosed the organization's needs.
2. The manager has correctly communicated those needs to the consultant.
3. The manager has accurately assessed the capabilities of the consultant to provide the information or the service.
4. The manager has considered the consequences of having the consultant gather such information and is willing to implement changes that may be recommended by the consultant.

Another weakness is the fact that the model is based on a "tell and sell" method by the expert and there is no "ownership" or commitment by the client.

Doctor–Patient Model A relationship between a consultant and an organization can be likened to that of a doctor and a patient. When an organization suffers symptoms such as declining sales or profits, low morale, or high turnover, a consultant may be brought in to check these problems. After the "checkup," the consultant prescribes what the organization needs to do to "get well" again. As Schein points out, this model places a great deal of power in the hands of the consultant in that he or she makes a diagnosis and also prescribes a treatment. The success of the model then depends on whether:

1. The initial client has accurately identified which person, group, or department is "sick."
2. The "patient" has revealed accurate information.
3. The "patient" accepts the prescription, that is, does what the "doctor" recommends.[14]

process consultation

A consultation model that involves others in making a joint diagnosis of the problem and eventually provides others with the skills and tools to make their own diagnoses.

Process Consultation Model In contrast to the other models, **process consultation** involves others in making a joint diagnosis and eventually provides others with the skills and tools to make their own diagnoses. Also, even though the consultant may be an expert in the area of consultation, he or she refrains from solving the problem for the client. The emphasis is on facilitating the process so the client learns problem-solving skills. Although the facilitator may make suggestions or raise questions that broaden the diagnosis or develop more alternatives, the client makes the ultimate decision and develops the action plan or remedy. The underlying assumptions of the process consultation model follow.

1. Clients/managers often do not know what is wrong and need special help in diagnosing what their problems actually are.
2. Clients/managers often do not know what kinds of help consultants can give to them; they need to be informed of what kinds of help to seek.
3. Most clients/managers have a constructive intent to improve things, but need help in identifying what to improve and how to improve it.
4. Most organizations can be more effective if they learn to diagnose and manage their own strengths and weaknesses.
5. A consultant probably cannot, without exhaustive and time-consuming study or actual participation in the client organization, learn enough about the culture of the organization to suggest reliable new courses of action. Therefore, unless remedies are worked out jointly with members of the organization, who do know what will and will not work in their culture, such remedies are likely either to be wrong or to be resisted because they come from an outsider.
6. Unless the client/manager learns to see the problem for himself or herself and thinks through the remedy, he or she will not be willing or able to implement the solution. More important, he or she will not learn how to fix such problems should they recur. The process consultant can provide alternatives, but decision making about such alternatives must remain in the hands of the client.

7. The essential function of process consultation, or PC, is to teach the skills of how to diagnose and fix organizational problems. In this way, the client is able to continue on his or her own to improve the organization.[15]

How do facilitators determine whether they are being effective? One group that facilitates partnering workshops always asks the participants to evaluate both the effectiveness of the workshop and the facilitator(s). The following comments demonstrate that the facilitator provided good process consultation skills.

"The facilitators did an excellent job in serving as catalysts for dialogue."

"The facilitator took the time to help each person or group with problem solving and with staying focused."

"The techniques of the workshop leader improved communications and helped us to solve our problems in a collaborative manner."

"The facilitator provided good, constructive, visionary thinking and identified personal and group blind spots."

"The facilitator was collaborative, but firm enough to keep things focused and keep things moving."

"The facilitator's people skills were exceptional. He was genuinely interested in the individual and group needs, which made the workshop most effective."

"The facilitator achieved the goal of allowing us to solve our problems."

"The facilitator kept us focused without inhibiting the interaction of the participants."[16]

In two of the skill builders at the end of the chapter, you will have an opportunity to develop your process consultation and facilitation skills. Increasingly, team leaders (supervisors) are asked to play facilitator roles that previously were the domain of outside consultants.

Facilitating Teleconferencing

10 *Specifically identify what can be done to make teleconferencing more effective.*

Sometimes because of the expense of bringing people from distant locations to a meeting, a facilitator needs to set up or make arrangements for a teleconference. Susan Fox, executive director of the Society of American Archivists, has developed some excellent tips for facilitators in both for-profit and nonprofit organizations. They are presented in Exhibit 10-12.

Stop & Think

Would Ms. Fox's tips apply or need any modifications to accommodate a hybrid tele/web conference using software that enabled your participants to simultaneously see and interact with a common desktop? Discuss.

Leadership Strategies

As a young child, were you ever entertained by blowing bubbles? If so, you might recall playing a game with friends to see whose bubble could last the longest, and thus be the winner! Facilitation can be likened to gently guiding and protecting a bubble to ensure it stays intact and does not pop! Learning effective facilitation skills can be quite

EXHIBIT 10-12

Tips for Facilitating Teleconferencing

Preparation

1. *Decide who will be in on the call.* The first thing you need to consider is who should participate in the call. Usually conference calls address a specific issue that requires discussion leading to consensus. Think about including members who hold information relevant to the topic at hand. This may or may not include the obvious participants. You will also want to include key representatives from constituencies potentially affected by the outcomes resulting from the call.

2. *Establish a clear set of desired outcomes.* Ask yourself these kinds of questions:

   - Is this call necessary?
   - Can the issue wait?
   - If not, what needs to occur as a result of our discussion?
   - How quickly?
   - Who should be involved?
   - What will be the chief result?

3. *Create and distribute an agenda.* Once you have the rationale and desired outcome firmly established, develop an agenda and distribute it to participants well in advance of the call, if at all possible. Remember to include clear instructions about how to dial into the call.

   All meetings, regardless of how they are convened, require an agenda. Don't try to cover too much ground. Keep the topic tightly focused, communicate your desired outcomes, and give each major agenda item a time limit. Cover minor items up front so that you can quickly move to items of substance. Conclude the agenda with next steps, which can be agreed on at the conclusion of the call.

Facilitation

Remember that a conference call is a cross between a face-to-face meeting and a telephone conversation. You will therefore need to draw on a number of skills. For example, similar to a face-to-face meeting, greet participants as they "check in," and engage those who are waiting for the quorum in small talk. Hold logistical and substantive topics until everyone is on line.

1. *Designate a timekeeper and note taker.* Once you have a quorum, ask one participant to be the timekeeper and another to take notes. You will, of course, take notes yourself, but having additional help will keep you focused on facilitation rather than dictation.

2. *Ask members to identify themselves each time they speak.* Because participants can't actually see one another, self-identification ultimately makes the discussion flow more easily. If a member forgets to identify himself or herself, take it upon yourself to make the identification as quickly and as unobtrusively as possible.

3. *Call on the silent.* Lack of visual clues can easily result in people stepping in on each other's conversation or, more likely, in one or two members dominating the discussion. It's up to you to provide balance and to call on those who remain quiet. You will need to ascertain whether their silence is the result of agreement, disagreement, or shyness.

4. *Poll each member.* It's up to you to solicit full participation. If you take a vote, register each participant. In fact, poll each member each time you reach a decision point. Bottom line, never assume.

5. *Watch the clock.* As in any meeting, work with your timekeeper. Groups naturally gravitate toward less difficult issues, which can quickly waste valuable time. Keep the discussion moving toward substantive issues and outcomes.

6. *Consider alternatives for difficult issues.* You may discover that the more difficult issues cannot be resolved on the telephone. If the group cannot reach consensus or engages in a heated disagreement, it may well be that a conference call is not the best communication mechanism for that particular issue. Acknowledge that fact and either give members time to reflect and eventually convene a second call or, if necessary, find another way to meet and work things out.

7. *Review assignments and close positively.* End the call on a positive note, then reiterate the tasks and deadlines and the individuals assigned to carry them out. Congratulate your colleagues on their fine work, and thank them for their time.

Follow-Up

As soon as the call is complete, prepare the to-do list with the deadlines and designees and send it out immediately. Within the week, if not sooner, gather your notes from the call and summarize the proceedings for all participants. Most of us tend to quickly forget what we say and promise to do, so this point can't be emphasized strongly enough.

It also helps to solicit feedback about how participants viewed the usefulness of the call. Did it accomplish its aims? Are there areas in which you can improve your facilitation skills? Most of us are unaware of our own telephone habits, and this kind of feedback can be enormously helpful.

challenging because of the complex blend of art and science. Fortunately, to become an expert facilitator, you simply need the proper training and experience.

Effective facilitation requires the supervisor to learn how to balance three key dimensions: process, relationships, and outcomes. The process must be open, achieve desirable results, ensure that participants feel safe, and guide—not lead—the group. With regard to maintaining effective relationships, participants must feel as if tension is managed appropriately, everyone has the opportunity to participate and contribute, and individuals listen respectfully. Ultimately, the facilitator's goal is for the group to accomplish its task or achieve its desired outcome.[17]

The authors' experience in working with organizations in strategic planning, partnering, team building, and organization development is that having effective internal facilitators is critical for success. Effective facilitators, in most instances, come from the supervisor/team leader ranks and are closest to where the real work of the organization takes place, whether it is constructing a building, making a product, or providing a service. Thus, there are a number of firms that either provide training for facilitators who then return to their own organizations or provide facilitator consultants who work with organizations in-house. The International Association of Facilitators (IAF), a nonprofit organization, provides opportunities for members (facilitators) to meet and exchange ideas to improve competencies in helping groups and organizations. The membership grew from 75 founding members in 1994 to over 1,100 members in 2005.

Chapter Review

1. **Explain how technology is enhancing meetings.**

   Electronic technology is enhancing meetings dramatically. As greater numbers of employees work at sites distant from their supervisor, electronic technologies such as cell phones, videoconferences, and the computer, have become valuable meeting tools. Moreover, face-to-face meetings are being enhanced through various computer software meeting-support programs, which include on-the-scene display of discussion points made, voting by members, actions taken, and on-the-scene meeting minutes.

2. **Explain the four basic purposes of meetings.**

   Meetings can serve four general purposes: (1) to give information, (2) to exchange information, (3) to find facts, and (4) to solve problems. Group consensus is an important process in many meetings, especially in problem-solving meetings where decisions are made by the group.

3. **Differentiate between the leader-controlled approach and the group-centered approach used in meetings.**

   With a leader-controlled approach to a meeting, the leader clearly runs the show and conducts a very structured meeting. The advantages of this approach are that it lends itself better to established timeframes, has more predictable outcomes, and is more appropriate for large groups. With a group-centered approach, more interaction occurs among members. This approach permits greater understanding, and the exchange of ideas is more apt to generate creative solutions.

4. **Identify the advantages and disadvantages of meetings.**

   The typical supervisor frequently must conduct meetings with his or her work group. Meetings have the following advantages over one-on-one contacts: (1) they save time, (2) they allow all present to hear exactly the same message, and (3) they lend a degree of formality. The disadvantages of meetings are that (1) they may result in watered-down decisions, (2) they may not be cost effective, and (3) they may become too impersonal.

5. **Describe the actions that a supervisor can take before, during, and after a meeting to make it effective.**

   A number of actions can help to make meetings more effective. *Before* the meeting, the supervisor should determine whether a meeting is necessary, establish a clear purpose for the meeting, and plan it. *During* the meeting, the supervisor should start promptly, designate someone to take minutes, clarify his or her expectations, provide leadership, encourage two-way communication, and see to it that closure is achieved on the items discussed. *After* the meeting, minutes of the meeting should be distributed, and agreed-on commitments should be followed up.

6. **Explain the process of consensus decision making in meetings.**

   Group consensus means that members agree to accept the decision made by the group, even though not all of them may agree with it.

7. **Define group facilitation.**

   Group facilitation is a process of intervening to help a group improve in goal setting, action planning, problem solving, conflict management, and decision making to increase the group's effectiveness.

8. **Explain the role of group facilitator.**

   Among the many roles facilitators play is that of process consultant. In carrying out that role, the effective facilitator is primarily a helper and wants the group to achieve long-term development and continuous process improvement.

9. **Differentiate between process consultation and other models of consultation.**

   In contrast to other approaches, process consultation involves others and eventually provides others with the skills to diagnose and solve their own problems.

10. **Specifically identify what can be done to make teleconferencing more effective.**

    Teleconferencing can be made more effective by following these guidelines:
    1. Include as participants those with information concerning the topic of the call and those affected by the outcome.
    2. Establish desired outcomes and keep the call short.
    3. Since the participants cannot see each other, involve all members and ask each to identify himself or herself before speaking; poll each member to ensure full participation.
    4. Consider alternative solutions for difficult issues and the possibility of another call or another way to meet.
    5. Review the tasks and deadlines and the individuals responsible for working on them.
    6. Finally, close on a positive note.

Key Terms

information-giving meeting, p. 296

information exchange meeting, p. 296

fact-finding meeting, p. 297

problem-solving meeting, p. 297

leader-controlled approach, p. 297

group-centered approach, p. 298

minutes, p. 304

consensus, p. 305

closure, p. 308

group facilitation, p. 310

process consultation, p. 312

Questions for Review & Discussion

1. Explain some of the ways that technology is impacting meetings.
2. Name the four basic purposes of meetings. Of these, which generally requires the most skill on the part of the leader?
3. Differentiate between the leader-controlled approach and the group-centered approach used in meetings.
4. What are the advantages and disadvantages of meetings?
5. Describe the actions that a supervisor can take before, during, and after a meeting to make it effective.
6. Discuss the purpose of group facilitation and the role of the facilitator.
7. How does process consultation differ from other models of consultation?

Resources

Interpersonal Skill

Skill Builder 10-1

Achieving Group Consensus (Group Activity)

The table below lists the qualities most valued in a leader. These qualities appear in no special order and do not represent an all-inclusive listing. You will be asked to rank these according to your personal view of what is most important to what is least important.

	QUALITY	RANK
a.	intelligent	____
b.	caring	____
c.	dependable	____
d.	inspiring	____
e.	mature	____
f.	forward-looking	____
g.	courageous	____
h.	honest	____
i.	fair-minded	____
j.	competent	____

Instructions:

1. Complete your personal ranking of the 10 qualities listed. Rate as "1" your most important, "2" your second most important, and so on, with "10" being the least important.

(Continued)

Information

Systems

2. Break into groups of seven to nine persons. The group will select a leader and two observers, who will follow additional instructions outlined below.
3. As a group, reread the discussion on the consensus process.
4. The allotted time for this instruction is 30 minutes. *As a group, your leader will conduct a team meeting in which the team uses a consensus approach that results in a team ranking of the items. Make sure you fully explore differences of opinion among your members about the way your team will proceed to develop its ranking, as well as selection of what the team feels is #1, #2, and so on. Try to avoid voting, which tends to restrict discussion of an issue. Make sure that all members "buy into" decisions of the group. It is not necessary that you complete the ranking in the time permitted for the task. It is more important that you reach consensus on that which you* do *achieve rather than totally completing the ranking of items. If you complete half or more of the items in the time allowed, the likelihood is that you have sacrificed consensus to do so.*

Instructions to the leader: Your team will have 30 minutes to work on the task. Remember, do not forge ahead without full discussion of all relevant issues. The consensus process takes time; make sure differences are fully explored and consensus achieved before moving along to the next issue. Your effectiveness as a leader and as a team is not based on how many items you rank, but rather the extent to which you effectively lead your group toward consensus.

Instructions to observers:

1. Your task is to observe the meeting, taking notes. Evaluate (a) the effectiveness of the leader's behavior in conducting the meeting and (b) the extent to which consensus was actually achieved by the group. Complete the leader assessment scale below.

		GOOD	FAIR	WEAK
a.	Clearly established the objective of the meeting.	____	____	____
b.	Kept discussion relevant.	____	____	____
c.	Made sure everyone participated.	____	____	____
d.	Used questioning techniques effectively.	____	____	____
e.	Kept the meeting moving along.	____	____	____
f.	Helped the group fully examine issues.	____	____	____
g.	Summarized key points thoroughly.	____	____	____
h.	Achieved closure for each item on the agenda.	____	____	____
i.	Maintained "consensus" approach within the group.	____	____	____

2. After the instructor calls time, or when the meeting is complete, whichever comes first, report your observations to the group. (Keep the report to five minutes.)

Interpersonal Skill

Skill Builder 10-2

Effective/Ineffective Meetings Survey (Group Activity)

Likely you have been a participant in numerous meetings, perhaps in your job or as a member of a social group or student organization. Some of these have been effective and others less so.

Instructions:

1. Identify a specific meeting in which you have participated that you would consider highly effective. Make a written list of the reasons why you considered the meeting "highly effective."
2. Identify a specific meeting in which you participated that you would consider "highly ineffective." Make a written list of the reasons why you considered the meeting "highly ineffective."
3. Form teams of three to five persons, compare your lists with those of other members, and discuss the two lists.
4. Select a spokesperson to present to the class a summary of your team's lists to discuss.
5. As a follow-up assignment, each team should visit http://www.iaf-world.org/i4a/pages/index.cfm?pageid=3387 and download the Basic Facilitation Primer. Based on your class lists, develop recommendations using the primer to ensure effective meetings in the future.

Information

Systems

Skill Builder 10-3

Meeting Facilitation Challenges (Group Activity)

Assume that you are the supervisor leading your work team in addressing an important issue. Each situation below represents an incident that crops up during the meeting.

1. Two of your team members, Jean Morton and Taylor Lester, are hard-nosed people who often compete for attention. They often argue with each other as a way to get the spotlight. This meeting you're conducting is no exception. After stating the problem and requesting alternatives from the group, you have a good idea who the first two to make comments will be. Morton gives the first alternative. Lester gives his alternative, which is, of course, quite different from Morton's. Morton mounts a counterattack by defending her own proposal. As she speaks, you can see by Lester's body language that he is preparing his own counteroffensive.
2. One of your team members, Ernie Statler, is especially long winded. He always stretches what could be said in 10 seconds to a minute or more. The meeting has now lasted about 10 minutes and Statler has already spoken four or five times. You can see the boredom on everyone's face as he interrupts another member and gets set to talk again. You must intervene.
3. As your meeting moves along, Ann Stiles and Harry Curran have become distracting. They have whispered a few comments to each other, and you have noted some other team members' raised eyebrows and glances cast in their direction. Harold Rodriguez, one of your quiet, soft-spoken members, has the

Technology

Resources

(Continued)

Interpersonal Skill

floor as Stiles and Curran continue their private conversation. It's time you intervened.

4. It's now about 35 minutes into the meeting, and someone in the group makes a comment about the upcoming big football game tomorrow between the state's two large college archrivals. Several members chime in with comments. Your group has some strong fans pulling for each school; several members are going as a group to see the game. They would obviously rather talk football than the subject at hand. You need to have them refocus.

5. At the start of the meeting, you told the group that you could live with any decision they made. It's now about 45 minutes into the meeting and your team has fully discussed four workable alternatives. You feel one alternative is the best, but you can truly live with any of the alternatives offered. You say, "Well, we seem to have done a good job discussing the alternatives; let's see if we can now make a decision." At that point, one of the members asks which of the alternatives you favor.

6. Based on the team's responses, considerable time has been spent discussing the pros and cons and the best choice of the four. It appears that seven of your nine members favor alternative 3. The other two members favor alternatives 2 and 4. You feel that everyone has had a chance to speak up and hear each other out. You say, "It appears that, having heard from everyone on this issue, this group strongly favors alternative 3. Is this alternative workable with everyone?" Rasheed Khan, one of the dissenting members, states, "No, it's not okay with me. I'm firmly convinced it's not workable. I refuse to vote for something I don't think is best."

Information

Systems

Instructions:

1. Indicate how you would handle each situation by writing down the exact words you would say.
2. In groups of four to six students, compare your responses to each situation. Select one for each situation that your group feels is best and read it to the rest of the class.

Interpersonal Skill

Skill Builder 10-4

Developing Skills as a Facilitator/Consultant (Group Activity)
In preparation for this exercise, reread the section on process consultation.
Keep in mind that the primary role of the facilitator/consultant is that of helper to an individual, a group, or an organization.

Instructions:

1. Each member of the class is to identify a problem or issue on which he or she needs help. It may be that you need help improving your study habits and grades. It may be that you are having a problem at work with your boss or with someone who works with you or for you. The guideline is that it must be a real problem or issue and that you "own" the problem.
2. The class is to be divided into groups of three. Each member of the trio will take turns being the client and receiving help from the other two members.

(Continued)

Information

Systems

Resources

Interpersonal Skill

Information

The client will start the process by stating the issue or problem and will have 20 minutes to receive help.

3. The other two members will ask questions to clarify, expand on, and sharpen the diagnosis. In carrying out the questioning, the facilitators will play an active listening role and ask questions that not only help them in understanding the problem, but also aid the individual being helped to better understand. Examples of such questions would be: "When did you first start having this problem? Can you expand on the history of your relationship with this coworker?"

4. Ask the client what steps, if any, have been initiated to solve the problem.

5. Move into a joint problem-solving framework where all three of you engage in brainstorming ideas on how to deal with the problem.

6. Put together an action plan using the best ideas on specific actions the client can take to solve the problem.

Skill Builder 10-5

Facilitator Training (Group Activity)

Assume you are in training to become an external facilitator/consultant and are faced with the following situations:

Your Task First you are to choose the correct answer from the three alternatives and write the letter (a, b, c) that corresponds to the answer provided under the heading "Your Answer." You will have 10 minutes to complete the task.

Team Task You will be assigned to a small team of trainees to develop a team answer. Although the team will arrive at its answer through consensus, remember that consensus does not always mean unanimity. It means everyone has an opportunity to have his or her views considered before a choice is made. You will have 30 minutes to complete the team task.

How would you handle the following situations if you were the facilitator?

1. You are the facilitator at a workshop with 35 participants. The participants have agreed on a common set of goals, and they have also identified five issues they need to deal with to achieve their goals. Five ad hoc subgroups of seven participants have been assigned to develop a plan to solve one of the top issues. The first step in the problem-solving process is to clearly state the problem. The members of one of the subgroups approach you as facilitator and state that they are having difficulty defining the problem and need your help.

   a. Tell them to do the best they can. (Your logic is that people learn from experience—success as well as failures.)

   b. Ask a few questions, and then write your version of the problem on the flipchart.

   c. Suggest that each person write a statement of the problem and then record all of them on the flipchart to see if one stands out or if there is a central theme.

   Your Answer   *Team's Answer*   *Expert's Answer*

   _____   _____   _____

(Continued)

Systems

2. You are facilitating a two-day workshop between the Navy and a contractor regarding the environmental clean-up progress of a Pacific island. Several former Navy personnel now work for the contractor. Toward the end of the first day, during a break, a public works civilian from the Navy approaches you and expresses a concern that a former Navy captain, who now works for the contractor, always begins a suggestion or recommendation with the following comment: "When I was Captain of XYZ installation and we were faced with this situation, we did so and so."

   a. Do nothing.
   b. As facilitator, talk with the former captain and level with him about the concern of a member of the Navy's group. Suggest he make recommendations without mentioning his former leadership positions in the Navy.
   c. As facilitator, mention the problem to the former captain's boss with the contractor. Leave it to him to decide whether or not he wants to say anything to the former captain.

   Your Answer   *Team's Answer*   *Expert's Answer*

   _____   _____   _____

3. You are facilitator for a group of 25 participants of two organizations who must work together to complete a major task such as building a dam. The two groups are having difficulties. As facilitator, you have taken them through a process where the group has identified and prioritized five issues they need to work on to ensure they will achieve their goals. After this task is completed, the group takes a short break before they start work on the priority issues. During the break, a key manager of one of the organizations comes to you and says that unless the lack of trust issue is addressed, very little progress will be made in resolving the other issues.

   a. Tell the key manager to trust the process and that by working on the five prioritized issues, team building will occur and trust will develop.
   b. Prior to reconvening, have a short meeting between four of the leaders, two from each organization, to gain their opinion on adding the trust issue to the list. Have the key manager present his case to them, and you, as facilitator, point out that developing trust is an important factor in successful teamwork and task accomplishment.
   c. When the group reconvenes, you, as facilitator, add the trust issue to the list to be worked on.

   Your Answer   *Team's Answer*   *Expert's Answer*

   _____   _____   _____

4. Assume you are facilitating a quarterly improvement meeting between representatives from the production and maintenance departments of a chemical plant. There are seven participants: four from production and three from maintenance. The meeting has become bogged down and is not making progress because of the strong views of two participants—one from production and one from maintenance. It appears to you that although both views have merit, neither participant is hearing what the other is saying, and each is strictly focusing on his or her own viewpoint.

(Continued)

    a. Intervene and remind the participants of the time constraints and suggest they move on to something else.

    b. Intervene and request to hear the views of the other participants.

    c. Intervene by asking the production representative to summarize the maintenance representative's viewpoint to be sure the viewpoint was understood correctly by the production representative; then reverse the process.

Your Answer   *Team's Answer*   *Expert's Answer*

_____   _____   _____

5. Assume you are the facilitator/consultant for two medical firms located in a U.S. city with a population of 300,000 people. The firms are considering a merger; there are a number of win–win outcomes from such a merger (lower costs, better offices and facilities, more complete medical coverage, etc.). You are facilitating an initial exploratory meeting with eight doctors (four from each firm). After three hours, the meeting is running into difficulties, despite several interventions by you to get things on track. The problem is that one of the doctors in the first firm is, from a leadership standpoint, very Theory X oriented and is strongly against the merger. It is obvious he basically does not trust the other doctors, and by voice tone and verbal and nonverbal actions, he is behaving in a very autocratic manner.

    a. Take a long break and have each group meet for an hour to decide if they really want to pursue the merger.

    b. Intervene by giving a short theory input on Theory X and Theory Y management philosophies, and for this discussion, suggest that a participative shared leadership style should prevail.

    c. Intervene by having all eight members respond on a 3 × 5 card to the following instructions:

- Evaluate on a five-point scale how well we've done in focusing on substantive issues and ways to achieve our joint goals of better patient care, service, and profits.
- Evaluate on a five-point scale how well we have done in carrying out good group dynamics of listening, supporting good ideas, sharing leadership, and differing without being disagreeable.
- Post the results and use them as a basis for the group to discuss how to improve the group's functioning and progress.

Your Answer   *Team's Answer*   *Expert's Answer*

_____   _____   _____

6. Assume you are the facilitator for a national sales organization that is changing its culture to a team approach from that of an individual entrepreneurial approach. The theme of the two-day workshop is "working together to grow stronger."

    After the national sales director reviews the overall company objectives and history, each regional team prioritizes issues, problems, and opportunities that they need to address to achieve overall company objectives. Next, each regional team works on an action plan involving the top-ranked item.

(Continued)

As facilitator, you visit the four regional breakout rooms and are quite pleased that three of the four regional teams are progressing well and demonstrating most of the characteristics of an effective team—shared leadership, good participation and listening, and so on. Unfortunately, the last regional team is having difficulty. After observing for some time, it is apparent the problem lies with the regional manager. He is doing 80 percent of the talking, cutting people off in midsentence who offer suggestions, and forcing his own viewpoint.

a. As facilitator, suggest that the team members brainstorm ideas and write them on the flipchart before evaluating them.
b. As facilitator, take over the leadership of the group by "playing traffic cop" and directing the flow of who talks when.
c. Privately provide some coaching to the regional manager on how the session could be more productive.

Your Answer   *Team's Answer*   *Expert's Answer*

_____   _____   _____

7. This situation is a bonus question and provides an opportunity to find an answer comparable to, or even better than, the expert's answer. The instructor, with class input, will decide if a bonus is deserved.

You have been asked as an outside facilitator to assist the chairperson of an appointed task force involving a department of the federal government. This department is moving into a new federal building under design and construction. The task force has been charged to determine such interior design questions as size and type of offices, paint color, size and number of conference rooms, and so forth.

The task force consists of 10 government employees and has had two meetings. There was no progress made in the meetings, however, primarily because of two disruptive task force members. One of the disruptive individuals is very skeptical about any new, innovative ideas and is playing the role of devil's advocate (challenger), to the point of causing frustration and unproductive meeting progress. The other individual obviously has no interest in being on the committee and has done paperwork during both meetings.

What advice would you give the meeting chairperson regarding how to handle this situation?

Your Answer   *Team's Answer*   *Expert's Answer*

_____   _____   _____

Source: This skill builder was developed by the Synergistic Group, 6 Schwaemmle Drive, Mobile, AL 36608

CASE 10-1

The Quiet Meeting

Debbie Ronson, sales supervisor, was just opening a meeting she had called for members of her department. Debbie did most of the talking for the first five minutes, recounting her group's performance over the past week. Then she asked, "Are there any questions?" No one responded.

Debbie then changed subjects. "As you know, in two weeks we'll be going to a new format for scheduling our calls. This was outlined in the memo from the vice president, copies of which I sent to each of you. This is going to alter your calling schedules and significantly change the way we've been doing things. I have some ideas on how we can best work into this new system. But before getting into that, I'd like to see if anyone here has any ideas … [pause]. Anyone care to contribute anything?" No one in the group responded.

Debbie continued, "Well, here's what I think we should do. …" She then spent eight minutes outlining her plan. After the meeting was over, Debbie discussed it with one of her fellow supervisors. "I don't know what it is," she said, "but I can never get my people to say much at meetings. I try to give them a chance, but I always end up doing most of the talking. It seems they're either shy or disinterested, but I really don't know if that's the reason or not. I just wish they'd contribute their ideas."

Instructions:

1. What might be some reasons for participants not saying much at Debbie's meetings?
2. Assume that you are a facilitation consultant. What advice would you give Debbie for encouraging participation in future meetings?

11

Coaching for Higher Performance

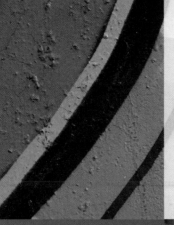

Ariel Skelley/Blend Images/Jupiter Images

Thanks to coaching from supervisors like Stacy Adelman, employees reach their highest level of achievement.

LEARNING OBJECTIVES

After reading and studying this chapter, you should be able to:

1. Explain the concept of coaching.

2. Identify the four major coaching functions.

3. Describe the important skills used in coaching.

4. Differentiate between general and pinpointed coaching statements.

5. Describe an "I" message.

6. Explain the extent to which a supervisor should counsel an employee about personal problems.

We grow because we struggle; we learn and overcome.

—R. C. Allen

The mediocre teacher tells; the good teacher explains; the superior teacher demonstrates. The great teacher inspires.

—William A. Ward

My ultimate goal for every player is performance at the highest possible level.

—Don Shula, Coauthor, Everyone's a Coach

Preview

STACY ADELMAN: PAINTBOX MANAGER Stacy Adelman has what she calls the perfect job as Paintbox manager for the world class Montage Resort Hotel in Laguna Beach, California. She loves how she spends her day—working with children of hotel guests daily. She also loves the Montage culture of "connecting with guests" that is the industry's envy. Then, there is also its strong commitment to employee training and development—the respect with which it treats employees and continuously supports their growth. Since its 2003 opening, the Montage has won rave reviews for its excellence; after just four short years, its CEO, Alan Fuerstman, was named Resort Executive of the Year by hospitality industry leaders.

Following graduation from Northern Arizona University with majors in elementary education and physical education, Stacy worked for international resort chain Club Med before joining the Montage in 2005 as its Paintbox manager. In Paintbox, Stacy and her associates deliver children's activities for guests of the 60-suite, 250-room resort, handling up to 40 children aged 2 to 12 years daily.

Let's examine some important roles she plays as Paintbox's leader. "First, everyone in our department must have a passion for children. When I hire a new associate, I'm looking for energy, enthusiasm, creativity, and caring for children. We want to be absolutely goofy with children," she states. Stacy uses "involvement," "enthusiasm," "energy," and "team" in describing Paintbox's culture and often uses the word "we" rather than "I" in describing Paintbox activities. A ritual is Stacy's weekly team meeting. "I pass along resortwide information that needs sharing. Then we go over what went well during the week and what we can work on the coming week. Everyone offers something to the team, be it their past week's work in a craft, an outdoor activity, or how they interacted with a child. We motivate each other. Our energy is contagious, especially with the children. When we have fun in Paintbox, they are having fun! We're responsible not only for their safety but also making sure they are entertained and constantly stimulated."

Stacy's associates range from two to seven in number, depending on the time of year. A newly hired associate completes a two-day orientation with other hires, called

"Mores," which begins imbuing them with the Montage culture. They interact with other new associates; learn the hotel's mission, philosophy, and operating procedures and all hotel functions; and meet key department managers. Following this, they join their respective assigned departments.

Stacy first spends time with new associates teaching them Paintbox's goals, priorities, and expectations. "I always start off with a quote of my dad's—cheesy, but so true: 'Children are like wet cement. Whatever marks you make on them leave a lasting impression.' We make a big impact on our children—we want to make sure that they have the best time and take home unforgettable memories. Our associates' goal is to become the best friend of every child and family which visits Paintbox." After discussing Paintbox procedures, such as room setup, how to greet and welcome parents and children, and key security/safety measures, Stacy says, "I then throw them right in with the children, usually teaming with an experienced associate. We all take responsibility for training someone new—they're part of our team and we want everyone to succeed."

Formal learning for associates doesn't end with "Mores" and on-the-job assignments. After two weeks, a new associate attends hotelwide "Listening and Language" and "Wow" classes, which teach how to listen and connect with guests. The resort's definition of a Wow is "a surprising personal gesture now." Each week, the top five Wows are recognized on a bulletin board that sits outside the associates' café. Stacy's associates have made the board a number of times. "We make a big deal of it when that happens," she notes.

When asked for a word that best describes her leadership approach with associates, Stacy chooses the term "cheerleader." She says, "I try to lead by example and be a great team member myself. I'm right there, pitching in with the children and leading activities just like my associates. I give performance feedback throughout the day, ranging from complimenting an associate about leading a beach game, putting together a scavenger hunt, or making a shy child feel comfortable. Or sometimes, it's a nudge like not to overlook that sunscreen...."

Because she has no office ("Paintbox is my office," she says), Stacy has the ultimate open door policy, usually working beside her associates. "I'm lucky in that I've never had a serious performance issue, perhaps because we work closely together and address things before they grow into larger ones. If one of my associates is having a personal issue I want to do what's best for them and even encourage time off as needed. You have to be 'on' all the time when working with children. They know it when an associate doesn't have the energy or focus—that's not something easily faked. And our children are number 1."

Each day, Stacy and her team review guests' surveys, which rank satisfaction with hotel services/amenities. "We're satisfied with nothing less than a perfect rating. Our goal is to become the best friend of every child and we love it when a parent mentions one of our names in the evaluations. Matter of fact, we've had parents tell us they've returned to the Montage at the urging of their children who've been in Paintbox. That's the best feedback we could ever get!"

The Montage is strongly committed to its managers' and staff development, with many key in-house promotions reflecting its policy. All managers complete, as has Stacy, a leadership course based on "The Seven Habits of Highly Effective People," and other courses in interviewing, coaching and counseling, train the trainer, and sexual harassment. Montage's Masters of Values in Practice (MVP) is a quarterly recognition that honors managers for extraordinary efforts as leaders, role models, and daily examples of Montage values. Stacy has been an MVP. One Paintbox associate has earned the Montage Masters Award, given to associates who reflect the highest standards, image, and ideals of Montage values.

Stacy sums up her perspective on Montage's emphasis on employee growth and development: "A highlight about working for a great hotel company like Montage is that it is new and growing. With that come opportunities for the associates that work here. As new properties develop, associates who demonstrate passion and commitment will either have opportunities at this Laguna Beach property as people move on to the new properties, or they may get the opportunity at other properties if willing to relocate there. That is why we take training and development of associates so seriously at Montage."

Source: Personal interview/correspondance with Stacy Adelman by Paul Pietri, July/August, 2009; Perry Garfinkel, "A Hotel's Secret: Treat the Guests Like Guests (Interview with Alan J. Fuerstman)" New York Times, August 23, 2008, p. C2.

What Is Coaching?

1 *Explain the concept of coaching.*

Did you ever play an organized sport, such as football, basketball, soccer, or volleyball, or take individual lessons in piano, karate, or math? In each case, you had a coach whose goal was to improve your performance. Golfer Tiger Woods, tenor Andrea Bocelli, and President Barack Obama have coaches. So do many top managers who employ professional coaches to help them with anything from better managing their time to softening an abrasive personality.[1] In fact, executive coaching has become a $1 billion industry.[2] The essence of supervisory coaching—just as in those situations—is helping individuals become more effective performers. In the Preview, much of Montage's culture is based on employee growth and development. Managers' jobs—like Stacy Adelman's—focus on helping team members learn, grow, and be the best they can be. That is the objective of this chapter—to help you learn more about coaching and the skills required to perform it effectively.

Tiger Woods is successful, in part, because of good coaching. Employees within an organization can benefit from the same type of coaching and support. Both the employee and the organization benefit from the employee's success.

coaching

Helping individuals reach their highest levels of performance.

Think of **coaching** as the interpersonal process that supervisors and managers use to help individuals continually reach their highest levels of performance.[3] It is a personal activity, a one-to-one relationship that starts when a new employee joins the team and continues throughout his or her tenure in your work unit. It may seem that new employees would be the primary focus of supervisory coaching. However, this is not true, given today's goals of *continuous* performance improvement. Supervisors continually coach individuals to help them achieve increasingly higher performance levels throughout their careers. As one well-known coaching expert puts it:

> *Coaching is the process by which managers stay in touch with subordinates. All the walking around in the world will not help managers get the best from their employees unless they are walking around as coaches. Coaching is "eyeball to eyeball" management. Every conversation between managers and employees is potentially a coaching conversation. It is a chance to clarify goals, priorities, and standards of performance. It is a chance to reaffirm and reinforce the group's core values. It is a chance to hear ideas and involve employees in the processes of planning and problem solving.*[4]

In the popular *Managing for Excellence*, Bradford and Cohen advocate that the days of the heroic leader who makes all key decisions and resolves all important problems are numbered. Given today's changing work environments, employees' greater competencies, and the need for employee "commitment" to excellence, the leader might be best served by using a "developer" leader style. The central orientation shifts from leader as primary decision maker to "how can each problem be solved in a way that further develops my subordinates' commitment and capabilities?"[5]

Coaching Is Performance Linked

The focus of coaching conversations is employee performance. The underlying assumption is that through effective coaching, a supervisor can help an employee become an increasingly effective performer, as shown in Exhibit 11-1. If a topic has a present or future impact on an employee's performance, then it should be considered suitable for a coaching situation. Some situations, such as helping an employee learn a new skill or addressing a problem of substandard work, are more obviously performance linked. Others are less directly performance related, such as helping an employee to prepare for advancement or to better understand and overcome insecurities. Notice the wide-reaching range of coaching situations shown in Exhibit 11-2 and how each is in some way performance linked. Quite a broad list, isn't it?

EXHIBIT 11-1
Performance-Linked Coaching

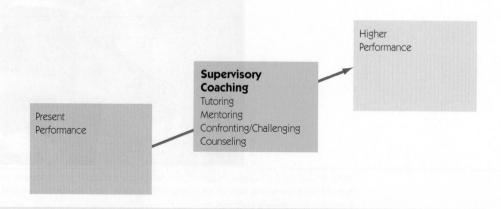

EXHIBIT 11-2

Examples of Coaching
Situations

- Assigning a new challenging task; reviewing results.
- Determining with an employee his/her training needs.
- Following up with an employee after his/her training events.
- Showing an employee how to perform a task.
- Discussing a plan for employee career advancement.
- Listening to an employee's fears of job cutbacks.
- Providing an employee insight into company politics.
- Helping an employee adapt psychologically to job changes.
- Discussing poor employee performance.
- Helping an employee manage stress.
- Discussing how a long-term, excellent employee can reach an even higher performance level.
- Conducting a disciplinary interview.
- Discussing a problem of poor work or failure to follow organization rules/policy.
- Conducting a performance appraisal.
- Allowing an employee to "blow off" some emotional "steam."

In the 1940s, a number of large organizations experimented by employing professionals to serve as organizationwide counselors. Their job was not to give advice, but essentially to become the organization's primary vehicle to listen to employees' job-related, personal, and emotional problems. Granted, it helped employees to vent their feelings about job frustrations and conflicts as well as personal problems, but the success of these programs was limited because the counselors worked outside of the formal chain of command. Today, although a number of large organizations employ full-time counselors, the individual supervisor often is considered the "first line" of counseling. She or he is best able to help an employee adjust to working conditions, work load and assignments, and employee–supervisor relationships. A team member's problems—be they job or personal—often affect his or her work performance (as well as the performance of others), but they also affect attendance, relationships with colleagues, and so on. Therefore, the supervisor has an immediate concern in these matters and assumes the legitimate role to address such employee problems. Supervisors cannot resolve personal problems such as poor health, substance abuse, or financial matters. However, they must at least understand the problem and urge the employee to seek adequate help if the problem has the potential to impact the employee's job performance negatively. The supervisor's role in these types of situations is discussed later in the chapter.

Stop & Think

Note in the chapter preview that when Paintbox manager Stacy Adelman feels an associate's personal problems may affect Paintbox's children, she encourages the associate to take time off to address the problem.

Current Emphasis on Coaching

Coaching gained momentum in the quality-driven 1990s and today is increasingly becoming the trademark in "best of class" organizations.[6] As the supervisor's role has evolved into one of being a developer of people and a facilitator whose job is to help team members maximize their potential, effective coaching is recognized as a powerful supervisory skill. At pension and investment company Skandia, a program has been installed that helps its managers learn how to have in-depth conversations with employees to identify what they both want. Following this, the conversation shifts to what support, coaching, and development the employee needs to commit to the goals. Skandia top managers attribute a large increase in employee motivation directly to these coaching conversations and their follow-up.[7]

Because organizations and work units have become more culturally diverse, managers and supervisors must understand their people as individuals, considering their needs, competencies, goals, attitudes, insecurities, and concerns. Coaching becomes an important vehicle by which a supervisor understands team members, which in turn better allows the supervisor to target his or her coaching efforts. Organizations recognize that coaching efforts should be tailored to the individual being coached. Coaching directed toward the younger, more insecure employee, who must learn many job essentials, differs dramatically from coaching directed toward the senior employee, who values advancement to the next level. And note, coaching is not limited in that it is only directed toward "B" and "C" level employees; it is also directed toward top performers.[8]

Why Supervisors Reject Coaching

Coaching appears to be a natural activity; however, in actual practice, many supervisors neglect their coaching role. First, many lack confidence. They may feel uncomfortable counseling employees and embarrassed to discuss problems of substandard performance.[9] There is always the risk that confronting a performance problem with an employee will create more problems than it resolves. Supervisors may have to deal with an employee's excuses, anger, or hurt feelings; the quality of a good relationship may be jeopardized. Ignoring a performance problem in the hope that it will resolve itself is often seen as a more desirable alternative.

Second, many supervisors view coaching as a passive process. They are more inclined through experience, and perhaps the expectation of their own managers, to have ready answers for everyone's problems and to deal with performance matters expeditiously. As one supervisor related in one of our coaching seminars:

> When people are not doing a job, you get on their case and they had better shape up. There's no way I can see myself sitting around saying "Oh, really, tell me more about that." My own boss would think I've lost it. I've always been direct with people—you tell them exactly what they're to do, see that they do it, and get on them when they don't. This is the best way to handle it.

We are all products of our past. Our parents told us what to do when we were young, as did our teachers or athletic coaches. If we had military experience, platoon leaders took over the telling. Then, when we went to work, our bosses told us what to do. When we become supervisors, it is only natural that we tend to become "tellers," which is an active, expeditious way to handle things. However, today's supervisory environment has changed considerably. The supportive relationship required for effective coaching involves more open two-way communication and greater emphasis on the supervisor's listening skills. As you will see throughout this chapter, coaching behavior always distinctly addresses continually improving performance.

Third, supervisors reject coaching because it takes considerable time. Faced by many pressures, supervisors are not prepared to abandon their heroic fire-fighting pace. Many are so immersed in managing "details" that they cannot effectively spare the time that coaching on a personal one-to-one level requires.

The Coaching Functions

2 *Identify the four major coaching functions.*

There are different ways to understand effective coaching. One is to examine *why* someone conducts a coaching session—that is, the *function* that coaching is intended to serve. Another is to examine what *skills* a coach uses during a coaching session. We will examine the functions first and then the skills. Coaching serves four fundamental functions: (1) tutoring, (2) mentoring, (3) confronting/challenging, and (4) counseling.[10]

Tutoring

tutoring

Helping team members gain knowledge, skill, and competency.

Tutoring involves a large range of coaching situations that help a team member gain knowledge, skill, and competency. Tutoring encourages team members to learn, grow, and develop. The goal is to avoid complacency with present skill levels and to develop a commitment to continuous learning. It also encourages members to put into practice those skills that are learned.

Stop & Think

Note in the chapter preview that Stacy performed tutoring when explaining to a new associate Paintbox priorities, rules, and procedures and when assigning the associate to team with an experienced Paintbox staff member. Put yourself in the job as Paintbox manager. What are some other ways of tutoring that you might develop?

Michael Newman / PhotoEdit

An important coaching function, *tutoring* is the guidance offered by a supervisor to help employees master the skills necessary to perform their jobs.

Mentoring

mentoring

Helping others develop careers.

Mentoring is the coaching activity that helps develop careers in others. Mentoring may teach political savvy, understanding of the organization's culture, and ways to advance one's career. It may also mean:

1. Helping an employee see the potentially negative impact of behavior he or she is considering.
2. Understanding how to approach and gain influence with powerful organization members.
3. Learning who key players are in given circumstances.
4. Understanding how relevant past or current events should influence the team member's actions and behavior.

Successful supervisory coaches help team members make key organizational contacts and develop their own networks. They aid in giving good career guidance, and they keep a watchful eye out for effective development of their team members' careers.

It is estimated that supervisors perform formal mentoring in about 75 percent of the companies listed as *Computerworld's* "Top 100 Best Places to Work." At companies such as Harrah's Entertainment, Lincoln Electric, and Avon Cosmetics, employees receive heavy doses of training to keep them challenged, satisfied, and employed. Mentoring comes into play by being more personal, practical, and job specific than training. It shows people shortcuts to using the skills learned in formal training. Or, as one manager puts it, mentoring shows people where the rocks and land mines are—how to avoid the mines and step on the rocks in moving toward career goals.[11]

Confronting/Challenging

confronting/ challenging

Establishing clear performance standards, comparing actual performance against those standards, and addressing performance that doesn't meet those standards.

The **confronting/challenging** coaching function is most directly performance related. Supervisory coaches establish clear performance standards, compare actual team member performance against those standards, and address performance that does not meet those standards. Through confronting/challenging, successful coaches help less-than-successful performers become successful and challenge successful ones to reach even higher levels.

Often, supervisors who are good, sensitive listeners and effective tutors and mentors experience difficulty in confronting and challenging team members regarding performance issues. They may find it uncomfortable to establish clear, concrete performance standards and to talk directly about performance. They may not be willing to address performance problems when a team member's behavior falls below standard. Confronting/challenging sessions, when finally held, may be superficial and apologetic and may skirt the poor performance problem. This issue is so important that we will discuss confronting/challenging in greater detail later in the chapter.

Counseling

counseling

Helping an individual recognize, talk about, and solve either real or perceived problems that affect performance.

Counseling is the coaching function whereby the supervisor helps an individual recognize, talk about, gain insight into, and solve either real or perceived problems that affect performance. The manager's role is essentially to help the individual determine his or her own course of action. Many supervisors feel inept and poorly trained to deal with employees' personal problems. Perhaps the most common mistake is the tendency to give advice rather than to help an employee think through, understand, and develop alternatives to problems.

In conducting counseling, it is especially important to show sensitivity and to help a team member understand how personal problems affect, or potentially affect, job performance. It is also important to help a team member gain confidence in his or her ability to handle problems. In serious cases—such as drug abuse, financial problems, or health

EXHIBIT 11-3
Outcomes of the Four
Coaching Functions

TUTORING	MENTORING
1. Increased technical know-how	1. Developing political understanding/savvy
2. Increased understanding of processes and systems	2. Sensitivity to the organization's culture
3. Increased pace of learning	3. Expanded personal networks
4. Movement to expert status	4. Increased sensitivity to key players' likes/ dislikes
5. Commitment to continual learning	5. Greater proaction in managing own career

CONFRONTING/CHALLENGING	COUNSELING
1. Clarification of performance expectations	1. Accurate descriptions of problems and their causes
2. Identification of performance shortcomings	2. Technical and organizational insight
3. Acceptance of more-difficult tasks	3. Ventilation of strong feelings
4. Strategies to improve future performance	4. Commitment to self-sufficiency
5. Commitment to continual performance improvement	5. Deeper personal insight about own feelings and behavior
	6. Changes in point of view

Source: Adapted from Dennis C. Kinlaw, Coaching for Commitment (San Diego, CA: Pfeiffer & Company, 1993), pp. 22–23.

issues—this would mean recommending that the individual seek help through the company's employee assistance program or an outside professional.

You can gain more insight into the four coaching functions by examining the different outcomes associated with each function, as shown in Exhibit 11-3.

Stop & Think

Which functions—tutoring, mentoring, confronting/challenging, and counseling—are reflected by each of the following coaching situations?
1. Helping an employee understand the political implications of his or her behavior.
2. Meeting with an employee to address his or her increased absenteeism.
3. Conducting an annual performance review with your top-rated employee.
4. Discussing with an employee her upcoming attendance at an advanced training course for which you nominated her.

All four functions have much in common and are often combined in a single coaching session. For example, when a new employee is struggling to perform, a single coaching session may involve confronting/challenging, counseling, and tutoring. Many of the skills and processes involved in all four functions are similar—the need for sensitivity, listening, and movement toward some form of closure.

Coaching and Understanding Diversity

Today's organizations reflect considerably more employee uniqueness and diversity than in past years. Perhaps in no other supervisory activity is recognition of individual differences as important to success as in coaching. Because coaching requires a highly personal, one-to-one relationship, a supervisor's ability to relate to and understand an employee's needs, sensitivities, and uniqueness and to reflect these concerns in his or her interactions is crucial to successful coaching.[12]

> Sharon Olds, marketing supervisor at AutoFin (see Chapter Preview, Chapter 7), supervises 12 associates. Her department reflects the wide diversity of employees found in organizations today. There are seven men and five women; seven Caucasians, three African Americans, one Asian, and one Hispanic. Their ages range from 23 to 59; three are single, never married; four are single and divorced or widowed. Half are college graduates, three never attended college, and three have completed some college or are presently attending college part time. Five different religions are represented, not to mention the differences in individual values, needs, interpersonal styles, and cultures. Sharon states, "I always thought that a correct saying was that you treat people the same way that you would like to be treated, or you treat people the same. I've learned that that's not true. Some people are so different. I have to be consistent and fair, but a key to being a good supervisor is being able to relate differently to the individual needs of my people."

Recall our earlier discussion in Chapter 7 about differences in motivating employees from the four generations. Coaching of Traditionalists will be quite different from coaching of younger Generation Yers. The differences in age, qualities, strengths, values, and style make coaching a highly personal, tailored activity rather than "one approach for all."[13]

The Coaching Skills

3 *Describe the important skills used in coaching.*

When a supervisor initiates a formal coaching session, he or she should have an objective to achieve and establish a basic framework for the session, adapted to the coaching function and the circumstances. However, the coaching process largely involves a number of spontaneous interactions that occur in a relaxed, personal setting. Many coaching interactions are initiated by the team member rather than the supervisor. These may include requests for help, advice, or informal discussion of a work-related matter. In some cases, such as those of a personal nature, work may not be directly involved.

A supervisor must create a supportive atmosphere that encourages contact. He or she must maintain a climate that makes people feel welcome, respects their views and feelings, and shows patience when communicating with them. A supportive climate exists when a supervisor understands what team members want to accomplish and when members are encouraged to try new approaches without fear of reprisal. It is difficult for many individuals to approach their supervisor for advice or to acknowledge job-related or personal problems that affect their job. Supervisors must establish an open, receptive communication climate, and effective listening is a critical coaching skill.

Coaching: The Core Skills

The core coaching skills are discussed in the following sections. A given coaching session may involve several or perhaps even most of these skills. As you read these skills, note the importance of an atmosphere of respect and understanding and the clear need for an outcome of the coaching effort.

acknowledging

Showing by nonevaluative verbal responses that you have listened to what the employee has stated.

attending

Showing through nonverbal behavior that you are listening in an open, nonjudgmental manner.

affirming

Communicating to an employee his or her value, strengths, and contributions.

confirming

Ensuring an employee understands what has been said or agreed upon.

pinpointing

Providing specific, tangible information about performance to an employee.

probing

Asking questions to obtain additional information.

reflecting

Stating your interpretation of what the employee has said.

Acknowledging is showing, through a range of nonevaluative verbal responses, that you have listened to what the employee has stated. These comments may range from a brief "uh-huh," "oh," "hmmm," or "I see," to longer phrases like "I can understand that" or "So that's how it happened." The acknowledging skill is designed to bounce the communication ball back to the employee and allow him or her to develop the information further.

Attending is showing through nonverbal behavior that you are listening in an open, nonjudgmental manner. In attending, your body language, such as alert posture, head nods, eye contact, and facial expressions, conveys full interest and attention. Nonattending behavior would include blank stares, nodding off, being distracted, glancing at your watch, or exhibiting other body language that displays uneasiness or disagreement with the topic being discussed. Effective attending behavior clearly communicates "I am interested and I am listening." A forest supervisor for a paper company offered one of the authors an interesting perspective on his attending environment: "When I have something personal I want to discuss with an operator, I can wait till the end of the day when I've an office setting. But I often prefer handling sensitive things directly in the field, which is less formal and likely more comfortable for my crew members. We might sit on a recently cut tree trunk, just the two of us, and I'll handle things right there, if possible."

Affirming is communicating to an employee his or her value, strengths, and contributions or other positive factors. An example might be "You have made excellent progress learning the new system" or "It always amazes me how quickly you catch on" or "I've always valued your willingness to share your feelings with me about things."

Confirming is making sure that an employee understands what has been said or agreed upon. The coach can do this by summarizing and repeating the key points or by requesting the person being coached to do so. The coach might ask, "How about going over these steps in your own words and telling me how you would proceed?" Confirming may also occur with an eye to the future: "How about modifying your estimates as we've discussed, using the highest quality materials available, and let's take a look at this at 3:00 p.m. tomorrow."

Pinpointing is providing specific, tangible information. For instance, "You did a poor job on the write-up" is a vague, general statement that covers wide territory. It is not as helpful as "The write-up used figures that were three years old, contained over 20 spelling and typographical errors, and lacked a specific recommendation." We will cover pinpointing in more detail in the next section.

Probing is asking questions to obtain additional information or exploring a topic at greater length, such as the following: "So you feel your group is ready to take on more responsibility. In what ways have they signaled this?" or "So you would do it differently next time, given what you now know. What would you do differently?"

Reflecting is stating in your own words your interpretation of what the employee has said or feels, such as "So you feel that you should have received more help from your teammates on this?" or "It seems like you're really upset with them for not helping out."

Resourcing Coaches should act as resources for their team members. **Resourcing** can be done by providing information, assistance, and advice: "I really wouldn't recommend

resourcing

Providing information, assistance, and advice to employees.

reviewing

Reinforcing key points at the end of a coaching session to ensure common understanding.

summarizing

Pausing in the coaching conversation to summarize key points.

bypassing Mason on this. It cost someone his job about five years ago when he did it" or "Talk to the human resources people. They should be able to answer your question" or "Let me show you how to do that."

Reviewing At the end of a coaching session, reinforcing key points to ensure common understanding is the skill of **reviewing.** This can be done by the coach as follows: "Let's pull this together. It seems we've identified three things you'll do with the survey data. First, you'll send your supervisors their individual results and the overall company results. Then you'll conduct one-on-one meetings with them to discuss their results. Following this, your supervisors will develop a written plan, accepted by you, as to what they'll do to improve." Another example is, "Let's make sure we're together on this. How about summarizing what you'll do with the survey results?"

Summarizing is pausing in the coaching conversation to summarize key points: "Let's see if I understand you. You believe two factors have hurt your sales performance: one, our promotion strategy was changed; and two, extra committee work has taken time away from your sales calls."

Note that some skills, such as acknowledging and attending, relate to the *atmosphere* or environment of the coaching session—its openness and the fact that the coach is interested and is listening. Other skills such as pinpointing, probing, and resourcing are more directly tied to the *content* of the session, or the issue(s) involved.

Fancy/Jupiter Images

Coaching involves several core communication skills, such as acknowledging, affirming, pinpointing, probing, and summarizing.

EXHIBIT 11-4
Suggestions for
Confronting Poor
Performance

1. Describe the performance situation in specific detail.
2. Seek and listen to the team member's point of view.
3. Get agreement on the problem.
4. Try to get the employee's involvement in determining a solution.
5. Agree on a plan of action to improve performance.
6. Summarize the agreement and reinforce the changed behavior.
7. Plan for follow-up, if needed.

Coaching for Improved Performance: Confronting and Challenging

One of the things supervisors must do, but often do poorly, is address performance problems. Many managers do it in a blunt, threatening way that may cause resentment. Too often, they blame, lecture, put down, warn, or coerce a person in attempting to make that person improve. It is questionable whether a good chewing-out is the best way to do this. Supervisors are not mind readers, and until you can understand the reason for poor performance, you cannot adequately coach someone to improve. It simply is not coaching to call someone in, read the riot act, and send that person away. Often, the result is no change, a half-hearted change, or resentment at having been "called on the carpet." By contrast, some supervisors dislike discussing poor performance and are reluctant to bring it up. They avoid confronting a poor performer only to find that the poor performance escalates, making the inevitable coaching meeting involve more serious stakes than if it had occurred earlier. An employee's poor performance can relate not only to actual on-the-job work performance, but to other types of behavior as well, such as attendance, safety, attitude, and adherence to various company rules and policies.

While individual situations may differ, the suggestions for dealing with substandard performance contained in Exhibit 11-4 are often effective.

It is essential that the issue of poor performance be addressed by the supervisor early in the meeting. Your comments should pinpoint the issue(s) specifically. For example, instead of telling an employee "Your job performance is poor," it is more informative to say, "You reached only 75 percent of your work goal," or "You have been absent three times in the past two weeks." In this way, the employee is given something concrete. Here are some further examples:

4 *Differentiate between general and pinpointed coaching statements.*

General	**Pinpointed**
1. Your attendance is poor.	1. You have missed a day in each of the past four pay periods.
2. You need to cooperate better with department heads.	2. Company policy is to give department heads the cost information when they request it.
3. You need to follow our safety rules.	3. This morning I saw you performing the job without wearing your safety goggles.
4. You haven't made the progress that you'd agreed to.	4. You and I agreed that you would complete the first draft by today, but you tell me you need two more days.

Stop & Think

How might you better pinpoint the following statement about an employee's performance? General statement: "You have a bad attitude."

Your pinpointed statement: _____

Note that a number of steps shown in Exhibit 11-4 require you to listen and/or to actively involve the team member in the discussion, especially step 2: Seek and listen to the team member's point of view; step 3: Get agreement on the problem; step 4: Try to get the employee's involvement in determining a solution; and step 5: Agree on a plan of action to improve performance.

Exhibit 11-5 illustrates a supervisor conducting a confronting/challenging coaching session. Note the supervisor's use of the steps involved in confronting poor performance, as well as many of the skills of pinpointing, acknowledging, reflecting, resourcing, and summarizing. The exchange also illustrates how, even while willing to listen to Bob's views, the supervisor remains focused on the performance issue.

EXHIBIT 11-5 Script of Confronting/ Challenging Coaching Session	**Sup 1**	Bob, I wanted to talk with you because I have a problem. I'd thought after we last talked about quitting time that you understood our policy and that you intended to stick to it. So, I was surprised yesterday to see you'd left a little after 5:00 and not 5:30. I'm upset about it.
	Bob 1	I've been trying hard not to leave before 5:30. I hadn't left early in about 2 months until this emergency.
	Sup 2	You've had a good record recently. So yesterday was something special?
	Bob 2	I had a call in the middle of the afternoon from the guy I ride with in my neighborhood. Said he had to leave a little before 5:30, and if I wasn't out on the street, he'd have to leave me.
	Sup 3	Put you in a bind, huh.
	Bob 3	You're right about that. Once when he was sick I took the bus, and it took me an hour and a half to get home.
	Sup 4	So you hated to use that alternative, huh.
	Bob 4	Yep. It only takes about 30 minutes driving with him.
	Sup 5	So you were torn between losing time getting home and sticking with our rule.
	Bob 5	Yeah, I looked around for you in the afternoon; you can ask Art. You were out of the office and I couldn't find you. Fifteen minutes didn't seem like such a big deal since I'd had a good record recently.
	Sup 6	So you hoped I'd approve, if you could ask me.
	Bob 6	I was sure of it.
	Sup 7	Apparently, you felt it was very important for you to go home and not miss your ride, even to the point of breaking a rule and our agreement.
	Bob 7	Well, it was a rare emergency that happens from time to time. Seems like a few minutes don't matter that much. I'm here working sometimes 20 minutes early in the morning.
	Sup 8	I understand that. You're always here on time, and I appreciate that. But we have two policies—one for getting here on time and one for staying until 5:30—and both must be kept.
	Bob 8	I wouldn't expect this to happen again, at least only very rarely.
	Sup 9	I felt that [way] after we had our last talk, Bob, but then something came up and it's happened again.
	Bob 9	I told him then that I have to stay until 5:30, so he usually waits, except for yesterday. At least he called me.
	Sup 10	Can you think of something you might do to avoid this happening in the future? Because this rule is not to be broken unless there is an emergency more serious than this. I don't consider this to be the type of emergency that would warrant your leaving early. Can you think of anything you could do to keep it from happening again?
	Bob 10	I could make sure that you know I'm leaving early, if he ever needs to leave again.
	Sup 11	That solution doesn't satisfy me—I don't think I could agree. I don't think I could give my permission for this.

EXHIBIT 11-5
continued

Bob 11	Not even for 10 or 15 minutes?
Sup 12	Not for that. We need a solution that will satisfy you and satisfy me and the company policy.
Bob 12	Maybe I'd have to ride a bus on those days.
Sup 13	In other words, you can take a bus if you have to.
Bob 13	Yeah, but it seems to me that the hour and a half it takes is a long time for just 10 or 15 minutes. Seems unreasonable to me, the policy, that is.
Sup 14	Seems to you like, if you keep the policy most of the time, it's all right to break it once in a while.
Bob 14	It seems that way to me.
Sup 15	If the 20 people working on our department took the same approach, almost every night someone would be leaving early. I wouldn't feel that would be fair. Would you?
Bob 15	Well, no. Maybe I could find someone right here who could drive me home on those days. I wouldn't even mind catching the bus and then walking a little way.
Sup 16	Think that would solve it, huh?
Bob 16	Yes, but how would I go about finding someone?
Sup 17	I'll bet Mr. Barrows has a list in the Human Resources department.
Bob 17	O.K., I'll drop over there today.
Sup 18	Bob, it's important that I can count on you to keep the rules by working through until 5:30. Thanks for discussing this with me, and I appreciate your working it out.

Source: Adapted from Thomas Gordon, Leader Effectiveness Training (L.E.T.) Copyright © 1977, 2001 Penguin Putnam. Reprinted by permission of the author.

5 *Describe an "I" message.*

"I" message

Attempt to change an employee's behavior by indicating the specific behavior, how it makes you feel as a supervisor, and the effect of the behavior.

Tom Gordon, a well-known writer on leadership and interpersonal issues, advocates the use of what he calls "I" messages when we want to effectively alter someone's behavior.[14] He says there are three major parts of an **"I" message:**

- *Feelings:* Indicate how you feel about the effects of the behavior (angry, embarrassed, frustrated, concerned, etc.).
- *Behavior:* Identify the specific behavior (absenteeism, not keeping appointments, not meeting quota, etc.).
- *Effect:* Spell out the end result of the behavior (poor example for others, making the work unit look unproductive, inconvenience to others in the unit, etc.).

When you send an "I" message, you appeal rather than demand that the other person change. Note in the following examples that the focus is the *behavior,* its *effect,* and how it makes you *feel.* Although no one likes being told his or her behavior is causing a problem, framing your displeasure in an "I" message addresses the problem more openly and tactfully and is more likely to pave the way toward a resolution in an objective, supportive manner.

"You" Message

1. You neglected to proofread that report, you should know better than to let a report go out like that.
2. You know I expect you to attend our regular meetings. You need to attend them from now on.

"I" Message

1. When I noticed the many typos in the report, I was really upset. It makes our unit look careless and unprofessional.
2. When you don't attend our regular meetings, I'm concerned that we miss your expertise and insight.

In using the "I" message, it is important to keep in mind the coaching skills from the previous section. Your goal as a supervisor is to correct the inadequate performance in a way that shields the employee's ego *and* maintains a positive relationship between you and the employee. Thus, the session should focus on the employee's *performance* rather than personality—in other words, the problem and not the person. Your use of "I" messages can be an important tool in focusing on the employee's behavior rather than on the employee's ego.

Stop & Think

Refer to Exhibit 11-5. Can you identify the supervisor's use of an "I" message?

Coaching: The Counseling Function

6 *Explain the extent to which a supervisor should counsel an employee about personal problems.*

Counseling, one of the four coaching functions, involves a broad range of emotional areas, ranging from an employee's frustrations, insecurities, anger, and resentment to his or her lack of commitment. The problem can be attributed to real or perceived factors and can be work related or personal. The objective of counseling is to help an employee better understand himself or herself and, when needed, to develop a plan of action to resolve the issue. The coach's job is to help the individual more fully discuss and understand the problem being experienced. Feelings, emotions, and attitudes may be exchanged. As shown in Exhibit 11-6, counseling attempts to identify and help both supervisor and team member better understand those "below-the-surface" factors that are influencing or may potentially influence the team member's performance. In counseling, the listening-related skills of attending, acknowledging, reflecting, and probing are especially essential.

A coach often has no advance notice as to when counseling is needed; these coaching opportunities are usually initiated by the team member. On other occasions, a team leader will plan to perform one of the other coaching functions, for instance, tutoring or confronting/challenging, when the need for counseling arises. The leader must be sufficiently flexible to shift gears and address counseling, as pointed out below.

What started as a routine tutoring session for supervisor Rosa Bender turned out quite differently when she learned that Rudy, a new technician, felt ignored by senior people in the department. Bender temporarily dropped her tutoring agenda and devoted

EXHIBIT 11-6
Iceberg Model of
Counseling

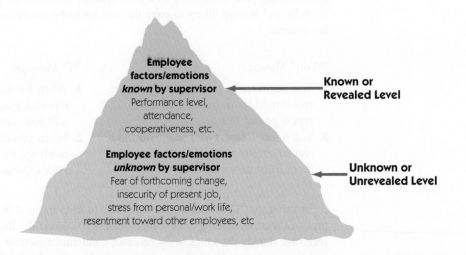

Employee factors/emotions *known* by supervisor
Performance level, attendance, cooperativeness, etc.

Known or Revealed Level

Employee factors/emotions *unknown* by supervisor
Fear of forthcoming change, insecurity of present job, stress from personal/work life, resentment toward other employees, etc

Unknown or Unrevealed Level

about 10 minutes to reflecting and probing why Rudy, the youngest and newest member of the team, felt this way. Learning that he felt slighted because senior employees offered him little help, Bender helped him understand that senior employees, while likely supportive, were independent performers who thoroughly immersed themselves in their own work. Although perhaps they hadn't offered help, they would gladly help if asked.

Rudy agreed to ask senior employees for help when he needed it and to communicate to Bender his degree of success. Satisfied that this addressed the immediate counseling issue, Bender then shifted back to the tutoring session she had originally planned.

Areas of Employee Counseling

Counseling is involved in virtually all aspects of the supervisor–employee relationship. It begins with the hiring phase and does not end until the employee leaves the company. Certain areas, though, are more likely to necessitate counseling than others.

Job Performance We have already indicated that counseling is often used in combination with the other four coaching functions. It is especially important in the area of job performance. Numerous factors, many of which the supervisor is unaware, influence employees' job performance. A good rule of thumb is to always be prepared to engage in counseling when addressing below-standard employee performance, especially for employees who have had no performance difficulties in the past or who have only recently engaged in negative job behavior. This would include performance changes in quality and quantity of work, absenteeism, adherence to policy and rules, and changes in cooperativeness and relationships with others, including the supervisor.

Physical and Emotional Illness Another common need for counseling arises because of physical and emotional illness. In some cases, these issues are initially addressed by the supervisor as performance problems, but in many cases, they may be initiated by the employee. Although the team leader must play a supportive, listening role in counseling, it is imperative that the employee clearly see the impact or potential impact of such problems upon performance.

When Avery Williard showed up late, his supervisor coincidentally happened to be present at Williard's work area. While Williard appeared quite uncomfortable and embarrassed, his supervisor expressed surprise because Williard was never late. It was then that the supervisor smelled alcohol. He asked Williard to join him in his office. Williard acknowledged that he had been drinking a lot lately because of "problems at home," but pledged he would not do it again. His supervisor listened patiently, noting that Williard didn't volunteer particulars. He praised Williard for his excellent work and dependability over the years, but reminded him that should it happen again, he would have no choice but to formally discipline him. Seeing that Williard was in no condition to work, his supervisor sent him home after setting a meeting for the next day. This meeting was to reinforce (1) his support for Williard and (2) the fact that Williard's behavior could not be tolerated again on the job. He also planned to strongly suggest that Williard consider referral to the company EAP (Employee Assistance Program) as a source of help.

Often it is difficult for a supervisor to diagnose an employee's substance abuse, especially when it is not accompanied by performance slippage. Behavior that differs from the norm may be the telltale sign. Note in Exhibit 11-7 the many behaviors, such as increased accidents, need for increased rest breaks, frequent off-the-job emergencies,

EXHIBIT 11-7
Profile of Typical
Substance Abusers

A 2007 national survey found that drug use remains a problem in the U.S. workplace, despite testing for illicit drugs. Self-reported impairment or actual use at work was 15.3 percent for alcohol and 3.1 percent for illegal drugs. Rates in some industries, such as food service and construction ranged up to 28 percent actual use in the workplace. Here are some characteristics of typical substance abusers.

- Four times more likely to have on-the-job accidents than nonabusers
- Four to six times more likely to have off-the-job accidents than nonabusers
- Five times the number of workers' compensation claims as nonabusers
- Five times the number of medical claims as nonabusers
- Two and a half times more absenteeism/tardiness than nonabusers, especially on Mondays and Fridays and before and after holidays
- Take extended breaks and lunch hours
- Have numerous restroom breaks
- Experience frequent off-job emergencies
- Experience frequent colds, flu, upset stomach, headaches, etc.
- Dramatic change in personality or work performance during the day, especially after breaks
- Deteriorating personal appearance and ability to get along with others
- Tendency to overreact to real or imagined criticism
- Experience difficulty handling instructions
- Depressed or anxious disposition
- Work at 67 percent of potential

Source: Chris O'Neill and Joel Bennett, "New Approaches to Drug Free Workplace Programs," The Journal of Employee Assistance, Oct 2008, 38, pp. 20–22; Janet Gemignani, "Substance Abusers: Terminate or Treat?" Business & Health 17(6), June 1999, pp. 32–37; Laura A. Lyons and Brian H. Kleiner, "Managing the Problem of Substance Abuse… Without Abusing Employees," HR Focus 69(4), April 1992, p. 9; Peter Ellis, "Substance Abuse and Work," Occupational Safety & Health 30(13), March 2000, pp. 38–41.

deteriorating personal appearance, and overreaction to criticism, that are indicators that substance abuse may be involved.

As in the preceding situation, supervisors are increasingly called on to counsel employees with many forms of physical and emotional problems. These problems range from substance abuse and job stress to debilitating physical illnesses, such as cancer, heart disease, and acquired immunodeficiency syndrome (AIDS). Moreover, the rash of corporate downsizings, mergers, and financial and ethical mismanagement has created unparalleled emotional anxiety, as reflected by present and former employees who commit acts of physical violence against employers.

Personal Problems To what extent should a supervisor counsel an employee with personal problems, such as financial, health, or marital problems? The answer depends largely on the extent to which the problem impacts present or future job performance. If it affects job performance, it is essential that the supervisor use counseling to understand the nature of the problem, if for nothing more than to help the employee appreciate the need for professional assistance. However, a supervisor should tread carefully before becoming entwined in personal problems, for several reasons:

Stop & Think

Note in Exhibit 11-5 that to fully address the performance issue (employee leaving work early), the supervisor helped the employee address his personal problem (transportation after work).

Sometimes superiors must counsel employees who have an emotional or physical illness or personal problems

1. Employees may feel resentful or embarrassed after "opening up" and disclosing highly personal matters. This may jeopardize their future job relationship with their supervisor.
2. If the supervisor makes too concerted an effort to probe into more than an employee cares to divulge, the employee may be resentful.
3. If the supervisor gives advice on personal problems—such as marital difficulties, problems with children, or buying and selling property—and the results turn out unsatisfactorily, the supervisor will be blamed. In addition, the supervisor and/or the company may be open to legal liability.

In general, supervisory counseling should be restricted to factors that affect job performance. Supervisors work hard to develop trusting, supportive relationships and are often placed in a position of counseling team members in problem areas only peripherally related to job performance. To reject the counseling opportunity outright may be perceived as lack of interest. The supervisor can always listen sufficiently to determine the nature of the employee's problem and then steer the individual toward a professional or other source of help. That is where an Employee Assistance Program enters the picture.

Role of Employee Assistance Programs in Counseling

Employee Assistance Programs (EAPs)

Professional counseling and other services for employees with unresolved personal or work-related problems.

From a handful of programs begun in the 1940s to address alcoholism, **Employee Assistance Programs (EAPs)** have emerged to extend professional counseling and other services to employees confronted by unresolved personal or work-related problems.[15] These may include counseling for substance abuse, emotional illnesses, marital issues, divorce, or stress. Many companies have broadened the counseling services available through their EAPS; at Comcast, employees and their families may receive counseling assistance in such wide-ranging areas as help with weight loss, smoking, budgeting, taxes, estate planning, legal matters, and even buying a car or house.[16] A program at Convergys' 1,600-employee Oklahoma City area call center provides employee assistance to newly hired employees who experience work scheduling conflicts for child care of personal reasons.[17] In cases where an EAP does not exist, a supervisor may refer an employee to counseling services provided within the community, most of which have public mental health or social service professional counseling available. However, most larger organizations do offer EAP support of some kind, and a Society of Human Resource Management survey of small firms with fewer than 100 employees showed that 70 percent provided EAP services.[18] Exhibit 11-8 gives you a good idea of the counseling services offered by one company's EAP.

EXHIBIT 11-8
Example of an Employee Assistance Program (EAP)

Most of the time, we like to think we are in control of our lives. All of us, however, occasionally experience personal crises that may cause us to feel out of control. These crises may be due to health problems, financial or legal difficulties, or emotional problems. Because we care about our employees, an Employee Assistance Program (EAP) has been implemented. The EAP will provide confidential, professional counseling and referral to employees who seek assistance with personal problems. Realizing that an employee may be affected by a family member's personal problem, the EAP is also available to the families of our employees.

What the EAP is:

- *Voluntary:* Employees or family members can contact the program directly. Participation in the program is always voluntary.
- *Independent:* The EAP is administered by Human Affairs Inc., a national company that provides assistance programs to many companies across the country.
- *Confidential:* Because of the two components mentioned above, EAP participants are assured that any information revealed to EAP staff will be held in the strictest professional confidence.
- *Professional:* All EAP staff are licensed Master's-level therapists and counselors.
- *Free:* All counseling and referral services provided by the EAP are free to employees and their families. If an EAP counselor does recommend that employees consult a special outside resource, the counselor can let employees know what part of that service may be covered by their other medical benefits.
- *Accessible:* EAP counselors are available for emergency situations 24 hours a day, 7 days a week. Appointments are made for non-emergency situations during day or evening hours.
- *A Valuable Resource:* The EAP can serve as a resource concerning counseling, information, and management consultation to employees, supervisors, and family members.

What the EAP is NOT:

- *A Branch of Human Resources:* The EAP is not designed to replace any personnel or management procedures.
- *A Refuge for Poor Job Performance:* Participation in the EAP will not protect employees from disciplinary action.

Procedures

- *Self-Referral:* An employee or an immediate family member may use the service by contacting Human Affairs Inc. directly in complete privacy whenever they would like to consult with the counselor. Self-referrals are both anonymous and completely confidential. Self-referrals will not affect job security or promotional opportunity.

EXHIBIT 11-8
continued

- *Supervisor/Management Referral:* A supervisor may recommend that an employee contact Human Affairs Inc. when there is a job performance or conduct problem which has not responded to ordinary supervisorial techniques. Whether or not the employee decides to contact Human Affairs Inc., it is the employee's responsibility to perform satisfactorily on the job; and if problems go unresolved and performance continues to deteriorate, disciplinary action up to and including discharge may result. Participation in the EAP is not a guarantee that these actions will not continue to occur, but improved performance often results from problem resolution.

The Company sincerely hopes that all staff and their dependents who might benefit from this service will take advantage of it.

Source: "Purpose of Company E.A.P." Personnel Policy Briefs, Sample Issue, n.d., p. 2, as found in Leon C. Megginson, Geralyn McLure Franklin, and M. Jane Byrd, Human Resource Management (Houston, TX: Dame Publications, Inc.), 1995, p. 296.

Where present, the EAP can be a big help to supervisors by handling referred cases at a professional level. Studies of EAP programs at Abbott Labs and McDonnell Douglas show that employees who participated had fewer absentee days and fewer terminations than other company employees in general.[19] Thus, it is in the supervisor's best interest to encourage employees to participate when necessary. Supervisors typically are given training and policy guidance in how and under what conditions to refer employees to a company's EAP, should one exist. Skill Builder 11-5 will give you insight into how the University of Maine provides a monthly newsletter to assist supervisors and managers in resolving EAP issues.

Chapter Review

1. **Explain the concept of coaching.**

   Coaching is the interpersonal process used by supervisors and managers to help individuals continually reach their highest levels of performance. Coaching is performance oriented, whether it helps a new employee gain new skills or accept challenges, or helps a seasoned employee reach even higher levels of performance. The current emphasis on coaching reflects the changing role of supervisors as facilitators and developers of people.

   Despite its importance, supervisors tend to experience difficulty in practicing effective coaching. Many lack the confidence in their communication skills, especially listening, to be an effective coach. Others see it as too passive and prefer to provide answers to employees rather than to work jointly with them to develop their own answers to problems. Still others are uncomfortable in spending the large amount of time that effective coaching requires.

2. **Identify the four major coaching functions.**

   There are four coaching functions. Tutoring helps a team member gain knowledge, skill, and competency. Mentoring develops political savvy, an understanding of key players, and the way to advance one's career. Confronting/challenging focuses directly upon performance itself—from setting clear objectives to follow-up meetings that discuss results. It can address performance problems and inspire top performers to continue to grow and improve. Counseling helps an individual recognize, talk about, and thereby gain insight into his or her real or perceived problems that may affect performance.

3. **Describe the important skills used in coaching.**

   Coaching is a one-to-one relationship that utilizes such skills as acknowledging, attending, affirming, confirming, pinpointing, probing, reflecting, resourcing, reviewing, and summarizing.

4. **Differentiate between general and pinpointed coaching statements.**

   In coaching designed to confront/challenge an employee with a performance problem, supervisors should pinpoint, in specific, concrete language, the employee's performance level, rather than using general terms.

5. **Describe an "I" message.**

   "I" messages, which indicate the problem behavior, its effect, and the supervisor's feelings, can be an effective way to focus on the performance problem. For example, "Your lunch break was in excess of an hour and a half. I was embarrassed when the plant manager came by looking for you on two occasions and found other people covering your work area."

6. **Explain the extent to which a supervisor should counsel an employee about personal problems.**

   In general, supervisors should restrict their counseling to factors that affect an employee's job performance. However, mny personal problems, such as physical and emotional health, substance abuse, and financial and family problems, actually affect or may affect future performance. The supervisor should focus counseling on the performance-related aspects of the problem. Many firms today have an Employee Assistance Program (EAP) to which supervisors can refer troubled employees.

Key Terms

coaching, p. 330

tutoring, p. 333

mentoring, p. 334

confronting/challenging, p. 334

counseling, p. 334

acknowledging, p. 337

attending, p. 337

affirming, p. 337

confirming, p. 337

pinpointing, p. 337

probing, p. 337

reflecting, p. 337

resourcing, p. 337

reviewing., p. 338

summarizing, p. 338

"I" message:, p. 341

Employee Assistance Programs (EAPs), p. 346

Questions for Review & Discussion

1. What is meant by coaching?
2. Of the four major coaching functions—tutoring, mentoring, confronting/challenging, and counseling—which do you feel is most difficult? Why?
3. Describe the following coaching skills and give an example of each:
   a. attending
   b. affirming
   c. resourcing
   d. reviewing

4. Give an example of a "general" coaching statement as contrasted to a "pinpointed" coaching statement. Which is more effective and why?
5. What is an "I" message? Why is it an effective way to confront someone's behavior? Give an example.
6. To what extent should a supervisor counsel an employee about the employee's personal problems?
7. What is an EAP?

Skill Builder 11-1

Information

Interpersonal
Skill

The Personal Trainer and Coaching

Given everyone's addiction to good health, physical fitness has experienced much popularity. One of the fastest growing professions has been that of personal fitness trainer. Consider the fitness trainer's job: Listen to the client's goals, outline a program of activities that will achieve the client's goals, and then, through coaching, help the client to achieve them. Once the client has learned the basics, the trainer's job essentially becomes one of encouraging, supporting, and giving feedback. You know the language: "That's it," "All the way down, now," "Tighten up a bit," "Way to go," "You can do it," "That's great," "Terrific," "That's the way to push yourself," "Hold that form, come through for me," "That's OK, you showed improvement, we'll get it next time," and so on.

Instructions:
Break into teams of four to six members. Select a spokesperson and discuss the following questions:

1. In what way are the roles of personal trainer and manager/supervisor similar? Dissimilar?
2. In what types of circumstances can all or most of the coaching behavior of personal trainers be applied to the manager/employee relationship? Give examples.
3. Have any team members worked for a manager/supervisor who functioned much like a personal trainer? In what ways?
4. Following discussion, the spokesperson will present to the class the results of the team's discussion.

Skill Builder 11-2

Information

Interpersonal
Skill

Practicing "I" Messages

In reading this chapter, you learned that an "I" message consists of (1) how someone's behavior makes you feel, (2) what the specific behavior is, and (3) the effect of the behavior. The following three situations show a need for an "I" message.

a. Four of your employees share a single telephone line. You are aware that one of them, Harry R., is especially long-winded on the phone and talks for as long as 15 minutes. This prevents others from placing outgoing calls and ties up the line, preventing customers from getting through.
b. It is a requirement that waiters at the upscale restaurant you manage wear white shirts and ties. One waiter has been loosening his tie, dropping the knot about two inches, and unbuttoning his shirt collar.
c. Coffee breaks for your office staff are normally 15 minutes. When someone occasionally takes a few minutes longer, it's not a big deal. Lately, however, one staff member has had three consecutive days when the break exceeded 20 minutes.

Instructions:
1. Write a hypothetical "I" message for each of the three situations.
2. Gather in groups of three to five students and share answers.
3. From your answers, select some good examples and present them to the rest of the class.

Information

**Interpersonal
Skill**

Skill Builder 11-3

Practicing Coaching Responses

Assume the role of shipping supervisor at Apex Company. One of your employees, Jason, has been an excellent performer for the past five years. However, during the past two weeks, Jason has not seemed himself. He was operating a forklift when a careless accident caused about $2,000 in damages. Moreover, Jason has punched in late twice. When you discussed these incidents, he apologized, attributing his tardiness to car trouble. Normally outgoing and energetic, he has appeared tired and edgy. Usually one of the liveliest contributors at meetings of your group, he said nothing at yesterday's safety meeting. During afternoon break on the loading dock today, Spud, another employee, made a joking comment about Jason's favorite college football team, which had been beaten handily by its cross-state rival this past weekend. Jason responded angrily with an expletive, then got up and left the area. Another employee commented, "What's been eating Jason, anyway?" Everyone shrugged their shoulders. You decide to have a coaching meeting with Jason.

It is about two hours later. Jason has just walked into your office. You stand, acknowledge him, and close the door behind him. Jason takes a seat, and as you move to sit down, he says, "So you wanted to see me about something."

a. **In the space below, write the opening statement you will make to Jason that pinpoints the reason for the meeting.**

Assume that following your statement, a discussion with Jason lasts for several minutes. He is very soft-spoken and avoids eye contact. Then he looks you in the eye and says, "I'm glad I have this chance to talk with you. I feel like so much is going on with me lately. I guess I've just taken on more than I should … and I don't know what to do about it."

b. **In the space below, write the statement you will make to Jason that demonstrates reflecting.**

Assume that the discussion continues. Jason is quite talkative now, volunteering information about financial problems brought on by a house addition, his son's college expenses, and a recent auto accident that cost him $750 to cover the deductible on his policy. To meet his financial needs, Jason tells you he has been moonlighting for 30 hours weekly as a security guard at a local hotel. He has gotten little sleep the past two weeks. He now worries that he can't sustain the pace, because his job performance at Apex is being affected. He says, "I know I haven't been much of a contributor around here lately."

c. **In the space below, write the statement you will make to Jason that demonstrates affirming, but also reinforces the need for him to improve performance.**

During the remaining discussion, Jason commits to making his present job performance his number one priority, despite his short-term financial needs. You discuss several alternatives that would allow him to do both, two of which he proposed: (1) reduce his hotel hours, with most of them being worked on weekends, and (2) getting a loan from the company credit union or a bank. A third idea—taking his two-week vacation now, which would allow him to work his full hotel hours for two weeks—was one you suggested he consider. You tell him you would look into waiving the normal two-week vacation notice. You also suggest he consider making an appointment with the company's EAP office, which can arrange for financial counseling for employees. Jason expresses interest in this.

You agree to let Jason know tomorrow about the vacation matter and to be available as needed to discuss things further should Jason need to talk. You note that Jason picks up his hard hat, which was placed on the floor, and says: "Well, I feel much better having talked with you about this. It's taken a lot off my mind, and it's helped me think some things through. Thanks for being so patient."

d. In the space below, write the statement you will make to Jason that demonstrates confirming/summarizing and closes the meeting.

e. Meet with other students and compare your responses.

Skill Builder 11-4

Information

Interpersonal Skill

Conducting a Coaching Meeting: Role Plays

In this exercise, you will break into small groups as determined by your instructor. The entire group should read the role for the manager/supervisor and the employee. One person should be designated to perform each role, with the others being observers. Several minutes of planning time should be allowed for players and observers to study their roles before beginning the actual coaching meeting.

General Instructions for Observers

Following each role play, you will lead a discussion of the manager's effectiveness in handling the performance coaching meeting. Use the pre–role play planning time to review some of the important coaching principles presented in the chapter to help evaluate the manager's performance. The following questions give insight into your critique of the meeting:

1. What do you feel was the objective of the meeting?
2. Were the steps in Exhibit 11-4, "Suggestions for Confronting Poor Performance" followed? Were any done especially well? Which might have been improved?
3. Which of the "Core Coaching Skills" such as acknowledging, attending, affirming, and so on, did the manager use in the meeting?
4. To what extent do you feel that the manager achieved the objective of the meeting?

Coaching Meeting 1: Assistant Principal and Teacher
(a) Role for Assistant Principal (to be read by all)
You are assistant principal at an elementary school. Twelve teachers report to you. One is Jan Wilson, who has been with you for three years. Jan teaches fourth grade. She has an excellent record as a teacher and is very well liked by her students' parents.

A well-known rule at your school deals with teacher absences—when a teacher will miss classes because of illness or emergency, your office should be notified so that a substitute teacher can be employed. Earlier in the year, Jan failed to show up for class and did not notify you until later in the day. You scurried to cover Jan's class, and when Jan returned the following day, you reminded her of the notification policy. You learned that her absence was related to a family emergency with one of her elderly parents.

Yesterday, it happened again. A teacher from an adjacent classroom notified you that Jan's class was unattended. Again, you had to exert much energy finding a temporary replacement for the rest of the day. Jan did leave a short voicemail at 10:30 a.m. yesterday for you in which she apologized for the inconvenience and said that she would be back in class today. No reason for her absence or late notification was offered.

Today, you made it a point to pass Jan's classroom shortly before class began. You asked if everything was okay, to which Jan responded, "Yes, thank you." You then asked Jan to drop by your office at 3:15 p.m. following dismissal of classes.

Instruction: In a few minutes, you will conduct a performance coaching session with Jan.
(b) Role for Teacher Jan (to be read by all)
Background facts for your role are presented in the "Role for Assistant Principal" as outlined in "a" above. In a few minutes, you will meet with your assistant principal. You expect that the subject will relate to your class absence yesterday. To develop your role, take a few minutes to determine a reason why you may have missed class and why you didn't notify the assistant principal earlier. Remember, you are a talented, conscientious teacher who has a good relationship with other teachers and your assistant principal. During the role play you may have to adapt your role as the discussion ensues.

Coaching Meeting 2: Restaurant Manager and Server
(a) Role for Manager (to be read by all)
You are manager of a well-known national casual dining restaurant in your area. You are reviewing customer comment cards that have been mailed by customers to your regional office, tabulated, and then forwarded to you each month. Results are compared to goals set for such important criteria as quality of service, food quality, and other factors. About 200 comment cards were returned to you from the past month. Your goal for server ratings is to average 85/100; during the past month, your restaurant's customers rated your 15 servers an average of 81/100. These scores ranged from a high of 95 to a low of 68.

Kelly's score of 68 is clearly poor! A new server like Kelly (presently in her second month) sometimes scores lower than more seasoned servers, but Kelly's is the lowest you have seen in the past year. Most customers rated her as "excellent" or "good." But Kelly bombed on five of 17 customers' cards, being rated as "unacceptable." Four of these found fault with Kelly's language—one labeling it as "foul mouthed," another as "profane." One mentioned some four-letter words attributed to Kelly: "hell," "damn," and "crap." This troubles you. Kelly's training has emphasized how important courtesy, pleasantness, and most assuredly nonoffensive language by servers is as part of a "quality" experience for your customers.

Much business is with Sunday and Wednesday churchgoers and with families with small children, so four-letter language is totally inappropriate. In her interview with you, Kelly displayed excellent interpersonal and rapport-building skills. Presently majoring in leisure services at the local university, she saw the server position as an excellent opportunity to help understand customer service.

Although you are clearly disappointed in the comment cards from Kelly's customers and with its impact on your restaurant's goals, Kelly has promise of becoming an excellent server. Clearly, however, she must clean up her language. You will conduct a coaching meeting with Kelly when she shows up for work this evening.

(b) Role for Server Kelly (to be read by all)

Read the background facts for your role as a server as presented in the "Role for Manager" outlined in "a" above. In a few minutes, you will meet with your manager, who has asked to see you. Take a few minutes to decide how you will respond in the role play to the likely things that your manager will bring up in the meeting. During the role play, you may have to adapt your role as the discussion proceeds.

Information

Skill Builder 11-5

Organizational EAP Newsletter: Help for Supervisors?

Organizations recognize that supervisors are key players in successful employee assistance program (EAP) services. In this exercise, you will visit and critique the EAP website of the University of Maine and examine its helpfulness to supervisors in resolving employee assistance issues.

1. Go to http://www.umaine.edu/eap/supervisor_resources.htm.
2. Read the text of "How Can EAP Be a Resource for Supervisors."
3. From the left margin menu, click "Supervisors," and read several copies of the *Frontline* supervisor newsletter.
4. On a scale of 1 to 5, with 1 being lowest and 5 highest, how helpful do you think the Newsletter is to the University of Maine supervisors? Why? What recommendations would you make to improve it?
5. In groups of three to five students, discuss your rating, explanation, and any recommendations for improvement.
6. Select a newsletter month/year and click.
7. Print and bring to class the *Frontline* supervisor newsletter for that month.
8. Be prepared to share with a team of three to five students the most critical EAP-related questions/issues addressed in the newsletter for that month.

Interpersonal Skill

Technology

CASE 11-1

Critiquing a Coaching Meeting

The following exchange took place between Charlene Rowe, human resources manager, and one of her senior team members, Leonard Busche.

Rowe 1: Come in, Leonard, have a seat. [Leonard sits down.] I suppose you're wondering why I wanted us to get together.

Busche 1: Yes, I guess I am, Charlene.

Rowe 2: Leonard, yesterday something happened that I want to know your feelings about. It's about the quality steering report I asked you to put together for my committee meeting yesterday afternoon.

Busche 2: [Somewhat defensively] What about it?

Rowe 3: To be quite frank, Leonard, I was too embarrassed to distribute it at the meeting. It just wasn't up to your usual standards. For one thing, it seemed superficial in that it described only a few of the programs we'd benchmarked, rather than all seven. Since this will be the major document the committee will be using as a reference, we needed coverage of *all* the visits we've made. Also, some of the most important processes were not included—like J&J's 360-degree feedback system and Motorola's team incentives.

Busche 3: [only half joking] Gee, it seems as if I may need a union steward in here with me. [Leonard is a salaried, nonunion employee.]

Rowe 4: No, Leonard, I don't mean to give that impression. It's just that this job isn't like you at all, and that concerned me. You've always done exceptional work in putting together material like this for me. For all I know, it might have been my own fault, a misunderstanding between us. I wanted to meet and get your perspective on the situation.

Busche 4: Well, there isn't much to say. I guess I should have figured it wouldn't be of much help. [Getting a little emotional] I wasn't tickled about it either.

Rowe 5: You weren't pleased with it yourself?

Busche 5: No, I wasn't. Charlene, that report would have taken about 8 to 10 hours for me to do it

up right. Do you know how long I had? About four hours, that's all. I couldn't do much in four hours.

Rowe 6: So you didn't get to put in the time on the report….

Busche 6: No, I didn't. In fact, you weren't the only one embarrassed by it. But I can't promise it'll be the last lousy job…. I just can't handle everything that comes my way. I know we're a service department [human resources], but we're not the little outfit we were five years ago. I just can't keep up.

Rowe 7: It sounds as if the quality report is only part of the problem.

Busche 7: That's exactly what I'm saying. I'm expected to do everybody's odds and ends besides my regular job in training and safety. I've got the two accidents we're investigating from two weeks ago and all that paperwork. We're approaching our deadlines on the new training manuals. I'm heading up the newsletter committee that puts out our first edition next month. Then, you gave me the quality report with one week's notice. I would have gotten it done, but last week Bushman [vice president and general manager] asked me to be his facilitator. I had to put in some eight hours observing his meetings with the budget committee. So the quality report was lousy, I know. But if things continue as they are, it won't be the last. I hate it more than you do.

Rowe 8: Leonard, you know how we've all come to expect so much from you. Granted, we are a service department, but in retrospect, I wish you'd confided in me about this. I could have simply pushed back my quality committee meeting, which is what I essentially did, anyway. What can we do to help you?

Busche 8: How can we help? [Flippant] Oh, give me an assistant.

Rowe 9: Is additional help the answer?

Busche 9: I don't know the answer to that. I think what's really got me upset is Bushman. He didn't *ask* me to facilitate, he *told* me to. I should have turned him down, but I guess I haven't got the guts to say "no" to a vice president. But then, I didn't want to let you down, either.

Rowe 10: I think it's terrific that Bushman values your abilities. Politically, it's in both of our interests for you to act as Bushman's facilitator. That is, if you want to do it.

Busche 10: Oh, I don't mind facilitating for Bushman. He needs a lot of help and he knows it. It would normally be a real compliment for me; it was just the timing that was bad.

Rowe 11: Leonard, you have a lot of things going on that I didn't know about. Maybe I'm the one who has to do some changing. I can see why, given your schedule the past two weeks, taking on that quality project was too much. It wasn't fair to you. Leonard, I need to feel confident that your work for me from now on will be what I can count on. What can we do to prevent this from happening again?

Busche 11: I could probably do a better job of letting you know what I've got going on. I could also be more honest with you. I just hate saying I can't do something, especially to my boss. You probably didn't know the newsletter was eating up my time last week, as were the safety problems. I guess I could keep you more up to date. I could also be more direct and tell you if I honestly don't have the time to take something on and do a good job. But it's hard for me to say no.

Rowe 12: Okay, let's give this a try. You'll give me a brief typed report on projects other than your normal training and safety activities. If you're skeptical about a commitment request from outside the department, you'll discuss it with me before taking it on. You're also agreeing to level with me about whether you have time to commit to special projects that I throw your way. We'll try this process for a month and see what happens. Is that acceptable?

Busche 12: Yep, that sounds acceptable. Hopefully, I'll not get caught up in a bind like this again.

INSTRUCTIONS:

1. What type of coaching function was reflected in Rowe's meeting with Busche?
2. In terms of effectiveness on a 1–10 scale, with 1 being "poor" and 10 being "excellent," what score would you assign to Rowe's handling of the session? Why?
3. Identify specific transcript comments by Rowe that reflect the following coaching skills: (a) reflecting, (b) pinpointing, (c) probing, (d) affirming, and (e) confirming.
4. To what extent did the meeting reflect the seven suggestions for confronting poor performance (Exhibit 11-4)?
5. Meet with a group of three to five other students, discuss your answers, and be prepared to report these to the rest of the class.

12
Managing Conflict, Stress, and Time

LEARNING OBJECTIVES

After reading and studying this chapter, you should be able to:

1. Identify the causes of conflict.

2. Discuss conflict management styles and identify when each would be appropriate.

3. Describe principled negotiation.

4. Explain why modern life makes us particularly vulnerable to stress.

5. Describe both the costs and the benefits of stress.

6. Explain the major causes of stress.

7. Compare and contrast Type A behavior and Type B behavior.

8. Elaborate on personal ways to cope with stress.

9. Discuss some ways to effectively manage time.

Brad Killer/istockphoto.com

As many management consultants will tell you, it can be challenging to establish trust and communicate clearly when most of the communication takes place electronically instead of face-to-face.

Nothing in life is to be feared. It is only to be understood.
—*Marie Curie*

Everything that irritates us about others can lead us to an understanding of ourselves.
—*Carl Jung*

Difficulties are meant to rouse, not discourage. The human spirit is to grow strong by conflict.
—*William Emery Channing*

Preview

THE FACILITATOR: DEVELOPING TRUSTING RELATIONSHIPS John Duncan* works for TSI Consultants* facilitating partnering workshops for large-scale construction projects. His job involves coordinating premeetings with the key stakeholders, who typically include the owner(s), architect(s), prime contractor(s), and key subcontractors, to determine the main issues and establish an agenda for the partnering meeting. John's task during the one- to three-day partnering retreat is to provide facilitation to the group such that they are able create a project management culture focused on joint problem solving. One particular project involved the U.S. Navy and the city of Honolulu on the Hawaiian island of Oahu. The Navy was in the process of transferring a particular piece of property to the city to be used for administrative office space. In his premeeting conversations with the key stakeholders, John did not detect any noticeable anger or conflict. Therefore, the agenda he devised primarily focused on establishing common goals, creating a project mission statement, identifying potential issues, and developing action plans to address each issue.

Although preliminary staging for the project had been underway for several weeks, the actual on-site work was just beginning. The one-day session started well, with the stakeholders getting to know each other better. However, during the early morning session, while developing the project mission statement reflecting important goals and values, John detected undercurrents of tension among some of the participants. One thing he had learned early in his career is that "if there are issues regarding trust, you better deal with them up front and openly. If not, it is not a question of if but when will the

*The names have been changed for privacy reasons.

train derail." Therefore, he decided to modify the meeting agenda to more quickly focus on the key issues facing the project management team.

After some time, the root cause of the tension became more apparent. The majority of the stakeholders were physically located in various areas of the island of Oahu. Thus, they relied on e-mails, faxes, and phone calls to disseminate and gather information because it saved time and money. This was causing an unforeseen problem. It was challenging to effectively encode and decode important, complex messages regarding contractual information without the assistance of verbal inflections and/or nonverbal signals. Thus, it was easier for the participants to fall into traps like making the wrong assumptions, having different interpretations, lacking sensitivity, and developing negative attitudes. Once they began to talk openly and candidly about specific instances, they realized the absurdity of it all. They had in essence created mountains out of mole hills!

The project management team's strategy to address the communication issue was to create a modular office facility on-site to house key members of each stakeholder group. This solution helped develop a project culture that allowed for and encouraged "richer" communication. The thought was that if the contractor's project manager has a question regarding a project specification, he or she could simply go down the hall and hash it out with the architect face-to-face. Once the team dealt with building trust through better communication, the remainder of the partnering session was very productive in terms of dealing with other important issues.

Source: Consulting experiences, The Synergistic Group, LLC, Mobile, AL 36608.

We have seen in the chapter preview that ineffective communication can result in interpersonal conflict, which is often very disruptive and damaging. A supervisor/team leader must possess a variety of skills. Two of the most critical are conflict and stress management. When stress is excessive, one's behavior can become dysfunctional. However, we must keep in mind that a certain amount of conflict and stress is healthy, because it can lead to more effective decision making.

For example, intrapersonal stress can motivate an individual to proactively make life changes for the better. When a certain amount of conflict is present, the status quo is examined. Individuals grapple with various solutions through their analysis of the situation. In many cases, this evaluation leads to better decisions.

Causes of Conflict

1 *Identify the causes of conflict.*

A supervisor/team leader must have a basic understanding of the causes of conflict before he or she can determine what is functional or dysfunctional. This section looks at some of those causes.

1. **Different goals or objectives.** If departments or individuals within an organization are working toward different goals, then conflict is almost always dysfunctional. It is important to develop a common set of goals that everyone supports.
2. **Communication.** Misunderstandings due to semantics, unfamiliar language, or ambiguous or incomplete information will surely lead to conflict.
3. **Structure.** Competition for scarce resources, power struggles between departments with conflicting objectives or reward systems, or interdependence of two or more groups to achieve their goals occur with organizational changes such as downsizing.
4. **Personal.** Incompatibility of personal goals or social values of employees with the role behavior required by their jobs will lead to conflict, as will certain personality

---

HISTORICAL INSIGHT

Mary Parker's Integration Process

One of the first to focus on conflict in organizations from a research/consultant standpoint was sociologist Mary Parker Follett (1869–1933). Ignored for a time, her ideas are found in many management and psychology textbooks today. One of her contributions was her analysis of how to deal with conflict. She believed that any conflict of interest could be resolved by (1) voluntary submission of one side, (2) struggle and victory of one side over the other, (3) compromise, or (4) integration (today, we call it joint problem solving).

Her preferred solution was the **integration process,** whereby everyone wins, as opposed to a win–lose situation, or a watered-down compromise by which neither side gets what it wants. An example Follett gave to illustrate the concept of integration was an incident that occurred when she was working in a small room in the Harvard library. The other person in the room wanted the window open, while Follett wanted it closed. After discussion, integration was achieved when they opened a window in the next room. This solution was not a compromise, since both got what they wanted: The other person got fresh air, and Follett did not have a cold draft on her back.

Follett also believed that the essence of collaboration and teamwork was creating the feeling of working *with* someone rather than *over* or *under* someone—the notion of "power with" rather than "power over."

Source: Oliver Sheldon, *The Philosophy of Management* (New York: Pitman, 1939; originally published in 1923), p. 2.

---

integration process

A conflict resolution strategy in which everyone wins.

characteristics, such as authoritarianism or dogmatism. Individual stress can also be a source of intrapersonal and interpersonal conflict.

5. **Change.** Fears associated with having to accomplish a task differently, job security, or the loss of personal power and prestige can cause abnormal behavior. Change can be threatening. Even change that is perceived to be positive can cause conflict when individuals are responsible for new duties and tasks.

Self–Check

How many of the previous causes of conflict were operative in the chapter preview?

Conflict Management Styles

2 *Discuss conflict management styles and identify when each would be appropriate.*

Individuals must cope with all forms of interpersonal and intergroup conflict. It is important to properly diagnose the conflict situation so that it can be dealt with in the most effective manner. Exhibit 12-1 is a diagram of five conflict-handling styles that are based on the concern an individual has for oneself and for others. The five styles, which were influenced by Mary Parker Follett's original model, are:

- **Avoiding.** Avoiding is an unassertive, uncooperative style in which the individual's concern for self and others is low. It is a useful style when dealing with trivial issues or when the negative consequences of confrontation outweigh the need for resolution.
- **Accommodating.** Accommodating is an unassertive, cooperative style in which the individual's concern for self is low while the concern for others is high. The accommodating approach downplays the parties' differences. It is an appropriate style to use when the issue is more important to the other party or the other party is right.

EXHIBIT 12-1
Interpersonal Conflict
Management Styles

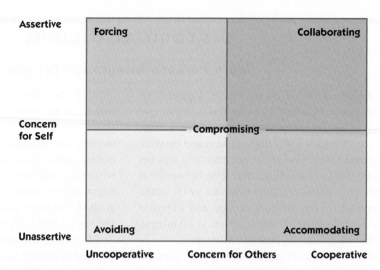

Source: Adapted from Thomas Ruble and Kenneth Thomas, "Support for a Two-Dimensional Model of Conflict Behavior," *Organizational Behavior and Human Performance*, Vol. 16 (1976), p. 145. Reprinted with permission from Elsevier.

- **Forcing.** Forcing is an assertive, uncooperative style in which the individual's concern for self is high while the concern for others is low. This approach uses power to resolve conflict. A forcing style is useful in an emergency, where quick decisions are necessary. It is also useful for correcting unethical behavior.
- **Compromising.** Compromising is a somewhat assertive, cooperative style in which the individual has a moderate amount of concern for both self and others. The objective is to find a middle ground. The compromising style is appropriate when the parties have reached an impasse due to mutually exclusive goals.
- **Collaborating.** Collaborating is an assertive, cooperative approach in which the individual has a high concern for self and others. Collaboration is a problem-solving style. It is effective when dealing with conflict "head on," trying to surface all of the pertinent issues, and attempting to interpret differing points of view.

Conflict management theory today supports collaboration as the appropriate approach to resolve conflict. Since collaboration in many cases leads to win–win outcomes, it is easy to discern why collaboration advocates support this approach as "the model" for handling conflict.

During the 1970s and 1980s, the contingency movement gained momentum. Proponents of this theory maintained that collaboration in all situations is unrealistic. For example, a management student, who is a member of a local emergency response team, made these observations when conflict management styles were covered in class.

The student's emergency response unit was activated shortly after a tragic train wreck occurred. The emergency response team prepares for these types of situations regularly. However, unanticipated problems arise that must be dealt with effectively as quickly as possible to save lives. Although the team members may utilize the collaborative approach during the planning stages, they do not have time to rely on this method while in the field. She indicated that the approach most often used by the team in the field was the forcing style, because it was the most effective.

Conflict management styles must be adapted to fit the situation at hand.

The avoiding, accommodating, forcing, and compromising conflict management styles are usually best used when dealing with tactical, day-to-day, short-term problems, whereas collaboration (and compromising, to a limited extent) is a conflict management style more appropriate for ad hoc task forces and long-term strategic problems.

Self-Check

In the chapter preview, what primary conflict management style(s) was/were used? Explain.

Using Principled Negotiation to Resolve Conflict

3 *Describe principled negotiation.*

A real breakthrough in conflict management and resolution is found in the concepts proposed by Roger Fisher and William Ury of the Harvard negotiation project. They emphasize that, whether negotiation involves a peace settlement among nations or a business contract, people often engage in *positional bargaining*. This common form of negotiation involves proposing and then giving up a sequence of positions. The idea is to give up things that are not important. Hence, proposals are "padded" initially. For this form of negotiation to succeed, it must meet three criteria of fair negotiation: "It should produce a wise agreement if agreement is possible; it should be efficient; and it should improve, or at least not damage, the relationship between the parties."[1]

When people bargain over positions, they tend to back themselves into corners defending their positions, which results in a number of either win–lose or lose–lose outcomes. Moreover, arguing over positions often endangers an ongoing relationship by straining and sometimes shattering relationships. In a marriage, this results in divorce; in business, the result can be the breakup of an otherwise successful operation. Many negotiations involve more than two parties, and in these cases, positional bargaining compounds the problem of negotiating an agreement.

principled
negotiation
_____

Negotiation on the
merits by separating the
people from the problem,
focusing on interests,
not positions, generating
a variety of possibilities
before deciding what to
do, and insisting that the
result be based on some
objective standard.

In their work with the Harvard negotiation project, Fisher and Ury developed an alternative to positional bargaining that they call **principled negotiation,** or negotiation on the merits. The four basic components of principled negotiation are as follows:

1. Separating the people from the problem.
2. Focusing on interests, not positions.
3. Generating a variety of possibilities before deciding what to do.
4. Insisting that the result be based on some objective standard.

Consultant facilitators for a number of joint ventures and partnerships involving multiple parties have noted that educating the joint venture parties in the concepts of principled negotiation has resulted in a high percentage of win–win resolutions in dispute settlements. Exhibit 12-2 illustrates the difference between positional bargaining and principled negotiation. Notice that in positional bargaining, one can either play "hardball" or "softball."

EXHIBIT 12-2
Contrast of Positional
Bargaining and
Principled Negotiation

PROBLEM: POSITIONAL BARGAINING: WHICH GAME SHOULD YOU PLAY?		SOLUTION: CHANGE THE GAME—NEGOTIATE ON THE MERITS
SOFTBALL	HARDBALL	PRINCIPLED
Participants are friends.	Participants are adversaries.	Participants are problem solvers.
The goal is agreement.	The goal is victory.	The goal is a wise outcome reached efficiently and amicably.
Make concessions to cultivate relationship.	Demand concessions as a condition of the relationship.	**Separate the people from the problem.**
Be soft on the people and the problem.	Be hard on the problem and the people.	Be soft on the people, hard on the problem.
Trust others.	Distrust others.	Proceed independent of trust.
Change your position easily.	Dig in to your position.	**Focus on interests, not positions.**
Make offers.	Make threats.	Explore interests.
Disclose your bottom line.	Mislead as to your bottom line.	Avoid having a bottom line.
Accept one-sided losses to reach agreement.	Demand one-sided gains as the price of agreement.	**Invent options for mutual gain.**
Search for the single answer: the one *they* will accept.	Search for the single answer: the one *you* will accept.	Develop multiple options to choose from; decide later.
Insist on agreement.	Insist on your position.	**Insist on using objective criteria.**
Try to avoid a contest of will.	Try to win a contest of will.	Try to reach a result based on standards independent of will.
Yield to pressure.	Apply pressure.	Reason and be open to reason; yield to principle, not pressure.

Overcoming Interpersonal Conflicts

The authors are convinced that principled negotiation is an excellent approach for dealing with conflicts among departments within an organization or resolving conflicts in joint ventures or partnerships. Perhaps a more pervasive challenge is managing interpersonal conflicts. This challenge has been accelerated because of fears of downsizing, mergers, and unknown organizational futures. Job insecurity fueled by these fears produces fertile ground for conflict. Dysfunctional interpersonal conflict can lead to a variety of negative outcomes, including poor morale, low productivity, increased absenteeism, and higher turnover. In fact, in exit interviews, 50 percent of individuals list unresolved conflict as their primary reason for leaving.[2]

Industrial psychologist and trainer Dr. Jack Singer makes a strong case that human resource professionals and supervisors must learn conflict resolution strategies and teach them to other employees. He recommends a three-step program for assessing and implementing a conflict resolution strategy, as shown in Exhibit 12-3. As

---

EXHIBIT 12-3

Three-Step Program for Conflict Resolution

STEP 1. EVALUATING CONFLICT STYLE

Several self-assessment questionnaires have been developed over the years that are geared toward offering participants insight into how they react in typical conflict situations. Consider using them. The insight they provide allows you to understand what "buttons" get pushed when a person is provoked, and becomes useful as a tool to reevaluate and enhance one's behavior.

STEP 2. IDENTIFYING CONFLICT BEHAVIORS

Nonproductive Behaviors. Confronting, dominating, defending, using sarcasm and hostile humor, repressing emotions, insisting on being right, stonewalling, blaming.

Neutral Behaviors. Avoiding, cooling off, apologizing, giving in, backing off to avoid confrontation.

Positive Behaviors. Active listening, empathizing, disarming, inquiring, using "I feel" statements, recognizing how internal dialogue impacts emotional reactions. The goal is to eliminate negative and neutral behaviors and practice positive confrontation reduction skills until they become new habits.

STEP 3. LEARNING POWERFUL CONFRONTATION REDUCTION SKILLS

Active Listening. The key to all interpersonal communications is genuine listening, as opposed to defensive listening, where you plan your retort *while* the other person is talking to you. To begin to really listen, set up a role-playing environment.

First, paraphrase what the other person says in your own words, without judging, agreeing, or disagreeing. Listen to and reflect upon the content, needs, and feelings of the other person.

Second, ask for feedback to determine whether you interpreted correctly. If you have not, ask for clarification.

Third, once you are sure you grasp the message and feelings of the other person, respond.

Fourth, the other person then should listen and paraphrase for you. This process continues until you have both clarified your positions.

Empathizing. This involves putting yourself in the other person's shoes and trying to see the world through his or her eyes, taking into account cultural, racial, gender, and experiential differences.

Disarming. The fastest way to defuse an argument is to find some truth in what the other person is saying, even if you do not agree with the basic criticism or complaint. For example, saying "*I can understand* how you'd feel angry with me since you believed that I started the rumor" acknowledges and validates the angry person's feelings without actually agreeing with what was said. This opens the door to clarification.

Inquiring. By asking for clarification of ideas, needs, and feelings *you* signal a feeling of working toward mutual understanding and compromise.

"I Feel" Statements. Expressing yourself with such statements as "I feel angry because you seem to be avoiding me" is much more productive than the accusatory, "*You* made me angry and it's *your* fault that I've had a bad day at work today." In the first scenario, *you* take responsibility for your own feelings and share them; in the second, you escalate the confrontation by blaming and putting the person on the defensive.

Source: Resources, Aberdeen Woods Conference Center, 201 Aberdeen Parkway, Peachtree City, GA 30269-1422. Jack N. Singer, *Personality Collisions* (Vol. 3, Issue 3, November 1997), pp. 5–6.

evidenced by the following example, conflict assessment and training can be quite effective.

> When Fernando Costa became divisional manufacturing manager at MM Kembla Products in Kembla, Australia, relationships between management, supervisory, and shop floor personnel had broken down, and interactions often resulted in confrontation. "Dialogues were nonexistent and threats were the acceptable way of putting a position forward. Any issue—no matter how trivial—would be addressed through union representatives," says Costa. The company decided to offer conflict resolution training, and, two years later, the benefits are evident. "There is a total change in the way people talk to each other today," Costa says. Union representatives no longer use abusive language to intimidate management, and management addresses problems more effectively, using the conflict resolution techniques they learned. Employees can resolve some issues without involving senior management, and without increasing tensions on the floor."[3]

Many interpersonal conflicts occur when one person finds another person's behavior uncomfortable, bullying, or irritating. Robert Bramson has identified basic types of difficult behavior, three of which are particularly troublesome when trying to resolve conflicts. Exhibit 12-4 identifies these three types and gives suggestions for coping with them.

EXHIBIT 12-4
Coping with Difficult Behavior

Hostile-Aggressives: Hostile-aggressive behavior occurs when individuals bully other people by bombarding them with cutting remarks, or by throwing a tantrum when things do not go their way. Their focus is on attacking the other party in a conflict. Openly emotional, they use these displays to create discomfort or surprise in their adversaries. Underlying their behavior is a strong sense of "shoulds," internal rules about the way things ought to be. A key to dealing with hostile-aggressive behavior is to recognize the behavior and not to be drawn into it yourself.

HOSTILE-AGGRESSIVES:
- Stand up for yourself.
- Give them time to run down.
- Use self-assertive language.
- Avoid a direct confrontation.

Complainers: Complainers gripe constantly but never take action about what they complain about, usually because they feel powerless or they do not want to take responsibility. You may want to hear complainers out and let them know you understand their feelings, but do not get drawn into pitying them. Use a problem-solving stance. For instance, a manager might say, "Joan, what do you want the outcome of our meeting to be? What action needs to be taken?" This focuses the complainer on solutions, not complaints.

COMPLAINERS:
- Listen attentively.
- Acknowledge their feelings.
- Avoid complaining with them.
- State the facts without apology.
- Use a problem-solving mode.

Clams: Clams are silent and unresponsive when asked for opinions. They react to conflict by closing up (like their namesakes) and refusing to discuss problems. The challenge in coping with clams is getting them to open up and talk. Open-ended questions are invaluable, as is patience in allowing them their silence for a reasonable time.

CLAMS:
- Ask open-ended questions.
- Be patient in waiting for a response.
- Ask more open-ended questions.
- If no response occurs, tell clams what you plan to do, because no discussion has taken place.

Source: Adapted from *Coping with Difficult People* by Robert M. Bramson, copyright © 1981 by Robert Bramson. Used by permission of Doubleday, a division of Random House, Inc.

What Is Stress?

4 *Explain why modern life makes us particularly vulnerable to stress.*

A number of concepts presented earlier in this chapter lend insight into how to manage stress. Organizations and supervisors can suffer serious consequences if stress is not understood and managed. We now examine the topic in more depth.

Definition of Stress

For many years, the medical community failed to take stress seriously. One of the reasons for this failure was the lack of an adequate definition of stress and of research into its effects. **Stress** can be defined as any external stimulus that causes wear and tear on one's psychological or physical well-being.[4]

stress

Any external stimulus that causes wear and tear on one's psychological or physical well-being.

Stress researchers point out that modern men and women sometimes react to the strains of work and everyday life the same way our primitive ancestors did. In the days of the caveman, when there was danger, a chemical reaction in the body geared our ancestors to either fight or flee. The problem for some modern men and women is that their bodies still react the same way to external stimuli, causing them to maintain a constant fight-or-flight readiness. The anxiety is similar to that of soldiers in combat, and it causes wear and tear on our bodies.

Jane Coleman was driving to work during the morning rush hour. An irresponsible driver nearly caused an accident by cutting into her lane. By the time Jane arrived at work, she was already tense; the problem was compounded when she discovered that one of her key employees was out with the flu. Two emergencies during the day caused her to end the day anxious and exhausted.

Ryan McVay/Photodisc/Getty images

Traffic is an external stimulus that can act as a common stressor. What is one example of an internal stimulus?

EXHIBIT 12-5
Equilibrium and
Disequilibrium

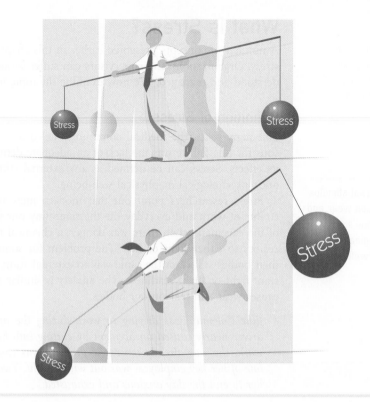

Many of us face situations similar to Jane's. Note that stress can be caused by an external stimulus, such as driving on the freeway, or by conditions on the job. An excellent definition of job stress is "a condition arising from the interaction of people and their jobs and characterized by changes within people that force them to deviate from their normal functioning."[5] Under normal conditions, our bodies and minds are in a state of equilibrium (see Exhibit 12-5). As a result of occurrences on or off the job, however, our equilibrium may be disrupted. In attempting to recover from this imbalance, we function differently and sometimes generate a fight-or-flight chemical reaction. Obviously, Jane, as a supervisor, cannot leave her job or pick a fight with someone, but the chemical reaction in her body occurs anyway.

The Costs of Stress

5 *Describe both the costs and the benefits of stress.*

It has been estimated that two thirds of all visits to physicians can be traced to stress-related symptoms. It is, for example, a major contributor to heart disease, cancer, lung problems, accidents, cirrhosis of the liver, and suicide. Even the common cold and skin rashes are sometimes related to a person's experiencing prolonged and severe stress. Industry leaders are aware that such symptoms play a major role in absenteeism, accidents, and lost productivity.

Certainly a person under severe and/or prolonged stressful conditions cannot function as effectively as a person leading a more balanced life. We are not implying that stress is all negative, however, because a certain amount adds zest to life.

The Positive Aspects of Stress

Some amount of stress is necessary to accomplish anything meaningful. The teams that play in the Super Bowl are certainly in a stressful situation. Anyone who has played a sport or spoken in front of a large group has been in a stressful situation. Without question, moderate amounts of stress improve performance. For example, difficult but attainable objectives motivate better than easy objectives. People who seek types of work and leisure that engage their skills find life zestful and interesting. The secret is to involve oneself in challenging work and active leisure accompanied by sufficient rest and retreat. Life is full of stressors that can stimulate, energize, and aid in such positive outcomes as individual health and high productivity. We call the constructive dimensions of positive stress *eustress*, which can be a powerful motivator. Examples of eustress include going to an athletic event or participating in sports.

Major Causes of Stress

6 *Explain the major causes of stress.*

A number of factors contribute to individual stress. Among these are (1) life events, (2) personal psychological makeup, and (3) organizational and work-related factors. Especially in the case of organizational and work-related factors, the result is likely to be burnout.

Life Events

life event

Anything that causes a person to deviate from normal functioning.

Stress occurs whenever we face situations that require changes in behavior and a higher level of activity. It would be impossible to list all of the situations that place stress on human beings, since the mere fact of living does so. However, researchers have identified major life events, both positive and negative, that require drastic changes in a person's behavior. If many of these events occur within a year's time, a person becomes particularly susceptible to unpleasant physical or psychological consequences of excessive stress.

Exhibit 12-6 lists a number of stress-provoking life events. A major **life event** is anything that causes a person to deviate from normal functioning. The events are ranked in

EXHIBIT 12-6
Sources of Stress

LIFE EVENT	POINTS
Death of a spouse	99
Divorce	91
Marriage	85
Death of close family member	84
Fired at work	83
Pregnancy	78
Marital separation	78
Jail term	72
Personal injury or illness	68
Death of close friend	68
Retirement	68
Change of financial state	61
Spouse begins or stops work	58
Marital reconciliation	57
Christmas	56
Change in health of family member	56

(Continued)

EXHIBIT 12-6
continued

LIFE EVENT	POINTS
Foreclosure of mortgage or loan	55
Sex difficulties	53
Addition of new family member	51
Change to different line of work	51
Business readjustment	50
Mortgage over $10,000 (Present-day amount of $80,000)	48
Change in residence	47
Change in number of arguments with spouse	46
Change in responsibilities at work	46
Begin or end school	45
Trouble with boss	45
Revision of personal habits	44
Trouble with in-laws	43
Vacation	43
Change in living conditions	42
Son or daughter leaving home	41
Outstanding personal achievement	38
Change in work hours or conditions	36
Change in school	36
Minor violations of law	30
Change in eating habits	29
Mortgage or loan less than $10,000 (Present-day amount of $80,000)	27
Change in sleeping habits	27
Change in recreation	26
Change in church activities	26
Change in number of family get-togethers	15

Source: Adapted from "The 1990s Stress Scale," *Albuquerque Journal*, December 16, 1991, p. B1. © McClatchy-Tribune Information Services. All Rights Reserved. Reprinted with permission.

order of impact on a person's life. The death of a spouse has the most impact; change in the number of family get-togethers causes the least stress. To obtain your score, record the points for each event you experienced in the past year. Add the events' points to get your total; anything above 300 points is the change level. Steps and action plans can be initiated to offset a high score and thus avoid adverse consequences. We discuss this later in the chapter.

Patrick Hogan was a 34-year-old supervisor who seemed to have it all. He had a good job, was happily married, had two children, and was on top of the world. At work, he was highly productive and outgoing and was considered a leading candidate for advancement.

In the course of a year, several events occurred in Patrick's life that completely disrupted his patterns of living. A long-time friend enticed him to invest in a steakhouse that the friend would operate. The restaurant lost money, and the friend left town, leaving Patrick responsible for the bank note. To save his investment, he started moonlighting at the restaurant, not getting home many nights until 1:00 a.m.

While Patrick was struggling with the restaurant, his mother died after a lingering illness. Two weeks after the funeral, his wife had an accident and was confined to bed with a slipped disk. For the first time in his life, Patrick had to prepare meals, wash clothes, and care for the children while at the same time carrying on with his regular job and struggling with the restaurant. At work, Patrick's behavior changed drastically. He was impatient with his employees and lost his temper quickly. He became depressed and found it difficult to reach decisions about matters that he had previously handled decisively.

Self–Check

Based on the description of what happened in Patrick Hogan's life within the past year, calculate his score from the life event table. Assume you are his supervisor, and Patrick comes to you to talk about his situation. What advice would you give him?

Personal Psychological Makeup

7 *Compare and contrast Type A behavior and Type B behavior.*

Americans have long been noted for their emphasis on work. The United States has a justifiable reputation as a country where individuals, through hard work, can achieve considerable economic success. Some people, however, have become so caught up in

Ryan McVay/Stone/Getty Images

Any major life event, even a positive one, can provoke stress since it causes an individual to deviate from normal functioning.

Type A behavior

Behavior pattern characterized by (a) trying to accomplish too much in a short time and (b) lacking patience and struggling against time and other people to accomplish one's ends.

Type B behavior

Behavior pattern characterized by (a) tending to be calmer than someone with Type A behavior, (b) devoting more time to exercise, and (c) being more realistic in estimating the time it takes to complete an assignment.

the work ethic that work becomes the end itself rather than the means to an end. New Zealanders say, "Americans live to work and New Zealanders work to live." Our point is that some Americans have become workaholics, and this excessiveness has behavioral consequences that take a toll over a period of time. Researchers have identified two basic types of behavior characterizing people in our society: Type A and Type B.

Type A Behavior Cardiologists Meyer Friedman and Roy Rosenman first defined the term **Type A behavior.** Individuals who exhibit Type A behavior tend to try to accomplish too many things in a short time. Lacking patience, they struggle against time and other people to accomplish their ends. As a consequence, they become irritated by trivial things. Type A people also tend to be workaholics. Because of their psychological makeup they may be subject to stress over prolonged periods. For this reason, Type A people have a much higher risk of heart disease than do Type B people.[6]

Type B Behavior People exhibiting **Type B behavior** tend to be calmer, to take more time to exercise, and to be more realistic than Type As in estimating the amount of time needed to complete an assignment. Type Bs also worry less and, in general, desire more satisfaction from their work.

Studies of Type A and B behaviors indicate that 60 percent of managers and supervisors fall into the category of Type A people (see Exhibit 12-7). Many supervisors respond to all events as if they were emergencies or life-threatening situations. Managers

EXHIBIT 12-7
Behavior-Type Quiz

To find out which behavior type you are, circle the number on the scale below for each trait that best characterizes your behavior.

Casual about appointments	1	2	3	4	5	6	7	8	Never late
Not competitive	1	2	3	4	5	6	7	8	Very competitive
Never feel rushed even under pressure	1	2	3	4	5	6	7	8	Always rushed
Take things one at a time	1	2	3	4	5	6	7	8	Try to do many things at once, think about what I'm going to do next
Slow doing things	1	2	3	4	5	6	7	8	Fast (eating, walking, etc.)
Express feelings	1	2	3	4	5	6	7	8	"Sit on" feelings
Many interests	1	2	3	4	5	6	7	8	Few interests outside work

Total score: _____ Total score multiplied by 3: _____

The interpretation is as follows:

NUMBER OF POINTS	TYPE OF PERSONALITY
Less than 90	B
90 to 99	B1
100 to 105	A2
106 to 119	A
120 or more	A1

Source: A. P. Brief, R. S. Schuler, and M. V. Sell, *Managing Job Stress* (Boston: Little, Brown & Co., 1981), p. 87. Reprinted by permission of Arthur P. Brief.

EXHIBIT 12-8
Organizational and
Work-Related Factors
that Cause Excessive
Stress

- A highly centralized organization with decision making concentrated at the top.
- Many levels and narrow spans of control.
- Excessive and continuous pressure from higher levels.
- Conflicting demands on lower levels.
- Lack of clarity with respect to organizational and work objectives.
- Widespread autocratic leadership and close supervision.
- Little or no participation in decision making by supervisor and workers.
- Inconsistent application of company policies.
- Favoritism in decisions regarding layoffs, salary increases, promotions, and the like.
- Poor working conditions.
- Poor communication.
- Lack of structure and job descriptions.
- Widespread permissive leadership.
- Technical glitches with computer interfaces.

and supervisors who exhibit extreme Type A behavior patterns tend to practice close supervision and find it difficult to delegate. They are concerned that errors might reflect on past achievements, and so they become excessively task oriented.[7]

Organizational and Work-Related Factors

We have discussed many organizational and work-related factors that may cause excessive stress. As shown in Exhibit 12-8, these range from having poorly defined job descriptions to having autocratic or permissive leadership. If these factors exist in an organization over a period of time, they will cause extensive damage in the form of dissatisfaction, high turnover, low productivity, incomplete goal accomplishment, and job burnout. As the following example shows, stress can even create an opportunity for union activity.

> *A union organizer approached several employees from the home office of XYZ Life & Casualty Insurance Company. He was quickly told that they were not interested in joining a union, since they had excellent pay, good working conditions, and a high regard for their supervisors.*
>
> *Six months later, a supervisor retired from the claims department. The new supervisor, after being on the job a month, called two long-time employees into the office and gave them dismissal notices without a reason for doing so. That night, five employees drove 90 miles to a meeting in another city with the union organizer. Upon their return, they obtained enough employee signatures to force an election to determine whether the union would represent employees in the XYZ home office.*

Burnout

burnout

A malady caused by
excessive stress in the
setting where people
invest most of their
time and energy.

One of the most common results of excessive stress is burnout. **Burnout** is a stress-related malady that generally originates in the setting where people invest most of their time and energy. This setting is usually the work environment, but it could just as well be the home or the golf course.

The seriousness of the burnout problem has been highlighted by researchers Robert Golembiewski and Robert Munzenrider. Using an adapted version of the *Maslach Burnout Inventory (MBI)*, they discovered that 40 percent of more than 12,000 respondents in 33 organizations suffered from advanced phases of burnout.[8] Exhibit 12-9 explains the

EXHIBIT 12-9
MBI Subclass and
Phases of Burnout

The adapted Maslach Burnout Inventory, or MBI, consists of 25 items, rated on a scale of 1 (very much *unlike* me) to 7 (very much *like* me). There are three subscales.

Depersonalization: Individuals with high scores on this subscale tend to view people as objects and to distance themselves from others. Example: "I worry that this job is hardening me emotionally."

Personal Accomplishment (reversed): Respondents with high scores on this subscale see themselves as not performing well on a task that they perceive as not being particularly worthwhile. Example: "I have accomplished few worthwhile things on this job."

Emotional Exhaustion: Individuals with high scores on this subscale see themselves as operating beyond comfortable coping limits and as approaching "the end of the rope" in psychological and emotional senses. Example: "I feel fatigued when I get up in the morning and have to face another day on the job."

Emotional exhaustion is considered most characteristic of advanced phases of burnout, and depersonalization is considered least virulent. Ratings of high or low on the three subscales determine the progressive phases of burnout, generating an eight-phase model of burnout:

	PROGRESSIVE PHASES OF BURNOUT							
	I	II	III	IV	V	VI	VII	VIII
Depersonalization	Low	High	Low	High	Low	High	Low	High
Personal accomplishment	Low	Low	High	High	Low	Low	High	High
Emotional exhaustion	Low	Low	Low	Low	High	High	High	High

Source: Adapted from Robert T. Golembiewski and Robert F. Munzenrider, *Phases of Burnout*, Copyright © 1988, pp. 19–28. Reproduced with permission of Greenwood Publishing Group, Inc. Westport, CT.

subscales used in the MBI and charts the eight phases of burnout. A person scoring in phase I would be highly energized and motivated by the positive aspects of stress. In Maslow's terms, such a person would be operating at the esteem and self-fulfillment level of the need hierarchy. To a lesser extent, the same would be true of a person in phases II, III, IV, and V. Difficulties occur when a person reaches phases VI, VII, and VIII, the advanced stages of burnout.

Candidates for job burnout have three distinguishing characteristics. First, they experience stress caused predominantly by job-related stressors. Second, they tend to be idealistic and/or self-motivated achievers. Third, they tend to seek unattainable goals.

Although over the long term the ideal way to deal with burnout is to address the factors that are causing it, in the short term, burnout can be managed through use of any of a variety of strategies for coping with stress. Some of the ways companies are preventing or attacking burnout are through providing an on-site fitness center or a subsidy program. Others, like Apple, Yahoo, and Google, offer increasingly popular on-site massage therapies and meditation classes. It is estimated that job stress and related problems cost companies an estimated $200 billion a year.[9]

Ways to Cope with Personal Stress

8 *Elaborate on personal ways to cope with stress.*

Four methods that have helped many supervisors cope with stress are (1) engaging in physical exercise, (2) practicing relaxation techniques, (3) gaining a sense of control, and (4) developing and maintaining good interpersonal relationships.

Physical Exercise

People who exercise a minimum of two or three times a week are much less prone to the adverse symptoms of stress than those who do not. The exercise should be vigorous to the point of inducing perspiration. A person's muscles and circulatory system are not designed for a life of inactivity. People who revitalize their bodies are much less likely to worry and become upset over events and problems. Exercise can take many forms—tennis, handball, jogging, walking, swimming, gardening, or workouts at a health and exercise spa.

Earlier in the chapter, we highlighted the problems that Patrick Hogan was facing and saw how the stress of dealing with these problems had drastically changed his behavior. Patrick's manager noticed the change and counseled him regarding the situation. After Patrick had discussed his circumstances, the manager asked him if he engaged in regular exercise. Patrick answered that he simply did not have the time as a result of having to moonlight at the restaurant.

Patrick's manager persuaded him to work out three times a week in the company exercise room. Within two weeks, Patrick's on-the-job behavior was back to normal, and he had begun developing a plan to cope with some of the problems outside of work.

Relaxation Techniques

Exhibit 12-10 summarizes several of the relaxation techniques that are easy to use and are effective. These techniques are particularly useful to supervisors/team leaders because they are neither time-consuming nor costly. Research shows that when practiced on a regular basis, these techniques enable one to deal more effectively with stress and may lower blood pressure and, in general, improve physical and emotional health.

Yoga is one option for both relaxation and physical exercise.

EXHIBIT 12-10
Relaxation Techniques

Relaxation Response. One of the best studied stress-relievers is the relaxation response, first described by Harvard's Herbert Benson, M.D., more than 20 years ago. Its great advantage is that it requires no special posture or place. Say you're stuck in traffic when you're expected at a meeting. Or you're having trouble falling asleep because your mind keeps replaying some awkward situation.

- Sit or recline comfortably. Close your eyes if you can, and relax your muscles.
- Breathe deeply. To make sure that you are breathing deeply, place one hand on your abdomen, the other on your chest. Breathe in slowly through your nose, and as you do you should feel your abdomen (not your chest) rise.
- Slowly exhale. As you do, focus on your breathing. Some people do better if they silently repeat the word *one* as they exhale; it helps clear the mind.
- If thoughts intrude, do not dwell on them; allow them to pass on and return to focusing on your breathing.

Although you can turn to this exercise any time you feel stressed, doing it regularly for 10 to 20 minutes at least once a day can put you in a generally calm mode that can see you through otherwise stressful situations.

Cleansing Breath. Epstein, who has searched the world literature for techniques people have claimed valuable for coping, focuses on those that are simple and powerful. He calls them "gems," devices that work through differing means, can be learned in minutes, can be done any time, anywhere, and have a pronounced physiologic effect. At the top of his list is the quickest of all—a cleansing breath.

Take a huge breath in. Hold it for three to four seconds. Then let it out v-e-r-y s-l-o-w-l-y. As you blow out, blow out all the tension in your body.

Relaxing Postures. "The research literature demonstrates that sitting in certain positions, all by itself, has a pronounced effect," says Epstein. Sit anywhere. Relax your shoulders so that they are comfortably rounded. Allow your arms to drop by your sides. Rest your hands, palm side up, on top of your thighs. With your knees comfortably bent, extend your legs and allow your feet, supported on the heels, to fall gently outward. Let your jaw drop. Close your eyes and breathe deeply for a minute or two.

Passive Stretches. It's possible to relax muscles without effort; gravity can do it all. Start with your neck and let your head fall forward to the right. Breathe in and out normally. With every breath out, allow your head to fall more. Do the same for shoulders, arms, back.

Imagery. Find a comfortable posture and close your eyes. Imagine the most relaxed place you've ever been. We all have a place like this and can call it to mind anywhere, any time. For everyone it is different. It may be a lake. It may be a mountain. It may be a cottage at the beach. Are you there?

Five—Count 'Em, Five—Tricks. Since you can never have too many tricks in your little bag, here are some "proven stress-busters" from Paul Rosch, M.D., president of the American Institute of Stress:

- Curl your toes against the soles of your feet as hard as you can for 15 seconds, then relax them. Progressively tense and relax the muscles in your legs, stomach, back, shoulders, neck.
- Visualize lying on a beach, listening to waves coming in and feeling the warm sun and gentle breezes on your back. Or, if you prefer, imagine floating, with your eyes closed while waves gently rock you back and forth.
- Set aside 20 to 30 minutes a day to do anything you want—even nothing.
- Take a brisk walk.
- Keep an iPod handy and loaded with relaxing, enjoyable music.

"Beating stress is a matter of removing yourself from the situation and taking a few breaths," says Rosch. "If I find myself getting stressed I ask myself 'is this going to matter to me in five years?' Usually the answer is no. If so, why get worked up over it?"

Source: Adapted from John Carpi, "A Smorgasbord of Stress-Stoppers", *Psychology Today* 29(1), January/February 1996, p. 39. Reprinted with permission from Psychology Today Magazine, Copyright © 1996 Sussex Publishers, LLC.

A Sense of Control

Supervisors who have a sense of control over their own lives handle stress much better than those who feel they are manipulated by life's events or by other people. If they have other interests, supervisors are better able to look at work as only one aspect of life. Many of them also have a deep faith in religion, which allows them to cope with adversity. Some ways to gain control are as follows:

1. Plan. Look ahead, identifying both long- and short-term goals. Also, identify causes of stress and ways to alleviate them.
2. Get to know and like yourself. Identify your strengths and interests and pursue activities that capitalize on your strengths.
3. Perceive situations as challenges rather than as problems.
4. Take a long vacation rather than a series of short vacations.
5. Do things for others, either through a religious group or by becoming involved in some kind of volunteer work or youth activities such as Boy or Girl Scouts, Big Brother or Big Sister, or Junior Achievement.
6. Provide yourself with positive reinforcement when you do a task well. Treat yourself to a reward when you accomplish something worthwhile.

Developing and Maintaining Good Interpersonal Relationships

It is most important for one's mental health and happiness to give priority to close relationships—family and friends. These relationships provide a base of mutual support where one can discuss success, opportunities, issues, and problems.

According to psychologist Alex Michalos, good interpersonal relationships are much more important to one's happiness and well-being than either income or looks. When one is facing a major challenge or problem, it is helpful to be able to discuss it with a spouse or friend. It is also important to maintain relationships and confront problems between yourself and loved ones and friends through discussion rather than through avoidance. Exhibit 12-11 provides a summary of strategies that help make you feel great. The second strategy, "take control of your time," is discussed next.

EXHIBIT 12-11
Strategies that Make You Feel Great

- Savor the moment. "Happiness," said Benjamin Franklin, "is produced not so much by great pieces of good fortune that seldom happen as by the little advantages that occur each day."
- Take control of your time. There is nevertheless a place for setting goals and managing time. Compared to those who've learned a sense of helplessness, those with an "internal locus of control" do better in school, cope better with stress, and live with greater well-being.
- Act happy. Study after study reveals three traits that mark happy people's lives: (1) They like themselves, (2) they are positive thinkers, and (3) they are outgoing. In experiments, people who feign high self-esteem begin feeling better about themselves.
- Seek work and leisure that engage your skills. Even if we make a lower but livable wage, it pays to seek work that we find interesting and challenging.
- Join the movement. A slew of recent studies reveal that aerobic exercise is an antidote for mild depression.
- Get rest. Happy people live active, vigorous lives, yet they reserve time for renewing sleep and solitude.
- Give priority to close relationships. People who can name several close, supportive friends—friends with whom they freely share their ups and downs—live with greater health and happiness.
- Take care of your soul. Actively religious people are much less likely than others to become delinquent, to abuse drugs and alcohol, to divorce, or to commit suicide. They're even physically healthier.

Source: Adapted from David G. Meyers, "Pursuing Happiness," Psychology Today, July–Aug, 1993, vol. 26, pp. 32–35 and 66–7.

Managing Your Time

time management

Ability to use one's time to get things done when they should be done.

Organizations have three types of resources—human, physical, and financial resources. Some management experts would include *time* as a fourth resource. *Make no mistake about it—time is one of the greatest resources a supervisor has.* Therefore, effective time management is essential for effective supervision. **Time management** is the ability to use one's time to get things done *when* they should be done. Another definition, which reflects planning and prioritizing, is "arranging to accomplish the things you choose to get done within the time available." Without this ability, all of your other management skills are for naught. Even if you have excellent human relations skills, poor time management can leave you too easily distracted to effectively listen to an employee's problems. Or pressures can keep you from thinking clearly enough to use your conceptual skills fully. You may not even be able to take the time to display your technical skills by showing a new employee the ropes. To be effective as a supervisor, then, you must make effective use of your time.

The Time Log: Where Your Time Goes

Time management experts say that the first step in making effective use of your time is to determine how your time is actually being spent. Conscientiously filling in a time log like the one shown in Exhibit 12-12 is an excellent way to get this information.

Setting Priorities: A "Must"

Once you know where your time is going, you can analyze whether it is going in the proper direction. Not everyone can do all that he or she wants to do. The secret, then, is to spend time on those activities that are most important and urgent and that contribute most significantly to your doing a top-notch job.

> *Hoi Mon Sol, whose time log is shown in Exhibit 12-12, said that he could not find enough time to do everything he wanted to do because he was so busy. Yet, when he got home, he looked back at his day and called his activities "wheel spinning." He didn't feel good about what he had accomplished. Sol, like many supervisors, typically spent his day handling many low-priority activities rather than the high-priority ones!*

To use a time log most effectively, one must establish a rating system for classifying the priority of activities to be performed in a given day, such as the following:

1. A activities are the most important—they are critical to your job.
2. B activities are of medium priority—important, but less so than A activities.
3. C activities are of low priority—routine and/or relatively unimportant.

The more efficient supervisor will spend a greater percentage of his or her time performing A activities.

Many of the "brush fires" to which supervisors devote a large percentage of their time are B or perhaps even C priority items. In the next section, we hope to help you learn to spend more of your time on your A activities!

Self–Check

Examine the list of activities shown in Exhibit 12-13. Identify an A activity and a C activity. On what types of activities did Sol spend most of his time?

EXHIBIT 12-12
Daily Time Log

	DAILY TIME LOG			

Name _____

Date _____ *March 1, 2010* _____

On this log record each activity that you performed during the workday. Make sure that you include every activity performed such as telephone calls, conversations, rest breaks, reading, and so on. Do this for a period of time long enough to reflect normal "workdays." A week should normally be sufficient.

From – To	Minutes	Type of Activity	People Involved	Priority A	B	C
8:00 – 8:05	5	Talked in hall	Dan, Patsy			
8:05 – 8:15	10	Read status report on work progress				
8:15 – 8:20	5	Checked progress on slow job	Ronald			
8:20 – 8:30	10	Prepared for supt. meeting				
8:30 – 9:30	60	Attended supt. meeting	Dept. heads & Supt.			
9:30 – 9:45	15	Coffee	Al, Peter, Karen			
9:45 – 9:50	5	Tried to return two phone calls -- no luck				
9:50 – 10:02	12	Completed questionnaire from Personnel Dept				
10:02 – 10:06	4	Went for mail				
10:06 – 10:20	14	Opened & read mail				
10:20 – 10:23	3	Called Purchasing Dept. to check status of order	Kawahara			
10:23 – 10:50	27	Discussion with Supt. about objectives for Dept.	McWilliams			
10:50 – 11:00	10	Visited Personnel office to check status of applicants	Alice			
11:00 – 11:55	55	Met with United Way Committee	too many!			
11:55 – 12:10	15	Began work on dept. budget proposal				
12:10 – 12:50	40	Lunch	Dan, Patsy, Al			
—						
—						

EXHIBIT 12-13
Eight Common
Supervisory Time
Wasters

- Distractions and interruptions
- Failure to set priorities
- Procrastination
- Doing routine work that subordinates could handle
- Indecision
- Personal disorganization
- Failure to delegate
- Excessive or unnecessary paperwork

Handling the Common Time Wasters

9 *Discuss some ways to effectively manage time.*

Many activities that you carry out during a typical day are time wasters—inefficient uses of your time (Exhibit 12-13). These may include doing routine work that someone else could handle, socializing excessively, or fighting a losing battle against paperwork.

Supervisory jobs vary a great deal in terms of the demands on the supervisor's time. That's why maintaining a time log (Exhibit 12-12) is an important first step in diagnosing your time management habits. Exhibit 12-14 is a broad list of "do's," which may help you to use your time more effectively.

EXHIBIT 12-14
How to Use Your Time More Effectively

1. *Set priorities.*
   a. Establish A, B, and C priorities.
   b. Determine daily priorities.
   c. Focus effort on high-priority items.
2. *Do not procrastinate.*
   a. Break big jobs into smaller parts.
   b. Get started, even if on a minor part of a job.
   c. Do the more unpleasant parts of a job first.
   d. Reward yourself for doing things on schedule.
3. *Manage e-mails effectively.*
   a. Handle all return e-mails at set times of the day.
   b. Prioritize e-mails based on importance and urgency.
4. *Manage the telephone effectively.*
   a. Have someone else take your calls and handle them if possible.
   b. Handle all return calls at set times of the day.
5. *Make your meetings effective.*
   a. Prepare and announce an agenda before the meeting.
   b. Begin meetings on time.
   c. Stick to the topics on the agenda.
   d. Make decisions or come to conclusions.
6. *Learn to delegate.*
   a. Delegate details that are time consuming.
   b. Delegate jobs that will help employees to develop.
   c. Delegate jobs that employees can perform better than you.
7. *Handle people who drop in.*
   a. Close your door for periods of time.
   b. Stand up and remain standing until the visitor leaves.
   c. Meet long-winded persons at their work area, so that you can leave when you are ready.
   d. Train your boss and work group to respect your time.
8. *Be decisive.*
   a. Set a personal deadline for making a decision.
   b. Once you have the facts, make the decision.
9. *Get organized.*
   a. Use a daily time planner.
   b. Implement a filing system.
   c. See 1b above.
10. *Stay on top of paperwork.*
    a. Handle papers only once!
    b. Handwrite short notes directly on original documents and forward them to the persons concerned.
    c. Have someone classify papers according to importance and route them for you.
11. *Avoid distractions and interruptions.*
    a. Keep a neat desk; work and papers piled on a desk are distracting.
    b. Try to set aside uninterrupted blocks of time.
    c. Face your desk away from the view of others.

Chapter Review

1. **Identify the causes of conflict.**

   A key skill needed by supervisors is that of conflict management. Two of the causes of conflict are having unclear or different objectives and communication breakdowns.

2. **Discuss conflict management styles and identify when each would be appropriate.**

   The five conflict management styles are avoiding, accommodating, forcing, compromising, and collaborating or joint problem solving. Two of the most widely used styles are forcing and collaborating. Collaborating seems to be most successful in dealing with conflicts caused by communication difficulties, whereas forcing is sometimes necessary when dealing with conflicts of personal values and personality.

3. **Describe principled negotiation.**

   Principled negotiation holds promise in keeping personalities out of conflict by focusing on the problem rather than the person.

4. **Explain why modern life makes us particularly vulnerable to stress.**

   Stress is any external stimulus that causes wear and tear on a person's psychological or physical well-being. Modern men and women react to stress as our primitive ancestors did, with a chemical reaction designed to ready the body for fight or flight. This chemical reaction is not helpful in normal situations today, so we need to develop ways to cope with and manage stress.

5. **Describe both the costs and the benefits of stress.**

   When we are unsuccessful in coping with stress, the costs are enormous. Stress is a major cause of many illnesses, from the common cold to heart disease. It plays a role in absenteeism, accidents, and lost productivity. Not all stress is negative, however. Small and great achievements occur as a result of moderate amounts of stress.

6. **Explain the major causes of stress.**

   Major causes of stress are life events, personal psychological makeup, and organizational and work-related factors. The death of a spouse or a divorce places tremendous stress on most individuals. Similarly, working in an extremely high-pressure environment under prolonged autocratic leadership can cause stress and job burnout.

7. **Compare and contrast Type A behavior and Type B behavior.**

   A person's psychological makeup influences how that person handles stress. Type A people try to accomplish too many things in a short time and tend to lack patience when dealing with people. Type B people tend to be calmer and more realistic in their assessment of the length of time needed to complete an assignment.

8. **Elaborate on personal ways to cope with stress.**

   Fortunately, many of us can do a better job of managing stress if we develop certain strategies and behaviors. On a personal level, we can (1) exercise, (2) practice relaxation techniques, (3) gain a sense of control over our lives, and (4) develop and maintain good interpersonal relationships. On the job, a supervisor can apply many of the concepts discussed throughout this book. Techniques particularly helpful in reducing stress in a work unit are to practice the concept of balance through participative management, when appropriate; to delegate effectively without losing control; and to control our time.

9. **Discuss some ways to effectively manage time.**

One of a supervisor's greatest resources is time. However, activities performed by supervisors vary in importance and urgency. The effective supervisor will concentrate on the more important and most urgent activities. Maintaining a time log is a necessary first step toward becoming a more efficient time manager. Such a log enables a supervisor to see exactly where his or her time is being spent. More effective supervisors spend a greater proportion of their time on A priorities—activities that are ranked number one in terms of importance to the effective performance of their jobs. The following time-saving tips can help you to make better use of your time: (1) Set priorities, (2) do not procrastinate, (3) manage the telephone effectively, (4) make meetings effective, (5) delegate to others, (6) handle people who drop in, (7) be decisive, (8) get organized, (9) stay on top of paperwork, and (10) avoid distractions and interruptions.

Key Terms

integration process, p. 359

principled negotiation, p. 362

stress, p. 365

life event, p. 367

Type A behavior, p. 370

Type B behavior, p. 370

burnout, p. 371

time management, p. 376

Questions for Review & Discussion

1. Identify the five conflict management styles and describe when each one would be appropriate.
2. Discuss what is involved in principled negotiation. How does it differ from hard or soft negotiation?
3. Compare and contrast Type A behavior and Type B behavior.
4. What are the major causes of stress on the job? Off the job?

5. Explain why exercise and relaxation techniques are helpful for coping with stress.
6. What can a supervisor do to prevent stress in his or her unit?
7. Why and how can time management help with stress and the achievement of effective results?

Information

Skill Builder 12-1

Up in Smoke—Are You Burned Out?

Answer each question on a scale of 1 to 5 (1 = never; 2 = rarely; 3 = sometimes; 4 = often; 5 = always).

Do you

- Feel less competent or effective than you used to feel in your work?
- Consider yourself unappreciated or "used"?
- Dread going to work?

Systems

- Feel overwhelmed in your work?
- Feel your work is pointless or unimportant?
- Watch the clock?
- Avoid conversations with others (coworkers, customers, and supervisors in the work setting; family members in the home)?
- Rigidly apply rules without considering creative solutions?
- Get frustrated by your work?
- Miss work often?
- Feel unchallenged by your work?

Does your work

- Overload you?
- Deny you rest periods—breaks, lunch time, sick leave, or vacation?
- Pay too little?
- Depend on uncertain funding sources?
- Provide inadequate support to accomplish the job (budget, equipment, tools, people, etc.)?
- Lack clear guidelines?
- Entail so many different tasks that you feel fragmented?
- Require you to deal with major or rapid changes?
- Lack access to a social or professional support group?
- Demand coping with a negative job image or angry people?
- Depress you?

Add up your scores for the test and record your total:

SCORES	CATEGORY
94–110	Burnout
76–93	Flame
58–75	Smoke
40–57	Sparks
22–39	No fire

The categories are interpreted as follows:

- **Burnout.** If your score is between 94 and 110, you are experiencing a very high level of stress in your work. Without some changes in yourself or your situation, your potential for stress-related illness is high. Consider seeking professional help for stress reduction and burnout prevention. Coping with stress at this level may also require help from others—supervisors, coworkers, and other associates at work and spouse and other family members at home.
- **Flame.** If you have a score between 76 and 93, you have a high amount of work-related stress and may have begun to burn out. Mark each question that you scored 4 or above, and rank them in order of their effect on you, beginning with the ones that bother you the most. For at least your top three, evaluate what you can do to reduce the stresses involved, and act to improve your attitude or situation. If your body is reflecting the stress, get a medical checkup.
- **Smoke.** Scores between 58 and 75 represent a certain amount of stress in your work and are a sign that you have a fair chance of burning out unless you take

corrective measures. For each question that you scored 4 or above, consider ways you can reduce the stresses involved. As soon as possible, take action to improve your attitude or the situation surrounding those things that trouble you most.

- **Sparks.** If your score is between 40 and 57, you have a low amount of work-related stress and are unlikely to burn out. Look over those questions that you scored 3 or above, and think about what you can do to reduce the stresses involved.
- **No fire.** People with scores of 22 through 39 are mellow in their work, with almost no job-related stress. As long as they continue at this level, they are practically burnout-proof.

For many people, both the job and the home have the potential to produce high stress and burnout. For this reason, having at least one "port in a storm" is important. Ideally, if things are going badly on the job, rest and comfort can be found in the home. Similarly, if home conditions involve pressure, conflict, and frustration, having a satisfying work life helps. The person who faces problems on the job and problems in the home at the same time is fighting a war on two fronts and is a prime candidate for stress overload and burnout.

Source: From Stress Without Distress: Rx for Burnout 1st edition by Manning/Curtis. 1988. South-Western, 1988. Copyright © 1988 by George Manning. Reprinted by permission of the author.

Skill Builder 12-2

Resources

A Planning Strategy to Cope with Stress

List the things that are causing stress in your life at the present time. Determine which factors are causing positive stress and which are potentially negative and harmful.

Develop an action plan that will enable you to cope with the negative factors more effectively. A good action plan looks ahead and deals with what, when, where, and how to solve the problem.

Skill Builder 12-3

Resources

A Personal Time Survey

To begin managing your time, you first need a clearer idea of how you use your time. The Personal Time Survey will help you to estimate how much time you currently spend in typical activities. To get a more accurate estimate, you might keep track of how you spend your time for a week. This will help you get a better idea of how much time you need to prepare for each subject. It will also help you identify your time wasters. But for now, complete the Personal Time Survey to get an estimate.

The following survey shows the amount of time you spend on various activities. When taking the survey, estimate the amount of time spent on each item. Once you have this amount, multiply it by seven. This will give you the total time spent on the activity in one week. After each item's weekly time has been calculated, add all

Information

Systems

these times for the grand total. Subtract this from 168, the total possible hours per week. Here we go:

1. Number of hours of sleep each night   × 7 =

2. Number of grooming hours per day   × 7 =

3. Number of hours for meals/snacks per day   × 7 = (include preparation time)

4a. Total travel time weekdays   × 7 =

4b. Total travel time weekends   × 7 =

5. Number of hours per week for regularly scheduled functions (clubs, religious services, get-togethers, etc.)

6. Number of hours per day for chores, errands, extra grooming, etc.   × 7 =

7. Number of hours of work per week

8. Number of hours in class per week

9. Number of average hours per week socializing, dates, etc. Be honest!

  Now add up the totals:

Subtract the above number from 168.   168 − X =

The remaining hours are the hours you have allowed yourself to study.

Study Hour Formula To determine how many hours you need to study each week to get A's, use the following rule of thumb. Study 2 hours per hour in class for an easy class, three hours per hour in class for an average class, and four hours per hour in class for a difficult class. For example, basket weaving 101 is a relatively easy 3-hour course. Usually, a person would not do more than 6 hours of work outside of class per week. Advanced calculus is usually considered a difficult course, so it might be best to study the proposed 12 hours a week. If more hours are needed, take away some hours from easier courses, i.e., basket weaving. Figure out the time that you need to study by using the previous formula for each of your classes.

Easy class credit hours   × 2 = Average class credit hours   × 3 =

Difficult class credit hours   × 4 =

Total

Compare this number to your time left from the survey. Now is the time when many students might find themselves a bit stressed. Just a note to ease your anxieties: It is not only the quantity of study time but also its quality. This formula is a general guideline. Try it for a week, and make adjustments as needed.

Source: Prepared by the Self-Development Center, a service of the Counseling and Student Development Center at George Mason University. Reprinted by permission.

The Entrepreneur

Sam Hinton Construction (SHC) is a small, entrepreneurial firm in a mid-sized city situated in the southeastern United States. SHC is run by Sam, the owner. Sam began the remodeling and repair business out of necessity when he couldn't find anyone to perform the needed work on his own home. External environmental changes, specifically the real estate and housing boom occurring across the nation due to monies being shifted from the stock markets to better investment opportunities in real estate, were impacting many communities just like Sam's. Add to this trend the impact of several years of active hurricane seasons in the southeastern region of the country, and it is no surprise that construction supplies—skilled labor, materials, equipment, and management—were harder and harder to obtain for reasonable prices. Based on this and other data, Sam saw an opportunity for a planned career change, and after talking the situation over with his wife, Ellen, he decided to make the transition and start his own business. Sam's initial vision for his small company was to make money to support his family while meeting the needs of his customers in a cost-effective way. Sam lacked significant up-front capital, relying on his family's savings to start operations, so marketing efforts were limited to advertising in the local yellow pages. Once under way, he relied heavily on word-of-mouth to grow his small firm. He was a one-man show that was determined to make the venture successful.

He was not as experienced as his competitors, so he took every opportunity to read, observe, learn, and acquire the competencies necessary for his new profession. Initially, Sam chose work opportunities based on his personal experiences with his own home. Thus, he was confident in the accuracy of his materials and labor estimates and his ability to complete a quality job on time. Sam's initial strategy paid off, because other contractors did not seem to want to fool with the small-sized jobs. Those that did were not reputable. However, as his business grew, he found himself bidding for work that he was not as familiar or comfortable with. More and more of Sam's training occurred on the job. Sam won a bid to remodel an older home built prior to 1950, which included extensive plumbing and structural work. Unfortunately, he underestimated the types of work, amount of time, and supplies needed to complete the job and was forced to use a significant amount of his savings to finish the job.

Sam soon began building this "learning cost" into future bids to ensure he stayed afloat and remained in a positive cash flow position. His estimates for more complex projects were more like guesstimates and tended to be higher than competitors' proposals. Sam decided to strategically reposition his small firm to survive. To justify the dollar difference to potential customers, Sam sold his firm as a quality renovating and remodeling operation—"You can go with the low bid, but you get what you pay for. My price is higher because I pay attention to the details."

He really liked getting new work and prided himself on his ability to interact and communicate with his potential clients. Sam also believed that he was quite adept at seeing the "vision" for a given project. For example, he could take a customer's rough ideas and create a detailed drawing of what the completed work would look like. Even if the clients were not sure what they wanted, Sam found that through dialogue and listening to his customers, he could better understand their wants and needs.

Sam was committed to providing his customers with the best service possible. As he generated additional work, he worked more hours to complete projects. Sam would routinely arise at 4:30 A.M. to begin his day. The first order of business was making sure that he had the proper materials and equipment for the job each day. Over time he had gotten much better at planning such that he rarely had to stop and leave the site for additional supplies. Because of his improved planning and efficiency, he found he finished jobs much more quickly than before, but he still felt as if he was always one step behind where he needed to be. Sam typically knocked off around 4:30 P.M., so that he could visit with potential clients. The early evening hours were spent providing bids to secure future work. Once he arrived home, it was time for a quick bite before doing paperwork, tracking costs, and preparing estimates.

Although Sam felt he had learned quite a bit during the past year and believed he had an effective strategy in place, he often found that he was stretched too thin with managing the work and finances and filling the pipeline with new jobs to manage the schedule, produce quality work, handle customers, and continuously develop his knowledge. As the months passed, Sam's wife, Ellen, noticed he was not as easygoing as he once had been, and she rarely got a chance to visit with him on the weekends, much less during the week. Ellen was also becoming concerned about his health. He rarely slept through the night anymore, often getting up several times a night. She was shocked one night when she awakened to find him at his desk at 2:00 A.M. buried in receipts and bills. In addition to problems sleeping, Sam was developing bad eating habits. Ellen knew he often worked through lunch to complete various stages of his projects, but now he rarely had time for evening meals. Ellen believed that Sam's sleep deprivation and poor eating habits were partly to blame for his increasingly short temper. Uncharacteristically, Sam was more on edge, flying off the handle at the smallest incidents. Ellen's feelings were confirmed when she got off the phone with one of Sam's clients. The client had called quite unhappy

with the way the project was going. The seams in the crown molding were unacceptable, the paint runs were unsightly, and when the client approached Sam about the imperfections, he got very gruff and defensive. As the customer complaints mounted, Ellen realized Sam was overwhelmed.

Questions

1. Divide into teams of three to five people. Each group is to assume the role of a consulting team that has been asked to help Sam Hinton get control of his company and his life.
2. Drawing from your own experiences and from what you have learned in this chapter, develop some alternatives for Sam.
3. Select the best alternative and present your recommendations to the rest of the class. Each class member will then vote for the team (excluding his or her own team) that he or she thinks had the best plan for SHC.

CASE 12-2

The Missed Promotion

Susan Williamson was worried. For the past six months, her husband, Paul, had been a different person from the man she married. Up until that time, Paul had been a cheerful and caring husband and father. He took an interest in their children, was active in church, and had a zest for day-to-day living. In recent months, he had been moody, abrupt, and withdrawn. He spent his time at home watching television and drinking beer. He never talked about his job as maintenance supervisor at the ABC Company as he once had. Recently Susan had asked if something at work was bothering him and, if so, whether he would discuss it with her. His reply was "No, there's nothing bothering me! You take care of the house and the children, and I'll take care of the job and making a living!"

Actually, the job had been bothering Paul for about a year. Before that, he was considered one of the outstanding maintenance supervisors. In those days, his two immediate supervisors, the maintenance superintendent and the maintenance manager, called on him frequently for advice and used him as a troubleshooter

within the plant. Although Paul did not have a college degree in engineering, the maintenance manager had strongly hinted that when the maintenance superintendent retired, Paul would be promoted to his position. The maintenance manager had told Paul that, despite having three engineering graduates in the supervision group, he considered Paul the best in the department.

A year ago, the maintenance manager was transferred to another plant. A new maintenance manager came aboard who, from the start, favored college graduates. Gradually Paul was used less and less for troubleshooting assignments, and his advice was rarely sought. Then, six months ago, the maintenance superintendent retired and a young engineering graduate named Bobbi, whom Paul had trained, was promoted to the superintendent's job. It was then that Paul's personality changed. He began sleeping longer each night, often falling asleep in front of the television set. He also developed a tightness in his stomach that was creating a burning sensation.

Bobbi, the engineer who had been promoted to maintenance superintendent, was worried. For the past several months, she had been concerned about the performance and health of one of her maintenance supervisors, Paul Williamson. Paul had been Bobbi's boss at one time, and she had always admired his ability as a supervisor and his knowledge of the maintenance area.

Recently, while attending a regional meeting of maintenance managers from different plants of the ABC Company, Bobbi ran into the former maintenance manager at her plant, who was now at another plant. He asked how Paul was doing. Bobbi, glad to share her concern with someone, said that she was really worried about him. "His performance has slipped, for one thing. Also, he used to have perfect attendance, but lately he's been calling in sick a lot."

The maintenance manager replied, "I wonder if disappointment over not being promoted to maintenance superintendent has affected his performance. No reflection on you, of course, but before I left, the plant manager and I had agreed that Paul would be pro-

moted to maintenance superintendent. Then the home office changed its corporate policy so that only college graduates could be promoted to superintendent. This made Paul ineligible, and you got the job instead."

Bobbi hadn't realized that Paul had been the first choice for the position she now held. Upon reflection, she decided to have a coaching and counseling session with him when she returned to the plant, as she certainly didn't want to lose him.

Questions

1. How should Bobbi approach Paul about the situation?
2. What do you think Paul's reaction(s) will be?
3. Do you agree with the company's policy of promoting only college graduates to the maintenance superintendent position? Why or why not?

13
Exercising Control

LEARNING OBJECTIVES

After reading and studying this chapter, you should be able to:

1. Define control and explain how it relates to planning.

2. Discuss the characteristics of effective control systems.

3. Discuss the three types of control systems.

4. Discuss the four steps in the control process.

5. Identify the different types of standards.

6. Explain the importance of strategic control points.

7. Discuss management by exception.

8. Discuss the impact of technology on control.

Thinkstock Images/Getty images/Jupiter images

In this work environment, informal communication among staff members helps the supervisors implement plans and exercise control.

We tried to make some adjustments at halftime. They just didn't pan out.
—*Pro Football Coach after His Team Was Beaten in the Playoffs*

Preview

CHANGING PERCEPTIONS AND ATTITUDES ONE DAY AT A TIME The health care industry is dramatically changing as costs continue to rise and the population gets older. Still, Beth Anderson, the administrator of a 406-bed acute care, urban hospital with over 900 employees believes that each day offers an opportunity to make a difference. Beth is aware of the daily challenges and her responsibility for ensuring quality care is provided and costs are managed so that the hospital remains viable long-term. To assist in accomplishing this goal, Beth hired outside consultants to conduct an employee opinion survey. The results were quite telling.

Overall, the employees enjoyed their jobs and felt committed to the hospital's mission. They really believed key services, such as the burn and trauma units, provided unique assistance to those in the community. However, they also perceived they were overworked and underpaid and that communications were inadequate. When asked whether their departments were adequately staffed, the employees' responses averaged a 2.2 on a 5-point scale. The perceived increased work demands were contributing to nonattendance issues. However, one of the more significant findings for Beth Anderson was that most of the respondents didn't believe that the hospital administration would act on the results. Beth and the assistant administrator, Elmer Sellers, were determined to initiate positive changes that would ultimately alter the employees' perceptions and attitudes.

The first step was to meet with department heads and staff to solicit input from these groups on the best ways to address the employees' concerns. A group of department heads actually initiated this effort when they approached Beth and shared their willingness to take on a leadership role as part of the organization's change effort. Over about a month, the group collected and tabulated 539 suggestions, of which many were implemented. For example, departments implemented flexible schedules for their employees to address concerns about work demand levels. Cross-training efforts were initiated for employees so that individuals could routinely be assigned to the highest work load areas during high-demand periods. The hospital also doubled the PRN pool over a 12-month period to alleviate concerns about staffing levels. In addition, the seventh-floor nurses' station was converted to a fully equipped exercise facility for employees to burn off stress! To address pay concerns, the employees were provided with raises and adjustments twice during the following year!

Beth and Elmer had succeeded in changing the employees' perceptions and attitudes, but the challenge became maintaining the momentum. The Speak Easy, a one-on-one communication process, was utilized for this purpose. Speak Easy, as the name implies, is an informal means of interpersonal communication that enables administrators to gather employee input, while providing important information throughout the ranks. These informal departmental meetings were announced in advance and communicated to individuals in the hospital in a variety of ways, including the intranet and screen-saver bulletin boards. Beth and Elmer chose this approach so that employees could prepare topics or questions in advance they wanted to share. The Speak Easys allowed Beth and Elmer to collect information "real time" so that appropriate actions could be taken without having to wait for the annual employee opinion survey results. The benefits were improved communication and trust building.

Source: Consulting and conversations with Beth Anderson and Elmer Sellers with the USAMC.

When an organization's activities "go according to plan," it is often the result of good planning, but it is just as frequently the result of good control in implementing the plans! In this chapter, we provide you with a broad overview of what is involved in the control function.

What Is Control?

1 *Define control and explain how it relates to planning.*

Have you ever been driving a car on a trip and had one of the dashboard warning lights come on? Perhaps it was the oil pressure or temperature light. Basically, the light indicates that something is wrong with the car. Without such a warning system, you would be caught by surprise when the car broke down, perhaps leaving you stranded far from home.

Managers and supervisors are often in a similar dilemma. They go along not knowing whether things are as they should be or not. Unfortunately, many of them find that things are not as they should be only when it is too late to do anything about it. They do not have the advantage of periodic feedback or warning lights to tell them whether they are on track. Thus, you might think of control as consisting of performance markers that tell you whether you and your unit's performance are moving in the right direction.

Controlling is defined as the management function that involves comparing actual performance with planned performance and taking corrective action, if needed, to ensure that objectives are achieved. Basically, control has three phases: (1) anticipating the things that could go wrong and taking preventive measures to see that they don't, (2) monitoring or measuring performance in some way to compare what is actually happening with what is supposed to be happening, and (3) correcting performance problems that occur. This last step is the therapeutic aspect of control.

Control's Close Links to Planning

Planning and controlling are so closely related. Planning "sets the ship's course," and controlling "keeps it on course." When a ship begins to veer off course, the navigator notices it and recommends a new heading designed to return the ship to its proper course. Essentially, supervisory control works the same way. You set goals and seek information on whether they are being reached as planned. If not, you make the adjustments necessary to achieve your goals. Thus, controlling may be thought of as the process that supervisors use to help carry out their plans.

Importance of Controls

Perhaps you have heard the old saying: "Things never go as planned." That truth is a primary reason supervisors need to perform the control function effectively. Control is important in view of the many variables that can put things off track. Murphy's laws (some of which are listed in Exhibit 13-1) seem to operate everywhere. Because anything involving humans is imperfect, supervisors must use control to monitor progress and to make intelligent adjustments as required.

Examples of Controls

We live in a world of controls. Circuit breakers in our homes and offices are examples of controls. When an electrical overload occurs, the system adjusts by shutting itself down. Security alarm systems send out signals when a protected area is violated. As mentioned earlier, the dashboard in your car contains numerous control signals to warn you when something is not the way it is supposed to be—low oil pressure, overheated engine, alternator malfunction, keys left in car, seat belt not on, and so on. Exhibit 13-2 illustrates a number of other common examples of control.

Characteristics of Effective Control Systems

2 *Discuss the characteristics of effective control systems.*

To be effective, a control system must have certain characteristics. Among them, these are the most important:

1. Controls need to focus on appropriate activities. Effective controls must focus on critical factors that affect both the individual's and the organization's abilities to achieve objectives. These critical objectives should include the essential areas of production and personnel activities, as well as related costs.
2. Controls should be timely. Information needed for comparisons and control purposes needs to be in a supervisor's hands for him or her to take effective corrective

---

EXHIBIT 13-1
Murphy's Laws

- Left to themselves, things always go from bad to worse.
- There's never time to do it right, but always time to do it over.
- If anything can go wrong, it will.
- Of the things that can go wrong, the one that will is capable of the most possible damage.
- If you think nothing can go wrong, you have obviously overlooked something.
- Of those things that "cannot" go wrong, the most unlikely one will.
- Inside every large problem are many small problems struggling to get out.
- Any object will fall so that it lands in the one spot where it is capable of doing the most damage.

EXHIBIT 13-2
Some Common Examples of Supervisory Control

- At the end of the workday, a production supervisor spends 30 minutes examining a printout showing each employee's output, quality, and scrap. The supervisor notes those employees whose performance is below par and makes plans to discuss their performance with them the next day.
- A nursing supervisor studies a survey completed by all patients who were housed in her ward in the past 6 months. The survey lists items such as nurses' friendliness, professionalism, appearance, and a number of other factors related to job performance.
- A maintenance supervisor tours the building, examining the progress of each worker or work team.
- After a college football game, the head defensive coach views the game films several times, assigning performance grades to each defensive player. Grades below 60 reflect areas to which the coach must devote special attention during upcoming practices.

action. Therefore, delays in generating, gathering, or disseminating information can prolong the occurrence—and extent—of deviations.

3. Controls must be cost-effective. The benefits of using appropriate controls should be worth the cost of their installation and operation. Too much control can be worse than too little. The key is that controls should be appropriate for the situation and provide savings greater than the costs involved. An example of this need was pointed out by former U.S. Senator William Cohen of Maine in the following statement:

> *The U.S. Department of Defense could save millions of dollars annually if it revamped regulations covering employee travel vouchers…. The system the Pentagon has created to protect itself against travel waste and fraud is the equivalent of assigning an armored division to guard an ATM machine…. The precautions cost more than the potential loss.*[1]

4. Controls should be accurate and concise. Controls must provide information about operations and people in sufficient quality and quantity to enable managers to make meaningful comparisons to operations standards. As with control, too much information can be as bad as too little.

5. Controls should be accepted by the people they affect. Controls and their applicability to specific situations should be communicated clearly to those responsible for implementing them and to those who will be governed by them.

Although all of these characteristics are important, a given control system need not have all of them in order to do the job for which it is designed.

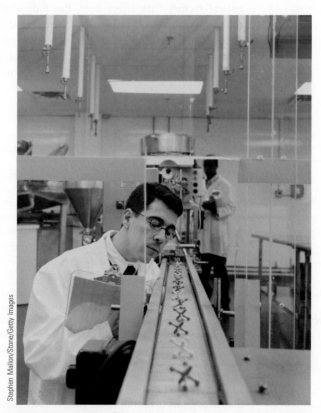

Stephen Mallon/Stone/Getty Images

Quality control inspection is one type of control system that provides timely and accurate feedback to the production line.

Types of Control Systems

3 *Discuss the three types of control systems.*

There are essentially three types of control systems. They are (1) feedforward controls, (2) concurrent controls, and (3) feedback controls.

Feedforward controls are preventive controls that try to anticipate problems and take corrective action before they occur. This type of control allows corrective action to be taken before a real problem develops. For example, Hart Schaffner Marx, a leading producer of quality clothing, inspects every bolt of cloth it plans to use in its tailored men's clothing before starting to cut pieces.

See Exhibit 13-3 for some tips on establishing preventive controls. Notice that the first step is to focus on your goals or plans. Again, you can see how closely linked the planning and controlling processes are.

Concurrent controls (sometimes called screening controls) occur while an activity is taking place. Thus, an inspector or an inspection system can check items on the assembly line to see if they are meeting standards. Production systems today are capable of providing operators with a wealth of information.

> *Carotek ECS offers a visual inspection system that can be used to trigger a shutdown of the production line if something looks amiss. First, "good" images are uploaded onto the system. Then, the cameras are trained on different points in the production line. The new images are automatically compared to the good images stored in the computer. If the images do not match, the system will either alert an operator or shut the system down entirely.*[2]

Feedback controls measure activities that have already been completed. Thus, corrections can take place after performance is over. Organizations evaluate their managers' performance levels in a variety of ways. For example, Marriott hotel managers' promotions and pay increases are dependent upon more than just hotel profitability. Guest satisfaction scores and staff ratings are factored in to a manager's overall performance score, thus providing a broader means of assessment. This evaluation process is critical for developing and coaching managerial talent, since most managers started as hourly workers. Even most of the executive team was promoted internally.[3]

feedforward controls

Preventive controls that try to anticipate problems and take corrective action before they occur.

concurrent controls

Sometimes called screening controls, these controls are used while an activity is taking place.

feedback controls

Controls that measure completed activities and then take corrective action if needed.

Self-Check

What type(s) of control were used in the chapter preview? Explain.

Steps in the Control Process

4 *Discuss the four steps in the control process.*

The steps in the control process are illustrated in Exhibit 13-4. Note that step 4 may require going back to any of the previous three steps. It may consist of modifying the original standard, changing the frequency and manner of measuring performance, or

EXHIBIT 13-3

Tips for Establishing Preventive Controls

1. Identify your department's major goals.
2. Identify those factors most crucial to accomplishing your department's major goals. These may be items such as properly running machinery and equipment, availability of raw materials, availability of key personnel, or a balanced demand for your department's services.
3. Determine the *most likely problems or circumstances* that could prevent the items in (2) from occurring. These could be factors such as machine breakdown or absence of key personnel.
4. Develop a plan for preventing the problems listed in (3). You might consider input from employees, staff personnel, your immediate supervisor, peers, and others in arriving at your preventive control plans.

EXHIBIT 13-4
The Process of Control

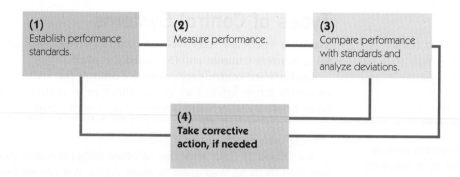

---

standard

A unit of measurement that can serve as a reference point for evaluating results.

tangible standards

Clear, concrete, specific, and generally measurable.

5 *Identify the different types of standards.*

numerical standards

Expressed in numbers.

monetary standards

Expressed in dollars and cents.

physical standards

Refer to quality, durability, size, and weight.

time standards

Expressed in terms of time.

intangible standards

Relate to human characteristics and are not expressed in terms of numbers, money, physical qualities, or time.

achieving more insight into the possible cause of the problem. Let us examine the details of each of these steps.

Step 1: Establishing Performance Standards

The first step of the controlling process is really a part of the planning step. You set your sights on something you want to accomplish. As a supervisor, you exercise control by comparing performance to some standard or goal. A **standard** is a unit of measurement that can serve as a reference point for evaluating results. Properly communicated and accepted by employees, standards become the bases for the supervisor's control activities.

Types of Standards   Standards can be either tangible or intangible. **Tangible standards** are standards that are quite clear, concrete, specific, and generally measurable. For instance, when you say, "I want the machine online by 3:00 P.M.," the goal is very specific and concrete. Either the machine is online at 3:00 P.M. or it is not.

Tangible standards can be further categorized as numerical, monetary, physical, or time related. **Numerical standards** are expressed in numbers, such as number of items produced, number of absences, percentage of successful sales calls, or number of personnel who successfully complete training. **Monetary standards** are expressed in dollars and cents. Examples of monetary standards are predetermined profit margins, payroll costs, scrap costs, and maintenance costs. **Physical standards** refer to quality, durability, size, weight, and other factors related to physical composition. **Time standards** refer to the speed with which the job should be done. Examples of time standards include printing deadlines, scheduled project completion dates, and rates of production.

Note that there may be some overlap among the types of tangible standards. For instance, when you say, "I want the machine online by 3:00 P.M.," you have obviously communicated a time standard, but the standard is expressed numerically. Monetary standards are also expressed numerically.

In contrast to tangible standards, **intangible standards** are not expressed in terms of numbers, money, physical qualities, or time because they relate to human characteristics that are difficult to measure. Examples of intangible standards are a desirable attitude, high morale, ethics, and cooperation (see Exhibit 13-5). Intangible standards pose special challenges to the supervisor, as the example illustrates.

Supervisor Maude Leyden of the State Employment Office overheard one of her newer employment counselors, David Hoffman, berating a job applicant. The tone of his voice was domineering, as though he were scolding a child, although the applicant was perhaps 30 years his senior. Maude heard David conclude the interview with the words, "Now don't come back here and bother us again until you've had someone fill this form out properly. That's not what I'm paid to do!"

EXHIBIT 13-5
Controlling Intangible
Standards

After the applicant left, Maude listened to David's explanation of what had just happened. He said he'd been under a lot of pressure that day and had grown very impatient, and he acknowledged his rudeness toward the applicant. Maude told him that he had not handled himself in a professional manner and discussed what he should have done differently. Later in the day, David was to call the applicant, apologize, and offer to be of further help.

He did call and apologize.

It is much more difficult to clearly explain an intangible standard, such as "interviewers must observe standards of professional conduct with clients," than to tell someone that the standard is "to service six malfunctioning computer systems each day." Just what is professional conduct? Is it patience, friendliness, courtesy, or keeping a level head? Certainly it is less specific than "servicing six computers daily." As difficult as it may be, every supervisor has to establish, communicate, and control some types of intangible job standards.

Self–Check

Employee cooperation, desirable employee attitude, appropriate employee personal hygiene, and mature employee behavior are some intangible standards that organizations and supervisors typically must control. Can you think of others?

How Standards Are Set Standards can be set in many ways. A supervisor will frequently set standards based on familiarity with the jobs being performed by his or her employees. The supervisor is generally knowledgeable about the time required to perform tasks, the quality necessary, and the expected employee behavior. This is especially true of supervisors who have been promoted through the ranks. If you are not technically knowledgeable about the work performed in your department, there are a number

EXHIBIT 13-6
Types of Standards for
Various Positions

POSITION	TYPE OF STANDARD
Bank teller	Monetary (balance), time (speed of teller line), physical (orderliness of work area)
Postal letter carrier	Time (hours taken to complete run)
Server in a large restaurant	Physical (appearance), time (speed), intangible (courtesy and friendliness)
Real estate salesperson	Monetary (volume), numerical (number of listings and closings)
Offensive-line football coach	Numerical (yards per game rushing), intangible (leadership of players)
Upholsterer in a manufacturing plant	Numerical (number of units completed), physical (quality of units)
Third-grade teacher	Intangible (appearance, classroom behavior), physical (quality of lesson plans)

of ways to become familiar with standards. You can gain insights from past records of performance, if available, and from fellow supervisors, employees, and your own boss. Exhibit 13-6 presents some types of standards for a variety of positions.

For many jobs, various staff departments will strongly influence the standards set. The industrial engineering department, for example, may utilize systematic studies of movements and speed of workers to set quantity and time standards. The quality control department may establish standards for finish, luster, or precision. Cost accounting may develop standards for material costs or scrap. Thus, many standards may already be established for the people you will supervise.

Staff departments may also have a hand in setting standards for supervisors. For example, the budget department may help determine standards regarding material and payroll costs. Personnel may establish standards regarding the quantity and quality of grievances and turnover in a department. The ability to meet your departmental standards, in turn, will determine the amount of control that your own boss will exercise over your activities.

Step 2: Measuring Performance

Setting standards is an essential first step in control, but by itself, it doesn't go far enough. A supervisor must monitor performance to ensure that it complies with the established standards. Two issues the supervisor must deal with are (1) how often to measure performance and (2) how to measure performance.

6 *Explain the importance of strategic control points.*

How Often to Measure Performance Determining how often to measure performance is an important control decision supervisors must make. Sometimes this decision has already been made by the system, as shown in the examples:

Kay Davis, sales manager of City Motors, need only look at the sales chart prominently displayed on the sales floor outside her office to see how her sales personnel are doing. The chart lists the number of new and used cars sold by each salesperson for the week and the month, as well as total sales volume for the entire company.

The production control room at DAVO Company provides a constant reading of activity on each of the production floor's operating machines. At any time, a production supervisor can visit the area and receive a printout of the work performed by any of the operators up to that time.

Sherwin Crasto/Reuters/Corbis

Customer service representatives are monitored against time standards such as how quickly they answer the telephone and how long it takes them to help each customer.

strategic control point

A performance measurement point located early in an activity to allow any corrective action to be taken.

Notice that in each of the preceding examples, performance is being constantly monitored. This does not mean that supervisors should spend the entire day monitoring performance. Instead, they should establish strategic control points. As shown in Exhibit 13-7, a **strategic control point** is a performance measurement point located sufficiently early in an activity to allow any necessary corrective actions to be taken to accomplish the objective. For each job, ask yourself: Considering the importance of this job, at what point do I need to know the progress being made so that I can make any required adjustments and still complete the job as planned?

EXHIBIT 13-7
Setting Strategic Control Points in the Control Process

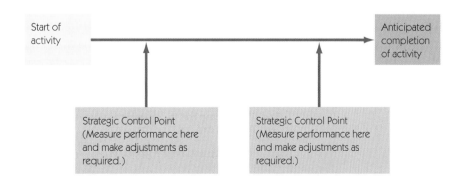

Certain types of jobs, such as maintenance, personnel, and sales, don't lend themselves to frequent measurement of progress. Measurement takes time, unless an automated system is in place. On the other hand, effective monitoring is crucial for some jobs. For example, the work of an emergency room nurse requires more careful monitoring than does the work of a sales representative or a clerical worker.

How to Measure A supervisor can measure performance in several basic ways:

1. Personal observation.
2. Written or oral reports by or about employees.
3. Automatic methods.
4. Inspections, tests, or samples.

Exhibit 13-8 is an example of the second method, which could be used frequently, at very little cost. Notice how precisely the information requested is stated.

EXHIBIT 13-8
Example of a Written Report about an Employee

Management Encourages Your Comments

Date **5/19/2007**

Waiter or waitress **Phyllis**

Please circle meal   Breakfast   (Lunch)   Dinner

	Yes	No
1. Were you greeted by host or hostess promptly and courteously?	✓	
2. Was your server prompt, courteous, and helpful?	✓	
3. Was the quality of food to your expectations?		✓
4. Was the table setting and condition of overall restaurant appearance pleasing and in good taste?	✓	
5. Will you return to our restaurant?		✓
6. Will you recommend our restaurant to your friends and associates?		✓

Comments
Food was overcooked. Potatoes were leftovers. Meat was tough. This was my second visit and I brought a friend with me. We were both very disappointed.

Name and address (if you desire)

Please drop this in our quality improvement box located near the exit.

Thank you and have a good day.

Self-Check

Can you suggest some instances or situations when each of these ways of measuring performance might be used?

In some jobs, supervisors and their employees work in the same area. The supervisor can easily move among the workers, observing their performance. In other departments, however, the supervisor may have workers spread out in various locations, which makes direct observation impractical. Consider a sanitation supervisor whose eight work crews collect garbage on various routes throughout the city. Such a supervisor must depend on written or oral reports or occasional inspections as the primary means of measurement. Here is what one sanitation supervisor said:

How do I know if my crews are doing the job properly? Mainly by the complaints I get from customers. Complaints range from garbage that isn't picked up on schedule to overturned trash cans, surrounded with litter. That's how I know what's going on in the field. Sometimes I will drive around and make a visual inspection. We also survey residents annually to see if our people are considered timely, friendly, and efficient.

Sales supervisors may seldom see their employees if the sales work takes them outside the office. As a result, salespersons are required to complete reports about number of calls made, sales results, travel expenses, customer comments, and numerous other matters. These reports are received by supervisors or the home office staff. Many salespersons, in fact, complain that they are required to do too much paperwork!

Supervisors who are not in frequent contact with their employees must come up with some meaningful, valid ways to measure results. They need to find some means of making sure the measurements are reliable. Because of pressures to conform to standards, employees may attempt to falsify reports to make themselves appear better.

Several years ago, a nationally respected youth organization set very high membership goals for its local offices. The results appeared spectacular until it was discovered that a number of local chapters had considerably inflated the number of new members enrolled to avoid looking bad.

In other words, you have to be careful about attempts to "beat" the control system. People may extort money, falsify documents, and distort oral reports to make themselves look good. For example, if you ask an employee to give you an oral report on a job's progress, he or she may tell you, "Everything's just fine, boss," when, in fact, it is not.

Step 3: Comparing Performance with Standards and Analyzing Deviations

Unfortunately, many supervisors receive information that demonstrates a serious departure from standards but make little effort to understand what caused the difference between planned and actual performance. Failure to meet standards may result from a variety of causes. A supervisor needs to understand the reasons for below-average performance. Many supervisors jump to conclusions about the causes of problems; as a result, the corrective action they take is ineffective.

Suppose that the quality control standard for producing a certain part is 99/100. This means that there should be no more than one defective product per hundred units produced by a worker. You just received notice from the quality department that of the last 200 units produced by employee Kevin Rae, almost 13 percent were defective.

What could have caused this problem? Could it have been poor materials? Could Rae's equipment be the cause? Is this like Rae's previous performance? What will you do about it? These are some questions you have to ask yourself. Simply giving Rae an oral or a written warning may be highly inappropriate and may not correct the problem!

It is also important to compare results that are substantially above standard to determine why they varied from standard. The supervisor should check to see if all operating procedures are being followed correctly, or if there is an improvement in operations that should be included in new standards.

It is important to find out the opinions of those close to a particular problem to determine why standards are not being met. For example, an employee's explanation or those of other employees or fellow supervisors might be obtained. Frequently, people in other departments can add insight. Here is what one supervisor said:

I was all set to really chew Emily out. She had an important job to complete for me this morning and didn't show up as scheduled. Fortunately, before I made a fool of myself, I learned from one of her friends that she'd gotten here early and the plant manager had asked her to do an even more important job. I checked this out with the plant manager, and, sure enough, that was the case. She was supposed to notify me but had just forgotten.

Step 4: Taking Corrective Action if Necessary

The final step in the control process is to take corrective action if needed. You have undoubtedly seen many athletic contests turn completely around after halftime. This change is often due to corrective action taken by the coach—the modifications, adjustments, and fine-tuning done in response to problems encountered earlier.

The supervisor's job is much like that of a coach. Adjustments, fine-tuning, and perhaps even drastic actions may be necessary to pull off important tasks or to maintain standards. Examples of corrective actions a supervisor might take include the following:

1. Making a decision to retrain a new operator whose performance has not progressed as expected.
2. Shifting several employees from their normal jobs to help meet a deadline on another job.
3. Counseling an employee whose performance has recently been below standard.
4. Reprimanding an employee for failure to adhere to safety rules.
5. Shutting down a piece of equipment for maintenance after defective output is traced to it.

7 *Discuss management by exception.*

management by exception

A supervisor focuses on critical control needs and allows employees to handle most routine deviations from the standard.

Management by Exception

Even under the best of circumstances, deviations from performance standards are bound to occur. Given the broad range of areas over which supervisors exert control, it is essential to distinguish between critical and less-critical deviations. The fact that many performance deviations are due to normal operating variances means that supervisors must exercise some discretion in distinguishing between variations that are relevant and those that are less so.

Under **management by exception,** a supervisor focuses on critical control needs and allows employees to handle most routine deviations from the standards. Exhibit 13-9 shows that the key issue is whether a deviation is exceptional.

AFP/Getty Images

When a quality control standard has not been met, a supervisor must investigate for possible causes.

EXHIBIT 13-9
Management by
Exception

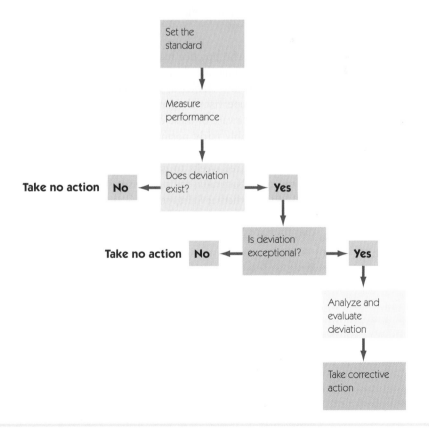

The idea is to set priorities for activities, depending on their importance, and to focus your efforts on top-priority items. Management by exception works essentially the same way. Your attention should be focused on exceptional, rather than routine, problems.

Self–Check

Suppose you are a sales supervisor and your departmental sales goal is 800 units weekly (or 3,200 units monthly). Each of your eight sales representatives, then, has a goal of 100 units weekly (or 400 units monthly). At the end of the first week, your sales results are as follows:

SALESPERSON	WEEKLY GOAL	UNITS SOLD
A	100	105
B	100	95
C	100	90
D	100	102
E	100	102
F	100	88
G	100	98
H	100	115
	Total = 800	795

What corrective action will you take?

Managers who practice management by exception might do absolutely nothing about the previous situation. "But wait!" you say. "Look at Salesperson C, who performed 10 percent below standard, and Salesperson F, who was 12 percent below standard. Shouldn't a supervisor do something about these two employees?" Of course, a supervisor should be aware of these deviations. However, recall that only the first week has gone by. It is probably fairly normal to find such variances in a single week; the more pertinent information is how performance compares to the monthly benchmark of 3,200 units. With three weeks to go, the supervisor who gets too upset after week 1 may be overreacting. Naturally, the supervisor should keep an eye on sales data in the upcoming weeks to see whether Salespersons C and F improve their performances. In this situation, the assumption of management by exception is that Salespersons B, C, F, and G realize that they are below standard and will be working to improve.

Self–Check

Suppose that at the end of the second week, sales results are as shown:

SALESPERSON	WEEKLY GOAL	WEEK 1	WEEK 2
A	100	105	107
B	100	95	101
C	100	90	97
D	100	102	101

SALESPERSON	WEEKLY GOAL	WEEK 1	WEEK 2
E	100	102	101
F	100	88	84
G	100	98	99
H	100	115	126
	Total = 800	795	816

What will you do now?

Sales have perked up, and, with the exception of Salesperson F, everyone is in reasonable shape. As supervisor, you'd be justified in entering the control process with Salesperson F, as the "red flag" is still up on this one. You may want to discuss this person's results, try to identify actions that produce below-standard results, and develop a plan of corrective action.

Note that Salesperson H has been setting the standards on fire, averaging more than 20 percent above standard the first two weeks. This performance is also an exceptional departure from standard. What is behind these results? Is Salesperson H using some techniques that will work for others? Is this person's territory so choice that it becomes easy to make the standard? Should you modify the standard for Salesperson H? Management by exception can be applied to both favorable and unfavorable deviations from standard.

The Impact of Technology on Control

8 *Discuss the impact of technology on control.*

As the world's economies—and their environments—continue to become more dynamic and complex, managers—including supervisors—must obtain, organize, and utilize huge amounts of information to make decisions and exercise control over them. Progressive managers are realizing that a high-speed information infrastructure is needed to cope with the rapid pace of operations in all types of economic activities.

One result of this "information revolution" is the redistribution of power in today's more advanced organizations. For example, decision making and control have now been shifted downward to lower levels of management, including the supervisory level. With practically unlimited types and sources of information at their fingertips, even operative employees no longer have to rely on others for facts and figures to make decisions. Thanks in part to networks and multimedia fusions, organizations such as Tiris are becoming more integrated. Tiris—a unit of Texas Instruments—is managed out of Bedford, England. Its line of low-frequency transponders is designed in Freising, Germany, and the units are produced in Kuala Lumpur, Malaysia, whence they are shipped to customers around the world.[4]

Organizations now have information and monitoring systems that permit supervisors to give instructions and control operations from a distance away from those activities.

For example, at the start of his workday at 8:30 each morning, Washington R., a delivery person for United Parcel Service (UPS), picks up a bulky brown box resembling an oversize computer game. He carries the box with him all day as he makes his deliveries and returns to home base at night. His personal box has a window in which he can view all the day's tasks, each one timed to the minute.

As he makes his deliveries, Washington keys the details into the box, which electronically transmits the data to his home depot. His supervisor can therefore determine at any time where he is and whether or not he is on schedule. At the end of the day, Washington hooks up his box to the UPS computer, and all the information he has accumulated during the day is automatically transferred to it.

UPS uses technology that allows the employee and supervisor to monitor and control desired results for their deliveries.

During the night, the computer downloads Washington's next day's itinerary and individual tasks into his box.[5]

Today's information technology makes possible—for better or for worse—this form of digital monitoring and control.

Chapter Review

1. **Define control and explain how it relates to planning.**

    Controlling is the supervisory process of making plans and following through on them. Because of the many variables involved in executing and carrying out plans, supervisory control is an essential part of the management process.

2. **Discuss the characteristics of effective control systems.**

    For control systems to be effective, they should (1) focus on appropriate activities, (2) be timely, (3) be cost-effective, (4) be accurate and concise, and (5) be accepted by people who will be controlled by them.

3. **Discuss the three types of control systems.**

    The three types of control systems are (1) feedforward controls, which try to anticipate problems and take corrective action before they occur; (2) concurrent controls, which are used while an activity is taking place; and (3) feedback controls, which measure activities that are completed and then take corrective action if needed.

4. **Discuss the four steps in the control process.**

    The four steps in the control process are: (1) Establish performance standards, (2) measure performance, (3) compare performance with standards and analyze deviations, and (4) take corrective action if needed.

5. **Identify the different types of standards.**

    There are several types of standards. They can be tangible (numerical, monetary, physical, and time) or intangible (attitudes, ethics, and morals). They can be set by supervisors or staff departments.

6. **Explain the importance of strategic control points.**

    It is important that the supervisor establish strategic control points. These points measure performance early enough in the process to permit sufficient adjustments or corrective actions to be made in order to achieve the goal. Supervisors measure performance through direct observation, by written or oral reports by or about employees, through automatic methods, and by inspections, samples, or tests.

7. **Discuss management by exception.**

    Management by exception focuses supervisory attention on exceptional departures from standard rather than on routine variances.

8. **Discuss the impact of technology on control.**

    The growth of information technology has redistributed power in organizations, thus enhancing the position of supervisors.

Key Terms

feedforward controls, p. 393

concurrent controls, p. 393

feedback controls, p. 393

tangible standards, p. 394

numerical standards, p. 394

monetary standards, p. 394

physical standards, p. 394

time standards, p. 394

intangible standards, p. 394

standard, p. 394

strategic control point, p. 397

management by exception, p. 400

Questions for Review & Discussion

1. In what ways are planning and controlling related?
2. Discuss the following statement made by a supervisor: "I don't have to worry much about controlling. My view is that, if you plan a job properly, things will go right; so you don't have to worry about control."
3. Name the primary characteristics of effective control systems.
4. Identify and explain each of the four steps in controlling.
5. Give an example of each type of standard:
   a. Numerical standard
   b. Monetary standard
   c. Physical standard
   d. Time standard
   e. Intangible standard
6. Name and explain the three types of control systems.
7. In management by exception, the supervisor focuses on exceptional deviations from the standard rather than on every deviation. Will employees grow lax when they realize that they can perform below standard as long as they are not too far below? Discuss.
8. Explain the impact technology has had on control.

Skill Builder 13-1

The Overcontrolling Supervisor

As a new operations supervisor, Clarise Rogers was very conscientious about wanting to do a good job and pleasing her boss. She spent a large part of the day watching her employees perform their jobs, moving from one workstation to another. She inquired how things were going and tried to engage in friendly small talk.

One day a senior operator asked to see Clarise in her office. The operator said, "We know you mean well, but there's no need for you to be constantly checking up on everybody. We had one of the best departments in this company under Morgan [the previous supervisor], and she stayed off our backs. We're professionals, and we don't need somebody constantly looking over our shoulders. We're going to do a good job for you. Just give us some breathing space."

Answer the following questions:

1. What should Clarise do?
2. Suppose Clarise had just taken over one of the poorest performing departments in the company. Would this make a difference in the control techniques she should use? How?

Systems

Skill Builder 13-2

Setting Standards and Measuring Performance (Group Activity)

Instructions: Form small groups to discuss each of the jobs listed below. Assume that each group member directly supervises that position. In each case, indicate the major type(s) of standard(s) that would be used (physical, monetary, time, or intangible) and the frequency and manner of measuring performance for each job.

Discuss with group members your ideas about how to handle each situation.

Interpersonal Skill

1. Bank teller
2. Postal letter carrier
3. Server in a large restaurant
4. Real estate salesperson
5. Offensive-line football coach
6. Upholsterer in a furniture manufacturing plant
7. Third-grade teacher in an elementary school

Systems

Skill Builder 13-3

Competitor Assessment (Group Activity)

Assemble into teams of three to five members. Choose two well-known direct competitors (e.g., Jimmy Johns and Firehouse, Walgreens and CVS, and Walmart and Target), and using the Internet, find information (articles, blogs, company websites, etc.) about each organization.

Instructions:

1. Specifically, your team should identify and classify (feedforward, concurrent, and feedback) the different types of control systems each competitor utilizes.
2. Pick one form of control for each company and evaluate its effectiveness based on the characteristics of effective control systems presented in this chapter. What improvements could each company make?
3. Prepare and give a 10-minute PowerPoint presentation of your overall findings to the class.

CASE 13-1

Controlling Absenteeism

Anna McIntyre had been named head nurse of the university hospital pediatrics department the previous day. She would officially begin her new job in one week, when Carla Smith, the present head nurse, would be reassigned to a new department. Anna reflected on the conversation she'd had with Gail Sutherland, director of nursing, when Gail offered her the position. "Anna," Gail had said, "you'll be taking over a department that has 8 percent absenteeism compared to only 2 percent for other nursing units in the hospital. This has always been a problem, and Carla never could handle it—that's a major reason she was transferred. I want you to make it your number 1 priority."

Anna reflected on Carla's performance as head nurse. Carla had always been a skilled, competent nurse, but since being promoted to head nurse in pediatrics, she had just been too soft. Many nurses had taken advantage of her good nature—Carla had found it impossible to discipline—and the situation in pediatrics had begun to deteriorate. Anna knew from her own experience that absenteeism had been high in the department. This was especially true of weekend work. Carla never took action, even when it was obvious that personnel were making petty excuses.

Questions

1. What additional information should Anna attempt to obtain regarding the absenteeism problem?
2. Advise Anna on the steps she should take to control absenteeism.
3. What types of standards should she use?
4. What strategic control points should she establish?

14

Controlling Productivity, Quality, and Safety

Sales "members" on the sales floor of Park Place Lexus help make it #1 in quality.

LEARNING OBJECTIVES

After reading and studying this chapter, you should be able to:

1. Explain the concept of productivity.

2. Identify and explain the ways in which management, government, unions, and employees affect productivity.

3. Describe some steps supervisors can take to increase productivity.

4. Differentiate between total quality and quality control.

5. Describe the role of variance in controlling quality.

6. Identify some important tools for controlling quality.

7. Explain what the Occupational Safety and Health Administration (OSHA) does.

8. Describe the supervisor's role in promoting safety.

You can never inspect quality into products. You can only build it into them.

—*Akio Morita, Co-founder, Sony Corporation*

Preview

PARK PLACE LEXUS: COMMITTED TO EXCELLENCE On the outskirts of Dallas, Texas, in Plano, is one special auto dealer, Park Place Lexus (PPL). PPL differs from other dealerships in many ways, and not just because of the feminine touch supplied by six of its sales "members," who just happen to be females. The differences also go beyond its putting green, cafe, Internet access, and portable DVD players with movies loaned to clients who wait for their cars to be serviced, all ideas that were suggested by customer focus groups.

Dealer-owner Ken Schnitzer explains his motive in making the commitment in 1995 to make PPL something special. "We wanted to distinguish ourselves among our competitors. We set out to prove that a 'car dealer,' can be run just as well and can be just as great a place to work as any other corporation in America." Jordan Case, Park Place dealership president and former quarterback of the Canadian Football League's Ottawa Rough Riders, states: "Buying a car doesn't rank up there with the top five things you like to do. So we try to make the experience different. We're always trying to raise the bar and think about how we can improve." For example, after attending a Lexus summit on best practices held at a Four Seasons Hotel, Case sent some of his own staffers to spend a weekend at a local Four Seasons. Hector Interiano, a lead PPL valet, was impressed when every Four Seasons staffer called him by name. Guess what? Now, when a car pulls up to PPL's service drive, valets can punch the vehicle ID number into a laptop that informs them of pertinent information, which allows the valets to call their clients by name.

Located in the Dallas suburbs, the company of more than 200 "members," as its personnel are called, has been very successful. Starting with its vision—"To be the unparalleled retail automotive group in the U.S."—PPL sets lofty goals, is committed to reaching them, and can be counted on to set them higher the following year. Name an activity that involves a client and you can bet a performance standard and tracking system is in place, ranging from requiring phones to be answered within three rings to e-mail response within 24 hours. Continuously improving is its mantra. Here are but a few of PPL's performance achievements:

- Customer satisfaction for new car clients approaches 100 percent; preowned vehicle clients' satisfaction approaches 96 percent.
- Customer satisfaction with service at the locations approaches 98 percent; 96 percent of service clients report their vehicle is ready when promised.
- Customer problems/complaints have dramatically been reduced. Over a three-year period, customer concerns that "promises were not met" dropped from 130 to 3; concerns about discourteous treatment dropped from 28 to 1, and concerns about misinformation dropped from 22 to 1.
- Seventy percent of customers say they will purchase their next vehicle from PPL.

To achieve these kinds of customer results, PPL is willing to commit resources. It has a human resources department, which is rare for an auto dealer. Its computer database includes all client interactions—needs and preferences, customer survey responses, follow-up interactions regarding sales and service, complaints, and special customer needs. Personnel in sales, service, parts, and accounting have this information available instantly from PPL's sophisticated information technology (IT) system. PPL's hiring process is stringent, including aptitude and personality testing, with special attention paid to integrity. New members follow a rigorous training plan that includes classroom training, on-the-job training, coaching, and mentoring to help them succeed. Everyone receives training in ethics, health, safety, wellness, quality improvement, documentation, reporting, and computer skills; English classes are offered to Hispanic employees with limited English skills. Member training has increased by 160 hours since 2001. Employee turnover runs at about 22 percent, which is half the typical rate of a large auto dealership.

To encourage member empowerment and motivation, a monthly "50-50 Meeting" is held, where half of the meeting focuses on ideas and concerns and half focuses on solutions. A recent solution authorized employees to spend up to $250 on the spot to resolve a client's concern.

PPL has zero tolerance regarding unethical or illegal behavior, with all managers receiving yearly ethics training in subjects ranging from sexual harassment to safety and health concerns. Leaders are expected to "walk the talk" as role models, with ethics commonly brought up at team meetings throughout the company. The company is active in the two communities its dealerships serve, one in Plano and the other in Grapevine, Texas. Each dealership generously donates funds to local charities throughout the year. It supports its members' volunteering time to support local programs.

PPL has been recognized not only by clients and competitors, but also by organizations that value excellence. General Mills, for one, has spent time benchmarking PPL's practices. The state of Texas awarded PPL its quality award for organizational excellence in 2002. In 2005, the company achieved national recognition when it was became one of six U.S. organizations to receive the Malcolm Baldrige National Quality Award for Organizational Excellence. As owner Schnitzer says, "The typical car dealer wakes up in the morning and says, 'How can I sell more cars today?' We wake up and say, 'How can we run the company better today?'"

Source: Julia Chang, "At Your Service: For Park Place Lexus, Treating Customers and Employees Right Led to National Recognition and Increased Sales," *Sales and Marketing Management* 158, June 2006, pp. 42–43.

Control is the management function that ensures that organizational plans are executed properly and that objectives are met. This chapter addresses several key areas of control, some of which were directly reflected in the scenario that you just read and that concern managers and supervisors: productivity and costs, quality, and safety.

Improving Productivity and Cost Control

1 *Explain the concept of productivity.*

Productivity has been an "in" word in American business for the past two decades. Another name for productivity is efficiency. We hear about productivity at work, read about it in magazines and newspapers, and see it discussed on television. It has become the subject of business- and government-sponsored seminars. "Productivity centers" have sprung up around the country to research the subject.

High U.S. Productivity: Mid-1990s to Present

On a global level, a country's productivity indicates how efficiently its human resources are utilized in producing goods and services. The productivity of U.S. workers has and continues to be high.

During the 1980s, a major concern was the United States' productivity stagnation (Exhibit 14-1). As U.S. productivity suffered, Japanese and other foreign competitors stole market share with their high-quality products in autos, steel, electronics, earth-moving equipment, appliances, and many others. Plenty of blame was tossed at management, government, unions, and employees. The 1990s saw a dramatic turnaround as U.S. companies grabbed back the initiative and built new facilities, upgraded technology, transformed production processes and work methods, and invested heavily in employee training. Since the mid-1990s, U.S. productivity has generally remained strong, helping firms keep costs low and enabling them to weather the recent global financial crises and economic storms.

EXHIBIT 14-1

U.S. Productivity Change in the Nonfarm Business Sector, 1947–2008

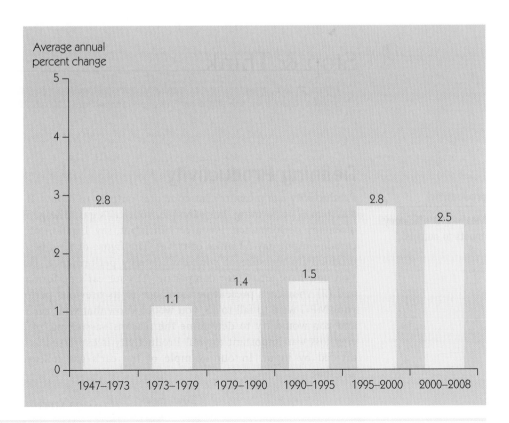

AP Photo/Koji Sasahara

Japanese workers, while highly productive, still don't approach the U.S. level of production.

Stop & Think

Although U.S. productivity has remained strong since the mid-1990s, what do you think are the reasons for the slight decline experienced from 2000 to 2008?

Defining Productivity

productivity

Measure of efficiency (inputs to outputs).

Productivity is a measure that compares outputs to inputs. It tells you how efficiently a system is performing. For example, your car's gas mileage is a productivity measure of energy performance. For a certain input, say 1 gallon of gas, your car achieves a certain output, say 22 miles of travel. The figure of 22 miles per gallon (MPG) is the productivity measure of your car's energy performance. How is this figure useful? You now have a basis for comparing (1) your car's performance to that of other cars and (2) your car's present performance to its previous performance. For example, if your MPG were to fall to 15, you would know that your car's performance had fallen, and you would try to determine the reasons—assuming, of course, that such an energy loss was important to you! Productivity is expressed as a ratio; that is, output is divided by input. In our example of the car's gas mileage, the ratio might look like this:

$$\frac{\text{Total miles (220)}}{\text{Number of gallons (10)}} = 22 \text{ MPG}$$

Stop & Think

What would be some meaningful input–output relationships for the following service organizations: restaurants, community colleges, beauty salons, insurance companies, and department stores?

The official productivity measure of the United States, as shown in Exhibit 14-2, is based on labor output and input per hour. This is the productivity that is announced each quarter by the government and discussed in the media. Basically, it is the ratio of the total output of the nation's goods and services to the total hours of labor that went into producing those goods and services. Business organizations use numerous input–output performance measures, some of which are shown in Exhibit 14-2. Generally, when people in business discuss improved productivity, they are talking about total costs and total goods or services produced. Assume that a department has a mandate from upper management to increase productivity by 15 percent in the next year or it will be shut down. Upper management's goal, then, is that at the end of the next 12-month period, the department's productivity ratio would look like this:

$$\frac{\text{Total output of goods/services}}{\text{Total costs}} = 15 \text{ percent more than previously accomplished}$$

Basically, there are three ways to accomplish the 15 percent productivity increase:

1. *Increase* the total output without changing the total costs.
2. *Decrease* the total input costs without changing the total output.
3. *Increase* the output and *decrease* the input costs.

Assume that the department produced 48,000 units (output) at a cost of $24,000 for raw materials, energy, and labor. The productivity ratio is as follows:

$$\frac{48,000 \text{ units (output)}}{\$24,000 \text{ (input)}} = 2.0 \text{ units/dollar}$$

To achieve a 15 percent increase in productivity, the department would need to raise the final ratio by 0.3 (that is, 2.0 × 15 percent). In other words, the department would

EXHIBIT 14-2

Examples of
Productivity
Measurements

INPUT	OUTPUT
Salesperson labor hours	Sales volume per salesperson
Energy used, in BTUs*	Number of pounds fabricated
Training hours for customer service personnel	Percent of error-free written orders
Number of hours of plant-wide safety meetings	Number of accident-free days
Labor hours spent on preventive maintenance	Number of hours without a machine breakdown
Cost of raw materials	Quantity of finished goods produced
Total labor hours of service personnel	Total quantity of services produced
Total labor hours of production workforce	Total quantity of goods produced
Total costs	Total number (or value) of goods or services produced

*BTU, British thermal unit.

need to produce 2.3 units per dollar to achieve a 15 percent productivity increase. There are three basic ways to achieve this, as discussed next.

Example 1: Increasing Output One approach to attaining the productivity increase is to hold the line on costs while increasing output. How much additional output would be needed to reach the new productivity rate of 2.3? This can be calculated by the following steps:

(a) $\dfrac{\text{Total units}}{\$24,000} = 2.3$ units per dollar

(b) Total units $= 2.3$ units per dollar $\times \$24,000$

(c) Total units $= 55,200$

Since the department is presently producing 48,000 units, it would have to produce 7,200 additional units without increasing costs to attain the 15 percent productivity increase.

Example 2: Decreasing Input Another approach is to maintain present output while reducing costs. By how much would the department need to reduce costs to attain the 15 percent increase? This can be calculated by the following steps:

(a) $\dfrac{48,000 \text{ units}}{\text{Costs}} = 2.3$ units per dollar

(b) Costs $= \dfrac{48,000 \text{ units}}{2.3 \text{ units per dollar}}$

(c) Costs $= \$20,870$

Producing the 48,000 units at a cost of $20,870 would provide the 15 percent productivity ratio improvement. The department would have to maintain production of 48,000 units while reducing costs by $3,130 (that is, $24,000 − $20,870).

Example 3: Increasing Output and Decreasing Input Suppose that the department could reduce costs by only $1,000. By how much would the department have to increase output to achieve the 15 percent productivity increase?

(a) $\dfrac{\text{Total units}}{\$24,000 - \$1,000} = 2.3$ units per dollar

(b) $\dfrac{\text{Total units}}{\$23,000} = 2.3$ units per dollar

(c) Total units $= 2.3$ units per dollar $\times \$23,000$

(d) Total units $= 52,900$

Thus, reducing costs by $1,000 and increasing output by 4,900 units (52,900 − 48,000) would also provide the 15 percent productivity increase.

Why Productivity Is Important

Productivity is important for several reasons. From an individual company's standpoint, increased productivity translates into lower prices, larger market share, and greater profits. The firm's stronger financial position enables it to invest in research and development, to utilize new advanced technology, to increase wages and benefits, to improve working conditions, and so on. Let us examine the following service-oriented business example:

> *Assume that you manage a steakhouse restaurant that uses seven waiters/waitresses. Their pay (including benefits but excluding tips) averages $10.00/hour. The maximum number of tables that they can serve effectively is five per hour. Thus, the labor cost for serving each table is $10/5, or $2 per table. Assume that business has picked up recently. The kitchen can handle the extra business, and, by rearranging tables, five new tables could be added. Since the current waiter/waitress maximum of five tables served per hour has already been reached, a new waiter/waitress must be hired to handle the extra workload. Before hiring another waitress, though, you pose the problem to your waiters and they come up with a plan.*

> *"We could each handle an extra table an hour if we didn't have to set each table," they say. "Couldn't the hostess who seats the party distribute the silverware and menus? Also, might we arrange each waiter's tables in a more compact area? This would reduce walking time among tables. The time saved with these two changes might allow us to effectively serve another table hourly (which, by the way, would mean an additional tip)."*

> *So you try it out, and behold, it works. Your waiters/waitresses handle the extra table per hour effectively. Let's calculate the effect on productivity—it has increased by one fifth, or 20 percent. Moreover, your labor costs have decreased from $2.00 per table to $1.67 per table ($10.00 ÷ 6 tables = $1.67 per table). Since labor costs typically account for 30 to 60 percent of a company's expenses, increasing the efficiency of labor is very important to an organization's success.*

Productivity is important for restaurants and other service-minded businesses.

On a larger scale, increased productivity greatly enhances the economic growth and health of the United States. In the international market, companies from the United States compete with firms from other nations. Increased productivity in the United States enhances the success of U.S. companies in international markets, keeps prices down, reduces inflation, and improves our standard of living.

Groups Influencing Productivity

2 *Identify and explain the ways in which management, government, unions, and employees affect productivity.*

As noted in Exhibit 14-1, the productivity growth rate of the United States picked up significant steam in the 1990s. But what caused the slowdown of U.S. companies' productivity in the 1980s? What is responsible for the impressive growth since the mid-1990s? Basically, four groups play important roles, as shown in Exhibit 14-3.

Management A major force in determining productivity is management. Many experts placed major blame on complacent, conservative management for the United States' deteriorating performance in the 1980s when U.S. companies lost ground to highly productive foreign producers, especially the Japanese, in such industries as steel and autos (see Exhibit 14-4).

EXHIBIT 14-3
Groups Influencing Productivity

EXHIBIT 14-4
Toyota's Production System

Toyota Production System

Toyota's philosophy and framework of organizing manufacturing facilities efficiently.

The global company with the strongest reputation for efficiency is unquestionably Toyota Motors. The **"Toyota Production System"** (TPS) has been admired, studied, and copied by most large manufacturers, including competitors. In fact, in Erlanger, Ohio, Toyota has created a training center to teach outside firms its TPS. The "system" refers to Toyota's philosophy and framework of organizing manufacturing facilities and having them interact with suppliers and customers in the most efficient way. TPS's goal is the elimination of waste—be it through defective materials, overproduction, inefficient logistics, or inventory buildup. The TPS requires a strong top management commitment and what for many companies is a dramatic change from their current ways of doing things.

One of the best known aspects of Toyota's approach to efficiency is its effort to continuously improve, called *kaizen*. Another is an *Andan*, part of every Toyota plant, which is a cord that any employee can pull to stop the production line when a problem or defect is spotted. The story is told of an American supervisor in Toyota's Georgetown, Kentucky, plant who feared for his job after one of his crew pulled the Andan, shutting the line down for 4 hours to trace and remedy the problem. Afterward, he was called to the desk of the Japanese plant executive where he nervously explained the problem and the solution. Only then did he learn he was summoned not to explain the problem and shutdown, but to receive recognition for his team having done it.

Source: Jingshan Li and Dennis Blumenfield, "Qualitative Analysis of a Transfer Production Line with Andan," *IIE Transactions* 38, October 2006, pp. 837–847. Dan Monk, "Productivity Machine," *Business Courier Serving Cincinnati-Northern Kentucky* 16, June 25, 1999, pp. 1–2.

Fortunately, a turnaround in the 1990s was fueled by management decisions to build more modern plants, upgrade equipment, improve processes, and train employees. However, some industries such as steel have never regained their dominant world market position.

Government Another important productivity player is government. For example, tax incentives can encourage business investment in new facilities and technology; government regulations also play an important role. During the 1980s, businesses spent huge amounts on the costs of compliance to satisfy, for instance, pollution and environmental controls, consumer protection requirements, and employee safety and health, to mention some of the more costly areas. This not only diverted expenditures from more efficient labor-saving technology, equipment, and plants, but it also required many new positions—such as equal employment opportunity (EEO) specialists, record keepers, and clerks—to meet government requirements. These personnel do not contribute directly to output. Although government regulation of business is necessary, the amount of regulation is a constant source of debate in this country as well as in others.

Individual Workers Another important productivity player is the individual worker. Employees' ability, motivation, and commitment strongly affect individual and team performance. The age and education of employees impact their skill: During the 1980s, the average age of workforce employees was much lower than in earlier years, which resulted in less-experienced, less-productive employees during that period. This situation has reversed itself and has fostered the United States' higher productivity during the 1990s to today.

Unions Unions also play a role in productivity by their posture toward technology enhancements, new work methods, and displacement of inefficient jobs. We read about cases in which unions resist labor-saving devices and efficiencies and protect jobs that are considered nonproductive. Many people tried to make unions the scapegoat of the 1980s' productivity crisis; however, during this period, union membership was decreasing, as is the case today. Moreover, in the retail and wholesale industry, which had practically no union strength, the decline in productivity was similar to that which occurred in the more traditionally unionized industries.

In summary, then, all of these groups play a role in productivity. However, management, which directly controls decisions about facilities, technology, research, and the company "productivity climate," is most responsible in that it strongly impacts relationships with its union and sets the stage in numerous ways for the productivity of individual employees.

The Supervisor's Role in Improving Productivity

3 *Describe some steps supervisors can take to increase productivity.*

Supervisors often have little control over spending for technology and equipment, but as the persons in direct contact with operating employees, they are very important players in the productivity issue. But how do you go about it? Suppose that you head a department of 20 employees who produced a total of 10,000 units last year. Under your plant manager's new mandate, you must increase production to 11,500 units. How would you do this? You could do some of the things listed in Exhibit 14-5.

The Supervisor's Role in Cost Control

As we pointed out earlier, the productivity of a department is based on its total outputs and total inputs. Upper management is cost conscious because costs represent major inputs. Supervisors direct the operating work of an organization; thus, they have a key role

EXHIBIT 14-5
How Supervisors Can
Improve Employee
Productivity

- Train employees. Can their abilities be upgraded?
- Clearly communicate the need for high standards so that workers understand what is expected of them.
- Use motivation techniques to inspire workers to increase output. Pride, ego, and security are several important motivators available.
- Eliminate idleness, extended breaks, and early quitting time.
- Build in quality the first time work is done. Productivity is lost when items are scrapped or need to be reworked to be salvaged.
- Work on improving attendance and turnover in your work group.
- Reduce accidents. Accidents normally result in time lost to investigations, meetings, and reports—even if the employee does not suffer a lost–work-time injury.
- Seek to improve production measures. Will process or work-flow improvements help?
- Try to eliminate or reduce equipment or machinery breakdowns. Preventive maintenance is important.
- Exercise good control techniques. Follow up on performance and take corrective action promptly.
- Involve your employees in the process of improvement. Select their ideas and suggestions for improvement. Form special productivity improvement teams.

in controlling a firm's cost in labor hours and efficiency, maintenance of machinery and equipment, supplies, energy, and other matters.

Budgets are one aid that can help supervisors to control costs. Different budgets are normally prepared for sales, production, scrap, equipment, grievances, lost–work-time accidents, and the like. Moreover, they may be set for different time periods such as a week, a month, a quarter, or a year. Since a budget reflects expected performance, it becomes a basis for evaluating a department's actual performance (see Exhibit 14-6).

Stop & Think

Assume that you are supervisor of the fabrication department in Exhibit 14-6. If you were really trying to tighten up costs, which activities in your department would you focus on? Why?

EXHIBIT 14-6
Performance Report

Name of department	Fabrication	Performance period	November 2006
Budgeted output	15,700 lbs.	**Budgeted scrap**	152 lbs.
Actual output	15,227 lbs.	**Actual scrap**	120 lbs.
Variance	−473 lbs.		+132 lbs.

ITEM	ACTUAL	BUDGETED	VARIANCE
Direct labor	$32,000	$32,000	$0
Overtime	1,500	1,000	−500
Supplies	500	385	−115
Maintenance and repairs	4,250	3,000	−1,250
Utilities	1,300	1,200	−100
Scrapped material	1,200	1,520	+320
Total	$40,750	$39,105	−$1,645

Note in Exhibit 14-6 that the supervisor's department has performed well in some cost areas and not so well in others. Output is off by 473 pounds, overtime is 50 percent higher than budgeted, and maintenance and repairs are also over budget. On the plus side, the department has been efficient in using raw materials.

Budgets are not carved in stone; there will always be unusual occurrences that affect performance. An investigation of the unfavorable variances in Exhibit 14-6 may reveal that the supervisor or team member could have done little to avoid them. For example, perhaps a crucial piece of equipment had faulty parts, causing the high repair costs; or perhaps the high overtime resulted from an unexpected weekend job thrust upon the supervisor. A budget does, however, serve as an important supervisory tool by signaling areas that may need attention. Such attention might take the form of combining certain jobs, reducing scrap, achieving better quality production, or focusing on large-cost items rather than numerous smaller ones.

Recently, advanced software technology has proved especially helpful to supervisors in achieving effective cost control. It is now possible for supervisors in some circumstances to have up-to-the-minute cost data on payroll, raw materials, utilities, and other costs as nearby as a computer monitor or printer.

Productivity Improvement Methods

In an effort to improve productivity, three productivity improvement measures have been introduced in manufacturing firms. These improvements, which are due to advances in computer and machinery technology, are (1) robotics, (2) just-in-time (JIT) inventory control, and (3) computer-assisted manufacturing (CAM).

robot

A machine that is controlled by a computer that can be programmed to perform a number of repetitive manipulations of tools or materials.

Robotics A **robot** is a machine, controlled by a computer, that can be programmed to perform a number of repetitive manipulations of tools or materials. Japan makes the greatest use of robots in the world, having about one third of the one million in use in the industrial world. The United States has fewer than half (about 162,000) of Japan's number, with most used in the automotive industry. However, robots are also finding increased acceptance in the semiconductor, electronics, food and beverage, pharmaceutical, consumer goods, and appliance industries, and in other industries where precision materials handling and packing are required. It is estimated that these machines—often called "steel-collar workers"—operate for about $5 an hour, considerably less than the $15 to $20 per hour (including benefits) or higher wages paid to many employees.[1]

Stop & Think

In addition to the $15 hourly payroll cost savings, can you think of any other advantages robots offer over human employees? Disadvantages?

just-in-time (JIT) inventory control

Materials arrive when they are needed in the production process.

Just-in-Time Inventory Control As pioneered by Toyota, under the **just-in-time (JIT) inventory control** system, needed materials arrive on the scene as close as is feasible to the time they are needed in the production process. Often, computers link the company with suppliers to keep them informed about the company's up-to-the-minute needs. With JIT, the proper components arrive in the right place at the right time. JIT allows an organization to minimize inventory holding and storage costs and to utilize the space previously occupied by inventory waiting to be used.

"Steel collar workers" operate at only $5 an hour, compared to their human counterparts at $15 to $20 per hour.

Toyota Motors has earned the reputation of being the best inventory manager around. Its Georgetown, Kentucky, plant operates with only 2.8 hours of inventory on hand at any one time, which saves millions. Parts from its suppliers, most located within 200 miles of the plant, are delivered some 16 times daily.[2]

The JIT approach has been used by many of the largest U.S. companies, such as Motorola, Chrysler, and other manufacturers. Retailers have also gotten into the act in a big way. Many large retail chains, such as Walmart and Home Depot, practice JIT inventory from their hundreds of suppliers. A good example can also be found at Dillard's, a leading department store chain throughout the Southeast and Midwest. A computer-driven "direct response" program allows items such as Gant dress shirts and Christian Dior lingerie to be ordered directly from the vendor each week—by computer—based on the previous week's sales.

computer-assisted manufacturing (CAM)

Special computers assist equipment in performing processes.

Computer-Assisted Manufacturing In **computer-assisted manufacturing (CAM)**, special computers assist automated equipment in performing the processes necessary for production. These computers can be reprogrammed to permit machinery to easily produce a product or part to different specifications. Whereas proper planning and

---

HISTORICAL INSIGHT

Evolution of the Quality Explosion in the United States

The background of today's surging quality movement in the United States can be traced to Japan. Following World War II, the words "Made in Japan" connoted cheap, inferior quality. As part of General MacArthur's program to help rebuild the country, 50-year-old W. Edwards Deming, a U.S. statistical quality control advocate, was brought to Japan to teach statistical quality control concepts. Deming addressed 21 top Japanese executives who were eager to learn and who represented the industrial leaders of the country. His theories formed the basis of **Deming's 85–15 rule**. This rule assumes that when things go wrong, 85 percent of the time the cause is attributed to elements controlled by management, such as machinery, materials, or processes, whereas only about 15 percent of the time, employees are at fault. Thus, Deming believed that management rather than the employee is to blame for most poor quality. The Japanese embraced Deming's message and transformed their industries by using his techniques. His "14 points for quality," as shown in Exhibit 14-7, are the actions he believed necessary for an organization to successfully make the quality "transformation."

Deming's contributions were recognized early by the Japanese. In 1951, the Deming Application Prize was instituted by the Union of Japanese Scientists and Engineers, and Deming was awarded the nation's highest honor, the Royal Order of the Sacred Treasure, from the Emperor of Japan. By the mid-1970s, the quality of Japan's products exceeded that of Western manufacturers, and Japanese companies made significant U.S. and global market penetration in areas such as autos, steel, computers, and electronics.

The United States' quality problem was first highlighted in a 1980 NBC program entitled, "If Japan Can ... Why Can't We?" The program introduced the then 80-year-old Deming who, although an American, was virtually unknown in this country. This program ignited a spark that awakened American executives and helped fuel a quality turnaround. Major companies, especially those that were threatened, embarked on extensive programs to improve quality. Ford Motors was among the first to invite Deming to help transform its operations. Within a few years, Ford's results improved dramatically; its profits became the highest for any company in automotive history. By 1992, its Ford Taurus unseated the Honda Accord as the best-selling domestic model.

In 1987, in an effort to encourage quality initiatives, the U.S. Congress established the Malcolm Baldrige National Quality Award (see Exhibit 14-8), which continues to generate remarkable interest in quality by American organizations.

The American quality story has been a successful one. Since the 1990s, the quality of U.S. goods and services has achieved a stunning turnaround, making "Made in the USA" again a symbol of world-class quality.

Deming's 85–15 rule

Assumes that when things go wrong, 85 percent of the time the cause is from elements controlled by management.

coordination would normally take hours, CAM equipment can be programmed to make adjustments within seconds. CAM is especially useful when small orders of customized products must be filled. Once the computer has been programmed, the electronic signals control the machine processor, resulting in the correct sequence of steps to properly complete the task.

For example, at carpet manufacturers, computer software programs control patterns, weaves, and the size of carpets being produced. At apparel manufacturers, such as Hart Schaffner and Marx, computer software programs determine optimum cutting of patterns and sizes to minimize waste and ensure perfect cuts.

Controlling Quality

In recent years, perhaps no other aspect of management has received as much attention of organizations as the effort to improve quality. As you have learned from the previous section, quality of an organization's products and services and the organization's productivity are intricately linked. That is one reason why organizations are so "quality"-oriented today. Quality expert Dr. Philip Crosby estimates that nonconformance—products and services that do not match up to requirements—cost the typical manufacturer about 20 percent of sales and the typical service firm 35 percent of sales. This includes the cost of scrapped materials, wasted time, costs of rework, and customers' exercise of warranties. Thus, quality directly affects the bottom line.

EXHIBIT 14-7
Deming's Fourteen Points for Quality

1. Top management should establish and publish a statement of the organization's purpose and commitment to quality products and services and continuous improvement.
2. Everyone throughout the organization should learn the new philosophy.
3. Dependence on "inspecting" quality into products should be shifted to an attitude of "expecting" quality by having it built into the system.
4. There must be a systematic way to select quality suppliers, rather than simply on the basis of cost.
5. The organization must be devoted to continuous improvement.
6. All employees should be trained in the most modern quality and problem-solving techniques.
7. Leadership techniques consistent with getting the most commitment from employees should be practiced throughout the entire organization.
8. Fear should be eliminated from the work environment.
9. Teams and work groups must work smoothly together; barriers between functional departments must be eliminated.
10. Exhortations, posters, and slogans asking for new levels of workforce productivity must be backed by providing the methods to achieve these.
11. Numerical production quotas should be eliminated. Constant improvement should be sought instead.
12. Barriers that deprive employees from pride in their work must be removed.
13. A vigorous program of education, retraining, and self-improvement for all employees must be instituted.
14. A structure in top management that will push the thirteen points above to achieve the transformation must be created.

Source: From *Out of the Crisis* by W. Edwards Deming, pp. 23–24. Reprinted by permission of the MIT Press.

EXHIBIT 14-8

The Malcolm Baldrige National Quality Award

The prize is only a gold-plated medal encased in a crystal column 14 inches tall. But since 1987, when Congress created the Malcolm Baldrige National Quality Award at the urging of business leaders, it has symbolized America's best in quality. Named for the much-admired former U.S. Secretary of Commerce, Malcolm Baldrige, who died in 1987, the award is administered by the National Institute of Standards and Technology, with endowments covering costs of administration and judging of applicants.

Applications are scored by examination teams drawn from senior ranks of business, consultants, and academics. The highest scoring applicants move on to stage two—a site visit by four to six examiners who verify the facts in the application and probe more deeply into organizational processes. They report back to a nine-judge panel, which recommends winners to the Secretary of Commerce. The White House makes the formal announcements.

Winning a Baldrige has proved tough. In 1988, the first year of eligibility, only three of 66 applicants were winners; in 1989, only two of 40. Organizations must observe eight essentials to win:

1. Establish a plan to seek improvement continuously in all phases of operations—not just manufacturing, but purchasing, sales, human relations, and other areas.
2. Put in place a system that accurately tracks and measures performance in those areas.
3. Establish a long-term strategic plan based on performance targets that compare with the world's best in that particular industry.
4. Link closely in a partnership with suppliers and customers in a way that provides needed feedback for continuous improvement.
5. Demonstrate a deep understanding of customers in order to convert their wants into products.
6. Establish and maintain long-lasting customer relationships, going beyond product manufacture and delivery to include sales, service, and ease of maintenance.
7. Focus on preventing mistakes instead of developing efficient ways to correct them; that is, feedforward control is a must.
8. Perhaps most difficult, but imperative, is to make a commitment to quality improvement throughout all levels of the organization, including top, middle, and bottom.

(Continued)

EXHIBIT 14-8
continued

Winners for 1998–2008 are:

2008	Manufacturing	Cargill Corn Milling North America		Service	Caterpillar Financial Services Corp.
	Education	Iredell-Statesville Schools		Small Business	Stoner, Inc.
	Health Care	Poudre Valley Health System		Education	Community Consolidated School District 15
2007	Small Business	PRO-TEC Coating Co.		Health Care	Baptist Hospital, Inc.
	Nonprofit	City of Coral Springs		Health Care	Saint Luke's Hospital of Kansas City
	Nonprofit	U.S. Army Armament Research, Development and Engineering Center	2002	Manufacturing	Motorola Commercial, Government, Industrial Solutions Division
	Health Care	Mercy Health Systems			
	Health Care	Sharp HealthCare		Small Business	Branch-Smith Printing Division,
2006	Service	Premier Inc.			
	Small Business	MESA Products, Inc.		Health Care	SSM Health Care
	Health Care	North Mississippi Medical Center	2001	Manufacturing	Clarke American Checks
				Small Business	Pal's Sudden Service
2005	Manufacturing	Sunny Fresh Foods, Inc.		Education	Chugach, AK School District
	Service	DynMcDermott Petroleum Operations			University of Wisconsin–Stout
					Pearl River, NY School District
	Small Business	Park Place Lexus	2000	Manufacturing	Dana Corp., Spicer Driveshaft Division, KARLEE Co.
	Education	Richland College			
	Education	Jenks Public Schools		Service	Operations Management Intl.
	Health Care	Bronson Methodist Hospital		Small Business	Los Alamos National Bank
2004	Manufacturing	The Bama Companies	1999	Manufacturing	STMicroelectronics, Inc.
	Small Business	Texas Nameplate Company, Inc.		Service	BI
					The Ritz-Carlton Hotel
	Education	Kenneth W. Monfort College of Business		Small Business	Sunny Fresh Foods
	Health Care	Robert Wood Johnson University Hospital Hamilton	1998	Manufacturing	Caterpillar Inc., Solar Turbines Division
2003	Manufacturing	Medrad, Inc.			Boeing Airlift & Tanker Programs
	Service	Boeing Aerospace Support			Texas Nameplate Co.

A second reason for quality consciousness is global competition (see Historical Insight). Many U.S. firms, such as Citigroup, 3M, Coca-Cola, Exxon, and others, earn over half of their revenues from foreign markets. Moreover, high-quality foreign firms, such as Michelin, Toyota, Seiko, Nokia, Nestlé, and others, compete vigorously, which requires U.S. firms to keep up or lose market share. In another reflection of globalization, many organizations require all supplier firms to achieve ISO 9000 certification—an assurance that they meet international quality standards in such areas as product design, manufacturing processes, testing, inspection, and service.

A third reason for greater quality emphasis is the increased information available to the public regarding product and service quality. Media coverage quickly informs potential consumers about safety problems, such as the abrupt tilting of a Princess Cruise ship that injured 240 passengers, contaminated beef from ConAgra Foods, or Dell Computers' recall of 6 million notebook computers that contained potentially hazardous Sony lithium batteries.[3] Additionally, independent quality ratings given by such organizations as JD Power and Associates (auto quality), AAA and Mobil (hotels and restaurants), and *Consumer Reports* (consumer products) significantly affect consumer behavior.

Total Quality and Quality Control

4 *Differentiate between total quality and quality control.*

Sometimes the terms *total quality* and *quality control* are used interchangeably. However, they are not the same. **Total quality** refers to an organization's overall quality effort that strives to achieve customer satisfaction through continuous improvement of the organization's products, services, and processes. The term *total* indicates its comprehensiveness, involving all management levels, employees, suppliers, and customers. It is based on the quality chain shown in Exhibit 14-9: Increased quality leads to more customers and increased market share, which enable greater profitability. It was this approach to quality that enabled Japanese firms to become so successful in the 1980s and such intense competitors today.

total quality

Refers to an organization's overall effort to achieve customer satisfaction through continuous improvement of products or services.

Stop & Think

In the chapter preview, note how Park Place Lexus used a total quality approach.

quality control

Defined measurements designed to check whether the desired quality standards are being met.

Quality control, on the other hand, is a narrower process, consisting of the measurement and analysis of quality performance and actions taken to correct quality problems. It occurs during or after performance and may include inspection, testing, sampling, and statistical analysis.

Understanding Variance in Controlling Quality

5 *Describe the role of variance in controlling quality.*

Every product and service is the output or result of a process. You might consider a process to be a set of related activities designed to accomplish a goal.

The nature of processes is to exhibit variation; for example, items produced in a machining or manufacturing process are not all exactly alike. Some measurable dimensions, such as length, diameter, or weight, will vary. These variations may be quite small and not perceivable by the naked eye, but sophisticated gauges or test equipment will reveal them. Similarly, service processes are also subject to variation. Fast-food customers wait different periods of time before being served. Some luggage checked on a commercial airline will not arrive with its owner. At a steakhouse, steaks prepared as "rare" may vary considerably.

EXHIBIT 14-9
The Total Quality Chain

Two types of variation exist: common cause and special cause. Let's use a classic example to illustrate process variation: writing. Note the variations of handwritten letters below, although each one was carefully written by the same author.

You don't need to use a magnifying glass to note that differences exist. The differences in each "p" are normal and to be expected. This we call *common cause variation.* Now look at each "a." Note that the middle one is clearly different from the others. Perhaps the writer was bumped, or the paper quality in that one spot was different, or a different pen was used. (Actually, it was made by the same writer but using the other hand.) The variation is not routine or expected; clearly, there was excessive variation, or *special cause variation.* Common cause variation is a general, routine variation that is built into the system. Special cause variation occurs intermittently and is associated with a specific event.

Effective control of quality can have two focuses: (1) reducing common cause variation and (2) reducing special cause variation. As Deming and other quality experts note, special causes can sometimes be addressed by individual workers, but common causes ordinarily can be corrected only through management action to improve the process. This might include such things as upgrading raw materials, using more sophisticated equipment, providing additional training, and so on. Importantly, much of the effort by organizations to seek continuous quality improvement is aimed at reducing common cause variation by improving processes.

Reducing special cause variation entails identifying the problem, isolating it, examining the cause, and remedying it. This might mean, for instance, replacing an erratic piece of equipment, reassigning an employee who cannot keep pace with job demands, or reassigning personnel to handle peak customer demand periods.

Six Sigma is a specific type of quality control technique that was developed at smaller companies and perfected at two large ones, Motorola and Allied Signal; Six Sigma is a specific methodology designed to slash the number of defects in a company's end-to-end process of producing, improving, selling, distributing, and servicing its products. Jack Welch and General Electric popularized Six Sigma in late 1995 with 200 projects. It grew to 6,000 projects by 1997. By the time of Jack's farewell annual meeting address in 2001, Welch was prepared to declare that "Six Sigma, originally focused on reducing waste and elevating the quality of our products and processes within the company, has delivered billions of dollars to GE's bottom line in savings."[4]

As a supervisor, it is important to understand variation and the extent to which different levels of quality performance can be attributed to normal or special cause variables. Statistical sampling is one useful tool for doing so but is beyond our scope here. However, we will examine some other important tools.

Some Tools for Controlling Quality

6 *Identify some important tools for controlling quality.*

A number of tools are available to assist in effective control of quality. Often, these are used by individuals who are part of special problem-solving or quality-improvement teams. Among the tools discussed here are flowcharts, histograms, run charts, Pareto charts, control charts, and fishbone diagrams. Some, such as histograms, run charts, and control charts, represent displays of the actual performance data that must be addressed. Keep in mind that these tools apply not just to the quality of manufacturing processes (although this is perhaps the most common application), but to service processes as well.

flowchart

Visual representation of the sequence of steps needed to complete a process.

Flowchart A **flowchart** is a visual representation of the sequence of steps needed to complete a process. Its purpose is to help individuals understand the *process* they are attempting to control. Flowcharts are frequently used by problem-solving teams to address quality issues involving processes with a number of sequential steps to complete (see Exhibit 14-10). Often such processes cut across departmental lines. The visual representation of the process enables team members to examine the relevant steps and note where improvements can be made, as reflected in the following example.

> *Boise Cascade's Timber and Wood Products Division formed a team of 11 people from diverse backgrounds in administration, marketing, and operations to improve customer claims processing. The group first created a flowchart of the process and discovered over 70 steps needed to process each claim within each division; combined division steps for the same customer claim often took hundreds of steps, taking months to resolve the claim. By studying systematically the steps involved in processing claims and addressing the concerns within each division, the team eliminated 70 percent of the steps in most claims.[5]*

EXHIBIT 14-10

Flowchart of a Fast-Food Drive-Through Process

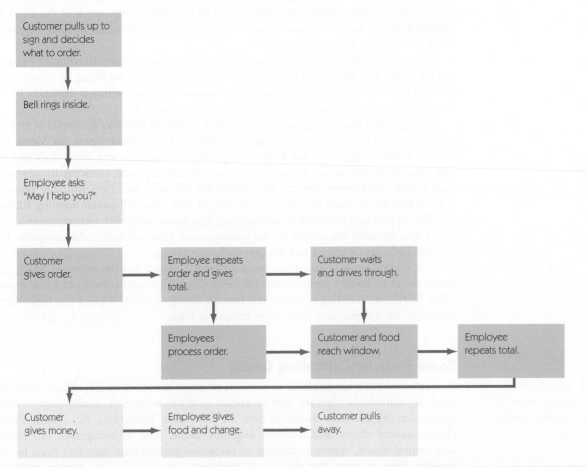

histogram

Graphical representation of the variation found in a set of data.

run chart

Data presentation showing results of a process plotted over time.

Pareto charts

Problem-analysis charts that use a histogram to illustrate sources of problems.

Histogram A **histogram** is a graphical representation of the variation found in a set of performance data. It can provide clues about the population's characteristics. The visual presentation reflects how the process's output varies and what proportion of output falls outside of the performance targets. The histogram in Exhibit 14-11 represents data on the length of time that it took a bank to process loan requests. Note how easy it is to see how the output of the process varies and what proportion falls outside of any specification limits.

Run Chart A process sometimes performs differently over a period of time. A **run chart** is a data presentation that shows the results of a process plotted over a period of time. It might be used to show the number of hotel checkouts per hour, the number of employee absentees per day, or the percentage of customers waiting in excess of one minute to be seated. Note in Exhibit 14-12 how the run chart points out specific patterns of behavior in the process. The percentage of patrons who have to wait falls into a definite pattern. A much larger percentage waits early in the week, with the percentage decreasing throughout the week.

Pareto Charts are problem-analysis charts that use a histogram to graphically illustrate the sources of problems. They typically list problem causes from left to right in descending order of seriousness. Named after Vilfredo Pareto, the economist who originated the use of such analyses, the Pareto chart helps problem solvers zero in on the dominant rather than trivial problem. For example, Exhibit 14-13 shows the results of an extensive survey of customer complaints in a restaurant over an extended period of time. The chart is a consistent reminder to the problem-solving team that its time would be best used by focusing on the complaints of customers waiting for seats and dealing with a poorly organized buffet table.

EXHIBIT 14-11
Histogram Showing Frequency and Length of Time Taken by Home Office to Process Loan Request

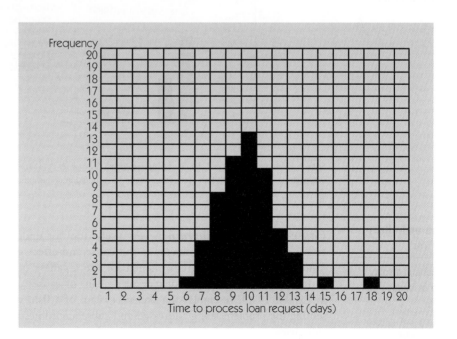

EXHIBIT 14-12

Run Chart of Percentage of Restaurant Customers Waiting in Excess of 1 Minute to Be Seated

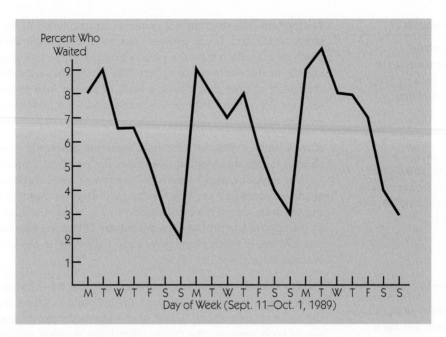

Source: From *Foundations of Total Quality Management: A Readings Book*, 1/e by Van Matre, p. 146. 0030078660. Copyright © 1995 by Joseph Van Matre. Reprinted with permission of the author.

EXHIBIT 14-13

Pareto Chart of Customers' Complaints about Restaurants

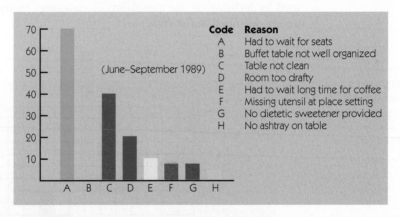

Source: From *Foundations of Total Quality Management: A Readings Book*, 1/e by Van Matre, p. 146. 0030078660. Copyright © 1995 by Joseph Van Matre. Reprinted with permission of the author.

cause-and-effect diagram

A graphical display of a chain of causes and effects.

control chart

Displays the "state of control" of a process.

Cause-and-Effect Diagram A very useful tool for understanding and identifying the causes of performance problems is the **cause-and-effect diagram.** This is also called a *fishbone* or *Ishikawa* diagram, named for the Japanese quality expert who popularized it. It represents a graphical display of a chain of causes and effects. The result, shown in Exhibit 14-14, resembles the skeletal system of a fish, with the horizontal line representing the problem being addressed and subsequent lines representing major causes and subcauses.

Control Chart The **control chart** is the "backbone" of statistical process control (SPC) and displays the "state of control" of a process. If a process is free from special cause

EXHIBIT 14-14

Cause-and-Effect Diagram for "Why Tables Are Not Cleared Quickly"

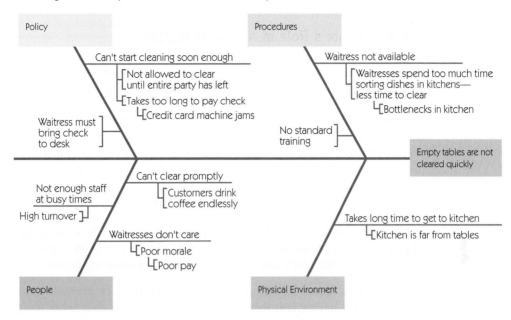

Source: From *Foundations of Total Quality Management: A Readings Book*, 1/e by Van Matre, p. 146. 0030078660. Copyright © 1995 by Joseph Van Matre. Reprinted with permission of the author.

variation, the process is said to be under control. An example of a control chart is shown in Exhibit 14-15. In the exhibit, time is measured in terms of days on the horizontal axis; the value of a variable is on the vertical axis. The central horizontal line corresponds to the average value of the characteristic measured. In this case, as long as the values fall between 97 percent and 89 percent and no unusual pattern exists (such as a succession

EXHIBIT 14-15

Example of a Control Chart

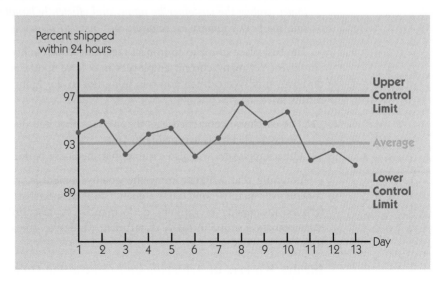

Source: From James W. Dean and James R. Evans. Total Quality, Management, Organization, and Strategy, 4th ed. Copyright © 2005 South-Western, a part of Cengage Learning, Inc. Reproduced by permission. www.cengage.com/permissions.

of decreasing values), it is likely that no special cause variation is present and that the process is "under control."

The Supervisor's Role in Achieving Quality

As you have noted throughout this chapter, upper management lays the foundation for achieving high quality by committing the organization's resources, communicating its values and norms, and creating rules and procedures. On a daily basis, though, lower-level managers and first-line supervisors have the critical role, because it is operating-level personnel who directly perform the activities of producing the goods or services that address customers' needs. One study confirmed the crucial role played by first-line supervisors. Written surveys of 3,500 employees in a food service company found that the quality of service that they felt they delivered was strongly impacted by the extent to which their first-line supervisor (1) emphasized the importance of high quality, (2) provided information and support to help employees achieve it, and (3) provided meaningful feedback.[6]

Motivating workers to perform high-quality work consistently is one of the most challenging jobs a supervisor faces. Two ways to do this are to (1) let employees know you expect quality performance and (2) involve workers in achieving quality.

Let Employees Know You Expect Quality Performance Many firms could be said to try to *inspect* quality into their product or service rather than *make it right* the first time. Fortunately, some companies and supervisors emphasize the right way from the start. They do this by stating their quality expectations for a job and including these expectations in their training of new personnel.

> *A large bank trains its new tellers not only in the technical aspects of the job, but also in how to interact with customers. In a number of trial runs, a "customer" walks up to the teller to complete a hypothetical transaction. The teller's actions are observed by a number of trainees and the trainer, and a critique is given of the way the customer was handled. Frequently, an experienced teller will demonstrate how the situation should have been handled. Included are such actions as smiling, looking directly at the customer, calling the customer by name, and efficiently handling the transaction. As a result, the bank's quality expectations are instilled in new tellers.*

The best place to make an impact regarding your quality expectations is with the new employee. Yet many current employees may have spotty quality records. What can you do about this? We can tell you one thing not to do! Ignoring poor-quality performance results in:

1. The employee concerned gets the message that you do not expect any better or that mediocre quality is acceptable to you.
2. Other employees will also assume that mediocre performance is acceptable.

Assuming that workers know the quality standards, you must exercise supervisory control over quality. Sometimes a quality control specialist will help a line supervisor determine the quality of workers' performance by presenting run charts, histograms, or other statistical units. In many departments, however, the supervisor must play the only role.

Involve Workers in Achieving and Controlling Quality You noted in the chapter preview that operative-level associates at Park Place Lexus played a key role in helping the company continuously improve its quality. As Peter Coors, CEO of Coors Brewing, puts it, "We're moving from an environment where the supervisor says, 'This is the way it is going to be done,' to an environment where the supervisor can grow with the changes, get his [or her] group together and say 'Look, you guys are operating the equipment. What do you think we ought to do?'"[7]

> *SSM Health Care (SSMHC), a St. Louis, Missouri, not-for-profit health system that won the first Baldrige given in the health care category (2002), makes extensive use of employee involvement teams. The company addresses such issues as developing standardized ways to care for SSMHC patients at its 24 hospitals and nursing homes in four states to improving outcomes of patients with congestive heart failure.[8]*

Quality teams are an important part of the quality scene. These may include special cross-functional teams, self-directed teams, or teams from within individual work groups. Problems (and opportunities) can be brought up by team members, team leaders, or higher management. Many companies allow these teams to call in staff experts for information or expertise as needed.

> *At Pella Windows, a standard team* kaizen *session—the Japanese term for continuous improvement—meets anywhere from one to five days to address important quality issues. Over a thousand such yearly sessions have been the norm for Pella's kaizen teams. A typical five-day schedule works like this: Get everyone thinking about the problem and how to attack it on Monday, come up with tentative solutions on Tuesday, and, if it's a production problem, move the machinery that night. Start working the new arrangement on Wednesday, tweaking as necessary. On Thursday, prove that it works, and on Friday show it off to everyone.[9]*

Exhibit 14-16 presents the overall characteristics of effective employee involvement teams. The kinds of teams we have been discussing are implemented formally and require top management's approval and commitment. *Individual supervisors may, however, capture the spirit of employee involvement on their own.* The following comments, from the manager of a hotel convention center, show what can be achieved by encouraging employees to become involved:

> *The best quality ideas come from the people who are directly involved in the work. Frequently, poor quality is not caused by something they directly control. We noted that many clients would show up for a meeting and say the room arrangement was not what they had requested. This often required hurriedly rearranging a stage, tables, and chairs for as many as 700 people. The clients would get flustered, as did our people.*

> *The problem was that our meeting coordinator would talk with the client, usually by phone, and take instructions as to how the meeting room needed to be set up. There was much room for interpretation as to just what the client wanted and last-minute changes would drive everyone nuts.*

EXHIBIT 14-16

Characteristics of Effective Employee Involvement Teams

- Managers at all levels, especially at the top, should be committed to the concept and give it their unqualified support.
- Projects undertaken should relate directly—or at least indirectly—to participants' work.
- Projects should be team efforts, not individual activities.
- Participants should be trained in quality-control, decision-making, and problem-solving techniques.
- Team leaders also should be trained in group dynamics and leadership of a group.
- Teams should be given feedback—in the form of results—regarding their recommendations and solutions.

We presented this problem to a team of four of our workers who met, studied the process used by our meeting coordinator, and learned that she usually took instructions by phone. This left much room for interpreting what the client wanted. They also learned that often the person who called in to make the booking wasn't the one who had responsibility for the event, but was perhaps a secretary or an assistant. This person's choice of room arrangement would then get overridden when the group arrived. Our team developed a form that graphically illustrates alternatives for arranging our rooms and audiovisual equipment we can provide. The client now selects the desired alternative, signs the form, and returns it to our coordinator. We now have something specific to go by, and our client is more committed to it. We'll still meet their last-minute needs or make adjustments if needed. But we've only had two such major cases all year.

The lesson here is to seek out workers' advice on how to improve the quality of their work. Since they are so directly involved in the work, they frequently have excellent suggestions.

Promoting Employee Safety

The final aspect of supervisory control that we will discuss in this chapter is employee safety. This subject has been in the business limelight since 1970, primarily as a result of the government's passage of the Occupational Safety and Health Act. But management has had an interest in employee safety for over a century because safety, efficiency, and productivity are closely related.

The results of poor safety are documented, and even though safety performance in the United States has improved in recent years, the costs of poor safety have gone in the opposite direction. According to the most recent cost data released, organizations made in excess of $42.6 billion in wage and medical payments to U.S. workers injured on the job in 2008 (see Exhibit 14-17).

Assume that a company has a 10 percent profit margin. An accident costing $5,000 in direct and indirect costs would translate into a need to generate $50,000 in sales just to cover costs of the accident.[10]

EXHIBIT 14-17
Workplace Injuries Cost
Billions

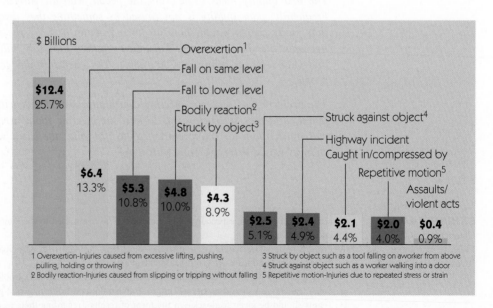

1 Overexertion-Injuries caused from excessive lifting, pushing, pulling, holding or throwing
2 Bodily reaction-Injuries caused from slipping or tripping without falling
3 Struck by object such as a tool falling on aworker from above
4 Struck against object such as a worker walking into a door
5 Repetitive motion-Injuries due to repeated stress or strain

Source: Liberty Mutual Research Institute for Safety, 2005 Annual Report, p. 10.

Stop & Think

Do such organizations as banks, supermarkets, and department stores really need to be concerned about occupational safety and health?

7 *Explain what the Occupational Safety and Health Administration (OSHA) does.*

OSHA

federal Occupational Safety and Health Administration, created by the Occupational Safety and Health Act in 1970 to ensure safe working conditions for employees.

What the Occupational Safety and Health Administration Does

The **Occupational Safety and Health Administration (OSHA)** is a federal agency that was created by the Occupational Safety and Health Act in 1970 and went into operation in April 1971. Previously, different states had different emphases on occupational health and safety. To ensure uniformity and enforcement, the federal government stepped into the picture. OSHA ensures that state governments, labor unions, and management provide consistently safer and healthier working conditions for employees.

OSHA requires organizations to keep safety logs and records of illnesses and injuries incurred on the job (see Exhibit 14-18). OSHA also has the right to develop standards, to conduct inspections to see that standards are met, and to enforce compliance by issuing citations and penalties against organizations that fail to comply. In addition, OSHA provides help by performing preinvestigations upon invitation from the organization.

Factors Influencing Safety

Several factors affect job safety. Among these are (1) the size of the organization, (2) the type of industry, and (3) the people.

Size of Organization The safest places to work are the smallest and largest organizations. Companies with fewer than 20 employees or more than 1,000 employees have had better safety statistics than medium-sized organizations.

Stop & Think

What do you think accounts for the fact that large companies of, say, 10,000 employees have better safety performance than those with 100 employees?

In a small firm, the owner or manager is more personally involved with employees and tends to take on the role of safety officer. Very large firms have more resources available, such as safety departments, whose sole mission is to improve employee safety. Medium-sized firms have neither the direct personal involvement of the top manager nor the resources to create full-fledged safety departments. Often, the person assigned to oversee the safety function has additional job responsibilities. The safety focus may therefore be diluted by other important assignments.

Type of Industry Some types of industry are safer than others. Exhibit 14-19 shows rates of occupational injury and illness for various industries. Note that the rates are highest for general medical and surgical hospitals, general merchandise stores, administrative and support services, and ambulatory health care services. But note also that safety issues affect a wide spectrum of service industries, such as limited-service and full-service restaurants, as well as supermarkets and grocery stores.

Also important is the seriousness of cases of the industries listed. General medical and surgical hospitals may have more serious accidents, resulting in a greater number of lost work days per incident.

EXHIBIT 14-18

Record Keeping Required by OSHA

OSHA's Form 301
Injury and Illness Incident Report

U.S. Department of Labor

Occupational Safety and Health Administration

Form approved OMB no. 1218-0176

This *Injury and Illness Incident Report* is one of the first forms you must fill out when a recordable work-related injury or illness has occurred. Together with the *Log of Work-Related Injuries and Illnesses* and the accompanying *Summary*, these forms help the employer and OSHA develop a picture of the extent and severity of work-related incidents.

Within 7 calendar days after you receive information that a recordable work-related injury or illness has occurred, you must fill out this form or an equivalent. Some state workers' compensation, insurance, or other reports may be acceptable substitutes. To be considered an equivalent form, any substitute must contain all the information asked for on this form.

According to Public Law 91-596 and 29 CFR 1904, OSHA's recordkeeping rule, you must keep this form on file for 5 years following the year to which it pertains.

If you need additional copies of this form, you may photocopy and use as many as you need.

Attention: This form contains information relating to employee health and must be used in a manner that protects the confidentiality of employees to the extent possible while the information is being used for occupational safety and health purposes.

Information about the employee

1) Full name _Robert L. Whitehall_

2) Street _707 Eighth St._

City _Sherman_ State _TX_ ZIP _75059_

3) Date of birth _12 / 01 / 68_

4) Date hired _3 / 14 / 99_

5) ☑ Male
   ☐ Female

Information about the physician or other health care professional

6) Name of physician or other health care professional
   Rita Sorenson, RN

7) If treatment was given away from the worksite, where was it given?

Facility _N/A_

Street

City _____ State _____ ZIP _____

8) Was employee treated in an emergency room?
   ☐ Yes
   ☐ No

9) Was employee hospitalized overnight as an in-patient?
   ☐ Yes
   ☑ No

Completed by _Joseph Dixon_

Title _Supervisor_

Phone _(903) 465 _ 1996_ Date _6 / 23 / 2005_

Information about the case

10) Case number from the Log _31_ *(Transfer the case number from the Log after you record the case.)*

11) Date of injury or illness _6 / 21 / 05_

12) Time employee began work _7:30_ AM/PM

13) Time of event _2:09_ AM/PM ☐ Check if time cannot be determined

14) **What was the employee doing just before the incident occurred?** Describe the activity, as well as the tools, equipment, or material the employee was using. Be specific. *Examples:* "climbing a ladder while carrying roofing materials"; "spraying chlorine from hand sprayer"; "daily computer key-entry."

Cleaning pipes in preparation for painting was standing on stepladder.

15) **What happened?** Tell us how the injury occurred. *Examples:* "When ladder slipped on wet floor, worker fell 20 feet"; "Worker was sprayed with chlorine when gasket broke during replacement"; "Worker developed soreness in wrist over time."

As he put stepladder down, sodium hypochlorite spilled inside face shield and entered right eye.

16) **What was the injury or illness?** Tell us the part of the body that was affected and how it was affected; be more specific than "hurt," "pain," or "sore." *Examples:* "strained back"; "chemical burn, hand"; "carpal tunnel syndrome."

Chemical burn in right eye.

17) **What object or substance directly harmed the employee?** *Examples:* "concrete floor"; "chlorine"; "radial arm saw." *If this question does not apply to the incident, leave it blank.*

Sodium Hypochlorate

18) **If the employee died, when did death occur?** Date of death _N/A_

Public reporting burden for this collection of information is estimated to average 22 minutes per response, including time for reviewing instructions, searching existing data sources, gathering and maintaining the data needed, and completing and reviewing the collection of information. Persons are not required to respond to the collection of information unless it displays a current valid OMB control number. If you have any comments about this estimate or any other aspects of this data collection, including suggestions for reducing this burden, contact: US Department of Labor, OSHA Office of Statistical Analysis, Room N-3644, 200 Constitution Avenue, NW, Washington, DC 20210. Do not send the completed forms to this office.

EXHIBIT 14-19
Occupational Injury and
Illness Rates: Selected
Industries, 2007

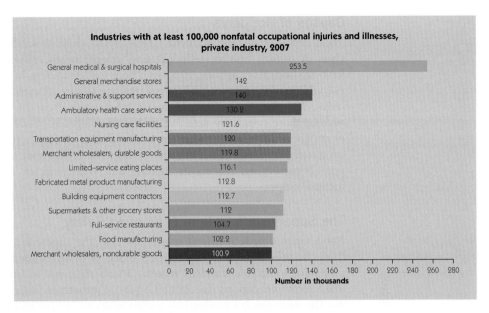

Industries with at least 100,000 nonfatal occupational injuries and illnesses, private industry, 2007

Industry	Number in thousands
General medical & surgical hospitals	253.5
General merchandise stores	142
Administrative & support services	140
Ambulatory health care services	130.2
Nursing care facilities	121.6
Transportation equipment manufacturing	120
Merchant wholesalers, durable goods	119.8
Limited–service eating places	116.1
Fabricated metal product manufacturing	112.8
Building equipment contractors	112.7
Supermarkets & other grocery stores	112
Full-service restaurants	104.7
Food manufacturing	102.2
Merchant wholesalers, nondurable goods	100.9

Source: U.S. Bureau of Labor Statistics. http://www.bls.gov/

Despite increased safety emphasis, some industries still suffer from a high incidence of employee lost workdays due to job-related injuries/illnesses.

People The attitudes of managers and supervisors strongly influence the safety of work performance. Moreover, employees' attitudinal, emotional, and physical factors definitely impact their safety performance.

Causes of Accidents

What causes on-the-job accidents? Basically, job-related accidents are caused by three types of factors: human, technical, and environmental. *Human factors* include carelessness, horseplay, fighting, drug use, poor understanding of equipment or processes, risk taking, poor attitudes, and fatigue. Human factors account for most work-related injuries. *Technical factors* include unsafe mechanical, chemical, and physical conditions, such as those caused by defective tools and equipment; poor mechanical construction or design; or improper personal protective equipment (safety shoes, glasses, or mechanical guards or shields). *Environmental factors* are factors that surround the job, such as poor housekeeping, inadequate lighting and ventilation, or management pressure to increase output.

The Supervisor's Role in Promoting Safety

8 *Describe the supervisor's role in promoting safety.*

Good safety practices among employees help the supervisor in many ways. For one thing, on-the-job injuries can take up much of a supervisor's time because he or she may have to fill out accident reports, attend meetings to investigate the injury, and make recommendations (see Exhibit 14-20). Furthermore, safety is linked to productivity. The work group's productivity suffers when an injured employee is being treated for or is recovering from an accident. Temporary or full-time replacements must be recruited, selected, and trained, and an inexperienced worker is unlikely to be as productive as the more experienced employee being replaced.

Because human factors are the major cause of work-related injuries, the supervisor, as top management's link with operating employees, plays a crucial role in employee safety.

EXHIBIT 14-20
Personal Injury
Investigation

Injured:	Fred Hanna
Position:	Lab Assistant
Presiding:	L. C. Smithson, Technical Supt.
Date of meeting:	4/15/2010
Time of meeting:	2:34 P.M.
Place of meeting:	Plant Conference Room
Present:	L. C. Smithson (Technical Supt.), Fred Hanna (injured), Jim Berry (Housekeeping), Tom Ahens (Safety Director), Kim Jernigan (Supervisor)
Nature of injury:	Fractured distal end of radius, right arm
Lost time:	42 days (estimated)
Accident time and date:	4/13/2010 at 7:15 A.M.
Cause of injury:	Floor was wet—appeared to be water. Investigation revealed that bags of Seperan (a synthetic polymer) had been rearranged during the 11:00 P.M.–7:00 A.M. shift. One bag was torn, and its contents had trickled onto the floor, causing it to be exceptionally slippery when washed at the end of the shift. Janitor noticed but did not flag it or attempt to remove hazard, as he noted at the end of his shift.

Corrective steps/recommendations:

1. Apply grit to slippery areas; mark with appropriate warning signs.
2. Remind incoming shift personnel of hazardous conditions.
3. Communicate to incoming shift personnel any job priorities.
4. Store Seperan in a more remote area of the plant.

He or she is accountable for safety, just as for output or quality. Good safety control by the supervisor begins with a positive attitude.

"Safety is very important at the company and especially in my work unit," said Vera Edwards, a machine tender for Supreme Manufacturing. "When you drive into the parking lot, a large sign shows our company's safety record for the week and the year. Our supervisor is always talking safety, we have safety meetings monthly, and there are posters and signs throughout the work area. Our supervisor also makes us toe the line in following safety rules. He can really be tough on you when he catches you bending a rule such as not using your goggles or failing to put on your machine guard."

Exhibit 14-21 shows a number of steps that supervisors can take to improve safety performance in their departments. Even though supervisors play a critical role in controlling safety, they cannot do it alone. Top management must be committed to such factors as proper plant layout and design, safe machinery and equipment, and good physical working conditions. Note how recognition by management plays a major role in reinforcing safety for UPS, which has over 2,400 nonmanagement employee Comprehensive Health and Safety Committees at its locations throughout the United States.

At UPS, drivers travel a million miles yearly with less than one avoidable accident! This performance is no coincidence; UPS strongly emphasizes driver safety. At 5-year intervals, drivers with no avoidable accidents are feted with ceremonies at the local level. Drivers with a 25-year unblemished record are inducted into the company's Circle of Honor at a national celebration dinner where they receive a camel-hair blazer and special plaque. Each year UPS publishes the names of its 2,700-plus Circle of Honor members in The Wall Street Journal *and in* USA Today.[11]

EXHIBIT 14-21 What Supervisors Can Do to Improve Safety	• Push for upgraded safety equipment and safer work methods. • Establish and communicate safety goals for the department. • Clearly communicate safety requirements to all employees. • Listen to employee job complaints about safety-related matters, including noise, fatigue, and working conditions. • Make sure new employees thoroughly understand equipment and safety rules. • Prohibit use of unsafe or damaged equipment. • Encourage safety suggestions from your workers. • Post safety bulletins, slogans, and posters to reinforce the need for safety. • Refuse to let rush jobs cause relaxed safety standards. • Set a proper example. Don't bend safety rules yourself. • Conduct periodic safety meetings, with demonstrations by employee safety specialists or insurance representatives. • Refuse to tolerate horseplay. • Compete with other departments in safety contests. • Report to employees any accidents that occur elsewhere in the company. • Review past accident records for trends and insights. • Encourage reporting of unsafe conditions. • Make regular safety inspections of all major equipment. • Enforce the rules when they are broken—take appropriate disciplinary action to demonstrate your safety commitment. • Look for signs of fatigue in employees, such as massaging shoulders, rubbing eyes, and stretching or shifting position to relieve pain or fatigue. In such a case, relief for the employee may be warranted. • Thoroughly investigate all accidents and attempt to remedy the causes. • Develop a system for rewarding or acknowledging excellent safety conduct.

Chapter Review

1. **Explain the concept of productivity.**

   This chapter examined three aspects of control that are important to supervisors: productivity, quality, and safety. Productivity is a measure of outputs compared to inputs. Companywide, it refers to the total value of the units or services a company produced as compared to the total cost of producing them. Productivity can be increased by increasing output with the same input, decreasing input and maintaining the same output, or increasing output while decreasing input.

2. **Identify and explain the ways in which management, government, unions, and employees affect productivity.**

   Four groups influence the productivity of U.S. firms. Management is considered by most experts to be the most influential group because it controls spending for new or upgraded facilities and technology. Government also plays a role through its policies that require financial outlays by companies to meet federal laws for air and water pollution, energy, safety, and other regulatory requirements. Unions play a role in that, while management's job is to increase efficiency through new labor-saving technology and work methods, the role of unions is to protect the jobs of their members. Finally, employees play a role through their skill levels, motivation, and job commitment.

3. **Describe some steps supervisors can take to increase productivity.**

   Actions that supervisors can take to increase productivity include upgrading workers' skills through training, improving worker motivation, using machinery and equipment better, improving quality, and preventing accidents.

   Cost control is an important measure of a supervisor's productivity. One helpful device is a budget, which shows expected outcome for a given period expressed in numbers. Robotics, just-in-time (JIT) inventory systems, and computer-assisted manufacturing (CAM) are three recent productivity enhancement measures.

4. **Differentiate between total quality and quality control.**

   A second major area discussed in this chapter was quality. Total quality is the entire system of policies, procedures, and guidelines an organization institutes to attain and maintain quality. Quality control, on the other hand, consists of after-the-fact measurements to see if quality standards are actually being met.

   Quality control consists of actions taken during or after the fact to measure, analyze, and, if necessary, correct quality problems. It is a much narrower concept than total quality, which is an organizationwide commitment to quality and includes such factors as top management commitment, employee training, relationships with customers and suppliers, continuous quality improvement, and employee involvement in the quality process.

5. **Describe the role of variance in controlling quality.**

   An understanding of variance is important in controlling quality. Common cause variance is built into organizational processes and is considered normal. Common causes can normally only be corrected through management action to improve a process through such things as upgrading raw materials, using more sophisticated equipment, or additional training. On the other hand, special cause variance is nonroutine and entails identifying the problem, isolating it, examining the cause, and remedying it. It might involve an erratic piece of equipment, damaged raw materials, or an employee who is not performing properly.

6. **Identify some important tools for controlling quality.**

   A number of tools are available to help in controlling quality. Often these tools are used by individuals who are part of special problem-solving or quality-improvement teams. These include such tools as flowcharts, histograms, run charts, Pareto charts, cause-and-effect diagrams, and control charts. These tools are applicable to a broad range of manufacturing and service-related situations.

7. **Explain what the Occupational Safety and Health Administration does.**

   Employee safety has become important to organizations in recent years, especially since the passage of the Occupational Safety and Health Act in 1970. The Occupational Safety and Health Administration (OSHA) is charged with enforcing compliance with the law. It sets standards and regulations, requires organizations to maintain safety logs and records, conducts inspections, and has the authority to issue citations and penalties for violations found.

8. **Describe the supervisor's role in promoting safety.**

   Supervisors play an important role in promoting safety. Because supervisors are the primary management link with operating employees, supervisory behavior greatly impacts employee safety performance. Supervisors do this in many ways, such as in setting departmental safety goals, ensuring that employees understand safety requirements and procedures, conducting safety meetings, encouraging safety suggestions from employees, thoroughly investigating accidents, and enforcing rules when they are broken.

Key Terms

productivity, p. 414

Toyota Production System, p. 418

robot, p. 421

just-in-time (JIT) inventory control, p. 421

computer-assisted manufacturing (CAM), p. 422

Deming's 85–15 rule, p. 423

total quality, p. 426

quality control, p. 426

flowchart, p. 428

histogram, p. 429

run chart, p. 429

Pareto charts, p. 429

cause-and-effect diagram, p. 430

control chart, p. 430

Occupational Safety and Health Administration (OSHA), p. 435

Questions for Review & Discussion

1. Explain what happened to productivity of U.S. firms in the 1990s.
2. Do you believe that management and unions must always be on opposite sides of the productivity issue? Why or why not?
3. Identify some of the steps that supervisors can take to improve their department's productivity.
4. How does quality control differ from total quality? Explain.
5. Describe the role of variance in controlling quality.
6. Identify each of the following tools for controlling quality: Pareto chart, run chart, and flowchart.
7. What does OSHA do?
8. Describe some ways in which supervisors impact safety performance.

Interpersonal Skill

Information

Resources

Information

Systems

Skill Builder 14-1

Determining Productivity Measurements

In this chapter, you learned that productivity is the ratio of inputs to outputs. Consider each of the following organizations:

(a) bank
(b) community college
(c) large laundry/dry cleaners
(d) hospital
(e) restaurant

Instructions:

1. For each of the organizations shown, identify some important productivity measures that managers could use to measure the efficiency of their organization. (Hint: Think broadly, including measures that go beyond profitability or cost measures.)
2. Meet with groups of four to six other students and discuss your items.
3. Present your results to the whole class.

Skill Builder 14-2

Quality Survey

Visit a local fast-food restaurant, such as McDonald's, Burger King, or Wendy's, and order a meal.

Instructions:

1. During your visit, perform a quality analysis of the store, including but not limited to:
   (a) external store appearance, including shrubbery, cleanliness, and upkeep of outer building and parking lot
   (b) drive-through, including ease, speed, and accuracy of service
   (c) cleanliness of inner store, including tables, floors, and restrooms
   (d) employee factors, including appearance, friendliness, and efficiency
   (e) service factors, including speed and accuracy
   (f) food quality, including taste, freshness, temperature, and portion size.
2. Assume that you are the store manager and want to improve the areas that you found to be weak. Outline the corrective actions that you would take.
3. Meet with other students in groups of five to six to discuss your findings.

Resources

Interpersonal Skill

Information

Systems

Skill Builder 14-3

Increasing Safety Performance

Assume the role of a newly appointed store manager of a regional food chain super-store. All stores in the chain have been pressured to turn a profit in this highly competitive industry. And, while the former store manager achieved his profit goal, he fell far short in another: the store's safety performance. You are expected to do much better.

Last year the store accident rate was twice that of other stores in the chain: 16 reportable incidents per 100 employees, 9 of which involved lost workdays. These involved cuts, burns, slips, and falls. Many cuts occurred in the meat and deli areas; two burns occurred in the bakery area. One bagger sustained a fall in the parking lot while riding an empty grocery cart, a clear violation of policy. But the most serious fall resulted when a janitor left puddles of wax in an aisle and failed to put up warning cones when his work was interrupted to clean up a spill in another area. Another employee slipped on the wax and fell, injuring his left leg and head. This injury resulted in nine months (and counting) of disability costs, nearly $200,000 in medical costs, and a reserve of about $150,000 for future rehabilitation payments. Analysis of the injury-causing incidents showed that all were caused by human error.

As the new store manager, you are expected to immediately address the safety issues with your employees.

Instructions:

1. Outline a plan for bringing your employees' safety performance next year up to the average of other stores in the chain. You may assume your boss has approved a one-time $1,000 safety budget allocation to spend as needed to help you achieve this goal.
2. Meet with a group of other students to share your ideas. Your instructor may ask you to select a spokesperson to summarize the ideas of your team members.

CASE 14-1

Using Quality Tools

Welz Business Machines sells and services a variety of copiers, computers, and other office equipment. The company receives many calls daily for service, sales, accounting, and other departments. All calls are handled centrally by customer service representatives and routed to other individuals as appropriate.

A number of customers had complained about long waits when calling for service. A market research study found that customers became irritated if the call was not answered within five rings. Scott Welz, the company president, authorized the customer service department manager, Tim Nagy, to study the problem and find a method to shorten the call-waiting time. Tim met with his service representatives who answered the calls (Robin Coder, Raul Venegas, LaMarr Jones, Mark Staley, and Nancy Shipe) to attempt to determine the reasons for long waiting times. The following conversation ensued:

Nagy: This is a serious problem. How a customer phone inquiry is answered is the first impression the customer receives from us. As you know, this company was founded on efficient and friendly service to all our customers. It's obvious why customers have to wait: You're on the phone with another customer. Can you think of any reasons that might keep you on the phone for an unnecessarily long time?

Coder: I've noticed quite often that the person to whom I need to route the call is not present. It takes time to transfer the call and to see if it is answered. If the person is not there, I end up apologizing and transferring the call to another extension.

Nagy: You're right, Robin. Sales personnel often are out of the office on sales calls, away on trips to preview new products, or away from their desks for a variety of reasons. What else might cause this problem?

Venegas: I get irritated at customers who spend a great deal of time complaining about a problem that I cannot do anything about except refer to someone else. Of course, I listen and sympathize with them, but this eats up a lot of time.

Jones: Some customers call so often, they think we're long-lost friends and strike up a personal conversation.

Nagy: That's not always a bad thing, you realize.

Jones: Sure, but it delays my answering other calls.

Shipe: It's not always the customer's fault. During lunch, we're not all available to answer the phone.

Venegas: Right after we open at 9 a.m., we get a rush of calls. I think that many of the delays are caused by these peak periods.

Coder: I've noticed the same thing between 4 and 5 p.m.

Nagy: I've had a few comments from department managers who received calls that didn't fall in their areas of responsibility and had to be transferred again.

Staley: But that doesn't cause delays at our end.

Shipe: That's right, Mark, but I just realized that sometimes I simply don't understand what the customer's problem really is. I spend a lot of time trying to get him or her to explain it better. Often, I have to route it to someone because other calls are waiting.

Venegas: Perhaps we need to have more knowledge of our products.

Nagy: Well, I think we've covered most of the major reasons why many customers have to wait. It seems to me that we have four major reasons: the phones are short-staffed, the receiving party is not present, the customer dominates the conversation, and you may not understand the customer's problem. Next, we need to collect some information about these possible causes. Raul, can you and Mark set up a data collection sheet that we can use to track some of these things?

The next day, Venegas and Staley produced a sheet that enabled the staff to record the data. Over the next two weeks, the staff collected data on the frequency of reasons why some callers had to wait. The results are summarized as follows:

Reason		Total Number
A	Operators short-staffed	172
B	Receiving party not present	73
C	Customer dominates conversation	19
D	Lack of operator understanding	61
E	Other reasons	10

Instructions: Form groups of three to five students and, based on the conversation between Nagy and his staff,

1. Draw a cause-and-effect diagram.
2. Perform a Pareto analysis of the data collected.
3. Develop some possible actions that the company might take to improve the situation.

Source: Adapted from "The Quest for Higher Quality: The Deming Prize and Quality Control," by RICOH of America, Inc., and presented in James W. Dean and James R. Evans, *Total Quality* (Mason, South-Western, 1994), pp. 96–98. Reprinted with permission of South-Western, a division of Thomson Learning: www.thomsonrights.com.

15

Selecting, Appraising, and Disciplining Employees

LEARNING OBJECTIVES

After reading and studying this chapter, you should be able to:

1. Explain who is responsible for selecting, appraising, and disciplining employees.

2. Describe the steps in the employee selection procedure, including the proper orientation of new employees.

3. Explain what employee performance appraisal is and who performs it.

4. State why performance-appraisal interviews are difficult for both the employee and the supervisor.

5. Define discipline and explain why it is necessary.

6. Describe how discipline is imposed under due process.

Mentoring the way Ron Blount has done for several of his employees can be an effective way to help develop and manage human resources.

Here lies a man who knew how to enlist in his service better men than himself.

—Andrew Carnegie's Epitaph

No one is free who cannot command himself.

—Pythagoras

Preview

RON BLOUNT: MENTORING TO ENSURE THE NEXT GENERATION IS PREPARED TO LEAD Ron Blount, the Project Director of Construction for the Retirement Systems of Alabama, is responsible for approximately $600 million of development. He has worked in the construction business for over 30 years and says the industry is in a state of "flux." Skilled leaders and laborers are not as plentiful as in years past, and Ron firmly believes effective mentoring can make a difference to ensure that a bright future exists for those who choose careers in this field. It made a difference for him, and it can make a difference for others.

Ron's first mentor, his father, helped him develop an appreciation for work. Ron's father worked two jobs to provide for his family and would typically awaken at 1:30 A.M. to deliver bundles of papers for distribution, getting a few additional hours of sleep prior to going to his regular job with the city of Atlanta, Georgia, where he managed several hundred employees. As a boy, Ron helped his dad with the early morning deliveries, but it wasn't until he was 15 that his dad gave him an opportunity to work for the city picking up leaves and rubbish on the side of the curbs. This was an attractive job for Ron because it paid adult wages. However, Ron's dad did not provide any preferential treatment to his son; rather, he made sure that Ron got up and came down each Saturday morning at 5:30 A.M. to stand in line to be chosen for the day's work assignments. His dad believed it was important to instill a sense of responsibility, commitment, and pride in his son at an early age.

After graduating from high school, Ron worked for a development company. Even though he was only employed with the firm for two years, his relationship with one of the company's principles, Don Carl, had a tremendous long-term impact. Don encouraged Ron to "think big" and attempt to do great things in his career. Having a vision for one's future is extremely important, but it wasn't until Ron went to work for Jim Curnyn at George Hyman Construction Company that he truly developed the confidence necessary to actually achieve great things.

Jim Curnyn hired Ron as an estimator to work on the Atlanta Airport, a $95-million construction project during the 1970s. Within two years, Ron was project manager. His career trajectory was due in no small part to Jim's excellent mentoring. Not only did Jim encourage and support Ron, but he also actively managed his growth and development. Jim made Ron go beyond problem recognition and continually asked Ron his opinion on issues. He wanted Ron to feel comfortable analyzing situations and making recommendations regardless of the cost associated with the situation.

A turning point in Ron's career came when Jim was a no-show for an important meeting. It is still unclear whether Jim was delayed for the meeting due to other business or whether there was a method to his madness! History shows (e.g., Winston Churchill) that many times an individual's true abilities shine when he or she is thrust into a challenging situation. Ron was prepared for the meeting with the joint venture partner, and over the next several days, successfully negotiated a multimillion dollar deal on the part of George Hyman Construction. Jim provided the opportunity for Ron to showcase his abilities. Once he proved to himself what he could accomplish, Ron began to negotiate $2 to $3 million contracts with major airlines on a regular basis. Ron states, "Jim was always there with a life preserver if I needed one, but ultimately he had confidence in me. Jim felt that I could handle challenges, solve problems, and basically, get it done."

Ron gained valuable insights from Don and Jim that have assisted in him becoming the great leader that he is today. When Ron was working for Avery Mays Construction in Dallas, Texas, as a project manager, he got the opportunity to apply the leadership insights he gained from his mentors. Tim Cary was a Harvard graduate and a school teacher prior to being selected for Avery Mays' executive management program. Soon thereafter, he was paired with Ron to "learn the business." Ron saw some of himself in Tim and tried to provide the type of guidance needed for Tim to thrive in his new career. As Ron states, "The relationship grew, and Tim became part of our family. He would eat at our house and spend time during holidays with us." Tim really blossomed under Ron's tutelage, and the last Ron had heard, Tim was executive vice president of a development company in Los Angeles, California.

Ron's second mentoring opportunity may be viewed by many as more challenging. Brent Clemens was the chief estimator at Avery Mays Construction. Not everyone got along with Brent, and it was believed he was about to be let go. Ron had always been gender neutral and color blind when it came to relationships. Therefore, he didn't hesitate when given the opportunity to accept the assignment of an African American as his project engineer. As Ron shares, "The job was a step down, but Brent has always approached every job he has had by giving 120 percent." In fact, Ron was so impressed with Brent's abilities and work ethic that when he was later managing a large project in Montgomery, Alabama, he hired Brent as his project manager. In the 92-year history of the Montgomery office of Algernon Blair, Inc., Brent was the first and only African American project manager. Ron showed the commitment and confidence in Brent that his mentors had shown him.

When the Montgomery job was winding down, Ron asked Brent, "Have you ever thought about going into business as a major contractor?" Brent admitted that he had not, but with Ron's encouragement, Brent struck out and opened his own company. Fifteen years later, Brent is evidence of what a great mentor can provide to an individual with raw talent, ability, and drive. Brent now owns and operates a very successful Atlanta-based construction company.

Source: Interview with Ron Blount with RSA.

In this chapter, we look at the processes of staffing, developing, appraising, and disciplining employees. When Art Linkletter, owner of over 75 companies, was asked the secret of his success, his answer was "I bet on people!" As the great industrialist Andrew Carnegie realized, an organization consists not merely of physical and financial resources but, most importantly, of people. Thus the supervisory challenge of the future will lie in properly selecting and developing people. Management must emphasize putting the right employees in the right jobs and then motivating them to perform well.

Candidates for a given job can be obtained from inside or outside the organization, but there must be some method of selection to find capable people. Then, the organization must improve employees' performance through training and developing their abilities adequately and then compensating them. Selecting, appraising, and disciplining employees are covered in this chapter.

We believe that supervisors need to "see the big picture" of the staffing process. Certainly not all supervisors are involved in the activities presented in this chapter, but, if they understand the total process of staffing, they will be in a better position to perform their part of this process.

Responsibility for Selecting, Appraising, and Disciplining Employees

1 *Explain who is responsible for selecting, appraising, and disciplining employees.*

An organization can be successful only if it has the right number and types of people to do the required work. Therefore, a primary duty of all supervisors is the proper selection, placement, training and development, compensation, and utilization of competent employees. How well—or poorly—supervisors perform these functions is a major factor in their success or failure.

A Shared Responsibility

Like almost all aspects of supervision, selecting, appraising, and disciplining employees are shared tasks, though the primary responsibility should be left to supervisors. In general, the responsibilities are divided as follows:

1. *Top managers* set human resources objectives, establish policies, and do long-range planning and organizing.
2. *Middle managers* control the operating procedures needed to achieve these objectives and carry out personnel policies.
3. *Supervisors* interpret policies for employees and carry out higher management's wishes as to selecting and training employees. Also, they interpret and transmit workers' interests to higher management.

With today's emphasis on *empowerment,* teams are often used at all three of these levels. It is especially important to have potential fellow employees involved in an advisory role, at least.

The Supervisor's Role

Operative employees usually have little contact with high-level managers. Therefore, they tend to think of their supervisor as being "management" or "the organization." Because employees interpret their supervisor's actions, attitudes, and methods as representing those of all managers, supervisors are probably the most important people in achieving an organization's human resources objectives. Supervisors usually have the final word in selecting, appraising, and disciplining employees. Then they supervise and control the employees' daily activities.

Self-Check

In the Johnson Company, a large department store, sales positions are filled directly by the personnel office. When a selection decision is made, the sales department supervisor is notified, and the new employee reports to her or him for a job assignment. Typically, the new employee first meets his or her supervisor on the first day of work. What are the pros and cons of this system?

Selecting Employees for Specific Jobs

2 *Describe the steps in the employee selection procedure, including the proper orientation of new employees.*

A suggested procedure for selecting employees is shown in Exhibit 15-1. Individual employers may find it desirable to modify this procedure—or depart from it—under certain conditions. In this section, each of the steps listed in the exhibit is briefly explained.

Requisition

Selection really begins with a requisition from the supervisor to the human resource department. This requisition, which is based on the previously prepared job description and specification, is the authorization the department needs to recruit applicants for the position(s) available. In many small and medium-sized firms, the supervisor makes an informal visit or phone call to the senior officer who is authorized to make the final job offer.

A reminder is needed at this point! If you, as a supervisor, are involved in recruiting and selecting job applicants, all aspects of your procedures must conform to the Equal Employment Opportunity Commission's (EEOC) *Uniform Guidelines on Employee Selection Procedures.* The guidelines cover *all selection procedures,* not just testing. Your procedures should also comply with your Affirmative Action Program (AAP) for hiring people from various groups. The human resource officer, in particular, should be certain that the selection procedure conforms to national and local laws and customs.

When Bryan Seibt accepted the position of Human Resources Director for the City of Fairhope, Alabama, personal referral was the primary recruiting source used to match individuals with vacant jobs throughout the city's various departments. He has worked for several years with the department heads to proactively broaden the applicant pool. A multisource strategy using the city's website, local and regional newspapers, the state's league of municipalities' network, and a variety of association groups has generated more diverse applicants. The result is more diversity within the city's departments.[1]

Preliminary Screening

Whether formal or informal, some form of preliminary screening helps weed out those persons who do not seem to meet the employer's needs—thus saving their time and yours. This step deals with such obvious factors as educational background, training, experience, physical appearance, grooming, and speech—if these are relevant to job

EXHIBIT 15-1

Flowchart of a Suggested Selection Procedure

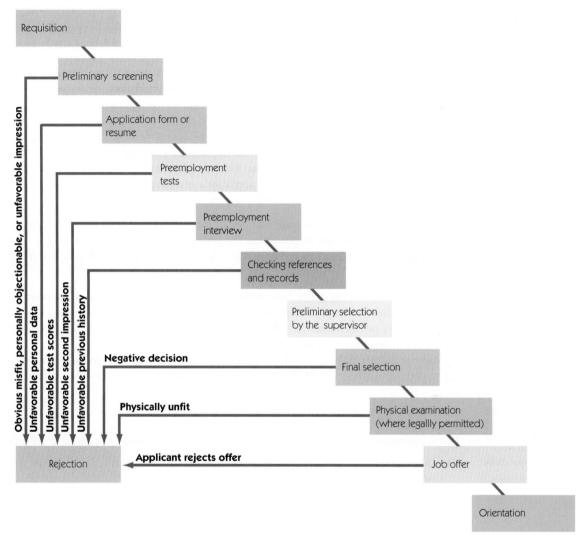

Source: From Figure 9-4, "Techniques for Gathering Information About Potential Employees," by Leon C. Megginson, Mary Jane Byrd and William L. Megginson, published in a 2003 issue of *Small Business Management: An Entrepreneur's Guidebook*, 4th Edition, p. 228. Reprinted by permission, uschamber.com, Sept. 2009. Copyright 2003, U.S. Chamber of Commerce and McGraw-Hill Companies.

performance. Also, the applicant should know something about the organization and the job being sought.

An early study found that 9 percent of college applicants were eliminated at this point for "personal reasons." Some of the reasons cited for not hiring were bad breath, dirty fingernails, and uncombed hair.[2]

Mike, a bright, young college student, applied at a local hotel for employment while home on summer break. He was rejected at the preliminary interview because his hair was below his collar—even though it was neatly pulled back. He was told that even the groundskeepers and dry cleaning plant workers had to have their hair above their collars. The next year, he was rejected by a grocery chain because he had a beard. Finally, he did find a lucrative job waiting tables at an English pub—with great tips and free meals.

Application Form or Résumé

After passing the preliminary screening, the job applicant usually completes an application form. (Some applications are submitted by e-mail, snail mail, or in person before preliminary screening.) The applicant usually lists such information as former employers, titles of jobs held, and length of employment with each one. Background, education, military status, and other useful data are listed. The form should be carefully designed to provide the information needed about the applicant's potential performance; it should not be a hodgepodge of irrelevant data. The completion of the form in longhand will provide you with a simple test of the applicant's neatness, thoroughness, ability to answer questions, and literacy, as the following example illustrates:

The manager of a tire store once told one of the authors that he requires all applicants to fill out an application in person on the premises. "When they ask to take it home," he said, "I can be almost sure they're illiterate and need help in reading it and filling it out."

The EEOC and many states have restrictions concerning the kinds of questions that may be included on an application form. Therefore, you should check any laws that your state may have on such practices. See Exhibit 15-2 for a list of topics to avoid on application forms and during interviews.

Many recruiters are now tending to react negatively to what showed signs of becoming a popular method of submitting résumés to potential employees—via e-mail. The

EXHIBIT 15-2
Topics to Avoid when Interviewing Applicants

Here is a summary of 10 of the most dangerous questions or topics you might raise during an interview.

1. *Children.* Do not ask applicants whether they have children, or plan to have children, or have child care.
2. *Age.* Do not ask an applicant's age.
3. *Disabilities.* Do not ask whether the candidate has a physical or mental disability that would interfere with doing the job.
4. *Physical Characteristics.* Do not ask for such identifying characteristics as height or weight on an application.
5. *Name.* Do not ask a female candidate for her maiden name.
6. *Citizenship.* Do not ask applicants about their citizenship. However, the Immigration Reform and Control Act does require business operators to determine that their employees have a legal right to work in the United States.
7. *Lawsuits.* Do not ask a job candidate whether he or she has ever filed a suit or a claim against a former employer.
8. *Arrest Records.* Do not ask applicants about their arrest records.
9. *Smoking.* Do not ask whether a candidate smokes. Although smokers are not protected under the Americans with Disabilities Act (ADA), asking applicants whether they smoke might lead to legal difficulties if an applicant is turned down because of fear that smoking would drive up the employer's health care costs.
10. *AIDS and HIV.* Never ask job candidates whether they have AIDS or are HIV-positive, because these questions violate the ADA and could violate state and federal civil rights laws.

Source: Originally published July 1992 in Nation's Business. Reprinted by permission, USChamber.com, November 2009. Copyright © 1992, U.S. Chamber of Commerce.

Workers' emotional adjustment and attitude will have a strong impact on work performance, especially those tasks requiring interpersonal skills.

IQ tests

Measure the applicant's capacity to learn, solve problems, and understand relationships.

aptitude tests

Predict how a person might perform on a given job.

vocational interest tests

Determine the applicant's areas of major work interest.

personality tests

Measure the applicant's emotional adjustment and attitude.

achievement, proficiency, or skill tests

Measure the applicant's knowledge of and ability to do a given job.

very success of the method led to its troubles. Some companies are getting thousands of résumés dumped into e-mail boxes each day. Not only is the volume overwhelming employers, but many of the résumés contain attachments that are difficult to open or decipher.[3]

Preemployment Testing

Various tests can be used to assess an applicant's intelligence quotient (IQ), skills, aptitudes, vocational interests, personality, and performance. Preemployment testing, especially "personality" or psychological testing, is growing in use by industry. These test(s) can minimize turnover because companies are now trying to hire for "fit" between the workers and employees, and testing can help them ensure that "fit." However, the tests must be approved by the EEOC and be valid and reliable. Only the most popular are discussed here.

Types of Tests **IQ tests** are designed to measure the applicant's capacity to learn, to solve problems, and to understand relationships. They are particularly useful in selecting employees for supervisory and managerial positions. **Aptitude tests** are used to predict how a person might perform on a given job and are most applicable to operative jobs. **Vocational interest tests** are designed to determine the applicant's areas of major work interest. Although interest does not guarantee competence, it can result in the employee working and trying harder. **Personality tests** are supposed to measure the applicant's emotional adjustment and attitude. These tests are often used to evaluate interpersonal relationships and to see how the person might fit into an organization.

Probably the most effective tests the supervisor can use in selecting operative employees are **achievement, proficiency,** or **skill tests.** These tests measure fairly accurately the applicant's knowledge of and ability to do a given job. They can also spot *trade bluffers—* people who claim job knowledge, skills, and experience that they don't really have. One

work sampling or work preview

A test in which the prospective employee must perform a task that is representative of the job.

type of proficiency test is a **work sampling** or **work preview**, in which the prospective employee is asked to do a task that is representative of the work usually done on the job. In addition to showing whether the person can actually do the job, the test gives the applicant more realistic expectations about the job.

Finally, some organizations now test for drug use, especially where the use of drugs by employees poses a serious safety risk, as in the case of machine operators or airplane pilots. Although such tests are controversial, they are legal in most states.[4]

Validity of Tests If tests are used in making the selection decision, employers must be prepared to demonstrate their validity. **Validity** is demonstrated by a high positive correlation between the applicant's test scores and some identifiable measure of performance on the job. Furthermore, the tests must be designed, administered, and interpreted by a professional (usually a licensed psychologist); be culturally neutral so that they don't discriminate against any ethnic group; and be in complete conformity with EEOC guidelines.[5] Tests must also have **reliability;** that is, the results will be the same if the test is given to the same person by different testers or by the same tester at different times. Care should be exercised in interpreting test results because some persons are adept at faking answers. Because of these and other problems, many firms are dropping testing in favor of other selection techniques.

validity

A high positive correlation between the applicant's test scores and some objective measure of job performance.

reliability

The probability that test results won't change if the test is given to the same person by different individuals.

It should be reemphasized at this point that *all selection techniques are subject to scrutiny by the EEOC*. It should also be mentioned that the most frequently used selection criteria are supervisory ratings and job performance.

Preemployment Interviewing

In preparing for the employment interview, which is the only two-way part of the selection procedure, you should use the information on the application form and the test results to learn as much as you can about the applicant. A list of questions prepared before the interview can help you avoid missing information that might be significant in judging the applicant. Compare your list of questions with the job specification to ensure that you are matching the individual's personal qualifications with the job requirements. Some specific questions you might ask are:

1. What did you do on your last job?
2. How did you do it?
3. Why did you do it?
4. Of the jobs you have had, which did you like best? Which the least?
5. Why did you leave your last job?
6. What do you consider your strong and weak points?
7. Why do you want to work for us?

structured interviews

Standardized and controlled with regard to questions asked, sequence of questions, interpretation of replies, and weight given to factors considered in making the hiring decision.

If you are observant and perceptive during the interview, you can obtain some impressions about the candidate's abilities, personality, appearance, speech, and attitudes toward work. You should also provide the applicant with information about the company and the job. Remember, the applicant needs facts to decide whether to accept or reject the job, just as you need information to decide whether to offer it.

The interview may be carried out individually by the supervisor or in cooperation with someone else—the human resource officer or some other senior manager. It may be structured or unstructured. **Structured interviews** are standardized and controlled with regard to questions asked, sequence of questions, interpretation of replies, and weight given to factors considered in making the value judgment as to whether or not to hire the person. In unstructured interviews, the pattern of questions asked, the conditions under which they are asked, and the basis for evaluating results are determined by the interviewer.

Not long ago, a former student started a new division within the family business. As part of the hiring process, she conducted numerous interviews to staff both clerical and production positions. At first, there wasn't a set structure to the interviews. She preferred for the interaction to unfold naturally. However, she quickly realized how difficult it was to make a decision by comparing the knowledge, skills, and abilities across applicants for a particular job using this approach. As a result, she structured her interviews, developing a list of questions to guide her actions. The structured interview setting helped her differentiate among applicants.

Checking References and Records

The importance of carefully checking applicants' references cannot be overemphasized.

Reference checks provide answers to questions concerning a candidate's performance on previous jobs. They are helpful in verifying information on the application form and other records, as well as statements made during the interviews. They are also useful in checking on possible omissions of information and in clarifying specific points. However,, a Robert Half survey found that 68 percent of employers now find that former employers, fearing lawsuits, tend to say nothing—or only nice things—about past employees.[6] In fact, most former employers will only give dates of employment and position(s) held.

Reference checks made in person or by telephone are greatly preferable to written ones because past employers are sometimes reluctant to commit to writing any uncomplimentary remarks about a former employee. Be sure to ask specific questions about the candidate's performance. The type of information you are allowed to seek is restricted by laws such as the Fair Credit Reporting Act and the Privacy Act. But you can check on dates and terms of employment, salary, whether termination was voluntary, and whether this employer would rehire the candidate. Many organizations are now using credit checks to obtain information about prospective employees. If this source is used and is the basis for rejecting a candidate, he or she has the right to see the report.

Preliminary Selection by the Supervisor

By this point in the selection process, you—the supervisor—have narrowed the number of candidates to one or a very few. If there is only one, the applicant can be hired on a trial basis. If you have more than one qualified candidate, a review of the information collected should reveal the best choice. Although your preliminary selection may be subject to approval by the human resource department or some higher authority, usually the person will be offered the job.

Final Selection

Human resource officers are usually brought in on the final hiring decision because of their expertise. They ensure that all laws and regulations, as well as company policies, are followed. Also, they have a voice in such questions as the salary and employee benefits to be offered to the applicant.

Physical Examination

Formerly, the final step in the selection procedure was a physical examination to see if the applicant could do the job. However, the Americans with Disabilities Act (ADA) has limited this part of the process. *Employers may not now require an exam before a preliminary job offer is made.*[7] *Then, when an exam is allowed, the exam may only determine whether the worker can do the job being sought, and no medical history may be taken.*[8]

Job Offer

Job offers to applicants for nonmanagerial and nonprofessional positions are usually made by the human resource office. They are often in writing and contain the terms and conditions of employment. At this point, the offer is either accepted or rejected. If it is rejected, an offer may be made to the next most qualified applicant. If there are no other qualified candidates, the selection procedure must start all over again.

After a candidate has accepted the job offer, those not hired should still be kept in mind for any possible future openings. It is common courtesy to notify them that someone else has been selected, and a diplomatic rejection will maintain their goodwill.

Self–Check

Have you ever applied for a job and been told, "We'll let you know within a week if we want you"? Even when the week was up, were you still hoping you might get a call, if only to say definitely that you had not been hired? How did this uncertainty make you feel toward the employer?

orientation

Procedures of familiarizing a new employee with the company surroundings, policies, and job responsibilities.

Orientation

The first day on a new job is confusing for anyone. Therefore, a new employee should be given a proper **orientation.** A job description should be given to him or her and explained in detail. Proper instructions, training, and observation will start the employee off on the right foot. A tour of the facilities and a look at the firm's product or service

Huntstock/Getty Images

Properly socializing employees who are new to an organization through orientation and other means can have a positive impact on employee retention.

will help the new employee understand where he or she fits into the scheme of things. The new employee needs to know the firm's objectives, policies, rules, and performance expectations. Frequent discussions should be held with him or her during the orientation program to answer questions and to ensure proper progress.

A formal interview with the new employee may be appropriate at some point during the first week. Other interviews can be held during the probationary period, which is usually from three to six months. The purpose of these interviews should be to correct any mistaken ideas the employee may have about the job and to determine whether he or she feels that you and your people are fulfilling your commitments.

After orientation is completed, a checklist is usually reviewed with the new employee. Then, the employee and a representative of the employer sign it, and it is placed in the employee's file as proof of knowledge of rules. If done properly by the supervisor, orientation should accelerate the building of a positive working relationship with the new employee.

> *A manufacturing company that one of the authors worked with was having employee retention problems. Even though turnover is relatively high in this particular industry, this firm seemed to have a higher-than-average rate of turnover. Examination of the problem identified a lack of proper socialization of new employees as one contributing factor. The company developed and implemented a detailed employee orientation program that includes an initial orientation day in which information about the company—policies, procedures, benefits, and so on—is communicated to all new employees. Each employee is given a "developmental book" during orientation to be used in conjunction with the supervisor to track the development of key task and performance objectives. The supervisor and the newly hired employee meet regularly each week during the first month to evaluate the employee's development and address any concerns. In addition, each person is informally paired with a more tenured employee within the work department who can be relied upon to answer questions and provide guidance. By implementing a multifaceted socialization process, the manufacturer cut its turnover in half.*

The Role of Performance Appraisals in Supervisory Management

3 *Explain what employee performance appraisal is and who performs it.*

Because performance appraisal is such an important part of the management process, enlightened managers are now trying to upgrade their appraisal programs. Most employers have already developed some kind of formal program for improving employee performance, growth, and development.

It should be strongly emphasized that performance appraisals—when properly designed, conducted, and discussed with the person being appraised—are beneficial to the employee as well as the organization. In other words, reviews can be positive and motivational if they are conducted with an attitude designed to improve performance and help each employee move toward maximizing his or her potential. Regardless of the appraisal method used, however, *the appraisal should be constructive* and future oriented.

performance appraisal *or* merit rating *or* efficiency rating *or* service rating *or* employee evaluation

Determines to what extent an employee is performing a job the way it was intended.

What Is a Performance Appraisal?

A **performance appraisal** is the process used to determine to what extent an employee is performing a job in the way it was intended to be done. Some other frequently used terms for this process are **merit rating, efficiency rating, service rating,** and **employee evaluation.** Regardless of the term used, the process always has the purpose of seeing how actual employee performance compares to the ideal or standard.[9]

EXHIBIT 15-3

How Performance Appraisals Operate

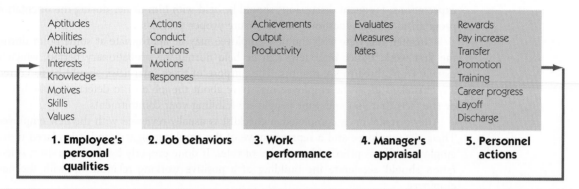

Aptitudes Abilities Attitudes Interests Knowledge Motives Skills Values	Actions Conduct Functions Motions Responses	Achievements Output Productivity	Evaluates Measures Rates	Rewards Pay increase Transfer Promotion Training Career progress Layoff Discharge
1. Employee's personal qualities	**2. Job behaviors**	**3. Work performance**	**4. Manager's appraisal**	**5. Personnel actions**

How a Performance Appraisal Operates

If employees' output can be physically measured, then their rewards can be based on their actual output and there is little need to formally appraise them. However, many jobs today do not lend themselves to physical measurement. Therefore, the supervisor tries to determine what personal characteristics an employee has that lead him or her to have satisfactory performance. As you can see from Exhibit 15-3, the process works as follows: An employee's personal qualities (1) lead to job behaviors (2) that result in work performance (3), which the manager appraises (4), and that appraisal results in some kind of personnel action (5).

An *employee's qualities* are his or her abilities, attitudes, interests, skills, knowledge, and values. These qualities lead the employee to take certain actions that result in output or productivity. The manager appraises the employee's performance and then may reward the employee through a pay increase, transfer, promotion, training and development, or career progress.

Most human resource departments now have computerized files on all employees. *These management staffing and development programs* should include appraisal criteria and ratings, along with consistent definitions of skills, level of experience, and development activity.[10]

Purposes of the Performance Appraisal

Some specific reasons for appraising employee performance are (1) to recognize "good" performance, (2) to point out areas that need improvement, especially if the employee hopes to progress in the organization, (3) to validate selection techniques to meet EEOC/AAP requirements, and (4) to provide a basis for administrative actions such as wage increases, promotions, transfers, layoffs, and/or discharges. Appraisal for these purposes is usually done by comparing the performance of one employee to that of others.

Administrative action sometimes takes the form of dealing with managers who are having problems, as well. A well-developed appraisal system can help detect "problem managers" in time to take appropriate action.[11]

Self-Check

Notice in Case 15-1 how Robert Trent manipulates the appraisal of Jane Smith to get her transferred. Although we do not condone the method he used, the case does show how a performance appraisal can be used as a basis for administrative action.

Performance appraisals can also be used for communications and motivational purposes, such as to provide a basis for giving advice, coaching, or counseling so that employees will have better expectations on the job or as a basis for career planning and development. When used for these purposes, performance appraisal is usually done by comparing employees' actual performance to some previously determined work standard(s). In such cases, the role of the supervisor is that of a counselor, a mentor, or an instructor, and the appraisal should serve to motivate employees by giving them a better understanding of their job responsibilities, of what is expected of them, and of their training needs.

The Role of the Appraisal Interview

4 *State why performance-appraisal interviews are difficult for both the employee and the supervisor.*

appraisal interview

Supervisor communicates the results of a performance appraisal to an employee.

Most organizations cannot afford poor performance, and workers cannot afford poor reviews. One way to satisfy both these requirements is for the supervisor to conduct an **appraisal interview** to communicate the results of a given performance appraisal to an employee. This method seems compatible with the objective of providing feedback on workers' progress and encouraging improvement on the job. However, conducting the appraisal interview is the job aspect that supervisors like least. This dislike, together with the poor way the appraisal interview is often handled, has caused this interview to be criticized heavily for damaging relationships between supervisors and employees. One of the main problems with such interviews is that too much is expected of them. The interview alone cannot improve performance, uncover training needs, and serve as the basis for pay increases, promotions, and so forth—but it can certainly help!

The appraisal interview is one of the most difficult duties required of a supervisor. Such an interview used to be along the lines of "Call Joe in and tell him what needs to be straightened out and what's expected of him." Today, however, interviewers are expected to aim for cooperation, constructiveness, and greater understanding.[12] Let us look at what tends to happen during the typical interview, even though it is conducted according to the rules of good performance-appraisal interviewing.

Once a year, Gloria Rogers calls her employees in one at a time for the appraisal interview. Both parties tend to "psych up" for this event. Rogers plans what she's going to say, and the employee tends to be apprehensive about what he or she is going to hear. At the beginning, Rogers tries to put the employee at ease by talking about the weather, the latest major league baseball game, or the employee's family. The employee knows that this is just the prelude to getting down to serious business—and tends to resent the delay.

Then Rogers explains her overall appraisal in broad terms. Initially, she'll mention some good aspects of the employee's performance and give the employee a chance to express his or her views. Next, she enumerates the employee's weaknesses and past failures. She allows the employee to explain these. Then, she explains what steps are needed to improve the employee's performance. At this point, she may ask for the employee's ideas on improvement. One variation of the procedure allows the employee to give his or her own self-evaluation and compare it with Rogers' evaluation after it is given.

The conventional approach to the appraisal interview is emotionally upsetting for both the supervisor and the employee. There is no doubt in the employee's mind that he or she is in the hot seat and that there's little point in disagreeing with the supervisor about her judgments. It's best simply to remain submissive and accept the criticism, even if the employee disagrees with it. Supervisors likewise tend to feel anxiety over performance appraisal, because, as management theorist Douglas McGregor points out,

Managers are uncomfortable when they are put in the position of "playing God." ... [We become] distressed when we must take responsibility for judging the personal worth of a fellow man. Yet the conventional approach to performance appraisal forces us not only to make such judgments and to see them acted upon, but also to communicate them to those we have judged. Small wonder we resist.[13]

It is fairly common practice for employers to require managers to discuss their appraisals with employees. The authors of this textbook have talked with numerous supervisors who suffer the double-barreled discomforts of performance appraisal. These supervisors dislike being appraised by their own bosses, and they dislike appraising their employees—or at least telling them the results. All this may lead to appraisal inflation. For example, in one company, when a policy was adopted requiring supervisors to give their appraisals to their employees, their appraisals of their employees suddenly jumped remarkably.[14] Another important aspect of performance appraisals is that they should contain aspects of career planning for the employee. In other words, the appraisal should help the employee plan for the future.

In summary, the appraisal interview presents both an opportunity and a potential danger for the supervisor, because both praise and constructive criticism must be communicated. A major effort should be made to emphasize the positive aspects of the employee's performance while also discussing ways to make needed improvements. One classic study showed that one group of employees, who took some form of constructive action as a result of performance appraisals, did so because of the way their supervisor had conducted the appraisal interview and discussion.[15] Exhibit 15-4 provides some helpful hints for conducting a more effective interview.

The Need for Discipline

5 *Define discipline and explain why it is necessary.*

Effective job performance requires that both managerial and nonmanagerial employees maintain discipline. Most employees would rather work with a group that is well organized, well trained, and well disciplined than with one that is not. Employees benefit from discipline and suffer from disorder. An early study found that, although workers do not necessarily want to be personally punished, they do want to be supervised "not too much—but also not too little."[16] Successful supervisors know how to find the "middle road" that allows their employees to know exactly what they may and may not do. These generalizations may lead to confusion unless the question, "What is discipline?" is answered.

EXHIBIT 15-4
Hints for the Appraisal Interview

DO	DON'T
• Prepare in advance.	• Lecture the employee.
• Focus on performance and development.	• Mix performance appraisal and salary or promotion issues.
• Be specific about reasons for ratings.	• Concentrate only on the negative.
• Decide about specific steps to be taken for improvement.	• Do all the talking.
• Consider your role in the employee's performance.	• Be overcritical or "harp on" a failing.
• Reinforce the behavior you want.	• Feel it is necessary that both of you agree on all areas.
• Focus on future performance.	• Compare the employee with others.

Source: From Mathis/Jackson. Human Resource Management, 12E, p. 318. © 2008 South-Western, a part of Cengage Learning, Inc. Reproduced by permission. www.cengage.com/permissions

What Is Discipline?

To start out, let us emphasize that good discipline is based on good leadership. On that assumption, the term *discipline* will be used in this chapter to refer to any of three concepts: (1) self-control, (2) conditions leading to orderly behavior in a work environment, or (3) punishment for improper behavior. Many companies say in their discipline policy that **discipline** is training that corrects, molds, or perfects knowledge, attitudes, behavior, or conduct. We agree with this overall definition.

discipline

Training that corrects and molds knowledge, attitudes, and behavior.

Discipline as Due Process

The Fourteenth Amendment to the U.S. Constitution guarantees every citizen due process under the law. Essentially, the following conditions ensure that an individual receives justice in the form of **due process:**

due process

Guarantees the individual accused of violating an established rule a hearing to determine the extent of guilt.

1. Rules or laws exist.
2. There are specific, fixed penalties for violating those rules, with progressive degrees in the severity of penalties.
3. Penalties are imposed only after a hearing has been conducted for the accused, at which time the extent of guilt is determined after considering the circumstances of the situation.

Unions have insisted that this same process be used within organizations in disciplining employees; even nonunion employers now use it. Today, most arbitrators will uphold a disciplinary action if it can be shown that (1) the rules are reasonable, (2) the penalty is related to the severity of the offense, and (3) the worker was given a fair hearing. Underlying the due process concept is the assumption that the employer has the right to maintain a well-disciplined work environment and the right to administer discipline when rules are violated. Of course, where there's a union, its representative wants to be present when a member is disciplined. At this point, we would like to emphasize that employers can avoid employee grievance proceedings by developing equitable and objective disciplinary procedures.[17]

How Disciplinary Due Process Operates

6 *Describe how discipline is imposed under due process.*

As indicated earlier, disciplinary due process involves three steps. First, rules are established. Second, fixed penalties are set for each infraction of a rule (the penalties usually vary according to the degree of severity of the offense and how many times the rule is broken). Third, the penalty is imposed only after the employee has been given a fair hearing.

Establishing Rules of Conduct If employees are to maintain self-discipline, they must know what they can and cannot do, and they must know it in advance. Therefore, most progressive organizations publish rules, usually in their employee handbook.

Determining Penalties The types of penalties, as well as the ways they are used, generally are determined in consultation with the union. What usually results is termed **progressive discipline,** because it involves a graduated scale of penalties. If there is no union, the penalties stem from management's philosophy of how to treat employees, as well as from its fear of the entry of a union or government action.

progressive discipline

Discipline that uses a graduated scale of penalties.

The normal steps in a progressive-discipline policy are:

1. *Oral warning* that does not go into the employee's record.
2. *Oral warning* that goes into the employee's record.
3. *Written reprimand,* which usually comes from some level above the supervisor.
4. *Suspension,* which usually consists of a layoff lasting from a day to a number of months.

5. *Discharge,* the ultimate penalty, which constitutes a break in service and wipes out the employee's seniority. Most supervisors are reluctant to use it because it is the economic equivalent of the death penalty and it affects the worker's family as well as the worker. Justification must be strictly established because discharge is almost always subject to the grievance procedure and arbitration.

Some other infrequently used penalties are demotions, transfers, and the withholding of benefits such as promotions, raises, or bonuses.

graduated scale of penalties

Penalties become progressively more severe each time the violation is repeated.

Unions, personnel managers, and most supervisors favor using a **graduated scale of penalties,** under which punishment for a given violation becomes progressively more severe each time the violation is repeated. The penalty may be, first, an oral warning; second, a written warning; third, suspension; and fourth, discharge. However, when the disciplinary problems are of such a drastic, dangerous, or illegal nature that they severely strain or endanger employment relationships, they are called **intolerable offenses,** and the first time one is committed, the employee is discharged.

intolerable offenses

Disciplinary problems of a drastic, dangerous, or illegal nature.

Imposing the Penalty Only after a Fair Hearing Supervisors must follow the correct procedure in taking any action against an employee. In other words, discipline must be properly administered in accordance with previously established and announced rules and procedures. Penalties should be based on specific charges, with notice given to the employee and the union, if there is one, usually in advance of management's attempt to take corrective action. The charges and their underlying reasons should be definite and provable. There should be provisions for a prompt hearing, witnesses, protests, and appeals. Finally, adequate remedies should be available to employees whose punishment has failed to meet the requirement of "fair play."

In summary, the main requirements for a proper disciplinary procedure are (1) to make definite charges; (2) to notify the employee (and union), in writing, of the offense; and (3) to have some provision for the employee to answer the charges either by protest or by appeal.

Martin Jenkinson/Alamy

Employees who understand exactly what is and what is not expected of them are better equipped to avoid unpleasant disciplinary measures.

The Supervisor and Discipline

7 *Explain the supervisor's disciplinary role.*

Regardless of whether supervisors work in unionized firms, they must exercise discretion when recommending or imposing penalties on employees. In dealing with mistakes, supervisors must consider what the mistakes were and under what circumstances they were made. Mistakes resulting from continued carelessness call for disciplinary action. Honest mistakes should be corrected by counseling and positive discipline, not by punishment. These should be corrected in a way that will help the employee learn from the mistakes and become a more proficient and valuable worker.

In light of recent incidences of violence in the workplace, supervisors need to be proactive in establishing boundaries, identifying problems, counseling employees, and taking corrective actions. Violent behaviors at work are not random acts. These types of behaviors are caused by a series of events that occur over time and that come to a head. In most cases, coworkers and supervisors were aware that it was just a matter of time before the person "snapped." First-line supervisors are the key to preventing workplace violence. How they choose to deal with issues and handle employees can have an impact.[18]

The Supervisor's Disciplinary Role

One of the primary duties of present-day supervisors is to maintain discipline. Top managers expect—and depend on—their supervisors not only to set disciplinary limits but also to enforce them. Only then does an organization operate effectively.

To achieve this goal, supervisors must instill a desire for self-discipline in employees. If employees are not required to face up to the realities of their jobs, their goals, their resources, and their potential, they are in a poor position to function properly and make their best contribution to the organization. It's surprising how quickly organizational problems melt away when interpersonal forthrightness is applied.

When applying discipline, a supervisor must consider these points:

1. Every job should carry with it a certain margin for error.
2. Being overly concerned with avoiding errors stifles initiative and encourages employees to postpone decisions or avoid making them altogether.
3. A different way of doing something should not be mistaken for the wrong way of doing it.

Supervisors are more likely than higher-level managers to avoid administering severe disciplinary action because of the likelihood of generating undesirable effects. Other managers, including some personnel managers, take a stronger—perhaps more punitive—position on matters of discipline. A possible explanation is that supervisory managers are inclined to give stronger consideration to individual circumstances and behavior than are top managers. Also, supervisors are somewhat reluctant to follow rules strictly for fear they'll lose the cooperation of their employees if they're too severe.

Principles of Effective Discipline: The Hot-Stove Rule

hot-stove rule

Compares a good disciplinary system to a hot stove.

Four important principles of effective discipline are discussed in this section. These principles are often referred to as the **hot-stove rule,** because they draw a comparison between touching a hot stove and experiencing discipline. Here are the four principles, as illustrated in Exhibit 15-5:

1. You know what will happen if you touch a hot stove (it carries a clear warning).
2. If you touch a hot stove, it burns you right away (it is immediate).
3. A hot stove always burns you if you touch it (it is consistent).
4. A hot stove doesn't care whom it burns (it is impersonal).

EXHIBIT 15-5
The Hot-Stove Rule

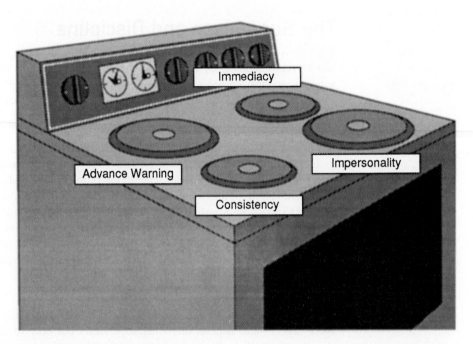

Source: Based on concepts in Theo Haimann and Raymond L. Hilgert, *Instructor's Manual-Supervision: Concepts and Practices of Management*, 6th ed. (Cincinnati: South-Western Publishing Co., 1995). Reprinted with permission of South-Western.

Discipline Carries a Clear Advance Warning Employees should know what is and what is not expected of them. This means that there must be clear warning that a given offense will lead to discipline, and there must be clear warning of the amount of discipline that will be imposed for an offense.

> *Supervisor C. D. Yates (name has been changed) had long ignored a safety rule that the employees wear short-sleeved shirts while operating their machines. In fact, for over a year, several employees had routinely worn long-sleeved shirts in the department. After learning of an injury in another department when an employee's long-sleeved shirt got caught in a conveyor belt, Yates immediately wrote up warnings to five employees in his department who were wearing long-sleeved shirts that day.*

Self–Check

If you were one of the five employees, would you consider Yates' action fair? Probably not. Since the safety rule was so openly ignored, it was the equivalent of no rule at all. For adequate warning to take place, Yates needed to communicate to his employees that, although the rule had been ignored in the past, it would now be enforced in the department. If you were an outside arbitrator, how would you rule? Why?

Discipline Is Immediate The supervisor should begin the disciplinary process as soon as possible after he or she notices a violation. This is important for several reasons:

1. An employee may feel that he or she is "putting one over" on the supervisor and may try to violate other rules.
2. An employee may assume that the supervisor is too weak to enforce the rules.

3. An employee may believe that the supervisor doesn't consider the rule important enough to be enforced. Thus, all the other employees may be encouraged to break or stretch the rule as well. It is not surprising to find an employee responding, "Well, I've been doing this for several days (or weeks) and nobody said anything about it to me before."

Discipline Is Consistent This principle means that for similar circumstances, similar discipline should be administered. If two people commit the same offense under the same circumstances, they should receive the same punishment.

> *Helen had a very high absenteeism record. Recently she missed work for two days without a legitimate excuse. Considering her past record, this offense would justify an immediate one-week suspension. However, her skills were badly needed by the supervisor, since the department was snowed under by a tremendous backlog of work. Helen was given only an oral warning.*

What will Helen's supervisor do when another worker misses work for two days without a legitimate excuse? If the supervisor is inconsistent, he or she will develop a reputation for playing favorites and losing credibility with employees. Does this mean a supervisor always has to dish out identical penalties for similar offenses? Note that we said the supervisor must be consistent as long as circumstances are similar. An employee's past record is a major factor to consider.

> *Two employees were caught drinking an alcoholic beverage on the job. The rules clearly prohibited this. For one employee, it was the first such offense; for the second worker, it was his third in the past year. Would the supervisor be justified in giving the second employee a more serious penalty than the first? You better believe it!*

Self-Check
What are the pros and cons of giving an employee a "break" regarding discipline?

Discipline Is Impersonal As a supervisor, you shouldn't get into personalities when administering discipline. You need to be as objective as possible. Moreover, after administering discipline to an employee, try to retain a normal relationship with that person. Two common mistakes supervisors make in imposing discipline are apologizing to employees and bawling out employees. Discipline the act, not the person. Your focus should be *on getting the employee's work behavior consistent with the rules.*

Applying Discipline
Two of the more unpleasant aspects of the supervisor's job are (1) laying off a worker for disciplinary reasons and (2) discharging an unsatisfactory employee.

Disciplinary Layoff If an employee has repeatedly committed major offenses and previous warnings have been ineffective, a **disciplinary layoff,** or **suspension,** is probably inevitable. Such a layoff involves a loss of time—and pay—for several days. This form of discipline usually comes as a rude shock to workers. It gets their attention! And generally it impresses on them the need to comply with the organization's rules.

Because this form of discipline is quite serious and involves a substantial penalty—loss of pay—most organizations limit the power to use it to managers who have attained at least the second level of management; often the human resources manager is involved as well. Yet supervisors have the right to recommend such action.

Not all managers believe the layoff is effective, and some seldom apply it as a disciplinary measure. First, they may need the worker to continue production. Second, they

disciplinary layoff *or* suspension

Time off without pay.

Photodisc/Jupiter Images

A supervisor may find it necessary to utilize a disciplinary layoff or suspension as means of redirecting an employee's behavior.

may feel that the worker will return with an even more negative attitude. Still, when properly used, it is an effective disciplinary tool.

termination-at-will rule

Right of an employer to dismiss an employee for any reason.

Discharge In 1884, a Tennessee court established the **termination-at-will rule,** whereby an employer could dismiss an employee for any reason—or even for no reason at all—unless there was an explicit contractual provision preventing such action.[19] The reasoning behind this decision was that if an employee can quit work for any reason, then the employer should be able to discharge for any reason.

Subsequent legislative enactments and court decisions, as well as union rules and public policy, have swung the pendulum of protection away from the employer and toward the employee by limiting the termination-at-will rule.[20] Most union agreements have a clause requiring "just cause" for disciplinary discharge and detailing the order in which employees can be laid off. EEO/AA regulations do essentially the same.

In general, court decisions suggest that the safest (legal) grounds for discharge include incompetent performance that does not respond to training or accommodation, gross or repeated insubordination, excessive unexcused absences, repeated and unexcused tardiness, verbal abuse of others, physical violence, falsification of records, drunkenness or drug abuse on the job, and theft.

Since discharge is so severe, supervisors can only recommend it. The discharge must be carried out by top management—usually with the advice and consent of the human resources manager.

Unions are quite involved in discipline when they represent the employees. Even many nonunionized organizations now follow the union's disciplinary procedure.

Supervisors' Personal Liability for Disciplining Employees

Recent court decisions holding supervisors personally liable for discharging disabled employees are making some supervisors reluctant to exercise their judgment in hiring, promoting, and firing employees. They are unwilling to take the punitive action indicated for unsatisfactory actions of employees if their personal assets, such as their houses or cars, can become subject to steep jury awards.

Supervisors have been held individually liable in some blatant and serious sex and race harassment cases.

Chapter Review

1. **Explain who is responsible for selecting, appraising, and disciplining employees.**

   This chapter has presented ways to select, appraise, and discipline employees. In general, the human resource department is responsible for overall planning, recruiting, and handling the details of staffing. The role of supervisors is to requisition needed workers, interview applicants, orient new employees, and appraise and discipline current employees.

2. **Describe the steps in the employee selection procedure, including the proper orientation of new employees.**

   The procedure for selecting employees for specific jobs includes (1) a requisition from the supervisor, (2) a preliminary screening-out of the obvious misfits, (3) the applicant's completion of an application form, (4) preemployment tests, (5) various interviews by the supervisor and human resource officer, (6) checking records and references, (7) a preliminary selection by the supervisor, (8) physical exam, if legal, and (9) a job offer. If the offer is accepted, the new employee is given a job orientation by the supervisor.

3. **Explain what employee performance appraisal is and who performs it.**

   An employee's performance is always being appraised, either formally or informally. The purpose of formal performance appraisals, however, is to compare employee performance to a standard or ideal—a sort of personnel quality control. Appraisal is more critical for employees whose output cannot be easily measured. Specific reasons for appraising employee performance are to provide a basis for some administrative action (such as a pay increase, promotion, transfer, layoff, discharge, or recommendation for training or development), to justify these actions for EEO/AA purposes, and to improve supervisor-employee relationships. Performance appraisals can be done by employees rating themselves, by employees rating supervisors, or by employees rating one another, but the immediate supervisors should be ultimately responsible, since they are most familiar with their employees' work.

4. **State why performance-appraisal interviews are difficult for both the employee and the supervisor.**

   One of the jobs supervisors like least is conducting the appraisal interview, which is used to communicate the results of the appraisal to the concerned employee. A supervisor's reluctance to criticize employees may lead to appraisal inflation.

5. **Define discipline and explain why it is necessary.**

   Another important supervisory activity is applying discipline. Because discipline is necessary for supervisory success, higher-level managers expect supervisors to set and enforce disciplinary limits. The three types of discipline are (1) self-control, (2) conditions for orderly behavior, and (3) punishment. Employee discipline is a process of control, either internally or externally imposed. As such, it is a method of maintaining management's authority—authority that is necessary to keep an organization operating effectively.

6. **Describe how discipline is imposed under due process.**

Although the right to discipline is still management's responsibility, today supervisors must be sure they follow due process, which requires (1) stated rules, (2) specific penalties, and (3) an orderly procedure for assessing guilt and punishment. The rules usually classify offenses as (1) minor infractions, (2) major violations, or (3) intolerable offenses. Penalties can include (1) oral warnings, (2) oral warnings with a written record, (3) written reprimands, (4) suspension, and (5) discharge. Usually a graduated scale of penalties is imposed, in which the penalty increases with the frequency and severity of violations.

7. **Explain the supervisor's disciplinary role.**

To be effective, discipline must be enforced. The manner of enforcement, in turn, affects the morale of the organization. One of the most difficult supervisory tasks is to strike an acceptable balance between severity and leniency in administering discipline. Four principles of effective discipline, collectively referred to as the "hot-stove rule," are that discipline should (1) carry a clear warning, (2) be immediate, (3) be consistent, and (4) be impersonal.

When lesser forms of discipline imposed by the supervisor are ineffective, it may be necessary to resort to layoff or discharge of the employee. Usually such action is carried out only by higher levels of management. In any case, it is important to be sure that due process has been observed and that there is just cause for such action.

Key Terms

IQ tests, p. 455

aptitude tests, p. 455

vocational interest tests, p. 455

personality tests, p. 455

achievement, proficiency, or skill tests, p. 455

work sampling or work preview, p. 456

validity, p. 456

reliability, p. 456

structured interviews, p. 456

orientation, p. 458

performance appraisal, p. 459

merit rating, efficiency rating, service rating, and employee evaluation, p. 459

appraisal interview, p. 461

discipline, p. 463

due process, p. 463

progressive discipline, p. 463

graduated scale of penalties, p. 464

intolerable offenses, p. 464

hot-stove rule, p. 465

disciplinary layoff, or suspension, p. 467

termination-at-will rule, p. 468

Questions for Review & Discussion

1. What is performance appraisal, and what are some of the other names for it?
2. Explain why performance appraisal is such an important part of the management process.
3. What are some of the purposes of performance appraisal? Explain.
4. Name and explain the steps in the suggested procedure for selecting workers for specific jobs.
5. What is discipline?

6. Why is discipline so important in organizations?
7. What is the due process of discipline, and why is it so important?
8. What is the union's role in the disciplinary process?
9. Why should disciplinary layoff and discharge decisions be restricted to higher levels of management?

Resources

Skill Builder 15-1

What Would You Do?

Three people have applied to you for an opening as a lathe operator. One is totally unqualified. One is experienced, but has a very poor attitude. The third lacks experience, but seems especially eager for the job; you think she would be a good worker if she had more experience, but you're not sure.

You have some rush work that you need to get out. Which of the following courses would you choose?

1. If the eager applicant has good references, hire her for a probationary period. But keep looking for a more qualified person in case she doesn't work out.
2. Pass up the three applicants. Keep looking.
3. Hire the experienced person, ignoring his attitude—you've got work to get out!

Information

Skill Builder 15-2

What Do You Want from Your Job?

Rank the employment factors in the following chart in order of their importance to you at three points in your career. In the first column, assume that you are about to graduate and are looking for your first full-time job. In the second column, assume that you have been gainfully employed for 5 to 10 years and are presently working for a reputable firm at the prevailing salary for the type of job and industry in which you work. In the third column, try to assume that 25 to 30 years from now you have found your niche in life and have been working for a reputable employer for several years. (Rank your first choice as "1," second as "2," and so forth, through "9.")

(Continued)

Resources

EMPLOYMENT FACTOR	YOUR RANKING		
	AS YOU SEEK YOUR FIRST FULL-TIME JOB	5–10 YEARS LATER	15–20 YEARS LATER
Employee benefits	_____	_____	_____
Fair adjustment of grievances	_____	_____	_____
Good job instruction and training	_____	_____	_____
Effective job supervision by your supervisor	_____	_____	_____
Promotion possibilities	_____	_____	_____
Job safety	_____	_____	_____
Job security (no threat of being dismissed or laid off)	_____	_____	_____
Good salary	_____	_____	_____
Good working conditions (nice office surroundings, good hours, and so on)	_____	_____	_____

Answer the following questions:

1. What does your ranking tell you about your motivation now?
2. Is there any change in the second and third periods?
3. What changes are there, and why did you make them?

Source: Donald Mosley, Paul H. Pietri, and Leon Megginson, *Management: Leadership in Action*, 5th ed., p. 386. Copyright 1996, Addison Wesley Longman, Inc. Reprinted by permission of Addison Wesley Longman.

Resources

Information

Skill Builder 15-3

Gloria Rogers Appraises Her Employees
Review the example of how Gloria Rogers conducts her performance appraisal interviews. Notice that they are "conducted according to the rules of good performance appraisal interviewing."

Instructions: Assume that you are Gloria's supervisor (manager). How would you advise her to improve her performance appraisals?

CASE 15-1

When the Transfer Backfires

Jane Smith abruptly rose and stormed out of the office of Robert Trent, the director of purchasing at a major eastern university. As she made her hasty exit, Trent began to wonder what had gone wrong with a seemingly perfect play—one that would have rid his department of a "problem" employee. How could his well-constructed plan, using the university's formal transfer system, have failed so miserably, leaving him with an even more unmanageable situation?

It had all begun in January, when Trent decided that something must be done about Smith's performance and attitude. The process was made a little more awkward by the university's not having a formal employee performance-appraisal policy and program. Each department was left with the right to develop and conduct its own employee appraisals. This meant that each department could choose whether or not to appraise an employee, as well as choose the format and procedure to be used.

In January, Trent decided to conduct an appraisal of Smith. After writing down some weaknesses in her performance and attitude, he called her in to discuss them. He cited the various weaknesses to her, but, admittedly, most were highly subjective in nature. In only a few instances did he give specific and objective references, and he did not give Smith a copy of his findings. During the appraisal interview, he even hinted that possibly she didn't "fit in" and that she "probably would be much happier in some other place." In any event, he was satisfied that he had begun the process for eventually ridding the department of her. He reasoned that, if all else failed, this pressure would ultimately force her to quit. At the time, he hardly noticed that she was strangely quiet through the whole meeting.

As time went by, Smith's attitude and performance did not improve. In March, Trent was elated to learn that an opening existed in another department and that Smith was most interested in transferring. The university's formal transfer policy required that Trent complete the Employee Transfer Evaluation Form—which he gladly did. As a matter of fact, he rated Smith mostly "outstanding" on the performance and attitude factors. He was so pleased at having the opportunity to use the transfer system that he called the other department manager and spoke glowingly of Smith's abilities and performance. Although he had been the purchas-

ing director for only eight months, having been recruited from another college, he even pointed with pride to Smith's five years of experience.

In April, much to Trent's dismay, it was announced that Smith had lost the transfer opportunity to a better qualified candidate. Robert Trent was shocked when Smith's transfer was turned down. To further complicate matters, Trent realized that he would have to face Smith in May when it would be time to discuss annual pay raises, which would include both merit pay considerations and a cost-of-living adjustment. This would be even more difficult because Smith's performance and attitude had not improved since the January appraisal. If anything, they were worse.

Trent had just finished the May meeting with Smith by telling her the bad news: Based on both performance and attitude, she should not be recommended for a cost-of-living or merit-pay increase for the new year beginning July 1. Smith, armed with the transfer evaluation forms (completed and given to her in March), threatened to use all internal and external systems for organizational justice due her.

As Trent pondered this dilemma, he fully recognized Smith's unique status within the university community. She was the wife of a distinguished, tenured professor of business, and this situation provided additional pressure. As if this were not enough, he had to contend with the office social process pivoting around a weekly coffee group that was greatly influenced by Smith. It was not unusual for the former director of purchasing (who had retired after 25 years of service) to attend these gatherings. Of course, Smith had kept this group fully apprised of her continuing troubles with "this new, young purchasing director who is hardly dry behind the ears."

Answer the following Questions

1. What are the facts Trent must consider now?
2. What avenues are now open to Trent? What does this case say to you about the need for supervisors to act morally?
3. Do you believe that some supervisors are untruthful where recommendations are concerned? Explain.
4. What three functions are salaries meant to perform?
5. To what extent should employee appraisals be used in salary adjustments? Explain.

Source: Prepared by M. T. Bledsoe, Associate Professor of Business, Meredith College, Raleigh, North Carolina.

Endnotes

Chapter 1

1. Interview with Jackie Schultz by Paul Pietri, May 28, 2009; "Panera Bread Beefs Up Menu to Boost Profit," Investor's Business Daily, April 22, 2998, p B03; "Panera Bread Managers Harvest Key Sales Data Via Intranet to Support Internal Marketing Goals," Nation's Restaurant News, November 3, 2008, p 12; "Not by Bread Alone," Fortune, June 10, 2006, p 126.

2. Andrea Priestland and Robert Hanig, "Developing First-Level Leaders," Harvard Business Review 83, June 2005, p. 112.

3. Gene A. Brewer, "In the Eye of the Storm: Frontline Supervisors and Federal Agency Performance," Journal of Public Administration Research and Theory, 15:4, October 2005, p. 519.

4. For more information about team leaders' roles in self-directed teams, see Peter R. Scholtes, Brian L. Joiner, and Barbara J. Streibel, The Team Handbook, 3rd ed. (Madison, WI: Oriel, Inc., 2003), Chapter 2, pp. 2–3.

5. Henry Mintzberg, "The Manager's Job: Folklore and Fact," Harvard Business Review, July-August 1975, pp. 489–561.

6. Pamela S. Lewis, Stephen H. Goodman, Patricia M. Fandt, and Joseph F. Mitshlisch, Management (Mason, OH: Thomson/South Western, 2007), p. 334.

7. See Rene Cordero, George F. Farris, and Nancy DiThomasco, IEEE Transactions of Engineering Management 51, February 2004, pp. 19–30. The authors studied over 2,000 technical professionals and found that for them to have a "stimulating" work environment, it was more important for their supervisors to possess people and administrative skills rather than technical skills. As the authors stated, "This appears a reversal from the traditional assumption that technical skills are the most important qualifications for promoting technical professionals into supervision."

8. Tiziano Casciaro, Migues Sousa, and Mark Lobo, "Competent Jerks, Lovable Fools, and the Formation of Social Networks," Harvard Business Review 83, June 2005, pp. 92–100.

9. Janice Klein and Pamela Posey, "Good Supervisors Are Good Supervisors—Anywhere," Harvard Business Review 64, November-December 1986, pp. 125–128.

10. Bureau of Labor Statistics. Table 10: Civilian Labor Force by Age, Sex, Race, and Hispanic Origin: 1996–2006–2016. http://www.bls.gov/news.release/ecopro.t10.htm.

11. Ibid.

12. See Ruth B. Lett, "Organizational Citizenship Behavior of Temporary Knowledge Workers," Organization Studies (29) , June 2008, pp. 849–866; Bureau of Labor Statistics. TED: The Editor's Desk: "Job Losses in Temporary Help Services," April, 2009. http://www.bls.gov/opub/ted/2009/apr/wk2/art02.htm.

13. James W. Dean and James R. Evans, Total Quality, 2nd ed. (Cincinnati, OH: South-Western College Publishing, 2000), p. 13.

14. Bruce Drake, Mark Meckler, and Debra Stevens, "Traditional

Ethics: Responsibilities of Supervisors for Supporting Employee Development," Journal of Business Ethics, June 2, 2002, pp. 141–155.

15. Nancy Hatch Woodward, "Lessons Learned from the Gulf Coast Can Help You Manage Employee Communication in the Aftermath of the Unthinkable," HR Magazine 50, December 2005, pp. 52–57.

Chapter 2

1. http://www.waterkeeper.org/ht/d/sp/i/181/pid/181 (retrieved 6/29/09).

2. http://www.waterkeeper.org (retrieved 6/29/09).

3. http://www.waterkeeper.org (retrieved 6/29/09).

4. http://www.waterkeeper.org (retrieved 6/29/09).

5. Consulting and conversations with Casi Callaway with MBK, by Don C. Mosley, Jr., 2004–2006.

6. Interview with Casi Callaway of MBK by Don C. Mosley, Jr., July 1, 2009.

7. Interviews with Chris Browning, Jennifer Fidler, James Gillespie, Dan McCrory, and Steve Seay by Don C. Mosley, Jr., May 2006.

8. Gene Marino, "Contingency Planning Essentials," Industrial Engineer, July 2003, p. 24.

9. Eileen Sullivan, "FEMA Tricks Out New Trailers for Next Disaster," http://abcnews.go.com/Politics/wireStory?id=7586106 (retrieved 8/18/09).

10. Interviews with Chris Browning, Jennifer Fidler, James Gillespie, Dan McCrory, and Steve Seay by Don C. Mosley, Jr., May 2006.

11. U.S. Pharmacist. http://www.uspharmacist.com/content/t/technology/c/10397/ (retrieved 6/29/09).

Chapter 3

1. Steven Levy, "Facebook Grows Up," Newsweek, August 27, 2007, pp. 40–46.

2. Ibid.

3. Facebook Factsheet, http://www.facebook.com/press/info.php?factsheet (retrieved 7/11/09); Steven Bertoni and Erin Gell, "By the Numbers: Billionaire Bachelors," http://www.forbes.com/2008/09/16/billionaire-bachelors-single-lists-cx_mm_0916bachelor_slide_11.html?thisSpeed=30000 (retrieved 7/11/09); Ellen McGirtTue, "Facebook's Mark Zuckerberg: Hacker. Dropout. CEO." http://www.fastcompany.com/magazine/115/open_features-hacker-dropout-ceo.html (retrieved 7/11/09); Steven Levy, "Facebook Grows Up," Newsweek, August 27, 2007, pp. 40–46.

4. Ellen McGirtTue, "Facebook's Mark Zuckerberg: Hacker. Dropout. CEO." http://www.fastcompany.com/magazine/115/open_features-hacker-dropout-ceo.html (retrieved 7/11/09).

5. Steven Bertoni and Erin Gell, "By the Numbers: Billionaire Bachelors," http://www.forbes.com/2008/09/16/billionaire-bachelors-single-lists-cx_mm_0916bachelor_slide_11.html?thisSpeed=30000 (retrieved 7/11/09).

6. Ibid.; Steven Levy, "Facebook Grows Up," Newsweek, August 27, 2007, pp. 40–46; Ellen McGirtTue, "Facebook's Mark Zuckerberg: Hacker. Dropout. CEO." http://www.fastcompany.

com/magazine/115/open_features-hacker-dropout-ceo.html (retrieved 7/11/09); Facebook Factsheet, http://www.facebook.com/press/info.php?factsheet (retrieved 7/11/09).

7. Ellen McGirtTue, "Facebook's Mark Zuckerberg: Hacker. Dropout. CEO." http://www.fastcompany.com/magazine/115/open_features-hacker-dropout-ceo.html (retrieved 7/11/09).

8. I. B. Myers and M. H. MCaulley, Manual: A Guide to the Development and Use of the Myers-Briggs Type Indicator (Palo Alto, CA: Consulting Psychologists Press, 1990).

9. V. H. Broom and A. H. Jago, The New Leadership: Managing Participation in Organizations (Englewood Cliffs, NJ: Prentice Hall, 1988).

10. T. L. Stanley, "Ethical Decision Making in Tough Times," Supervision 70.3, March 2009, p. 3. Academic OneFile. Gale.: University of South Alabama (AVL). 7 July 2009.

11. See Mortimer R. Feinberg and Aaron L. Wenstein, "How Do You Know When to Rely on Your Intuition?" The Wall Street Journal, June 21, 1982, p. 16.

12. Prepared by Julia Allen, from various sources, including "Persons of the Year," Time, December 30, 2002/January 6, 2003, pp. 30–31.

13. Ethisphere, "2008 World's Most Ethical Companies," http://ethisphere.com/wme2008/ (retrieved 7/9/09).

14. Marc Orlitzky, Frank L. Schmidt, and Sara L. Rynes, "Corporate Social and Financial Performance: A Meta-Analysis,"

Organization Studies 24, March 2003, pp. 403–441.

15. Andrew Caffrey, "FBI Takes Up Heavy Load of Corporate Fraud Probes," Boston Globe, May 6, 2003, p. Al.

16. Ethisphere, "2008 World's Most Ethical Companies," http://ethisphere.com/wme2008/ (retrieved 7/9/09).

17. Ibid.

18. Ibid.

19. Ibid.

Chapter 4

1. Microsoft Press Pass, http://www.microsoft.com/presspass/exec/leadership/default.aspx; The Microsoft Blog, http://blog.seattlepi.com/microsoft/archives/160111.asp; Microsoft's Business, http://www.microsoft.com/about/companyinformation/ourbusinesses/business.mspx (retrieved 7/12/09).

2. Peter Drucker, "The Coming of the New Organization," Harvard Business Review 76, January-February 1988, pp. 45–53.

3. Richard L. Bunning, "The Dynamics of Downsizing," Personnel Journal 69, September 1990, p. 69.

4. Phillip R. Nienstedt, "Effective Downsizing Management Structures," Human Resources Planning 12, 1989, p. 156.

5. Bunning, "The Dynamics of Downsizing," Personnel Journal 69, September 1990, p. 70.

6. Ronald Henkoff, "Getting Beyond Downsizing," Fortune, January 10, 1994, p. 58.

7. Wayne F. Cascio, "Downsizing: What Do We Know? What Have We Learned?" Academy of Management Executive 2(1), February 1993, p. 95.

8. This section adapted from Michael Hammer and James Champy, Reengineering the Corporation (New York: Harper Business, 1993).

9. Ibid., p. 31.

10. Ibid., p. 32.

11. Frank Ostroff, The Horizontal Organization (New York: Oxford University Press, 1999), pp. 22–24.

12. Bloomberg.com, http://www.bloomberg.com/apps/news?pid=newsarchive&sid=a54WN3jQ6TEs; Nordstrom 2008 Annual Report, https://materials.proxyvote.com/Approved/655664/20090311/AR_38144/HTML2/nordstrom-ar2008_0002.htm (retrieved 7/12/09).

13. Nancy K. Austin, "Reorganizing the Organization Chart," Working Woman, September 1993, p. 24.

14. Interviews and discussions with Vernon Mason, Assistant Manager with Family Dollar, by Don C. Mosley, Jr., June and July 2009.

15. Rensis Likert, New Patterns of Management (New York: McGraw-Hill, 1961); Rensis Likert, The Human Organization (New York: McGraw-Hill, 1967).

16. George Benson "Why the Ritz Is the Ritz," Georgia Trend 15, August 2000, p. 99.

17. Excerpts from handout from the Ritz-Carlton, Island of Maui, Hawaii; Edwin McDowell, "Ritz-Carlton Keys to Good Service," New York Times, March 31, 1993, pp. C1–C3; Portrait: The Ritz-Carlton Hotel Company; interviews and discussions with Lenny Litz, General Manager, and staff of Ritz-Carlton, Maui; discussion with Sue Musselman,

assistant to the Vice President of Quality, Ritz-Carlton Hotel Company, Atlanta, GA; and Mark Memmot, by Donald C. Mosley, Sr., June 1994; "The Quality Quest," USA Today, June 28, 1993, p. 2B.

Chapter 5

1. Peter M. Senge, The Fifth Discipline: The Art and Practice of the Learning Organization (New York: Doubleday, 1990), p. 4.

2. With Carl Moore, currently Dean of the Mitchell College of Business, the University of South Alabama.

3. Interview with Dan Burns by Donald C. Mosley, Sr., Summer, 1988.

4. Interview with Larry Bonine by Donald C. Mosley, Sr., Partnering News, Arizona Department of Transportation, Summer, 1993.

5. Interview with Larry Bonine by Donald C. Mosley, Sr., June 2003.

6. Chester Barnard, The Functions of the Executive (Cambridge, MA: Harvard University Press, 1938).

7. Personal experience as related to one of the authors.

8. Personal experience as related to one of the authors.

9. J.R.P. French, Jr., and Bertram Raven, "The Bases of Social Power," Studies in Social Power, ed. D. Cartwright (Ann Arbor, MI: Institute for Social Research, 1959).

10. Excerpts from Polly Labarre, "The Agenda—Grassroots Leadership," Fast Company Magazine 23, April 1999, p. 114.

11. Jeffrey Pfeffer, Robert B. Cialdini, Benjamin Hanna, and

Kathleen Knopoff, "Faith in Supervision and the Self-Enhancement Bias: Two Psychological Reasons Why Managers Don't Empower Workers," Basic and Applied Social Psychology 20, 1998, pp. 313–321.

12. Gary Yuki and Ping Ping Fu, "Determinants of Delegation and Consultation by Managers," Journal of Organizational Behavior 20, 1999, pp. 219–212.

13. J. Richard Hackman and Greg Oldham, "Development of the Job Diagnostic Survey," Journal of Applied Psychology 60, 1975, pp. 159–170.

14. Ronald A. Heifetz, Leadership Without Easy Answers (Cambridge, MA: Belknap Press of Harvard University Press, 1994).

15. Ronald A. Heifetz and Donald L. Laurie, "The Work of Leadership," Harvard Business Review, January-February 1997, p. 124.

16. Partnering: The Central Artery/ Tunnel Manual (Boston: Massachusetts Highway Department, 1993), p. 2.

17. Stephen E. Amrose, Eisenhower, Soldier and President (New York: Simon and Schuster, 1990), pp. 39–40.

18. Stephen E. Ambrose, Soldier, General of the Army, President-Elect, 1890–1952 (New York: Simon and Schuster, 1983), p. 77.

19. Ibid., p. 78.

20. Ibid., p. 79.

21. Sidney Finkelstein, "7 Habits of Spectacularly Unsuccessful Executives," Fast Company, July 2003, pp. 86–89.

22. Ibid., p. 86.

Chapter 6

1. Interview with Bob Greim by Paul Pietri, July 9, 2009.

2. Richard L. Daft, Management, 7th ed. (Mason, OH: Thomson/ South-Western, 2004), pp. 328–329.

3. Interview with Amanda Phillips by Paul Pietri, May 18, 2006.

4. Don Hellriegel and John W. Slocum, Jr., Organizational Behavior, 11th ed. (Mason, OH: Thomson/South-Western, 2007), p. 339.

5. "Ten Killer Job Search Mistakes," National Business Employment Weekly, Winter-Spring 1995, p. 5.

6. "'Why Am I Here?' Cosmic Question Gets Frequently Asked at Work," Training 43, April 2006, p. 13.

7. Yvonne Brunetto and Rod Farr-Wharton, "Importance of Effective Organizational Relationships for Nurses: A Social Capital Perspective," International Journal of Human Resource Development 6, July 18, 2006, pp. 232–236.

8. One recent study showed the circumstances in which high-disclosing supervisors are especially valued by team members. Employees whose jobs involve working with people outside the organization in unstructured, often ambiguous circumstances and who were physically remotely located from their supervisor (such as salespeople, customer service workers, etc.) rated as "most supportive" those supervisors considered to be "high disclosers." See Mark C. Johite and Dale F. Dohan, "Supervisory Communication Practice and Boundary Spanner Role Ambiguity," Journal of Managerial Issues 13, Spring 2001, pp. 87–103.

9. See Lisa A. Burke and Jessica M. Wise, "The Effective Care, Handling, and Pruning of the Office Grapevine," Business Horizons 71, May/June 2003, pp. 71–76.

10. Jeff Forest, "The Space Shuttle Challenger Disaster," http:// www.dssresources.com/cases/ spaceshuttlechallenger/index. html; also Paul Singer, "Brown's Flood of Criticism," National Journal 38, March 3, 2006, pp. 2–5.

11. Margery Weinstein, "Extreme Makeover: Training Edition," Training 46, March 2009; p. 20; Charlotte Huff, "Powering Up a Hispanic Workforce," Workforce Management 88, May 2009, pp. 25–29.

12. "Language Barriers in Firefighting: Rising Number of Hispanics Fight Western Wildfires," The South Bend Tribune, August 31, 2003, A6.

13. Mark Hinrichs, "Como Se Dice? Break Down the Language Barrier Between You and Your Employees," Entrepreneur 33, December 2005, pp. 113–114.

14. Donald Fishman, "ValueJet Flt 592: Crisis Communication Theory Blended and Extended," Communication Quarterly 47, Fall 1999, pp. 345–356.

15. Eric Eisenbert and H. Lloyd Goodall, Jr., Organizational Communication, 4th ed. (Boston: Beford/St Martin's, 2004), p. 261.

16. Deborah Tannen, "Language, Sex, and Power: Women and Men in the Workplace," Training and Development, September 1997, pp. 34–40.

17. Edward Wong, "A Stinging Office Memo Boomerangs," New York Times, April 5, 2001, p. C1.
18. Stephen R. Covey, The Seven Habits of Highly Effective People (New York: Simon and Schuster, 1990), pp. 34–40.
19. Mary Ellen Guffey, Business Communication: Process and Product, 6th ed. (Mason, OH: South-Western Cengage Learning, 2008), p. 50.

Chapter 7

1. Holly Dolzeak, "Sick Day or Just Sick and Tired," Training 42, December 2005, p. 8.
2. Matthew Boyle, "Motivating without Money," Business Week Online, April 27, 2009, p. 18; Gerald H. Siejts and Dan Crim, "What Engages Workers the Most or the Ten Cs of Employee Engagement," Ivey Business Journal (online), March-April 2006, pp. 1–5.
3. "Motivation: A Management Challenge," Training and Development, November 2006, p. 17.
4. Saul W. Gellerman, Motivation and Productivity (New York: American Management Association, 1963), pp. 20–22; Daniel A. Wren, The Evolution of Management Thought (New York: Ronald Press Co., 1972), pp. 275–281.
5. Jennifer M. George and Gareth R. Jones, Organizational Behavior, 3rd ed. (Upper Saddle River, NJ: Prentice-Hall, 2002), p. 182.
6. Reported in Thomas J. Peters and Robert Waterman, In Search of Excellence: Lessons from America's Best Run Companies (New York: Harper and Row, 1982), p. xxi.
7. Gareth R. Jones and Jennifer M. George, Contemporary Management, 3rd ed. (New York: McGraw-Hill, 2003), p. 411.
8. "Talk about Job Security: Clune," Crain's Chicago Business 32, March 2, 2009, p. 21; Clune Construction Company, http://www.clunegc.com/overview.html.
9. William A. Cohen, The Art of the Leader (Englewood Cliffs, NJ: Prentice-Hall, 1990), pp. 18–19.
10. See Jody G. Hoffer, The Southwest Airlines Way (New York: McGraw-Hill, 2005); "Train to Retain," Incentive, September 12, 2007.
11. See Frederick Herzberg, "One More Time: How Do You Motivate Employees?" Harvard Business Review 81, January 2003, pp. 41–47.
12. "Enjoyment is the Top Motivator," Personnel Today, April 8, 2003, p. 55.
13. See Michael Byrne, "The Implications of Herzberg's Motivation-Hygiene Theory for Management in the Irish Health Care Sector," The Health Care Manager 25, January-March, 2006, pp. 4–12.
14. Stephanie Armour, "Cash or Critiques: Which Is Best?" USA Today, December 16, 1998, p. 6b.
15. Fred Luthans, Organizational Behavior, 7th ed. (New York: McGraw Hill, 1995), p. 156.
16. Bob Nelson, "Making the Job Meaningful Down the Line," Business Week, May 1, 2006, p. 60.
17. E. A. Locke and G.P. Latham, A Theory of Goal Setting and Task Performance (Englewood Cliffs, NJ: Prentice-Hall, 1990).
18. M. Sixel, "Driven by Boss' Challenge," Houston Chronicle, May 20, 2006.
19. Condensed from Peters and Waterman, In Search of Excellence, p. 68.
20. Samantha Oller, American Printer, October 1, 2002.
21. Kevin McManus, "A Simple Thank You," Industrial Engineer 37, February 2005, p. 19.
22. As cited in Alan Zaremba, Organizational Communication (Mason, OH: South-Western, 2003), p. 34.
23. J. R. Hackman and G. R. Oldham, "Motivation through the Design of Work: Test of a Theory," Organizational Behavior and Human Performance, August 1976, pp. 250–279; Jennifer M. George and Gareth R. Jones, Organizational Behavior, 4th ed. (Upper Saddle River, NJ: Pearson Prentice-Hall, 2005), pp. 208–214.
24. Example adapted from Chuck Williams, Management, 4th ed. (Mason, OH: Thomson/South-Western , 2007), p. 287.
25. Susan Eisner, "Managing Generation Y," SAM Advanced Management Journal 70, August 2005, p. 4.
26. "Six Steps to Guaranteeing Generation Y Productivity," Supervision 68, July 2007, pp. 6–8.
27. Lynn Curry, "Managing the Gen X/Y Employee," Alaska Business Monthly 19, November 2003, p. 31.
28. Glenn Bakers, "The Young Ones: So You Want to Attract More Young Talent to Your Business, But Don't Know How? You Need to Understand a Generation before You Can Successfully Recruit and Manage It," NZ Business 20, April 2006, pp. 24–30.
29. Dave Hotler, "21st Century Management and the Quest

for Excellence," Supervision 63, October 2002, pp. 3–7.

Chapter 8

1. Jimmy John's, http://www.jimmyjohns.com.
2. Ibid.
3. Interview with Jimmy Burckhartt by Don C. Mosley, Jr., July 2009.
4. Ibid.
5. Douglas McGregor, The Human Side of Enterprise (New York: McGraw-Hill Book Co., 1960), pp. 33–42.
6. Notes from Workshop on Process Consultation conducted by Edgar Schein, Albert Einstein Institute, Cape Cod, August 1991.
7. Interview with Jimmy Burckhartt by Don C. Mosley, Jr., July 2009.
8. Interview with Dr. Paul Hersey, Trainer's Bookshelf (San Diego, CA: Learning Resources Corporation, 1982).
9. Robert R. Blake and Jane S. Mouton, The Managerial Grid III: The Key to Leadership Excellence (Houston, TX: Gulf Publishing, 1985).
10. Paul Hersey and Kenneth H. Blanchard, Management of Organizational Behavior: Utilizing Human Resources, 3rd ed. (Englewood Cliffs, NJ: Prentice-Hall, 1977), pp. 161–162.
11. Hersey and Blanchard acknowledge that they were strongly influenced by William J. Reddins, "3-D Management Style Theory," found in William J. Reddins, Management Effectiveness (New York: McGraw-Hill, 1970). We use Hersey and Blanchard's model because it is better known.
12. Robert Tannenbaum and Warren Schmidt, "How to Choose a Leadership Pattern," Harvard Business Review 51, May–June 1973, pp. 162–180.
13. Leonard M. Apcar, "Middle Managers and Supervisors Resist Moves to More Participatory Management," The Wall Street Journal, September 16, 1985, p. 25.
14. David L. Bradford and Allen R. Cohen, Managing for Excellence (New York: John Wiley & Sons, 1984), pp. 71–98.
15. Interviews with Dale Roberts and Jimmy Burckhartt by Don C. Mosley, Jr., July 2009.
16. John MacGregor Burns, Leadership (New York: Harper and Row, 1978).
17. Bernard Bass, Leadership and Performance beyond Expectations (New York: The Free Press, 1985).
18. B. M. Bass, B. J. Avolio, and L. Goodheim, "Biography and the Assessment of Transformational Leadership at the World Class Level," Journal of Management 13, Spring 1987, p. 7.
19. Ibid., p. 16.
20. George R. McAleer, "Leadership in the Military Environment," Association for Psychological Type, Special Topic Symposium, Type and Leadership, Crystal City, VA, March 5–7, 1993.
21. Ronald A. Heifetz, Leadership Without Easy Answers (Cambridge, MA: Belknap Press of Harvard University Press, 1994); Martin Linsky and Ronald A. Heifetz, Leadership on the Line: Staying Alive through the Dangers of Leading (Cambridge, MA: Belknap Press of Harvard University Press, 2002); Ronald A. Heifetz, Martin Linsky, and Alexander Grashow, The Practice of Adaptive Leadership: Tools and Practices for Changing Your Organization and the World (Cambridge, MA: Belknap Press of Harvard University Press, 2009).
22. Loren Gary, "Thought Leadership; Ronald Heifetz—The Challenge of Adaptive Leadership," New Zealand Management, August 1, 2005. http://findarticles.com/p/articles/mi_qn5305/is_20050801/ai_n24914910/?tag=content;col1 (retrieved 7/25/09).
23. Interview with Amanda Kohn by Don C. Mosley, Jr., July 2009.
24. Loren Gary, "Thought Leadership; Ronald Heifetz—The Challenge of Adaptive Leadership," New Zealand Management, August 1, 2005. http://findarticles.com/p/articles/mi_qn5305/is_20050801/ai_n24914910/?tag=content;col1 (retrieved 7/25/09).
25. Bennett J. Sims, Servanthood—Leadership for the Third Millennium (Boston: Cowley Publications, 1997).
26. Operation Sagebrush, Fall 1955, experienced by Donald C. Mosley, Sr.
27. Robert K. Greenleaf, Servant Leadership (Mahwah, NJ: Paulist Press, 1991), p. 3.
28. Ibid., p. 21.
29. William D. Hitt, "The Model Leader: A Fully Functioning Person," Leadership and Organization Development Journal 14(7), December 1993, p. 10.
30. Interview with Bill Donaldson, hospital middle-level manager, by Donald C. Mosley, Sr., Cape Cod Institute's Leadership Course, July 1–4, 2003.
31. Kenneth Cloke and Joan Goldsmith, The End of

Management and the Rise of Organizational Democracy (San Francisco: Jossey-Bass/John Wiley & Sons, 2002), p.179.

32. Interview with Maureen McNamara by Donald C. Mosley, Sr., Cape Cod Institute's Leadership Course, July 1–4, 2003.

33. Interviews with Dale Roberts, Amanda Kohn, and Jimmy Burckhartt by Don C. Mosley, Jr., July 2009.

34. Daniel Goleman, "What Makes a Leader?" Harvard Business Review, November-December 1998, pp. 93–94.

35. J. D. Mayer and P. Salovey, "What is emotional intelligence?" P. Salovey and D. Sluyter, eds., Emotional Development and Emotional Intelligence: Implications for Educators (New York: Basic Books, 1997), pp. 3–31.

36. Emotional Intelligence Information, "The Four Branch Model of Emotional Intelligence," Durham, NH: University of New Hampshire. http://www.unh.edu/emotional_intelligence/ei%20What%20is%20EI/ei%20fourbranch.htm (retrieved 7/31/09).

37. Ibid.

38. Doris Kearns Goodwin, "The Master of the Game," Time, July 4, 2005, pp. 48–54.

39. Doris Kearns Goodwin, Team of Rivals; the Political Genius of Abraham Lincoln (New York: Simon and Schuster, 2005).

40. Richard E. Boyatzis and Ellen van Oosten, "A Leadership Imperative: Building the Emotionally Intelligent Organization," Ivey Business Journal, January/February 2003, pp. 1–5.

41. Ibid., p. 2.

42. Ibid., p. 5.

Chapter 9

1. Family Dollar History, http://familydollar.com/history.aspx (retrieved 8/1/09).

2. Fortune 500, http://money.cnn.com/magazines/fortune/fortune 500/2008/full_list/ (retrieved 8/1/09); Family Dollar Investors, http://familydollar.com/investors.aspx (retrieved 8/1/09).

3. Interviews with Margaret Gibson and Vernon Mason by Don C. Mosley, Jr., July 2009.

4. B. W. Tuckman, "Developmental Sequence in Small Groups," Psychological Bulletin, May 1965, pp. 384–399.

5. See, for example, F. Steven Heinen and Eugene Jacobson, "A Model of Task Group Development in Complex Organizations and Strategy of Implementation," Academy of Management Review 1, October 1976, pp. 98–111.

6. Don Hellreigel, John W. Slocum, Jr., and Richard Woodman, Organizational Behavior, 5th ed. (Mason, OH: South-Western Publishing, 1989), p. 210.

7. R. Bruce McAfee and Paul J. Champage, Organizational Behavior: A Manager's View (Mason, OH: South-Western Publishing, 1987), p. 250.

8. Don Hellreigel and John W. Slocum, Jr., Management (Reading, MA: Addison-Wesley, 1986), pp. 539–542.

9. W. Allen Randolph, Understanding and Managing Organizational Behavior (Homewood, IL: Richard D. Irwin, 1985), p. 399.

10. William C. Dyer, Team Building: Issues and Alternatives (Reading, MA: Addison-Wesley, 1977), p. 4.

11. Don Hellriegel and John W. Slocum, Jr., Management, 7th ed. (Mason, OH: South-Western, 1995), p. 52.

12. Observation of team meeting by Donald C. Mosley, Sr., and discussion with Matt Callan after the meeting on October 27, 2005.

13. Interviews with Resort Quest members by Donald C. Mosley, Sr., October 2005.

14. Penelope McClenny, "Cancer Fighters Join Hands," Mobile Press-Register, July 27, 2006, pp. 1A, 4A.

15. Interviews with doctors and staff at the Providence Hospital and Sacred Heart Hospital Cancer Center by Donald C. Mosley, Sr., June-October 2005.

16. Charles C. Manz and Henry P. Sims, Jr., "Superleadership: Leading Others to Lead Themselves to Excellence," in Jan L. Pierce and John W. Newstrom, eds., The Manager's Bookshelf (New York: Harper & Row, 1988), p. 328.

17. Interviews with Mike Odom, Kay Montgomery, and others, by Donald C. Mosley, Sr., November 2002.

18. About SEI, http://www.seic.com/enUS/about.htm (retrieved 8/3/09).

19. Google Finance, http://www.google.com/finance?q=NASDAQ:SEIC (retrieved 8/3/09).

20. Alfred West, Jr., and Yoram Wind, "Putting the Organization on Wheels: Workplace Design at SEI," California Management Review 49(2), Winter 2007, pp. 138–153.

Chapter 10

1. Kitty Locker and Stephen Kyo Kaczamarek, Business Communication, 3rd ed. (New York: McGraw-Hill/Irwin, 2007), p. 323.
2. Interview with Chris Sholler by Don C. Mosley, Jr., July and August 2009.
3. Daniel L. Plung and Tracy Montgomery, Professional Communication: The Corporate Insider's Approach (Mason, OH: South-Western, 2004), p. 237.
4. Ibid.
5. Daniel McGinn, "Mired in Meetings," Newsweek, October 16, 2000, p. 152.
6. Ibid.
7. Heera Singh, "Ensuring Effective Meetings," Asia African Intelligence Wire, November 12, 2005.
8. Alan Zaremba, Organizational Communication (Mason, OH: South-Western, 2003), p. 142.
9. Zaremba, Organizational Communication, p. 199.
10. Daniel McGinn, "Mired in Meetings," Newsweek, October 16, 2000, p. 152.
11. Ibid.
12. Cited in Robyn D. Clarke, "Whipping Up a Great Meeting," Black Enterprise 31, December 2000, p. 82.
13. John V. Thill and Courtland I. Bovee, "Chapter NaN: Communicating in Teams; Collaboration, Listening, Nonverbal, and Meeting Skills," in Excellence in Business Communication, 5th ed. (Upper Saddle River, NJ: Prentice-Hall, 2002), p. 29.
14. Edgar H. Schein, Process Consultation, vol. 1, 2nd ed. (Reading, MA: Addison-Wesley, 1988), p. 6.
15. Ibid., p. 9.
16. Client evaluation feedback to the Synergistic Group, Mobile, Alabama.
17. Journal of Extension, http://www.joe.org/joe/2006april/tt5.php (retrieved 8/22/09).

Chapter 11

1. JoAnn Greco, "Hey Coach," Journal of Business Strategy 22(2), March 2001, p. 28.
2. Kathleen Kingsbury, "New Shrink Gig: Executive Coach," Time, February 13, 2006, Bonus Section, p. A17.3.
3. D. T. Hall, K. L. Otrazo, and G. P. Hollenbeck, "Behind Closed Doors: What Really Happens in Executive Coaching," Organizational Dynamics 27(3), 1999.
4. Dennis Kinlaw, Coaching for Commitment (San Diego, CA: Pfeiffer & Co., l993), p. 19.
5. David L. Bradford and Allan R. Cohen, Managing for Excellence (New York: John Wiley & Sons, 1984), pp. 62–63.
6. Sukhant Bal, "Staff Motivation: Holding Deeper Conversation Can Help Drive Motivation," Personnel Today.Com, July 22, 2008.
7. "Use these 10 Tips to Brush Up Your Coaching Skills," Pay for Performance Report, January 2002, p. 10
8. Julie Barker, "Too Good to Ignore: Getting More Out of Top Producers: That's Right, 'A' Players Need Coaching, Too," Sales and Marketing Management 157, March 2005, pp. 38–41.
9. K. R. Phillips, "The Achilles Heel of Coaching," Training and Development 52(3), March 1998, pp. 41–46.
10. Dennis C. Kinlaw, Coaching Skills Inventory (San Diego, CA: Pfeiffer & Co., 1993), pp. 1–13.
11. David Bicknell, "Keep It Personal and Keep Your Staff," Computer Weekly, July 8, 1999, p. 2.
12. See Marcus Buckingham, "What Great Managers Do," Harvard Business Review 83, March 2005, pp. 70–79.
13. Tip Fallon, "Retain and Motivate the Next Generation: 7 Ways to Get the Most Out of Your Millennial Workers," Supervision 70, May 2009, pp. 5–7.
14. Thomas Gordon, Leader Effectiveness Training (New York: Wyden Books, 1977), pp. 92–107.
15. George Bohlander and Scott George, Managing Human Resources, 15th ed. (Mason, OH: South-Western Cengage Learning, 2010), p. 551.
16. Steve Davold, "Comcast Employees Tune into Employee Assistance Programs," Employee Benefit News 20, April 2006, pp. 57–59.
17. Jim Stafford, "Employee Assistance Program Helps in Worker Retention," Daily Oklahoman (Oklahoma City, OK), March 27, 2007.
18. "Small Companies Fuel Rising Use of EAPs," HR Magazine 24, September 2007, p. 1.
19. "It's Your Problem Too," Business Week 3670, February 29, 2000, p. 26.

Chapter 12

1. Roger Fisher and William Ury, Getting to Yes (New York: Penquin, 1993), pp. 3–4.
2. Kathryn Tyler, "Extending the Olive Branch: Conflict Resolution Training Helps Employees and Managers Defuse

Skirmishes," HR Magazine, November 2002, p. 47.

3. Ibid.

4. A. P. Brief, R. S. Schuler, and M. W. Sell, Managing Job Stress (Boston: Little, Brown, & Co., 1981), p. 2.

5. "The Road to Happiness," Psychology Today 27(4), July-August 1994, p. 34.

6. Claudia Wallis, "Stress: Can We Cope?" Time, June 6, 1983, p. 52.

7. W. W. Suoganen and Donald R. Hudson, "Coping with Stress and Addictive Work Behavior," Business (Atlanta, GA: College of Business Administration, Georgia State University,) 31, January-February 1980, p. 11.

8. Robert T. Golembiewski and Robert F. Munzenrider, Phases of Burnout (New York: Praeger, 1988), p. 220.

9. M. Hovanesian, "Zen and the Art of Corporate Productivity," BusinessWeek, July 28, 2003 (retrieved 8/22/09 from Academic Search Premier database).

Chapter 13

1. "Pentagon Travel Costs," USA Today, March 28, 1995, p. 4A.

2. Andres Kaplan, "Mission Control: Systems for Monitoring Beverage Production Can Keep Lines Running as Smoothly as Possible, While Trimming Excess Costs at the Same Time," Beverage World 122, July 15, 2003.

3. Marc Gunther, "Marriott Gets a Wake-Up Call," Fortune, July 6, 2009, pp. 62–66.

4. Myron Magnet, "Who's Winning the Information Revolution," Fortune, November 30, 1992, pp. 110–111.

5. Simon Head, "Big Brother in a Black Box," Civilization, August/September 1999, pp. 52–55.

Chapter 14

1. Tim Kelly, "The Robots Are Coming," Forbes Global, September 4, 2006, vol. 2, p. 120; John Teresko, "Robots Revolution," Industry Week 251, September 2002, pp. 24–28.

2. N. Shirouzi, "Why Toyota Wins Such High Marks on Quality Surveys," The Wall Street Journal, March 15, 2001, p. A1.

3. Machingo Nakamoto, "Battery Trouble Hinders Sony Bid for Global Brand Supremacy," The Financial Times, August 26, 2006, p. 19.

4. James W. Robinson and Jack Welch, Leadership (Roseville, CA: Prima Publishing Co., 2001), pp. 129–130.

5. James R. Evans and William Lindsay, The Management and Control of Quality, 5th ed. (Mason, OH: South-Western, 2002), pp. 604–605.

6. Deanne N. Den Hartog and Robert M. Verburg, "Service Excellence from the Employees' Point of View: The Role of First Line Supervisors," Managing Service Quality 3, 2000, pp. 159–164.

7. Quoted in Evans and Lindsay, The Management and Control of Quality, p. 301.

8. Malcolm Baldrige National Quality Award Profile, http://www.nist.gov/public_affairs/releases/ssmhealth.htm (retrieved 11/22/02).

9. Philip Seikman, "Glass Act: How a Window Maker Rebuilt Itself; Not Waiting for Perfect Answers, Pella Conducted Thousands of Kaisen or Continuous Improvement Sessions," Fortune 142(11), November 13, 2000, p. 384.

10. Bureau of Labor Statistics, "Industries with at Least 100,000 Non-Fatal Occupational Injuries and Illnesses, 2004," http://www.bls.gov/iif/oshwc/osh/os/osbl0015.pdf.

11. "National Safety Council Lauds UPS Safety Program," U.S. Newswire, June 24, 2002, p. 1008175.

Chapter 15

1. Interview with Bryan Seibt by Don C. Mosley, Jr., October, 2006.

2. "Taking Advantage," WGN TV station (Chicago, IL), February 19, 1984.

3. Stephanie Armour, "Employers: Enough Already with the e-Résumés," USA Today, July 15, 1999, p. IB.

4. "Drug Testing: The Things People Will Say," American Salesman, March 2001, pp. 20–24.

5. See "Adoption by Four Agencies of Uniform Guidelines on Employee Selection Procedures (1978)," Federal Register 43, August 1978, pp. 290–315.

6. "Labor Report," The Wall Street Journal, February 23, 1993, p. Al.

7. Julia Lawlor, "Disabilities No Longer a Job Barrier," USA Today, June 22, 1993, pp. 1A and IB.

8. Michael A. Verespej, "How Will You Know Whom To Hire? No More Questions about Medical History," Industry Week, September 17, 1990, p. 70.

9. Robert Cyr, "Seven Steps to Better Performance Appraisals," Training and Development 47, January 1993, pp. 18–19.

10. Ren Nardoni, "Corporatewide Management Staffing," Personnel Journal 69, April 1990, pp. 52–58.

11. Kenneth M. Golden, "Dealing with the Problem Managers," Personnel 66, August 1989, pp. 54–59.

12. Mary Mavis, "Painless Performance Evaluations," Training and Development 48, October 1994, pp. 40–44.

13. Douglas McGregor, "An Uneasy Look at Performance Appraisals," Harvard Business Review 35, May-June 1957, p. 90.

14. L. Stockford and W. H. Bissell, "Factors Involved in Establishing a Merit Rating Scale," Personnel 26, September 1949, p. 97.

15. H. H. Meyer and W. B. Walker, "A Study of Factors Relating to the Effectiveness of a Performance Appraisal Program," Personnel Psychology 14, August 1961, pp. 291–298.

16. For further details, see Irwin H. McMaster, "Universal Aspects of Discipline," Supervision 36, April 1974, p. 19.

17. M. Michael Markowich, "A Positive Approach to Discipline," Personnel 66, August 1989, pp. 60–65.

18. Jennifer Gatewood, "Attacking Violence: Former Hostage Negotiator Warns Workplace Violence Won't Go Away until Managers Take an Aggressive Approach," Risk & Insurance, March 14, 2003.

19. Payne v. Western & A.R.P. Co., 81 Term, 507 (1884).

20. S. A. Youngblood and G. L. Tidwel, "Termination-at-Will: Some Changes in the Wind," Personnel 58, May-June 1981, p. 24.

Chapter 16

1. Mary-Kathryn Zachary, "Labor Law for Supervisors, Discrimination without Intent," Supervision 70(4), 2009, pp. 23–26; http://web.ebscohost.com/ehost/detail?vid=6&hid=9&sid=eb956c64-c50c-48c3-ba25-cf166908d011%40sessionmgr4&bdata=JmxvZ2lucGFnZT1Mb2dpbi5hc3Amc2l0ZT1laG9zdC1saXZlJnNjb3BlPXNpdGU%3d#db=buh&AN=37000093 (retrieved 9/9/09).

2. Ibid.

3. "Are Unions Striking Out?" U. S. News and World Report, June 12, 1995, p. 26.

4. "Unions on the Ropes," USA Today, June 14, 1995, p. 12A.

5. Leon C. Megginson, Mary Jane Byrd, and William L. Megginson, Small Business Management: An Entrepreneur's Guidebook (New York: McGraw Hill/Irwin, 2003), p. 290.

6. Ibid.

7. Joseph P. Cangemi, et al., "Differences between Pro-Union and Pro-Company Employees," Personnel Journal 55, September 1976, pp. 451–453.

8. Philip Ash, "The Parties to the Grievance," Personnel Psychology 23, Spring 1970, pp. 13–37.

9. NIOSH Safety and Health Topic, Occupational Violence, http://www.cdc.gov/niosh/topics/violence/ (retrieved 10/18/06).

10. Tony Mauro, "Sex Bias Ruling Is 'Mixed,'" USA Today, June 23, 1999, p. 3A.

11. Equal Employment Opportunity Commission, Guidelines on Discrimination Because of Sex, 29 C.F.R., Section 1064.11, July 1, 1992.

12. Equal Employment Opportunity Commission Enforcement Statistics, http://www.eeoc.gov/stats/harass.html.

13. Equal Employment Opportunity Commission, "Rampant Sex Harassment Costs Lowe's 1.7 Million in Settlement of EEOC Lawuit," http://www.eeoc.gov/press/8-21-09.html.

14. George Ming, "All the Points of Comparable Worth," Personnel Journal 69, November 1990, p. 99.

Glossary

acceptance theory of authority A manager's authority originates only when it has been accepted by the group or individual over whom it is being exercised.

accountability The obligation that is created when an employee accepts the leader's delegation of authority.

achievement, proficiency, or skill tests Measure the applicant's knowledge of and ability to do a given job.

acknowledging Showing by non-evaluative verbal responses that you have listened to what the employee has stated.

active listening A listening technique for understanding others and encouraging open feedback.

adaptive leadership Organizational members take a hard look at the past to identify what to hold on to, while deciding what needs to go. Employee participation in the change process is the key.

administrative skills Establishing and following procedures to process paperwork in an orderly manner.

advisory authority Authority of most staff departments to serve and advise line departments.

affirmative action programs (AAPs) Programs to put the principle of equal employment opportunity into practice.

affirming Communicating to an employee his or her value, strengths, and contributions.

agency shop All employees must pay union dues even if they choose not to join the union.

agreement or contract Prepared when an accord has been reached to bind the company, union, and workers to specific clauses in it.

alternatives Possible courses of action that can satisfy a need or solve a problem.

appraisal interview Supervisor communicates the results of a performance appraisal to an employee.

aptitude tests Predict how a person might perform on a given job.

arbitrator Will make a binding decision when collective bargaining reaches an impasse.

attending Showing through non-verbal behavior that you are listening in an open, nonjudgmental manner.

authority compliance The leader has a high concern for production results and uses a directive approach.

authority Given the right to act in a specified manner in order to reach organizational objectives; the right to tell others how to act to reach objectives.

Baby Boomers Workforce generation born between 1945 and 1964.

body signals Nonverbal signals communicated by body action.

brainstorming Freely thinking of ideas without evaluating the ideas as they are generated.

budget A forecast of expected financial performance over time.

burnout A malady caused by excessive stress in the setting where people invest most of their time and energy.

cause-and-effect diagram A graphical display of a chain of causes and effects.

channel   The means used to pass a message.

closed shop   All prospective employees must be members of the recognized union before they can be employed.

closure   Successfully accomplishing the objective for a given item on the agenda.

coaching and selling style   Used with individuals or groups that have potential but haven't realized it fully.

coaching   Helping individuals reach their highest levels of performance.

collective bargaining   Conferring in good faith over wages, hours, and other terms and conditions of employment.

communication process model   Model of the five components of communication and their relationships.

comparable worth or pay equity   Jobs with equal points for the amount of education, effort, skills, and responsibility have equal pay.

computer-assisted manufacturing (CAM)   Special computers assist equipment in performing processes.

conceptual skills   Mental ability to become aware of and identify relationships among different pieces of information.

concurrent controls   Sometimes called screening controls, these controls are used while an activity is taking place.

confirming   Ensuring an employee understands what has been said or agreed upon.

confronting/challenging   Establishing clear performance standards, comparing actual performance against those standards, and addressing performance that doesn't meet those standards.

consensus   The acceptance by all members of the decision reached.

contingency planning   Thinking in advance about possible problems or changes that might arise and having anticipated solutions available.

continuum of leadership behavior   The full range of leadership behaviors in terms of the relationship between a supervisor's use of authority and employees' freedom.

control chart   Displays the "state of control" of a process.

controlling   Comparing actual performance with planned action and taking corrective action if needed.

cost leadership strategy   Attempts to lower costs below competitors by focusing on creating efficiencies within organizational systems.

cost/benefit analysis   Estimating and comparing the costs and benefits of alternatives.

counseling   Helping an individual recognize, talk about, and solve either real or perceived problems that affect performance.

country club management   High concern for people.

craft unions   Workers in a specific skill, craft, or trade.

Crawford Slip technique   Makes use of two elements that are important in achieving creativity—fluency and flexibility.

creativity   Creativity is the process of developing something unique or original.

critical path   The series of activities in a PERT network that comprise the longest route, in terms of time, to complete the job.

decentralization   The extent to which authority is delegated from one unit of the organization to another.

decision making   Considering and selecting a course of action from among alternatives.

delegating style   Used with exceptionally ready and capable individuals and groups.

delegation of authority   The process by which leaders distribute and entrust activities and related authority to other people in an organization. The three key aspects of organization are (1) granting authority, (2) assigning duties and responsibilities, (3) requiring accountability.

Deming's 85–15 rule   Assumes that when things go wrong, 85 percent of the time the cause is from elements controlled by management.

departmentalization   The organizational process of determining how activities are to be grouped.

developmental leadership   An approach that helps groups to evolve effectively and to achieve highly supportive, open, creative, committed, high-performing membership.

differentiation strategy   Used by managers to gain a competitive advantage through goods and/or services that are clearly unique or different from the competition.

disciplinary layoff *or* suspension   Time off without pay.

discipline   Training that corrects and molds knowledge, attitudes, and behavior.

dissatisfier or hygiene factors
Factors that employees said most affected them negatively or dissatisfied them about their job, including low pay, low benefits, and unfavorable working conditions.

diversity Refers to the wide range of distinguishing employee characteristics, such as sex, age, race, ethnic origin, and other factors.

downsizing Eliminating unnecessary levels of management; striving to become leaner and more efficient by reducing the workforce and consolidating departments and work groups.

downward communication
Flows that originate with supervisors and are passed down to employees.

due process Guarantees the individual accused of violating an established rule a hearing to determine the extent of guilt.

e-mail Refers to messages and documents created, transmitted, and read entirely on computer.

ego or esteem need The need for self-confidence, independence, appreciation, and status.

emotional intelligence (EI) The capacity to recognize and accurately perceive one's own and others' emotions, to understand the significance of these emotions, and to influence one's actions based on this analysis; an assortment of skills and characteristics that influence a person's ability to succeed as a leader.

Employee Assistance Programs (EAPs) Professional counseling and other services for employees with unresolved personal or work-related problems.

employee associations Organizations that function as labor unions.

employees' bill of rights Protects employees from possible abuse by unscrupulous managers and union leaders.

empowerment Granting employees authority to make key decisions within their enlarged areas of responsibility.

equity theory Theory that when people perceive themselves in situations of inequity or unfairness, they are motivated to act in ways to change their circumstances.

ethical dilemmas Situations in which the supervisor is not certain of the correct behavior.

ethical organizations Organizations composed of three pillars: ethical individuals, ethical leaders, and sound structures and systems.

ethics Are the standards used to judge the "rightness" or the "wrongness" of one person's behavior toward others.

exclusive bargaining agent Deals exclusively with management over questions of wages, hours, and other terms and conditions of employment.

exempt employees Employees not covered by the provisions of the Fair Labor Standards Act.

expectancy theory Views an individual's motivation as a conscious effort involving the expectancy that a reward will be given for a good result.

experience rating Determining, from the record of unemployed workers, the amount the employer must pay into the state's unemployment insurance fund.

experiential learning Using an integrated process of experiencing, identifying, analyzing, and generalizing to gain insights in learning.

external change forces Forces outside the organization that have a great impact on organizational change. Management has little control over these numerous external forces.

extrinsic motivation Behavior performed not for its own sake, but for the consequences associated with it. The consequences can include pay, benefits, job security, and working conditions.

facial signals Nonverbal messages sent by facial expression.

fact-finding meeting Held to seek out relevant facts about a problem or situation.

feedback controls Controls that measure completed activities and then take corrective action if needed.

feedback The response that a communicator receives.

feedforward controls Preventive controls that try to anticipate problems and take corrective action before they occur.

financial resources The money, capital, and credit an organization requires for operations.

financing Providing or using funds to produce and distribute an organization's product or service.

flexibility The ability to use free association to generate or classify ideas in categories.

flowchart Visual representation of the sequence of steps needed to complete a process.

fluency The ability to let ideas flow out of your head like water over a waterfall.

formal group Group prescribed and/or established by the organization.

formal theory of authority Authority exists because someone was granted it.

functional authority A staff person's limited line authority over a given function.

functional departmentalization A form of departmentalization that groups together common functions or similar activities to form an organizational unit.

Gantt chart Identifies work stages and scheduled completion dates.

Generation Xers Workforce generation born between 1965 and 1980.

Generation Yers Youngest workforce generation, born since 1981.

glass ceiling Invisible barrier that limits women from advancing in an organization.

goal-setting theory Theory that task goals, properly set and managed, can be an important employee motivator.

graduated scale of penalties Penalties become progressively more severe each time the violation is repeated.

grapevine Informal flow of communication in organizations.

grievance procedure A formal way of handling employees' complaints.

group cohesiveness The mutual liking and team feeling in a group.

group facilitation The process of intervening to help a group improve in goal setting, action planning, problem solving, conflict management, and decision making in order to increase the group's effectiveness.

group-centered approach Used at meetings in which group members interact freely and address and question one another.

group Two or more people who communicate and work together regularly in pursuit of one or more common objectives.

heroic managers Managers who have a great need for control or influence and who want to run things.

hierarchy of needs Arrangement of people's needs in a hierarchy, or ranking, of importance.

hierarchy of objectives A network with broad goals at the top level of the organization and narrower goals for individual divisions, departments, or employees.

histogram Graphical representation of thevariation found in aset of data.

hot-stove rule Compares a good disciplinary system to a hot stove.

human relations skills Understanding other people and interacting effectively.

human resources The people an organization requires for operations.

"I" message Attempt to change an employee's behavior by indicating the specific behavior, how it makes you feel as a supervisor, and the effect of the behavior.

impoverished management Management with little concern for people or production.

industrial unions Unions composed of all the workers in an industry.

informal communication Separate from a formal, established communication system.

informal group A group that evolves out of the formal organization but is not formed by management or shown in the organization's structure.

information exchange meeting Held to obtain information from group members.

information richness Amount of verbal and nonverbal information that a channel carries.

information-giving meeting Held to announce new programs and policies or to update present ones.

instant message (IM) Use of intranet or Internet technology that allows people to receive messages in real time.

intangible standards Relate to human characteristics and are not expressed in terms of numbers, money, physical qualities, or time.

integration process A conflict resolution strategy in which everyone wins.

internal change forces Pressures for change within the organization such as cultures and objectives.

intolerable offenses Disciplinary problems of a drastic, dangerous, or illegal nature.

intrinsic motivation Behavior that an individual produces because of the pleasant experiences associated with the behavior itself.

inverted pyramid A structure widest at the top and narrowing as it funnels down.

IQ tests Measure the applicant's capacity to learn, solve problems, and understand relationships.

job characteristics model Approach to job design that focuses on five core job elements that lead to intrinsic motivation and then positive work outcomes.

job descriptions Provide information to employees about the important job-related tasks.

just-in-time (JIT) inventory control Materials arrive when they are needed in the production process.

labor relations or union–management relations or industrial relations The relationship between an employer and unionized employees.

labor union An organization of workers banded together to achieve economic goals.

lateral–diagonal communication Flows between individuals in the same department or different departments.

leader-controlled approach Used at meetings of large groups in which the leader clearly runs the show and the open flow of information is impeded.

Leadership Grid Categorizes leadership styles according to concern for people and concern for production results.

leadership Influencing individual and group activities toward goal achievement.

leading Guiding, influencing, and motivating employees in the performance of their duties and responsibilities.

life event Anything that causes a person to deviate from normal functioning.

life-cycle theory of leadership Leadership behaviors should be based on the readiness level of employees.

line authority Power to directly command or exact performance from others.

line organization An organization concerned with the primary functions of the firm—in this case, production, sales, and finance.

line personnel Carry out the primary activities of a business.

line-and-staff organization An organization structure in which staff positions are added to serve the basic line departments and help them accomplish the organization objectives more effectively.

lockout A closing of a company's premises to the employees and refusing to let them work.

maintenance-of-membership clause An employee who has joined the union must maintain that membership as a condition of employment.

management by exception A supervisor focuses on critical control needs and allows employees to handle most routine deviations from the standard.

management Working with people to achieve objectives by effective decision making and coordinating available resources.

managerial functions Broad classification of activities that all managers perform.

marketing Selling and distributing an organization's product or service.

matrix departmentalization A hybrid type of departmentalization in which personnel from several specialties are brought together to complete limited-life tasks.

mediator Tries to bring the parties together when collective bargaining has reached an impasse.

mentor An experienced manager who acts as an advocate and teacher for a younger, less experienced manager.

mentoring Helping others develop careers.

messages Words and/or nonverbal expressions that transmit meaning.

middle management Responsible for a substantial part of the organization.

middle-of-the-road management Places equal emphasis on people and production.

minutes A written record of the important points discussed and agreed on at a meeting.

mission Defines the purpose the organization serves and identifies its services, products, and customers.

monetary standards Expressed in dollars and cents.

motivation Willingness to work to achieve the organization's objectives.

Myers-Briggs Type Indicator® (MBTI®) Helps identify an individual's personal style related to decision-making and problem solving.

network structure Sometimes referred to as a modular structure; includes a central business unit, or "hub," that is linked to a network of external suppliers and contractors.

nominal grouping technique (NGT) A structured group technique for generating ideas through round-robin individual responses, group sharing without criticism, and written balloting.

nonexempt employees Employees covered by the provisions of the Fair Labor Standards Act.

norms Rules of behavior developed by group members to provide guidance for group activities.

numerical standards Expressed in numbers.

object signals Nonverbal messages sent by physical objects.

objectives The purposes, goals, and desired results for the organization and its parts.

operational planning Consists of intermediate- and short-term planning.

operations Producing an organization's product or service.

opportunity A chance for development or advancement.

organization A group of people working together in a structured situation for a common objective.

organizational effectiveness The result of activities that improve the organization's structure, technology, and people.

organizing Deciding what activities are needed to reach goals and dividing human resources into work groups to achieve them.

orientation Procedures of familiarizing a new employee with the company surroundings, policies, and job responsibilities.

OSHA federal Occupational Safety and Health Administration, created by the Occupational Safety and Health Act in 1970 to ensure safe working conditions for employees.

Pareto charts Problem-analysis charts that use a histogram to illustrate sources of problems.

participating and supporting style Best used with ready individuals or groups.

perception How one selects, organizes, and gives meaning to his or her world.

performance appraisal *or* **merit rating** *or* **efficiency rating** *or* **service rating** *or* **employee evaluation** Determines to what extent an employee is performing a job the way it was intended.

personality tests Measure the applicant's emotional adjustment and attitude.

physical resources Items an organization requires for operations.

physical standards Refer to quality, durability, size, and weight.

physiological or biological need The need for food, water, air, and other physical necessities.

picketing Walking back and forth outside the place of employment, usually carrying a sign.

pinpointing Providing specific, tangible information about performance to an employee.

planning Selecting future courses of action and deciding how to achieve the desired results.

policy Provides consistency among decision makers.

power the ability to influence individuals, groups, events, and decisions.

prevailing wage rate Approximates the union wage scale for the area in the given type of work.

principled negotiation Negotiation on the merits by separating the people from the problem, focusing on interests, not positions, generating a variety of possibilities before deciding what to do, and insisting that the result be based on some objective standard.

probe Directs attention to a particular aspect of the speaker's message.

probing Asking questions to obtain additional information.

problem-solving meeting Held to identify the problem, to discuss alternative solutions, and to decide on the proper action to take.

problem An existing unsatisfactory situation causing anxiety or distress.

procedure Steps to be performed when a particular course of action is taken.

process consultation A consultation model that involves others in making a joint diagnosis of the problem and eventually provides others with the skills and tools to make their own diagnoses.

product departmentalization A form of departmentalization that groups together all the functions associated with a single product line.

productivity Measure of efficiency (inputs to outputs).

Program Evaluation and Review Technique (PERT) Shows relationships among a network of activities to determine the completion time of a project.

program A large-scale plan composed of a mix of objectives, policies, rules, and projects.

programmed decisions Routine and repetitive decisions.

progressive discipline Discipline that uses a graduated scale of penalties.

project A distinct part of a program.

quality control Defined measurements designed to check

whether the desired quality standards are being met.

readiness level The state of a person's drive or need for achievement.

receiver The ultimate destination of the sender's message.

reengineering "It means starting over…. It means asking and answering this question: If I were creating this company today, given what I know and given current technology, what would it look like?"
Rethinking and redesigning processes to improve dramatically cost, quality, service, and speed.

reflecting Stating your interpretation of what the employee has said.

reflective statement The listener repeats, in a summarizing way, what the speaker has just said.

reframing Examining the situation from multiple vantage points to develop a holistic picture.

reinforcement theory Based on the law of effect, holds that behaviors that meet with pleasant consequences tend to be repeated, whereas behaviors that meet with unpleasant consequences tend not to be repeated, and rewards and punishments are used as a way to shape the individual.

reinventing Organizations dramatically changing such elements as their size, organizational structure, and markets.

relationship behaviors Providing people with support and asking for their opinions.

relationships network The major individuals and groups with whom the supervisor interacts.

reliability The probability that test results won't change if the test is given to the same person by different individuals.

resourcing Providing information, assistance, and advice to employees.

responsibility Occurs when key tasks associated with a particular job are specified.
The obligation of an employee to accept a manager's delegated authority.

reviewing Reinforcing key points at the end of a coaching session to ensure common understanding.

right-to-work laws Protects the right of employees to join or refuse to join a union without being fired.

risk The possibility of defeat, disadvantage, injury, or loss.

robot A machine that is controlled by a computer that can be programmed to perform a number of repetitive manipulations of tools or materials.

roles Parts played by managers in the performance of their functions.

rule A policy that is invariably enforced. Rules are inflexible requirements and are much stronger than guidelines. It is important for supervisors to know when they can be flexible in promoting the objectives of their company and when they have to enforce rules.

run chart Data presentation showing results of a process plotted over time.

safety or security need The need for protection from danger, threat, or deprivation.

satisfier or motivator factors Factors that employees said turned them on about their job, such as

recognition, advancement, achievement, challenging work, and being one's own boss.

scenario planning Anticipating alternative future situations and developing courses of action for each alternative.

schedule A plan of activities to be performed and their timing.

self-fulfillment or self-actualization need The need concerned with realizing one's potential, self-development, and creativity.

self-managing work teams Groups that tend to operate by member consensus rather than management direction.

sender Originates and sends a message.

seniority An employee's length of service in a company; provides the basis for promotion and other benefits.

servant leadership Defines success as giving and measures achievement by devotion to serving and leading. Winning becomes the creation of community through collaboration and team building.

sexual harassment Unwelcome sexual advances that create a hostile, offensive, or intimidating work environment.

single-use plans Developed to accomplish a specific purpose and then discarded after use.

Situational Leadership Model Shows the relationship between the readiness of followers and the leadership style.

social or belonging need The need for belonging, acceptance by colleagues, friendship, and love.

space signals Nonverbal messages sent based on physical distance between people.

span of control principle   States that there is a limit to the number of people a person can supervise effectively.

span of management   The number of immediate employees a manager can supervise effectively.

staff personnel   Have the expertise to assist line people and aid top management.

staffing   Recruiting, training, promoting, and rewarding people to do the organization's work.

standard   A unit of measurement that can serve as a reference point for evaluating results.

standing plans or repeat-use plans   Plans that are used repeatedly over a period of time.

stereotyping   The tendency to put similar things in the same categories to make them easier to deal with.

strategic control point   A performance measurement point located early in an activity to allow any corrective action to be taken.

strategic planning   Has longer time horizons, affects the entire organization, and deals with its interface to its external environment.

strategies   The activities by which the organization adapts to its environment to achieve its objectives.

stress   Any external stimulus that causes wear and tear on one's psychological or physical well-being.

strike   When employees withhold their services from an employer.

structured interviews   Standardized and controlled with regard to questions asked, sequence of questions, interpretation of replies, and weight given to factors considered in making the hiring decision.

structuring and telling style   Used with individuals or groups relatively less ready for a given task.

summarizing   Pausing in the coaching conversation to summarize key points.

supervisory management   Controls operations of smaller organizational units.

synergy   The whole is greater than the sum of the parts.

synergy   The concept that two or more people working together in a cooperative, coordinated way can accomplish more than the sum of their independent efforts.

tangible standards   Clear, concrete, specific, and generally measurable.

task behaviors   Clarifying a job, telling people what to do and how and when to do it, providing follow-up, and taking corrective action.

team advisors   Share responsibility with team for cost, quality, and prompt delivery of products.

team management   High concern for both people and production.

team structure   Utilizes permanent and temporary cross-functional teams to improve horizontal coordination and cooperation.

team   A collection of people who must rely on group cooperation.

technical skills   Understanding and being able to supervise effectively specific processes required.

termination-at-will rule   Right of an employer to dismiss an employee for any reason.

text message   A written message sent by cell phone that uses abbreviations.

Theory X   The average person has an inherent dislike of work and wishes to avoid responsibility.

Theory Y   Work is as natural as play or rest.

time management   Ability to use one's time to get things done when they should be done.

time signals   Nonverbal messages sent by time actions.

time standards   Expressed in terms of time.

top management   Responsible for the entire or a major segment of the organization.

total quality   Refers to an organization's overall effort to achieve customer satisfaction through continuous improvement of products or services.

touching signals   Nonverbal messages sent by body contact.

Toyota Production System   Toyota's philosophy and framework of organizing manufacturing facilities efficiently.

traditionalists   Workforce generation born before 1945.

transactional leadership   Leaders identify desired performance standards and recognize what types of rewards employees want from their work.

transformational leadership   Converts followers into leaders and may convert leaders into moral agents.

tutoring   Helping team members gain knowledge, skill, and competency.

Type A behavior   Behavior pattern characterized by (a) trying to accomplish too much in a short time and (b) lacking patience and struggling against time and other people to accomplish one's ends.

Type B behavior Behavior pattern characterized by (a) tending to be calmer than someone with Type A behavior, (b) devoting more time to exercise, and (c) being more realistic in estimating the time it takes to complete an assignment.

unfair labor practices Specific acts that management may not commit against the workers and the union.

unified planning Coordinating departments to ensure harmony rather than conflict or competition.

union authorization card Authorizes a particular union to be an employee's collective bargaining representative.

union shop All employees must join the union within a specified period.

union steward A union member elected by other members to represent their interests in relations with management.

unity of command principle States that everyone should report to and be accountable to only one boss.

unprogrammed decisions Decisions that occur infrequently and require a different response each time.

upward communication Communication that flows from lower to upper organizational levels.

validity A high positive correlation between the applicant's test

scores and some objective measure of job performance.

vocational interest tests Determine the applicant's areas of major work interest.

voice signals Signals sent by placing emphasis on certain words, pauses, or the tone of voice used.

Vroom-Yetton model Provides guidelines on the extent to which subordinates are involved in decision making or problem solving.

wagon wheel An organization form with a hub, a series of spokes radiating from the hub, and the outer rim.

work sampling or work preview A test in which the prospective employee must perform a task that is representative of the job.

Index

Acknowledgements

The content of this text has been adapted from the following product(s):

Case 1.15 - Travel Expenses: A Chance for Extra Income
ISBN-10: (1-426-64514-7)
ISBN-13: (978-1-426-64514-3)

Module 1 - Traveler Import Cars, Inc. - Buller/Schuler
ISBN-10: (0-324-38570-6)
ISBN-13: (978-0-324-38570-0)

Module 8 - Motor Parts Corporation - Buller/Schuler
ISBN-10: (0-324-61616-3)
ISBN-13: (978-0-324-61616-3)

Case 3.6 - Adelphia: Good Works via a Hand in the Till
ISBN-10: (1-426-64527-9)
ISBN-13: (978-1-426-64527-3)

Module 1 - The Marketing Campaign and ChemCorp - Buller/Schuler
ISBN-10: (0-324-38569-2)
ISBN-13: (978-0-324-38569-4)

Module 3 - Microsoft: Adapting to New Challenges
ISBN-10: (0-324-31474-4)
ISBN-13: (978-0-324-31474-8)

Module 6 - Propco, Inc.
ISBN-10: (0-324-31477-9)
ISBN-13: (978-0-324-31477-9)

Module 1 - Custom Chip, Inc. - Buller/Schuler
ISBN-10: (0-324-38567-6)
ISBN-13: (978-0-324-38567-0)

Module 4 - Conflict Management
ISBN-10: (0-324-31475-2)
ISBN-13: (978-0-324-31475-5)

Case 10.6 - Paul Wolfowitz and the World Bank
ISBN-10: (1-426-64627-5)
ISBN-13: (978-1-426-64627-0)

Table Of Contents

BULLER │ SCHULER   1

Managing Organizations and People

A Resource for Cases in Management, Organizational Behavior, and Human Resource Management

Abstract

The continued rapid growth of Microsoft Corporation has caused a variety of management, structural, and legal challenges for the company. In addition, changing technology, particularly the rise of the Internet, has caused Microsoft to transform its strategy and operations to remain competitive. This case describes how Microsoft has adapted to these challenges by developing an organization that can respond quickly in a dynamic environment.

Microsoft: Adapting to New Challenges

Between 1993 and 1997, Microsoft Corporation continued its historically dramatic growth. Revenue more than quadrupled from $2.75 billion in 1993 to $11.36 billion in 1997, reflecting a compounded annual growth rate over 43%. Net income likewise grew from $708 million to $3.45 billion over the same period.[1] Asset levels rose from $3.8 billion in 1993 to $14.4 billion in 1997, while the number of employees increased to approximately 25,000 worldwide. The company's continuing success in the development and marketing of operating system and personal productivity applications software drove most of this growth. Microsoft's MS/DOS and Windows 3.1 operating systems together with its MS Office Suite of personal productivity applications had commanding market shares in their respective segments.[2]

The rapid growth generated by Microsoft's success, however, began to create coordination, management and legal problems. Coordination problems surfaced in the form of delays in software rewrites and product introductions. Windows 95, for instance, was introduced over one year after the original rollout date.[3] Management of the company's various projects also grew more complex and unwieldy. In fact, between 1982 and 1992, Microsoft went through a series of presidents until Chairman William "Bill" Gates ultimately decided to create an Office of the President in which three senior executives would jointly hold the post.[4] Lastly, legal problems cropped up as government officials from the Antitrust Division of the U.S. Department of Justice began investigating whether or not Microsoft's dominant market position was an impediment to competition in certain segments of the computer software market. In fact, in mid-1995, the Justice Department successfully blocked Microsoft from pursuing its planned acquisition of rival software maker

Intuit on the grounds that such an action would consolidate too much market power and consequently reduce market competition within the product segment.[5]

In response to these challenges, Gates introduced a number of incremental structural and organizational changes. The coordination problems were partially addressed by continued enhancement of the company's internal communication capabilities. Microsoft used a number of formal and informal methods for facilitating information flows such as frequent project team meetings, internal newsletters, and prodigious E-mail usage. As noted above, on the dismissal of company President Michael Hallman, Gates created the Office of the President to be shared by the three chief operating heads: Michael Maples, who headed the applications systems business; Steve Ballmer, who headed the operating systems business; and Francis Gaudette, Microsoft's chief financial officer.[6] In May of 1995, this group was augmented by Pete Higgins, head of desktop applications, and Nathan Myhrvold, head of advanced technology.[7] By creating the senior committee, Gates freed himself from supervising daily operations in order to focus on broader strategic concerns. Lastly, in terms of the antitrust issues, Microsoft retreated from the proposed merger with Intuit.[8]

Further structural adjustments were made as the three divisions under Maples, Higgins, and Myhrvold were reorganized into two groups. Maples would continue to oversee the Platforms Group, while Higgins and Myhrvold would jointly run the Applications and Content Group. Microsoft's other two divisions were the Sales and Support Group, which continued to manage customer relationships, and the Operations Group, which supervised the manufacturing and delivery of products.[9]

Internet

The Internet is a global network of computer servers providing an alternate communications platform for the private, public, and government sectors. The term "Internet" was coined in the early 1980s as university researchers developed a common computing language to link a loose collection of networks called the Arpanet.[10] The Arpanet, a 1960s product of Department of the Defense, evolved into a research tool to promote data sharing and the remote access of super-computers among researchers in the United States.[11]

The boom in inexpensive personal computers and network-ready servers in the 1980s allowed many companies and universities to join the rapidly growing Internet.[12] By the early 1990s, rapid innovations gave rise to the World Wide Web, which allowed users to navigate the Internet with "point-and-click" ease.[13] In 1993, Mosaic, the first Web browser, provided a user-friendly interface to the Internet.[14]

During this period, the growth in the use of the Internet soared. Between 1987 and 1997, the number of Internet hosts grew from 10,000 to over five million.[15] In 1993, traffic on the Internet expanded at a 341,634% annual rate.[16] By 1996, analysts estimated that over 20 million people used the Internet regularly.[17] Growth has been so rapid that the Internet is believed to have doubled in size every year since 1988.[18] Studies also suggest that over $1.0 billion per year changes hands at Internet shopping malls.[19]

In order to meet this growing demand, a number of companies such as Cisco Systems, Sun Microsystems, Netscape Communications, and Oracle Corporation made significant investments in developing and marketing hardware and software applications for the Internet.[20] Microsoft, on the other hand, initially questioned the Internet's commercial viability and therefore postponed committing significant resources for research and development of Internet-friendly applications.

As the Internet's popularity continued to grow, industry analysts began to forecast the possibility that the Internet could supersede Windows as the de facto operating system for personal computers.[21] The principal concern was the fact that competing firms were developing systems, such as Sun Microsystem's NC computer, that could operate without the industry-standard Windows operating system or other resident applications. Instead, these so-called network computers would be linked to the Internet via high-speed servers in a central location and would operate like PCs.[22] By concentrating computing power and software applications in a central computer, many of the costs and hassles of operating in a PC environment would be significantly reduced.

Development of such a scenario would free consumers from the need to purchase operating systems or software applications. Instead, consumers could rely upon the applications and operating systems resident in the servers of their online service provider. As a result, Microsoft's cash generating capabilities would be severely diminished since the licensing and sale of the company's operating system and personal productivity applications account for the majority of its revenues. Microsoft's principal business of developing operating systems and personal productivity applications would be seriously compromised.[23]

The Response

During the mid-1990s, much of Gates' attention was focused on the development and launch of Windows 95, a new operating system developed to replace Microsoft's popular Windows 3.1 system.[24] With its 15 million lines of computer code, Windows 95 was billed as the operating system that would finally give the PC the ease of use associated with Apple's Macintosh System.[25] Analysts expected Microsoft to take in $1.0 billion on Windows 95 upgrades in year one alone.[26]

In the midst of Windows 95 development, a small band of programmers at Microsoft led by Steven Sinofsky campaigned for the company to articulate a more deliberate strategy for developing Internet-based applications. Sinofsky, one of Gates' technical assistants, sparked an interest in the Internet during a company recruiting visit to Cornell in early 1994. He was surprised to note the popularity of E-mail and the Internet amongst the students and faculty of the university.[27]

Together with programmer J. Allard, Sinofsky began peppering Gates and his technical staff with E-mail messages about the Internet and its potential commercial promise.[28] Both men pointed to the rapidly growing popularity of the Internet with both private and corporate users. In fact, by 1994, analysts estimated that there were some 21,700 commercial Web sites, up from only 9,000 in 1991.[29] Sinofsky and Allard were alarmed at the possibility that Microsoft, which at this point was almost entirely focused on the rewrite of the Windows operating system, might miss the significance of this dramatic development in information technology. Sinofsky was determined to focus management's attention on this issue despite the fact that the technological implications for Microsoft's own operating system and applications software business were still unclear.

After two months of incessant drum beating, senior executives from Microsoft convened for an executive retreat to focus on the Internet. Retreats were commonly used at Microsoft to help executives focus on specific issues and challenges. Gates and his top executives reviewed documents prepared by Sinofsky outlining the critical issues. A second retreat followed during which Gates penned a memo outlining the company's first shades of a formal—albeit tepid—commitment to the Internet. Gates wrote, "We want to and will invest resources to be a leader in Internet support."[30] During the months that followed, however, the intense focus on Windows 95 and Windows NT, which was designed specifically for the corporate market, derailed much of the initial momentum.

By May 1995, with work on Windows 95 rapidly approaching completion, Gates issued a memo declaring the Internet as the "most important single development" since the advent of the personal computer.[31] Benjamin J. Slivka, who was the project leader for Microsoft Explorer, an Internet browser developed to compete with Netscape Communication's Navigator, followed up with his own memo suggesting that an Internet-based platform could potentially supercede Windows as the de facto operating system for the personal computer.[32] This memo was notable because it was one of the first formal, public acknowledgments from Microsoft's senior management of the fundamental threat presented by the Internet. This realization prompted another round of brainstorming sessions for Gates and his colleagues.

On August 24, 1995, after a delay of more than one year, Microsoft officially launched Windows 95. Analysts and industry players alike confirmed the success of the operating system's introduction.[33] While corporate customers generally postponed purchases of the new system in anticipation of the Windows NT operating system, most retail consumers and original equipment manufacturers adopted Windows 95 as the de facto standard.

The success of Windows 95 notwithstanding, on November 16, 1995, Goldman Sachs & Co., the New York investment bank, withdrew Microsoft from its recommended purchase list due to concerns that the company did not have an adequate strategy for coping with the Internet.[34] Despite multiple memos and brainstorming sessions, the company had failed to articulate a comprehensive and convincing response to the threat presented by the Internet.

Subsequent to the ratings downgrade, Steve Ballmer, Microsoft's Executive Vice President, adamantly pushed for the company to solidify its strategic plans. Ultimately, December 7, 1995 was the deadline set for the announcement of Microsoft's wide ranging Internet strategy which called for browsers, Web servers, consumer and content applications, and the Microsoft Network (a new proprietary online service provider), among others. In front of an estimated 300 analysts and reporters, Bill Gates announced that Microsoft was "hard-core about the Internet."[35]

Internet Strategy

Microsoft's vision regarding the Internet extended beyond the immediate competitive threat it presented to the company's virtual monopoly in operating systems and applications software. Gates believed that the Internet would be the principal communications platform of the future, just as the MS/DOS and Windows operating systems are today's dominant platform for personal computing.[36] The Internet offered a cost-effective medium for capturing, analyzing, and transmitting millions of bits of information. Specifically, however, the Internet was a powerful tool for collecting information on consumer practices and behavior. Gates believed that the company that could cost-effectively collect, sift through, and capitalize on information such as purchasing habits, product interests, and hobbies would attain a significant competitive advantage.[37] Consequently, capturing and controlling the key interfaces for the Internet became a critical aspect of the company's overall strategy.[38]

Microsoft announced its intention to develop a broad array of Internet-related applications and software. The company began positioning itself in most of the Web-related market segments by using a variety of tactics from joint ventures and acquisitions to internally funded research and development. As of fiscal year 1996, the company had a cash balance in excess of $8.0 billion that was available to fund their various initiatives.[39] On the hardware segment, Microsoft entered into a joint venture with Intel Corporation, Hewlett Packard, and Compaq in order to develop the NetPC, an Internet PC computer that would be positioned against the NC computer from Sun Microsystems, Oracle, and IBM. The NetPC would make use of both Intel's microprocessor and Microsoft's operating system.[40]

For the software market, Microsoft has allocated significant resources for developing applications for corporate Intranets. An Intranet is similar to the Internet, but it includes networked computers within a single company. Microsoft believes that control of this particular market segment is critical since Intranet applications will effectively act as the de facto operating system for networked computers. The company has also made an effort to transform many of its more popular personal productivity products into Intranet-friendly applications. For example, in 1997 the company introduced Office 97, an upgrade of its widely popular MS Office Suite. Office 97 includes an interface with the World Wide Web.[41]

What Microsoft is unable to create in-house, it attempts to buy. Within a $1^1/_2$ year time frame, Microsoft either acquired or entered into joint ventures with UUNET Technologies Inc., Vermeer Technologies Inc., Colusa Software Inc., eshop Inc., and Electric Gravity Inc.[42] Licensing of software and advanced technology was also frequently used. Notable amongst its recent deals was Microsoft's licensing agreement with chief rival Sun Microsystems for the use of Sun's Java computing language.[43]

For the content segment of the market, Microsoft has embarked on a number of joint ventures with established players in the media, publishing, and telecommunications industry in order to create content for display through a variety of interactive devices. These initiatives included computer equipment, television, and printed publications. For example, to address the needs in the consumer segment of the content market, Microsoft worked with Dreamworks SKG to develop a line of 3-D computer games.[44] Dreamworks provided the creative talent for the venture while Microsoft furnished technical expertise. Microsoft also has allocated a significant portion of its cash reserves to purchase fledgling content development firms. For the business segment of the content market, Microsoft's principal efforts focused on the development of MSNBC, a 24-hour business news channel distributed both via cable networks and the Internet.[45] MSNBC is a joint venture with General Electric's NBC television subsidiary.[46]

While preparing the launch of Windows 95, Microsoft's programmers were also putting the finishing touches on the company's new proprietary online service provider, the Microsoft Network (MSN).[47] The principal business of an online service provider is to provide subscribers access to the Internet. America Online, CompuServe, and Prodigy were among the first companies to actively package and market Internet access.[48] Microsoft began development of MSN in December 1992, in part due to the success of America Online, which rapidly became the world's largest proprietary online service provider.

Results

Jeffrey Katzenberg, principal of Dreamworks SKG, noted, "I cannot think of one corporation that has had this kind of success and after 20 years, just stopped and decided to reinvent itself from the ground up. What they are doing is decisive, quick, breathtaking."[49] A Microsoft employee adds that Bill Gates has taken a booming $11 billion company with 25,000 employees and turned the "battleship around as if it were a PT boat."[50]

Within a one-year period, Gates and his team achieved what many industry analysts said was impossible. Essentially, Microsoft took what was the world's largest and most prolific operating software and personal productivity application developer and transformed it into a dominant Internet-focused company with significant ventures in the hardware, software, and content segments of the market. In fiscal year 1996, total sales revenues grew 46% from $5.96 billion in 1995 to $8.67 billion.[51] Net income grew over 40% from $1.5 billion to $2.2 billion.[52] Perhaps even more telling about the company's future are its plans to dramatically raise its investment in new technologies. Over the next year alone, the company will deploy its financial resources to fund over $2.0 billion worth of research and development, which is almost half of the total $4.4 billion that it has spent over its 22-year history. Employment applications are still flooding in at a rate of 15,000 per month, giving Microsoft the enviable advantage of picking from the best and the brightest.

Government and Competitor Reactions

By packaging MSN together with Windows 95, Microsoft intended to create a system whose features would be seamlessly blended together. While the product was delivered on schedule in November 1995, an antitrust investigation by the Justice Department ultimately forced the company to reassess its approach. The principal issue investigated by the government was whether Microsoft's packaging plan would constitute an unfair advantage over its competitors.[53] While no formal charges were filed during the investigation, Microsoft moved to adjust aspects of its original plan in order to address some of the government's concerns.

In October 1997, Microsoft again came under government scrutiny for tying its Internet browser, known as Internet Explorer (IE), to the upgraded version of Windows 95. The Justice Department sued Microsoft for "trying to use its overwhelming dominance in computer operating systems to compete unfairly in the browser market."[54] Microsoft considers Windows 95 to be an integrated program, which means that a wide variety of features are built into the software. The company was requiring computer manufacturers to install IE as a condition of licensing Windows 95 on new PCs. As such, computers that come with Windows 95 preinstalled would automatically have the IE icon on the desktop. Further,

[s]worn statements from computer manufacturers . . . show exactly how Microsoft ruthlessly used its control over what appears on the PC desktop as the means to displace Netscape's Navigator with its own Internet Explorer browser. Although 'end-users' were free to adapt their desktops, the computer manufacturers had to ensure, as a condition of

*their Windows license, that when a machine was switched on for the first time the desktop
had every icon on it that Microsoft decreed. Faced with the threat . . . that they would lose
their Windows license and thus their business if they removed the IE icon, PC makers all
meekly fell into line.[55]*

In December 1997, the government ordered Microsoft to offer PC manufacturers the
choice of whether or not to include IE on the system. Microsoft responded by offering PC
manufacturers two alternatives to the combined Windows and IE system: 1) an outdated
version of Windows that predated IE, or 2) a version of Windows with IE disabled. The
problem with the second option was that the software would not function properly without IE fully activated. Neither option was accepted by any OEM manufacturers.

The government was outraged by Microsoft's response. Since Windows is the de facto
standard for operating systems, the government maintained that Microsoft was "using its
near-monopoly in operating system software to restrict competition in the market for Internet browsing software, where its main competitor is Netscape Communications Corporation."[56] Microsoft, on the other hand, maintained that Windows and IE had become a
single integrated product. In addition, Microsoft feared that government interference
would hamper the company's strategy of blending Internet capabilities into all of its new
products.[57]

In addition to complaints from the government and Windows licensees, Microsoft's
competitors in the software arena have actively voiced concerns about the company's
growing market power. Both Netscape and Sun Microsystems "have suggested that Microsoft's aggressive tactics in the software marketplace border on the tyrannical."[58]
Netscape, the current leader for Internet browsers with a 60% market share, has steadily
been losing ground, and attributes its losses to Microsoft's policy of bundling IE with the
Windows operating system.

Until January 1998, Microsoft continued to insist that IE and Windows were so intricately integrated that Windows simply could not operate without IE. In order to avoid
being found in contempt of court, however, Microsoft ultimately gave in to government
demands by agreeing to make Windows available with the Internet browser icon hidden or
partially removed from the computer desktop. A moderately knowledgeable consumer can
easily install the icon on the desktop.

Addressing Government Concerns

Throughout the 1970s and 1980s, while in its infancy, Microsoft had no need to be concerned with government matters. Rapidly increasing market power, however, has caused
the government to pay attention to the now large corporation. While Gates maintains that
he has done nothing more than remain responsive to consumer demands, the company's
ability to influence industry standards has led to intense government scrutiny. Specifically,
the Justice Department fears that Microsoft's control of industry standards could impede
innovation, leaving competing technologies little chance to survive. Too much government
interference, however, could have potentially devastating effects on Microsoft's strategy.

In 1996 Gates began to hire lobbyists, including Washington lawyer Jack Krumholtz,
in order to defend his company against government attacks. "We've increased our [politi-
cal giving] efforts in response to the very concerted campaign by our competitors to use
the government against us rather than to compete in the marketplace," says Krumholtz.[59]
Until recently, the company made few political contributions and preferred to lobby in
Washington through the Business Software Alliance—an industry trade group whose mission is "to advocate free and open world trade for legitimate business software"[60]—and
its own law firm, Preston Gates Ellis & Rouvelas Meeds.

Even Gates himself has begun to spend more time in government matters. Although
he rarely visits Capitol Hill, Microsoft's chief executive has been inviting more and
more politicians to both the company's corporate headquarters and his private home. Microsoft has also increased its campaign contributions. In 1996, for example, the company
donated $236,784 to candidates for office, as compared to only $105,484 just two years
earlier.[61]

**Public
Relations**

As Microsoft's market power has increased since its humble beginnings, the company's tremendous success has coincided with a shift in Gates's image as a 'quintessential nerd' to one who uses brute force to dominate the marketplace, stifling innovation by controlling industry standards. Indeed, "Microsoft has been able to crush competitors—eliminating competition and perhaps innovation, which could harm consumers."[62] To further promote this negative image, it has been said that Microsoft has taken a "combative stance" in government courtroom confrontations, during which the company, "usually so sure footed, has appeared at times to be throwing a temper tantrum, picking fights with a Federal judge and the Justice Department."[63]

In a campaign beginning in March 1998, Bill Gates became a celebrity endorser for a line of golf clubs. The campaign consisted of a television commercial and print advertisement, and featured Gates as an enthusiastic new golf player. Gates added his role as an endorser to his resume "at a time when he seems to be engaged in a frenetic series of activities intended to change perceptions of him as a rapacious cyber capitalist bent on dominating the information industry."[64] Corporate identity and brand image consultant Clay Timon commended the move, stating, "It will make [Gates] seem human after all."[65] In additional public relations activities, Gates paid tribute to the Wright brothers at *Time* magazine's 75th anniversary party, presented a $640,000 gift to the New York Library, and visited a sixth grade class.

Structure

Microsoft's Internet-focused strategy had dramatic implications for both the company and its employees. New product groups were formed and divisions were reorganized in order to focus on a variety of product initiatives. As previously noted, Microsoft was organized into four main business groups: 1) the Platforms Products Group; 2) the Applications and Content Product Group; 3) the Sales and Support Group; and 4) the Operations Group.[66] In February 1996, both the Platforms Products Group and the Applications and Content Product Group were reorganized in conjunction with company's efforts to enhance its Internet capabilities.

The Platforms Group, headed by Group Vice President Paul Maritz, was organized into three divisions: 1) the Personal and Business Systems Division (which develops and markets applications such as Windows 3.x, Windows 95, Windows NT, and the BackOffice applications, etc.); 2) the Consumer Devices and Public Networks Division (handheld devices, set-top boxes, etc.); and 3) the Internet Platforms Division (focusing on Web browsers, shell and multimedia technology, developer tools, online service commerce technology, etc.)[67]

The Applications and Content Product Group, run by Group Vice Presidents Nathan Myhrvold and Pete Higgins, was likewise reorganized into three divisions. The Desktop Applications Division focuses on personal productivity and consumer applications (e.g., Microsoft Office).[68] The Interactive Media Division develops online and CD-ROM based versions of consumer and business software while overseeing development of content for MSN. The Advanced Technology and Research Division focuses on emerging technologies such as speech recognition and artificial intelligence.[69]

The Sales and Support Group, headed by EVP Ballmer, is responsible for "building long-term business relationships with customers."[70] This group is structured to focus on three customer types: end users, organizations, and original equipment manufacturers (OEMs).

The Operations Group, headed by EVP and COO Bob Herbold, is responsible for managing business operations. This includes processing, manufacturing, and delivering finished goods, licenses, subscriptions, and overall business planning.[71]

In reorganizing the Platforms Products Group and the Applications and Content Product Group, Microsoft was able to capitalize on its loosely structured team approach to software development. Teams of software developers and marketers frequently are used to develop specific software applications. Because the team concept is so pervasive, management was readily able to reshape both business groups by adding and eliminating product teams according to management's assessment of their strategic value. A variety of new units were created to focus on discrete aspects of the company's overall Internet strategy.

Microsoft was reorganized again in early 1998. The move placed three product groups under Paul Mafitz, Group Vice President for Platforms and Operations. The groups are: 1) Personal and Business Systems, 2) Consumer Platforms, and 3) Applications and Tools. The move also shifted responsibility for Internet Explorer into the Personal and Business Systems Group, which is the unit that develops and markets Windows. David Readerman, a financial analyst at Nationsbanc Montgomery Securities Inc., supports the move, stating that "Internet Explorer is an integrated product. You better integrate the reporting responsibilities." The reorganization came less than one month after the company agreed to make Windows available without the Internet Explorer icon present on the desktop. Due to this timing, it has been said that the move "is certain to raise eyebrows in light of the Microsoft Corporation's antitrust battle with the United States Government."[72]

Conclusion

Now that Microsoft represents the dominant force in the computer software industry, Bill Gates claims to have trouble comprehending the nature of the allegations being thrown at his company. He says that rivals should pay more attention to their own businesses and less time obsessing about Microsoft's competitive position. After all, the technology markets are fast paced, and there are no guarantees that Microsoft will remain the industry leader. In fact, it has been said that the Justice Department "faces an extraordinary challenge in keeping . . . in step with the fast-changing Internet software market and Microsoft's quickly shifting tactics."[73] Gates even cites the emergence of Netscape's Navigator and Sun Microsystem's Java programming language as evidence of the highly competitive and threatening nature of the industry. However, there is little opposition to the point that Microsoft virtually owns the future of computing. In fact, it has been said that if Gates can extend Microsoft's dominance to the Internet browser realm, "the little software company he co-founded in 1975 could come to dominate the nexus of computing and communications well into the 21st century."[74]

Endnotes

1. http://www.microsoft.com
2. Hingorani, Sanjiv G. and Sheela Chandrashekhara, "Microsoft Corporation—The Renaissance at Redmond: From DOS to the Web," Furman Selz LLC, August 1996.
3. Staff, Windows 95, *Business Week*, August 1995.
4. Lohr, Steve, "Three Named to Microsoft's Top Management," *The New York Times*, 5/22/95.
5. Staff, *The New York Times*, 5/7/95.
6. Lohr, Steve, "Three Named to Microsoft's Top Management," *The New York Times*, 5/22/95.
7. Ibid.
8. Staff, *The New York Times*, 5/7/95.
9. Lohr, Steve, "Three Named to Microsoft's Top Management," *The New York Times*, 5/22/95.
10. http://www.PBS.org/internet/history
11. Ibid.
12. Ibid.
13. Ibid.
14. Ibid.
15. http://www.economist.com/surveys/internet/intro.html
16. http://www.PBS.org/internet/history
17. http://www.economist.com/surveys/internet/intro.html
18. Ibid.
19. http://www.PBS.org/internet/history
20. Flynn, Mary Kathleen, "The Battle for the Net," *US News and World Report*, 12/18/95.
21. Cortese, Amy, "Win 95 Lose 96," *Business Week*, 12/18/95.
22. Reinhardt, Andy, "Intel Inside the Net," *Business Week*, 11/18/96.
23. Hingorani, Sanjiv G. and Sheela Chandrashekhara, "Microsoft Corporation—The Renaissance at Redmond: From DOS to the Web," Furman Selz LLC, August 1996.
24. Rebello, Kathy, "Inside Microsoft: The Untold Story of How the Internet Forced Bill Gates to Reverse Course," *Business Week*, 7/15/96.

25. Staff, Windows 95, *Business Week*, August 1995.
26. Ibid.
27. Rebello, Kathy, "Inside Microsoft: The Untold Story of How the Internet Forced Bill Gates to Reverse Course," *Business Week*, 7/15/96.
28. Ibid.
29. Ibid.
30. Ibid.
31. Ibid.
32. Cortese, Amy, "Win 95 Lose 96," *Business Week*, 12/18/95.
33. Hingorani, Sanjiv G. and Sheela Chandrashekhara, "Microsoft Corporation—The Renaissance at Redmond: From DOS to the Web," Furman Selz LLC, August 1996.
34. Rebello, Kathy, "Inside Microsoft: The Untold Story of How the Internet Forced Bill Gates to Reverse Course," *Business Week*, 7/15/96.
35. Flynn, Mary Kathleen, "The Battle for the Net," *US News and World Report*, December 18, 1995.
36. Hafner, Katie, "Microsoft Century," *Newsweek*, 12/2/96.
37. Ibid.
38. Gleick, James, "Making Microsoft Safe for Capitalism," *The New York Times Magazine*, 11/5/95.
39. Annual Report—Fiscal Year 1996, Microsoft Corporation.
40. Reinhardt, Andy, "Intel Inside the Net," *Business Week*, 11/18/96.
41. Rebello, Kathy, "Microsoft's Suite Spot," *Business Week*, 11/25/96.
42. Hingorani, Sanjiv G. and Sheela Chandrashekhara, "Microsoft Corporation—The Renaissance at Redmond: From DOS to the Web," Furman Selz LLC, August 1996.
43. Flynn, Mary Kathleen, "The Battle for the Net," *US News and World Report*, 12/18/95.
44. Hingorani, Sanjiv G. and Sheela Chandrashekhara, "Microsoft Corporation—The Renaissance at Redmond: From DOS to the Web," Furman Selz LLC, August 1996.
45. Ibid.
46. Ibid.

47. Rebello, Kathy, "Inside Microsoft: The Untold Story of How the Internet Forced Bill Gates to Reverse Course," *Business Week*, July 15, 1996.

48. Hingorani, Sanjiv G. and Sheela Chandrashekhara, "Microsoft Corporation—The Renaissance at Redmond: From DOS to the Web," Furman Selz LLC, August 1996.

49. Rebello, Kathy, "Inside Microsoft: The Untold Story of How the Internet Forced Bill Gates to Reverse Course," *Business Week*, 7/15/96.

50. Ibid.

51. Annual Report—Fiscal Year 1996, Microsoft Corporation.

52. Ibid.

53. Markoff, John, "US Won't Challenge Microsoft Network Before Its Debut," *The New York Times*, 8/5/95.

54. Brinkley, Joel, "Microsoft Gives in to a Federal Order on Internet Browser," *The New York Times*, 1/23/98.

55. _____, "Microsoft is Fighting its Competitors and the Justice Department Tooth and Nail. Is it Driven by Strategy or Nature?" *The Economist*, 1/31/98, p. 65.

56. Lohr, Steve and John Markoff, "Why Microsoft is Taking a Hard Line with the Government," *The New York Times*, 1/12/98, p. D1.

57. Hamm, Steve, Amy Cortese and Susan Garland, "Microsoft's Future," *Business Week*, 1/19/98, p. 58.

58. Westneat, Danny and James Grimaldi, "Gates to Testify: Will Star Power Work on Senate? Meek Lessons Suggested for Microsoft Chief," *The Seattle Times*, 3/1/98, p. A1.

59. Yang, Catherine, Amy Borrus, Susan Garland and Steve Hamm, "Microsoft Goes Low-Tech in Washington," *Business Week*, 12/22/97.

60. http://www.bsa.org/info/aboutbsa.html

61. Yang, Catherine, Amy Borrus, Susan Garland and Steve Hamm, "Microsoft Goes Low-Tech in Washington," *Business Week*, 12/22/97.

62. Lohr, Steve and John Markoff, "Why Microsoft is Taking a Hard Line with the Government," *The New York Times*, 1/12/98, p. D1.

63. Ibid.

64. Elliot, Stuart, "Bill Gates is Tiger Woods? Well, He's Doing a Commercial," *The New York Times*, 3/6/98, p. D5.

65. Ibid.

67. Hingorani, Sanjiv G. and Sheela Chandrashekhara, "Microsoft Corporation—The Renaissance at Redmond: From DOS to the Web," Furman Selz LLC, August 1996.

68. Ibid.

69. Ibid.

70. Ibid.

71. Ibid.

72. Markoff, John, "Microsoft Shifts Web Unit to Windows Group," *The New York Times*, 2/6/98, p. D3.

73. Lohr, Steve, "US Facing Lightning Technology Shifts in Microsoft Case," *The New York Times*, 3/30/98, p. D1.

74. Hamm, Steve, Amy Cortese and Susan Garland, "Microsoft's Future," *Business Week*, 1/19/98, p. 58.

BULLER | SCHULER   2

Managing Organizations and People

A Resource for Cases in Management, Organizational Behavior, and Human Resource Management

Abstract

The Custom Chip, Inc. case provides students with an opportunity to understand and explore the complexity of a manager's job. The case, set in the semiconductor industry, describes a middle level engineering manager's activities over the course of a day. Students see that this manager—Frank Questin—is faced with a never-ending stream of organizational situations and opportunities to which he can respond. The primary issue in this case is Frank Questin's effectiveness as a manager. The interplay of his personality, job requirements, and environment make the assessment of his effectiveness a challenging task for the students.

Custom Chip, Inc.

Introduction

It was 7:50 on Monday morning. Frank Questin, Product Engineering Manager at Custom Chip, Inc. was sitting in his office making a TO DO list for the day. From 8:00 to 9:30 A.M. he would have his weekly meeting with his staff of engineers. After the meeting, Frank thought he would begin developing a proposal for solving what he called "Custom Chip's manufacturing documentation problem"—inadequate technical information regarding the steps to manufacture many of the company's products. Before he could finish his TO DO list, he answered a phone call from Custom Chip's human resource manager, who asked him about the status of two overdue performance appraisals and reminded him that this day marked Bill Lazarus' fifth year anniversary with the company. Following this call, Frank hurried off to the Monday morning meeting with his staff.

Frank had been Product Engineering Manager at Custom Chip for 14 months. This was his first management position, and he sometimes questioned his effectiveness as a manager. Often he could not complete the tasks he set out for himself due to interruptions and problems brought to his attention by others. Even though he had not been told exactly what results he was supposed to accomplish, he had a nagging feeling that he should have achieved more after these 14 months. On the other hand, he thought maybe he was functioning pretty well in some of his areas of responsibility given the complexity of the problems his group handled and the unpredictable changes in the semiconductor industry—changes caused not only by rapid advances in technology, but also by increased foreign competition and a recent downturn in demand.

Company Background

Custom Chip, Inc. was a semiconductor manufacturer specializing in custom chips and components used in radars, satellite transmitters, and other radio frequency devices. The company had been founded in 1977 and had grown rapidly with sales exceeding $25 million in 1986. Most of the company's 300 employees were located in the main plant in Silicon Valley, but overseas manufacturing facilities in Europe and the Far East were growing in size and importance. These overseas facilities assembled the less complex, higher volume products. New products and the more complex ones were assembled in the main plant. Approximately one-third of the assembly employees were in overseas facilities.

While the specialized products and markets of Custom Chip provided a market niche that had thus far shielded the company from the major downturn in the semiconductor industry, growth had come to a standstill. Because of this, cost reduction had become a high priority.

The Manufacturing Process

Manufacturers of standard chips have long production runs of a few products. Their cost per unit is low and cost control is a primary determinant of success. In contrast, manufacturers of custom chips have extensive product lines and produce small production runs for special applications. Custom Chip, Inc., for example, manufactured over 2000 different products in the last five years. In any one quarter the company might schedule 300 production runs for different products, as many as one-third of which might be new or modified products which the company had not made before. Because they must be efficient in designing and manufacturing many product lines, all custom chip manufacturers are highly dependent on their engineers. Customers are often first concerned with whether Custom Chip can design and manufacture the needed product *at all*, secondly with whether they can deliver it on time, and only thirdly with cost.

After designing a product, there are two phases to the manufacturing process. (See Figure 1.) The first is wafer fabrication. This is a complex process in which circuits are etched onto the various layers added to a silicon wafer. The number of steps that the wafer goes through plus inherent problems in controlling various chemical processes make it very difficult to meet the exacting specifications required for the final wafer. The wafers, which are typically "just a few" inches in diameter when the fabrication process is complete, contain hundreds, sometimes thousands of tiny identical die. Once the wafer has been tested and sliced up to produce these die, each die will be used as a circuit component.

If the completed wafer passes the various quality tests, it moves on to the assembly phase. In assembly, the die from the wafers, very small wires and other components are attached to a circuit in a series of precise operations. This finished circuit is the final product of Custom Chip, Inc.

Each product goes through many independent and delicate operations, and each step is subject to operator or machine error. Due to the number of steps and tests involved, the wafer fabrication takes 8 to 12 weeks and the assembly process takes 4 to 6 weeks. Because of the exacting specifications, products are rejected for the slightest flaw. The likelihood that every product starting the run will make it through all of the processes and still meet specifications is often quite low. For some products, average yield[1] is as low as 40 percent, and actual yields can vary considerably from one run to another. At Custom Chip, the average yield for all products is in the 60 to 70 percent range.

Because it takes so long to make a custom chip, it is especially important to have some control of these yields. For example, if a customer orders one thousand units of a product and typical yields for that product average 50 percent, Custom Chip will schedule a starting batch of 2200 units. With this approach, even if the yield falls as low as 45.4 percent (45.4% of 2200 is 1000) the company can still meet the order. If the actual yield falls below 45.4 percent, the order will not be completed in that run, and a very small, costly run of the item will be needed to complete the order. The only way the company can effectively control these yields and stay on schedule is for the engineering groups and operations to cooperate and coordinate their efforts efficiently.

FIGURE 1
Manufacturing
Process

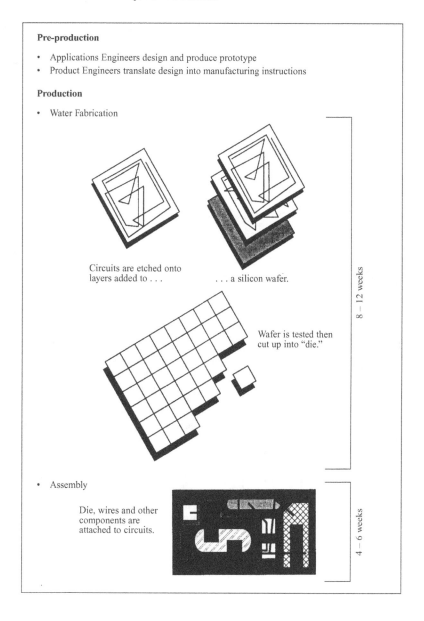

Pre-production

- Applications Engineers design and produce prototype
- Product Engineers translate design into manufacturing instructions

Production

- Water Fabrication

Circuits are etched onto
layers added to . . .   . . . a silicon wafer.

Wafer is tested then
cut up into "die."

8 – 12 weeks

- Assembly

Die, wires and other
components are
attached to circuits.

4 – 6 weeks

Role of the Product Engineer

The product engineer's job is defined by its relationship to application engineering and operations. The applications engineers are responsible for designing and developing prototypes when incoming orders are for new or modified products. The product engineer's role is to translate the application engineering group's design into a set of manufacturing instructions, then to work alongside manufacturing to make sure that engineering related problems get solved. The product engineers' effectiveness is ultimately measured by their ability to control yields on their assigned products. The organization chart in Figure 2 shows the engineering and operations departments. Figure 3 summarizes the roles and objectives of manufacturing, application engineering, and product engineering.

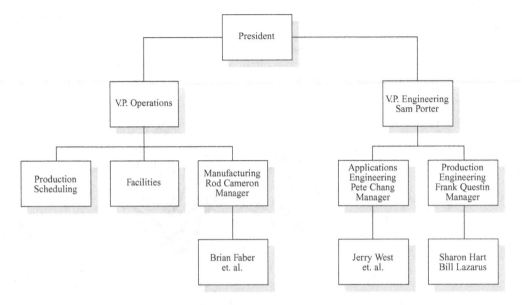

FIGURE 2
Custom Chip, Inc.
Partial Organization
Chart

The product engineers estimate that 70 to 80 percent of their time is spent in solving day-to-day manufacturing problems. The product engineers have cubicles in a room directly across the hall from the manufacturing facility. If a manufacturing supervisor has a question regarding how to build a product during a run, that supervisor will call the engineer assigned to that product. If the engineer is available, he or she will go to the manufacturing floor to help answer the question. If the engineer is not available, the production run may be stopped and the product put aside so that other orders can be manufactured. This results in delays and added costs. One reason that product engineers are consulted is that documentation—the instructions for manufacturing the product—is unclear or incomplete.

The product engineer will also be called if a product is tested and fails to meet specifications. If a product fails to meet test specifications, production stops, and the engineer must diagnose the problem and attempt to find a solution. Otherwise, the order for that product may be only partially met. Test failures are a very serious problem, which can result in considerable cost increases and schedule delays for customers. Products do not test properly for many reasons, including operator errors, poor materials, a design that

FIGURE 3
Departmental Roles
and Objectives

Department	Role	Primary Objective
Applications Engineering	Design and develop prototypes for new or modified products	Satisfy customer needs through innovative designs
Product Engineering	Translates designs into manufacturing instructions and works alongside manufacturing to solve "engineering related" problems	Maintain and control yields on assigned products
Manufacturing	Executes designs	Meet productivity standards and time schedules

is very difficult to manufacture, a design that provides too little margin for error, or a combination of these.

On a typical day, the product engineer may respond to half a dozen questions from the manufacturing floor, and two to four calls to the testing stations. When interviewed, the engineers expressed a frustration with this situation. They thought they spent too much time solving short-term problems, and consequently they were neglecting other important parts of their jobs. In particular, they felt they had little time in which to:

- **Coordinate with applications engineers during the design phase.** The product engineers stated that their knowledge of manufacturing could provide valuable input to the applications engineer. Together they could improve the manufacturability and thus, the yields, of the new or modified product.
- **Engage in yield improvement projects.** This would involve an in-depth study of the existing process for a specific product in conjunction with an analysis of past product failures.
- **Accurately document the manufacturing steps for their assigned products, especially for those which tend to have large or repeat orders.** They said that the current state of the documentation is very poor. Operators often have to build products using only a drawing showing the final circuit, along with a few notes scribbled in the margins. While experienced operators and supervisors may be able to work with this information, they often make incorrect guesses and assumptions. Inexperienced operators may not be able to proceed with certain products because of this poor documentation.

Weekly Meeting

As manager of the product engineering group, Frank Questin had eight engineers reporting to him, each responsible for a different set of Custom Chip products. According to Frank:

When I took over as manager, the product engineers were not spending much time together as a group. They were required to handle operation problems on short notice. This made it difficult for the entire group to meet due to constant requests for assistance from the manufacturing area.

I thought that my engineers could be of more assistance and support to each other if they all spent more time together as a group, so one of my first actions as a manager was to institute a regularly scheduled weekly meeting. I let the manufacturing people know that my staff would not respond to requests for assistance during the meeting.

The meeting on this particular Monday morning followed the usual pattern. Frank talked about upcoming company plans, projects and other news that might be of interest to the group. He then provided data about current yields for each product and commended those engineers who had maintained or improved yields on most of their products. This initial phase of the meeting lasted until about 8:30 A.M. The remainder of the meeting was a meandering discussion of a variety of topics. Since there was no agenda, engineers felt comfortable in raising issues of concern to them.

The discussion started with one of the engineers describing a technical problem in the assembly of one of his products. He was asked a number of questions and given some advice. Another engineer raised the topic of a need for new testing equipment and described a test unit he had seen at a recent demonstration. He claimed the savings in labor and improved yields from this machine would allow it to pay for itself in less than nine months. Frank immediately replied that budget limitations made such a purchase unfeasible, and the discussion moved into another area. They briefly discussed the increasing inaccessibility of the application engineers, then talked about a few other topics.

In general, the engineers valued these meetings. One commented that:

The Monday meetings give me a chance to hear what's on everyone's mind and to find out about and discuss company wide news. It's hard to reach any conclusions because the meeting is a freewheeling discussion. But I really appreciate the friendly atmosphere with my peers.

Coordination with Applications Engineers

Following the meeting that morning, an event occurred that highlighted the issue of the inaccessibility of the applications engineers. An order of 300 units of custom chip 1210A for a major customer was already overdue. Because the projected yield of this product was 70 percent, they had started with a run of 500 units. A sample tested at one of the early assembly points indicated a major performance problem that could drop the yield to below 50 percent. Bill Lazarus, the product engineer assigned to the 1210A, examined the sample and determined that the problem could be solved by redesigning the writing. Jerry West, the application engineer assigned to that product category was responsible for revising the design. Bill tried to contact Jerry, but he was not immediately available, and didn't get back to Bill until later in the day. Jerry explained that he was on a tight schedule trying to finish a design for a customer who was coming into town in two days, and could not get to "Bill's problem" for a while.

Jerry's attitude that the problem belonged to product engineering was typical of the applications engineers. From their point of view there were a number of reasons for making the product engineers needs for assistance a lower priority. In the first place, applications engineers were rewarded and acknowledged primarily for satisfying customer needs through designing new and modified products. They got little recognition for solving manufacturing problems. Secondly, applications engineering was perceived to be more glamorous than product engineering because of opportunities to be credited with innovative and ground breaking designs. Finally, the size of the applications engineering group had declined over the past year, causing the workload on each engineer to increase considerably. Now they had even less time to respond to the product engineer's requests.

When Bill Lazarus told Frank about the situation, Frank acted quickly. He wanted this order to be in process again by tomorrow and he knew manufacturing was also trying to meet this goal. He walked over to see Pete Chang, head of applications engineering (see Organization Chart in Figure 2). Meetings like this with Pete to discuss and resolve interdepartmental issues were common.

Frank found Pete at a workbench talking with one of his engineers. He asked Pete if he could talk to him in private and they walked to Pete's office.

Frank: We've got a problem in manufacturing in getting out an order of 1210A's. Bill Lazarus is getting little or no assistance from Jerry West. I'm hoping you can get Jerry to pitch in and help Bill. It should take no more than a few hours of his time.

Pete: I do have Jerry on a short leash trying to keep him focused on getting out a design for Teletronics. We can't afford to show up empty handed at our meeting with them in two days.

Frank: Well, we are going to end up losing one customer in trying to please another. Can't we satisfy everyone here?

Pete: Do you have an idea?

Frank: Can't you give Jerry some additional support on the Teletronics design?

Pete: Let's get Jerry in here to see what we can do.

Pete brought Jerry back to the office, and together they discussed the issues and possible solutions. When Pete made it clear to Jerry that he considered the problem with the 1210A's a priority, Jerry offered to work on the 1210A problem with Bill. He said, "This will mean I'll have to stay a few hours past 5:00 this evening, but I'll do what's required to get the job done."

Frank was glad he had developed a collaborative relationship with Pete. He had always made it a point to keep Pete informed about activities in the Product Engineering group that might affect the applications engineers. In addition, he would often chat with Pete informally over coffee or lunch in the company cafeteria. This relationship with Pete made Frank's job easier. He wished he had the same rapport with Rod Cameron, the Manufacturing Manager.

Coordination with Manufacturing

The product engineers worked closely on a day-to-day basis with the manufacturing supervisors and workers. The problems between these two groups stemmed from an inherent conflict between their objectives (see Figure 3). The objective of the product engineers was to maintain and improve yields. They had the authority to stop production of any run that did not test properly. Manufacturing, on the other hand, was trying to meet productivity standards and time schedules. When a product engineer stopped a manufacturing run, he was possibly preventing the manufacturing group from reaching its objectives.

Rod Cameron, the current manufacturing manager, had been promoted from his position as a manufacturing supervisor a year ago. His views on the product engineers:

The product engineers are perfectionists. The minute a test result looks a little suspicious they want to shut down the factory. I'm under a lot of pressure to get products out the door. If they pull a few $50,000 orders off the line when they are within a few days of reaching shipping, I'm liable to miss my numbers by $100,000 that month.

Besides that, they are doing a lousy job of documenting the manufacturing steps. I've got a lot of turnover, and my new operators need to be told or shown exactly what to do for each product. The instructions for a lot of our products are a joke.

At first, Frank found Rod very difficult to deal with. Rod found fault with the product engineers for many problems and sometimes seemed rude to Frank when they talked. For example, Rod might tell Frank to "make it quick, I haven't got much time." Frank tried not to take Rod's actions personally, and through persistence was able to develop a more amicable relationship with him. According to Frank:

Sometimes, my people will stop work on a product because it doesn't meet test results at that stage of manufacturing. If we study the situation, we might be able to maintain yields or even save an entire run by adjusting the manufacturing procedures. Rod tries to bully me into changing my engineers' decisions. He yells at me or criticizes the competence of my people, but I don't allow his temper or ravings to influence my best judgment in a situation. My strategy in dealing with Rod is to try not to respond defensively to him. Eventually he cools down, and we can have a reasonable discussion of the situation.

Despite this strategy, Frank could not always resolve his problems with Rod. On these occasions, Frank took the issue to his own boss, Sam Porter, the Vice President in charge of engineering. However, Frank was not satisfied with the support he got from Sam. Frank said:

Sam avoids confrontations with the Operations VP. He doesn't have the influence or clout with the other VPs or the president to do justice to engineering's needs in the organization.

Early that afternoon, Frank again found himself trying to resolve a conflict between engineering and manufacturing. Sharon Hart, one of his most effective product engineers was responsible for a series of products used in radars—the 3805A–3808A series. Today she had stopped a large run of 3806A's. The manufacturing supervisor, Brian Faber, went to Rod Cameron to complain about the impact of this stoppage on his group's productivity. Brian felt that yields were low on that particular product because the production instructions were confusing to his operators, and that even with clearer instructions, his operators would need additional training to build it satisfactorily. He stressed that the product engineer's responsibility was to adequately document the production instructions and provide training. For these reasons, Brian asserted that product engineering, and not manufacturing, should be accountable for the productivity loss in the case of these 3806A's.

Rod called Frank to his office, where he joined the discussion with Sharon, Brian and Rod. After listening to the issues, Frank conceded that product engineering had responsibility for documenting and training. He also explained, even though everyone was aware of it, that the product engineering group had been operating with reduced staff for over a year now, so training and documentation were lower priorities. Because of this staffing situation, Frank suggested that manufacturing and product engineering work together and pool their limited resources to solve the documentation and training problem. He was especially interested in using a few of the long-term experienced workers to assist in training newer workers. Rod and Brian opposed his suggestion. They did not want to take experienced operators off of the line because it would decrease productivity. The meeting ended when Brian stormed out, saying that Sharon had better get the 3806A's up and running again that morning.

Frank was particularly frustrated by this episode with manufacturing. He knew perfectly well that his group had primary responsibility for documenting the manufacturing steps for each product. A year ago he told Sam Porter that the product engineers needed to update and standardize all of the documentation for manufacturing products. At that time, Sam told Frank that he would support his efforts to develop the documentation, but would not increase his staff. In fact, Sam had withheld authorization to fill a recently vacated product engineering slot. Frank was reluctant to push the staffing issue because of Sam's adamance about reducing costs. "Perhaps," Frank thought, "if I develop a proposal clearly showing the benefits of a documentation program in manufacturing and detailing the steps and resources required to implement the program, I might be able to convince Sam to provide us with more resources." But Frank could never find the time to develop that proposal. And so he remained frustrated.

Later in the Day

Frank was reflecting on the complexity of his job when Sharon came to the doorway to see if he had a few moments. Before he could say "come in," the phone rang. He looked at the clock. It was 4:10 P.M. Pete was on the other end of the line with an idea he wanted to try out on Frank, so Frank said he could call him back shortly. Sharon was upset, and told him that she was thinking of quitting because the job was not satisfying for her.

Sharon said that although she very much enjoyed working on yield improvement projects, she could find no time for them. She was tired of the application engineers acting like "prima donnas," too busy to help her solve what they seemed to think were mundane day-to-day manufacturing problems. She also thought that many of the day-to-day problems she handled wouldn't exist if there was enough time to document manufacturing procedures to begin with.

Frank didn't want to lose Sharon, so he tried to get into a frame of mind where he could be empathetic to her. He listened to her and told her that he could understand her frustration in this situation. He told her the situation would change as industry conditions improved. He told her that he was pleased that she felt comfortable in venting her frustrations with him, and he hoped she would stay with Custom Chip.

After Sharon left, Frank realized that he had told Pete that he would call back. He glanced at the TO DO list he had never completed, and realized that he hadn't spent time on his top priority—developing a proposal relating to solving the documentation problem in manufacturing. Then, he remembered that he had forgotten to acknowledge Bill Lazarus' fifth year anniversary with the company. He thought to himself that his job felt like a roller coaster ride, and once again he pondered his effectiveness as a manager.

Endnote

1. Yield refers to the ratio of finished products that meet specifications relative to the number that initially entered the manufacturing process.

BULLER | SCHULER   3

Managing Organizations and People

A Resource for Cases in Management, Organizational Behavior, and Human Resource Management

Abstract

Propco, a subsidiary of a large, diversified manufacturer of advanced technology products, is a leading U.S. producer of a variety of marine systems products. Due to a dramatic decline in defense spending beginning in the later 1980s, Propco has been seeking ways to reduce its costs. One of the primary strategies has been to cut spending through employee layoffs. In 1991, Propco had a work force of about 14,000 people, 3.2 percent of which were minorities. By January 1, 1993, the firm's employees totaled about 10,000 with just under 1.1 percent comprised of minorities. This case provides an "inside" look at the human impact of downsizing strategies and corporate diversity programs. In particular, it highlights the challenges of attracting and maintaining a diverse work force in a declining business.

Propco, Inc.

Allied Technologies Corporation (ATC)

Founded in 1918, Allied Technologies is a diversified designer and manufacturer of advanced technology products and is one of the largest private employers in the state of Rhode Island. Headed by Joseph R. Wagner, the company is comprised of 10 operating units. These units conduct their businesses within four principal industry segments or lines of business—Marine Systems, Construction, Power, and Motor Parts. During 1991, the major business units within these four segments held, in most instances, rankings of either number one, two, or three in their major lines of business.

Revenues for 1991 totaled $16,427 million, with an operating income of $892 million. Non-U.S. operations accounted for 41 percent of sales in 1991, while U.S. Government business comprised 23 percent of sales.

Historically, at least half of ATC's revenues were derived from the military sector. Cuts in defense budgets for marine products (e.g., submarine engines, screw propellers, and environmental control systems), both in the U.S. and in other developed countries,

■ This case was written by Richard D. Freedman, Stern School of Business, New York University. Reprinted with permission. This case is based upon a real situation, certain facts have been changed, and the names of the corporations and the names and titles of individuals have been disguised.

have reduced requirements for military submarines and ships and related equipment from U.S. suppliers. Total U.S. defense spending peaked in 1985, and current budget requests indicate a further 4 percent decline in spending by 1993.

Wagner stated:

Beyond the problems in the military business, the plant closings and layoffs are intended to make the company more efficient. We have begun a transformation more profound and more potent than any single event in the corporation's recent history . . . sadly, though, 13,900 jobs must be eliminated in order to attain this efficiency.

Consequently, according to many experts, diversification of their operations into non-military marine areas is one of the most promising strategies for survival. In fact, ATC is following a diversification strategy. ATC has grown from a narrowly focused marine company in the 1970s with revenues of less than $2 billion, to what is today a $16 billion enterprise. Based on 1991 sales, the firm is one of the largest U.S. industrial companies, and one of the tenth largest U.S. exporters.

According to Wagner,

We have built the Company in order to be profitable in the face of declining Pentagon expenditures; the firm is reducing its reliance on defense contracts. We are now selling more products overseas. The Company is very strong and viable.

But some of ATC's operating units—such as Propco—whose primary task was to develop and construct military equipment, have suffered extensive financial losses because of the reductions in the military budget in the post-cold-war era.

Overall, the Corporation's earnings for the first nine months of 1991 were down 65 percent from the equivalent period of 1990. In 1991 ATC suffered its first annual operating loss in three decades.

Propco

Propco was the creation of a 1929 consolidation of HLL Vessels and the Excelsior Screw Propeller Company. At that time, Propco was the largest manufacturer of marine propellers in the world. Its specialty was the development and construction of screw propellers for submarines. A major risk to submarines is their location by enemies using instruments that detect the sounds and signals they make. Propellor screws are a major source of such "noise." Consequently the design and manufacture of better screw propellers is a significant issue in submarine development. Propco is renowned for its leadership in screw propellor development.

Although the advent of the jet age did not eliminate ocean-travel, it did reduce their commercial business and require that the company acquire other types of businesses. In the 1950s, with the development of an electronics group and a new engineering group, the division diversified into other marine and space systems especially in the defense industry.

At present, under the leadership of Malden K. Ruhn, Propco is a leading domestic producer of a number of Marine Systems products. Its major production programs include engine controls, environmental controls, marine-engine controls, and propellers for commercial and military boats.

The Marine Systems business is affected by many different factors: rapid changes in technology; lengthy and costly development cycles; heavy dependence on a small number of products and programs; changes in legislation and in government procurement and other regulations and procurement practices; licensing or other arrangements; substantial competition from a large number of companies; and changes in economic, industrial and international conditions. In addition, the principal methods of competition in the Marine Systems business are price, delivery schedules, product performance, service, and other terms and conditions of sale. Consequently, in times of recession and reduced government spending, firms heavily involved in the production of these systems must seek to reduce production and cut costs in order to remain profitable.

One primary way in which the company sought to cut spending is through employee layoffs. In 1991, Propco had a workforce of approximately 14,000 people, 3.2 percent of which were minorities. As of January 1, 1993, the firm's employees totaled 10,000 with just under 1.1 percent comprised of minorities.

Corporate Restructuring

In 1991 there was a sharp decline in ocean traffic, construction, and engine production. This marked the first time that ATC's core commercial markets simultaneously hit the bottom of their industry cycles. In addition, government reassessments of the military threat from the former Soviet Union—and efforts to reduce the U.S. deficit—resulted in fewer defense procurement contracts being awarded.

Consequently, in early 1992, ATC management announced that it would eliminate 15,297 jobs, including 8,143 in Rhode Island, by the end of 1994. At the time of this announcement, the Company had over 50,000 employees based in Rhode Island. The proposed cuts represent over 7.5 percent of the over 100,000 workers employed worldwide by the sprawling company—virtually all parts of the company will be affected. The largest job losses will be in the divisions that produce defense products.

According to CEO Wagner,

The Corporation is embarking on a sea of change that will produce a leaner, tougher-minded company capable of enduring the current recession, and seizing opportunities as they arise in the future. The harsh reality is that a shrinking military budget means fewer orders for the company's military marine equipment and sophisticated electronics.

The goal of the restructuring plan is to reduce costs by $1.2 billion a year by 1994 in order to improve the Company's financial performance. The Company has said that the layoffs would save $500 million a year; closing plants will add another $400 million by early 1993; and improvements in design, engineering and manufacturing will add an additional $500 million in projected savings.

Repercussions for Propco Employees

As part of the reorganization announcement by ATC, Propco was instructed to lay off 925 employees. According to corporate spokespeople, most of the reductions are being accomplished through severance and enhanced early retirement programs. The official statement released by Propco's public relations department is:

We understand the difficulties that our employees are under during this time of restructuring; however, it is in Propco's long-term interests to become a much leaner and more flexible organization. In order for our Company to compete effectively and efficiently, we must cut costs where possible. It is our understanding that the reorganization will be completed soon.

But while ATC executives emphasize the necessity for the layoffs and paint a positive picture of the Corporation's recent balance sheet performance, Propco employees appear to be much more pessimistic about this latest round of employee firings. Below are the comments of some of Propco's former and current employees who have witnessed, and experienced, the effects of the restructuring program.

Vincent S.

(Vincent is a White, 33-year-old Operations Center Manager at Propco. He received his MBA in Operations by attending school at night while working for the company. Vincent is married and is the father of newborn twins. He has been with the company for six years.)

Propco has been laying off people for close to two years now. Each new quarter we receive fewer Marine Systems orders. Unfortunately, this leads to another round of layoffs. It's not that our people don't know how to project orders. Look, the entire industry is suffering and our customers have had to cut back, most times at the last minute. They have to look out for their bottom line, just like we do.

It's frustrating. It's frustrating as hell. My men look to me for answers as to when this is all going to end, but I know little more than they do about future economic performance. Of course morale is very low. "Was the last layoff the last?" is the most unanswered question among the guys. Every time a new wave of layoffs comes around you can feel the tension. People barely speak to each other, and no one wants to speak to me. You can see the fear in people's eyes.

I'm scared too. I'm not really afraid of losing my job. I'm afraid that someone is going to take their anger out on me. Every time my boss calls a meeting I'm scared that I have to lay off more men. In December I had to lay off 50 people right after Christmas. I was told that would be the last of the reduction from my unit. But two weeks ago I was told to reduce my numbers by another 20 men. You have no idea how hard it is to tell a man who is old enough to be your father, that he's fired. It really is hard. Men have cried and begged for their jobs. Let me tell you, I don't sleep well at night when I have to do this. I don't park my car in the employee parking lot when I lay people off. Some of the manager's cars have been scratched or dented after they lay off people. Telling people who have worked for a company for 20 or 30 years that they are no longer needed is one of the hardest things I have had to do in my life. I hope this all ends soon.

These constant layoffs have been really hard on everyone here. At first the unions took a hard-line stance—an "us vs. them" mentality. But after the fourth round of layoffs they decided to cooperate in order to make the firm more competitive. They know that in the long run this is what's best. Because union leadership decided to cooperate, we were able to adopt many Japanese-style manufacturing models. This has not prevented layoffs, but it has resulted in a more accurate determination of the number of employees that should be dismissed.

The bottom line is that everyone wants Propco to remain competitive so that when things get better, corporate headquarters will keep Propco in Rhode Island.

The layoffs have caused the level of distrust between the hourly employees and senior management to increase a great deal. Hourlys think management is incapable of saving the company, is not making any sacrifices (for example they recently received bonuses), and sees them as process components instead of human beings. Senior management thinks that hourlys are incapable of understanding the market situation, are not helping to regain competitiveness, and are spoiled union babies. I'm sort of in the middle of all this since I'm not a part of senior management, and I'm not an hourly employee. I'm the guy that gets the job of actually laying off my workers.

Richard C.

(Richard is a White, 48-year-old Manager of Central Purchasing. He received his undergraduate degree in Finance from an Ivy League university. He is married and a father of three teenagers. Richard has been with the company for 27 years.)

I was laid off right before Christmas. I can honestly say that I had no idea whatsoever that I would be let go. I mean, I have been with Propco for 27 years. It's home to me, and the people there are my family. Or so I thought. I guess I got too complacent. You figure, "I'm part of management. I make $85,000 a year. I'm secure." Do you know that my boss wouldn't even look me in the eye when he told me? I really thought we were friends. We used to be a team in the company golf tournaments. I'm sure it was hard on him, but at least he still has his job.

At first they offered me an early retirement package last November. The package included a payment of $15,000 and, get this, three months of medical before my benefits would run out. At first I turned the package down, but my boss told me that if I didn't take it I would be fired anyway. Some choice.

I understand that the economy is in a recession, but you figure that if you put in as much time as I did with a company, nothing will ever happen. You'll retire and receive a good pension. Now I'm mailing out resumes and cover letters, something I never thought I would have to do again. Propco is a great company to work for; I loved it there. But apparently the feeling was not mutual. Do you know that the company did not give me any career counseling? At least the hourly workers get that.

What went wrong? Who knows? I guess the company screwed up. It's not my concern now. The only thing on my mind now is how to take care of my family. My wife works, but we need to have a second income. I made some connections with other firms in the industry while I was at Propco. Hopefully something comes through soon.

Carl G.

(Carl is a 35-year-old, African-American former screw propeller grinder. He was employed at Propco for 12 years. Carl has taken courses toward an undergraduate degree in Sociology from a local university. He is divorced.)

Yeah, I was a grinder at Propco for 12 years before the layoff. I made $15.22 an hour to grind metal off of a military screw forging. Sounds really hard, but it was just manual labor; a lot of lifting and hard work, but it was easy once you got used to it. I have to say, though, that most of the unit's grinders were Black. I used to hear some of the White union guys joking and calling our area "the plantation," saying what we did was "slave labor." They weren't lying. I was there for 12 years and I never could seem to get promoted out of that area. Most of the time, new Black guys were put in our area. Not to say that Propco has a lot of Black workers—they don't. That's a different story, though, but it seems strange to me that a company that is 15 minutes from Hartford and 50 minutes from New Haven has so few minorities in their plant.

Out of the 10 Blacks in my section, 4 have been laid off. You see, union people know when they will be laid off because its done by seniority. Those people with the most years don't have to worry. But since most of the Black guys are what they call "recent hires," they are the first to be fired. You know the old saying. That's the name of the game.

What was it like to be Black at Propco? Well, you never quite feel comfortable there. You feel like what you are, an outsider. The foreman watches you all the time. He's never as easy with you as he is with the White guys. He checks your time card. He calls you at home to make sure that's where you are, when you call in sick. When the rest of the guys go play golf, you're never invited. They just assume you don't know how to play. Or else they just don't want you around. When there's some kind of party, either you're not invited, or they invite you at the last minute. The White guys talk to you when they want to know how to do something. Otherwise, for the most part, they act like you're not there. There are some White guys who are cool; they try to get to know you. But for the most part, you are looked down at, even though they are doing the same kind of work.

The Black guys in my area were lucky, though, because we had each other. We laughed and talked and told stories. We did our own thing. We covered for each other, and helped out when someone fell behind. We had our own parties. We went out together. We helped each other.

Propco has diversity meetings all the time. They say they're trying to find ways to hire more minorities and women. I haven't seen any real progress. It seems more like talk to me. Sometimes I think that they only had the Blacks that they did there because of the government contracts. You see, whenever you do work for the government, you have to have a certain number of minorities. It could be that Propco only hired the minorities that it did because of that.

Don't get me wrong, Propco is a pretty good company to work for. You get health, dental, a savings plan, and free education. Even after the layoff my benefits will last for one year. Also, the union gave us job counseling and assistance. I received one week's pay for every year of employment as severance pay. But, there is no doubt that a lot of people in management are prejudiced. I used to hear jokes all the time about minorities. You know, sexual jokes, stupid jokes, that type of thing. Usually you try to ignore it. It's hard. I guess I'm lucky. I just found another job. Most everyone I know is still looking. Maybe things are getting better.

Samuel L.   *(Samuel is a White, 36-year-old foam machinist. He recently received a B.A. in Psychology from a local college by attending night school. He is married and has two children. Samuel was employed at Propco for 14 years.)*

I knew it was coming, but I prayed that the economy would get better before it was my time to get the pink slip. In a way it's a relief that it finally happened. Every time layoffs were announced, I couldn't sleep. I couldn't eat. I yelled at my family. I was very difficult to live with. The waiting got to be too much. Even being at work was hard. The guys walked around like someone had just died. It was real uneasy there. Guys who used to be friends, barely spoke to each other. I guess it was the tension. Everyone looked at each other like they were enemies. Like the next guy would take their jobs from them. It was really rough.

I was a foam machinist at Propco; I put a regional blade spar into a die machine and injected high pressure foam that forms an X-10 screw shape. Big deal. I doubt that I can find another job doing the same thing. Not that I would want to, but what else can I do? I have a degree, but what do you do with it? Psychology. What a useless degree unless you go back to school. I can't do that now. I guess I'm lucky since my wife makes a pretty good salary, and she can support the family until I can find another job.

I made good money at Propco—$15.35 an hour. But management sure as heck makes a lot more. And you don't see too many of them getting laid off. It's always the same. Management gets paid a lot of money to "manage," but the people who actually do the work get $15.00 an hour. Then when management messes up the company, they fire the people who work and keep the people who think. Does this make any sense to you? They could fire a couple of "thinkers" and save more money than if they fired 20 of us. But, hey, what do I know? I'm just an hourly.

Race relations at Propco? What about it? There were a few Black guys there not a whole lot though. I never had any problem with them. They were just like any of the other guys to me. I mean they worked hard. Everyone at Propco did. I heard a few guys telling race jokes. But they told other kinds of jokes too. You know, like jokes about Polish people, Italian people, women, sex. The people who told those jokes were jerks. I don't have a problem working with Black people. As long as the guy does his work, he's all right with me.

The Black guys sure did stick together. They ate lunch together. Clocked in and out together. I guess I understand. There just weren't that many of them. I'm sure I would be like that too. But you know, the Italian guys were sort of like that too. Strength in numbers I guess.

I feel sorry for all of us now. I know that the economy has been bad, but Allied Technologies is a rich company. It's huge. Something else could be done. They could work with the governor; maybe negotiate tax breaks. They could try lots of things. You're damn right I'm angry. I worked at that place for 14 years. And what do they do for me? They fire me to save themselves.

Steven H.   *(Steven is a 38-year-old, African-American Division Manager at one of Allied Technologies Corporation's other operating units. Prior to his present position, he was assigned to corporate headquarters where he had frequent interaction with Propco managers. He has an engineering degree from an Ivy League university and advanced studies in business and Human Resources. He has been with the company for eight years. Steven is married.)*

Out of over 3,000 people at Propco, there are only 81 Black salaried workers. When I say salaried, that includes clerks, buyers, and secretaries, as well as unit managers. Out of that 81, only 7 are actually managers of people. And after the next round of layoffs, I expect that number to drop. Black managers are an endangered species here at Propco, and in fact throughout ATC.

It's just a fact that Black salaried workers have a higher propensity of getting laid off. Propco's culture—like other ATC operating units—is one of institutional racism. For example, in one of their units there are 400 employees. Only 15 of those people are Black. That was last October. Now I understand that there is only one Black salaried employee. And he's there because somebody high up likes him.

The bottom line is that Black employees at Propco don't have a support network. There is a lot of nepotism there, so that when it comes time to lay off salaried workers, those who don't have real friends often find themselves on the unemployment line. Face it, people don't lay off their friends and family. This situation generally applies to salaried workers, since hourly workers are laid off based upon seniority.

To further exacerbate matters, it is difficult for Black employees to take additional training and education classes that would assist in making them more competitive. I am not saying that these individuals are not already highly qualified. Management does not tend to hire minorities unless they are superior achievers. It is just that it is essential for a manager's career to always look like he is trying to improve his leadership skills.

But then again even education is no safety net. Here is a classic example. There was a Black employee at Propco who had started as an hourly and had worked his way up to a position as a $40,000 a year manufacturing engineer. When his mentor left, he was demoted back to an hourly worker as a dispatcher. And this guy had an engineering degree. It goes without saying that he left Propco.

Is Propco consciously racist? I tend to think so. I can't tell you how many diversity meetings friends of mine have attended where someone from upper management would say, "we can't find qualified minority candidates to fill our positions." That whole argument is ridiculous. Propco participates in a program where minority college students are given summer internships at the company. They are also assigned a mentor from the management ranks. These kids are not dumb. Their grade point averages are in the 3.3 range. How many are with the company now? None. This is despite the fact that over 90 percent of the interns get superior ratings on their summer performance. I think this speaks for itself.

I believe that something has to be done to address the racist mentality around the entire corporation. I hate being the one who has to defend my race all of the time, but there are very few others that care. I'm doing what I can, but I can't fix the problem alone.

Do I see a future for myself here? ATC is doing great things. I think that if I hang in here long enough, I can make a difference. I want to help qualified minorities—not just Blacks—get into these large firms. ATC has a lot to offer employees. But if it gets too tough for me, I don't think I'll have a problem finding another position somewhere else.

Propco's Human Resource Policies

The ATC Human Resources Department has issued policy statements over time regarding layoffs, diversity, and minorities that the company indicates are the basis for its layoff decisions. All divisions have to rigorously adhere to these policies. All of them have been developed with the direct involvement and approval of the CEO, Joseph R. Wagner. Wagner has given numerous speeches stressing the importance of diversity in corporate life in general and ATC in particular. ATC donates considerable money to civil rights organizations and Wagner himself has received several humanitarian awards.

It is the position of Allied Technologies Corporation to hire qualified candidates regardless of race, creed, color, sex, or ethnic origin. We have an ongoing diversity program in place in which we hope to devise ways to introduce more minorities and women into our businesses. For the past two years the Company has participated in an internship program in which minority college students are given the opportunity to work in some of our business units during the summer. It is our hope that the students will learn from, and enjoy, their intern experience and consider working for ATC upon graduation.[1]

As far as industry standards are concerned, the Company is on an even keel with other firms of its size when it comes to the number of minority employees that it employs.

There is a concerted effort on the part of the executives at ATC to hire the best people for the job, and that is what we do.

In laying off union workers, we adhere to the union contract and lay them off in order of seniority.

Endnote

1. As of now, Propco does not have any of the former interns in its employ, although some have graduated from college.

Edited by Paul F. Buller, Gonzaga University, and Randall S. Schuler, Rutgers University

BULLER | SCHULER   4

Managing Organizations and People

A Resource for Cases in Management, Organizational Behavior, and Human Resource Management

Abstract

As workforces become more diverse, they begin to face many new human resource issues. The Barden Corporation case illustrates four people-related business concerns: the influx of immigrants, the need for skilled workers, the increasing number of older workers, and the growing number of employees who are out of shape that results in safety and health concerns. The case setting is the Precision Bearing Division of the Barden Corporation in Danbury, Connecticut.

Managing Workforce Diversity: People Related Issues at the Barden Corporation

Introduction

The largest segment of the business at the Barden Corporation is the Precision Bearings Division. It manufactures high-precision ball bearings in a range of sizes for machine tools, aircraft instruments and accessories, aircraft engines, computer peripherals, textile spindles, and medical and dental equipment. Presently, the division employs about 1,000 people, which includes a marketing department and a small corporate staff. It was founded during World War II to manufacture the special bearings needed for the Norden bombsight. It has been non-union since that time (which gives you a hint about the culture). The following description is told by Mr. Donald Brush, Vice President and General Manager of the Precision Bearings Division.

Background

Reporting directly to me is a small staff comprising a manufacturing manager, a quality manager, an engineering manager, a director of manufacturing planning, and a director of industrial relations (see Exhibit 1). We meet together several times a week to discuss current problems, as well as short- and long-range opportunities and needs. On alternate weeks we augment this group by including the supervisory personnel who report to the senior managers listed above. I might interject here that all supervisors meet with hourly employees on either a weekly or bi-weekly basis to review specific departmental successes and failures, and otherwise to keep employees informed about the business and to encourage ownership of their own jobs. The managers themselves meet on call as the

■ This case was prepared by Randall S. Schuler, Rutgers University, who expresses his appreciation for the cooperation of Donald Brush.

EXHIBIT 1
Precision Bearings Division

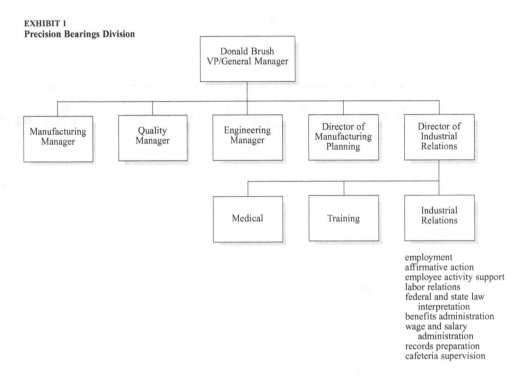

employment
affirmative action
employee activity support
labor relations
federal and state law
   interpretation
benefits administration
wage and salary
   administration
records preparation
cafeteria supervision

Employee Relations Committee to discuss and recommend approval on a wide range of issues that include the evaluation and audit of hourly and salaried positions, as well as the creation or modification of all divisional personnel policies.

A few words about our Personnel (or Industrial Relations) Department. (You will notice that the term "Human Resources" does not yet roll off our tongues easily, but we understand what it means.) There are six employees who together provide the basic services of employment, affirmative action, employee activity support, labor relations, interpretation of the plethora of federal and state laws, benefits administration, wage and salary administration, records preparation and maintenance, cafeteria supervision, and so on. There are, in addition, two people who coordinate our rather extensive training activities.

As presently organized, the Medical Department comes under the supervision of the director of industrial relations. Its authorized staff includes a medical director, the manager of employee health and safety (who is an occupational health nurse), a staff nurse, a safety specialist, and a secretary/clerk.

The development and execution of plans and programs, including those of a strategic nature, almost invariably involve the active participation of Personnel. And that's how we want it to be. On the other hand, the Personnel Department doesn't run the business. By this I mean they don't hire or fire, promote, or demote. They don't write job descriptions or determine salaries or wages, etc., etc. All these things are done by the line managers with the Personnel Department providing a framework to ensure consistency and that all actions are appropriate to company goals. You might say that Personnel is our "Jiminy Cricket"—they are there for advice, consent and, importantly, as a conscience.

During the past several months we have been running into many issues that are affecting the very essence of our business: growth, profits, survival, and competitiveness. Because the issues involve our human resources, we call them people-related business issues. Would you please give us your experience, expertise, and suggestions as to how we can solve them? Thanks! The following briefly describes the nature of each of the four issues.

Issue: Recruiting and Training New Hourly Employees

The need to recruit and train approximately 125 new hourly workers to respond to a surge in business in a high cost of living area at a time when the unemployment rate is no more than 2.5% is very challenging. By mid-1989 it had become evident that we had an opportunity to significantly increase our business. In order to achieve otherwise attainable goals, we have to increase our hourly workforce by a net of about 125 employees (that is, in addition to normal turnover, retirements, etc.) in one year. I have asked Personnel to test the waters, recognizing the unemployment in the Danbury labor market has reached an unprecedented low of about 2.5%.

Issue: Safety and Occupational Health Issues

The need to create a heightened awareness by the workforce for safety and occupational health considerations is very important. This is an evolving mission born of a dissatisfaction on our part about "safety as usual." Over the years, Barden employees have assumed that, because we are a metal working shop, people were just going to get hurt. But we cannot afford to have people get hurt and miss work anymore. Yet, as our workforce ages, the employees seem to get out of shape and become more injury and illness prone.

Issue: Spiraling Health Costs of an Aging Population

The spiraling health costs of an aging and sometimes out-of-shape workforce are very costly. All employers face this. Barden's problem is a little unique in that hourly employees tend to stay with the company and retire from the company. For example, we still have several employees whose careers began with us 45 years ago shortly after the company was founded. Our average age approaches 45 for employees and their dependent spouses. Generally, our jobs do not require much physical effort, and it's easy to become out of shape and overfed. As a consequence, they get sick, use hospitals, and have accidents.

Issue: New Machines and the Development of Qualified Workers

The technological evolution of increasingly complex machinery and related manufacturing equipment and the development of trained workers to operate and maintain these machines and equipment, are important facts of life. This process is unceasing and requires a good deal of planning for both the short and the long run. For example, where will we be next year or five years out in order to remain competitive in terms of cost, quality, and service? Buying and rebuilding machines is part of the story. Running them efficiently is quite another. As you know, modern equipment of this sort requires operational people who are not only knowledgeable about the turning or grinding of metals, but also conversant with computerized numerical controls. The employee who sets up and operates a $500,000 machine must be well-trained. Yet having trained people is getting more difficult.

Summary

Mr. Brush knows that these four people-related business issues all reflect the increasing diversity of the workforce. Because of this, he knows that these issues will be around for a long time. Therefore, he requests that you provide him with action plans that can offer long lasting solutions (if at all possible!). He would also appreciate having any more facts related to the four issues identified.

5

CASE 3.6
Adelphia: Good Works via a Hand in the Till

John Rigas opened his first business in 1952 in Coudersport, Pennsylvania, an old-fashioned movie theater, something he still would own at the time he would be indicted for fraud and other felonies in running Adelphia, the giant cable firm that would spring from this small beginning in media entertainment.

His foray into cable began when he and his brother bought a cable franchise for $300, also in 1952. They chose the name "Adelphia" for their new company, a name which is Greek for "brothers."[12] Early in the 1980s, John bought out his brother's interest in Adelphia and began bringing his now-grown sons into the business. By 2002, Adelphia was operating cable companies in 32 states and had 5.7 million subscribers. At its peak, Adelphia was the sixth largest cable company in the United States. Adelphia claimed that its aggressive marketing was partially responsible for its amazing growth and earnings.[13] Adelphia's annual reports also touted its "clustering strategy," something others in the cable industry did not really understand.[14] Many doubted the existence of such a strategy and questioned Adelphia's performance, but when it went public, its stock skyrocketed.

The Rigas family was respected, indeed revered, in Coudersport. John Rigas was often called "a Greek god" by the locals for his stunning looks as well as his generosity with everyone from employees to the needy. However, subsequent investigations would show that the Rigases had "borrowed" over $3 billion from the corporation for personal investments in hockey teams, golf courses, and even the independent film company created by daughter Ellen Rigas Venetis (married to Peter Venetis who was also an officer of Adelphia).[15]

There were also webs of transactions between the Rigas family and Adelphia. For example, John Rigas owned a furniture store from which Adelphia purchased all of its office furniture. However, Adelphia then gave the furniture store free ads on its cable and Internet services. A seasoned federal investigator was quite taken aback by what the Justice Department's review of corporate records uncovered, "We've never seen anything like this. The level of self-dealing is quite serious."[16] Mrs. John Rigas, Doris, was paid $12.8 million for her work as a designer and decorator for Adelphia offices. The Rigas family farm, billed as a honey farm in local literature, really just provided landscaping, maintenance and snow removal services to Adelphia, for a fee.[17] Adelphia invested $3 million in "Songcatcher," a film produced by Ellen Rigas Venetis.[18]

The family managed to conceal the self-dealing quite well from its auditors. When the financial statements were finally restated, cash flow had to be reduced by about $50 million per quarter. In total, the Rigases had concealed $3 billion of takings from the company from its external auditor, Deloitte Touche.[19] Timothy Werth, who was Adelphia's director of accounting, entered a guilty plea to fraud, securities fraud, wire fraud, conspiracy, and other crimes related to the concealment as well as the falsification

---

[12] *Id.* Eric Dash, "Sorrow Mixed with Disbelief for Patrons of a Community," *New York Times*, July 9, 2004, pp. A1, A5.
[13] www.adelphia.com/investors relations.
[14] www.adelphia.com/relations/1999.
[15] Robert Frank and Deborah Solomon, "Adelphia and Rigas Family Had a Vast Network of Business Ties," *Wall Street Journal*, May 24, 2002, pp. A1, A5.
[16] *Id.*
[17] Susan Pulliam and Deborah Solomon, "Adelphia Faces Irate Shareholders," *Wall Street Journal*, April 4, 2002, pp. C1, C2. Geraldine Fabrikant, "A Family Affair at Adelphia Communications," *New York Times*, April 4, 2002, p. C1.
[18] Geraldine Fabrikant, "A Family Affair at Adelphia Communications," *New York Times*, April 4, 2002, p. C1. Geraldine Fabrikant, "New Questions on Auditors for Adelphia," *New York Times*, May 25, 2002, p. B1, at B4.
[19] Christine Nuzum, "Adelphia's 'Accounting Magic' Fooled Auditors, Witness Says," *Wall Street Journal*, May 5, 2004, p. C5.

of earnings.[20] In his statement of facts for his guilty plea, Mr. Werth said that he had been cooking the books from the time he first joined Adelphia when he was 30 years old, some ten years.

The Rigases owned 20% of Adelphia stock, and, as a result, held 60% of the voting shares of the company. Because of their share control, the board consisted of 60% Rigas family affiliates, including John Rigas, sons Michael, James, and Timothy, and son-in-law, Peter Venetis.[21] The family also did business with Adelphia in other ways, and the transactions always seemed to net a nice profit for the Rigases. For example, Adelphia paid $25 million for the timber rights to a piece of property that it then sold to the Rigas family for $500,000.[22] There were substantial loans made to members of the Rigas family by the corporation, some used for business investments and some used to keep them from selling Adelphia shares to satisfy personal investment responsibilities. There were also conflicts galore among officers, board members and the Rigas family with the officers and board members actually competing with Adelphia for the purchase of cable systems, and with something that takes the term chutzpah to a new level, the company providing the credit, collateral and financing for the family members to make the purchases for themselves. The total amount of the loans to the Rigas family was $2.3 billion, much of that amount concealed from the board and auditors through off-the-book entities.[23] It was when a financial analyst uncovered at least $1 billion in off-the-book debts, that the board filed an 9-K disclosure statement and investigators came calling.[24]

The Rigases also owned finance companies that purchased cable services and then those finance companies entered into contracts to sell cable services to Adelphia.[25] Adelphia was required to purchase the cable services at full retail prices from the Rigas firms. Nell Minow, a renowned corporate governance expert and head of The Corporate Library said the following about these arrangements, "Even the existence of a credit line that allows the family to buy cable systems raises conflict-of-interest questions because the company was actually funding the family's ability to compete for properties."[26]

One accounting and financial expert said the conduct by the Rigases at Adelphia was just "plain-vanilla-old-fashioned self-dealing."[27] Many referred to the Rigases' conduct as not clever and nothing more than a classic "personal piggy bank" case.[28] The lines between Rigas activities and ownership and Adelphia's ownership were so blurred that local tax records showed that Adelphia paid the real estate taxes for all of the Rigas families and their 12 homes with one check.[29] Adelphia also fronted $12.8 million for the construction of a golf course owned by the Rigas family.[30]

Wayne Carlin, the regional director for the SEC's northeast division said, "The thing that makes this case stand out is the scope and magnitude of the looting of the company on the part of the Rigas family. In terms of brazenness and the sheer amount of dollars yanked out of this public company and yanked out of the pockets of investors, it's really quite stunning. It's even stunning to someone like me who is in the business of unraveling these kinds of schemes."[31]

[20] "Former Adelphia Executive Enters a Guilty Plea," *New York Times*, November 3, 2003, p. B3.
[21] This information was taken from the proxy for Adelphia for 2001.
[22] Nuzum, *Id.*
[23] www.sec.gov/edgar. March 27, 2002 8-K filing.
[24] Geraldine Fabrikant, "Adelphia Fails to Make Note Payment," *New York Times*, May 17, 2002, p. C1.
[25] Geraldine Fabrikant, "New Questions on Auditors for Adelphia," *New York Times*, May 25, 2002, p. B1, at B4.
[26] Geraldine Fabrikant, "New Questions on Auditors for Adelphia," *New York Times*, May 25, 2002, p. B1, at B4.
[27] Geraldine Fabrikant, "New Questions on Auditors for Adelphia," *New York Times*, May 25, 2002, p. B1, at B4.
[28] *Id.*
[29] Devin Leonard, Adelphia, *Fortune*, August 12, 2002, p. 137, at 146.
[30] Jerry Markon and Robert Frank, "Five Adelphia Officials Arrested on Fraud Charges," *Wall Street Journal*, July 25, 2002, p. A3.
[31] Jerry Markon and Robert Frank, "Five Adelphia Officials Arrested on Fraud Charges," *Wall Street Journal*, July 25, 2002, p. A3.

Adelphia was, however, a godsend, as it were, to Pennsylvania.[32] Suffering from declines in the coal and steel industries, the Pennsylvania economy was greatly depressed during Adelphia's rise. Because it was a company in a growing industry, nearly everyone in Coudersport would work directly for Adelphia or would benefit indirectly as their businesses picked up because of the company's growth. Rigas was so respected and beloved in the small central Pennsylvania town that it would often take him one hour to walk one block along Main Street because so many people stopped to talk with him, and mostly to thank him for what he had done with the company as well as for them personally.[33] The Rigas family also benefited local business because of their profligate spending on homes, events, help, and decorating.[34] At least 20 Adelphia employees worked personally for the Rigas family. One of those employees served as a chef for the Rigas family.[35] Country folklore holds that the local drycleaner had the following exchange with Mr. Rigas about his wife, Doris, and her spending, "That woman is costing you millions." To which Mr. Rigas replied, "Well, sometimes it's worth it. Because when she's bothering [the contractors], she's not bothering me."[36]

The Rigas family was very generous with the people of Coudersport. Mr. Rigas donated to the Coudersport fire department and paid $50,000 so that the veteran's monument in the town could have the worn-away names of the veterans restored. He gave the necessary funds to McDonald's and Subway so that they could change the outward appearances of their businesses to look more like the Main Street USA image that the Rigases wanted to preserve in Coudersport.[37] The Rigas family threw the Coudersport Christmas party. Doris decorated two large Christmas trees for the party with 16,000 lights each.[38] Mr. Rigas used the original theater that began his business career to allow more people to attend the movies. The prices at the Rigas Coudersport theater: Adelphia employees admitted for free; others for $4; candy for 60 cents and popcorn in a tub for $2.25.[39]

Adelphia's philanthropic program was called, "Because we're concerned," and donations went to Boy Scouts and Girl Scouts of America, the March of Dimes, Ronald McDonald House, YMWC, YWCA, Habitat for Humanity, Leukemia Society of America, Lupus Foundation of America, Meals on Wheels and Toys for Tots.[40] The Tennessee Titans' stadium was named "Adelphia Field." (The stadium is now LP Field.)

But Rigas' philanthropy went beyond these large public actions and donations. When John Rigas read a story in the local paper about someone experiencing financial difficulties, he would send them a check and a note that read, "I read your story in the newspaper."[41] Mr. Rigas offered the company jet to employees and family members who needed to go out-of-state for medical care. Mr. Rigas would even follow up with personal phone calls to these beneficiaries of the corporate jet by calling to see how the treatment had gone.[42] Mr. Rigas was inducted into the Cable Television Hall of Fame for his good works in Coudersport and the other communities served by Adelphia.[43]

The reaction in Coudersport to the Adelphia collapse and all of the indictments of the Rigas family was one of utter shock and disbelief. One Adelphia officer said that he

[32] *Id.* David Lieberman, "Adelphia's woes 'a total shock' to many," *USA Today*, April 5, 2002, p. 3B.
[33] Deborah Solomon and Robert Frank, "Adelphia Story: Founding Family Retreats in Crisis," *Wall Street Journal*, April 5, 2002, pp. B1, B4.
[34] Devin Leonard, "Adelphia," *Fortune*, Aug. 12, 2002, p. 137.
[35] Geraldine Fabrikant, "Adelphia Said to Inflate Customers and Cash Flow," *New York Times*, June 8, 2002, pp. B1, B3.
[36] Devin Leonard, "Adelphia," *Fortune*, Aug. 12, 2002, p. 137, at 146.
[37] John Schwartz, "In Hometown of Adelphia, Pride, But Worry About the Future, Too," *New York Times*, May 28, 2002, p. C1
[38] Devin Leonard, "Adelphia," *Fortune*, August 12, 2002, p. 137 at 138.
[39] John Schwartz, "In Hometown of *Adelphia*, Pride, But Worry About the Future, Too," *New York Times*, May 28, 2002, p. C1.
[40] www.adelphia.com/investors—see annual reports for 1999 and 2000.
[41] Devin Leonard, "Adelphia," *Fortune*, August 12, 2002, p. 137 at 146.
[42] John Schwartz, "In Hometown of Adelphia, Pride, But Worry About the Future, Too," *New York Times*, May 28, 2002, p. C1 at C6.
[43] *Id.*

"hasn't heard Rigas utter a slur or profanity in 32 years. The whole story isn't known. That's part of the problem."[44] One town member explained, "Whatever has to be done to make it right, they'll do. People don't know the real John Rigas."[45]

John Rigas and his son, Timothy, were convicted of bank fraud, securities fraud and conspiracy. Michael Rigas was acquitted of conspiracy and wire fraud, but there was a hung jury on securities and bank fraud. The judge declared a mistrial.[46] John Rigas was originally sentenced to 15 years, but with an intervening U.S. Supreme Court decision on the proper application of the sentencing guidelines, Mr. Rigas was resentenced in 2007. However, his sentence remained at 15 years because the federal judge noted that were it not for Mr. Rigas's age and failing health, he would have imposed a longer sentence. Because he was 82 at the time of the sentencing, Mr. Rigas will spend his life in prison unless he is able to show through a doctor's report that he is within six months of death. He will be released if and when that medical certification can be made. The judge also said he would review the sentence again when and if Mr. Rigas has served two years.

Discussion Questions

1. Does using money for good deeds excuse violations of the law or accounting principles? Is John Rigas a Robin Hood?

2. Why do you think the officers got so comfortable with the conflicts and mixing together of personal and company business interests? Did the philanthropy and good for Pennsylvania provide their justification?

Compare & Contrast

1. What principles of social responsibility do you develop from this case? Are virtue ethics different from the issues raised in social responsibility? Was the Rigas family socially responsible? Were they ethical? Was Adelphia a socially responsible company? Was its conduct fair to its shareholders?

2. When he was indicted, Mr. Rigas issued the following statement: "We did nothing wrong; My conscience is clear about that."[47] He also attributed all of the government indictments as well as the shareholders' litigation against him as "a big P.R. effort on the part of the outside directors and their lawyers to shift responsibility."[48] Given Mr. Rigas's convictions, why did he remain so defiant and unwilling to acknowledge the misconduct? As you study other cases in the book, note how many other convicted CEOs express the same sentiments. Offer some reasons they might feel so diametrically different from those who have prosecuted them or sought recovery for their losses.

---

[44] David Lieberman, "Adelphia's woes 'a total shock' to many," *USA Today*, April 5, 2002, p. 3B.
[45] *Id.*
[46] Barry Meier, "Michael Rigas Is Free for Now after Mistrial Declared," *New York Times*, July 16, 2004, p. B1.
[47] From *Business: Its Legal, Ethical and Global Environment*, 6th ed., by Marianne Jennings, 46–47. Copyright © 2003. Reprinted with permission by South-Western, a division of Cengage Learning.
[48] Andrew Ross Sorkin, "Fallen Founder of Adelphia Tries to Explain," *New York Times*, April 7, 2003, p. C1.

BULLER | SCHULER   6

Managing Organizations and People

A Resource for Cases in Management, Organizational Behavior, and Human Resource Management

Abstract

Jim Wallace, the Vice President of Sales at ChemCorp, is being faced with a difficult situation. His boss has just asked him to market a product line that is likely to be banned because of its link with cancer. Jim's boss, Art Jackson, tells Jim that he has to market the product and present him with a marketing plan by the next morning. Because Jim is in the Midwest, it is likely that his customers will not know about the harmful effects of Agri-Coat, a product produced by another West Coast subsidiary. The firm's real intent is to unload the inventory before the federal ban is official and known to customers.

The Marketing Campaign at ChemCorp

Jim Wallace stood at the window of his 8th floor office looking out over a city about to be engulfed by dusk. He had just come back from a meeting with Art Jackson, President of ChemCorp, an agricultural chemical and fertilizer company. Unlike other meetings with Art, this one left Jim with a feeling of uneasiness.

Art had proposed that Jim, in his position as Vice President of Sales, develop a sales campaign for AgriCoat, a pesticide to be shipped from Western Fertilizers and Chemicals, a California company. The President had asked that this project be given top priority because of its importance to both ChemCorp and its parent company, CCA. But the circumstances surrounding the request made it difficult for Jim to start designing the campaign right away. He struggled to find the reasons for his reluctance.

Background of ChemCorp

ChemCorp was founded in the early 1920s by two chemical engineers as a small chemical company with a focus on the market in the southeastern part of the United States. With a limited product line but a reputation for quality and service, it became a very successful company, weathering both the Great Depression and World War II. The booming post-war economy found ChemCorp poised for expansion within the emerging agricultural industry in the Southeast. Agricultural cooperatives and larger farmers became the primary customers who fueled its growth as they came to rely on ChemCorp to meet their needs.

The small core of managers who had guided the company through its early period gave way to a new group of managers in the 1950s who brought new sophistication to both

■ This case was written by D. Jeffrey Lenn, School of Business and Public Management at The George Washington University. While it portrays an actual situation, names and places have been changed to maintain confidentiality for the managers involved. Reprinted by permission.

production and marketing. ChemCorp expanded its production capacity by building new plants in a number of small towns in the Southeast. An aggressive marketing strategy was inaugurated through a well-trained sales force, an expanded product line, and a substantial research and development program designed to create products suited to the needs of farmers. Growth never clouded ChemCorp's fundamental mission of retaining a reputation for product quality and customer service.

Art Jackson became president 10 years ago, the first outsider to take over the reins of the company. Well-established in the industry as a divisional vice president of a major chemical company, Art found a new home at ChemCorp. He quickly surrounded himself with a new executive group and set his sights on consolidating the position of ChemCorp as a regional leader in the agricultural chemical industry.

Four years ago, ChemCorp was taken over by CCA, a diversified conglomerate headquartered in the Northeast. CCA was searching to expand its portfolio of small and medium companies with excellent cash flow and established market share in the agricultural industry. ChemCorp was a prime candidate to round out a new CCA division which already included two other small chemical and several agricultural product companies. While reluctant initially to sell, the ChemCorp board took Art's advice that the price was right. CCA's promise to maintain an arms-length management relationship while providing capital infusion was important also in the board's decision. They sold to CCA with the understanding that top management would stay and the thrust of the business would be maintained.

Jackson's forecast had been correct. CCA was liberal in its capital expenditure policy as it approved a large initial capital budget proposed by the President. This led to a full revamping of the ChemCorp plants with the latest in technology built into the production process. The inclusion of ChemCorp in a national division provided the basis for further integration into a broader marketing strategy in which ChemCorp was expected to play a major role over the next few years.

Jim Wallace's Career at ChemCorp

Jim started as a chemical engineer with ChemCorp right out of college. He worked in the production side for nearly 7 years but became a little frustrated with the highly technical aspects of his job. When an opening in the sales department came up, he jumped at it. His first two years were rocky ones as he just met his sales quota each year. He found that his engineering training had not equipped him very well to handle the day-to-day contacts with customers. While he could help them understand the technical characteristics of the products, he was not always sure just how to convince them to buy these products.

But he worked hard, and with the help of an excellent regional sales manager, began to learn how to couple his product knowledge with customer knowledge to become a highly successful salesman. When a regional manager's position opened up, his own manager recommended him highly. Jim proved his ability in this new position because of his sales expertise and his management experience. An earlier stint as an engineering manager had helped set the stage for this success.

Five years ago, when Art Jackson had reorganized, he had chosen Jim as his new Vice President of Sales. The CEO saw in Jim someone with executive talent. He had fine experience in the field and an excellent reputation with key customers and the sales force. He had acquired good product knowledge through his years in engineering. And most of all, he had developed a good sense of the importance of overall corporate objectives with his exposure to both sales and production. Art recognized that the informal grooming process for executive talent in ChemCorp had produced a fine candidate for this position.

Jim took to the position nicely. Sales volume increased as well as the customer base during his tenure. He worked hard to shape the sales force into a cohesive unit through his hiring practices, a new incentive program, and a personal touch, where he was in touch with top producers on a quarterly basis. His department developed a new sense of pride which led to even greater productivity.

Jim fostered a good working relationship with the engineering department. He worked closely with them to develop new products which were responsive to farmers' needs for fertilizers and pesticides. One of these new products, Gro-Go, was developed nearly three years ago in response to growers' concerns about environmentally safe products. Gro-Go was a breakthrough in a market which was now demanding pesticides which could both control insects and not be harmful to the ultimate consumer. In its first two full years on the market, Gro-Go established itself as a strong product with an excellent future.

At 42, Jim recognized that he had become a successful executive. His relationship with Art made him a key member of the ChemCorp executive team. His hard work and full commitment to his staff had increased his stature within the sales department as well as within other departments. He was pleased with his ability to forge a career which incorporated both production and sales skills rather than simply being defined as a narrow advocate of one or the other of the corporate functions. He was optimistic about his future career.

The Meeting with Art Jackson

Jim was puzzled by the hastily arranged meeting with Art Jackson. He was disturbed by the CEO's manner as they sat across the large oak desk in Art's office. Art's words seemed to be more carefully chosen than usual as he explained that the CCA Group Vice President had called yesterday with a proposal for ChemCorp.

The proposal detailed that ChemCorp would add AgriCoat, a pesticide produced by Western Fertilizers and Chemicals, another subsidiary of CCA on the West Coast, to its product line. The CCA Vice President indicated that the full inventory of AgriCoat would be shipped within the next two weeks and ChemCorp should be prepared to sell it to its customers over the next six months. It suggested that AgriCoat might be heavily discounted or coupled with other promotions to move it quickly into the market in light of such a short time horizon.

While Art was covering some of the financial details, Jim sifted through his knowledge of AgriCoat. He originally had considered adding it to the ChemCorp line but decided that another pesticide would be better suited to his market. His decision to develop Gro-Go had been prompted by customer interest in the environmental aspect. Art had been supportive of this decision even though he recognized that the research and development costs would be higher. Jim's strategy had paid off in terms of the sales figures for Gro-Go. Thus, Art's acceptance of the current CCA proposal was all the more surprising because it appeared that AgriCoat would be in direct competition with Gro-Go.

As Jackson started to outline some of his own ideas about a sales campaign, Wallace interrupted: "But Art, why the big push for AgriCoat now? Sales for Gro-Go are excellent, and we are just beginning to see the early signs of our campaign to build its image as a pesticide which is effective while safe. Introducing AgriCoat would work at cross purposes with what my sales force is doing right now."

Art stumbled a little as he explained the importance of the AgriCoat campaign. Then he paused and looked Jim in the eye: "I wasn't supposed to tell you this, but we have worked together too long not to be honest with each other. CCA staff has found out from inside sources that the U.S. Government has decided from confidential studies that a number of pesticides should be banned from the market. These studies show a direct link between these pesticides and cancer in laboratory animals. The implication is that they also cause cancer in human beings. AgriCoat is one of these pesticides."

"CCA will join with other chemical companies to appeal the ban but expects that it will be unsuccessful. Western is already in shaky financial condition with a heavy inventory of AgriCoat. A California newspaper has leaked a state environmental agency report which questions the safety of this product in particular. Sales have begun to drop off, so CCA has decided that Western will discontinue production of AgriCoat in a week and ship their full inventory to us for marketing here. The Group Vice President estimates that the federal ban will finally take effect in six months. In the meantime, there is little likelihood of much controversy here in our market as nobody knows anything about AgriCoat."

The CEO moved quickly to the point of the meeting: "Jim, I know that the arms-length relationship with CCA has been beneficial to ChemCorp. Now it is time that we begin to see ourselves as part of the larger company by assuming some of the burden from another subsidiary. You are in charge of this operation and I have full confidence that you will be successful.

"We need tell nobody else about the real reason for taking on AgriCoat. Let's just position it as part of our product line. I can understand your difficulties in light of the strength of Gro-Go, but this is only temporary. We really have no choice on this one, as it comes from the top. Your work on this campaign will be important to me and to CCA. This is a big one for your career as well. Those guys at headquarters will be watching us on this one.

"Remember, Jim, we have to move it! In fact, that might be a good start on your campaign with the sales force—'Move it!' I will need a general outline of your campaign by tomorrow morning so I can call CCA. We can finalize the details by the end of the week."

The Decision on the AgriCoat Campaign

Having called home to say he would be working late, Jim settled down to review the CCA proposal. He began to think through a strategy for the campaign with Art's words of "Move it!" echoing in his ears. He realized that marketing in a highly competitive industry took a lot of creativity. But there was something which nagged at him on this campaign. He had always been able to overcome his uncertain feelings in the past and work out a successful strategy. But there was some deep uncertainty about this one, something which he could not put a label on.

BULLER | SCHULER   7

Managing Organizations and People

A Resource for Cases in Management, Organizational Behavior, and Human Resource Management

Abstract

Seeking to make the topic of whistleblowing personally relevant and meaningful to undergraduates, we have developed a brief case exercise, based on the fictionalized and embellished experience of a former student of the first author. The decision of the prospective whistleblower, a part-time business student working as a first-line supervisor at a restaurant, (1) involves an organizational scenario in which students can readily picture themselves and (2) does matter, to a number of stakeholders, including the supervisor's friend (knowing the victim of wrongdoing may increase the likelihood of whistleblowing). The protagonist merely suspects her manager of stealing, until she hears concrete evidence of it from her assistant manager, who does *not* want to take action. This case therefore asks students to think about the extent to which it is ethically appropriate for a prospective whistleblower to force another member of his or her organization to become an unwilling collaborator in the reporting of misconduct. Also, the supervisor perceives that their company has an old boys' network, and her assistant manager presumes that their miscreant male manager has allies in high places. The case thus also addresses political aspects of whistleblowing decisions and outcomes.

Unsavory Problems at Tasty's: A Case Exercise About Whistleblowing

Emily Brown, a part-time business administration student, has been supporting herself and paying tuition at Teaberry University for the past five years by working at Tasty's, a family-style restaurant. During the last three years, she has been a supervisor there. Tasty's, which runs 37 franchises in the northeastern U.S., has experienced some financial difficulties in the last year. About six months ago, as a result of declining revenues, Tasty's closed several stores in the district where Emily works. Many employees lost their jobs; their more fortunate co-workers were offered jobs at stores that remained open. Emily's store survived the recent spate of closings, but her general manager, Connie O'Hare, was transferred to a store outside the district. Before her transfer, Connie had been general manager at Emily's store for eight years. Her subordinates had enjoyed their jobs and worked hard. They were proud that their Tasty's was one of the strongest performers in the district, and attributed their store's continuing viability in large part to Connie's managerial talent.

■ Debra Comer, Hofstra University, and Gina Vega, Merrimack College.

Replacing Connie as their general manager was John Tadmore. John had been the general manager at another Tasty's for barely two years at the time of his transfer to Emily's store. John, whose own store had closed, was delighted by the transfer, which cut his commute in half. Emily, for her part, was infuriated that John was actually benefiting from the closing of his store, whereas Connie was being shuffled around without any regard for what she—or her subordinates—wanted. She chalked up Connie's transfer to the old boys' network at Tasty's, which has no female division managers and only a handful of women at the level of district manager (see Figure 1). The scarcity of women in top leadership positions had been the only feature of the company that bothered Emily, who, until recently, had otherwise considered Tasty's an ideal employer.

Within the first month of John's arrival, the store was showing signs of neglect. Orders weren't placed on time, the employee schedule was always finished late and frequently contained gaps and/or overlaps, and the level of grime and grunge had hit an all-time high. Perhaps most troubling, money seemed to be disappearing. Registers were short on a regular basis by twenty dollars or more, the change fund (kept in the safe) was often missing money, and bank bags were coming up short. In her five years at Tasty's, Emily had never witnessed a situation like this one. Despite her lack of any solid evidence, she suspected John of stealing from the store. Meanwhile, John was accusing others. He blamed a light bank bag on a new employee, and a $40 register shortage on Martin Pine,

FIGURE 1
Organization
Chart of Tasty's

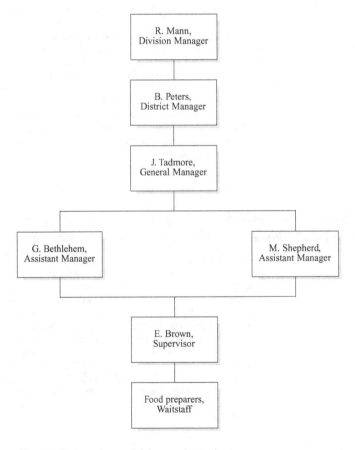

Note: Emily Brown is one of eight supervisors at her store.

one of Emily's closest colleagues. Perturbed and feeling helpless, Emily turned to Ginger Bethlehem, one of her assistant managers.

E: *Ginger, I need to talk to someone about what's been going on in the store.*

G: *O.K. Have a seat. I'm listening.*

E: *Since Connie left, everything's been going down hill. Scheduling is a mess, the store is not as clean as it should be, and, of course, there's the mysterious disappearing money. John has been blaming other people of stealing, but I think he is the real thief!*

G: *Emily, I've never seen you so upset!*

E: *Well, John has been unfairly accusing innocent people. Martin is a good friend of mine. I've known him for more than three years and I know he would never steal period, let alone from the store. He loves his job as much as I do, or, as much as I did, anyway. Did you know Marty was thinking about leaving?*

G: *No, I didn't know that. That's too bad. He's a solid performer.*

E: *I can't prove anything, Ginger, but I'd bet that John is the culprit. I mean, the way he's so quick to blame others. You're an assistant manager; can you talk to him about this?*

G: *What could I say that would make a difference? Listen to me, Emily. Last week, at the end of the night, John and I were getting ready to close up. I was exhausted, so I headed toward the ladies' room to splash some water on my face to perk up for my drive home. But I noticed my right earring was missing, so I started crawling around, looking for it. When I finally found it, I heard some sounds at the register. I stayed crouched down, so John couldn't see me. But I could see him. He took three bills from the stack of twenties and stuffed them in his back pocket.*

E: *John thought he could get away with it because he thought you were in the bathroom.*

G: *Exactly.*

E: *What did John say when you told him?*

G: *Told him?!?! What, are you kidding me? John is doing my performance review next month, and I'm not going to say or do anything to ruin my chances of getting the raise I deserve.*

E: *Have you spoken with Blake Peters?*

G: *The district manager! Why do you want me to stir up trouble? Besides, Emily, Blake and John went to college together. I could be wrong, but I'm guessing that that's how John got to be our general manager after his store was closed.*

E: *But you don't know for sure. Don't you think Blake should know? John's getting away with stealing, and he's ruining our store and driving away capable employees. It's not fair!*

G: *Who told you life is fair? Well, I have to get back to my paperwork now. Please, Emily, do us both a favor and forget I told you anything.*

Emily left Ginger's office, more upset and confused than she'd been before entering. She recognized that maybe Ginger was right that it wouldn't accomplish anything to speak with Blake. But knowing that John was hurting the store and people in it was eating away at her. She couldn't respect Ginger's decision to keep quiet. She wondered whether she should try talking to Blake, or whether it made more sense to go over Blake's head and speak with Richard Mann, her division manager. For years, Emily had loved working at Tasty's. Now, she dreaded going to work. She knew one thing for sure: She had to do something, even if it meant resigning. She didn't think she could stay at Tasty's if the current situation continued.

CASE **10.6**
Paul Wolfowitz and the World Bank

Paul Wolfowitz was the head of the World Bank from June 1, 2005 until May 17, 2007. Mr. Wolfowitz was romantically involved with an executive at the bank, Shaza Riza. Mr. Wolfowitz went to the board with an ethics question about their relationship and her continuing employment. The bank board advised that Ms. Riza be relocated to a position beyond Mr. Wolfowitz's influence because of their relationship and also because she could no longer be promoted at the bank. On August 11, 2005, Mr. Wolfowitz wrote a memo to Xavier Coll, the bank's vice president of human resources, and suggested the following:

I now direct you to agree to a proposal which includes the following terms and conditions:

The terms and conditions included her future at the bank when Mr. Wolfowitz was no longer heading it as well as an obligation to find her other employment. Ms. Riza now earns $193,590 per year at a nonprofit organization, following a stint at the State Department at World Bank expense. She earned $132,000 at the World Bank (a salary that was tax-free because of diplomatic status).

In response to the questions raised about his relationship and the memo, Mr. Wolfowitz posted the following explanation on the World Bank website:

Let me just say a few words about the issue on everyone's mind. Two years ago, when I came to the Bank, I raised the issue of a potential conflict of interest and asked to be recused from the matter. I took the issue to the Ethics Committee and after extensive discussions with the Chairman, the Committee's advice was to promote and relocate Ms. Shaha Riza.

I made a good faith effort to implement my understanding of that advice, and it was done in order to take responsibility for settling an issue that I believed had potential to harm the institution. In hindsight, I wish I had trusted my original instincts and kept myself out of the negotiations. I made a mistake, for which I am sorry.

Let me also ask for some understanding. Not only was this a painful personal dilemma, but I also had to deal with it when I was new to this institution and I was trying to navigate in uncharted waters. The situation was unprecedented and exceptional. This was an involuntary reassignment and I believed there was a legal risk if this was not resolved by mutual agreement. I take full responsibility for the details. I did not attempt to hide my actions nor make anyone else responsible.

I proposed to the Board that they establish some mechanism to judge whether the agreement reached was a reasonable outcome. I will accept any remedies they propose.

In the larger scheme of things, we have much more important work to focus on. For those people who disagree with the things that they associate me with in my previous job, I'm not in my previous job. I'm not working for the U.S. government, I'm working for this institution and its 185 shareholders. I believe deeply in the mission of the institution and have a passion for it. I think the challenge of reducing poverty is of enormous importance. I think the opportunities in Africa are potentially historic. We have really been able to call attention to the progress that's possible in Africa, and not just the despair and misery in the poorest countries. I think together we've made some progress in enabling this institution to respond more effectively and rapidly both in poor countries and in middle income countries to carry on the fight against poverty. I also believe—even more strongly now than when I came to this job—that the world needs an effective multilateral institution like this one that can responsibly and credibly manage common funds for common purposes, whether it is fighting poverty or dealing with climate change or responding to avian flu. I ask that I be judged for what I'm doing now and what we can do together moving forward.

Discussion Questions

1. What ethical issues do you see?

2. Did Mr. Wolfowitz act properly?

3. What should the board have done?

Compare & Contrast

The overarching goal of Mr. Wolfowitz's tenure as head of the World Bank has been eliminating corruption in all countries that deal with the bank. In fact, Mr. Wolfowitz had been very effective in eliminating corruption by insisting that countries install online payment mechanisms for government fees and licenses. The result of these Internet transactions was that the in-person demand for additional fees by government officials was halted. The Internet transactions also provided a complete accounting system that could not be altered for purposes of siphoning funds. What effect does his personal conduct have on that goal?

Sources:

Krishna Guha, "World Bank Staff Group Queries 'Misleading' Website Extracts," *Financial Times*, April 16, 2007, p. 3.

Krishna Guha, Javier Blas, Eoin Callan, and Scheherazade Daneshkhu, "Division Emerge as Wolfowitz Fights on," *Financial Times*, April 16, 2007, p. 1.

Greg Hitt, "Wolfowitz Digs in as Criticism Intensifies Within World Bank," *Wall Street Journal*, April 16, 2007, p. A3.

Greg Hitt, "Wolfowitz Memo, Dictating Raises Given to Friend, Now Haunts Him," *Wall Street Journal*, April 14, 2007, p. A1, A5.

9

CASE **1.15**
Travel Expenses: A Chance for Extra Income

The *New York Times Magazine* profiled the problems with employees' submissions for travel and entertainment expenses reimbursement. American Express reported that employees spend $156 billion annually on travel and entertainment related to business. Internal auditors at companies listed types of expenses for which employees have sought reimbursement: hairdresser, traffic tickets, and kennel fees.

Although the IRS raised the amount allowable for undocumented expenses to $75, most companies keep their limit for employees at $25. One company auditor commented that all taxi cab rides now cost $24.97 and if the company went with the IRS limit, the cab fares would climb to $74.65.

Some of the horror stories submitted by auditors on travel and entertainment expenses submitted by employees:

One employee submitted a bill for $12 for a tin of cookies. When questioned, he could not explain how it had been used but asked for reimbursement anyway because all he would have to do is "make up" a couple of taxi rides to get it back anyway;

$225 for three hockey tickets, except that the names on the tickets were the employee's family members;

$625 for wallpapering. The employee had included it with her other travel expenses and even had the wallpaper receipt written in a different language in order to throw off any questions; and

$275 sports jacket submitted as a restaurant bill. The travel office called the number listed on the receipt and asked if food was sold there. The response was, "No, we're a men's clothing store."[25]

Discussion Questions

1. The auditors noted that employees who are confronted often respond with similar justifications:

   "The company owes it to me."
   "It doesn't really hurt anyone."
   "Everybody does this."
   Are these justifications or rationalizations?

2. Why do employees risk questionable expenses?

3. Who is harmed by dishonest expense submissions?

4. There is a book called "How to Pad Your Expense Report ... and Get Away with It!" by Employee X. Employee X says that he offers these suggestions because of the "obscene salaries" of executives. Employee X also notes that he has been cheating on his expenses for so long that he doesn't even think about it anymore. Can you see any of the rationalizations in Employee X's views? What critical point do you discern from habit and ethics working together?

[25] Paul Burnham Finney, "Hey, It's on the Company!" *The New York Times Magazine*, March 8, 1998, pp. 99–100.

BULLER | SCHULER 10

Managing Organizations and People

A Resource for Cases in Management, Organizational Behavior, and Human Resource Management

Abstract

Bob Marvin, president of Motor Parts Corporation (MPC), feels a great deal of conflict and frustration about how to deal with the behavior of one of his vice presidents, Al Shepherd. Al's wife, Ruth, has recently had a recurrence of a malignant brain tumor, and Al is spending more and more time away from work to be with her. Bob believes that Al's increasing absence from work and his preoccupation with his wife's problem is causing Al's performance to suffer. In addition, Bob thinks Al's behavior is beginning to affect the morale and performance of others who work with Al. Bob is even beginning to question Al's commitment to the organization.

Bob has chosen not to confront Al directly because he does not want to seem insensitive. Instead, he has asked Mike Jones, a management professor and planning consultant to MPC, as well as a good friend to both Al and Bob, to speak with Al. Al was quite open about his feelings with Bob. Al believed that he was performing his job duties adequately and expressed his loyalty to the company.

When Mike Jones reports the results of his conversation with Al, Bob becomes more puzzled about what to do. Later, when Bob finds out that Al is in Detroit at his mother's house (who is ill), he becomes really frustrated. (What Bob does not know is that Al is in Detroit closing the deal on a major account for MPC.) Mike asks Bob to talk to Al in a more straightforward way.

Motor Parts Corporation

Bob Marvin, president of Motor Parts Corp. (MPC), felt a great deal of conflict and frustration as he chaired the strategic planning meeting of his senior management team. Al Shepherd, his executive vice president, had just arose from the conference table and excused himself, saying:

I'm sorry but we have had a change in our chemotherapy appointment and I have to meet Ruth.

■ This case was written by Richard D. Freedman, Stern School of Business, New York University. Copyright ©1995 by Richard D. Freedman. Reprinted with permission.

Ruth, Al's wife, had just recently learned that she had a recurrence of a malignant brain tumor. The prior bout, over only two years ago, had been difficult. Al was completely involved with his wife's fight against her illness. He had become about as expert as a layman could become on the disease, the many methods of fighting it, and the best institutions and physicians. He had accompanied her to virtually all medical appointments and procedures. When asked about her condition he would report to colleagues at great length and in technical detail. He was consumed by her situation. It had been a year since she had been given a clean bill of health when they were devastated to learn about her relapse. Now, the odds were against her. The doctors suggested a variety of alternative treatments, but at best her chances of surviving two years were less than one in three.

Bob, with great self-restraint, did not want to react at the meeting, and as hard as it was he tried to work around some of the issues that most directly affected Al.

Bob couldn't help but notice increasing, and less subtle references by others in the meeting to problems they had working around Al. After all, the organization had to go on. They all had their jobs to do, and while none had problems as severe as Al, many of them had their own serious problems. Jay Unger, VP Marketing had a son who had recently been expelled from college and was in rehabilitation with a drug dependency problem. Pete Arnell, was in the middle of a divorce. Bob himself, had his own problems, real problems.

At the end of the meeting he asked Mike Jones, who had happened to be at the meeting to return with him to his office. Mike is a management professor at the university and a consultant to MPC on planning issues.

What am I going to do about Al? As you know, after me, he has the most important job in this company. In fact, on a day-to-day basis he probably has the most critical job since all functions except for Finance, Legal, and Public Relations report directly to him. For the past few months he has been out of the office as much as he has been in it. Even worse, numerous meetings have been set to coincide with his schedule only to be aborted at the last second because he had to leave to take his wife to a medical appointment.

Now I just heard that our national sales meeting that has to be set up months in advance can't be scheduled because he is not certain about a procedure she has scheduled for about that time period.

His job requires considerable travel to regional offices and he just has not been doing enough of it. We have a number of new regional managers who are not getting enough guidance. We have some regional managers who are not doing a good job. They require closer supervision, if not replacement. Instead of dealing with these issues directly he is delegating supervisory chores to the two senior staff people in his department. For example, I know Joe Roderick is a great planner and earlier in his career he was a regional manager at Major Parts, but he is not their boss. I don't want lines of authority confused. I told that to Al when we created those staff positions.

You know that I try to keep in contact with our major customers. I have picked up hints that some of our regional people are just not performing adequately. He is not on top of things. Just look at how poor some of our regions are performing—Detroit and San Francisco are good examples. Our business is as dependent on service as price and quality. We can't afford not to be on top of things.

Just think about today. Here we are under all of this pressure from our Board to develop a new five-year plan. Even though our performance has been, on a relative basis, the best in the industry, they keep warning me that a company of our size has to do even better if it is going to avoid a takeover.

And you know we haven't been cheap. Salaries have risen around here faster than any place in the industry. I think that is only fair given performance. No one has done better than Al in the eight years that he has been here. He started at a rather low pay level and now is the highest paid executive in a comparable position in the industry.

Even though I have always had problems with his attention to detail and some of the people he has hired, I have no complaint about overall results. But we have to continue to improve.

By the way, you know that this is only part of the problem with Al. He's got to be one of the softest guys I've ever met. He stays home when he's got a bad cold, when there's a few inches of snow in his driveway. He was out a week last year with an ear infection. He is out about as much as any senior manager I've ever known.

You really have to wonder sometimes about his commitment. Some Board members have picked this up. To be honest, if something happened to me I don't think he would be a serious candidate for my job, even though they think he is very talented.

Mike couldn't help but think while Bob was talking. "If someone didn't know Bob they would think him quite callous if they overheard what he just said, but Bob is really a good person in his own way." He had known Bob for over 20 years. Their careers ran in parallels. Mike had been a consultant for three organizations that employed Bob, each watched the other move up their respective professions.

Bob was a rather shy person who frequently had to work in public. So he masked his shyness in formality. Although he encouraged subordinates to demonstrate initiative, he tended to carefully scrutinize their work, even the work of those in whom he had developed considerable confidence. He wanted things done the "right" way. He was often characterized as a perfectionist. He was as meticulous in his dress as his work. Despite his success, he was quite insecure. He worried most of the time.

Bob held himself to the same standard as others. It was an unusual evening or weekend that he would not spend much of his time working on the thick pile of papers he would take home and dictating one of the dozen or so memos that he would send to subordinates every day. He tried to overcome his natural reticence in public by carefully developed presentations. There were times that he could spend half a day preparing a 10-minute presentation to his Board. One problem with the approach was that he came across to some as stiff and cold. People who did not know him well thought of him as a rather dry and formal person, even bureaucratic. Bob had few friends. Those few who managed to get close to him over the years know him as a caring and brilliant executive.

Bob said little to Al because he wanted to be supportive, and he certainly did not want to be perceived by Al as not caring or putting his job ahead of his family. After all, no one spent more time thinking about family issues than Bob. So what he did was constantly send Al reminders about unresolved issues, press him for dates, and urge him to make trips in the field.

Well what have you said to him?" asked Mike.

I have stressed to him how important some of the meetings are and I have tried to alert him to some of the critical issues he has to handle."

He has indicated that he has been working on many of the problems at home and over the phone. He says he is in constant contact with his people over the telephone and that there are very few problems that he is not able to deal with. But that is simply not true.

You've known him for a long time. Why don't you talk to him and give me your assessment?"

The next week Mike asked Al out to lunch after they worked on the planning issues. Before lunch Mike couldn't help but review his impressions of Al. Al was like many people he had known who came up through sales. He was one of the most enjoyable people you could want to be around. He had an endless supply of the latest jokes—although he could be somewhat indiscreet as to who he told what joke. He was warm and friendly and showed great interest in the problems of the people he worked with—including his subordinates. He genuinely enjoyed helping his subordinates, although he was so busy that the lack of contact with him was a constant source of complaint. While this was a significant problem before the recurrence of Ruth's malignancy, now it was serious. Being liked was important to Al. His feelings would be hurt when he would hear about or sense the disapproval of a colleague. An ongoing source of conflict between Bob and Al was the fact that while Bob thought rules and regulations were meant to be followed, Al was inclined to overlook the rules, both for himself and others if the job was being done. Al was basically an optimistic person; he tended not to worry about the future, unless he had a specific problem he was forced to confront. He felt no need to control his subordinates if they were producing. After all, he had said to Mike many times what is the difference if he took time off if the job was being done?

After chatting for a while about issues that they were working on together Mike turned the conversation to Ruth's health. Al was quite hopeful about a new treatment available at the Morris Clinic. In fact, he had pulled strings with influential people and had a famous expert examine her. He advised an operation that would give her a one chance in three probability for surviving three years. Without the operation she had about a 15 percent probability. The operation would be in two months and she would have to remain at the hospital for a month. Of course, he would stay with her.

Mike asked about other relatives who could share the load. Their two children were away at college and he did not think it would be right to ask them. They were under enough stress at school and with their mother's illness. She had one sister who had two young teenagers so she could not help. Of course, he would not even consider leaving her alone.

Mike then asked: "Given all of the important issues you are working on and the people who look to you for supervision, how will you deal with your work responsibilities?"

Al said. "No problem, I've thought it through. First, I will set up in the regional office. I will try to be available for three hours a day, when I can leave Ruth. When there are significant problems with regional managers I'll fly them in to see me. After all, what's the difference if I fly out to see them or they come in to see me? As you know we hired Joe Roderick to handle major staff responsibilities like planning and executive development. He's had many years of supervisory experience, so he can handle any other issues that come up. So you can see that we ought to be able to handle the problems.

"I guess I ought to tell you that this illness has been very troubling, very difficult for me to handle. I haven't been sleeping well for weeks. The same thing happened the last time. So I've been getting up at 3 or 4:00 a.m. every day. I have been using that time very productively. It is incredible how much work you can get done through the computer tie in to the office when everything is so quiet."

Mike had the feeling that there was a lot more to the story than he was getting from Al, so he responded that, "It is clear that you've given this a lot of thought. But don't tell me what your plans are, tell me how you feel about things. The fact that you are having trouble sleeping is understandable, but it's also suggestive of deeper issues."

Al replied that, "It is very difficult for me now. I know that I am not 100 percent into my job. But let me remind you about what happened about a year-and-a-half ago. The presidency of Delta Corp., our major competitor, opened when Arnie Wyman had the sudden heart attack. Their Board hired that executive search firm to find candidates, and the partner managing the account knew me and wanted me to go on their short list. You'll surely remember that I came to you as a friend and discussed the situation with you. Everyone said I would be the prime candidate for the job.

"After thinking it over I decided not to interview with them. There were a lot of factors involved, of course. But in the end the determining factor was how MPC, and Bob in particular, treated me when we were having all those health problems. I felt, and I feel, part of a family. Families take care of their own in times of trouble. Mike, money can't buy that."

Mike later spoke to Bob about his lunch with Al. He tried to be descriptive and non-evaluative, urging Bob to speak to Al directly. Yet, after the discussion Bob seemed fixated on one point. He wondered whether Al's reference to being recruited away was a cryptic warning or a genuine statement of emotion. Or was it some combination?

Two weeks later Mike was in the office working with managers on some rather complex planning issues when he was called out of a meeting to take a long distance call from Al. Al was calling from Detroit where MPC had one of its most important regional offices and which happened to be his home town. While going over some of the planning issues Al interrupted the conversation, saying "Mike, I have to interrupt, I'm so excited, you'll never guess what happened last night. You know how long and hard we've been working on the Delta Corp. account. Tim Reynolds, our Detroit regional manager, finally set things up and we met with Delta's senior management team. We got the account! It will be at least $15,000,000 this year—almost 2% of our sales goal! Don't tell Bob, I want to break the news to him. This account was a real high priority for him."

A few hours later, toward the end of the day, Mike was just completing a meeting with Bob, when Bob said to him:

"You'll never guess the latest with Al. He is in Detroit. I tried to get him in the office yesterday morning on a very important issue, but Tim Reynolds said that he hadn't been in. He said that Al was at his mother's house. You remember that his dad died last year and his mother is alone and is in the early stages of Alzheimer's. He didn't get back to me until the late afternoon. Then he told me that he had to cancel some important meetings back here because he had to spend Friday in Detroit. It's obvious that he is taking advantage again. On top of everything else. I'm really frustrated."

"Well," Mike said, "Why don't you think about discussing it with him in a more straightforward way?"

Bob replied, "What's the use? You heard what he said. He has us over a barrel. He is staying with us because we treat him like family."

"Bob, are you being sarcastic?"

BULLER | SCHULER   11

Managing Organizations and People

A Resource for Cases in Management, Organizational Behavior, and Human Resource Management

Abstract

This case describes the conflict between two groups that appears to be anchored in the personality of a manager of one of the groups. The manager over both groups, John, is faced with the questions of what are the real causes of the conflict and what to do about the conflict. As with groups in conflict, each makes strong statements about the other that makes it difficult to determined the source of the conflict. A primary challenge of this case is to develop the means and sources of data collection to determine the causes.

Conflict Management

Area Manager John H. was surprised and astounded by the conversation he had just heard if you could call it a conversation! He could hardly believe that two of his key managers could be involved in such a bitter feud. One accused the other of trying to undermine his department by stealing his best people and the other accused in rebuttal that the other manager was simply finding excuses for his bad management. There had been accusation and counter-accusation followed by hot denials and bitter recrimination. He finally decided there was nothing to be gained by further outbursts and sent both men back to their departments. This, he hoped, would give them a cooling off period and himself a chance to try and sort it all out.

It wasn't unusual for Technical Development and Product Engineering to have these differences, but they rarely took on such a heated aspect. John's thoughts turned to Ralph, Manager of Technical Development. He had come highly recommended by the president of another division. He had been very successful in development work and seemed well suited to this assignment. In his six months on the job he had reorganized several sections and initiated new projects. It wasn't spectacular but it appeared competent from all John could see. There had been a few gripes that he was too aloof and reserved, but that was

■ This case was prepared by James C. Conant, School of Business Administration and Economics, California State University, and is used here with his permission. Copyright © James C. Conant.

natural in view of the man he had replaced. It always took a little time for these management transitions to settle down. It appeared Ralph was aware of his problem since he had inserted a new manager under him (Frank) who was effective in personal relationships. It was too early to tell how that was working out but it seemed a wise move.

John knew there were problems, however. He had talked with Personnel after the recent Opinion Survey and learned the morale in Ralph's group was down from its usual mark. There seemed to be more employee apathy, more lateness and absences, and more transfer requests. This latter issue was the most surprising since there were few such requests usually. It was odd to find morale at such a low ebb since the group was well knit and had strong group identity. Personnel had talked informally with a few of the people and their view was (1) the work load was too low and they didn't feel meaningfully utilized and (2) they felt their present management was too distant and reserved.

It was difficult to put these in perspective. From Ralph's viewpoint the low work load was directly traceable to the "game" George was playing. He contended one of George's people would request a "sizing" for a particular job. His people would carefully give cost, technology, and schedule estimates, but then nothing happened. One of his people would call over to find out where the work requisition was and would be told the job had been canceled by George. His manager would be offered a much smaller job—provided they transferred the people key to the former job request—"to help keep your people busy." When this finally came to Ralph's attention he "hit the roof" and this is what led to the recent confrontation. George's views varied greatly, hence the hot argument.

George had been in the department longer than Ralph. He was known as an effective, "hard-nosed" manager who got the job done. He was ambitious and had grown rather rapidly over the last two years. He was adaptable as shown by the fact that he had made the transition from Chemistry to Product Engineering. The Product Engineering Department had a poor reputation prior to George's moving over and he had been instrumental in changing its image to a very positive one. As a result the department had grown considerably under George. All in all it was a good record.

George contended Ralph was an inefficient manager, with too much fat in his organization, who was unwilling to cut back to a reasonable level. As a result Ralph was pricing himself out of the business. He had to cancel jobs because the costs were prohibitive. George laid some of the blame on the previous manager, Henry, claiming it was Henry's doing that caused the lab to reach the present ridiculous size. George felt Ralph should reevaluate his situation and curtail the department size and become competitive again. If the cost problem had merit as an argument it could go back to Henry. There was nothing to indicate Ralph's costs were out of line with past history.

George freely admitted to wanting several of Ralph's people. He felt they would be better placed and better utilized in his area, but he hotly denied he had "played any games" to get them. The pressure of the new releases had caused a backlog in his department and he could use expert help.

John wondered why George steadfastly refused to use the Technology group. He was slipping schedules and the overtime costs would eventually overtake the claimed excessive costs of Ralph's group. He wasn't in any serious trouble as yet and might be gambling he could pull his chestnuts out by the transfer of a few key people. If this was his gamble he might be trying to force Ralph's hand.

John decided he had better talk to Henry in order to clarify this matter further. After that was concluded he sorted out the following impressions. Henry had no love for Ralph. He felt it was still his "shop" and Ralph was doing a poor job of taking over. On the other hand Henry supported Ralph's contentions about George. He indicated he had similar problems in the past and had called him on it a number of times. He flatly denied that the group was too large and indicated it would function well if George didn't feel he had to save the managership of all operations necessary to his function. The conversation left John more puzzled than edified.

Well, there it was. All made good points. If George is correct an overhaul is in order and Ralph should get his costs in line. If Ralph is right George must be stopped from disrupting the department and risking full project success for the sake of his own gain. In all probability both have valid points and the problem will be how to respond appropriately to both managers.

Ralph's Viewpoint

Ralph was transferred into this division after several successful projects in Engineering Development. He came highly recommended by the president of another division, under whom he had worked, and was deemed a candidate for higher management in the near future.

There was little doubt about his technical competence. He was informed and innovative. He preferred small groups to large, complex ones, and this was a partial reason for giving him this assignment. Higher growth would depend on his ability to handle larger groups. For this reason the job had been enlarged to encompass additional functions. This meant Ralph had a substantially larger group to manage than his predecessor.

Although Ralph never commented on his reaction to this change in operations for him, he appeared a little overwhelmed by it. He spent considerable time in his office planning and integrating the various functions. He only rarely met with the Lab people and had staff meetings on an irregular basis. It must be emphasized he had been in the job only about six months and still was getting his feet on the ground.

He had never been much of a delegator. Some of this was by temperament and some from the nature of the reward structure. He had been heard to comment: "I do my business in the halls. When I run into the Division President and he asks about my project I can get away with maybe one 'I don't know' and after that I'm known as an 'I don't know guy.'" The result was a tendency to know details that usually are reserved for subordinates. The new job stretched him to the point that he had greater difficulty doing this, but it may account for the inordinate amount of time he spent in his office.

In his approach to others he was direct and confronting. People knew where they stood, and in general their comments indicated they liked this style of managing. He was aware he interacted somewhat stiffly with others and this had occasioned the insertion of Frank at the Lab level. In addition he was planning to change some of the procedures Henry had instituted, and he felt Henry would be an obstacle to these plans. Frank would be a major factor in assuring that the new procedures went as smoothly as possible.

His relationship to Henry was cordial but distant. He had no particular dislike for Henry, but felt the group could be more effectively organized. He was in the process of developing these plans when the problem broke.

His relationship with John, the Director, was essentially OK as far as one could tell. On the whole his "clout" with John was undeveloped, as was his impact on his peers. He seemed to be regarded as an unknown quantity—perhaps something of a threat in view of his reputation.

He was disappointed with the way the meeting turned out. He didn't like shouting matches but he wasn't going to stand by and have George put him or his Lab group down. He was sure they were effective and as soon as he completed some of the new project planning he knew their work load would be more than adequate. He was familiar with people trying the kind of thing George was doing and the only way to avert it was through direct confrontation. He only wished he could better predict John's reaction.

Henry's Viewpoint

Henry was an "old timer" and had been the Lab's Manager for many years. He was affable and outgoing, walking the shop regularly and on a first-name basis with virtually everyone in the Lab. It had been his assignment to create and staff the Lab, and over the several years he managed it he exercised care in the selection and placement of the staff. It had been generally conceded the Lab was staffed with topnotch people.

The Lab group had strong ties with one another. There were a few who had turned down promotions in order to remain with the group. That it was not all one big happy family was indicated by a few dissidents who felt they had been passed over for promotion. On the whole, however, they worked well together and enjoyed a favorable reputation by all concerned.

As Henry had indicated, George had tried to lure some of his better talent away during the recent past. Henry learned of these rather quickly because of his close relationship to the group and he effectively aborted each of these. George had finally given up on this and had gone to outside recruiting for the talent he wanted. This meant a slower indoctrination process for him and slowed down his growth potential. It was Henry who first became aware that George was up to his "old tricks."

He probably should have gone to Ralph with the information about George but he felt at odds with Ralph's methods. He resented the staff role into which he had been put, even though medical advice was the basis for the move. He sensed that Ralph was planning changes and he had not been consulted. When Frank was brought in he felt even more resentful. He regarded his assignment as a "make work" one and did not feel meaningfully utilized. He still felt a strong proprietary interest in the Lab group and would take whatever measures he could to prevent its disruption.

Given a choice of choosing between Ralph or George he would choose Ralph, and eventually this choice had to be made. In his meetings with John he had been fully candid regarding George's tactics and hoped this once John would put a stop to them. He did it more to ensure the Lab remaining intact than because of Ralph. He certainly didn't want to see the Lab destroyed after all the years he'd spent building it to its present state.

George's Viewpoint

George was dynamic, energetic, and technically proficient. He had taken over the Product Engineering group when it was regarded with disfavor and had steadily built into its present respectable state. He had ambition and sought to enlarge his sphere of influence whenever possible. He viewed the situation in this way. "I like this environment. It is highly fluid and I have a lot of freedom to do things the way I believe they should be done. I get reprimanded when I make a mistake—and that's only fair as far as I'm concerned. My attitude is to take over and operate any group I can. If I'm successful it will soon come under my jurisdiction. I keep pushing until I'm told to stop by someone who can make it stick."

This had been George's method of operation as long as he had been a manager. It had paid off handsomely for him, and from the Company's standpoint they had benefited too. His group was well-managed, competently staffed, and morale was at least as good as one could find in the Division. His people were loyal to him and respected his ability. He had considerable "clout" because of his past success and had more than the usual influence with the Director.

He had no personal antipathy for Ralph. He was anxious to secure some of the key Lab people and honestly believed they would be more effective in his organization. He felt this would be better for the Company and would provide the people with greater opportunities for growth. There was some accuracy to the latter, but the former was a matter of opinion.

As he regarded the Lab group he felt they were overstaffed and underutilized. He didn't think Ralph was effective in moving to reorganize the department and felt the people were fair game for his managerial approach.

(It was interesting to this observer that direct methods were never utilized. The ground rules permitted making offers to people in other departments, through promotions, raises, etc. Why George never did was unclear.)

George felt he was an effective manager, better than his peers (possibly including the Director). He felt Ralph was running a country club and that it needed effective management. If possible he wanted to absorb the Lab into his operation, but that would require a restructuring of the organization. Since the Lab served many groups in addition to his, his functions would have to be broadened, an unlikely move at this time.

He was taking a calculated risk in not using the Lab for some of his immediate jobs because he might well get into a last minute "crunch" and, failing to meet schedule, lose some of the ground he had gained. On the other hand if he could secure some key people, he could come in on schedule and be in a position to take over other Lab functions that would arise later. In the meantime it would appear as if the Lab was not as necessary because of the low work load. He, at this time, was the major user of the Lab—although this was not always the case. This depended on the development cycle, which was at a low ebb for other groups, but would probably pick up fairly soon.

All in all George was satisfied with his progress and felt he had a good chance at the Director's job when John was promoted. He wasn't happy about this current situation with Ralph, but felt he could weather it and perhaps make Ralph appear foolish or somewhat less competent. It would be a good time for a put-down, his being new and all. The last meeting with John left him uncertain as to where each stood. He was sure he had not heard the last of the situation.

BULLER | SCHULER   12

Managing Organizations and People

A Resource for Cases in Management, Organizational Behavior, and Human Resource Management

Abstract

Many small- and medium-sized firms experience growth problems due to the absence or dearth of professional supervisors/managers. This is the nub of the Traveler Import Cars case. The company, a car dealership, was started by a capable and ambitious married couple. The dealership experienced immediate fast growth due to its location, the quality of its products, and the customer-oriented climate in the company. However, fast growth of the dealership, and several related acquisitions, created a number of problems in the company. Randy and Beryl hired new managers to help them gain control, and the organization structure became more complex. The case illustrates some of the problems of growth—such as a lack of clear goals, poor communication, and lack of control—that are largely caused by lack of skilled management.

Traveler Import Cars, Incorporated

Background

Randy Traveler had been a partner in Capitol Imports, one of the most prosperous foreign car dealerships in greater Columbus, Ohio, selling expensive European automobiles. His wife, Beryl, a holder of an MBA degree from a respected private university, was a consultant specializing in automobile dealerships.

In 1979, Randy and Beryl decided to go into business for themselves. Since between the two of them they had four decades of automobile dealership experience, they elected to acquire their own dealership. With some luck, they obtained a dealership selling a brand of Japanese cars that had become known in the United States for its very high quality. Randy became president and Beryl executive vice-president.

Evolution of the Firm

Stage 1. After obtaining the Japanese dealership, Randy and Beryl decided to locate it approximately two miles from Capitol Imports. The decision was made on the basis of immediate availability of a suitable facility. This location, however, was several miles from a major shopping area of any kind, and the closest automobile dealership was Capitol Imports. Furthermore, the location was approximately three miles from the nearest interchange of a major interstate highway. Nonetheless, the dealership was located on a busy street within easy access to half a dozen upper-middle-class-to-affluent neighborhoods with residents predisposed to purchasing foreign automobiles with a high-quality image.

A number of key employees were enticed by Randy and Beryl to leave Capitol Imports and join Traveler Import Cars. Stuart Graham, who was in charge of Finance and Insurance at Capitol Imports, became general manager at Traveler Import Cars. Before specializing in finance and insurance, Graham was a car salesman. Several mechanics and car salesmen also left Capitol Imports to join Traveler Import Cars. As a rule, the policies and procedures that pertained at Capitol Imports were relied on at Traveler Import Cars, Inc. for the first five years of operations.

No one at Traveler Import Cars was unionized, but the mechanics were given everything that unionized mechanics received at other dealerships in order to remove the incentive to unionize. By everything, it is meant direct compensation, indirect compensation (fringe benefits), and work rules.

Randy and Beryl viewed their dealership as a family. This was in some measure due to the fact that the dealership was part of a Japanese Corporation (which viewed its employees as family), and partly due to the beliefs that Randy and Beryl shared about organizations. Randy and Beryl made every effort to involve subordinates in day-to-day decision-making. As tangible evidence of her commitment to democratic leadership, Beryl decided to introduce a quality circle into Traveler Import Cars, Incorporated. This was done by selecting five non-supervisory employees (one from each part of the organization) to meet once a month with Beryl and Stuart Graham in order to discuss problems, possible solutions, and implementation strategies. No training whatsoever regarding quality circles was provided anyone involved with the so-called "quality circle," and this includes Beryl and Stuart.

Stuart Graham, on the other hand, was a benevolent autocrat, although he tried to create the facade of a democratic leader because he understood well Randy and Beryl's leadership preferences. Most employees agreed with Randy and Beryl that Traveler Import Cars was a family. Furthermore, most employees felt free to voice an opinion on anything to Randy, Beryl, and Graham, or to any other supervisor or manager, for that matter.

Stage 2. As long as the dealership was small everything went well, largely because Randy and Beryl made all key decisions, provided daily direction to supervisors and managers (including the general manager—Stuart Graham, who should have been running the dealership on a day-to-day basis), and resolved problems through face-to-face communications with the involved individuals. As the dealership grew and prospered, it generated enough money for growth. Expanding the dealership rapidly was impractical because of the limited allotment of cars due in large measure to the so-called "voluntary" import quotas by the Japanese car manufacturers. The demand for these cars was so great that cars were even sold from the showroom floor, leaving at times few models for new customers to view.

The first acquisition that Randy and Beryl made was a car leasing company, which they located next to the dealership. Randy elected to spend most of his time building up the car leasing company, leaving the operations of the dealership to Beryl. The second acquisition consisted of another car dealership located approximately ten miles from the original one. The new dealership sold another make of Japanese cars and an expensive European make. The newly acquired dealership was located in the midst of automobile dealerships on a main road, but was housed in inadequate facilities and beset by many problems. Beryl became the chief operating officer of the second dealership as well. Soon after acquiring the second dealership, Randy and Beryl decided to construct new facilities adjacent to the existing ones.

Stage 3. The newly acquired dealership created a great deal of additional work for Beryl, but she understood and accepted that reality because she and Randy knowingly acquired a business that had been plagued by problems prior to acquisition. What bewildered and frustrated Beryl was the fact that the operation of Traveler Import Cars, Inc. took so much of her time as well as physical and psychic energies. After all, it had been five years since she and Randy purchased that dealership. Many key supervisory and managerial personnel now have five years of experience with the dealership, yet the task of running Traveler Import Cars is just as consuming at this time as it was when the dealership was new. Frequently, Beryl would tell one of the managers to do something, but it wouldn't get done. Decisions were reached at management meetings, but they did not get implemented. Programs were initiated, but were frequently permitted to drift and disappear. Important deadlines were being missed with increasing frequency. Mechanics and salesmen were coming to work late and taking excessive lunch breaks with greater frequency. Beryl knew that these problems were not due to insubordination or lack of motivation. Yet, if she did not directly oversee implementation of an important decision, it did not get implemented.

In order to relieve herself of some of the work load, Beryl hired two experienced managers. In order to justify their salaries, however, they spent half of their time at Traveler Import Cars and the other half at the newly acquired dealership. The newly hired managers had good ideas, yet Beryl was working just as hard as ever, and the problems that motivated Beryl to hire two experienced managers remained practically unchanged. In spite of the problems, the dealership grew as rapidly as the increase in the quota of cars that was allotted to the dealership by the manufacturer permitted. In addition, Traveler Import Cars began wholesaling parts to service stations and car repair shops, and started to lease cars in direct competition with the leasing operation managed by Randy. Although an organizational chart did not exist, it would look like Figure 1, if Randy and Beryl bothered to construct one.

About this time, Randy and Beryl's marriage had come undone, and Randy remarried a lady considerably his junior. Even so, Beryl and Randy maintained their business relationship, and were able to work together professionally without visible acrimony. Beryl now had more money than she knew what to do with, and was about to make much more because the newly acquired dealership was being turned around rapidly, largely due to Beryl's considerable talents, the new facility, and the rapidly recovering economy. Yet Beryl no longer wanted to work as hard as she had in the past.

Beryl understood that Stuart Graham lacked the right stuff to be general manager of a car dealership in a metropolitan area, and she approached Randy on the matter. His response was: "Stuart Graham is too valuable of an asset because Traveler Import Cars, Inc. had generated a $500,000 after tax profit last year. He must be doing something right."

Even though Beryl had been a consultant to automobile dealerships for twenty years, she decided nonetheless to retain a consultant. Beryl was fortunate to contact a particularly astute consultant by the name of J.P. Muzak. Her request was that Muzak straighten out the quality circle, which she felt wasn't living up to her expectations. Muzak, however, was reluctant to get involved unless he was permitted to conduct a thorough needs analysis before selecting any kind of intervention strategy. Beryl, after thinking the matter through, assented to Muzak's proposal. The organizational needs analysis relied on confidential structured interviews with all the managers, supervisors, and select non-supervisory personnel. The summary of Muzak's organization needs analysis follows.

Possible Problem Areas

Goals. Although general goals (such as providing the best customer service possible) exist at the organizational level, many individuals report that what is expected of them, in terms of specific and measurable objectives, isn't clearly defined. It is difficult to make a superior happy if the subordinate isn't sure just what it is that the boss wants.

Also, there does not appear to be a philosophy for setting goals. For example, should goals and objectives be imposed unilaterally by the superior on the subordinate, or should the goals and objectives be set jointly between the superior and subordinate?

Organizational Structure. The organizational structure in a number of instances appears to be confusing. Specifically, a number of individuals appear to be reporting to two or more superiors. Irma Krupp reports to David Chapel and Stuart Graham. Tom Tucker reports to Sam Carney and Stuart Graham. Charles Spikes reports to Tom Tucker, Sam

FIGURE 1
Organizational
Chart of Traveler
Import Cars, Inc.

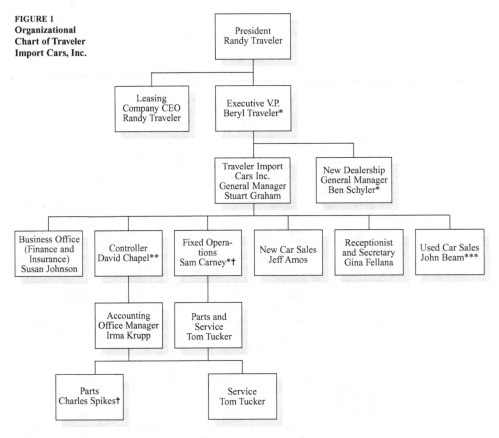

* These individuals spent approximately one-half of their time at Traveler Import Cars and one-half at the new dealership.

** David Chapel is the controller for Traveler Import Cars, the new dealership, and the leasing company. He spends about one-half of his time at Traveler Import Cars and one-half at the new dealership.

*** John Beam frequently is asked by Randy Traveler to assist with matters pertaining to the leasing company.

† Sam Carney owned and operated his own small business prior to joining Traveler Import Cars, Inc. Charles Spikes was a supervisor at a local office of a national automobile parts distributor before coming to work for Traveler Import Cars, Inc.

Carney, and Stuart Graham. John Beam had Susan Johnson's jobs before he became manager of used cars. David Chapel believes that he reports to the two general managers, to Beryl, and to Randy. Gina Fellana appears to report to everyone.

There is the perception that few managers know what they can do on their own authority and what they must get approved and by whom.

Communications. There appear to be too many meetings and they do not seem to be as productive as they could be. On this point there is a consensus.

A paper flow problem exists in several areas. The Accounting Office at times does not receive properly filled out forms from the Business Office. It appears that Susan Johnson does not have the time to fill out carefully and on a timely basis all the forms and attend to her other finance and insurance duties. The Accounting Office at times does not receive the necessary paper work from New Car Sales. The Parts Department at times doesn't receive on a timely basis the necessary information from New Car Sales.

Some individuals complain that their superiors do not keep them informed. Everything is a secret.

Training and Development. A number of individuals have risen through the ranks into supervisory and managerial positions. Since these individuals have never received formal managerial training, the void must be filled by coaching. In a number of cases, the void has not been filled by coaching, and these persons are learning through trial and error—an expensive and time-consuming way of learning, indeed.

The consensus is that the computer equipment is adequate to the task, but the operators need additional training to realize the potential of the equipment. The mechanics receive the latest training from the manufacturer.

Performance Appraisal. Many people reported that they do not receive a periodic formal appraisal. Thus, their need for performance feedback is frustrated.

Wage and Salary Administration. Numerous individuals have reported that it is the subordinate who has to initiate a wage or salary increase. Most individuals report that they would like to see the superior initiate wage and salary action at least annually. Moreover, a number of individuals are not sure on what basis they are remunerated. The absence of a systematic periodic performance appraisal is responsible, in part, for this perception.

Discipline. In a number of instances, individuals arrive late, take extended lunch breaks, and violate rules with impunity. This creates a demoralizing effect on others.

Control System. The financial control system at the top of the organization appears to be satisfactory. The operational control systems in the rest of the organization are problematic.

Morale. While there is still the feeling that the organization is a family and the best place the employees have ever worked, the feeling is starting to diminish.

Sundry Problems.

1. Quality circle may need restructuring along traditional lines.
2. The time it takes to make decisions should be shortened.
3. The organization has difficulty implementing decisions that have been made.
4. Lack of follow-up presents serious problems.
5. Policies and programs are permitted to drift and disappear (motivator board is an example).
6. Managers may not be delegating enough.
7. New car salesmen do not always turn customers over to the Business Office, resulting in loss of revenue to the dealership.
8. Service desk is crucial and it has been a revolving door.

At a meeting, Muzak presented the findings of his needs analysis to the management team of Traveler Import Cars, Inc., and a discussion ensued regarding each of the possible problem areas. Randy Traveler did not attend since he relegated the operation of the dealership to Beryl. At the end of the discussion, the management team agreed that all the problems uncovered by Muzak were real and, if anything, understated.

Muzak did not present at the meeting his assessment of the potential of the key managers. This he did in a private discussion with Beryl. In summary, Muzak concluded that Stuart Graham was too set in his ways to change. Moreover, he displayed too much emotion publicly, and lacked the respect of his subordinates. Jeff Amos was considered by his subordinates to be a nice guy, but was indecisive, lacked firmness, was manipulated by subordinates, and did not enjoy the respect of his subordinates. Tom Tucker was probably in over his head in his present position. He was only a high school graduate, he was not a mechanic, was unsure of himself, and lacked the confidence of his subordinates. Lastly, he was quite impulsive. His previous experience was as a service desk writer (the person to whom the customer explains the car problems and who writes the work order). All the other managers and supervisors were thought to possess the necessary potential which could be realized through training and experience.